THE REAL LIFE GUIDE TO ACCOUNTING RESEARCH

RESEARCH

A BEHIND THE SCENES VIEW OF USING QUALITATIVE RESEARCH METHODS

THE REAL LIFE GUIDE TO ACCOUNTING RESEARCH
A BEHIND THE SCENES VIEW OF USING QUALITATIVE RESEARCH METHODS

EDITED BY

CHRISTOPHER HUMPHREY

Manchester School of Accounting & Finance, University Manchester, UK

BILL LEE

Sheffield University Management School, Sheffield, UK

ELSEVIER

AMSTERDAM • BOSTON • HEIDELBERG • LONDON
NEW YORK • OXFORD • PARIS • SAN DIEGO
SAN FRANCISCO • SINGAPORE • SYDNEY • TOKYO

CIMA Publishing is an imprint of Elsevier

PUBLISHING

CIMA Publishing is an imprint of Elsevier
Linacre House, Jordan Hill, Oxford OX2 8DP
30 Corporate Drive, Suite 400, Burlington, MA 01803, USA

First edition 2004

British Library Cataloguing in Publication Data
A catalogue record for this book is available from the British Library

ISBN   978 0 0804 8992 6

For information on all CIMA publications
visit our website at books.elsevier.com

Printed and bound in Hungary

Dedication

Thank you to those people whose lives were affected by us 'having to work' on this book, to those who came along during its preparation and changed our lives in wonderful ways and to those whose memories will always remain fond ones.

To Kendra, Cameron, Jacqueline, Cathy and the memories of Bob, Nell and Doreen.

Acknowledgements

The idea for this book first originated from a qualitative research conference held in Portsmouth in 1996. Sheena Murdoch and Bernard Williams played an important role in the conception of that conference. The conference was only able to take place because of the financial support provided by the Institute of Chartered Accountants in England and Wales (ICAEW) and the determination of the, then, secretary of the research board of the ICAEW, Des Wright. A number of people — Michelle Brooks, Mike Page, John Prescott and Pippa Wilmer — helped with the organization of the conference. The attendees at the conference gave initial impetus to the idea for this book, although some, such as our former colleague Christine Flint, are no longer here to witness its publication. The publishers and staff — particularly Sammye Haigh and Neil Boon — merit our thanks for their faith in the idea and their advice when requested. Our biggest debt, however, is to the authors — some of whom have remained with the idea of the book since the conference and others who have subsequently agreed to fill in important gaps — for contributing their chapters. We hope that the collection does justice to their thoughts and efforts.

Contents

Authors' Biographies

Thomas Ahrens Ph.D., is a Senior Lecturer in Accounting at the London School of Economics where he has been working since 1996. His research is mostly qualitative. It is broadly concerned with accounting and organisational process. Thomas has compared management accounting practices in contemporary British and German firms and studied the uses of performance measurement systems in a large U.K. restaurant chain. He has also written on comparative and case study research in accounting. Thomas' latest research project is investigating performance measurement in British and German banks. He is on the editorial board of the *European Accounting Review*.

Fiona Anderson-Gough BA, Ph.D. has a background in Philosophy and Psychology and worked for several years as a research analyst for a consultancy business, which specialised in analyses using theories and techniques from Social Psychology, before developing an academic interest and career in accounting. Her research interests are the practices of expertise and the development of knowledgeable, accountable selves particularly in the context of accounting knowledge and practices. She has worked and published in the area of professional identity, socialisation and accountancy education and training. A number of the joint research projects she has undertaken have attracted funding from the Institute of Chartered Accountants in England and Wales (ICAEW). At the time of writing the chapter in this book Fiona was a Lecturer in Accounting at Warwick Business School. She is now a Senior Lecturer in Critical Accounting and Management at the University of Leicester.

Jean Bédard Ph.D., CA is a Professor of Accounting at the Université Laval in Canada. His main research interests are in the area of auditing, internal control and audit committees. Jean is currently on the editorial advisory boards of *Contemporary Accounting Research* and the *International Journal of Auditing*.

Anthony J. Berry began his professional life in the U.K. and U.S. aircraft industry. His Ph.D., at Manchester Business School, in 1976 was based upon a case study of management control in the electricity industry. After 25 years at MBS he moved to become Professor of Management Control at Sheffield Hallam University. Tony Berry has published in a variety of research journals and has edited several volumes on Management Control with Jane Broadbent and David Otley. Tony's current research interests include cost management, risk, financial management in small firms, management control and accounting change. He is a former editor of *Management*

Education and Development and for ten years has edited the *Leadership and Organisational Development Journal.*

Frank Birkin BSc, ACMA, ARSM is a Senior Lecturer at the Management School of the University of Sheffield. His research interests include environmental accounting, social accounting and accounting for sustainable development. Frank has obtained funding from the European Union for several international research projects and has usually played a significant managerial role on them.

Jane Broadbent BA, MA, Ph.D., FCCA, started her career in the NHS where she qualified as an accountant, gaining experience in all aspects of NHS finance. In 1981 she returned to full-time education completing a first degree in sociology as a mature student at the University of York. Jane held posts at Leeds Polytechnic and the Universities of Sheffield and Essex before being appointed as Professor of Accounting at Royal Holloway, University of London in 1997. During her time at Royal Holloway she has served as Dean of History and Social Sciences before taking the post of Vice-Principal (Academic Affairs) in 2002. Jane has a wide range of refereed publications aligned to management and accounting change in the public sector and methodological issues and is joint editor of three books, two of which are in the area of management control, the third relating to the changing role of the professions. Her research has attracted external funding from bodies such as the ESRC and CIMA. She is the Associate Editor of *Public Money and Management* and an editorial board number on other international journals.

John Burns Ph.D. is a Senior Lecturer in Management Accounting at the Manchester School of Accounting and Finance, having also previously been an Associate Professor at the University of Colorado (Denver). His main research interests are in the areas of changing management accounting practices, the roles of accountants in business, and institutional theories. He is an Associate Editor of *Management Accounting Research.*

Catherine Cassell Ph.D., C.Psychol. is a Professor of Organizational Psychology and Director of Research at the University of Sheffield Management School. She is also a Chartered Occupational Psychologist. Cathy's research interests are in the area of organizational change and development. She also retains an ongoing interest in issues of research methodology, particularly in relation to the use of qualitative methods in organizational and management research, where she has collaborated and published widely with Gillian Symon over many years.

Harry Collins is Distinguished Research Professor of Sociology and Director of the Centre for the Study of Knowledge, Expertise and Science (KES) at Cardiff University. His main research area is the sociology of scientific knowledge, publishing *Changing Order: Replication and Induction in Scientific Practice* in 1985 (2nd edition 1992) and with Trevor Pinch, a popular series about science and technology which so far has two volumes *The Golem: What you should know about Science* and *The Golem at Large: What you should know about Technology.* He has worked on the nature of artificial intelligence, publishing two books on the topic: *Artificial Experts: Social Knowledge and Intelligent Machine* (1990) and, with Martin Kusch, *The Shape of Actions: What Humans and Machines Can Do* (1998). In 2001 University of Chicago Press published his co-edited (with Jay Labinger) book, *The One Culture?: A Conversation about Science*. This is a debate between scientists and social scientists about the nature of science. His pioneering work has won a number of academic prizes and his latest text comes out in 2004, when the University of Chicago Press will publish his monograph, *Gravity's Shadow: The Search for Gravitational Waves*.

John Cullen is Professor of Management Accounting at Sheffield Hallam University and is a Fellow of the Chartered Institute of Management Accountants. His main research interests are in the area of supply chain accounting, management control, corporate governance and accounting education. John's research is mainly case study based and has focused on both small and large organisations in the public and private sectors. He actively uses case studies in his teaching, which covers a range of undergraduate, postgraduate, professional and management development programmes. John is on the Executive of the Committee of the Heads of Accounting. He is also a Subject Specialist Reviewer for the QAA and is involved in accreditation reviews for the Chartered Institute of Management Accountants.

Kevin Dowd BA, MA, Ph.D., is Professor of Financial Risk Management at Nottingham University Business School. He taught previously at Sheffield Hallam University and the University of Sheffield. His research interests are in risk management, financial and monetary economics, and political economy.

Masaya Fujita Ph.D. (Econ.) is a Professor at the Graduate School of Economics, Kyushu University, Japan. He is interested in the epistemology of accounting and the methodology of accounting theory. He has recently published related work in *Critical Perspectives on Accounting*.

María Antonia García-Benau Ph.D. is a Professor of Accounting at the University of Valencia, Spain. Her main research interests are in the areas of auditing and international accounting. Her work has been published in several international accounting research journals including the *European Accounting Review, Accounting History* and the *International Journal of Accounting*.

Yves Gendron Ph.D., CA is Professor of Accounting at the University of Alberta, Canada. Most of his research focuses on the examination of auditing-related phenomena, informed by sociological perspectives of analysis. Yves is particularly interested in developing a better understanding of the ways in which professional work is carried out in actual practice and the process by which professional work is legitimized in the eyes of relevant audiences. Yves has published his work in research journals such as *Accounting, Auditing & Accountability Journal, Accounting Organizations and Society, Auditing: A Journal of Practice & Theory, Contemporary Accounting Research* and *Critical Perspectives on Accounting*.

Rob Gray BSc (Econ.), MA (Econ.), FCA, FCCA is Professor of Accounting and Director of the Centre for Social and Environmental Accounting Research at the University of Glasgow. He is a qualified chartered accountant, editor of *Social and Environmental Accounting Journal* and joint editor of the *BAR Research Register*. He has published extensively in the areas of social and environmental accounting, sustainability, social responsibility and education. His books include *Accounting for the Environment*; *Financial Accounting: Practice and Principles* and *Accounting and Accountability: Changes and Challenges in Corporate Social and Environmental Reporting*. He is a member of numerous editorial boards and, in 2001, was chosen as the British Accounting Association's Distinguished Academic Fellow.

James Guthrie held posts at the University of New South Wales and Deakin University prior to taking up his Professorship at the Macquarie Graduate School of Management, Sydney, Australia in 1995. For the past 16 years James has been joint founding editor of the international research journal, *Accounting, Auditing and Accountability Journal*. Together with Lee Parker, he was awarded Editor of the Year in 1993 and 2001 and received the quality award of Leading Editor for MCB University Press in 1994. James is on the editorial board of numerous international research journals and was awarded the prestigious Chartered Institute of Management Accountants (CIMA) Research Foundation International Visiting Professorship for 2000. He has published in a wide range of refereed and professional journals and has co-edited six public sector management and accounting books.

Treasa Hayes DPA, BA, B.Comm M.Litt, Ph.D. is a Lecturer in Organisation Theory and Management in Dublin City University Business School. Before taking up her academic post, she worked as a management consultant. Her current research interests include: management in third sector/voluntary organisations; corporate social responsibility; the learning organisation and knowledge management.

John Holland BSc, MBA, Ph.D. is a Professor of Finance at Glasgow University in the Department of Accounting and Finance. His main research interests are in the areas of corporate disclosure, intangibles, corporate governance, fund management and banking.

Joanne Horton Ph.D. studied at the University of Wales, Aberystwyth where she gained her Ph.D. degree for research into changes in life assurance accounting and subsequently became a Lecturer in Accounting. After experience with KPMG in London she was appointed as a Lecturer in Accounting at Bristol University before moving to the London School of Economics. Her main research interests relate to financial reporting and financial institutions.

Christopher Humphrey B.Com, MA (Econ.), Ph.D., ACA is a Professor of Accounting and currently Head of School at the Manchester School of Accounting and Finance. His main research interests are in the areas of auditing, public sector financial management and accounting education. He is an associate editor of the *European Accounting Review* and is on the editorial advisory boards of a number of other academic accounting journals.

Yoshiaki Jinnai is a Professor of Accounting at the Department of Business Administration, Tokyo Keizai University, Japan. His main research interests are in the areas of methodology of accounting theory, financial reporting and the history of accounting. He is a managing director of the Japan Society for the Social Science of Accounting and is on the editorial boards of *Critical Perspectives on Accounting* and the *Pacific Accounting Review*.

Naoko Komori is an Associate Professor in the Faculty of Economics, University of Wakayama, Japan and a part-time doctoral student at the University of Sheffield Management School. Her main research interests are in the areas of gender and accounting, the social significance of the accounting profession and the comparative role of accounting in private and public spheres.

José Antonio Laínez-Gadea Ph.D. is a Professor of Accounting at the University of Zaragoza, Spain and currently the head of the Department of Accounting and Finance in the Faculty of Economics and Business Studies. His main research interests are in the areas of financial reporting, accounting and capital markets and international accounting. He has published in several international accounting research journals including *The International Journal of Accounting*.

Irvine Lapsley B.Com., Ph.D., CA is Professor of Accounting and Director of the Institute of Public Sector Accounting Research at the University of Edinburgh Management School. He is also Head of the Management School. He is editor of *Financial Accountability and Management*, and is on the editorial board of other leading accounting journals in the UK, USA and Australia. He is a co-chair of the EIASM's Third Sector Workshop and of its Public Sector Conference. He is interested in all aspects of the public sector and has undertaken externally funded research sponsored by the ESRC, CIMA, ICAS, Leverhulme and Nuffield, into health care, local and central government.

Richard Laughlin M.Soc.Sc., Ph.D., FCA, FRSA worked in professional accounting practice and as a consultant accountant before joining the University of Sheffield in 1973. He left Sheffield to join the University of Essex in 1995 before moving to his current position as Professor of Accounting in The Management Centre at King's College, University of London in 1999 where he has been Head of Department until recently. Richard's numerous publications in accounting, management, organisation and political science refereed journals and books relate to methodological issues and to enhancing understanding of the organisational and human effects of changes in accounting, finance and management systems. His research projects have received external sponsorship from bodies such as the ESRC and CIMA. Richard is Associate Editor of the *Accounting, Auditing and Accountability Journal* and on the editorial board of a number of other international journals.

Bill Lee BSc, Ph.D., F.I. Manf. is a Lecturer in Accounting and Financial Management at the University of Sheffield Management School. His publications cover issues in auditing, accounting education and the relationship between accounting and technological change. His current research interests include the role of accounting in local exchange and trading schemes and the financing of vocational training initiatives.

Tom Lee MSc, D.Litt, CA, CIT is Professor Emeritus of Accountancy at the University of Alabama following his retirement as Culverhouse Endowed Chair of Accountancy and State of Alabama Endowed Scholar in Accountancy in 2001. He received the university's premiere award for scholarship, the Burnum Distinguished Faculty Award, in 1997 and headed its doctoral programme in accountancy from 1991 until his retirement. He was previously Professor of Accountancy and Finance and head of the

Department of Accounting and Business Method at the University of Edinburgh and Professor of Accountancy at the University of Liverpool. Tom is a chartered accountant and graduate of the University of Strathclyde. He specializes in corporate financial reporting and auditing research, with particular reference to income and cash flow accounting, corporate auditing, and the sociology and history of the public accountancy profession. He has published extensively in both academic and professional arenas. He has held various professional appointments in the United Kingdom and the United States including the director of accounting and auditing at ICAS, president of the Academy of Accounting Historians, and editorial board membership on a number of leading research journals.

Anne Loft Ph.D. is a Professor of Auditing at the Copenhagen Business School in Denmark and part-time Professor of Accounting at Lund University in Sweden. Her main research interests are in the following areas: the globalisation of the accountancy profession and global trade in accounting services, the regulation of auditors, gender in accounting and the history of accounting in the twentieth century. She is on the editorial board of a number of academic journals including *Accounting, Organizations and Society* and for nine years served as the joint founding editor of *European Accounting Review*. Anne frequently participates as faculty in international doctoral workshops and organises doctoral courses.

Kari Lukka Ph.D. is a Professor of Accounting at the Turku School of Economics and Business Administration, Finland. Kari's research interests as well as his international publication record cover a wide range of topics in management accounting, accounting theory and research methodology. He is currently the Editor of *European Accounting Review* and a Professor at the EIASM. Within that context, Kari organizes and chairs, jointly with Michael Shields, the biannual conference on *New Directions in Management Accounting* and is the coordinator and faculty member of the EDEN doctoral course on *Case-based Research in Management Accounting*. He also co-edited, jointly with Tom Groot, a leading book on *Cases in Management Accounting: Current Practices in European Companies* (2000).

Richard Macve MA, MSc, FCA Hon, FIA is Professor of Accounting at the London School of Economics and Honorary Visiting Professor of Accounting at the University of Wales, Aberystwyth. He has been a Council Member of the ICAEW and is Academic Advisor to the ICAEW's Centre for Business Performance. His main research interests relate to the conceptual framework of financial accounting and reporting, financial reporting in the insurance industry and the historical development of accounting.

David E. W. Marginson BA, MA, Ph.D. Lectures in Management Accounting and Control at the Manchester School of Management, UMIST. His main research interests include: the relationship between management control systems and the strategy process, modern methods of management control, management control and media selection, the psychology of management control, and empowerment and accountability.

Ruth Mattimoe B.A.(Mod.), Dip. Stats., FCA, Ph.D. is a Lecturer in Management Accounting and Financial Statement Analysis at Dublin City University Business School. A science graduate, she qualified as a chartered accountant with Price

Waterhouse Cooper in Dublin, obtaining second place in Ireland in the Professional Two examination of the Institute of Chartered Accountants in Ireland (ICAI). Having worked as a management accountant in the electronics industry, she entered academic life and recently completed her Ph.D. at the Manchester School of Accounting and Finance. Her main research interests include pricing and marketing in the hotel and tourism sector, accounting issues in service industries, institutional economics and data analysis for executives. She is a former Examiner and Author for the Professional Two and Three examinations of the ICAI.

Brendan McSweeney B.Comm, Ph.D., FRSA is Professor of Management, Royal Holloway, University of London. Prior to that appointment he was Professor of Accounting and Director of Research at the Department of Accounting, Finance & Management, University of Essex. Before he became an academic he had a variety of jobs including railway porter, trade union official, and director of a venture capital organisation. He has published articles in a wide variety of scholarly journals including: *Accounting, Organizations & Society, Human Relations, Journal of International Business Studies*, and *The Political Quarterly*. He is a member of the editorial board of *Organization Studies* and of the advisory board of a major Japanese company.

Brendan O'Dwyer B.Comm, MBS, DPA, Ph.D., ACA is College Lecturer in Accountancy at the Michael Smurfit Graduate School of Business, University College Dublin and, currently, the Director of its Accounting Master's programme. He holds a Ph.D. in Accounting from the University of Dundee. Brendan's main research interests encompass: corporate social accountability; social and ethical accounting and reporting; corporate governance, professional ethics; audit education; and qualitative research methods. His work has been published in a number of international accounting research journals. He is a member of the editorial board of *Accounting, Auditing and Accountability Journal* and a Founding Fellow of the Institute of Social Auditors in Ireland. He is also a member of the judging panels for the ACCA Irish and European Sustainability reporting awards schemes. Prior to entering academia, Brendan worked as a chartered accountant with Ernst and Young in Dublin.

David T. Otley MA, M.Tech, Ph.D., FBAM is Professor of Accounting and Management and associate dean for resources at Lancaster University Management School. His research interests have centred on issues of management control, management accounting and performance measurement. He has been a consistent user of case-based research methods and published extensively, both in international research journals and in book form. He was the founding editor of the British Journal of Management and is on the editorial board of several other international accounting and management journals. He has made a very extensive contribution to the last three Research Assessment Exercises (RAE's) in the U.K., including chairing the Accounting and Finance assessment panel for RAE 2001. In 2002, he was elected the British Accounting Association Distinguished Academic Fellow. He is also a management board member of the ICAEW's Centre for Business Performance and, was the director of the Accounting and Finance doctoral programme at Lancaster.

David Owen is Professor of Social and Environmental Accounting at Nottingham University Business School. He has previously taught at the universities of Huddersfield, Salford, Manchester, Leeds and Sheffield. Dave's main research interests lie in the field of social and environmental accounting, auditing and reporting. He has written extensively on social investment, corporate social audit, corporate social and environmental disclosure practice and social and environmental accounting education. His most recent work has focused on corporate capture of the 'sustainability' agenda and the appropriation of its potential radical edge by managerial interests. Dave is an associate editor of the *British Accounting Review* and is on the editorial boards of several leading journals. He is also an Associate Director of the Centre for Social and Environmental Accounting Research at the University of Glasgow and has been a member of the short-listing and judging panels for the Association of Chartered Certified Accountants Environmental and Sustainability Awards Scheme since its inception in 1991. He is a co-author of the leading texts *Corporate Social Reporting: Accounting and Accountability (1987)* and *Accounting and Accountability: Changes and Challenges in Corporate Social and Environmental Reporting (1996).*

Lee D. Parker BEC, M.Phil, Ph.D., FCA, FCPA, FAIM is Professor of Commerce and Associate Dean (Research) in the School of Commerce at Adelaide University, South Australia. Prior to this he held positions at the Universities of Glasgow, Dundee, Monash, Griffith and Flinders. He has published widely on management and accounting issues. Lee is joint founding editor of the international research journal *Accounting, Auditing and Accountability Journal* and serves on numerous other journal editorial boards. He is also a founding Fellow of the Centre for Social and Environmental Accounting Research at the University of Glasgow (Scotland) and was an international advisor to the Accountancy Panel for the 1996 and 2001 British universities' Research Assessment Exercises. Lee is past president of the Academy of Accounting Historians (USA) and the American Accounting Association Public Interest section. He teaches in strategic management, international management, management accounting and auditing and his research interests include strategic management, public/non-profit sector management and accounting, corporate governance, social and environmental accountability, and accounting and management history.

Sue Richardson BA is a Lecturer in Accounting and Financial Management at Sheffield University Management School. Her main research interests are in the areas of smaller business governance, accounting and change in the public sector, and accounting education. Sue was recently appointed as an assessor for the Association of Chartered Certified Accountants.

Alan Sangster BA, MSc, Cert TESOL, CA is a Professor of Accounting and currently Head of Department at the Open University Business School. His main research interests are in the areas of accounting education and accounting systems. He is a past chair of the Artifical Intelligence/Emerging Technologies section of the American Accounting Association. He has published widely and is an active reviewer for, and member of the editorial boards of, a number of academic research journals.

Robert W. Scapens Ph.D., MA (Econ.), FCA is Professor of Accounting at the University of Manchester. He is also a visiting professor at the University of Groningen in the Netherlands. He has published 15 books and numerous papers on various aspects of accounting and, especially, management accounting. He has also written extensively on research methodology and on methods of case research. He is the Editor-in-chief of *Management Accounting Research* and has extensive experience of research into various aspects of management accounting theory and practice — based primarily on case study research. In addition, he has supervised a substantial number of doctoral students who have conducted case studies in their own research, and he has lectured in many countries on doing case study research. He is one of the authors (together with R. J. Ryan and M. Theobald) of the successful book entitled *Research Methods and Methodology in Accounting and Finance*, the second edition of which was published by Thomson in 2002.

Greg Stoner BSc, FCA is a Lecturer in Accounting and Information Systems at the University of Glasgow. In addition to his research interests in the use and flows of information and the use of qualitative research methodologies Greg has a long established practical and research-oriented involvement in the application of information technology in education.

Geert Struyven MBA, Ph.D., ACA studied in Belgium and at the University of Wales, Aberystwyth where he gained his Ph.D. degree for research into changes in insurance accounting in the European Union and became a Lecturer in Accounting. He qualified as a chartered accountant with Arthur Andersen and is now Director, Corporate Finance with BDO Stoy Hayward.

Gillian Symon Ph.D., C.Psychol. is Senior Lecturer in Organizational Psychology in the Department of Organizational Psychology, Birkbeck College, University of London. Her main research interests lie in the areas of technological change at work and research practice. She and Catherine Cassell have collaborated over many years in producing articles, book chapters and conference papers that challenge traditional research practices in their discipline and seek to encourage both reflexivity in research and the use of innovative research methods.

Stuart Turley MA(Econ.), CA is the KPMG Professor of Accounting at the University of Manchester. He is also currently an academic member of the Auditing Practices Board for the U.K. and Ireland. His research interests include contemporary developments in audit methodologies, the role and impact of audit committees and the international development of the auditing and accounting profession.

David E. Tyrrall MSc, MA, FCMA, FCCA is a Lecturer in Accounting at Cass Business School, City University, London. His main research interests are in the areas of accounting, organisations and economics.

Stephen P. Walker BA, Ph.D., CA is a Professor of Accounting and member of the Accounting and Business History Research Unit at Cardiff Business School. His main research interests are in accounting history. Specifically, the history of: the accountancy profession; accounting in social institutions; accounting and gender; and accounting and trade associations. He is currently editor of *The Accounting Historians Journal*. He is also on the editorial boards of a number of academic journals and is a member of the Research Committee of the Institute of Chartered Accountants of Scotland.

Introduction

The first thing that we need to do in this book is to explain why it was considered necessary and how we came to be its editors. As with many of the projects reported in the book, the book's history has not been straightforward. We first met each other in the process of co-organising an Institute of Chartered Accountants in England and Wales' (ICAEW) sponsored conference entitled *Beneath the Numbers: Reflections on the Use of Qualitative Methods in Accounting Research*, held at Portsmouth Business School in 1996. The conference provided a unique forum for the exploration and understanding of a wide range of experiential issues that had arisen from the growing application of qualitative approaches in accounting research. A large number of delegates expressed the need for a book that shared the objectives of the conference and provided a practical guide that could be used in the course of the 'real life' research process.

Impressed by the response to the conference, we made the commitment to pursue the possibility of a book. Originally this was going to be something very simple, such as a ring-bound compilation of the various papers presented at the conference. However, people started to suggest that such a book could be something rather more significant and encouraged us to move from a quick and cheap reproduction format to pursuing a proper book contract with an international publisher. The envisaged book's contents were felt to be deserving of a wider audience.

While it was nice (and motivating) to receive compliments, securing a book contract and putting together a contents package that suited an international publisher did not prove to be that simple. Why did we want to just cover qualitative research, rather than including quantitative research as well? Why were we not just using the work and reflections of high-profile, senior academics? Were we simply reproducing conference papers that could not be published elsewhere? Was this a legitimate dimension of academic research, having people talk about doing research? Was the subject matter credible? Were we credible editors? What was the market and likely sales forecasts for the book? And possibly the most difficult hurdle to overcome — were we really asking people to write about their qualitative research experiences in accounting! Now there might be an interest in qualitative research in sociology or social policy but accounting, a book providing a behind-the-scenes view of qualitative research in accounting? What would that amount to and who would be interested in it? Would it be discussions over how to do double-entry bookkeeping, or how to ask questions of the payroll clerk or other accounting officers, or how someone came to write their masterpiece on the different available methods of depreciation or accounting for fixed assets? Maybe such behind the scenes stuff was best left unspoken — rather than being brought front stage in a reflective research methods book?

We did not accept some of the scepticism expressed by an initial group of publishing houses. We were well aware that the increasing relevance of accounting to a wide range of social and organisational contexts had led to accounting research becoming increasingly interdisciplinary with recognition being given to the insights that such research may bring to, and gain from, fields such as Business Studies, Management, Sociology, Social Policy, Politics, Public Administration, and Social Anthropology. We knew that as accounting researchers had widened their focus beyond the direct construction of accounting techniques, there had been a greater emphasis on qualitative research. Accountants were seeking understanding of the organisational, social and political roles and influences of accounting practice. Articles could easily be found in journals such as *Accounting, Organizations and Society*, *Accounting, Auditing and Accountability Journal*, *Critical Perspectives in Accounting*, and *European Accounting Review* questioning traditionally accepted histories of, and standpoints on, accounting development.

We continued to pursue the idea of a book that could serve as a practical and intellectual companion for those undertaking research on the role of accounting in organisations and society, particularly one that offered some unique insights into the rarely discussed practical, day-to-day world of accounting research. Accordingly, we were delighted when Elsevier stepped in with a serious offer of interest. The initial conference had generated a considerable amount of excitement and now we had the chance both to capture that and to develop a number of ideas first raised there. We still had a long way to go, however, from an initial expression of contractual interest to securing the contract and then producing the final manuscript.

One big issue was that we had to meet book reviewers' fears that the inner-thoughts (if not ramblings) of accounting academics would not have much credibility if such academics were not already famous and were only from the U.K. But famous, international academics are often very busy and are they going to want potentially to put at risk their reputations by talking candidly about the realities of the research process — potentially demystifying it and revealing inner dilemmas and worries about their own work? Why disrupt a process that has served them well? At the same time, there was the danger that if we excluded researchers drawn from the junior end of the academic community, we would be selling out on the original ideas and motivations for the project by effectively providing a voice-piece for the senior 'men in suits' who are supposed to control editorial processes and much of the way in which academic knowledge develops in the subject area.

Fortunately, we were able to arrive at a nice balance between senior and junior staff and between U.K. and international academics and to get people who were fully signed up to the importance of talking more about the accounting research process and the nature of accounting knowledge. We have also managed to attract authors from the disciplines of economics, sociology and psychology to help put the experience of accounting researchers using qualitative research methods into a broader context.

So with the book contract signed and the contents agreed in outline, what, in more detailed terms was it really going to say? What is it all about? Although the title of the book may suggest that it is about a particular ontological position — i.e. that of realism — our intention was neither to nail our flags to a particular philosophical mast, nor to regurgitate philosophical debates that could be found elsewhere. Our main motivation was to try to do something that was different and fresh in discussions of accounting research methodology. Many methodological texts provide standard, almost acontextual, descriptions of the various available research methods and tools, but with limited exceptions they usually give you very little nitty-gritty, practical advice on how to do a case study or how to respond to unanticipated events in the course of a research project. It is one thing, so to speak, to know the 'highway code' — it is another to be able to drive a car. We were also struck by how often people's advice on how to obtain an external research grant appeared overly formulaic and deterministic — make sure that your chosen methodology is the 'right' one and that it allows the chosen research questions 'to be answered'. It is perhaps not surprising that methodology chapters in postgraduate dissertations and theses are often the most formal, if not staid and boring — providing some general, almost official, descriptions of qualitative and quantitative research methods and their relative strengths and weaknesses.

Accordingly, we have sought to produce an edited collection which moves beyond dry, abstract outlines of research methods, and seeks to bring research methodology to life, by giving insights into the motivations and disappointments, concerns and interests, triumphs and failings, disappointments and joys of the researcher. We wanted the book to contain a wide range of original, 'real life' accounts of **what is accounting research**, rather than the simple typical prescriptive accounts of **what research should be**.

We were also aware of a frequently acknowledged lack of confidence in the mechanisms for doing such work. Or what we labelled as the 'we're not worthy' syndrome seemingly embedded in qualitative researchers. Classic worry number one — case studies are interesting but they are not academic. They are more like journalism than legitimate academic research. Indeed, academic accounting research should contain more numbers and calculations, it shouldn't just be a load of quotes and narrative. Classic worry number two — case studies do not add to knowledge. They provide a nice story but not a representative one. They simply provide a one-off anecdotal event that is not generalisable, too descriptive and either short on theory or they use a whole bundle of theories to make false claims about the international relevance of the case. Classic worry number three — case studies are too difficult and too hard to get published or to merit the award of a doctorate, that they are not worth the risk. Its better to do something quantitative, like working with databases of stock prices. At least then you don't have worries of access or of the organisation being researched trying to control what you write.

Across all these worries, there can be a seeming unwillingness or reluctance to talk about methodological issues. Indeed, such concerns could be used as a way of preventing discussion of research issues, of putting someone in their place. How does a supervisor stop a doctoral student from bothering them — just ask the student what is their theoretical perspective? In what way are they going to contribute to existing accounting knowledge? 'Come back and see me when you have sorted it out'.

Methodological issues almost assume a sense of mystery and illusiveness. Sorting out your methodological concerns can become a rite of passage through which doctoral students and young accounting academic staff have to pass before they may be regarded as fully-fledged academics. As one supervisor-student conversation went: Supervisor — 'I have been thinking about your research project and how to address the issues in which you are interested and I have cracked it'. 'Great' said the inquiring student, 'what do I do'. 'Ah well' said the supervisor, 'that is for you to find out. It is your thesis not mine'.

For those students and staff who choose to stick with a qualitative research project, there are a whole number of hoops and hurdles through and over which they will have to jump. There is the literature that has to be identified, assimilated and ultimately mastered. This can be quite daunting, both in terms of the sheer volume of what to read and also when to decide that you have read enough and when it is time to go out in the field. Subsequently, you have to decide what sort of research access that you have to secure or negotiate. What do you need to survey or consult? Whom do you need to interview or seek opinions from? What questions are you going to ask of yourself or to other people? Are you going to get exposed for not knowing enough? Are you going to get caught out by an unanticipated comment or request when the research subject stops answering questions and starts questioning you? At some subsequent point in time, you have to decide that you have done enough fieldwork but how do you determine that? When do you know when to stop reading or interviewing and when to start writing? And then when to stop writing? Is a Ph.D. thesis judged on weight or content quality? Will more pages help you disguise a weak study? Should you highlight weaknesses or let the external examiner dig them out? Finally, how do you get from a raw package of research interviews or even a completed doctoral thesis to an academic article? The latter can look so polished and finished that they can almost seem out of reach, written by infinitely cleverer people. What really do you need to do to get something published in a refereed journal? What is the right journal? Is a good idea sufficient? Does the methodology have to be foolproof? Have all angles been covered? How do you respond to referees' comments? Do you get angry if the comments are critical and tell the editor just how bad you feel? Or do you take it on the chin and get on with revising the paper?

Go into a bookshop and for all these questions, there is potentially some methodological text that will look like it can help to provide you with the answers. However, they often give you something in a rather more formal and hypothetical way than you really want. There is a level of detail and practicalities into which they often do not go. You can read all about the various ways and typologies for conducting an interview, yet it is one thing knowing them and another to decide when to challenge and question what someone is saying to you in an interview. Typically, texts will tell you not to be too dominating in an interview, to ask questions mainly in a neutral fashion, which neither threatens the interviewee or unduly leads them to say what you wanted them to say. There is much in that and we have both seen cases where a challenged interviewee has clammed up and basically not said anything else in the interview. However, we have also seen cases where explicit statements of belief (for example 'I do not believe that you have any moral authority to provide such a service unless you know how it has impacted upon the service recipient') have brought forth a whole series of responses (if not confessions) which would not have been forthcoming from a gentler interview style. Further, what standard methodology textbook is going to help you in dealing with an interviewee whose hairpiece starts to slide backwards, bit by bit, as they nod in response to questions or scratch their head as they think through what they want to say? Do you tell them or ignore it? Can you pull yourself away from watching the movement of the hairpiece? Can you remember the questions you wanted to ask?

Similarly, what do you do in a case study when you know that people are not telling the truth or restricting your access to key documents and meetings, when such access had been previously promised? When is the right time to walk away? What do you do when you can see that a case study is not going the way that the organisation really wanted it to go? What do you do if you find things that do not fit with the line that senior management has told you and which they expect to come out of the case? What do you do when you realise that the confidentiality clause that you have signed is going to prevent you from saying what really needs saying about the case and effectively enables the organisation to sit on your findings? What do you do when interviewees confide in you and when you feel a bond developing between the two of you? Will this make you write your research report in a different way? Will you be less critical than you would otherwise have been?

In raising these issues, we have to be very clear from the start that this book is not going to provide explicit and comprehensive answers for every problem. This is not a cookbook guide to doing qualitative research but then there has to be serious doubts as to the practical benefits that can be passed on by any cookbook approach to research. Many research skills and answers to problems can really only be learned through experience — but experience does not come quickly and there are many heartfelt incidents that some researchers will never experience but from which they could gain much in terms of understanding, research awareness and reassurance that stems from a knowledge that others have not only survived but benefited from what might initially appear as at best upsetting and at worst, insurmountable problems. This book seeks to pass on just such experiences. For instance, just some of the incidents discussed include: travelling several hundred miles only to find out that the documents that you wanted to examine had been destroyed decades before: discovering a huge hole in your logic after having conducted most of your fieldwork; and having the people who invited you to conduct an independent enquiry engaging in actions that challenge your very independence.

By encouraging the provision of what we have labelled as a behind-the-scenes view of accounting research, we have sought to get both young and established researchers talking about the things that they would not generally discuss in formal academic articles; the encounters that they have had in the research arena, the joys and frustrations, the problems and good fortune that have helped to develop and improve their research skills. In so doing, we hope to instil confidence in young researchers and help them deal with the unexpected. We also hope to raise a number of important, methodological issues in the minds of experienced researchers — using thoughts and reflections on processes and experiences that are usually left unsaid — to stimulate new research questions.

The primary intention here is to try and unpick or unpack what is often bound up as a single entity, package or achievement — the qualitative research project, the explanatory case study which looks so structured, logical and organised when it is presented in its final published form but which might have been anything but in the process of planning the project, conducting the fieldwork and writing up the main research findings. There are real dangers in trying to unpick things of beauty, trying to appreciate the complexity inherent in the deceptively simple. Finished items should be respected for what they are rather than dissected in some form of academic autopsy. There is always the risk that any 'expert' reflection on 'real life' research experiences could be regarded as self-praiseworthy lectures by the moderately able or serve to depress the reader by highlighting the sheer gap in skill between the naturally gifted and the grafter to whom little comes easily. However, overall, we believe the benefits offered by behind-the-scenes reflections and analyses far outweigh the risks involved.

It is one thing to wish to provide much needed 'real life' reflections on accounting research and to draw directly from the experiences of academics personally involved with, or connected to, the international accounting research community. It is another, and much bigger editorial task to try and bring such wishes to fruition, to identify suitable contributors and to get them to talk, in a personal way, about their research experiences. Ultimately, it is for the reader to determine how successful we have been at this task and no matter how many grand claims are made in the introduction to this book, its impact will very much depend on what people make of the thirty commissioned chapters.

In selecting authors we strove to achieve a good balance from the academic community, not only in terms of seniority with the added interdisciplinary representation discussed above, but also in terms of international composition. We also sought to ensure that we provided a good coverage of the research process and, indeed, we have chosen to structure the book so that it progresses from issues concerning the meaning of research to the general construction and management of research projects, the collection and analysis of data and the publication/dissemination of research findings. The book closes with three specific, but quite different, interdisciplinary reflections on the research process.

In determining or structuring what authors would write about, we gave everybody some basic guidelines, stressing that as much as possible, we wished them to provide: (a) candid, 'behind the scenes' accounts of the research process; and (b) some clear, salient observations on what lessons others may take from their research experiences. With each author we discussed, in some detail, the specific content of their chapter, offering them some initial suggestions as to what we felt they were best positioned to write (taking into consideration their position and experience and the other chapters that we had already commissioned, or were considering commissioning) and then agreeing a general outline. All chapters went through at least two stages of revision, following the receipt of editorial comments from the two of us. The review process was particularly important in that it not only sought to develop or tighten the internal consistency of analysis and arguments in individual chapters but enabled us to ensure as much as possible that overlaps between chapters were kept to a minimum and that important related themes were suitably developed.

As noted earlier, we anticipated that one of our key editorial tasks, given the desired tone and flavour of the book, would be to encourage contributors to talk as frankly and openly as possible about their personal experiences. In the early stages, this involved some quite basic matters, such as reminding people to write in the first person rather than referring to themselves as 'the authors' or only talking about themselves through formal citations to their published work. There was also a learning experience for some authors in having to talk more about the process of conducting their research, rather than just their formal method and the results of their work. Similarly, it was important for chapter recommendations to go beyond the standard type of practical tip (for example, use new batteries at the start of each taped interview) to more complex issues such as how to maintain fieldwork access in troublesome situations or extract information from hesitant interviewees and, even, to draw implications from commentaries that were of more practical significance than the author originally realised. In some cases, we understood that it was obviously difficult to talk too openly as their real life reflections could well become rather public exposés of awkward colleagues (unhappy, for example, that their article has not been accepted for publication in an international journal).

Initially, we had some worries that certain chapters might not turn out to be as real life as we had hoped. However, as the drafts developed, it became clear that there were many ways of looking at 'real life' issues, many possible practical suggestions to younger researchers and various problematic methodological concerns worthy of further academic debate. For instance, some authors chose to write in a chronological way, aligning their comments very closely to quite personal changes in their life as they progressed through the various stages of a Ph.D. Others wrote in a fashion more focused on a particular research project and the ways in which they try to manage day-to-day interactions in the workplace. A number of authors also chose to provide analyses (if not typologies) of certain qualitative research methods or provided the reader with a review of where the literature in a particular field had developed and what currently were the most pressing research questions. At first sight, some chapters might not seem that 'real life' but they are and reflect very much the way in which particular authors view their research discipline and frame/construct their research work. It is clear, for example, that some authors are very relaxed (almost laid back) about issues of ontology and epistemology, while for others, such issues clearly dominate how they approach a research project. Some authors appear to work very much in the gaps or interfaces between theories and elements of the accounting discipline, while others see things through a very clearly specified research agenda in their chosen field. Accordingly, 'real life' issues are both presented and reviewed very much from the research framework applied by individual authors and should not be expected to appear in any, one, standard form. This is perhaps most noticeable when considering chapters written by authors for whom English is a second language, with such chapters raising quite diverse reflections — from analyses which emphasise the significant scale of differences in research cultures and agendas to those which reveal in quite emotional ways how research is wrapped up closely with day-to-day life outside of the standard working environment. The chapters written from an interdisciplinary perspective serve a useful closing set of notes, in highlighting interesting parallels with experiences in accounting research and showing how much of what is possible in research, depends on the personal outlook and mindset of the researcher. From a range of 'real life' perspectives, it becomes apparent that the research process is full of life, diversity and real opportunities and challenges.

In summary terms, we have sought to produce a book that is neither a conventional research methods textbook, nor a routine edited collection of papers. Rather, it is an original set of contributions intended to represent a practical and thought-provoking research guide. We hope that the book will be of particular use to those already committed to the field of qualitative accounting research, although we also hope that its challenging content will be attractive to those who are just beginning to think of venturing beyond traditional quantitative methodological approaches in management and related social science disciplines.

We provide a brief introduction and overview of each of the book's five sections in order to give the reader a basic positioning in terms of content. However, it is the experiences and writings of our contributors that we hope will provide the 'real' guide for the reader as they work through the different stages of the research process. Taken together, their stories will provide personal accounts of: the trials and tribulations involved in doing research; the daily thrills and spills; the things to do and what to avoid; the dilemmas and ethical questions posed and overcome; the various modes of communicating research findings; the relationship between teaching and research and between the researcher and accounting practitioners; the perceived impact and effect of accounting research on both researchers and research subjects; and other agendas for the future. We hope that the willingness of the chapters' authors to share their experiences will appeal not only to research students, but also to established academics who want to gain a fuller understanding of such things as research projects that have outputs with which they are familiar, journals in which they have published or the commitment necessary to benefit from research opportunities offered by public practice and the professional accounting institutes. Above all, we hope you enjoy the journey!

Christopher Humphrey
Bill Lee
Editors

Section One: The Meaning of Research

When conventional books about research methods discuss the meaning of research, they tend to focus on issues of the meaning of 'truth' or the validity of data and how different ontological and epistemological traditions would lead researchers to perceive the meanings of such terms in different ways when they are attached to their research findings. In compiling this collection, we started by prioritising a different set of considerations. That is not to say that we do not accept that researchers are often asked to comment on the underlying philosophical assumptions that inform their work. What was at the forefront of our minds was a recognition that the everyday experiences of choosing and conducting a qualitative research project often involve a wider range of considerations and broader sets of meanings than the formal research traditions in which researchers choose to locate their work. We thought that prospective researchers might like to know more about the personal research experiences of people working in a qualitative research tradition and the ways in which such experiences have influenced those researchers' understanding of the research process.

In compiling this section on the meaning of research, we have chosen deliberately not to focus on ontological and epistemological debates. These can be found easily elsewhere. Instead, we have asked contributors to talk about the nature of the everyday choices and experiences involved in their research and how such choices and experiences have subsequently affected them. The chapters in this section can be divided into three general types. Firstly, there are chapters that provide an insight into the real-life environment of the work tasks and research agenda in a particular area of accounting research. Secondly, there are chapters that address the environment of research by focusing primarily on the different power relationships that people may encounter and will have to work within. Finally, there are chapters that discuss the relationship between the individual and a particular type of research project, the Ph.D. and how the project and the researcher are mutually transformed.

When deciding on an area to research, people will be confronted with a number of choices. These include whether to explore an existing area? Whether to seek to establish a new area of research? Whether to attempt to address an established area from a new perspective, or to introduce a new method for compiling data that is capable of generating new insights? Such choices will influence how they then spend a considerable part of their working life, whether reviewing a particular body of literature that addresses a specific set of issues, or employing certain types of research methods in a specific environmental context with an associated set of working conditions. The three chapters that discuss particular areas of accounting research to which qualitative research methods have been applied come from three markedly different areas of accounting research — Accounting History, Social and Environmental Accounting and Auditing, and Finance. There is a range of other areas of accounting research that we could have included, such as Management Accounting, Financial Reporting, Accounting Education or Public Sector Accounting. However, the crucial things with the chapters is not so much the chosen subject area but what the authors reveal about the nature of research and what they feel they have learned about the research process. Examining how they have approached their work, the difficulties and rewards that they have encountered along the way and assessing what had been achieved and what could still be achieved in their specialist area, each chapter gives an inside view of the way in which research agendas are shaped and offers a number of suggestions as to how to respond to and work within such agendas. In commissioning each chapter, we invited authors whose work has made important contributions to their respective areas, as we felt they would be best placed to give the type of overview and informed assessment that we were looking for.

Chapter one is by Stephen Walker who discusses the breadth of opportunities for research and publication that exists in accounting history, the types of research that exist in that field and a description of the culture, environs, methods, frustrations and satisfaction that may be encountered in the course of such research. He provides some valuable guidance as to the key values and methods that researchers must hold dear to in relation to their work. Chapter two is by David Owen, one of the pioneers of Social and Environmental Accounting and Auditing Research (SEAAR). David discusses the focus and history of SEAAR, reviewing current areas of research, the different contributions made by critical theorists and those more willing to engage in SEAAR. He also considers the extent to which academics in SEAAR have succeeded in contributing to change of companies' practices and potential areas of investigation and other advice for researchers new to the area. Chapter three is by John Holland and Greg Stoner who have been influential in introducing case studies to the area of Finance. Noting the relatively limited amount of qualitative research in Finance, especially in comparison to the areas covered by the preceding two chapters, John and Greg discuss why they chose to use case studies in an area where such methods had not been employed historically. They consider the problems that they encountered in doing such qualitative research, how these were overcome and the potential for future qualitative research in the finance arena.

John and Greg's chapter is suggestive of an unequal relationship between quantitative and qualitative research in finance. That said, there are many other ways in which unequal relationships may materialise in the course of a research project. Unequal relationships are manifest in: the relationship between traditional and new universities; the different terms and conditions experienced by permanent staff and those on fixed term contracts; the domination of different academic traditions over others in departments, journals or at research conferences; the capacity of particular people to sway journal editors or interview panels in varying ways; and the ability (or good fortune) of some people to write in their native tongue for the most prestigious journals while others have to write in a second language. Many such disadvantages can be denied, or sub-consciously downplayed, by those who benefit most from them.

In identifying contributors to discuss the ways in which disadvantages and discrimination may materialise in everyday problems, we sought researchers who had first hand experience or knowledge of such issues. Chapter four is by Tom Lee, an English academic who has spent a large part of his career working in the USA where more quantitative, positivist traditions dominate academic life and where — as in the U.K. — greater weight is given to the importance of research than is given to teaching. Tom's chapter describes how doctoral studies in the typical career path of American accountants tends to promote the adoption of quantitative research methods and the impact of the Ph.D. on future career prospects. From a context of the description of élite institutions and journals, Tom details how the primacy of research over teaching and the domination of quantitative research that may be conducted in a short period has a consequence on the education that is received daily by students, the quality of articles that are produced, the pattern of submissions to journals, publication and research strategies of academics and levels of career success. Lessons are drawn for those in Europe. Chapter five is written by two Spanish academics, María Antonia García-Benau and José Antonio Laínez Gadea. Their chapter highlights two forms of inequality. The first — which is shared by many researchers at new universities in the U.K. — is the late stage at which their institutions started to recognise research and the disadvantage at which this places them *vis-à-vis* researchers at institutions that have had a research tradition for a far longer period. The second form of inequality — which is shared by researchers from other non-English speaking countries — is the difficulty of writing for top academic journals that are all almost exclusively written in a language that is not their native tongue. María Antonia and José Antonio reflect on the level of success that they and other Spanish academics have had in the pursuit of international publications and recognition and the steps that need to be taken, both in Spain and by the wider international academic community to enable such academics to participate on equal terms.

Conducting research is always likely to have a significant impact on the individual researcher. Often, an important first major project for a new researcher is that which leads to a Ph.D. The Ph.D. provides a *rite-de-passage*, a process through which people assimilate and become competent in research methods and experts in an area of research. It is by design a formal process of transformation for researchers. Yet, in the course of this formal process, there are many (unintended and unanticipated) events and informal processes that can impact on the researcher. When identifying authors to comment on the consequences of doing a Ph.D. we sought people who would be able to tell stories packed with real life incident but who could also relate these to the formal transformation process through which many academics go and identify critical pieces of advice for students currently registered for, or contemplating undertaking, a Ph.D. We have included chapters by Anne Loft and Naoko Komori who have conducted their doctoral studies in contrasting situations. Both have striking stories to tell. Unlike many U.K. undergraduates, Anne commenced her doctoral studies after deciding to stop training as a Chartered Accountant. Her love for the British Library helped her to avoid a bomb attack in London and she ended up having some of her doctoral work published in *Accounting, Organizations and Society*, with the article being cited extensively ever since. Naoko, like many doctoral students, came from overseas to study for her Ph.D. in England. She also has published work from her thesis and, like Anne, also encountered many ups and downs during her doctoral studies. Naoko had to overcome some striking cultural differences in studying as a Japanese student in the U.K. and conducting fieldwork in Japan as a student from a British University. She also has had to overcome a serious car accident in Japan and her story is very much of the inter-relationship between the Ph.D. process and one's everyday life and personal beliefs.

Anne's chapter describes how her thesis evolved from an intention to explore processes of accounting for research and development expenditure to a study in accounting history, involving the application of the ideas of Michel Foucault to an examination of the increasing significance of cost accounting during the First World War and its immediate aftermath. In describing her sojourn, Anne's chapter highlights how the formal process of writing a Ph.D. that builds on extant work and ideas interacts with the relationships that exists with senior members of the academic community into which the doctoral student is being socialised, student peers with whom many experiences are shared and one's own self. One of the notable dimensions of Anne's tale — although a whole lot more common than is often acknowledged — is that the process of generating knowledge in a particular way is often dependent on the chance everyday events affecting the personal history of the researcher. In Anne's case, these included a broken relationship, a letter to a professor not yet known, a reluctance to take a particular day off work and a comment at an academic presentation or from a fellow doctoral student. Naoko's doctoral research is about gender relations in accounting in Japan. Her chapter identifies how studying for a Ph.D. helped to transform her life in terms of leading her to learn about different cultures and to view her own, national, culture in a different light. She explores how she sought to develop her knowledge and understanding in her chosen subject area and the particular importance of critical thinking and persistence. Her chapter illustrates the very unexpected ways in which a doctoral project, and associated lifestyle, can change — and, in the case of her car accident, almost cease. She discusses the importance of viewing and trying to understand gender and other cultural relations from different perspectives and the need to recognise a clear interaction between work and social life, whether in the Japanese accounting profession or in the day-to-day experiences of a doctoral student. Naoko also shows how her research has provided an important *raison d'etre* at critical stages of her life and the key lessons she has learned, to date, with respect to undertaking and seeking to complete her Ph.D.

Chapter 1

The Search for Clues in Accounting History

Stephen P. Walker

Introduction

History is fundamental to an understanding of accounting. The practices and issues of today inevitably have a past. Our comprehension of that past can colour the formulation of research questions, the application of appropriate methodologies and the interpretation of results. Some form of historical context is likely to feature in most types of accounting research — it is usually found in an early chapter of a Ph.D. thesis. This chapter focuses on the work of those who pursue historical research as their principal activity and seek to publish in that field, that is, the practitioners of accounting history. In particular it examines the practice of data collection in the archive — the activity which most distinguishes historians from other researchers in accounting.

In recent years history has come to feature prominently in the canon of accounting research. Accounting history flourishes as a sub-discipline in its own right and offers considerable opportunities for new entrants to the field. As the authors of one introduction to the subject have stated: "The greatest appeal of accounting history research, aside from its general interest to those who do it, lies in the substantial possibility for publication that exists in a plethora of journal outlets" (Fleischman *et al.* 1996). There are currently three journals devoted to the specialism: *The Accounting Historians Journal* (which commenced in 1974 and is the publication of The Academy of Accounting Historians), *Accounting, Business and Financial History* (1990) and *Accounting History* (NS 1996). Journals in business, management, financial and economic history are also outlets for the fruits of accounting history research. In addition, the mainstream accounting journals (and those in other specialisms) also periodically publish special issues on historical themes (most recently *Accounting, Organizations and Society* (1991); *Accounting, Auditing and Accountability Journal* (1996); *Critical Perspectives on Accounting* (1998) and *European Accounting Review* (2002)). These journals also contain accounting history papers outside of thematic numbers.

The Real Life Guide to Accounting Research: A Behind-the-Scenes View of Using Qualitative Research Methods
Copyright © 2004 by Elsevier Ltd.
All rights of reproduction in any form reserved.
ISBN: 0-08-043972-1

The growth of research in this area is reflected in the numerous gatherings of accounting historians. An annual conference at Cardiff Business School is associated with *Accounting, Business and Financial History.* A biennial international conference is convened under the auspices of *Accounting History.* The Academy of Accounting Historians organises an annual research conference in the USA and a World Congress of Accounting Historians every four years. There is an annual conference on accounting and management history in France and the EIASM convenes workshops on the history of accounting and management practice. Accounting history features also at national and international accounting conferences as well as gatherings which focus on interdisciplinary and critical perspectives on accounting. It has been known for some professional organisations to encourage historical research. Most notably, ICAS has supported accounting history research projects since 1971 and published a number of books and monographs on the subject.

The subjects that accounting historians research are potentially as broad as accounting itself. Characterised by their study of the past, accounting historians are not usually classified according to their interest in particular sub-disciplines such as management accounting, financial accounting, auditing, public sector accounting, international accounting, or the accountancy profession. Neither do they wear the commonplace badges usually applied to historians based on periodisation, such as 'modernist' or 'medievalist'. While, most accounting historians inevitably specialise, the labels which attach to them tend to echo their positioning in debates about the nature and direction of historical research. Hence, there are a number of entangled descriptors and identities which serve as emblems proudly worn (sometimes temporarily) or sources of disparagement. These include 'new' or 'traditional' accounting historian, armchair theorist, antiquarian, archival historian, 'critical' historian and 'con-textualiser'. An additional level of classification is often introduced where the historian is motivated by the work of a particular social philosopher and designations can also be earned (often to the surprise of their recipient) by the appearance of published output in certain accounting journals. Such designations reflect divergent notions of the purpose and conduct of historical research in accounting and these are expressed in lively discussion of accounting historiography and methodology. However, it would be useful for those new to accounting history to convey something of the subject-themes which are in vogue. In this we may refer to recent papers which have surveyed the field of accounting history scholarship.

A major landmark in the passage of time usually has an energising effect on historians as well as the audiences for their work. During the late 1990s the impending dawn of both a new century and a new millennium offered irresistible encouragement to some notable accounting historians to reflect on the state of the discipline and muse about its future. Carnegie & Napier (1996) suggested a number of research directions and approaches, many of which were contiguous with themes articulated by earlier writers (Previts *et al.* 1990). These include studies of the history of accounting in (corporate and non-corporate) business organisations (to analyse accounting practices, policies and the diverse uses made of accounting information); contextualised biographical and collective biographical studies (of persons involved in professionalisation, the development of accounting thought, practice and its regulation); critical histories of accounting institutions (such as professional organisations, accountancy firms and regulatory authorities); histories of accounting in the public sector (particularly in local and central government); comparative international accounting history (explanations for cross-national variations and the diffusion of accounting practices and institutional structures); and the exploration of innovative research methods (oral history).

An analysis of articles published in these areas in the three specialist accounting history journals is provided in Carnegie & Potter (2000). The year 2000 also marked the 25th anniversary of *Accounting, Organizations and Society*. During a conference to celebrate that event Napier (2000) presented a most insightful assessment of the state of 'new' accounting history. In this he identified the following principal themes: histories of 'accounting, power and knowledge', 'the accountant and the lure of profession-alization' and histories of the 'fundamentals of financial reporting'.

Parker (1999) also discussed the state of accounting history, and future research directions and approaches. He is one of a number of scholars who has urged the reassertion of narrative in history (Funnell 1998) — encouraging an approach to research and writing which not only seeks to describe past events but also to interpret and explain them in innovative and engaging ways. Parker calls for further 'critical' studies which draw on manifold theoretical approaches to reveal the multifaceted nature and richness of accounting in history. He also encourages social histories which uncover the operation and impacts of accounting in the everyday and on dispossessed groups; and, the use of oral and visual history to capture the experiences of the persons who practiced accounting at various levels and those who were affected by it. Carnegie, Napier and Parker's retrospective and prospective papers on accounting history themes concede that these foci are by no means exhaustive. The annual listings of (English language) publications in accounting history printed in *Accounting, Business and Financial History, Accounting History* and *The Accounting Historians' Notebook* (and in *Business History*) attest to the plurality of subjects and approaches. Ongoing research activity in U.K. accounting history can also be identified from entries in the index of *The British Accounting Review Research Register*, published biennially.

As the foregoing suggests, when compared to practitioners of the wider craft of history, accounting historians expend considerable effort discussing the merits and demerits of different approaches to historical research, analysing publication outputs, and reflecting on the state and direction of the discipline and its relationship to other branches of history, especially business history (see, for example, the papers in *Critical Perspectives on Accounting* 1998, Volume 9 No. 6). Divergent views, particularly on subjects such as theory-driven vs. archival-based research reflect the individual accounting historian's adherence to particular ideologies, his/her education, direct experiences of conducting historical research and ideas about what history is, its purpose and how it should be done. They are symptomatic of the diverse pathways through which accounting academics have arrived at accounting history. Some combine history with other streams of accounting research, others make a fleeting appearance and leave the stage, producing a single offering born of research into the background to a contemporary topic. An increasing number pursue accounting history as their major research activity and build their careers in the field.

The capacity for career-building varies considerably according to the status of accounting history research in particular countries and institutions. Accounting historians currently contrast the differential rates of progress in the discipline in certain European and Australasian countries, where accounting history is well entrenched, and the USA where, despite calls for its greater presence in accounting research and teaching, career-building in the subject is difficult amid claims that it remains peripheral and lacking in methodological rigour (Slocum & Sriram 2001). The author is fortunate to have a research career in accounting history. What follows reflects his experiences in arriving at that blissful state and of working in this field.

The Search for Clues

I began my research career as a doctoral student in social and demographic history and discovered accounting history almost by accident. My thesis was an investigation of the impact of fertility decline on self-recruitment and social mobility in the professions during the late nineteenth century. The research focused on the case of chartered accountants in Edinburgh (Walker 1988). This choice of case was my first acquaintance with the history of accounting. Doctoral studies were not, however, my first encounter with historical research. As an undergraduate of economic and social history I was introduced, albeit briefly, to the historian's sources and methods. There was little scope in the undergraduate programme for actually conducting historical research based on primary sources. The principal vehicle for instilling the skills of the historian was the historical essay, based on the scrutiny of secondary sources.

Foremost among the social historians whose work I encountered at university was Harold Perkin. In 1970 Perkin wrote an essay on 'The Uses of History' as part of a guide to history for intending students. Although I first read this essay as an undergraduate, it was not until I began work on a Ph.D. that his description of historical research seemed to resonate with my own experiences. Although the editors of this book requested that contributors desist from offering a prescribed view of research I will incur their displeasure and quote Perkin. I do so because his words encapsulate the practice of empirically-based historical research. Perkin (1970: 12–13) wrote:

> Historical research is like crime detection: it addresses itself to solving problems, to finding out not merely the critical ordering of the relevant facts but their meaning and interconnection, the aims and motives of the protagonists, the constraints and pressures of the surrounding circumstances, the place of accident and coincidence, the part played by human charity or malice, skill or clumsiness, success or failure. Like detection, it does this by taking one problem at a time and studying it in depth: the microscope is more informative than the telescope, a prowl round the garden more relevant than a world cruise. Like detection, too, it is a kind of multi-factorial analysis: it cannot afford to ignore any factor, any kind of clue, whatever level of experience it comes from, whether it is labelled political, social, economic, religious, moral, intellectual, technological,

scientific, medical, psychological, or just plain human, frivolous or whimsical.

There are various aspects of Perkin's populist analogy with crime detection which I have found germane to my experiences as an accounting historian. First is his reference to multi-factorial analysis and the permeable boundaries between history and auxiliary disciplines. This eclectic view of historical research has its parallel in accounting in the guise of the employment of a pluralisation of methodologies (Miller *et al.* 1991) and a strong tendency to contextualisation. These are characteristics of the 'new' accounting history which has enlivened the subject and lifted it from a primary concern with the technical (Carnegie & Napier 1996). Napier (2001: 21) has recently stated that the 'new' accounting history "is a sociological history written by social scientists". Despite its impact on advancing accounting history, there is a tendency among some to set the subject in opposition to social science (Mills 1993; Fleischman *et al.* 1996).

Another attractive feature of Perkin's approach in 'The Uses of History' is its implication that historical research is about seeking explanations and causes as opposed to a superficial search for artefacts. It also refers to the intensity of historical research. It is in the interest of furthering knowledge that the researcher conducts exhaustive investigations. This is not to suggest that contributions to the subject are purely empirical. As one whose roots are in social history (where theory features more than in other branches of history) and having researched social structure and social mobility, I recognise the importance of conceptual innovation in stimulating historical research and find it difficult to comprehend that a historian can investigate the role of accounting in industrial and post-industrial society without some comprehension of the major theories which have been advanced to understand it.

Indeed, it is also clear to most accounting historians that the research agenda has been substantially energised by such interventions as Foucauldian explorations into the emergence and use of costing and management techniques; Marxist interpretations of the relationship between capitalism and double entry bookkeeping; and Weberian approaches to the study of professional organisations. All such contributions have been key to the formulation of research questions and the generation of controversies in accounting history. Controversies, in turn, have stimulated further research, and broadened and deepened our understanding about the history of accounting. In terms of practical realist research, theoretical perspectives (broadly defined) in accounting history are important in providing organising and analytical frameworks for projects, in suggesting hypotheses, delimiting research objectives and the attendant scope of evidence-gathering, in offering coherence to writing and in the formulation of conclusions. The least promising ventures in accounting history are those devoid of either theoretical underpinning, hypotheses or research questions. In these situations the search for clues becomes meandering and illimitable. Working within institutional contexts which emphasise quality publication outputs and journal editors who usually discourage papers which merely report the discovery of accounting artefacts, accounting historians do not have the luxury of aimless wanderings in the archive.

In the search for research questions, accounting historians have not only pursued issues arising from published work in their own field, they have also found the work of economic and business historians fertile ground. They have been inspired to test assertions about accounting made in major theses by authors such as Chandler (1977) and Pollard (1968) on the history of management in the U.S. and U.K. respectively. Others are stirred to investigate the antecedents of a modern day accounting issue. Illustrating the modern-day relevance of a historical subject can be important to funding bodies such as professional organisations. In pursuing such projects the historian has to be alert to the perils of exploring and interpreting the past in terms of the present.

It will have become apparent already that the search for clues involves quite a physical and intellectual excursus. However, the time consuming nature of major research projects in accounting history is rather discordant with schedule of the agencies which assess its quality. The criteria set by U.K. Research Assessment Exercise panels in Accounting and Finance and Business and Management Studies have not been particularly conducive to generalised wanderings, imprecise research objectives and the pursuit of meta histories of accounting. The system encourages 'salami slicing' — the dispersal of publication outputs as opposed to coherent presentation in a single authoritative book. Some slices are cut thickly, others are wafer-thin. In the 2001 exercise the Accounting and Finance panel considered that four items of research output was "a normal level of activity" and required explanations for the submission of less than that number. The Business and Management panel recognised that there might be circumstances in which less than four items would be cited (again, the reasons were to be disclosed) but encouraged "the submission of the maximum number of [four] outputs". The assessment period of both panels was five years. By contrast, colleagues working within the jurisdiction of the RAE panel in History were favoured by greater sensitivity to the character of historical research. There were "no automatic penalties" for the submission of less than four pieces of work, and judgments were made on the basis of "the quality of the best work assessed" covering a period of seven years (www.rae.ac.uk).

In accounting history, disputes about the role of theory have been compounded because searches of primary source material have often been limited in theory-driven work. Controversies persist about accounting historiography and methodology (Fleischman & Tyson 1997; Oldroyd 1999) and calls have been made for greater dialogue between theoreticians and archival historians, or between critical and traditional historians (Merino & Mayper 1993; Fleischman & Radcliffe 2000). Napier has argued that the distinction between 'theoretical' and 'archival' researchers is probably a false dichotomy and is also unhelpful. He notes that many contributions to the new accounting history "are thoroughly based on punctilious use of archival material in a manner that would surely be complimented by any mainstream historian. It is easy to forget, faced with the more polemic objections to the new accounting history that the work of inspiring theorists such as Foucault and Marx was thoroughly grounded in the archive" (2000).

Arguably, the most potent contributions to accounting history have been essentially constructionist, emerging where the historian applies concepts to understand evidence gathered about the past. Here, there is convergence between the theoretical and archival approaches in devising hypotheses and research questions, identifying the specific sources necessary to address them, interpreting the evidence and writing history within conceptual frames. Accounting history papers of this type are most likely to find a home in high-ranking journals. Research which is purely driven by the convenience of a local archive (from which it is hoped a research question will emerge) are potentially risky ventures especially if the resulting output is a purely descriptive reconstruction of a past practice or technique. Even worse if the paper is not connected to themes in the literature and its contribution is elusive.

Taken in this context, personal adherence to theories and ideologies is only problematic in accounting history when it impedes (through prescription or otherwise) the inclination of the researcher to pursue high quality history. At this point, and at the risk of once more incurring the wrath of the editors, I will revert to some guidance offered by works on historical study. Marwick (1989: 329–330) puts it bluntly: "the final and really meaningful distinction is not between feminist and non-feminist, or Marxist and non-Marxist, but between competent historians and incompetent ones". Tosh considers that provided a hypothesis is clearly articulated and the available evidence is collected to evaluate its acceptance, rejection or modification then the 'fitting' of findings to expectations can be guarded against (2000: 132). He nicely summarises the relationship between theory and empirics in (accounting) history: "The business of historians is to apply theory, to refine it, and to develop new theory, always in the light of the evidence most broadly concerned. And they do so not in pursuit of the ultimate theory or 'law' which will 'solve' this or that problem of explanation, but because without theory they cannot come to grips with the really significant questions in history" (2000: 159). In her book on *History in Practice*, Jordanova argues for the historian to be balanced and self-aware and states that "passions and values should . . . be constantly subjected to scrutiny: they need to be tempered by evidence — for a conviction to be heartfelt need not imply it is unreflexive" (2000: xiv). This emphasis on evidence returns us to Perkin and the search for clues.

Perkin's statement in 'The Uses of History' seemed to resonate with my experiences as a student chartered accountant. Readers will be distressed to learn that I found intellectual solace (at least temporarily) in the unlikely world of the corporate audit. As a history graduate and post-doctoral CA student in a 'big 8' firm, I was a rather enthusiastic and diligent auditor. Not for me the cerebral dark age of ticking and bashing. I claimed the analytical review section of the audit file as my own. This bizarre counter-cultural behaviour was attributed to the affinity between the historical research process and the work of the auditor. My staff partner noted this unlikely connection. It was immediately apparent on opening an audit manual: "Auditing is a happy mixture of a number of things — gathering information, probing, observing, checking, enquiry, evaluation, interpretations, assessment and review".

During my professional training I was introduced to David Hatherly's book on *The Audit Evidence Process*. This began with the statement "As far as auditing is concerned evidence is at the centre of the stage" (1980: vii). Indeed, Hatherly (1980: 2–4) argued that deficiencies in the collection and evaluation of evidence had contributed to nothing less than a crisis in the audit profession. The Auditor's Operational Standard referred to the need for the auditor to plan, control and record work and to obtain relevant and reliable evidence. Concerns about the sufficiency, reliability and relevance of evidence, and the use of evidence as a basis for exercising judgements and reporting opinions were akin to the practical concerns of the historian and resonated with the life-course of a historical research project. Both auditor and historian were engaged in the examination of records about past events. There were mutual concerns with the relative quality of oral and documentary evidence, with not accepting explanations at their face value, with the need for corroboration, drawing conclusions on the basis of different types of evidence and with the circumstances surrounding the creation of evidence.

At this juncture it should be pointed out that like the disputes between 'traditional' and 'critical' approaches to accounting history, this focus on the centrality of evidence is controversial. It takes us into the territory of historiography where disputes rage about the fundamentals of the historian's craft. On the one hand postmodernists challenge empiricism and contend that historical writing constitutes little more than competing fictional discourses; that the quest for truth based on documents is futile, and original sources are mere 'traces' whose value as representations of the past is nullified when communicated through the subjective medium of the historian (Jenkins 1991, 1999). On the other hand there are those who, while guarding against a 'fetishism of documents', argue that history is more than creative writing, is about the systematic use of sources in the quest for "substantiable truth", that the results of evidence gathering provides the lifeblood of historical debate, is the link between the historian and the past, and the process of discovering and analysing sources demands high academic skill (Marwick 1993). Vincent begins his provocative book *An Intelligent Person's Guide to History* with the following uncompromising assertion: "History is about evidence. It is also about other things: hunches, imagination, interpretation, guesswork. First and foremost, though, comes evidence: no evidence, no history" (2001: 9).

Whatever the merits and demerits of these strongly held views, this volume is concerned with *real-life* accounting research. The remainder of the current chapter is accordingly devoted to 'doing' evidence gathering (primarily written evidence) — the distinguishing research activity of most accounting historians. This is apparent not only from the bibliographies of their published work but also in the conversations of accounting historians during social interludes at academic conferences. Once the customary gossip has been exhausted, sharing tales from the archives tend to feature large. The richness of the material in Paradise Record Office, the excellent assistance offered by the staff in the library at Elysium, the use of digital cameras in the Nirvana Archive. Conversely, the uncatalogued morass in Abaddon, the punitive cost of photocopying in Hades, restricted access to key material in Tartarus. Or, worst of all, the discovery that the rival Dr Evil has already collected the same data from Paradise Record Office. Such comments allude to the pathways, obstacles and frustrations in the search for clues.

What Perkin's definition of historical research does not convey is the roller-coaster ride which is the process of evidence gathering. This essentially derives from the fact that documentary evidence is usually deposited in archives and libraries, is organised and catalogued in ways which are not always congruent with the specific research question and involve entering an arena where there is likely to be much *potentially* useful material and many tempting diversions. The search for evidence, which (in audit parlance) is sufficient, reliable and relevant, requires that the historian travel to where the evidence is kept (often more than one location), sift through the relevant catalogue entries and consult the material. Like detective work this process can be replete with the frustration of dead ends, uncooperative witnesses and poor quality evidence. It can include bouts of tedium. For example, in waiting for material to be retrieved in an archive; wading through endless boxes of papers in a vain search for pertinent clues; in the routine of copying, preparing and processing data. Conversely, the researcher may encounter the exhilaration of an unexpected find which challenges conventional wisdom; a lead which poses a new research question; or opens pathways to unexplored sources pertinent to the current research question. This is the thrill, as Lord Acton, a leading figure in the Cambridge School of History, put it, of discovering clues which evidence "the crumbling of an idol or the disclosure of a skeleton".

Perkin's view of historical research also gives the impression that while the historian-detective is cognisant of the world around him, he conducts his enquiries as a solitary, companionless introvert. However, like the detective, the historian is heavily dependent on others in his search for clues. Read the prefaces of major works of history and they invariably contain a list of credits to rival a Hollywood production. This is because the gathering of evidence is invariably dependent on the support, patience and goodwill of various parties. Like other forms of research, historical research is, as Bell and Newby observed, "a deeply social process" and is conducted in real-life political contexts (1977: 10). It involves interaction and support from joint researchers, academic colleagues, possibly research assistants, funding bodies, family and friends, and publishers. It can involve conflicts with the same.

While these relationships are common to most accounting researchers, the historian, has a particular engagement with another set of characters. These are the gatekeepers to the sources of evidence: archivists, librarians and their assistants - individuals who are key players in the successful completion of a history project. It is my experiences of evidence gathering, its irritations and pleasures, and of the relationship with archivists that feature in the following sections. It should also be pointed out that the emphasis in what follows is on investigating the written record. This is not intended to denigrate the wealth of other sources which may be utilised in historical research such as oral testimony (see Collins & Bloom 1991; Hammond & Sikka 1996; Matthews 2000). But it is assumed that the real-life experiences of interviewing in accounting research will feature in other chapters of this book. Further, it is the investigation of documentary remains of the past which tend to predominate in the practice of clue searching.

Irritations in the Search for Clues

Let me relate some of my more frustrating experiences of archival research and the lessons which were learnt from them. First, it should be recognised that the nature of the site in which the documents are stored and consulted can vary enormously. Like the auditor, the accounting historian has to be prepared to gather evidence from a variety of different locations: from the large scale public institution such as a national record office with its computerised catalogue and resident experts, to the small private firm where the documents are kept in a cardboard box in the basement and the office cleaner is the party most knowledgeable about its contents. There may be occasions when no-one seems to know whether documents exist or where they might be located. I once embarked on a hunt for the minute books of a bank which had been placed in a document store amidst mountains of other papers, broken furniture and ephemera and without the benefit of an inventory.

The researcher is likely to encounter varying degrees of bureaucracy when visiting a public archive. In the Public Record Office, London, for example, the first experience is of applying for a reader's ticket, attending a new reader induction course, making sense of the layout of the place and understanding the ordering system. The institutional environment can also vary considerably. From the imposing surroundings and surveillance systems of a national archive or library (I was once admonished for distracting readers by making too much noise when turning the crisped pages of a nineteenth century journal) to the unobserved freedom of movement and endless cups of tea in a local firm staffed by employees pleased to welcome such an unusual visitor.

Once access to material has been obtained the researcher can often be content that a major hurdle has been successfully negotiated. But not always. I once gained permission to examine records, travelled 300 miles to their location only to find that the granting of permission had not been communicated to the individual on duty. I also arrived at a record office to examine a gifted deposit to learn that it was recently returned to its owner in the Outer Hebrides. I recall being very excited about discovering a source in the British Library Catalogue which had escaped the attention of other researchers. Having placed an order over the phone in advance of a visit, I travelled from Edinburgh to London only to discover that the material could not be found. It was explained that the books were probably lost in the Library's move from Bloomsbury to St Pancras, or the catalogue was incorrect and had never been amended. I also have fond memories of being assured by the staff of a local professional society that its minute books were available for my inspection. Having travelled some distance to examine them I was informed that they had actually been destroyed during an air raid in 1941.

The ordering and delivery of documents can also be a source of frustration. I have experiences of placing orders for microfilm reels which were out to repair and not available for several weeks; of material which was temporarily unavailable having been loaned for an exhibition; of finding that the record ordered was being consulted by another reader. The experience of archival research can also be conditioned by the speed at which attendants process orders, retrieve and deliver material to reading rooms. Be prepared for waiting times. In one repository it was not advised to place orders for material on a Friday afternoon as the attendants were routinely the worse for a liquid lunch. It is often the case that the historian needs to search through numerous boxes/ volumes of material until the clues for which she/he is searching are discovered. This may result in upsetting archive attendants whose patience is stretched by the velocity with which material is ordered and returned. I have succeeded in frustrating some attendants to the extent that they refused to collect the next order until I had finished consulting material currently on the desk. This arrangement appeared as a device for delaying the processing of my requests until the bell was rung for last orders.

In addition to delays in delivering documents, the number of items that can be ordered at any time can also impact on the duration of a visit to the archive. The most significant exercise in data collection for my doctoral research was to examine 3,000 extracts from the census enumerators' books. On my first visit to General Register House, Edinburgh, I placed a single order slip for the first twenty volumes. The repository assistant picked up the order, gazed at it mysteriously, burst into laughter and proceeded to share the joke with a colleague. He then authoritatively explained that readers were required to complete a separate production slip for each volume and a maximum of three orders could be placed at a time. In a depressing instant I recognised that the period it would take to complete the data collection for my Ph.D. had been extended by several months.

When the material is delivered for consultation, the historian is gripped by a sense of expectation. Is this set of papers to contain rich evidence in support of one's thesis or will it confirm the opposite? Dejection sets in on discovering that the promising description of an item in the catalogue contains nothing more than a solitary note, the file cover itself, or worse still, has been lost altogether. Enthusiasm can also be checked when the documents are torn, stained, faded or otherwise illegible, require a knowledge of Latin, are written in handwriting styles which would confound a palaeographer, or are full of the incomprehensible legal jargon of a past age. By contrast, there may be occasions where the documents are almost too voluminous and contain material which is incidental to the subject of research. Without some self-discipline and constant reminders of the research objective time allocated to the search for clues can be exhausted by pursuing interesting diversions. Most historians agree that searches of newspapers can be especially deadly. If the reader is engaged in scanning a periodical for pertinent material it is difficult not to be beguiled by headlines such as 'Appalling Railway Accident in Hertfordshire', or 'Extraordinary Occurrence on Sheep Farm'. One's attention can often stray to contemporary accounts of murders, scandals, momentous political debates or the football results. These subjects seldom fall within the broadest notion of contextualisation in accounting history.

Facilitating the Search for Clues

As mentioned above, in addition to the stoic support and perseverance of their close kin, historians invariably acknowledge the role played by the custodians of the archives in accomplishing their research. According to one authority, the general relationship between academic historians and archivists has deteriorated as the latter have attempted to define a distinctive professional territory and prioritised the servicing of the increasing clientele of family history enthusiasts (Moss 1997). Indeed, at the personal level, most experienced historians have encountered the officious librarian or protective archivist whose role as gatekeeper appears to translate into keeping the doors shut or only partly open. It is more usual, however, for archivists to be key players at several junctures in the search for primary evidence. This ranges from gaining permission to access records (some repositories are not open to the public and records within public archives may have restricted access), to determining which classes of record would most profitably be searched. The whole experience of a visit to an archive can be conditioned by the researcher's relationship with archivists and associated staff. It is, therefore, advisable not to assume an antagonistic stance and to reveal that one has thoroughly prepared for the visit. It is worth remembering that, depending on the record office, the academic researcher is likely to have a firmer grasp of the specific subject being investigated. This is especially so in accounting history which can be something of a mystery to some archivists.

In specialist libraries or repositories, the archivist may take an active interest in the research and seek out unexplored material or indicate new leads. In larger record offices, locating accounting records can be difficult as these are invariably listed within the collections of government departments, companies, estates, or individuals and are not separately identified as a major catalogue heading. Experienced archivists are likely to be of considerable assistance in identifying those collections which might be targeted and explored for accounting material. The message, therefore, is to use the knowledge of these experts.

Advances in information technology are revolutionising the search for material and the accounting historian's ability to plan visits to the archive. In rare instances, physical attendance may not be necessary at all. Original documents are increasingly being scanned and made available over the Internet, though the impact of this innovation should not be overestimated. Only a small proportion of the total material in archives is likely to be available in such convenient forms in the foreseeable future. In some cases historical data may be accessed on compact disc and read on the researcher's own pc. More important to the practical concerns of accounting historians is the increasing availability online of up-to-date information about admission criteria, how to plan a visit, and procedures for ordering material. Of especial significance to the search for relevant material is the availability online of finding aids such as the catalogues of major libraries and archives. This represents a substantial, time-saving advance on wading through card systems to locate relevant sources. For example, the British Library Public Catalogue (http://blpc.bl.uk/) offers 24 hour access to the vast contents (including c.10 million books) of one of the foremost research libraries in the world. The search options enable the compilation of subject-specific bibliographies, an invaluable facility for any researcher of an accounting topic in the U.K. Similarly, the catalogue of 90 miles of material in the Public Record Office (PRO), London, can be searched using PROCAT (http://www.pro.gov.uk/). This excellent facility, part of the PRO's programme to achieve full electronic access to services and records during the twenty first century, permits multi-level searches and online ordering. Considerable progress is being made towards creating a national archives network on line (http://www.nationalarchives. gov.uk/).

These Internet-based resources represent embryonic stages in the development of the 'global archive', and together with electronic indexes and databases greatly assist the historian's ability to organise projects and search for evidence. Even where such information is not available via the World Wide Web, it is strongly advised to plan the visit to the archive as much as possible in order to avoid the frustrations of document searches. Given the significance of evidence gathering the availability of sources is a key constraint to empirical research in accounting history. Determining the extent of the sources is an early task in the feasibility and design of a project. It is advisable to make a preliminary visit to the archive to ascertain the extent of the material likely to be searched. In contrast to the advice of guides to historical methodology, primary sources ought to be consulted early in the genesis of a project. The historian is usually engaged in an ongoing search for evidence drawn from both primary and secondary sources. Findings in original documents may reveal unexpected themes. These incite further explorations of the published literature.

As the negative experiences related previously suggest, many of the problems confronting the researcher in the search for clues can be prevented by good planning. Before embarking for a repository it is advisable to gather basic information relating to the following: opening hours (look out for annual stocktakes when the archive is closed for several days); conditions of admission (proof of identity may be necessary); whether special permission is necessary to access documents; for recent material ensure that the papers do not fall within a thirty year (or longer) closure rule; the location of the archive; accommodation arrangements (you may need to book a seat or a microfilm reader); the possibility of ordering material in advance of your visit (by phone, fax, email or letter); and, whether the material is kept at an outstore (in which case it may take days to be produced).

Having identified the existence of relevant records it is advisable to learn as much as possible about them before viewing. There may be printed catalogues or guides to the classes of documents you intend to consult. Discover as much as possible about systems of referencing and ordering prior to the visit. There may be specialist advisers on your subject at the archive who can be contacted when arranging your visit (e-mail or letter are usually preferred). The National Archives of Scotland suggest that such communication is most effective when the reader is specific about the information/ document being sought, when references are made to any earlier correspondence and when sources in the archive already consulted are referred to. Check out the availability and cost of reprographic services (including arrangements for gaining permission and reproducing material in publications). It may prove to be more economical for the researcher to pay for a microfilm copy of documents than travel long distances to read them on site.

Before arriving, be aware of the regulations of the archive and remember that the mission of archivists is to preserve documents as well as making them available to researchers. Be ready to wear white gloves (in an Australian archive I was asked to don these in order to read a book published in the 1930s), use book cushions, polystyrene supports, acid-free bookmarks, and don't forget a pencil and a note pad. Any implement or activity which poses a threat to documents are strictly forbidden in public archives. Use of pens, coloured pencils, correction fluid, cameras and scanners as well as smoking, eating and drinking are capital offences in search rooms. Neither are mobile phones popular. Be prepared to leave coats and bags in a locker (for which you may need a coin) or cloakroom. Check out the facilities for using laptop or handheld computers and the location of the nearest supply of coffee or something stronger if it all goes wrong.

Work through orders for documents (production slips) in a systematic way. Experienced archival researchers work up a head of steam to reduce waiting time, though, as mentioned earlier, be aware of the potential to overload those who process orders and physically retrieve the material. The waiting period for documents can vary considerably between archives, and within one place according to the number of readers and the availability of repository staff. If possible, order your first batch of material before arrival and reduce the effect of waiting times by placing orders in a way which ensures a flow of material when you are ready for it. When taking notes do not forget to take full catalogue references, the exact titles of documents and their date. There is nothing worse than having a paper accepted for publication subject to completing missing references which had not been noted while at a distant archive.

Finding Clues to Other Crimes

For those with a fetishism for documents, the thrill of archival work comes from merely working with material which represent a physical survival from a past age. For those engaged in academic historical research the kick comes from discovering clues which support one's thesis, opens a research question, provides evidence which overturns accepted understandings, or offers an alternative solution to the crime. The most rewarding episode of this kind, in my experience, was in identifying the likely reasons for the formation of the first modern accountancy organisation in Scotland in 1853. During the late 1980s and early 1990s new explanations on this subject were being presented by Macdonald (a sociologist) and Kedslie (an accountant). A heated debate ensued in the pages of the *British Journal of Sociology*. Neither of these researchers seemed to offer wholly convincing arguments and their searches of the archives seemed less than exhaustive. In particular, no one had examined the socio-legal context of contemporary debates about Scottish bankruptcy, despite its accepted relevance. I ventured to the libraries of the law societies, identified the key participants in the discourse on professional formation and located the media through which they conducted it. A rather different story emerged from those advanced in earlier studies and the results were published as a paper in *Accounting, Organizations and Society* in 1995.

It is through the pursuit of depth contextualised research that new questions are usually suggested and exciting times flow for the accounting historian. Historians will claim that their discoveries are entirely founded on a deep understanding of the period concerned, their awareness of relevant sources, and the pursuit of comprehensively planned and informed research. This is invariably the case. Most will submit, however, that even the most exhaustive searches can result in dead ends: the clues may run out and the crime cannot be solved. Such adversities reiterate the need for an early evaluation of available evidence. These disappointments can also be compensated by chance discoveries arising out of a search for material relating to another project. As historians may privately concede, some of their greatest successes are entirely serendipitous. More commonly, these fortunate events are explained as a consequence of Pasteur's maxim that "chance favours only the prepared mind". What is important is the capacity to identify the relevance of a chance discovery to a historical debate, for testing a theory, for devising new research questions, for forming the springboard for future research.

An example follows which is unusually illustrative of the accounting historian as investigator of crimes and searcher of clues. I was researching the consequences for auditing of the foremost financial scandal of the nineteenth century, the City of Glasgow

Bank failure of 1878, in the archives of the Royal Bank of Scotland in Edinburgh. While waiting for material to be delivered, I wandered across to an exhibition on the history of the Royal Bank. Among the items on display was a copy of a poster issued by the Edinburgh City Police. This read in bold print '£100 Reward. Donald Smith Peddie'. This dubious character was wanted for forging bills and promissory notes. Now, I knew from my previous research on the history of the accountancy profession that Mr Peddie was a founding member of the Society of Accountants in Edinburgh whose name was removed from the roll in 1883 for committing an undisclosed but highly publicised misdemeanour. I was also aware that there was an emerging interest in the literature on ethics and white collar crime. With this enticing lead and these themes in mind, the newspapers, court records and other documents were searched for clues about the intriguing Mr Peddie. These sources revealed a compelling story of blackmail, divorce and sexual impropriety and much about the discordance between the 'public' face of the Victorian accountant and his private life. It also offered insights into the emergence of disciplinary codes in the early chartered accountancy profession. The research, emanating from a chance discovery formed the raw material for what was to be a prize-winning paper! (Walker 1996).

Conclusions

With three specialist journals in the field as well as outlets in business history, management history and the mainstream accounting journals, the publication opportunities in accounting history have never been better. Not to mention other output genre. When submitting work authors should, however be alert to the character of the history which tends to feature in particular journals (importance may be attached to theory-informed work, 'critical' studies, particular geographical emphases, or topics relevant to modern-day issues). As a reviewer I am constantly surprised by the extent to which authors submit history papers which fall outside the stated scope, aims and objectives of the journal concerned and are so insensitive to the destination of their work that they neglect to apply the house style. Most editors and reviewers of accounting history journals are increasingly alert to the need for papers to offer much more than the descriptive antiquarianism which characterised some of the earlier work in this field. Pure description is unlikely to generate publications which will impress RAE panels. In 2001 the Accounting and Finance panel identified the following attributes of quality: significance to the intellectual development of the subject, rigorous evidence gathering and interpretation, capacity to set the intellectual or policy agenda, and recognition as high quality by those in the subject community.

The aversion to pure description has also been indicated by editors of *The Accounting Historians Journal*. In 1990 they took the unusual step of reporting why it was that of the 40 papers submitted in the previous year only six had been accepted for publication. They identified poor writing, boring subject matter, exclusive reliance on secondary sources, and weak methodology as among the reasons for the rejection of manuscripts (Flesher & Samson 1990). They also reported that "the biggest criticism that reviewers have made relate to the fact that many papers are merely descriptive" adding that, "papers must be more than just a description of some old accounting records". On assuming the editorship of the same journal in 2001 I soon found it necessary to repeat the same message.

Flesher and Samson also noted that some authors seemed oblivious to the qualities of 'good' historical research. We may conclude by summarising some of these characteristics. The most successful empirically-based accounting history papers tend to have clear objectives and scope, be fully conversant with the previous literature on the subject, display a cognisance of patterns of scholarship in the field, identify the potential contribution which they make, apply and discuss appropriate theoretical frameworks and methodologies, are well researched in primary and secondary sources, narrate and analyse the evidence, identify pertinent contexts, seek explanation as opposed to pure description and explore the implications of their findings. This is a tall order and to pursue historical research in this way can be a time consuming, exhausting and frustrating business. But it can also be elating, and more likely to produce the high quality publications which serve to satisfy personal career objectives and advance the discipline of accounting history itself.

References

Bell, C., & Newby, H. (1977). Introduction: The rise of methodological pluralism. In: C. Bell & H. Newby (Eds), *Doing sociological research* (pp. 9–29). London: George Allen and Unwin.

Carnegie, G. D., & Napier, C. J. (1996). Critical and interpretive histories: insights into accounting's present and future through its past. *Accounting, Auditing and Accountability Journal, 9*(3), 7–39.

Carnegie, G. D., & Potter, B. (2000). Publishing patterns in specialist accounting history journals in the English language 1996–1999. *The Accounting Historians' Journal, 27*(2), 177–198.

Chandler, A. D., Jr. (1977). *The visible hand: The managerial revolution in American business.* Cambridge MA: Belknap Press.

Collins, R., & Bloom (1991). The role of oral history in accounting. *Accounting, Auditing and Accountability Journal, 4*(4), 23–31.

Fleischman, R. K., & Radcliffe, V. S. (2000). Divergent themes of accounting history: a review and call for confluence. *Proceedings of the Sixth Interdisciplinary Perspectives on Accounting Conference*, July, Manchester.

Fleischman, R. K., & Tyson, T. (1997). Archival researchers: An endangered species? *The Accounting Historians' Journal, 24*(2), 91–109.

Fleischman, R. K., Mills, P. A., & Tyson, T. N. (1996). A theoretical primer for evaluating and conducting historical research in accounting. *Accounting History, NS, 1*(1), 55–75.

Flesher, D. L., & Samson, W. D. (1990). What is publishable accounting history research: an editorial view. *The Accounting Historians' Journal, 17*(1), 1–4.

Funnell, W. (1998). The narrative and its place in the new accounting history: The rise of the counternarrative. *Accounting, Auditing and Accountability Journal, 11*(2), 99–109.

Hammond, T., & Sikka, P. (1996). Radicalizing accounting history: The potential of oral history. *Accounting, Auditing and Accountability Journal, 9*(3), 79–97.

Hatherly, D. (1980). *The audit evidence process.* Anderson Keenan Publishing.

Jenkins, K. (1991). *Re-thinking history.* London: Routledge.

Jenkins, K. (1999). *Why history? Reflections on the possible end of history and ethics under the impact of the postmodern*. London: Routledge.

Jordanova, L. (2000). *History in practice*. London: Arnold.

Marwick, A. (1989). *The nature of history* (3rd ed.). Basingstoke: Macmillan.

Marwick, A. (1993): 'A fetishism of documents'? The salience of source-based history. In: H. Kozicki (Ed.), *Developments in modern historiography* (pp. 107–138). Basingstoke: Macmillan Press.

Matthews, D. (2000). Oral history, accounting history and an interview with Sir John Grenside. *Accounting, Business and Financial History, 10*(1), 57–84.

Merino, B. G., & Mayper, A. G. (1993). Accounting history and empirical research. *The Accounting Historians' Journal, 20*(2), 237–267.

Miller, P., Hopper, T., & Laughlin, R. (1991). The new accounting history: An introduction. *Accounting, Organizations and Society, 16*(5/6), 395–403.

Mills, P. A. (1993). Accounting history as social science: A cautionary note. *Accounting, Organizations and Society, 18*(7/8), 801–803.

Moss, M. (1997). Archives, the historian and the future. In: M. Bentley (Ed.), *Companion to historiography*. London: Routledge.

Napier, C. (2000). Accounts of change. Paper presented at the *Accounting, Organizations and Society 25th Anniversary Conference*, 26–29 July, Oxford.

Napier, C. (2001). Accounting history and accounting progress. *Accounting History, NS, 6*(2), 7–31.

Oldroyd, D. (1999). Historiography, causality, and positioning: an unsystematic view of accounting history. *The Accounting Historians' Journal, 26*(1), 83–102.

Parker, L. D. (1999). Historiography for the new millennium: adventures in accounting and management. *Accounting History, NS, 4*(2), 11–42.

Perkin, H. (1970). The uses of history. In: H. Perkin (Ed.), *History: An introduction for the intending student*. London: Routledge and Kegan Paul.

Pollard, S. (1965). *The genesis of modern management*. Cambridge MA: Harvard University Press.

Previts, G. J., Parker, L. D., & Coffman, E. N. (1990). An accounting historiography: Subject matter and methodology. *Abacus, 26*(2), 136–158.

RAE (2001). Panels' Criteria and Working Methods, UoAs 43, 44, 59. (http://www.rae.ac.uk/Pubs/5_99/ByUoA).

Slocum, E. L., & Sriram, R. S. (2001). Accounting history: A survey of academic interest in the U.S. *The Accounting Historians Journal, 28*(1), 111–130.

The British Accounting Review Research Register (biennial), London: Academic Press and ICAEW.

Tosh, J. (2000). *The pursuit of history* (3rd ed.). Harlow: Pearson Educational Ltd.

Vincent, J. (2001). *An intelligent person's guide to history*. London: Duckbacks.

Walker, S. P. (1988). *The society of accountants in Edinburgh 1854–1914. A study of recruitment to a new profession*. New York: Garland Publishing Inc.

Walker, S. P. (1995). The genesis of professional organization in Scotland: A contextual analysis. *Accounting, Organizations and Society, 20*(4), 285–310.

Walker, S. P. (1996). The criminal upperworld and the emergence of a disciplinary code in the early chartered accountancy profession. *Accounting History, NS, 1*(2), 7–36.

Chapter 2

Adventures in Social and Environmental Acccounting and Auditing Research: A Personal Reflection

David Owen

Introduction

My purpose in this chapter is a straightforward one, being simply to encourage colleagues new to academia to direct their research (and teaching) efforts towards the exciting, and challenging, field of social and environmental accounting and auditing (SEAA). To this end, I will begin by very briefly outlining how research in the area has developed over the past thirty years, whilst additionally offering a personal viewpoint of the direction current leading edge research is heading. In particular, I seek to demonstrate how SEAA research has not only become much more theoretically informed over the years, but has also acquired an explicit campaigning edge as researchers look to critically engage with an ever growing corporate and professional interest in issues of social and environmental accounting and accountability. Critical engagement provides the challenge and excitement that characterises so much current SEAA research activity but is, of course, far from easy to pursue in an academic environment where short term pressures to publish have never been greater. In a bid to allay the understandable fears of researchers new to the area, the chapter therefore concludes with some practical tips drawn from personal experiences acquired over the twenty plus years I have so far spent in academia.

An Introduction and Brief History of SEAA

Perhaps as a good starting point as any is to begin with a fairly broad definition of social and environmental accounting and auditing as being:

> ... the process of communicating the social and environmental effects of organisations' economic actions to particular interest groups within

The Real Life Guide to Accounting Research: A Behind-the-Scenes View of Using Qualitative
Research Methods
ISBN: 0-08-043972-1

society and to society at large. As such, it involves extending the accountability of organisations (particularly companies) beyond the traditional role of providing a financial account to the owners of capital, in particular shareholders. Such an extension is predicated upon the assumption that companies do have wider responsibilities than simply to make money for their shareholders (Gray *et al.* 1987: ix).

At the outset it should be clearly understood that modern SEAA research is avowedly normative in nature. It is largely predicated on the notion that conventional accounting practice, with its overriding focus on the interests of wealthy capital providers in (predominantly) western nations, is fundamentally flawed and pernicious in its influence. In simple terms, conventional accounting's pre-occupation with financial performance as the sole yardstick of organisational success leads inevitably to its implication in the environmental destruction, social dislocation and exploitation of the weakest members of society consequent upon such a narrow interpretation of 'success'. Research in SEAA is, therefore, largely concerned with critiquing current accounting practice and searching for more emancipatory alternatives that may improve the situation, in terms of delivering greater levels of organisational accountability. In carrying out these tasks the researcher inevitably has to expose his, or her, ethical, moral and indeed political value systems, not always a comfortable task!

Clearly it is impossible in this short chapter to do more than give a very sketchy overview of the rich thirty year history of SEAA research. What follows is simply an attempt to draw out the key strands of research endeavour during this time period.[1] SEAA first came to real prominence in the early 1970s as a natural consequence of the debate then raging concerning the role of the corporation in society at a time of rising societal expectations and emerging environmental awareness. More perceptive managements, particularly those of prominent corporations in environmentally or socially sensitive sectors, speedily grasped the public relations benefits in producing, at least rudimentary, social reports which attempted to convey a picture of corporate responsiveness to key societal concerns.

Research during the first decade of SEAA was largely directed towards predominantly descriptive empirical work charting the emergence of this new practice together with normative attempts at model building in order to improve such practice. Generally, work in the area was theoretically undeveloped, with little attention paid to corporate motives for disclosure, except for the beginnings of what became somewhat of a cottage industry in the 1980s and beyond — empirical studies seeking to investigate links between social disclosure and financial or stock market performance. A rare exception to the conservative orientation of much SEAA research during this time was provided by the work of the independent research and lobbying organisation Social Audit Limited. Adopting an uncompromising normative stance of holding to public

---

[1] I draw heavily here on Reg Mathews excellent 1997 paper. Readers looking for a fuller analysis are referred to Gray *et al.*'s (1996) work. In the interests of readability, references in the text are kept to a bare minimum and the interested reader is referred to the comprehensive bibliographies contained in Mathews and Gray *et al.* together with the more analytical review of the 'social accounting project' and its development over the past 25 years presented by Gray (2002).

account the activities of powerful economic entities, Social Audit Limited conducted a number of critical exposés (audits) of the social and environmental performance of major commercial organisations which to this day provide a fund of ideas and tools for researchers (see Gray *et al.* 1996, Chapter 9).

The 1980s and early 1990s heralded the coming of age of SEAA as an area of scholarly enquiry, perhaps best exemplified by the appearance of the journals *Accounting, Auditing and Accountability*, *Advances in Public Interest Accounting* and *Critical Perspectives on Accounting* which joined the longer established (1976) *Accounting, Organizations and Society* as major outlets for publication in the field. Greater attention started to be paid to methodological issues, with empirical studies increasingly having a basis in rigorous content analysis, whilst research became much more theoretically informed. In particular, perspectives drawn from legitimacy, stakeholder and political economy theories began to be employed in attempts to explain, rather than simply describe, SEAA practice, an approach that has persisted to the present day.

However, without doubt the most significant theoretical contribution to the SEAA debate came from the newly emerging critical (or radical) perspective, notably represented in the work of Tony Tinker, Tony Puxty, David Cooper and sundry colleagues. Emanating from a socialist, largely Marxist, tradition,[2] the work of these scholars not only lambasted conventional accounting practice but also took extant SEAA research to task for its failure to recognise social conflict as endemic to society and consequent adoption of a stance of political quietism concerning itself with simply the symptoms, rather than the causes, of environmental and social degradation.[3] Indeed, in the course of a particularly noteworthy polemical broadside, Puxty (1991: 107) characterised social and environmental accounting as amounting to merely ". . . re-arranging the deck chairs on the Titanic".

Towards the end of the 1980s SEAA research underwent something of a transformation, with environmental accounting and auditing taking centre stage and driving the research agenda into the 1990s. The plethora of special issues of academic journals devoted to the topic — perhaps most notably *Accounting, Auditing and Accountability Journal* (Vol. 4, No. 3 1991), *Accounting, Organizations and Society* (Vol. 17, No. 5 1992), and *Accounting Forum* (Vol. 19, No. 2/3 1995) — bear clear testimony to this trend. Largely influenced by a growing corporate and professional led agenda, initial research in environmental accounting and auditing tended to privilege the physical environmental dimension to the almost complete displacement of the social. Whereas some elements of this tradition still persist, notably in research addressing the implications for management information systems design of growing corporate environmental awareness, a more critical slant to research in the area quickly made an appearance.

---

[2] Later work in the critical tradition has also been informed by the perspectives of deep ecology (Maunders & Burritt 1991) and radical feminism (Cooper 1992).
[3] For a particularly cogent, and personally painful, critique in this context see the seminal paper by Tinker *et al.* (1991).

Researchers, for example, began to critique a perceived professional 'capture' of the field and to highlight the dubious ecological credentials of corporate and professional led initiatives. Insightful analysis of the former phenomenon has, for example, been provided by Mike Power (see Power 1991) whilst in the latter context the work of Frank Birkin is particularly noteworthy, heralding as it does something of a return to the normative model building initiatives of the 1970s (see Birkin 1996, 2000). Most fundamentally, a concern with the concept of sustainability, and recognition that its pursuit encompassed an eco-justice dimension, concerned with issues of inter and intra generational equity, as well as one of eco-efficiency, led to a re-introduction of the social into the environmental accounting and auditing project (see, particularly, Gray 1992).

Significantly, and perhaps largely because the term lends itself to numerous different interpretations, sustainability has become a generally accepted public policy goal, seemingly subscribed to by an increasing number of major corporations. This is particularly evident in the way that the companies who pioneered environmental reporting practice are now incorporating the social dimension via the production of reports variously entitled 'Ethical', 'Social', 'Corporate Responsibility' and 'Sustainability'. Intriguingly, the concept of corporate social audit largely dormant since its heyday in the early to mid-1970s has been given a new lease of life with a growing corporate (and professional) interest in the practice of what is generally termed social and ethical accounting, auditing and reporting. However, a concern for the practice's efficacy in enhancing corporate reputation and controlling risk appears to have largely displaced its public accountability dimension which so centrally informed the work of *Social Audit Limited*. This shift in emphasis is, as we shall see, increasingly attracting the attention of researchers.

Where Are We Today?

The above overview of thirty years of SEAA research endeavour is, as acknowledged at the outset, sketchy and also highly selective in its identification of major research strands.[4] The following assessment of where the field is at at the present time, and identification of interesting and significant research agendas to pursue, is also the product, of course, of personal idiosyncrasy.

Two strands of SEAA research referred to in the foregoing historical overview still attract considerable attention from researchers. Particularly popular in the U.S. literature are the market based studies which seek to establish associations between corporate social (including environmental) disclosure and/or performance and financial or stock market variables. To the extent that establishing some clear links between the social and financial performance dimensions of corporate activity might be of some use in

---

[4] For example, I have omitted any consideration of human resource accounting, which was much debated in the 1970s (see the special issue of *Accounting Organizations and Society*, Vol. 1, No. 2/3, 1976) and is enjoying some renaissance today in the guise of accounting for intellectual capital (see, for example, *Accounting, Auditing and Accountability Journal*, Vol. 1, 14, No. 4, 2001) or the role of accounting in collective bargaining. Whereas I would consider these topics as being very marginal in the context of SEAA, many researchers will disagree!

persuading companies of the efficacy of SEAA such studies may be considered worthwhile. However, from my reading, it appears increasingly clear that analytical sophistication and the playing of statistical games have become the overriding obsession of researchers in the area and hence such studies, rooted as they are within the prevailing economic and political status quo, can be largely considered as exercises in irrelevance as far as advancing the SEAA agenda is concerned.

Of much greater interest are studies that continue to probe corporate motivations in disclosing social and environmental information. As has been noted, initially researchers focussed their attention on published corporate reports, employing content analysis methodology in order to evaluate the explanatory power of widely touted theories (notably legitimacy and stakeholder theories) of disclosure. There is still scope for ongoing work within the genre and anyone looking to pursue this line of research is particularly referred to Rob Gray *et al.*'s (1995a, b) seminal contribution to the literature as a pointer to guide their own efforts.[5] More recently researchers have begun to probe managerial motivations for embarking on SEAA initiatives more directly, via utilising questionnaire and interview methods. At the forefront of work in this area are Jan Bebbington and Craig Deegan. Jan's ongoing investigation of what corporate managers understand the concept of sustainability to entail makes for particularly fascinating, if at times worrying, reading (see, for example, Bebbington & Thomson 1996), whilst Craig over recent years has produced a steady stream of deeply perceptive and exceedingly well-designed studies which probe not only managerial motivations but also user (or stakeholder) needs and perceptions as regards SEAA disclosure (see, for example, Deegan & Rankin 1997, 1999). The issue of stakeholder needs and perceptions, albeit with attention focussed solely on the investor stakeholder group, has been further addressed in a fascinating series of papers by Markus Milne and colleagues which employ experimental methodologies to investigate investor reactions to corporate environmental and social disclosure practice (see Milne & Chan 1999; Chan & Milne 1999; Milne & Patten 2002). Again, new researchers in the SEAA field can learn much to guide their future endeavours from a careful perusal of the work of Bebbington, Deegan and Milne.

Work directly evaluating corporate practices and motivations concerning SEAA or studying stakeholder needs and perceptions is reflective of the major thrust of much leading edge research in SEAA today, that of a desire for 'engagement'. As Bebbington (1997: 366) points out, the idea here is to critically engage with practice in an attempt to transform it, often in ways which practice itself is reluctant to develop. "It is this question of engagement which is at the core of [SEAA] as an enabling form of research."

As those of us pursuing the engagement line have to clearly admit, a major danger we face is that of our efforts being 'captured' by powerful managerial and professional interests. Certainly, it is far from easy to break free from the economic and risk based language of professional accounting expertise, so that one becomes fixated upon issues such as how conventional accounting systems can be (marginally) adjusted to cope with

---

[5] An additional piece of absolutely essential reading prior to dabbling in content analysis is provided by Milne & Adler (1999).

the SEAA agenda. For example, research referred to earlier that investigates the potential for management accounting system modification to take on board corporate environmental concerns, in my view, largely falls into this trap, notwithstanding the no doubt admirable intentions of the researchers concerned (see, for example, Bennett & James 1998). Equally 'captured' is a strand of research popular in the 1990s that essentially sought to tweak traditional financial accounting concepts so as to encapsulate an environmental dimension (see, for example, Macve & Carey 1992; Wambsganns & Sanford 1996).

Without doubt, the contributions of the critical theorists referred to earlier have been invaluable in forcing researchers in SEAA to closely re-examine their own work for hitherto undetected signs of capture and to fundamentally re-appraise (or at least clarify) the ethical, social and political beliefs driving their efforts.[6] This has led, I believe, to a far more overt campaigning flavour underpinning current leading edge SEAA research. This research exhibits two major strands. Firstly, there is a growing volume of work that rigorously critiques the steadily increasing number of corporate SEAA initiatives, both in terms of analysing the reports produced by companies and teasing out the real motivations underlying them. Secondly, researchers are demonstrating a growing willingness to, where the opportunity arises, work with organisations in developing new accounting systems that, rather than seeking to fit the social and environmental dimension into the straitjacket of existing generally accepted accounting principles and conventions, are able to offer a fundamentally different conceptualisation of corporate performance.

Prominent within the former strand is Rob Gray's work on 'silent' social accounts. Observing that, despite the hostility that SEAA has experienced from prominent corporate and institutional interests over the past thirty years, there are some legally mandated social disclosure requirements, together with a growing volume of voluntary disclosure, Gray has been experimenting with drawing together such material (generally scattered throughout published corporate reports) in order to produce a coherent social statement (see Gray 1997). This exercise serves two purposes. Firstly, it helps to socially re-construct the organisation as more than simply an economic entity. Secondly, and more fundamentally, the exercise enables one to identify gaps in information provided which it might be expected that a fully accountable organisation would provide and thereby critique its social, ethical and environmental stance and performance.

Recent work by Carol Adams which rigorously analyses ICI's SEAA reporting initiatives in recent years, with the aim of assessing the credibility and completeness of the company's endeavours, further, and most effectively, picks up the latter theme. Significantly, Adams is able, by painstakingly comparing company generated disclosure with information gleaned from other, more independent sources, to point to a reporting-performance portrayal gap which certainly calls into question the accountability credentials of the former (see Adams, forthcoming). There appears the potential for much further work in similar mode and I would refer aspiring researchers to Adams and Laing's (2000) excellent article providing guidance as to how one can go about conducting this type of research. Finally, on a personal note, I should add that much of

---

[6] For examples of such soul searching, see Bebbington (1997) and Owen *et al.* (1997).

my own recent work is set very much within the theme of critiquing current corporate SEAA initiatives. This has included, for example, analysing environmental verification statements appended to corporate environmental reports with a view to assess as to whether or not they are worth the paper they are printed on (Ball *et al.* 2000). Additionally, I have been involved in carrying out a series of interviews with leading practitioners and opinion formulators in the social and ethical accounting, auditing and reporting area in order to investigate whether notions of accountability and transparency, or managerial capture of the agenda, best describe what is going on (see Owen *et al.* 2000, 2001).

An excellent example of research that goes beyond mere critique and actively engages with the organisation in the development of new accounting systems is that of Colin Dey (Dey *et al.* 1995; Dey 2000). Dey's work, indeed, displays two important facets. Firstly, there is a purely practical element — the development of a systematic formal social book keeping system at the U.K. fair trade organisation, *Traidcraft plc*, designed to underpin the ongoing external social reporting function. Secondly, a fascinating theoretical dimension based on ethnographic research methods is employed which seeks to understand and interpret the particular cultural system within that organisation (Dey 2002). Essentially, this entailed the researcher immersing himself within the day-to-day operations of the organisation over a long time period, thereby allowing a reflective stance to be adopted in which the nature and consequences of the organisational social accounting and accountability system as a whole (of which the book keeping system is the key technical element) could be studied.

A further major ongoing project centring on organisational engagement is the attempt by Jan Bebbington and Rob Gray to construct a formal account of the sustainability of the operations of Landcare Research New Zealand Limited, a government sponsored research organisation concerned with developing knowledge of how land eco-systems may be sustainably managed. The central thrust of Bebbington and Gray's work lies in the development of a sustainable cost calculation. Drawing on earlier theoretical work by Gray (1992) this aims to measure the additional costs to be borne by the organisation if its activities are not to leave the planet worse off at the end of an accounting period.[7] Bebbington & Gray (2001) provide a fascinating account of both the practical and conceptual reasons for their efforts proving, so far, unsuccessful, hence offering a graphic illustration of the challenges faced in carrying out leading edge SEAA research referred to at the beginning of this chapter.

Two key reasons for the failure of the sustainable cost calculation attempt are most instructive. Firstly, our present state of knowledge does not enable us to specify what 'sustainable' organisational performance might be — hence we are currently limited to producing accounts of unsustainability. Secondly, struggle as one might, it is monumentally difficult in a case study context to move away from, an at least implicit, 'business as usual' scenario as macro level market constraints and perceived economic 'realities' greatly limit the range of more sustainable practices organisations feel able to practically contemplate. However, as Bebbington & Gray (2001: 583) so rightly point

---

[7] For fuller analysis of theoretical and practical issues to be addressed in developing such a form of 'full cost' accounting, see Bebbington *et al.* (2001).

out "if business and society are to undertake a [sustainable development} path it will not be business as usual". These two issues clearly represent formidable obstacles for researchers working towards changing the 'factual universe' of the organisation, the task which above all symbolises the SEAA project. The struggle continues!

Whilst initiating research that seeks to engage with practice in order to promote change is a far from easy task, the excitement and challenge it provides to the researcher certainly makes the effort most worthwhile. In particular, it offers the opportunity to engage in public policy debate over the key social and environmental problems facing humankind, something that certainly cannot be said of safer, more conventional accounting research (unless I am missing something!). In a nutshell, what is going on at the cutting edge of SEAA research today amply demonstrates that accounting research does not necessarily have to be an exercise in boredom, rooted in the trivial and arcane, that merely serves to accumulate academic brownie points.

There are, of course, many potential points of 'engagement' for the new researcher in SEAA to pursue, and it is certainly not for me to prescribe a comprehensive agenda. Nevertheless, for what it is worth, I would offer the following two 'hot' topics as providing clear opportunities to make a meaningful contribution to both the literature and ongoing policy debate.

Firstly, the area of ethical, or social, investment, whilst being far from something new in research terms, has now a much heightened profile in the public policy arena. This is as a result of, amongst other things, the provision introduced into the 2000 Pensions Act that funds must disclose their policy, if any, towards taking on board social and environmental issues in making investment decisions. A smattering of work in the past (see, for example, Rockness & Williams 1988; Harte *et al.* 1991) began to look at the information requirements and decision processes of the pioneering ethical investment mutual funds and unit trusts. This work has been recently built on by Niklas Kreander (2001) in his investigation of the decision making processes of European ethical funds which draws on a rich programme of interviews carried out with leading fund managers and ethical researchers. However, much remains to be done now that ethical investment is apparently entering the mainstream. For example, we know very little about how investment decision-making processes and operations generally are being affected in more mainstream funds by the injection of a social and environmental dimension. In particular, how are financial and social performance imperatives being reconciled? Equally fundamentally, what are the implications for the corporate reporting function and governance structures of the funds themselves? Without doubt, a rich research agenda presents itself here.

Purely on the grounds of personal inclination I would suggest that the rejuvenated (or re-invented?) area of corporate social audit, now operating in the guise of social and ethical accounting auditing and reporting (SEAAR), offers even more in terms of engagement opportunities. Certainly, much is happening at the moment. The corporate reporting initiatives referred to earlier have been accompanied by a growing interest on the part of professional accounting firms and institutional efforts to begin to standardise practice. Particularly noteworthy in the latter context have been the Sustainability Reporting Guidelines, issued under the auspices of the Global Reporting Initiative (GRI), and the work of the Institute of Social and Ethical Accountability (ISEA) in attempting to standardise principles and processes to be followed for securing quality SEAAR.[8]

Much current SEAAR theory and practice is rooted in notions of stakeholder dialogue and engagement, whereby stakeholder views on corporate social policies and performance are actively elicited and fed into the reporting process. In this way, it is argued, stakeholder accountability on the part of the company is established. It is this claim in particular that engages my attention as a researcher. Drawing on a long established interest in the area — dating back to my exposure to the work of Social Audit Limited as an undergraduate in the 1970s and further informed by my work with George Harte (see Harte & Owen 1987) on the role of local government social audit initiatives in combating de-industrialisation — I have severe reservations concerning what is now going on. To my jaundiced eye, growing corporate and professional capture of the field has led to public relations imperatives and a desire to control for risk and enhance reputation via effective stakeholder management displacing any meaningful concern with notions of accountability. A number of fascinating research issues present themselves in this context. We have, for example, so far only scratched the surface in terms of investigating how, if at all, SEAAR influences corporate culture and how stakeholder concerns can be both effectively fed into corporate decision-making processes and addressed in terms of information provision. The most encouraging, and generous, response of companies, institutions and individuals pushing forward the SEAAR agenda to my own attempts at engagement, despite our apparently irreconcilable differences, has served to greatly reinforce my confidence as to the potential richness of research in this area.[9] I can but only encourage new researchers to enter the fray.

Get Stuck In! A Personal Slant on Pursuing SEAA Research

In common with the experience of many of my contemporaries at the time, I entered academia (in the late 1970s) straight from the accounting profession without having experienced the benefit of any research training whatsoever. This is a deficiency I have never really made good and have instead adopted a, no doubt, somewhat naïve approach of 'learning by doing'. I am, therefore, certainly not in the position of being able to offer the aspiring researcher any advice whatsoever concerning matters of research methodology! Indeed, whilst obviously not wishing to play down the importance of employing appropriate methodology in a suitably rigorous fashion, if good quality research is to be produced, I would argue that an obsession with issues of research method is likely to be counter-productive. One has only to skim through the pages of the so-called prestigious American journals, notably *The Journal of Accounting Research*

---

[8] The work of the GRI and ISEA is very much ongoing. At the time of writing these bodies latest recommendations are to be found in GRI (2002) and ISEA (1999).

[9] Worth of particular mention here is the work of ISEA which most effectively fulfils the role of a forum bringing together corporate, professional, NGO and academic interests in promoting experimentation with SEAAR practice and moving towards standardisation of such practice.

and *Accounting Review* to illustrate this point. Here we simply have, to paraphrase Tony Tinker, numerous examples of increasingly sophisticated techniques being employed to annihilate increasingly trivial problems. For those wishing to make their mark in the SEAA research arena, the problem being studied, and the motivations underpinning the work, are infinitely more important factors, in my view, than issues of methodological intricacy.

The one over-riding attribute of the leading edge SEAA research we have just been looking at is that of the personal commitment of the researcher. In a nutshell:

> For most environmental (and social) accountants their choice of research represents a central and fundamental part of who they are and how they wish to serve their community. Such beliefs are often amongst the most important elements of the researcher's existence (Owen *et al.* 1997: 181).[10]

It is pertinent to point out here that for many prominent SEAA researchers their commitment, and desire for engagement, is not simply confined to the research arena but is carried forward also into the realm of teaching. Individual experiences concerning the problems and potentialities of introducing SEAA material into the accounting curriculum featured regularly in the accounting education research literature throughout the 1990's and still form the subject of debate today. (See, for example, the collection of papers in *Accounting Education*, Vol. 10, No. 4 2001 featuring a particularly thought provoking piece by Reg Mathews, who has long championed the cause of social and environmental accounting education). Many writers draw attention in particular to the efficacy of courses in SEAA for offering an insight into the flimsy conceptual framework and taken for granted assumptions that underpin conventional accounting theory. Moreover, such courses enable students to develop deeper understandings of the extent to which accounting is implicated in processes of social and political control (see Humphrey *et al.* 1996). Crucially, teaching SEAA material offers the opportunity of influencing the next generation of accountants, whether they be future practitioners or researchers, and hence is a central component of any engagement strategy designed to bring about change. To add a personal note here, I was greatly influenced by exposure as an undergraduate at the University of Kent in the mid-1970s to a pioneering course in Social Responsibility Accounting. Suddenly, I was able to begin to make a connection between my deeply rooted traditional socialist political beliefs,[11] and the academic specialism I was following, something that had completely passed me by when studying profit and loss accounts, balance sheets and discounted cash flow techniques!

In addition to commitment, one other absolutely essential pre-requisite for pursuing meaningful research in SEAA is that of taking the time and trouble to thoroughly acquaint oneself with the literature. Knowledge of what has been written in the past can be invaluable in critiquing current theoretical and practical initiatives, as for example noted earlier in the field of corporate social audit, as well as avoiding the danger of

---

[10] This does not, of course, preclude pursuing other less academic obsessions — in my case greyhound racing and following the (usually disastrous) fortunes of Barnsley Football Club.

[11] In U.K. parlance these beliefs would be described as 'Old Labour'.

perpetually 'reinventing wheels'. The latter phenomenon was, indeed, particularly apparent in professional-led research (or perhaps more appropriately termed, consultancy) initiatives in the environmental accounting boom of the 1990s, where all too many authors seemed blithely unaware of the practical experiments and normative model building efforts of the 1970s that they were unwittingly drawing upon. Research in SEAA, like in any other field, is incremental in nature and rests on sound scholarship with, unfortunately, no short-cuts allowed!

Of course, it has to be recognised that sound scholarship is not particularly encouraged in the short term atmosphere prevailing in U.K. academic accounting today, brought about largely by the pernicious influence of a regular cycle of research assessment exercises (the dreaded RAE!). This has been particularly brought home to me over the past few years in refereeing articles submitted to a range of academic journals. All too often a 'quick and easy' literature review is a precursor for an empirical exercise that, whilst often competently planned and executed, is trivial in scope, or simply refines what has been done before, and thereby adds nothing of value whatsoever to the literature. I cannot think I am alone in finding it easy to recommend rejection of the paper in such cases.

Whilst resisting the pressure to achieve short term results is far from easy for the new academic, it may help to bear in mind two points. Firstly, the RAE has very little to do with promoting research excellence and is much more a convenient tool of control and means of administering ongoing cuts to the academic resource base. Secondly, despite the ethos promoted by the RAE of pitching institution against institution and colleague against colleague (particularly those working in other universities) we are part of an academic community. Nowhere is this more true than the field of SEAA. A particular resource in fostering our particular community is the Centre for Social and Environmental Accounting Research (CSEAR) directed by Rob Gray and based at the University of Glasgow. Amongst other activities, CSEAR publishes its own bi-annual journal and has for the past ten years run a highly successful series of summer schools which have provided the opportunity for new academics to expose their early research efforts to peer review and comment in a highly supportive atmosphere. I can offer those just embarking on careers in SEAA research no better advice than to join CSEAR and play a full part in the Centre's activities.[12]

Of course, resisting pressure to achieve short-term results does not mean that publication of good quality work should not be the aim of any accounting academic. Whilst many myths prevail about the obstructive role of academic 'gatekeepers' and the difficulties new academics have in breaking into the charmed circle of those publishing in the top journals, this, in my experience, is not true of the SEAA field. In my formative years in academia, Anthony Hopwood, the Editor of *Accounting, Organizations and Society*, offered tremendous encouragement and was instrumental in me publishing in that journal at a comparatively early stage of my career. Anthony has indeed performed a similar supportive role for numerous young academics over the years, an example that

---

[12] Full contact details for CSEAR are: Department of Accounting and Finance, University of Glasgow, 65–73 Southpark Avenue, Glasgow G12 8LE; telephone +44 (0)141 330 6315; fax +44 (0) 141 330 4442; email: csear@accfin.gla.ac.uk; web www.gla.ac.uk/departments/accounting/csear.

has been admirably followed by Lee Parker and James Guthrie of *Accounting, Auditing and Accountability Journal*, David Cooper and Tony Tinker of *Critical Perspectives on Accounting* and Glen Lehman of *Accounting Forum*. Indeed, theirs is a lead I myself have tried to follow in my role as Associate Editor dealing with SEAA submissions to the *British Accounting Review*. In sum, the spirit of community prevalent within the field of SEAA research extends to the journal submission process, and there really is very little to fear for those committed to their research and the ideals of sound scholarship.

In conclusion, my advice to the aspiring SEAA researcher is therefore to:

• seek to fully engage with education and practice;
• whilst not dismissing its importance altogether, do not get too hung up on issues of methodology;
• take the time to get fully acquainted with the literature;
• resist pressures towards short-termism and the 'quick fix';
• take full advantage of the networking and support mechanisms available to you in the SEAA research community.

As this chapter has possibly made only too clear, undertaking research in SEAA is highly unlikely to provide an entirely smooth ride career wise but certainly for me it has provided fascination, challenge and ultimate satisfaction. I have had the opportunity to work with some excellent colleagues who have become close personal friends as well as research collaborators. I can do no more than wish you the same from your careers.

References

Adams, C. A. (forthcoming). The reporting — performance portrayal gap in ICI. *Abacus*.

Adams, C. A., & Laing, Y. (2000). How to research a company. *Social and Environmental Accounting*, *20*(2), 6–11.

Ball, A., Owen, D. L., & Gray, R. H. (2000). External transparency or internal capture? The role of third party statements in adding value to corporate environmental reports. *Business Strategy and the Environment*, *9*(1), 1–23.

Bebbington, J. (1997). Engagement, education and sustainability: A review essay on environmental accounting. *Accounting, Auditing and Accountability Journal*, *10*(3), 365–381.

Bebbington, J., & Gray, R. H. (2001). An account of sustainability: Failure, success and a reconceptualization. *Critical Perspectives on Accounting*, *12*(5), 557–587.

Bebbington, J., & Thomson, I. (1996). *Business conceptions of sustainability and the implications for accountancy*. London: ACCA.

Bebbington, J., Gray, R. H., Hibbitt, C., & Kirk, E. (2001). *Full cost accounting: An agenda for action*. London: ACCA.

Bennett, M., & James, P. (Eds) (1998). *The green bottom line: Environmental accounting for management*. Sheffield: Greenleaf.

Birkin, F. (1996). The ecological accountant: From the cogito to thinking like a mountain. *Critical Perspectives on Accounting*, *7*(3), 231–257.

Birkin, F. (2000). The art of accounting for science: a pre-requisite for sustainable development. *Critical Perspectives on Accounting*, *11*(3), 289–309.

Chan, C. C. C., & Milne, M. J. (1999). Investor reactions to corporate environmental saints and sinners: an experimental analysis. *Accounting and Business Research*, *29*(4), 265–279.

Cooper, C. (1992). The non and nom of accounting for (m)other nature. *Accounting, Auditing and Accountability Journal, 5*(3), 16–39.

Deegan, C., & Rankin, M. (1997). The materiality of environmental information to users of annual reports. *Accounting, Auditing and Accountability Journal, 10*(4), 562–583.

Deegan, C., & Rankin, M. (1999). The environmental reporting expectations gap: Australian evidence. *British Accounting Review, 3*(5), 313–346.

Dey, C. R. (2002). The use of critical ethnography as an active research methodology. *Accounting Auditing and Accountability Journal, 15*(1), 106–121.

Dey, C. R., Evans, R., & Gray, R. H. (1995). Towards social information systems and bookkeeping: A note on developing the mechanisms for social accounting and audit. *Journal of Applied Accounting Research, 2*(3), 33–67.

Global Reporting Initiative (GRI) (2002). *Sustainability reporting guidelines*. Boston MA: GRI.

Gray, R. H. (1992). Accounting and environmentalism: An exploration of the challenge of gently accounting for accountability, transparency and sustainability. *Accounting, Organizations and Society, 17*(5), 399–425.

Gray, R. H. (1997). The silent practice of social accounting and corporate social reporting in companies. In: S. Zadek, R. Evans & P. Pruzan (Eds), *Building Corporate Accountability: Emerging Practices in Social and Ethical Accounting, Auditing and Reporting* (pp. 201–217). London: Earthscan.

Gray, R. H. (2002). The social accounting project and Accounting Organizations and Society: Privileging engagement, imaginings, new accountings and pragmatism over critique? *Accounting, Organizations and Society, 27*(7), 687–708.

Gray, R. H., Kouhy, R., & Lavers, S. (1995a). Corporate social and environmental reporting: a review of the literature and a longitudinal study of U.K. disclosure. *Accounting Auditing and Accountability Journal, 8*(2), 47–77.

Gray, R. H., Kouhy, R., & Lavers, S. (1995b). Constructing a research database of social and environmental reporting by U.K. companies: A methodological note. *Accounting, Auditing and Accountability Journal, 8*(2), 78–101.

Gray, R. H., Owen, D. L., & Maunders, K. T. (1987). *Corporate social reporting: Accounting and accountability*. Hemel-Hempstead, Prentice Hall.

Gray, R. H., Owen, D. L., & Adams, C. A. (1996). *Accounting and accountability: Changes and challenges in corporate social and environmental reporting*. London: Prentice Hall.

Harte, G., & Owen, D. L. (1987). Fighting de-industrialisation: The role of local government social audits. *Accounting, Organizations and Society, 12*(3), 123–141.

Humphrey, C., Lewis, L., & Owen, D. L. (1996). Still too distant voices? Conversations and reflections on the social relevance of accounting education! *Critical Perspectives on Accounting, 7*(1/2), 77–99.

Institute of Social and Ethical Accountability (ISEA) (1999). *Accountability 1000*. London: ISEA.

Kreander, N. (2001). *An analysis of European ethical funds*. London: ACCA.

Macve, R., & Carey, A. (Eds) (1992). *Business, accountancy and the environment: A policy and research agenda*. London: ICAEW.

Mathews, M. R. (1997). Twenty-five years of social and environmental accounting research: Is there a silver jubilee to celebrate? *Accounting, Auditing and Accountability Journal, 10*(4), 481–531.

Mathews, M. R. (2001). Some thoughts on social and environmental accounting education. *Accounting Education, 10*(4), 335–352.

Maunders, K. T., & Burritt, R. L. (1991). Accounting and ecological crisis. *Accounting, Auditing and Accountability Journal, 4*(3), 9–26.

Milne, M. J., & Adler, R. (1999). Exploring the reliability of social and environmental disclosures content analysis. *Accounting, Auditing and Accountability Journal, 12*(2), 237–256.

Milne, M. J., & Chan, C. C. C. (1999). Narrative corporate social disclosures: how much of a difference do they make to investment decision making? *British Accounting Review, 31*(4), 439–457.

Milne, M. J., & Patten, D. M. (1992). Securing organisational legitimacy: An experimental decision case examining the impact of environmental disclosures. *Accounting, Auditing and Accountability Journal, 15*(3), 372–405.

Owen, D. L., Gray, R. H., & Bebbington, J. (1997). Green accounting: Cosmetic irrelevance or radical agenda for change? *Asia Pacific Journal of Accounting, 4*(2), 175–198.

Owen, D. L., Swift, T. A., Humphrey, C., & Bowerman, M. (2000). The new social audits: accountability, managerial capture or the agenda of social champions? *The European Accounting Review, 9*(1), 81–98.

Owen, D. L., Swift, T. A., & Hunt, K. (2001). Questioning the role of stakeholder engagement in social and ethical accounting, auditing and reporting. *Accounting Forum, 25*(3), 264–282.

Power, M. (1991). Auditing and environmental expertise: between protest and professionalisation. *Accounting, Auditing and Accountability Journal, 4*(3), 30–42.

Puxty, A. G. (1991). Social accountability and universal pragmatics. *Advances in Public Interest Accounting, 4*, 35–45.

Rockness, J., & Williams, P. F. (1988). A descriptive study of social responsibility mutual funds. *Accounting, Organizations and Society, 13*(4), 397–411.

Tinker, T., Neimark, M., & Lehman, C. (1991). Falling down the hole in the middle of the road: Political quietism in corporate social reporting. *Accounting Auditing and Accountability Journal, 4*(2), 28–54.

Wambsganns, J. R., & Sanford, B. (1996). The problem with reporting pollution allowances. *Critical Perspectives in Accounting, 7*(6), 643–652.

Chapter 3

Using Case Studies in Finance Research

Greg Stoner and John Holland

Introduction

This chapter discusses how qualitative, case research can make an important contribution to finance, and accounting, research and explores the problems faced by the authors when investigating a set of issues arising at the boundary between companies and their suppliers of capital. These issues included corporate disclosure, the corporate release of price sensitive information, and financial institutions' use of close corporate contacts to acquire information and to influence company management. Interview case data from contacts within companies and financial institutions provided the basis for developing insight into these issues. The case based research findings were further interpreted using conventional finance theory. The chapter draws on the experience of the authors when conducting the research, writing up the results, and seeking publication outlets.

Positivism and normative approaches to finance had developed in the 1950s (mainly in the U.S.) in response to the unstructured and unsystematic nature of prior finance research and theory. Since then the prevailing emphasis has been on markets, transactions and decisions. However, the world of finance has changed much since this conceptual framework became dominant. In particular, the institutional world has altered radically, especially in a European and City of London context. This, in part, explains the need to expand the conceptual and research framework of finance to include the interactions between companies and financial institutions in a more formal way. The expanded and changing phenomena also plays a role in increasing the need for variety in research and theorising in finance and related fields of accounting. Qualitative case research methods were established elsewhere in the social sciences and were recognised by the authors as practical ways of directly exploring the how and why of such complex finance phenomena.

The Real Life Guide to Accounting Research: A Behind-the-Scenes View of Using Qualitative Research Methods
© 2004 Published by Elsevier Ltd.
ISBN: 0-08-043972-1

Use of Case Studies in Finance Research

Though case study based research is not uncommon in managerial and organisational accounting studies, at the time of the research that formed the basis on which this chapter is based, case based research in the field of finance was rare. This chapter reports on this initial research — i.e. Holland & Stoner (1996) on price sensitive information disclosure and Holland & Doran (1998) on fund management. It also briefly draws on more recent research by one of the authors. In particular, research on corporate voluntary disclosure (Holland 1998a, b, 2002b), on fund management (Holland 2002c) and on corporate governance by fund managers (Holland 1998c, 1999, 2001a, 2002a). This work has evolved over time, and it was only by the early 1990s that it established a clear focus on the boundary area between companies and their suppliers of capital.

The Initial Studies

The initial studies investigated two related areas: The dissemination of price sensitive information and management of voluntary corporate disclosure (Holland & Stoner 1996), and: Financial institutions, their equity investment decisions and the role of company relationships (Holland & Doran 1998). The first of these (Holland & Stoner 1996) aimed to describe and analyse how twenty-seven large U.K. companies sought to adapt their City and stock market disclosure policies to cope with the changes brought about by the publication in March 1994 of the Stock Exchange's 'Guidance on the dissemination of price sensitive information'. This research used the corporate case interview data to describe models of corporate behaviour and to investigate how the case companies dealt with the interpretation of legislation and other regulation in the price sensitive information (PSI) area. In terms of communications and disclosure the themes identified in the data gave rise to the following concerns: The limitations of regulation in providing clear concepts and boundaries for corporate behaviour when communicating with the City, and: How the research relates to the major field study on voluntary corporate disclosure of Gibbins *et al.* (1990). This research also lead to a variety of other questions, and indicators of possible relationships worthy of further research, including; the lack of congruence between corporate City communications policy and the information flows and practices assumed in traditional finance theory, and; the creation and utilisation of policies and structures to protect companies and executives from the uncertainties inherent in the extant regulation of PSI and information dissemination within the financial markets.

The second study (Holland & Doran 1998) described how twenty-seven large U.K. financial institutions sought to acquire an information, knowledge, and influence advantage with the relationship component of their portfolio of investee companies. The financial institutions invested much time and effort cultivating links and contacts. The primary aim of this relationship investment decision was to produce added value in stock selection and asset allocation decisions. The resulting fund performance was the means for financial institutions to satisfy a fiduciary duty to supply their clients with their preferred mix of return, diversification and liquidity (Pozen 1994). This problem area was further investigated by using financial institutional case data to describe simple models of financial institution behaviour when interacting with their relationship investee companies. The research project ended by analysing the case data and case structures through the perspective of finance theory. This reveals that fund managers employed practical concepts of downside risk at individual stock and portfolio levels and these were in sharp contrast to theoretical views.

Holland further developed the corporate voluntary disclosure case research in Holland (1998a, b, 2002b). These studies have elaborate the nature of the private and public disclosure agenda, related it to the literature on intellectual capital, and identified corporate preferences for secrecy over private disclosure and over public disclosure. Holland (2002) also extended the case research on fund management and also broadened the analysis of fund manager use of the private agenda information on intangibles in stock selection and asset allocation decisions. The same fund manager case data was also employed to extend models of corporate governance by fund managers (Holland 1998c, 1999, 2001a, 2002a).

In the following sections, the initial studies on PSI (Holland & Stoner 1996) and on fund management in financial institutions (Holland & Doran 1998), will be used as the main examples to explore issues concerning how such case research was and can be conducted, the obstacles and problems in doing the research, the way they were overcome, and the use and potential of case studies in the finance area. The subsequent set of studies by Holland also reflects the same set of issues and will be used as further examples throughout the chapter.

Key Steps and Methods in Case Research: How We Carried Out The Research

The company research on PSI set out to explore the following questions.

- How do company executives define and disclose price sensitive information?
- How do they operate within the uncertain environment of externally defined standards of behaviour concerning the dissemination of price sensitive information?

The financial institutional research set out to explore the following questions.

- How do fund managers acquire information from their investee companies?
- How do they use this information in their decisions?
- How do they influence their investee companies?

The analysis of these two issues was only part of the use to which the interview data is being used. Issues of self-regulation, corporate governance and the nature of corporate and institutional links are also being explored. In order to reveal potential answers to the first set of research questions a series of interviews were undertaken with twenty-seven large U.K. listed companies. The interviews were conducted in the period August 1993 to March 1994 and covered a large part of the 'year of uncertainty' concerning price sensitive information (PSI) issues in the U.K., during which there was an extensive public debate. As a result the case participants were concerned about the PSI debate and were developing their own approaches to its management. In each case the initial contact was by telephone, and this was the point at which the general aim of the research programme was discussed. This was followed up by a letter providing more detail and the questions. The subject of PSI was highly topical at the time and of strong interest to managers. Access was established in twenty-seven companies out of thirty-three approached, a success rate of 82%.

The second leg of the research programme involved twenty-seven confidential case studies prepared from interviews with senior directors and fund managers in U.K. based financial institutions (FIs). The interviews were conducted in the period June 1993 to March 1994; the same period as the company interviews. The case FIs constituted twenty-seven out of the thirty five largest U.K. FIs (by managed and own funds) and included Life Insurance, Pension Fund, Unit trust and Investment trust FIs. The focus of the research was on large U.K. companies and fund managers in large U.K. FIs. A sample of twenty-seven from the top one hundred FTSE companies and twenty-seven out the top fifty FIs meant that a significant portion of the market for information was covered. It also meant that cross checking was possible on the private company and FI exchanges. However to some extent the size of the samples was opportunistic and heavily dependent on the practical issue of gaining access.

In both the company and institutional cases, the interview questions were semi structured and designed to allow the participants to interpret and describe the phenomena in their own way. The research letter and research questions were designed by surveying the literature on qualitative research and by adapting interview instruments published in this literature (Bryman 1988; Buchanan *et al.* 1988; Buchanan 1993). The interview questions focussed on the broad nature of links between companies, financial institutions and the market, as well as the flow of information through these links and directly to the market. This was the limit of the structure imposed on the interview process.

Each participant had the generalised interview questions for at least a month before the interview and all appeared well prepared to explain their own views in considerable detail. However, there was little opportunity for rehearsal of answers relating to the specific research questions addressed in these papers as the questions were deliberately general, and designed to capture data on several related issues, some of which are discussed in other papers. Thus the interviewer's main roles were to record subjects' views and to empathise with interviewees so that a trusting, open atmosphere prevailed. At the start of the interview the participants were asked to talk freely about the questions and to discuss them from their own experiences. Their commentary was not disrupted. It was only in the last ten minutes of a one and half or two hour interview that specific questions were posed and this was only done if a major aspect of the research questions had been omitted.

The research design appeared to work very well in that most participants were very forthcoming and a high success rate was achieved in securing interview access. Subjects also provided considerable breadth of coverage in their views on the research questions, reflecting the topicality of the issues and the semi structured nature of the questions. The interview case data has been used in the research reports in two broad ways. Firstly, as the basis for developing an understanding of the participants understanding of the issues of interest and thereby to build models of corporate and institutional behaviour concerning the communication of price and non-price sensitive information. Secondly, to provide short cases and quotes to enliven and illustrate the concepts and decision processes identified.

An iterative approach was taken to the analysis of the large volume of case interview data, based on the seven stage approach described by Easterby-Smith *et al.* (1991). The seven stages they describe are case familiarisation, reflection on the contents, conceptualisation, cataloguing of concepts, recoding, linking, and re-evaluation. In essence the approach is one of sifting through the data in order to compare the interview responses of the various subjects and thereby to identify common themes and relationships, indicating inter-subjective understandings of the research issues: Under-standings that we compared to our own priors and extant literature. The approach was iterative in that the data and analysis was revisited on several occasions over an extended period of time. The iteration is an important element of the method, showing similarities to Kohak's phenomenological methods:

> ". . . a matter of looking, looking again, then again, each time with greater precision, until we reach a clear evident grasp" (Kohak 1978: 23).

Acquiring this degree of access to key corporate and institutional decision makers is rare in research in financial management. The initial research was unique in the field of inside information, the dissemination of PSI, and in fund management. The subsequent research on corporate disclosure, and corporate governance was also quite distinct. This uniqueness stems from the access obtained and from the focus on enterprise level decision processes in the little observed and little understood interactions between companies, financial institutions and analysts. The research method has provided an illuminating study of how decisions are conducted at the level of individual firms.

Why We Used These Methods: Research Methodology

The research methods adopted were designed to delve into the real worlds of the interviewees, in order to gain insights into how they saw their actions within the contexts of the financial markets of which they are a part. The case study method was adopted because of the limited prior research and because this research method allows rich insight into new research fields (Scapens 1990). As we were interested in the way in which the company executives and fund managers defined and dealt with these issues it was important to use a methodology that was focused on the individual and which would minimise the imposition of the researchers' priors on the subjects. To this end the data for analysis was collected via the use of general questions in a semi-structured interview context. The questions focused on the character of the relationships between companies and financial institutions and the reasons for such interactions. The questions were posed in a climate of uncertainty and debate about the nature and function of such interactions. These questions were relied on to raise the research issues and to generate novel case data independent of the researcher's prior views.

The method adopted was to use a non-invasive naturalistic interview method in order to focus on the reflected verbalised thoughts of the interview subjects, thereby providing valuable insights into the subjective understanding of the individuals' life worlds. Neutral and non-detailed and non leading questions were asked and interviewees were allowed to respond in their own time without interruption. The interviews occurred within the company and FI contexts. The interviewees and interviewers shared a common understanding and perception that the focus was on corporate disclosure, fund manager research, and private company and fund manager exchanges. Other similar interviews by the authors had indicated that this approach would create a sufficient degree of structure to ensure that the research questions would be addressed whilst minimising the risk of pre-sensitisation and biased interview responses.

It can be seen therefore that the qualitative methods that we have adopted in this research were designed to allow rich insight into new research fields and provide the basis for the establishment of understandings of the interpersonal and social construction of everyday decisions and action of the participants in and creators of the boundary between the company and corporate financial markets. For examples, see Morgan & Smircich (1980), Tomkins & Groves (1980), Hopwood (1983), Scapens (1990) and Easterby-Smith (1991). Methodologically we have advanced the importance of the experiences of the case interviewees, rejecting the notion that we can objectively observe what they are doing and thinking when they are operating at the corporate/ market interface. However, we have not taken an extreme subjectivist stance as we have sought to relate subjects' individual reflections with each other in order to explore commonalities of experience and to search for evidence of shared understandings amongst the case subjects. Further, we have attempted to synthesis these reflections and understandings with our own projections of the nature of the corporate market interface, in order to describe some tentative "models" of the nature of corporate/market information flows.

We have accepted that, at least in part, the information flows between corporate and market "sides" of the market cannot be abstracted from individual participants, as it is the participants that create information through their interpretations and understanding of the messages that are created (the inward forming of in-formation, Boland 1987). As such we are adopting an ontological stance somewhat similar to the assumption of 'Reality as Symbolic Discourse' as elaborated by Morgan & Smircich (1980: 494). Much of modern finance theory seems to depreciate the role of individuals in the operation of the market, by relying on concepts of aggregate market reactions, ideas of market equilibrium and positive predictive methodologies. These highly positivistic approaches have a tendency to assume, or imply, that individual market participants' actions are largely determined by 'higher forces' possibly derived from 'rules of nature'. What we have attempted to do is to research what is happening at the corporate/market interface, an interface that intimately involves individuals. In many institutions these individuals are recruited and paid for this specific task — indicating that the institutions accept a role for individuals, implicitly thereby rejecting notions consistent with deterministic assumptions of human nature, unless all free will is denied.

As we have focused on the role of individuals we have implicitly rejected the (extreme) objective stances on the role of human nature. It is tempting (particularly given the importance of notions of information in our research) to accept that we have adopted the mildly objective assumption of 'humans as information processors' (Morgan & Smircich 1980: 495). However our stance on the nature of 'in-formation' (above) suggests a more subjectivistic stance — accepting that the giving and receiving of messages involves social interaction, via the "utilis[ation] of language, labels, routines, and other modes of culturally specific action". From Morgan & Smircich's (1980: 494) description of the assumption of 'humans as social actors'.

In our initial analysis we have attempted to record, read, understand and interpret the verbalised reflections of corporate and market participants. Thus emphasising the importance of attempting to understand the world through the understandings of those enmeshed in its creation. Indeed our approach here is consistent with a subjectivist anti-positivistic epistemology and is in outline form close to the suggested methodology derived from the phenomenological sociology of Schutz (1967) — see for example, Burgoyne & Hodgeson (1983), Huczyski & Mmobuosi (1985) and Stoner (1987). However, our latter analysis shows evidence of the latent positivistic element within us (the researchers), as we have attempted to look for causal relationships, or at least for models of linkages between precedent factors, actions and outcomes. In the context of our broadly subjectivist approach the "models" of flows and interactions that we have presented within the research have to be considered as our understandings of the ways in which the subjects of our research had articulated their own understandings of their work worlds: How they seem to have understood their roles and actions and the information flows and barriers that they encountered, established and maintained in their everyday experiences.

Pragmatic Compromises

Subjectivist approaches such as that adopted here emphases the importance of the experiences of the subject, rather than our own "external observations". In this context the principal questions of research reliability and validity revolve around the following questions:

- How do we (and the readers of the research) know that we have elicited and "captured" valid subjects' reflections/thoughts?
- How do we know that we have faithfully reflected the subjects' understandings in our analysis of their verbalised reflections, in particular that we have avoided researcher bias, imposing of our own views?

In short we can't be sure that we have done so, though the methods described in the previous section were designed to obtain reasonable levels of assurance on these questions within the practical constraints of this research project.

If we had adhered to the strict methods derived from phenomenological sociology (Burgoyne & Hodgeson 1983; Huczyski & Mmobuosi 1985; Stoner 1987), a degree of assurance to both of these questions would be assured. However our methods diverge from those methods in two principle ways. Firstly, we did not use tape recorders to record the case interviews and therefore did not base our analysis on verbatim transcripts. Secondly we did not carry out formal phenomenological protocol analysis to identify the nomatic elements of the verbalised recall. The effect of each of these divergences is addressed below.

We did not use tape recorders to record the interviews (for the production of verbatim transcripts). We accept that many researchers (including one of the authors) have argued that tape recording of interviews need not effect the validity of subjects' responses, however it was felt that the area of the studies were particularly sensitive, especially given the potential illegality of passing/receiving inside information. A view supported by our experiences of trying to obtain confirmation of case notes (see the section on practical difficulties, below). Hence our view was that the potential loss in research rigour and validity was acceptable in order to obtain data that would not be possible were we to adhere to the purer forms of phenomenological interview research.

The possibility of secretly recording interviews was rejected on two grounds. Firstly the ethical position of doing so would be highly suspect. Secondly, the adverse effects of discovery would have been grave both for us and for other researchers, a problem exacerbated by the impossibility of reporting the fact in order to obtain additional perceived research validity. Though we are happy with the accuracy of our case interview notes they are not verbatim scripts and are not therefore susceptible to the formal protocol analysis suggested by phenomenological interview research, nor to other forms of protocol, content or similar forms of formal analysis. Instead we have relied on the independent analysis of the joint researchers to provide a degree of corroboration of the analysis.

In order to internally validate the research interpretations the co-researchers reviewed the interview data and discussed differences of interpretation and analysis. Full independent coding and analysis of the interview data has not been undertaken. Though independent analysis would increase the internal validity of the research findings the investment entailed was not deemed to be practical given the constraints of the research environment. We recognise this methodological weakness which is reflected in the tentative nature of the research claims made. Cross checking of companies and FIs views of the same events and phenomena, the use of archival sources for further assurance checks, and further repeat interviews with companies and FIs over successive research cycles, also provided further levels of assurance.

The justifications of our relatively informal approach to methods, whilst staying within this broadly subjectivist/ideographic methodological sphere, are based on the balance of access, practicality, reliability and validity. Clearly we have traded off the potential research reliability and validity of our results on grounds of practicality in order to obtain access to the rich data sources that we have obtained. In terms of the generalisations that can be drawn from this research it is important to recognise that it is problematic to generalise beyond the case study subjects. Despite the coverage of major U.K. companies and institutions the research reports do not claim to be representative studies of all large U.K. companies and institutions. However, the findings of this research do form a basis for further research of this phenomenon. The short cases and quotes have been edited to preserve the confidentiality of the sources.

Developments of the Method and Methodology

The cumulative effect of conducting grounded theory case research with companies and fund managers in five distinct phases over the period 1992 to 2001 had an important impact on the nature of grounded theory generated and in the way in which the case based grounded research was conducted and conceived. In the first case, many of the case based grounded theory concepts (axial coding) changed over the successive phases of fieldwork and data process. In particular they changed as: company and FM participants began to change their behaviour; the prior grounded theory was used to probe the changing phenomenon and to investigate the core phenomena in greater depth; and new literature and comments of other academics increased the theoretical sensitivity of the work.

For example, many of these grounded concepts began to change again in the second round of company and FI interviews in 1997–2001 as the participants began to change their behaviour. Thus, the formal private information agenda was the basis for most company presentations in 1993/1994. By 1998 and 1999, the FIs were using their own conceptual framework for deriving questions and for driving the private meeting agenda with companies. The 'formal agenda' construct was still relevant but was a lower priority in the meetings.

A similar change in the macro concepts occurred in the second round of company and FI interviews in 1997–2001 as the prior grounded theory was used to probe the corporate value creation, disclosure process, and the fund manager investment and governance processes, in much greater depth. These areas had been identified as central in the previous fieldwork and grounded theory generation, and the new data stimulated the generation of more advanced grounded theory. Thus, the 1997–2001 company and FM case data was used to deepen existing concepts such as 'management quality' and to expand the range of case based concepts to be observed in such corporate and FM decision processes. New case derived concepts in the 2000–2001 company cases included concepts concerning key categories of knowledge intensive assets and their role in a value creation process, three elements of value creation, the horizontal value creation process, the vertical value creation process, and the network value creation process. They also included concepts of how the market valued the company, and new insights into disclosure content and behaviour.

A third area of change in concepts over 1993–2001 research phases occurred as the new academic literature and the cumulative comments of other academics came into play. These were very useful at this stage to sensitising the work both in terms of similarities and differences to extant theory. For example, in the 1990s, the author became aware of the debate on 'intellectual capital' and its relationship to the private agenda. Theoretical and empirical concepts of intellectual capital became very influential in 1997–2001 in sensitising the researcher to more complete and comprehensive ways of categorising the qualitative information which lay at the heart of the private agenda, private disclosure by companies, and the use of such private information in fund manager investment and governance decisions. The literature was used to develop broader, more comprehensive categories to describe this wider set of macro concepts for qualitative information developed in the company and FM cases.

The use of a broader set of existing theories was an important means to see links between several conceptual categories. Theory was therefore used as a stimulant to keep an open mind, and care was taken to avoid closing down the generation of new concepts by relying on existing theory constructs. However, the area of study was firmly within the accounting and finance field, and where possible, attempts were made to relate to existing theory and empirical work. This cumulative learning during the casework and subsequent data processing and theory generation changed the way in which the researchers conceived and conducted the case based grounded research. The nature of the case research varied over the period 1992 to 2001 depending on whether it involved generating initial grounded theory work or was concerned with exploring and developing more established grounded theory work. As indicated above, during initial grounded theory work involving case work in 1993–1994, it was necessary to take considerable care with use of extant finance theory to sensitise the researcher during data collection and analysis. It was very easy to fall into the 'theoretical dogmatism' trap and only see the phenomena through extant finance theory.

However, during subsequent case work in 1995/1996 (with companies) and 1997–2001 (FIs), and 2000–2001 (companies), prior grounded theory (generated by the authors and others) was used to establish a richer grounded theory. In these situations, the researchers were now able to establish a deeper dialogue and debate between more established grounded theory and extant orthodox theory. This proved to be a very fruitful form of theoretical sensitivity. For example, over a ten year period, simple initial models of corporate disclosure (Holland 1998a) were developed into more comprehensive grounded theory of corporate disclosure (Holland 2002b) and the policy implications of such private disclosure in new world of economic change. Initial grounded theory work on the corporate governance role of fund managers (Holland 1995) developed into comprehensive theory of institutional governance and the major policy implications of such FI activity in terms of economic and social and environmental aims (Holland 2002a). In both cases, the central role of intangibles in corporate valuation became clearer over the cycles of case work and emerged as central explanation for the valuation and disclosure crises observed in stock markets in 1997–2002. All of these process based, field research results, produced novel insights into corporate and FI practices that were not forthcoming from positivist or normative finance traditions. However, it became possible with the more advanced grounded theory to establish a dialogue with extant finance theory. For example, differing concepts of 'value relevant information' arose in the fieldwork compared to extant finance theory and these insights generated new possibilities for research. As a result of the above case based learning, the research method was adapted over ten years, from a more judgmental and less structured approach as advocated by Glaser & Strauss (1967). It subsequently moved towards a more systematic and structured approach advocated by

Corbin & Strauss (1990). The full details of this change in methods and methodology are outlined in Holland (2001b).

Obstacles and Practical Difficulties Encountered in Finance Case Research

Many practical difficulties were faced in the research and these imposed some constraints in implementing the ideal research method. The main method/methodological compromises and changes are discussed in the sections above. This section deals with practical and organisational difficulties.

The research costs incurred for company visits involved extensive travel and hotel costs. The research bodies cut this expenditure to the bare minimum. This influenced research choices limiting the number of company visits, the time spent on each visit, and the number of researchers involved. The choice was made to maximize the breadth of coverage of the corporate and institutional sector at the expense of using one rather than multiple researchers for site visits. This led to subsequent problems of validity.

Case study research requires absence from the University. The twenty-five to thirty companies and institutions case studies each involved up to six working weeks of absence. This created problems for teaching and administration. Other academics, particularly those who use readily available databases and orthodox econometric models in finance, find it difficult to understand the need for long periods of absence. Thus, case research can be seen as a leisurely form of research that lacks the substance of conventional finance research methods. Persuading colleagues that this is an important way of collecting new types of finance related data can at times be difficult. Professional and social pressures therefore severely limit the time available to conduct case study work.

Access to companies and institutions did not turn out to be a problem in this research as the researchers gained access to fifty-eight of sixty-four enterprises approached. This success was based on a 'seed and network' approach to building contacts with companies and institutions. The specific interview access was normally based on previous contact with a company or institution. Research money was spent on attending expensive corporate and financial institution conferences in order to establish contact 'seeds'. These were then used to identify or gain access to others in the corporate and institutional network. In other cases, the ploy was to write direct to the superior of an individual the researchers wished to interview. Thus, the plan was to write to the Chairman or Chief Executive if we wished to gain access to the Finance Director. The senior executives were happy to 'pass the buck' to their junior colleagues and the latter were in difficult position to refuse.

A major problem, and benefit, of the research was that the researchers were always collecting data in sensitive situations surrounding the interviews. This meant that the interviews often spontaneously produced new insights into the situations and events. It also made the interviewees very cautious about producing concrete records of their views and ideas. Thus, creating difficulties in collecting case data during the interviews. Taping was difficult because of the above and the interviewees preferred note taking.

The latter was seen more as the interviewer's property rather than the interviewees. This approach built the confidence of interviewees and they were very frank in comments, dispelling our initial concern that subjects would censor their views.

The case or interview notes were written up immediately after the interviews and most were between 7,500 to 10,000 words in length. There was inevitably some loss of case data if, for example, an individual spoke very fast. However, this loss was not thought to exceed 20% even in the worst cases. Normally, it was possible to make a near verbatim copy of what was said. The original notes were in black pen and the interviewer memory recalls were in red, with the latter forming a very small part of the text. Initially, attempts were made to feed back interview notes to Chief Executives, Finance Directors, and top Fund Managers. They rarely responded to this and indicated that they had little time to comment. Generally they also indicated that they did not like to see the written word compared to private spoken word and were not prepared to confirm what had been said. They preferred a situation where everything they had said was deniable. This feedback approach was quickly abandoned as it became clear that it could affect future contact with the interviewees. We recognised that this would in effect be a different research method allowing subjects to censor the data after the event, as the interviewees changed to their now more public views. Thus the process of attempting to validate the interview data 'cost' more than it added: The richness and private reflections of the subjects being lost for the additional but illusory validity that it offers.

Though analysis problems were created by the difficulty of eliminating the researchers priors and individualistic and personalised structures of the interview response, these two problems were counterbalanced by two positive factors. Firstly, the researchers were continually learning through the experience of conducting cumulative cases. General patterns in the data were absorbed through direct observation during the cumulative interviews, and it became easier to see general themes as the work progressed. The repeated experience and discussion of the same phenomena over many similar cases over a short period of time gave the researcher opportunities for insights that were generally unavailable to others. This was particularly useful if a relevant corporate, FI, or regulatory, event was occurring at the same time as the interviews. This enhanced researcher understanding of PSI issues during 1993 regulatory change, corporate governance issues during and after the Cadbury and Hampel reports, and of corporate disclosure issues during the 1997–2000 'dot.com' boom. Secondly, despite the personalised nature of the structure of each case, it was possible for individual managers to identify managerial theories or constructs from individual cases that had broad applicability to many cases. Thus, a case may be unstructured in many respects but at the same time the managers articulated unifying ideas that were subsequently seen to be applicable to other cases. Thus we can see that in both of these examples, interpretation of the case data was going on before the formal interpretation process was begun with the completed set of cases. Both the researcher and the participants were identifying themes and patterns before this process began, with the case participants playing a major role here. It was difficult to avoid this but major attempts were made to ensure that it did not bias data collection. Both of these examples created a potential bias problem in that earlier cases could have effected the conducted of subsequent cases. This was controlled for by the researcher trying to maintain the same format throughout all interviews and, especially, seeking to avoid body language that might have pushed the interviewees in directions learnt from previous interviews.

A final, possibly mundane problem encountered was that writing up and interpreting the research results as described was a long and laborious task given the amount of text that had to be manipulated, processed, condensed and summarised. Computing technology can ease this somewhat but not to the same extent that it can in more orthodox finance research.

The difficulties and problems of conducting case study research, such as those noted in this section, may explain, in part, why so little qualitative research is conducted in this way in the field of finance.

How our Work has been Received

As authors of novel case research in finance we had many interesting experiences in getting case studies in finance refereed, accepted and published. In general, commentators on our papers (referees, conference participants and other colleagues) have been very sympathetic to both the new ideas generated by the research (regarding PSI release, company disclosure, fund manager corporate governance influence, and fund manager use of private information for stock selection and asset allocation) and the novel relationship focus of the research. Numerous commentators have also been very supportive in helping the researchers to locate the research in its wider finance, financial management and financial reporting contexts. However, several commentators have dwelt on "problems" with the research methodology and methods that we have adopted, particularly on issues of reliability and validity. As one reviewer noted "We are left with the researcher's views and there is . . . no way that the reader can validate or assess these." (Anonymous referee on our first journal submission of one of the papers, commenting on the lack of "formal analysis of the interviews".)

We, the researchers, have a degree of empathy with these criticisms. However, in many ways similar points could be, but often aren't, made with respect to many 'more rigorous' quantitative research reports. At the core of this comment is the fact that in this research we ask the reader to trust our analysis and conclusions and trust that we have carried out the research as described. Whilst it is true that, as we explicitly recognise, our analysis has involved a degree of judgment it is common feature of all research that researcher judgements play an important role. The choice of methods and tests is in the hands of the researchers, as is the selection of what is and is not chosen for inclusion in research submissions. However, we should also note that many of the authors' early findings on disclosure have been corroborated by other researchers using different mixtures of qualitative and quantitative methods (Marston 1993; Barker 1997). The authors' early findings on fund manager influence and governance of companies has also been corroborated by researchers such as Black & Coffee (1994) and Stapledon

(1996). Such confirmation of research results suggest that the underlying phenomena is robust and can be investigated successfully using a variety of qualitative methods (interviews, observation, archival research) in combination with more conventional research methods such as questionnaires.

It should be noted that accounting and finance academics operate primarily as one academic body in the U.K. The accounting academics have long been sympathetic to a qualitative research tradition. In addition, within a European context, many research traditions are evident. This has meant that there has been a supportive climate in the U.K. and Europe for a qualitative approach to finance and accounting related research. It has therefore been possible to argue for the value of this approach with U.K. and European journal editors and with conference organisers. The novelty of the findings, and the targeting of journals, special issues, and conferences, with an interest in new approaches to finance questions and research, all helped to ensure successful publication.

Another area of difficulty in qualitative and exploratory research of the type reported here is how should the research be presented? There is considerable debate about the appropriate 'formulae' for the conduct and writing up of qualitative research reports.' Further, it is difficult to convincingly present qualitative research within the 'accepted' quasi-scientific structure that is used for the majority of the published work in the disciplines of finance and accounting market studies. It is indeed arguable that any rigid standardisation/ 'formularisation' of qualitative research reports and methods should be avoided in the early stages of case based qualitative research. As a result, the less structured and more open Glaser & Strauss (1967) concept of grounded theory was adopted in the early stages (1993–1996) of this case research and care was taken to ensure that extant finance theory was not imposed on the processing stages with the case data. By 1997, case based grounded theory was available to the researchers and the more structured Strauss & Corbin (1990) approach was used in the processing of case data and in extending and deepening the grounded theory. In addition, a fruitful dialogue with extant finance theory was established. Both the explicit reflection and learning about research methods (Holland 2001b) and the independent corroboration of results by other researchers provide some means to resolve the problems of validity and trust outlined above.

Additional practical difficulties arise in reporting qualitative research within the confines of a standard length research article. By its nature qualitative data is voluminous and, unlike quantitative data, is difficult to summarise in an accepted and 'objective' way. There is no equivalent of the mean and standard deviation of a qualitative data set. Further, there are few standard shorthand descriptions (jargon) of the methods or tests used in qualitative research that is readily recognised by the accounting and finance community, at least not that is widely accepted. Therefore, there is an essential conflict between brevity (conciseness) and the provision of convincing evidence and methodological support — a conflict that is exacerbated by the problems of inertia when attempting to break away from the dominant paradigm of quantitative research within the domains of finance and market studies. The more structured Strauss & Corbin (1990) approach has however provided some means to resolve this issue.

Potential of Case Studies in Finance Research

The boundary area between companies (executives) and financial institutions (fund managers), analyst, the financial press, is the source of many debates in the related fields of financial management, financial reporting, and the functioning of financial markets. Many issues of public concern arise concerning the role of these links in creating and using private and public information and in the accountability and control of the network participants. It is difficult to see how a conventional finance framework alone can deal with these issues. Indeed the conventional response is that these problems do not exist or should not exist. Further, the market study based research on the utility of financial reporting is premised on the notion that financial report data is a prime source of information to the market, yet it is possible by looking beneath the reporting event to the communication flows and structures at the market interface to explore the role of reporting practices at this boundary. To ask questions that could not otherwise be approached, such as: Is the value of public financial reports that it enhances the reliability, and therefore value, of previously 'known' information? Does the publication of financial reports provide a way of 'legitimising' the trading on PSI (before 'outsiders' can do so)? Does the publication of financial reports provide a benchmark or baseline from which company-institutional communications begin? Does the latter reveal the outer limits of financial reporting or the route to further development? Is there a wider model of disclosure including secrecy, private disclosure, as well as public disclosure? What private information advantages do fund managers seek? How do they use these in their investment decisions, and in their governance decisions?

This 'boundary' research work and direct interview method does not fit neatly into the prevailing paradigm in finance and banking or financial reporting. Finance theory and it market based approach has probably been the big success story in economics in the past forty years. The primary relationship recognised between the company and banking/finance markets involves 'market forces' in the form of efficient markets and 'fair' pricing of risk. The focus has been on individual transactions and their pricing in these markets. Principal-agency models and other contracting theory may not cope well with this boundary phenomenon. In contrast, practitioners have been actively using the institutional-company boundary area for a variety of (multiple) transacting, control and learning purposes. They have been constructing relationships and other structures that appear to be central to corporate financial management, institutional investing and bank lending tasks. These boundary activities appear to have been encouraged, fashioned and moulded by larger social forces that are quite different in character to 'market forces'. The resulting networks appear to have functions that are much broader than those required by financial decision making alone.

It may be difficult to persuade finance academics to recognise the importance of this boundary zone even when it is clear that there are major issues and problems to be investigated here. The research projects on the 'Corporate control over the release and the use of inside and price sensitive information', and 'Institutional equity investing in relationship context' have been used as the two main examples of how new kinds of finance related research can be conducted in this area. However, as we have seen this research has been already been extended to broader models of corporate disclosure, of

fund management, and of corporate governance. We can also add new and related topics such as 'Corporate financing with relationship banks and institutions', 'Self regulation in financial markets', and 'Bank lending in a relationship context'. The long-term research strategy here is to unravel parts of the company-institutional networks over time and to illustrate their significance to major issues in the fields of finance and financial reporting. The hope is to be able eventually to tie together parts of the network and the associated finance and financial reporting issues into a larger, more complete, picture. The aim of such research would be to establish a broader grounded theory which connects corporate disclosure decision and corporate financing and market related decisions to activities in the market for information — by fund managers and analysts to security market states such as market efficiency. This grounded theory would have the explicit aim to develop such grounded theory based on the underlying case phenomena and networks and information flows. It would also seek to explicitly link with extant finance theory in an explicit search for wider understandings of these quite complex phenomena.

This research appears to be related to sociological work in some dimensions (for example, Scott 1993). However, there are major differences in aims and perspectives. It seems to be working from the 'bottom up', or from micro institutional-company relationships, to understand the role of networking and relationships in information markets, in security markets, in banking markets and in corporate and institutional decisions. In contrast, sociology seems to be working from the 'top down' and trying to understand the larger finance related social structures, their broader social purpose, and the way in which they shape our lives. Despite these differences, these research programmes do seem to offer opportunities for useful exchange. The work of sociologists is very useful for situating these observations of financial networks and the associated decision issues into a broader theoretical and empirical debate.

Conclusion

This chapter has set out how we have conducted and reported two related research projects, why we believe that the methods and methodologies that we have used are valid and justifiable, and to help others to learn from or successes and failures. We do not contend that these approaches are relevant in all situations or that they are acceptable to all readers/researchers. We do however suggest that the adoption of these types of research strategies are justifiable as they enable us to delve into questions that can not even be posed within the mathematical quantitative paradigms that have traditionally been accepted in this boundary area of finance theory and that any imperfections of the methods and methodology are worth accepting given the insights offered by the research that are unlikely to be generated using more rigorous "scientific" methods. Essentially, the research methods utilised in this research reflect a compromise between the ideals of research methodology and what is practically possible within the context of both the research environment and the resources available to the researchers. The constraints on the research that mitigate against the adoption of such methods fall into two related groups, resource constraints and aspects of the environment of the research. The resource constraints included limited research funds and researchers time and constrained management access time and access quality. The environment included the difficulties of breaking new ground and of persuading others (peers, referees etc) to accept the focus and the method of the research.

In addition, there has been considerable learning over the period 1992–2002 on how to effectively employ a case based grounded theory research approach in finance. This has led to changing assumptions and choices about the research methods. This was reflected in the switch from the less structured and more open Glaser & Strauss (1967) grounded theory approach adopted in the early stages (1993–1996), to the more structured and systematic Strauss & Corbin (1990) approach used in 1997–2001. This learning whilst doing case research and whilst generating grounded theory provided the experience to make informed and open judgements about compromises made between the ideals of research methodology and what is practically possible in case based research in the world of finance. The major benefits of such an approach have been the novel insights into the uncharted territories in finance, followed by the opportunity to develop wider grounded theory in the boundary areas between companies, fund managers, analysts, and security markets. This in turn has begun to create novel opportunities for a new dialogue and agenda in finance which connects such phenomena with extant finance theory. These developments create many new exciting opportunities for case based researchers in the field of finance in the new millennium.

This research work and the many publications arising from it indicate that many of the social and professional barriers to the use of grounded theory and other qualitative research methods in finance have been overcome. The crises observed in 1997–2002 concerning corporate disclosure to stock markets, of valuation of companies, of governance of companies, all suggest that such research approaches have much to offer in the decades ahead. A focus on such policy related areas in finance are likely to yield the insights necessary to understand these issues. Such highly significant policy research is also likely to find a home in reputable finance and related accounting and management journals.

References

Arnold, J., & Moizer, P. (1984). A survey of the methods used by U.K. investment analysts to appraise investments in ordinary shares. *Accounting and Business Research, 14*(55), 195–207.

Arnold, J., Moizer, P., & Noreen, E. (1984). Investment appraisal methods of financial analysts — a comparative study of U.S. and U.K. practices. *The International Journal of Accounting, 19*(2), 1–18.

Black, B. S., & Coffee, J. C. (1994). Hail Britannia? Institutional investor behaviour under limited regulation. *Michigan Law Review, 92*(7), 1997–2087.

Barker, R. (1997). Accounting information, corporate governance, and stock market efficiency: A study of information flows between finance directors, analysts and fund managers. Paper presented at *British Accounting Association*, Birmingham, March 21st.

Boland, R. J. (1987). The In-formation of information systems. In: R. J. Boland & R. A. Hirschheim (Eds), *Critical Issues in Information Systems Research* (pp. 363–379). Chichester: John Wiley.

Burgoyne, J. G., & Hodgson, V. E. (1983). An experimental approach to understanding managerial action. *Seventh Biennial Conference on Leadership and Management Behaviour.* Oxford.

Burgoyne, J. G., & Hodgson, V. E. (1983). Natural learning and managerial action: A phenomenological study in the field setting. *Journal of Management Studies, 20*(3), 387–399.

Burrel, G., & Morgan, G. (1979). *Sociological paradigms of organisational analysis.* London: Heinemann.

Bryman, A. (Ed.) (1988). *Doing research in organisations.* London: Routledge.

Buchanan, D. (1993). Recruitment mode affecting informant response. *Journal of Management Studies, 30*(2), 297–313.

Buchanan, D., Boddy, D., & McCalman, J. (1988). Getting in, getting on, getting out, and getting back. In: A. Bryman (Ed.), *op cit.* (pp. 53–57).

Chugh, L., & Meador, J. (1984). The stock valuation process: The analysts view. *Financial Analysts Journal, 40*(6), 41–48.

Easterby-Smith, M., Thorpe, R., & Lowe, A. (1991). *Management research — An introduction.* London: Sage.

Eden, C., Jones, S., & Sims, D. (1983). *Messing about in problems.* Oxford: Pergamon Press.

Financial Aspects of Corporate Governance (The Cadbury report), December 1992, London: The Committee on the Financial Aspects of Corporate Governance and Gee and Co.

Gibbins, M., Richardson, A., & Waterhouse, J. (1990). The management of corporate financial disclosures: opportunism, ritualism, policies and processes. *Journal of Accounting Research, 28*(1), 121–143.

Glaser, D. G., & Strauss, A. L. (1967). *The discovery of grounded theory: Strategies for qualitative research.* New York: Aldine.

Guidance on the Dissemination of Price Sensitive Information (1994). London Stock Exchange, February.

Holland, J. B. (1995). *The corporate governance role of financial institutions in their investee companies.* London: Chartered Association of Certified Accountants, (ACCA), Research Report 46.

Holland, J. B. (1998a). Private corporate disclosure, financial intermediation, and market efficiency. *Journal of Business Finance and Accounting, 25*(1 and 2), 29–68.

Holland, J. B. (1998b). Private disclosure and financial reporting. *Accounting and Business Research, 28*(4), 255–269.

Holland, J. B. (1998c). Influence and intervention by financial institutions in their investee companies. *Corporate Governance, 6*(4), 249–264.

Holland, J. B. (1999). Financial reporting, private disclosure, and the corporate governance role of financial institutions. *The Journal of Management and Governance, 3*(2), 161–187.

Holland, J. B. (2001a). Financial institutions, intangibles, and corporate governance. *Accounting, Auditing, and Accountability Journal, 14*(4), 497–529.

Holland, J. B. (2001b). Qualitative research in finance and accounting: Developing a grounded theory of the market for information and governance. Working paper, University of Glasgow Department of Accounting, Finance, and Management.

Holland, J. B. (2002a). *Financial institutions and corporate governance: A dynamic model of corporate governance.* CIMA research report, London: CIMA.

Holland, J. B. (2002b). Corporate intangibles, value relevance, and disclosure content. Working paper, University of Glasgow Department of Accounting, Finance, and Management.

Holland, J. B. (2002c). Fund management, intellectual capital, intangibles and private disclosure. Working paper, University of Glasgow Department of Accounting, Finance, and Management.

Holland, J. B., & Stoner, G. (1996). Dissemination of price sensitive information and management of voluntary corporate disclosure. *Accounting and Business Research, 26*(4), 295–313.

Holland, J. B., & Doran, P. (1998). Financial institutions, private acquisition of corporate information, and fund management. *European Journal of Finance, 4*(2), 129–155.

Huczynski, A. A., & Mmobuosi, I. B. (1983). Introduction to phenomenology and its application to social science research. Unpublished manuscript, University of Glasgow.

Huczynski, A. A., & Mmobuosi, I. B. (1985). A phenomenological approach to organisational research. Unpublished manuscript, University of Glasgow.

Kelly, G. A. (1955). *The psychology of personal constructs*, New York: Norton.

Kelly, G. A. (1972). *A theory of personality.* New York: Norton.

Kohak, E. (1978). *Idea and experience: Husserl's project of phenomenology in ideas.* Chicago: Chicago University Press.

Lakonishok, J., Shleifer, A., & Vishny, R. (1994). Contrarian investment, extrapolation, and risk. *Journal of Finance, XLIX*(5), 1541–1577.

Marsh, P. (1992). Short termism. In: P. Newman, M. Milgate & J. Eatwell (Eds), *The new palgrave dictionary on money and finance* (Vol. 2, pp. 446–453). London: Macmillan.

Madut, A. M. (1985). Phenomenology: An alternative research approach. *Graduate Management Research* (Autumn/Winter), 32–41.

Marston, C. (1993). Company communications with analysts and fund managers. Unpublished Ph.D. thesis, University of Glasgow.

Mayer, C. (1995). Corporate governance in the U.K.: Is there a problem? Centre for Economic Policy Research, Lunchtime meeting 21st March 1995, hosted by the Royal Society of Edinburgh.

Moizer, P., & Arnold, J. (1984). Share appraisal by investment analysts: A comparison of the techniques used by portfolio vs. non-portfolio managers. *Accounting and Business Research, 14*(56), 341–348.

Morgan, G. (1983). Social science and accounting research: A commentary on Tomkins and Groves. *Accounting, Organizations and Society, 10*(4), 385–388.

Morgan, G., & Smircich, L. (1980). The case for qualitative research. *Academy of Management Review, 5*(4), 491–500.

Pozen, R. C. (1994). Institutional investors: The reluctant activists. *Harvard Business Review* (January-February), 140–149.

Scapens, R. W. (1990). Researching management accounting practice: The role of case study methods. *British Accounting Review, 22*(3), 259–281.

Schutz, A. (1967). *The phenomenology of the social world.* Evanston: Northwestern University Press.

Scott, J. (1993). Corporate groups and network structures. Chapter 16 in: J. McCahery, S. Picciotto & C. Scott (Eds), *Corporate control and accountability.* Oxford: Clarendon Press.

Stapledon, G. P. (1996). *Institutional investors and corporate governance.* Oxford: Clarendon Press.

Strauss, A., & Corbin, J (1990). *Basics of qualitative research.* Newbury Park, CA: Sage.

Stoner, G. N. (1987). The use of a phenomenological methodology to investigate the organisational; flows and uses of information: Some observations from a study of bank exposure management. Paper presented to the Management Control Association, June, Sheffield.

Tomkins, C., & Groves, R. (1983). The everyday accountant and researching his reality. *Accounting, Organizations and Society, 8*(4), 361–374.

Tomkins, C., & Groves, R. (1983a). The everyday accountant and researching his reality: further thoughts. *Accounting, Organizations and Society, 8*(4), 407–415.

Willmott, H. C. (1983). Paradigms for accounting research: critical reflections on Tomkins and Groves' "Everyday accountant and researching his reality". *Accounting, Organizations and Society, 8*(4), 361–374.

Walmsley, P., & Yadav, W. R. (1992). The information content of the company meeting programme of the society of Investment analysts: 1985–1990. *Journal of Business Finance and Accounting, 19*(4), 571–584.

The Wilson Committee (1980). *Report on the functioning of financial institutions.* Cmnd 7939, HSMO, London.

Chapter 4

Accounting and Auditing Research in the United States

Tom A. Lee

Introduction

This essay was written at the end of an eleven-year period of residence in the U.S. I had been employed full-time at a large state university with an explicit research mission[1] and its school of accountancy was ranked nationally. It had the only accounting doctoral programme in the state.[2] My duties included directing the programme for ten years and I held offices and other positions in several research organizations in the U.S., Canada, Australia, and the U.K. I believe these experiences together with twenty-four years as a researcher in the U.K. prior to 1991 give me a relatively unique perspective of American accounting and auditing research (henceforth "research").

The purpose of my chapter is to discuss some observations I can make of American research. The observations are focused its main characteristics and prefaced with a warning that other academics with similar experiences might make different observations. My commentary is a critical analysis of research and dependent on personal experience and may be biased by either what I have or have not observed or the value system that I bring deliberately to the analysis. I have always seen research as a sub-set of professional accountancy practice and directed at improving the utility of practitioner services. I therefore do not believe that research is a function that exists solely for the benefit of academics.[3]

[1] In the U.S., state government provides only a minority of the resources needed to fund the research of most universities. The shortfall comes from private sources for which there are generous tax incentives for donors. However, despite their minority funding status, legislators typically mandate teaching requirements for state-funded universities and are often critical of faculty time devoted to research.

[2] There are less than one hundred active doctoral programmes in the U.S. (Hasselback 2001). The annual doctoral graduate output in recent times has been between one hundred to one hundred and fifty individuals. However, over the last year or so, this number has fallen to less than twenty and indicates current recruitment problems and future faculty staffing crises.

[3] Such a closed system is effectively what research has become in the U.S. and elsewhere and has been analyzed by writers such as Sterling (1979), Zeff (1989), Lee (1990), and Brinn et al. (2001).

The Real Life Guide to Accounting Research: A Behind-the-Scenes View of Using Qualitative Research Methods
Copyright © 2004 by Elsevier Ltd.
All rights of reproduction in any form reserved.
ISBN: 0-08-043972-1

My analysis is not based solely on my employment at specific American universities. Instead, I am attempting to examine a contemporary situation that involves all U.S. universities concerned with research. In addition, my criticisms of research should not be regarded as unique to America. The problems I am commenting on are of a global nature. They are arguably more pronounced in the U.S. than anywhere else at the present time. However, there is recent evidence that the gap between American and British research is closing.[4] In this respect, I believe that the separation of practitioners and academics in the U.S. beyond economically-inspired alumni contacts has particularly contributed to the problems I describe.[5] The consequences of this situation appear to me to have been largely ignored by American practitioners and researchers and both groups need to respond to the challenge of making research relevant to the needs of practice.

Typical Career Path

It is helpful in this analysis to understand the career path of a typical researcher in the U.S. The main employment requirement is a research-based doctorate. Acquiring such a qualification involves attendance for several years at a university with an accredited graduate school. This is usually made possible because of scholarships guaranteed for at least four years. Tuition fees are effectively waived and the scholarships are usually sufficient to live on, although recipients are expected to undertake teaching and research support activities in return. Funding of scholarships and tuition fee waivers are made possible by private donations from alumni and public accountancy firms.

A doctoral programme in accounting typically consists of two or three years of study in the classroom and one or two years writing a dissertation based on a defined project. Classroom work is largely focused on research design and methodology taken from economics, finance or psychology. The dissertation that follows is typically based on an accounting or auditing project that uses theoretical arguments derived or adapted from one of these non-accounting disciplines. It is prepared with guidance from a committee chaired by a faculty member who acts as the main supervisor.[6]

The dissertation proposal is usually presented for approval to all full-time faculty members. This means that non-researchers can have the same vote as researchers. Faculty with no interest or knowledge of the dissertation topic can therefore influence whether or not it is accepted and this can create understandable tensions during the presentation process. Not all non-researchers are aware of how outdated their knowledge of research can be. Once approved, however, the dissertation proposal becomes a legal contract in which the sole requirement is that the completed research is consistent with the accepted proposal. It therefore does not matter if the research relates to what proves to be a non-issue. If the proposal has been accepted, and the promised research process has been followed, that is the end of the matter. Only

---

[4] This is evident in Brinn *et al.* (2001) and Zeff (1989).
[5] See Lee (1990) for a U.K. analysis and Bricker & Previts (1990) for a U.S. equivalent.
[6] The doctoral supervisor is an essential influence in the career of an American researcher and Haskins & Williams (1986) and Fleming *et al.* (1991) provide some historical evidence of this.

members of the dissertation committee vote on the acceptability of the research completed in these terms.

A further, and arguably more substantial effect of the above system, is that the doctoral candidate has no incentive to refine or redefine the project in light of research findings after the dissertation topic has been approved. This is not only a severe constraint on creativity in research but also explains why American doctoral research is almost always based on quantitative models in which a limited number of variables are defined and statistically manipulated (for example, as in capital markets and agency, and judgment and decision making projects). It certainly rules out research in which the process of research in large part defines and shapes the project (for example, as in field-based work, history, and critical studies). In addition, the commitment to significant funding of doctoral students places obvious pressure on faculty and staff to complete doctorates in the minimum time possible. The U.S. is not a place to do qualitative research under these conditions.

Following presentation of the dissertation proposal, a doctoral student wishing to work in the U.S. seeks employment as a faculty member for a probationary period of six years.[7] The search for a faculty position can involve visits to several universities at which the main task is the presentation of the dissertation proposal or completed dissertation. There is also the strong possibility that probationary employment will mean moving several hundred miles to an unfamiliar state, city and university. Considerable time therefore has to be spent getting to know a new locality, university, faculty and staff. Often the local culture is different and the familiarization process leaves little time for research. However, immediately following the end of the fifth year of the probationary period, a decision is made by all tenured faculty members on the probationer's suitability for tenure and promotion to associate professor. Again this involves researching and non-researching faculty. A negative decision means termination of employment but a positive decision provides a job for life. The name of the game for five years, therefore, is to perform a number of tasks that will assist in a positive decision. These include keeping students content,[8] providing visible committee service and, most importantly, creating a portfolio of published research in quality journals when probationary employment is with a research-orientated university.[9] There are no figures publicly available concerning termination rates for probationers. However, personal experience at several U.S. universities suggests to me that a conservative figure would be between 25% and 33%.

---

[7] The availability of doctoral student funding in the U.S. is attractive to foreign students and raises debate within the American community on whether significant investment is made in students who will not work in the U.S. Because of a shortage of home-based students, American doctoral programmes typically contain a number of non-U.S. students.

[8] This means receiving good evaluations from students by not being too demanding of their time and intellect and giving them expected high grades.

[9] Studies reveal that accounting academics in the U.S. are reluctant to rate anything other than American journals as top quality (see, for example, Howard & Nikolai 1983). Little or no attention goes to specialist journals other than those dealing with economics-related empirical and behavioural research methodologies (Lee 1997).

Much of this employment process makes little sense to me for a variety of reasons argued later. But perhaps the most curious aspect is that, despite ten or more years of research training, relatively few tenured faculty members in the U.S. seriously practice as researchers after the tenure decision is made.[10] This paradox seems to me to have less to do with having a job for life than the fact that most faculty members do not want to be researchers when they enter their doctoral programmes. Indeed, I found few students with a serious ambition to be a career-long researcher. They want to teach. However, doctoral programmes are not designed to train teachers.[11] A typical accounting faculty member in the U.S. therefore trains to practice a profession that he or she is involved in at best for only a few years in order to obtain tenured employment. An accounting doctorate in the U.S. appears to be nothing more than a symbol of academic respectability and a job ticket.

Doctoral Degree Pedigree

The reputation of the accounting doctorate in the U.S. is crucial to the career of a potential faculty member because it determines which career doors open and which remain closed. The better the reputation of the degree, the more prestigious the employing institution and the larger the compensation package negotiated. It is therefore important that students choose their doctoral programmes carefully. This is particularly the case for those who wish to make research a major part of their career. The American academy is a rigid hierarchical structure and it is rare for faculty to move up the pyramid but exceedingly easy to move down it.[12]

The argument typically given to excuse this élitist system suggests that first-class universities only admit first-class students to their doctoral programmes. Second or third class students go to second or third-class doctoral programmes. Although this logic may be true in some cases, I do not believe that it reflects a universal truth in practice. Doctoral programmes perceived to be first-class typically graduate their fare share of second-class faculty and so-called second-class programmes regularly produce first-class researchers. However, the rigid hierarchy in the U.S. academy cannot cope with such anomalies. The remainder of my essay is concerned with examining such contradictions.

Research is Superior to Teaching and Service

The greatest rewards to U.S. faculty come from research-based activities. Reputations rely on research-related publications, offices, and awards rather than excellence in the

---

[10] A majority of accounting faculty never publishes and only a very tiny percentage produces more than ten journal articles in a lifetime career (Chung *et al.* 1992).

[11] A doctoral student in the U.S. typically receives free tuition and a stipend and benefits in return for service as a teaching or research assistant. This financial support is a cheap means of providing teaching support for full-time faculty.

[12] See Lee (1995), Lee (1997) and Lee (1999).

classroom or service on committees. Teaching and service can definitely augment a research record, but cannot diminish it significantly. Research is therefore the glamour part of academic activity and researchers are on public display. Pay increases and tenure and promotion decisions in research-based universities are typically associated with the number of 'hits' achieved in research journals. The most valued 'hits' are those in perceived 'top' journals. The objective in effect is to maximize the number of 'top journal hits'.

Unsurprisingly in this type of environment, researchers become preoccupied with research from an early stage in their careers. They learn to cope with inevitable constraints on research time caused by teaching and service. Some senior researchers negotiate contracts in which teaching and service activities reduce to a minimum to allow time for research. Graduate students usually undertake teaching in these situations. Faculty maintain service activities, however, if they are of an external variety and relate to research. These include appointments with professional bodies such as the American Accounting Association and editorial boards of 'top' journals such as *The Accounting Review* and the *Journal of Accounting Research*. These services augment a successful research career in the U.S.

Research-biased faculty contracts usually are found at private universities and can give rise to criticism from students that too much of their instruction is by graduate students rather than full-time faculty members. In public universities, research-biased contracts exist if faculty have exceptional national or international research reputations. Most researchers at public universities teach a specific number of courses annually because legislators mandate this. Inevitably, this creates situations in which ambitious researchers put less effort into teaching and service in order to create more time for research. Students therefore suffer from sub-standard or undemanding teaching, and university administrators do not fully benefit from the experience of these researchers.

Research is a major focus in decisions about promotion and tenure. Despite explicit stipulations from university administrators that teaching and research are equal in worth, I found that there is an almost universal bias to research in faculty discussions. This is unsurprising because research is a faculty activity that can be 'measured' according to seemingly objective criteria. The latter include input indicators such as research funds and output indicators such as journal publications, research awards, and citations.[13] The same argument is not relevant to teaching performance in the U.S. Classroom activities have an invisible existence in terms of relevance, quality, and influence. Teaching in American universities is remarkably free of monitoring or accountability. Apart from faculty decisions on outline proposals for new courses, there are relatively few checks on what happens in the classroom. The sole output measure is the written evaluation of faculty by students and faculty manipulate this process with undemanding syllabi and grade inflation. There are virtually no reviews of syllabus content, classroom performance, and grading. A course taught by more than one faculty member is a rarity and external examiners are unknown in my experience. Researchers teach the same

---

[13] Primary emphasis is given to research journal articles. Other forms of research publication such as texts, monographs, and contributions to texts are generally regarded as secondary. See Zeff (1989) for an American comment on this issue. Brinn *et al.* (2001) contains British evidence of this distinction.

course several times a year for many years to avoid preparation time. Courses are constructed around textbook packages that eliminate the need to prepare classroom and examination materials. It is therefore easy for a researcher to comply with mandated teaching requirements with minimal effort. It is also remarkably undemanding of students.

Only Doctors of Philosophy Need Apply

Since the 1960s, the terminal qualification for faculty in the U.S. has been the doctorate.[14] In order to teach at degree-awarding institutions, faculty members train as researchers. As previously stated, this situation is one where most faculty therefore train to practice something they have no intention of practicing. It also creates a number of other curious side effects. First, in my experience American researchers are usually better trained in quantitative research methods compared to researchers in other countries.[15] This is particularly true with respect to research design in projects using theories of economic and psychological behaviour. Even the worst American student can have acceptable quantitative design and methodology skills. This seems to me to provide American researchers with a considerable advantage when submitting papers for review at research journals. The other side to this particular coin, however, is that non-U.S. researchers are better able to deal with qualitative research because American researchers rarely see it or, indeed, know of its existence. But this limits the publication opportunities for non-U.S. researchers. It is a matter of fact that few researchers not trained in American universities publish in American research journals.[16]

Researchers in the U.S., on the other hand, appear to me to be less creative than their non-American equivalents with respect to identifying significant issues for research purposes. The reason for this difference is complex and related to two problems. The first is that faculty in the U.S. study little or no accounting or auditing in their doctoral programmes. The classroom focus is predominantly on methodological issues necessary to complete the dissertation project. Outside the U.S., however, accounting researchers typically identify a researchable issue before studying a compatible methodology. American researchers therefore seem less aware of accounting and auditing issues than do their international counterparts.[17] This is also a consequence of uncritical undergraduate teaching of accounting and auditing in the U.S. Despite the need to study practice problems within theoretical frameworks, theory is not discussed. Such discussion requires detailed study by faculty to provide clarity and understanding. However, studies of theories of accounting or auditing are incompatible with a professional career designed to maximize research time by minimizing classroom time.

---

[14] See Committee on Doctoral Programs (1965).

[15] This is a matter of growing concern in countries such as the U.K. where research is driven by issues rather than methodologies (Brinn *et al.* 2001).

[16] See Brinn *et al.* (2001).

[17] This is hard to imagine because of the media coverage of accounting and auditing problems of the largest companies in the U.S. In very recent times, these have included Cendant, Enron, Global Crossing, Sunbeam, Waste Management, America Online, and WorldCom.

Accounting or auditing theory courses that are taught in the U.S. tend to be advanced and "packaged" explanations of generally accepted accounting principles or auditing standards.[18]

Third, doctoral programmes in the U.S. are constructed in such a way that students are significantly influenced by the researchable issues and methodologies they are exposed to by faculty. Teaching and supervising in doctoral programmes inevitably point students only to issues and research designs with which their supervising members have experience, competence, and interest. This continuity of thinking and practice in research has the benefit of building on experience and prior research with the disadvantages of indoctrination and examining specific issues to the point of irrelevance. An example of this phenomenon is several decades of research and writing on the relation of accounting and auditing to agency theory that has done nothing to address the poverty of financial reporting in the marketplace. It is also unsurprising that research in the U.S. is dominated by a design built on the statistical manipulation of economic and financial databases. Most American researchers of the last thirty years have been trained in it because it is compatible with the need to maximize the number of journal 'hits' in a short period of time. It can be completed conveniently in the summer semester.

Research for Academics Rather Than Practitioners

Several decades ago, research was concerned primarily with normative prescriptions to improve the quality of accounting and auditing practices. Different forms of accounting practice and audit technique were offered, explained, discussed, and criticized. Research projects arose from problems identified in practice. Research careers and reputations were made and broken by normative research. However, the 'publish or perish' culture and the emergence of computerized economic and financial databases changed this world. Research, particularly in the U.S. where there was sufficient funding, was quickly dominated by empirical research projects based on economic or finance theories and the use of economic or financial data. Doctoral students in economics and finance gravitated to accounting because they were using accounting data in their projects, and job opportunities and compensation in accounting were more accessible than in economics or finance. The use of accounting data by these researchers, however, did not mean that they comprehended its nature or limitations. Major research journals focused largely on issues concerning capital markets and economic agency. A similar but much smaller emphasis in auditing was also evident with respect to cognitive psychology generally and human judgment and decision-making.[19] With the exception of critical

---

[18] The writer's American experience of theory-based examinations was typically of spending hours of preparation on potential questions and problems, and days of grading student answers. Colleagues, in contrast, would usually offer 'packaged' questions and answers from the prescribed text that could be processed in a fraction of the time.

[19] No one has convincingly explained to me why it is necessary for relatively untrained accountants to conduct studies on market and human behaviour rather than leave these matters to trained economists and psychologists. In addition, there is little evidence in the economics or psychology literatures that research by accountants is used or cited. Such lack of impact would concern me if I was working in these areas.

research, normative projects in accounting and auditing disappeared completely in the 1990s and so did the relevance of much of research to practice. Instead of research journals full of prescriptions to improve practice, their contents were and remain directed at predominantly informing researchers rather than practitioners about complex research designs and self-evident issues and solutions.

In my opinion, the self-evident nature of contemporary research in the U.S. can be summarized as follows. The behaviour of capital markets and individual actors in these markets is affected by the absence or presence of relevant accounting information. A recent scandal such as Enron clearly illustrates this.[20] It also signals the failure of researchers to advocate solutions to lapses in corporate accounting, disclosure, and audit.[21] The question of what is relevant and reliable accounting and auditing has been ignored by American researchers for several decades, despite the presence of leading researchers in standard setting. To me it is as if medical researchers were interested only in the behaviour of doctors rather than the detection, prevention and cure of illnesses and diseases. Unsurprisingly, therefore, the quality of reported information is increasingly found to be suspect and the work of auditors of such information is declared to be unimpressive. In my opinion these conditions will persist until the American research community gets back to the basics of helping practitioners provide dependable services rather than conducting anthropological studies of markets and their participants.

Normative Research is Not Research

As I suggested earlier, the 1950s and 1960s can be characterized as a golden age of normative accounting research in the U.S. and elsewhere. The major research journals of the times such as *The Accounting Review* and *Journal of Accounting Research* were composed of extensively argued prescriptions. The latter were typically constructed by the comparative analysis of alternative prescriptions for a defined accounting or auditing issue. The alternatives were systematically eliminated until the preferred solution was revealed.[22] Particular prescriptions often sparked published responses. Less frequently, prescriptions were tested by practitioners.[23] Most normative accounting researchers were therefore aware that their arguments could affect practice.[24] Nevertheless, towards the end of the 1960s, concerns about the subjectivity of normative research began to emerge in the U.S. It was declared to be non-scientific (Watts & Zimmerman 1986).

---

[20] Enron is an American energy trading company. At its collapse in 2001, it was the seventh largest company in the U.S. Its auditor was Arthur Andersen. The executives, directors, and auditor of Enron face accusations of removing billions of dollars of debt from its balance sheet.

[21] Researchers such as Watts & Zimmerman (1986) believe that to offer solutions to problems is unscientific and therefore unacceptable as research. This attitude beggars belief.

[22] See, for example, Sterling, 1970.

[23] See, for example, American Institute of Certified Public Accountants (1969).

[24] Cash flow accounting is an example of this phenomenon (Lee 1993).

This new approach to research started with the publication of several economics-based accounting studies using computerized databases of reported financial data.[25] The quantitative nature of these studies and their dependence on accepted economic theories gave them a quasi-scientific appearance that is not apparent in a normative study. The divide between normative and empirical research was exacerbated by many researchers being trained in economics or finance rather than accounting. Statistical manipulation of reported accounting data, however, does not necessarily provide reliable science. In my experience, identifying and understanding accounting issues is the key to meaningful research. This applies to both normative and empirical research.

During the 1970s and 1980s, the complexity of the empirical research design being applied to accounting projects began to demand sophisticated training in the manipulation of computer databases and the use of advanced statistical techniques to test data relationships. Increasing time was devoted in accounting doctoral programmes to this training and the study of accounting and auditing issues was steadily reduced until it disappeared. Major research journals began to fill with empirical studies and their editorial boards were dominated by empirical researchers.[26] Normative research publications ceased to be published during the 1980s and 1990s and effectively a division was created between accounting practitioners and researchers. Practitioners were unable to read and understand research publications and researchers appeared uninterested in finding better ways to account and audit. Some researchers protested about this unnecessary separation, but most adapted to the new form or retired from research. For those in influential roles in the research community in the U.S., normative research was unscientific and therefore not to be trusted. Put simply, their view was that such research was speculative opinion. Unless an accounting research project was designed to pose a question and seek an answer by quantitative means, it was not to be regarded as research. This is the current position of most American researchers. Few doctoral students are able to use normative or non-quantitative research designs in their dissertation.

American Research is Best

Few American researchers appear to me to be aware of research undertaken outside the U.S. This is partly due to a national insularity but has mainly resulted from training in doctoral programmes. American students read previous research only to the extent they need to use it in a particular project. American researchers — and probably other researchers — do not read widely and only study in their narrow specialty. Buried within this problem of a lack of general knowledge is a specific bias towards American journals because these are regarded in the U.S. as the 'top' outlets for research. Few, if

---

[25] The acknowledged trigger for this phase of accounting history was the Ball & Brown (1968) paper that studied the effect of the public release of accounting information on stock market prices.
[26] Dyckman & Zeff (1984) provide a detailed analysis of these points in relation to the *Journal of Accounting Research*.

any, non-American journals are ranked as highly as American journals.[27] The editorial requirement in journals such as *The Accounting Review, Journal of Accounting Research*, and *Journal of Accounting and Economics* is that contributors demonstrate a comprehensive awareness of previous research in these journals. Such awareness is typically established by means of a search of computerized databases. My experience as a researcher, reviewer, and editor is that there does not appear to be such a narrow requirement in non-American journals.

American researchers, however, turn to non-American journals when their papers are rejected by American journals. In these circumstances, the switch in publishing intention is usually detectable by the insertion of non-American citations in the literature review — particularly publications in the journal to which the paper has been submitted. In other words, research outside of the U.S. becomes of significance to American researchers when they are unable to publish their work in the U.S. Despite the questionable ethics of this situation, many American researchers appear on the editorial boards of non-American journals. Most have not and will not publish in them and often remain listed on the boards for many years. What this suggests to me is that the reputation of American researchers is being used as a marketing device to improve the apparent quality of non-American journals and attract American submissions, subscribers, and readers. In my opinion, this tactic has done little to improve American awareness of the non-American literature or enhance American researchers' perceptions of the quality of non-American journals. In fact, it is a strategy that can accentuate perceptions of the second-class status of non-American accounting journals in the U.S. community.

Practicing Single Research

As previously mentioned, the name of the game in American research is the number of publication 'hits' achieved. The more 'hits' the bigger the economic and social rewards for the researcher. With this in mind, the simplest way of maximizing 'hits' is to work in teams of researchers. A typical team contains two members. However, teams as large as five or six appear in the American literature. Teams are often initially constructed from the research relationship between a faculty member and a doctoral student. Doctoral dissertations lead to publications in which faculty supervisors are co-authors. Often these relationships continue for many years. Teams also reflect divisions of skills. Some researchers specialize in literature reviews and theory constructions. Others deal with database constructions and manipulations. Statistical testing of data forms a further specialty task.

Team research provides obvious benefits for researchers. It allows different skills to be brought together in a collective effort. It is particularly suited to research where there is only a short period available to design, argue, collect, test and write. American researchers usually research in the summer and devote the remainder of the year to

---

[27] The only exception is *Accounting, Organizations and Society* edited by a graduate of the University of Chicago and with several American members on its editorial board.

teaching and service. Thus, particularly for probationary faculty, team research is vital if productivity is to provide a necessary number of 'hits' to satisfy faculty colleagues at the end of five years of probationary work. There are also disadvantages of team research. First, researchers become skilled in a small number of tasks but never become proficient in them all. This should make it difficult to judge the quality and proficiency of a researcher for purposes of promotion, tenure, pay increases, and job applications. Sadly, however, these judgments appear to me to be made as if there was overall proficiency. Second, it is the American practice in decisions relating to these matters to ignore the team and treat each author as if he or she was the only author. For example, if there are four authors separately applying for promotion and tenure, their joint paper will appear in each of their records. It is then counted in each case as a single rather than one-quarter publication. Third, it is tempting to have a team of several researchers where only a subset works on an individual project. Different subsets are responsible for each paper produced but each paper bears the name of every researcher and credit is given to each individual. In my experience, these practices are endemic in the U.S. but no doubt also exist in other countries. The contrast of the considerable reluctance of American faculty to teach in teams is an enduring paradox for me.

Elite Rule OK

There is social closure in the U.S. accounting academy.[28] It is structured as a hierarchy with élite schools, programmes, and faculty at the top. The remainder of the community is spread in several social layers of perceived quality. Generally speaking, those at the top of the pyramid are at institutions that were the earliest members of the community. Universities such as California at Berkeley, Chicago, Illinois, Michigan, Ohio State, Stanford, and Texas therefore have a disproportionate presence in academic offices, awards and honours lists, and editorial appointments. This suggests that, with few exceptions, only researchers who are doctoral graduates of these institutions are worthy of these offices, awards and appointments. Alternatively, graduates from other programmes are unworthy. In my view, such arguments are spurious and the facts relate to a biased system of power and patronage. The hierarchy is self-perpetuating, faculty accept it, and there is no need for deliberate conspiracies to create social closure. The original creators of the structure reproduced and perpetuated the positions of power and influence at the American Accounting Association and journals such as *The Accounting Review*. Their successors today know of no other world. It is the divine right of these editors and presidents to rule.

The problem with this closed system is that it is hard to conceive of ways in which it could be overcome. Opinion surveys of American faculty through the decades have persistently reported that élite and non-élite faculty members agree on what are the 'top' doctoral programmes and journals. This is unsurprising to me. A MORI opinion poll in the Middle Ages would have achieved the same result — both peasants and nobility

---

[28] I have researched this issue in a number of recent papers (Lee 1995, 1997, 1999, and 2000; Lee & Williams 1999).

knew their place in the pecking order. However, the consistency of these results should not be taken as justification for closing offices, awards, and journal appointments to graduates of non-élite programmes. Nor should it be used to regard only the research of the élite as legitimate. The most obvious closure in this respect exists at *The Accounting Review*. This is the flagship journal of the American Accounting Association. As such, it should reflect the Association's membership in terms of editors and contents. That it does not is arguably one of the reasons for the current dwindling membership of the Association. Editorial board members since the *Review*'s inception in 1927 have been disproportionately élite and its contemporary content is heavily biased to economic empirical research.[29] Historical, organizational, and sociological research studies are rarely published in the *Review* and editorial board members do not reflect these research interests. Behavioural research has also suffered a diminished appearance in the *Review*. Of course it can be argued that there are specialist journals for these different research designs. But that in my view is not the point. The *Review* is intended as a general journal according to its published statement of purpose. Elitism prevents that mission being accomplished.

The Only Good Research is Elite Research

A further consequence of élitism in the U.S. research community is the relegation to a secondary status of several types of research with respect to decisions about promotion, tenure, and pay increases. First, research publications are judged in terms of perceived journal quality rather than content relevance to practical issues. A publication in a 'top' journal such as *The Accounting Review* is unquestionably assumed to be of high quality. An article in a 'lesser' journal is usually regarded to be of lesser value irrespective of the actual relevance or reliability of the study. The name of the journal is more important than the research. The brand name is apparently more significant than the contents of the package. 'Top hits' also receive disproportionate rewards in the academic accounting community in the U.S. For example, a publication in an élite journal will typically be treated as equivalent to several papers in non-élite journals with little or no reference being made to the actual research or its impact. This means that a faculty member publishing in non-élite journals has to complete several research projects compared to one study (or a share in one study) by a colleague who publishes in an élite journal (e.g. five papers in *Critical Perspectives on Accounting* could be regarded as equivalent to a one-fifth authorship in a paper in *The Accounting Review*). The argument for this unfairness that I have heard repeatedly made in its justification is that it is 'difficult' to publish in an elite journal and 'easy' to get into non-élite journals. As someone who has published, reviewed, and edited in both types of journal, I can categorically state the argument is nonsensical and uninformed.

A further unfairness exists when research is published in professional or education journals in the U.S. It is typically weighted downwards even more than non-élite journal publications. It is possible that practice and education papers are given little value in

---

[29] See Lee (1997, 2000).

many academic organizations and, once more, is a problem created by concerns about the perceived quality of the journal outlet rather than the quality of the research or its practical utility. The raw unfairness of these separations based on surface perceptions and judgments is relatively obvious. It is certain that a researcher who infrequently and jointly publishes research of little use to practitioners will be rewarded to a much greater degree than a researcher who publishes frequently and singly in the practice and education literatures. In my opinion, it is a system that discourages young researchers from becoming involved in research of use to practitioners. A more rational approach with respect to career and rewards is to focus on research that is only of interest to fellow researchers.

Conclusions

Despite private concerns about the American research community and its practices there are few public challenges to it. Most academics in the U.S. are relatively well paid and do not want to research. They do not read the research literature and the latter is rarely part of the public accountancy curriculum in universities. Elite begat élite and get away with the practice of social closure. But a heavy price is paid. Current research is irrelevant to practice and the latter is patently in need of reform in both accounting and auditing. Companies and their shareholders are persistently hurt by poor financial reporting and auditing. Eventually someone in power is going to ask the basic question of why, with all the private and public investment in research, the returns are negligible in terms of better accounting and auditing products and practitioners. A credible answer will be very difficult to make.

And what of the implications of these comments for non-American researchers generally and those in Europe particularly? The first thing I would say is that the current situation is unhealthy. There is a need for wider recognition of the value of all types of research. No particular paradigm has primacy at this time. Americans need to widen their horizons to cover non-quantitative research types in their doctoral programmes, faculty activities, and research journals. Non-Americans need to become better skilled at quantitative work and recognize the important part it has to play in the search for a better accounting practice. In other words, neither group should regard the other as either stronger or weaker. Both have significant contributions to make to knowledge generally and the work of the accountancy profession particularly. The immediate issue is to start to remove the current division of 'us' and 'them'.

This process cannot be achieved by isolation. All journals that profess to be general in their coverage (for example, *The Accounting Review* and *Journal of Accounting Research* in the U.S.) must be open to all research paradigms and methodologies or amend their constitutions and policies accordingly. Doctoral programmes and faculty promotion and tenure decisions in all countries should embrace all paradigms and methodologies. To do otherwise is, at least in my view, to be anti-intellectual and contrary to the fundamental ethos of universities. It is therefore imperative that Americans and non-Americans work unceasingly at ways to welcome and involve all paradigms and methodologies. This is not an easy option nor is it one for the inexperienced. Indeed, I would argue that collaborative research, including comparative work, is best done in the first instance by senior faculty who do not have the same career risks to face as do junior faculty. But, hopefully, senior collaborations would lead to better understanding and tolerance would feed down into doctoral programmes, dissertations, promotion and tenure decisions, journal editing and reviewing, and research assessment exercises. Exchanges and collaborations are essential and these should be built on existing contacts. There are qualitative researchers in the U.S. and there is a public interest section of the American Accounting Association. The Academy of Accounting Historians largely comprises North American members. The British and European Accounting Associations should continue to build on existing relations and explore the possibilities of American doctoral students studying in Europe and vice versa. Exchanges of faculty should also be considered in terms of sponsored programmes to deal with any economic inequalities that currently exist between the U.S. and Europe.

It is particularly important to re-assess a world dominated by spurious league tables and rankings, and superficial assessments of the apparent quality of the 'kennels' (for example, the doctoral programme, university, or research journal) rather than the quality of the kennel product (for example, the doctoral graduate, faculty member, or journal article content). Using this analogy, anyone with the remotest knowledge of dogs knows that intensive and isolated inbreeding within a pedigree creates long-term and undesirable defects and issues. Paradoxically, man's best friend is typically the crossbreed or 'mutt' built on the strengths of several pedigrees (i.e. a constant reminder of the doctrine of the survival of the fittest). Research assessment exercises, no matter how well meaning, are almost inevitably likely to lead to kennel rankings based on the perceptions of the assessors. And if the assessors do not represent an adequate cross-section of kennels, then a danger exists that biases will emerge in their deliberations and judgments. They judge in terms of what they are familiar and comfortable. There is a French phrase that captures best what I am trying to say about the future — 'vive la difference!'

References

American Institute of Certified Public Accountants (1969). General price-level accounting. *Accounting Principles Board Opinion, 3.* New York, NY: AICPA.

Ball, R., & Brown, P. (1968). An empirical evaluation of accounting income numbers. *Journal of Accounting Research, 6*(3), 159–78.

Bricker, R., & Previts, G. (1990). The sociology of accountancy: a study of academic and practice community schisms. *Accounting Horizons, 4*(1), 1–14.

Brinn, T., Jones, M. J., & Pendlebury, M. (2001). The impact of the Research Assessment Exercise on U.K. accounting and finance faculty. *British Accounting Review, 33*(3), 333–355.

Chung, K. E., Pak, H. S., & Cox, R. E. K. (1992). Patterns of research output in the accounting literature: a study of bibliometric distributions. *Abacus, 28*(2), 168–185.

Committee on Doctoral Programs (1965). Doctoral programs in accounting. *The Accounting Review, 40*(2), 414–421.

Dyckman, T., & Zeff, S. A. (1984). Two decades of the Journal of Accounting Research. *Journal of Accounting Research, 22*(1), 225–297.

Fleming, R. J., Graci, S. P., & Thomson, J. E. (1991). Tracing the evolution of research in The Accounting Review through its leading authors: The 1946–1965 period. *The Accounting Historians Journal, 18*(1), 28–53.

Haskins, M. E., & Williams, D. D. (1986). A genealogy of today's contributors to accounting research. *The Accounting Historians Journal, 13*(2), 93–101.

Hasselback, J. (2001). *Accounting faculty 2001.* Englewood Cliffs, NJ: Prentice Hall.

Howard, T. P., & Nikolai, L. (1983). Attitude measurement and perceptions of accounting faculty publication outlets. *The Accounting Review, 58*(4), 765–776.

Lee, T. A. (1990). Education, practice and research in accounting: Gaps, closed loops, bridges and magic accounting. *Accounting and Business Research, 19*(753), 237–254.

Lee, T. A. (1993). *Cash flow reporting: A recent history of an accounting practice.* New York, NY: Garland Publishing.

Lee, T. A. (1995). Shaping the U.S. academic accounting research profession: The American Accounting Association and the social construction of a professional élite. *Critical Perspectives on Accounting, 6*(3), 241–261.

Lee, T. A. (1997). The editorial gatekeepers of the accounting academy. *Accounting, Auditing and Accountability Journal, 10*(1), 11–30.

Lee, T. A. (1999). Anatomy of an élite: A history of the executive committee of the American Accounting Association 1917–1996. *Critical Perspectives on Accounting, 10*(2), 247–266.

Lee, T. A. (2000). Sustaining a *habitus* in U.S. accounting research. *Advances in Public Interest Accounting, 10,* 177–194.

Lee, T. A., & Williams, P. W. (1999). Accounting from the inside: Legitimizing the accounting academic élite. *Critical Perspectives on Accounting, 10*(6), 867–895.

Sterling, R. R. (1970). *Theory of the measurement of enterprise income.* Kansas City, KS: University of Kansas Press.

Watts, R., & Zimmerman, J. L. (1986). *Positive accounting theory.* Englewood Cliffs, NJ: Prentice Hall.

Zeff, S. A. (1989). Recent trends in the USA: Implications for the U.K. *British Accounting Review, 21*(2), 159–176.

Chapter 5

Forever Destined to be Extras in a Broadway Show? A Discussion on the Status of National Accounting Research in an International Arena

María Antonia García-Benau and José Antonio Laínez-Gadea

Introduction: Why are We Writing this Paper?

When we attend a show in a Broadway theatre and see the actors completely at home in their roles, we are captivated by the setting. Everything seems so easy that we dream of becoming actors performing before an expectant public. But in fact, although we are part of the supporting cast, nobody notices us at rehearsals. We make an effort to attract attention, but to no avail. We painstakingly prepare ourselves to achieve a small part in one of the magnificent plays that are going to be put on. The truth is that on many occasions, directors might give us a walk-on part in the show. We are often assailed by doubts and deep down we think, "How can we do this if English isn't even our first (or, in many cases, second) language?" The theatre is magic, but how much effort does each scene in each act call for? One day, we might see our effort rewarded? Maybe one day we will get to become stars of a Broadway show, or are we forever destined to be extras?

For those of us born in Spain, the above serves as a simile to express what it takes for us to attain a certain status on the international scene. Rehearsals, for us, are the presentation of papers in English before a diverse and lively audience but which is, all too often, just a group of Spanish colleagues. We dream of being published in prestigious international journals, as proof that our work does have some relevance, but our reality is that most of our efforts in research never gain an audience. If only we could play on Broadway some day!

When the editors of this book suggested that we write this chapter, we thought it would be interesting to tell colleagues in other countries of our experience in accounting research. It is a fact that each country's progress and development in accounting

The Real Life Guide to Accounting Research: A Behind-the-Scenes View of Using Qualitative Research Methods
© 2004 Published by Elsevier Ltd.
ISBN: 0-08-043972-1

research is different. Economic, cultural and social differences mean that we are faced with a heterogeneous world, despite the effects of globalisation and the wish to standardise many of the customs, norms and even traditions of many countries. The Spanish experience in accounting research has been somewhat different to that of English-speaking countries. As there has barely been any tradition of accounting research in Spain, this has meant that we have had to intensify our efforts and the fruits have not been as bountiful as we should have wished. In other words, we as accounting researchers all share a common objective, but the difficulties we come up against are not the same: it depends crucially on the country in which you are born and where you decide to make your life.

As academics, we have personally been providing our services to the Spanish University system for twenty years now and our experience might be summed up as the quest for excellence in research and 'making our mark' on the international scene. Fortunately, the situation in Spanish universities at the beginning of the 21st century is very different from that of twenty years ago, and therefore our experience is now past history, but we hope that this chapter will help to clarify what the last twenty years have been like for us in terms of research and to give some personal insights on the current times in which we are living. For, in spite of the progress made in accounting research in the last few years, the actual situation is not ideal. Many things need to be done and many answers have to be found. In particular, important efforts have to be made to reach a proper balance in the international accounting research community.

This chapter deals with four issues. Firstly, we set the scene for the situation in Spain, discussing the development of higher education in our country and the impact on the Spanish academic accounting profession. We also explain the motives that drive us to take part in the world of research (dreaming of Broadway or doing it because we have to?). Secondly, the chapter considers movements towards some form of assimilation of the Spanish academic accounting community into the international community. Thirdly, the paper assesses the extent to which the Spanish academic community has received recognition from the rest of the international community. We then talk about our experiences in the last fifteen or twenty years and how we have started to find our feet in the international milieu (or, rather, a small role in a Broadway show), by striving for quality in accounting research. We conclude with a look at the future and speculate what it holds for us.

Beyond Teaching: The Growing Interest in Research

In this section, we will explain the motives that have led us to conduct research projects. It is important to recognise that in the last few years intensive research in accounting has been carried out in Spain. We will address the constant institutional pressure that has linked employment stability with the obtaining of a doctorate, as well as the strong personal motivations to contribute to accounting knowledge.

By 1975, the year of Franco's death, Spain had lived for forty years under a military dictatorship and had become isolated from the rest of the world. This had an effect on many aspects of Spanish life including, of course, the university system. There were no research links with Europe: during the Franco era, one was not allowed even to think about research collaboration with other countries. And yet, Spain copied the accounting norms issued by France, although this fact should not be taken the wrong way, since the norms were copied without prior debate or comparison with what was being done in countries with a long tradition of preparing and publishing accounts. The 1973 General Accounting Plan, while not compulsory, was virtually sacrosanct. Accounting was required to follow the rules expressed therein, and the teaching of accounting was planned entirely around this General Plan.

The Franco era was a very dark stage in Spain's history. However, the period that we shall be referring to in this paper really begins in 1983, the year in which the University Reform Act was passed under the socialist government of Felipe González — this Act has, consciously or unconsciously, influenced and steered most of our actions.

Institutional Pressures Imposed in the Last Twenty Years: The Marrying of the Quest for Knowledge with One's Academic Career

The Spanish university system has traditionally been based on instruction rather than education, so that teaching has been the principal driving force for university activities. To a large extent, this has been due to the fact that the basic purpose of education was to give a large part of the population the chance to enter university, coupled with the relative absence of a tradition of academic excellence (especially when compared to English-speaking countries). In Spain, accounting was a technical component within the study of Economics. Accounting education of a more conceptual nature only started to develop in the last few decades of the 20th century, albeit still following the line of training students for the profession (see Martínez Churiaque 1992), and the idea that accounting theory and practice should go closely together (see, for example, De Fuentes *et al.* 1994; García-Ayuso & Sierra 1994; García-Benau *et al.* 1996). And yet, the Spanish university system's emphasis on professional practice gave rise to a strange paradox, because in spite of the important pragmatic aspect of accounting teaching, the academic and the professional worlds remained apart. For instance, it was very rare for a University to receive professional commissions from the business sector.

In the field of accounting research, there remained much to do. The only research being carried out in Spain in the late 1970s/early 1980s was not research in the strictest sense of the word; it was limited to using certain *ad hoc* premises to resolve short-term, practical business problems that required an immediate solution. The university was acting almost as a business advisory branch, a situation that was not conducive to scientific and technological progress. Basic research was too difficult to assess and rarely undertaken. However, unlike the situation in many of Spain's closest neighbours, it was understood that to conduct research one had to have a doctorate and the ability to manage the resources required for such research to be carried out efficiently. This aspect of educational policy had a singular effect on research, in that young teachers defended their doctoral theses in the early stages of their career, when often they had not received all the training that one might reasonably expect.

The 1983 University Reform Act turned university teachers into public servants. This meant that they had to take State competitive exams in which the tribunal gave extra credit for any research conducted. Thus:

> ... it is a fact that nowadays the prestige and social and professional recognition of university teaching staff, and therefore their salaries and academic rank, will be conditioned by their performance in the field of research, rather than by their teaching . . . (Larrán *et al.* 1996).

Consequently, institutional pressures served as an incentive for conducting accounting research. However, not all lecturers remained active in the research field once they had attained the status of public servant, although, these days, more and more lecturers are committed to research projects, as a result of self-imposed challenges and the commitments they acquire during research. Without any doubt, it is because of these personal goals rather than legal requirements or regulations that has caused Spanish accounting research to spread its wings on the national as well as international scene.

The 1983 University Reform Act was repealed by the centre-right, *Partido Popular*, government under José María Aznar in late 2001, when it passed the Universities Act (*Ley Orgánica de Universidades — LOU*). This Act now governs university activity in Spain. It has reiterated that research is an essential function of universities and is recognised as a basis of teaching, a means for the advancement of the community and a medium for the social transfer of knowledge (art. 39.1). Since the Act was passed, there has been a flood of regulations and laws from the government that have been introduced despite being strongly criticised. There are currently a good many issues still to be resolved in detail, and there are only draft regulations on the table, but all the signs are that a highly regimented university system is being planned, in which all the power is to be concentrated among certain groups of researchers.

We would like to highlight one particularly controversial issue. Barely fifteen years ago, the Spanish university system established some components designated as '*sexenios de investigación*' (research sexennials), whereby university teachers submit their research (every six years) for evaluation by a national committee. This is voluntary, and some teachers were not in favour of letting anybody issue positive or negative assessments of their research work. However, there were no academic repercussions to distinguish between teachers with research sexennials and those without. Achieving this complement[1] has been interpreted during this time as being an important merit, although many Spanish academics have kept it secret as they have not wanted to reveal the number of positively-evaluated research sexennials obtained. And yet, with the reform imposed by Aznar's government, research sexennials are now playing a major role for any academic, since a good many doors are being closed on teachers whose research has not been positively evaluated via several research sexennials. For example, a certain number of sexennials are required if an individual is to become a member of a competitive exam tribunal, to assess doctoral theses or to supervise a master's thesis, etc.

---

[1] Teachers may attain a maximum of six research sexennials, which means that 36 years of their research work will have been positively evaluated.

This has caused certain ill-feeling among some academic people who argue that something that had been voluntary is now being used as an element of discrimination.

Research Concerns (The Process by which Research was Undertaken)

An important question for aspiring researchers in Spain was how to tackle the changes required for carrying out accounting research in a society that felt that the university system was basically orientated towards teaching and publishing textbooks? How were we to work in a country that was opening up to research but where such a high dedication to teaching, and in some cases, administration, was required? What type of research could be conducted in a society which saw accounting as being little more than a way of keeping registers? To show the scenario in place in the early 1990s, we indicate below the distribution of teachers' *actual and ideal working time*. The data to illustrate this point is from a study conducted in Spain by García Benau *et al.* (1997).

The most important result of this study is that accounting academics in Spain distribute their working time in the following way: 62% to teaching, 27% doing research and 11% carrying out administrative tasks. However, there is a discrepancy between the activities actually carried out by university accounting teachers and what they would want to carry out. The desirable distribution would double the percentage of time devoted by staff to research (to 53%), while the teaching percentage would be reduced by a third (to 40%). In the case of administrative tasks, the percentage is also reduced by almost half, although in recent years, university administration has undergone gradual change, from pure administrative tasks to duties relating to teaching and research decision-making.

In seeking to understand such results, it is worth pointing out that the 1980s saw a massive intake of students into the Spanish university system. The number of students was extremely high and there was an unfavourable student-teacher ratio. For example, there were nearly 200 students in each lecture hall for classes. Obviously, all this caused a chain reaction, involving long teaching hours, made up of student consultations, a large number of exams to be assessed, etc. As we see it, the distribution of *ideal* time declared by teachers tallies with the current system of promotion (recently modified by the *LOU*) that puts increasing emphasis on research. With regard to teaching, the little weight it carries in the process of turning teachers into public servants might explain the wish for teaching hours to be reduced. This amounts to confirming, in the words of Donoso (1991), "the almost total absence of academic recognition of teaching activity, which has led on many occasions to comments from our colleagues on the need to concentrate on our research activity, since this is the only way to attain professional recognition, and this directly implies the abandonment, to a certain extent, of our focus on teaching, and thus low motivation". The strong willingness by teachers to carry out research, however, also needs to be kept in perspective in that the actual time being spent by Spanish academics on research activities (27%) is well below that in other countries (where at least 40% of a full-time academic staff's workload is officially allocated to research activity).

As far as we are concerned, it has not been easy to break into the world of accounting research. A lack of support, stimulus and supervision have all proved important obstacles to development. However, despite the hostile atmosphere in Spain twenty years ago, there has been a gradual and growing interest in carrying out good quality research — so much so, that in the last few years, research has taken on an important role in Spanish university life.

In our opinion, various factors have had a major influence on the development of research. The first, and perhaps most important factor was the publication in the early 1980s of the aforementioned University Reform Act, whereby the only chance of making an academic career and promotion was to get involved in research projects. To obtain the post of a permanent teacher in the Spanish university system, one needed to have a doctorate (for two of the three types of post envisaged), and this qualification became one way of attaining employment stability. This gave rise to a certain perverse effect in Spain since, in many cases, researchers were not researchers in the strict sense of the term; instead, they just published certain papers to justify the minimum requirement to become a public servant. The passing of the 2001 Universities Act has not changed this philosophy, although it has changed the way one can become a member of the body of university teachers.

The second factor was the great personal commitment made by some Spanish teachers. One of the first measures we took in our interest to get involved in high quality research was to spend time in foreign universities. This was a major step, because we did not have outside funding and had to meet all the costs from our own pockets. This was a major commitment and in addition, during our stays, we received very little attention from foreign researchers (a criticism levelled by quite a few Spanish colleagues).

The third factor was Spain's entry into the European Union in 1986 and the subsequent increase, in the 1990s, of grants to promote research in financial topics. The resulting modernisation imposed on Spanish society and the fact that Spain had found itself among a group of more advanced, democratic countries meant that Spanish legislation adapted surprisingly quickly to EU Company Law directives. Being a member of the then twelve member states was really important for accounting research. Spain's adaptation to the Company Law directives was completed in 1989 and it became fashionable to compare Spain's adaptation with that of the rest of the member states. These comparative studies were extremely hard work, particularly because of the difficulty in obtaining (and understanding) information from certain countries most notably, Greece and Denmark — it was impossible for us to read Greek or Danish!). However, the desire to publish and collaborate in international research was noticeable among a good many teachers in Spain. There was a desire to become leaders on the world stage, even though the research process kept throwing up new problems and new difficulties, some of which seemed practically insurmountable. We began to concentrate more on quality than quantity, and we realised that it was not necessary to analyse all the member states, just one or two of them. Thus our research was to become more detailed and our work more fruitful. Currently in Spain, funds are being devoted to financing accounting research projects, and this will enable us to take on more complex research.

The fourth factor has been the availability of databases that facilitate the conduct of empirical research. Until very recently, we did not have data at our disposal to tackle certain research projects. Spain's entry into what was then the European Economic Community introduced a large dose of modernisation into our country and we began to find it easier to obtain financial information from Spanish companies, something unthinkable up to then. Accounting information and financial data were no longer closed books. Currently there is a strong interest and a major increase in applied research. We have databases at our disposal with which we can carry out empirical studies to show certain comportments and reactions when financial information is published. In this respect, we should underline the fact that financial information has only been considered to be in the public domain for the last fifteen years; in fact, at the beginning of this period, the only way of obtaining company information was to consult the mercantile register and photocopy the annual accounts. The effort was arduous and somewhat unproductive and it was not until the beginning of the 1990s that we really began to realise the research benefits of having access to databases - and realising the potential to conduct empirical accounting research that might be of real relevance to the international scene.

Progress over the Last Fifteen Years: A Long Learning Process

Spanish Presence at International Conferences

Writing our respective doctoral theses were the first serious research projects that we ever did. The general perception in the 1980s was that nothing of the doctoral thesis should be revealed until it was defended before the tribunal that would judge it. Presenting part of your research in conferences precluded it from the final text, and so we would have to hide our work until defending our thesis (this was *'el secreto major guardado'*, our best kept secret). In addition, presenting papers in national conferences did not have much appeal because the papers were hardly, if ever, reviewed. This lack of constructive criticism meant that, together with the absence of supervision, the non-existence of research groups and the methodological shortcomings we possessed, we had to teach ourselves how to conduct research.

In fact, we started attending international conferences before we had gained the necessary experience in our own country. The presentation of our research in international conferences has been gradually adapting itself to the international scene. However the small problems experienced by our English-speaking colleagues became huge for us. How could we take part in a crash course that would enable us to take our place in the international milieu if we had little experience (looking back, we had practically none), and we were faced with a highly consolidated international collective? Presenting a paper in an international conference meant months of preparation, just to present it (after having written the paper). Often we would have two or three hours of English classes per week, dreaming of attaining a fluency that was really unattainable, although we would be capable of presenting our paper and perhaps understanding the different accents of our English-speaking colleagues. We often asked ourselves: "What were they doing while we were studying English?" The public presentation of our research in international conferences had its own big drawback. How were we to know whether what we were doing was interesting or whether it had methodological problems if we had never heard criticism of our work? And what if the audience talked about some research method or model that we had never heard of? Help!

Spanish presence at international conferences (particularly European conferences) began to make itself known from 1990 onwards. In the early 1990s our main objective was just to survive, making sure that the work was done on time and that we could get through the long questions from English-speakers (were they trying to ask us something or were they simply making a comment? That was something we would nervously ask ourselves with great frequency). Our experience in these international conferences was very useful for us. We realised that we were doing something wrong and we began to learn to speak a new language. We began using criteria of scientific relevance for qualifying a research topic, becoming aware of the existence of a scientific problem and research methodology. And of course, we learnt to accept strong criticism of our research projects.

All these issues and uncomfortable situations did not deter us from endeavouring to publish high quality research. Furthermore, the Spanish journal, *Revista Española de Financiación y Contabilidad*, introduced external evaluation of submitted papers and a positive trend has been established because the journal has reached an important level of quality; in many ways it compares favourably with international journals.

The Importance of where Research is Published (Things that we had to learn)

Our way of reviewing the literature and comparing theoretical postures go a long way towards explaining the Spanish situation as it was in the mid-1980s. We used to study articles published in international journals, and practically pull them apart, but we never fully understood the editorial stance of the journals. We were not very aware of the fact that one had to be extremely cautious when analysing the sources that we consulted, since our interpretation and criticism to a certain extent depended on their value. Another important issue for us was learning which medium to seek publication, since in Spain, the main medium was books (although it was not really research but, in the words of Gonzalo (1999), '*docencia escrita*', written teaching). We started to appreciate the value of academic literature, the author's knowledge, the originality of the work and its overall, scientific value. Accordingly, we began to replace books with international journals as the desired mode of publication.

We soon came up against the problem of measuring the journal's quality and we learnt that there was a link between the quality of the medium and that of the article (see Carmona *et al.* 1999). However, in view of the mechanisms established for ensuring the quality of publications (usually, evaluation by various anonymous reviewers), we accepted that there was certainly a strong correlation between one aspect and the other. One of the most frequent mechanisms for measuring journal quality has been via questionnaires to academics. Another way of tackling the issue has been through impact indices, mainly citations in other journals. However, the use of citation analyses poses certain problems. As Jones *et al.* (1996) show, it is not only good papers that are referenced, but also bad articles, while there is also the problem of citation 'networks'. One also has to add that very few accounting journals are included in citation indices, specifically the Social Science Citation Index.

One of our major concerns was finding a measure to help us distinguish what was considered to be of good quality on the international scene, and so the choice of an area of research was very important (see, for example, Cea 1996). At first we mainly used bibliometric indicators, and soon began to associate various authors and their methodologies and use their opinions as a quality indicator. In this respect, it was particularly useful for us to read opinions such as those expressed by Tinker & Puxty (1995), when they said that quality was a broad concept that could mean very different things. Tinker (1985) stated that accounting could not expect to be discovered like an atomic particle; much of what happened in accounting research was related to the interpretation of existing knowledge. Brinn *et al.* (1996) compared quality of research with an elephant when they said that "you know it when you see it" (although we often could not see it!).

However, these opinions did not provide us with an objective criterion for understanding what was seen in the international context as quality in research. Whittington (1993) was in favour of finding more objective criteria to define quality, since it was understood that publication in quality journals was an accepted criterion for assessing the level of a piece of research. And yet this criterion cannot be considered universal either, since the prestige of a journal depends on the reputation of the editorial board (Ryan *et al.* 2002), the number of articles published that have made an important contribution to the literature and the number of citations from that journal quoted in others. This path eventually led us to articles that were to have a great influence on us (including McRae 1974; Brown & Gardner 1985; Brown *et al.* 1987; Bricker 1988; Smith & Krogstal 1991). Also high up on our list were, among others, works by Beaver 1968; Ball & Brown 1968; Zeff 1978; Watts & Zimmerman 1978; Flint & Shaw 1981; Laughlin 1981; Tinker *et al.* 1982; Tinker 1985; Loft 1986; Whittington 1986, 1987; Hopwood 1987; Beaver *et al.* 1987; Cooper & Hopper 1990. While having the greatest influence on our research and a significant influence more generally in Spanish academic accounting circles, not all the above studies had the same impact in Spain. A significant majority of Spanish researchers still chose to 'play it safe' and opted for more traditional accounting research based on positive empirical methodology and centred on the capital market.

Having imported the positions and methodology of prestigious authors on the international scene, we sought to imitate them by trying to publish articles in international journals. The Spanish journals at the time offered us no opening since, among other reasons, they did not have much of a research tradition, and those that had been on the market for years were orientated towards accountancy practice. Perhaps it is difficult, for an international reader to understand why we have not included research published by Spanish researchers in our list of the most influential papers on our research. It is easy to provide an answer. Spanish publications were orientated towards explanations of professional accountancy practice; so, it was necessary to look for references in other countries with more established traditions in accounting research.

Besides, we needed papers across a broad range of research in order to establish and debate theoretical and methodological perspectives.

From our point of view, the above was real evidence of a change in the way that accounting research was understood in Spain. The momentum continued at the beginning of the 1990s, as we started to attend European conferences. To gain some visibility in these congresses was really important for our academic life as accounting researchers. Following the lines of the international literature available to us by that time, we were able us to make presentations of our papers at international conferences and, step by step, get to know how to locate the authors from other countries in different conceptual positions. Hence, we began to meet with international colleagues and to exchange ideas as well as methodological and conceptual approaches with them. In fact, we could say that European conferences helped us to find our own position in the different ways of understanding accounting research in the world. Since then, we have been more selective in the choice of the studies we have read and we have been able to define better our chosen areas of research, participating in more specific accounting debate with researchers from other countries.

In spite of the progress achieved to date, there is still a long way to go. In this sense, most of the papers presented by Spanish authors in collaboration with foreign people, still deal with Spanish cases. The political Spanish situation (change from a dictatorship to a democracy), the new international image of Spain (entrance to the EU), the new demand for, and availability of, financial information presented by Spanish companies (compulsory auditing, publication of financial statements etc.) have all helped to make made Spain attractive for academic researchers from other countries. This situation has led to the publication, in general, of two different kinds of papers: (i) papers that follow a developing international line of research by providing a Spanish example/case of the phenomenon being studied (for example, efficient capital markets), and (ii) papers that seek to contribute more directly from a Spanish perspective, by means of enhancing our understanding of the accounting activity and particular/special traditions in Spain (for example, historical analyses of the development of Spanish accounting practices).

Our ówn experience shows that it is difficult to introduce many changes and new research methodologies into our country. For instance, we have been doing research in auditing, focused on the effects of the financial scandals in Spain (such as the Banesto case in the early 1990s), the political nature of auditing, or the role of the big auditing firms. These papers have had an important impact in Spain, albeit on just a few groups of researchers. However, we will be missing something very important if Spanish research does not start to try and gain further knowledge about audit practice. In our opinion, this will help us evaluate such things as the impact of the Enron scandal in Spain and the loss of credibility of the auditing profession.

Establishing the Boundaries of Accounting Traditions and Research Methods (Goal Reached: Our papers are published in international accounting journals)

We began to become familiar with the currents of research in accounting in the late 1980s/early 1990s. At that time, an awareness of the bibliography and the theories contained therein became a decisive step in our attempt to make a contribution to research. We became aware of the traditions of accounting research and the delimitation of the two very strong traditions that were dominating the literature. Firstly, positivism, and its particular way of looking at realism through the question of 'what is', took root in Spain. Most of the research carried out in Spain and the highest number of papers published in recent years lies within this current of research (see, for example, Sánchez Segura 1994; Monterrey 1996; Vico & Pucheta 2001; De Fuentes & Pucheta 2002). However, the second tradition in research, centred on the interpretation of practical reality and/or on a tradition of thought that is strongly relativist in orientation, has had fewer followers in Spain, although it may be found in the odd study (see Ruíz 1996; Vico 1997; Larrinaga 1999).

Spanish researchers have concentrated more on the finance field and the forecasting of economic variables based on certain hypotheses. Market-based accounting research, focused on the impact of investors' decisions on market security prices, found favour with a group of Spanish researchers who examined the predictive ability of accounting information and wanted to know the usefulness of financial reports in predicting variables of interest to decision-makers (for instance, future cash flows, predicting corporate failure). There was also a fair amount of capital market research into the relationships between accounting information and share prices, to determine the way in which the stock market reacts to different types of accounting information (although the Spanish stock market was fairly opaque, and many studies concluded that the market did not react to financial news).

However, studies based on explanation and which considered philosophical perspectives also brought together a group of Spanish researchers, albeit fewer in number than the previously mentioned group. The journal, *Accounting, Organizations and Society* (*AOS*) and its emphasis on social theory really started to be discovered in Spain in the 1990s. Spain's extraordinary history of the last fifty years, in which we experienced diametrically opposed situations, from dictatorship to democracy and incorporation into the European Union, meant that we sought to amplify the conditions of social life, which in turn increased our interest in this type of research. Nevertheless, introducing this type of research into Spain has not been easy, especially because of the reticence expressed by some of our older colleagues, who felt that research from this domain was more like a 'novel' (or a soap opera) and not quality research (in the sense that accounting research should of necessity be 'dull' and packed with suitably handled data).

In addition, as databases were more readily available in the 1990s, descriptive studies started to give way to empirical research. Series of hypotheses were proposed which needed to be generated and validated, with the initial stage being the identification of what might be termed the research question. The interpretations of positive research, together with case study research methods were introduced into Spain in the 1990s. Empirical research using questionnaires met many obstacles in Spain because of the low response rate – often around 10% – in comparison with other countries. Further, case study research, often quite common in management accounting research, struggled to make a significant impact in Spain. Often it was not properly understood that case studies offered an understanding of accounting in practice/action; it was usually classified as soft research, ignoring the fact that, in Yin's words (1984), ". . . paradoxically, the 'softer' a research technique, the harder it is to do". However, at the end of the 1990s, Spanish management accounting researchers were generally showing greater interest in case studies methods to examine the nature of accounting practices within organisations.

And yet, regardless of the research method followed and the research current it is contained in, we feel that a large number of Spanish case studies rather too faithfully follow certain English-written papers, and this is just one more piece of evidence to show that, in spite of our efforts, we are still taking our first steps in accounting research. More specifically, our view would be Spanish empirical research to date has been largely based on the positive methodological approach, while approaches based on behavioural and social theories have not developed that significantly. In this respect, we should like to highlight the fact that a good many research studies have been based on forecasting rather than explanation. The relative lack of Spanish accounting research on behavioural and social issues is a pity because Spain has a very social nature. But this may be why for many colleagues it is not seen as quality research — because it is almost too much like Spain and (old) Spanish traditions and not 'scientific' enough.

García-Benau & Giner (2000) provide Figures for the percentage of empirical research published in a group of international journals in the 1990s. Obviously, there are significant differences between journals; for example the study shows that in the *Journal of Accounting and Economics*, 80% of the published works are of an empirical nature, while in *Critical Perspectives on Accounting*, this figure is 14%. However, while we do not have exact Figures for empirical studies published in Spanish journals, we should like to point out that practically all of them are published in the *Revista Española de Financiación y Contabilidad* and in the recently launched *Revista de Contabilidad* (first published in 1998).

A major obstacle for us was how to get published in some of the above-mentioned international journals. How were we to get accepted by a journal whose editorial board was basically dominated by native English-speakers, a journal which often belonged to a specific school? Our experience here has been interesting. Usually the reviewers began by saying that the English was very bad, and sometimes we were advised that the results of an empirical study conducted in Spain were of little interest.

Getting to publish a paper in an international journal has been really important for us. We often joke about this, saying (when a paper is accepted for publication) *'he tocado el cielo'* (I've touched the stars), as a way of expressing the sense of joy and reward received for the work done. However, this struggle to open up a presence in the most prestigious accountancy journals is so hard that many Spanish researchers have been left stranded and given up because of the constant obstacles placed in their way. For example, to be lucky enough to have a study accepted in an international journal, we have to send numerous drafts of papers and read various reviews by English speakers, with an English-speaking mentality, who can be quite unaware at times of what is happening in non-English-speaking countries. However, even though Spanish participation in international journals is not high compared to that of other countries, some works have been published, as can be seen in Table 1, showing the number of articles published during the 1990s in a group of international journals.

Table 1: Spanish presence in certain international journals (García-Benau & Giner 2000).

Journal	Number of Spanish articles
Abacus	0
Accounting, Organizations and Society	3
Accounting and Business Research	1
Accounting, Auditing & Accountability Journal	0
Accounting History	1
Critical Perspectives on Accounting	0
European Accounting Review	16
International Journal of Accounting	5
Journal of Accounting and Economics	0
The Accounting Review	0
Total	26

As may be seen, Spanish participation, although fairly low, has begun to be slightly significant in certain journals, particularly *European Accounting Review*, *The International Journal of Accounting* and *Accounting, Organizations and Society*. Spanish participation is more concentrated in the latter part of the 1990s. It is also worth mentioning that, in addition to the papers shown in Table 1, there are some papers written by Spanish academic people in other international journals. For instance, there was a special issue dedicated to Spain in the *Journal of Accounting, Business and Financial History* in July 2002 (Vol. 12, No. 2).

A recent study by Laínez & Martínez García (2002), centring on accountancy research produced by Spanish authors in areas reflecting the principal changes arising from the new international scenario (the new economy and new business models, information quality, intangible assets, the internationalisation of accounting information, the problems of accounting information in capital markets, company and environmental information and audits), clearly shows a growing publication record. Laínez & Martínez García (2002) concluded that Spanish authors are beginning to spread to other foreign journals such as: *European Business Review*, *Akrôpolis*, *Management Accounting*, *Journal of Accounting, Auditing and Taxation*, *Journal of Accounting Literature*, *IMPS-2000 Proceedings* and *The International Journal of Digital Accounting Research*.

However, many Spanish papers still do not realise their objective of being published. Loft *et al.* (2002) reported that in the *European Accounting Review* (one of the main targets for Spanish papers), Spain stood second in terms of number of submissions (9.5% of the papers submitted from the end of 1991 to the end of 1999). However, "of the articles submitted from 1991 to the end of 1994, only *one* was ultimately accepted out of sixteen submissions" (Loft *et al.* 2002: 69). The situation, though, is gradually improving (although the cost/benefit ratio is still too high) and "the quality of the articles coming from Spain academics improved radically over the 1990s" (Loft *et al.* 2002: 69) and ". . . in 1998 and 1999 almost half of the articles were accepted".

The Future — What Would We Like to Change? What Can We Expect?

In the quest for improved quality in our research, along a road often blocked by difficulties that we have encountered around us, and by our own personal limitations, we have been learning from our mistakes and from the models that have been provided by the work of some of our foreign colleagues. The preparation of this paper has enabled us to look back over our starting out point years ago, the process and stages of our learning, our habits, institutional conditions, resources, dreams, personal commitments and many other factors that have influenced our development.

It is not our intention to give the impression that the academics who went through this stage in the evolution of research in Spain underwent some form of 'martyrdom' in the quest for a more important role in the 'accounting' theatrical play showing on the national and international stage. On the contrary, it is just that an over-viewing historical perspective can make things seem that way. The daily excitement about what we were doing, the enthusiasm with which we tackled our projects and our eagerness to cope with problems easily outshone all this. Even so, once the problems had been surmounted, and our effort was rewarded with the 'success' of publication, we did celebrate with a glass of wine or a beer. This is why, when they see the current situation without this historical perspective, some of our colleagues who have joined us more recently and have encountered a very different reality might think, with a modicum of pity, 'poor things', or perhaps, 'what are they talking about? I haven't experienced any of this'. So, when the editors of this book invited us to write this chapter about our actual experience in the field of research, we accepted the challenge since it enabled us to commit our reality to these pages, stripped of many formalities or external constraints.

In concluding, we wish to note some ideas for the future that our experience over the years has enabled us to formulate, and which we would like to be the hub of the evolution of our research. They are not just expectations of change, but the hope, or even conviction, that only through them can we one day look back with the immense satisfaction of someone who has seen their dreams come true.

The Role of the Institutions

The institutional framework surrounding university research must change. After a period in which academic people had to devote most of their time to teaching, with a large number of students to attend to, Spanish universities have managed to reduce this number, and this should enable research to play a greater role in university activities, as is the case in other countries. This should be complemented by a greater professionalisation of university administration, something that is still highly bureaucratic and currently in the hands of researchers. It is often difficult to concentrate on research when you have a diary full of meetings to discuss administrative and financial problems affecting the Department, Faculty or the very university that employs us. This task should be removed from the activities of the researcher and placed in the hands of qualified staff employed for this purpose.

Universities should also clearly define the boundaries between research and teaching activities, with staff posts devoted to both or just one of these activities, with real incentives for those who opt for research. In this context, we feel that the current system does not sufficiently reward the effort of teachers who, with the same teaching load, invest extra effort in research. This might deter those who are attracted by activities that are better paid. Regular assessment of research, by the departments and universities, as well as at a national level, accompanied by incentives that reward effort and results, should be a constant feature to be promoted in our academic environment. Without these stimuli, complacency — a natural human quality — could imperil the promising future of a good many Spanish researchers.

We also feel that it is necessary for stronger links in research with the business and public sectors. Research cannot ignore the needs of business and other entities. They should explain and communicate their needs to the research groups that can meet them. The research groups should in turn inform them of their research potential. Thus, universities should create the necessary channels for this interflow of applied research supply and demand, through research publication systems, researchers' and company fora, etc.

Research has Become Globalised Too

When everything around us is being globalised, researchers must follow suit to adapt their activities to this new scenario. There is no point in going on researching if we ignore this process. We need to integrate into our teams, researchers from similar (and not so similar) disciplines, who will widen our field of vision and provide new techniques that will make the result of our own effort easier. We must also insist on collaborating with colleagues from other countries. The feedback obtained from this experience is vital for improving the quality of our work. Those of us who have done this are fully aware of the know-how generated through such exposure.

Mobility of researchers is equally necessary both with regard to Spanish colleagues spending time in prestigious universities in other countries, as well as promoting visits by foreign researchers to Spanish universities. Indeed, we would go so far as to say that it should become a habitual practice for everyone. So often, the coming together of people from different cultures and traditions gives rise to an alternative view of the nature of the problems we come up against in our research, and of the objectives, scope and even the methods to tackle them.

In the last few years, we have begun to see Spanish researchers on the Editorial Board of certain international journals. We would like to see this presence gradually increasing as an indicator of the international community's recognition of the evolution of our level of research. If this happens, we will be able to say that Spanish research has moved up a rung on the international scene.

We also wish to stress that research should be the way to progress accounting knowledge. We sometimes feel disappointed that colleagues from other countries seem to value us more because we are bi-lingual and can facilitate their contacts and networks rather than because of any current or potential contribution to knowledge that we might have made. Reaching a good communication flow among researchers from different countries is not that difficult and so hopefully in the future we will be able to mutually interesting critical and constructive research studies (and only giving language the degree of importance that it deserves).

A Firm Commitment to International Diffusion of Research

Because of the problems explained above, it was not until the early 1990s that Spanish researchers began to express an interest in presenting research in international fora. Nowadays, Spanish conference participation is quite significant — being noticeably prevalent in the last few *European Accounting Association* conferences. We like to think that this has not been, as we say here, 'una nube de verano' (a summer cloud). On the contrary, we trust that this presence will be maintained and intensified, and that international workshops that take place in other European countries, will be organised more regularly in Spain.

All of this is helped by the fact that, nowadays, most young Spanish researchers speak fluent English. This makes an enormous difference since, for example, they can profit much more from conferences and workshops, develop their personal contacts with academics from other countries, and thus gradually become integrated into key international networks of researchers. This will be a great advance on previous years and, hopefully their efforts will bear much more fruit. Certainly, the starting out point is sufficiently different to that of fifteen or twenty years ago for us to be extremely optimistic in this respect. Naturally, there has been another influential factor here — namely, the internet. Communication has been enormously enhanced because of the internet, and with that, the opportunities to conduct joint research projects.

Special mention should also be made of our hope that there are more papers published by Spanish authors in international journals. In spite of the obstacles mentioned previously, the progress that has been made, particularly since the mid-1990s, gives us cause for optimism. There are currently in Spain only two academic accounting research journals, with just six issues published a year between the two of them. The current delay in publishing accepted works is considerable. This is why trying to publish in English has become a virtual necessity for all those who are seeking an outlet for their research, not to mention the consequences that may result from being published in an international journal.

This pressure to publish in English is also playing its part in deciding the topics of research in Spain; thus we see that the field of concern is not centred on Spain, but has been transferred to other areas of international interest. Case studies that may be worth researching in Spain in the fields of creative accounting, accounting information and the stock market, or auditing, for example, have been abandoned partly because of the scant interest they are perceived to arouse in international journals. Spanish researchers are now concentrating on topics that concern the international scene: the adaptation of IASB standards in Europe, corporate government and the quality of information, the new economy and business models, intangible assets, the problems of accounting information in the principal capital markets, and company and environmental information, to name the main topics.

Finally, we are convinced that, in spite of the ever-present language barrier, once we have overcome our old habits and acquired methods of setting objectives with a suitable methodology, we can gradually see works by Spanish authors cited in the main international journals. Today, there are still many people who think that for a paper to be accepted for publication in one of these journals, one of the required conditions is that no work in Spanish should be included in the bibliographical references, because of the prejudice that the evaluator might have with regard to the nationality of the authors.

Self-Criticism, the Basis for Improvement

Although it is important to contrast the quality and progress of our research against external benchmarks, positive self-criticism must be omnipresent. This is why we believe that self-criticism must govern all presentations of papers, be it in departmental seminars, workshops or parallel sessions. The exercise of self-criticism is a healthy habit which will help to improve our quality standards. As we have pointed out, this practice is not usual in our presentations, and so contributions by our colleagues are usually scarce. Normally, our works are submitted to external opinion for the first time when we send them for assessment for publication in a journal. Naturally, as they have not been discussed publicly before colleagues, they have not received critical and constructive analysis. Consequently, when we send in our papers for assessment to a journal, they are still often at the first draft stage, and the assessment we receive often discourages us. This is why it is only through constructive discussions, in which we receive the critical view of our colleagues, that we can enhance the possibility that one day our papers will more regularly grace the pages of international journals.

The Importance of Resources

It is said that resources for research are insufficient because we always want more. There is a certain amount of truth in that, and we feel that without a suitable level of resources, the desired results will not be forthcoming. This is why, from a human as well as material and financial point of view, availability of resources at a certain level is an essential condition for carrying out research activity. Great strides have been made here in Spain over the last few years, but we cannot afford to be complacent. On the contrary, we need to continue giving suitable training to young researchers, incorporating them into consolidated teams, wherever they are working. This is why it is extremely important to follow the lead, initiated several years ago by some Spanish universities, of sending young people who are learning about the purpose, methods and techniques of research to certain prestigious Universities at home and abroad. European doctorates, which some of our young researchers now hold, are just one instance of this pattern of development.

Claiming public and private financial resources to ensure the success of our activity is something else we consider essential. We cannot expect to achieve notable progress in any of the quality indicators of our research without resources, for instance, to pay for attending conferences or organising workshops. People cannot be expected to do all this for free. Any improvement, as well as a change in the policy promoted by those at the top, and in the habits and attitudes of researchers, requires financial resources to get these measures, and others on which scientific progress depends, off the ground.

Finally, with the putting into practice of these and other measures, we believe that our research can continue to evolve and help us, in the not too distant future, to enjoy a supporting or maybe lead role (dreams are free) in the great Broadway theatre of dreams. Let us hope so.

A Few Tips for Researchers

The situation of accounting researchers, as we have illustrated in this chapter, can depend significantly on their respective country's geography, experience and history. Spain is a country geographically located *al sur*[2] (in the South) of Europe. This means that we are also 'in the South' in a broad sense, which unfortunately includes accounting research. However, even though the United Kingdom is one of the European countries more clearly *al norte* (in the North), accounting research also needs studies from the other European countries. Political and social frameworks differ significantly across European countries. If it was difficult for us to compare the twelve EU countries in the early nineties, with the new incorporations to the European Union especially the new one of ten countries, the situation is now far more complex and heterogeneous from an accounting research perspective. The number of groupings of countries within the EU are growing, as are the different issues that social science research is expected to cover. From our personal experience, could we make a contribution so as to help young researchers address the challenge of giving answers to the questions that accounting has to face nowadays?

The authors of this paper have worked together in some research projects yet we also have distinctive research styles and areas of interest. We think that people must try and work on topics where they have a strong interest, although it is always good to be sociable and listen to presentations of other researchers and the ideas they want to share with us. Lastly, it is worthwhile to point out that we think that you can never be very deterministic in planning research collaboration since, many times, a lot of factors can influence how and whom you work with. We have met very nice people, we have been very lucky!

---

[2] In addition to the geographical reference, in Spanish the expressions 'north' and 'south' are also often used to indicate the higher or lower social and economic development of regions, respectively.

References

Ball, R., & Brown, P. (1968). An empirical evaluation of accounting income numbers. *Journal of Accounting Research, 6* (Autumn), 159–178.

Beaver, W. T. (1968). The information content of annual earning announcements. *Journal of Accounting Research, 6* (Suppl.), 67–92.

Beaver, W. H., Lambert, R. A., & Ryan, S. G. (1987). The information content of security prices: a second look. *Journal of Accounting and Economics, 9* (July), 139–157.

Bricker, R. (1988). Knowledge preservation in accounting: A citational study. *Abacus, 24* (September), 120–131.

Brinn, T., Jones, M. J., & Pendlebury, M. (1996). U.K. accountants' perceptions of research journal quality. *Accounting and Business Research, 26*(3), 265–278.

Brown, L. D., & Gardner, J. C. (1985). Applying citation analysis to evaluate the research contributions of accounting faculty and doctoral programs. *The Accounting Review, 60* (April), 262–277.

Brown, L. D., Griffin, P. A., Hagerman, R. L., & Zmijewski, M. E. (1987). An evaluation of the alternative proxies for the market's assessment of unexpected earnings. *Journal of Accounting and Economics, 9* (March), 159–193.

Carmona, S., Gutierrez, I., & Camara, M. (1999). A profile of European accounting research: evidence from leading research journals. *European Accounting Review, 8*(3), 463–480.

Cea García, J. L. (1996). *La Búsqueda de la Racionalidad Económico-Financiera. Imperativo Prioritario para la Investigación Contable.* Madrid: Instituto de Contabilidad y Auditoría de Cuentas.

Cooper, D. J., & Hopper, T. (1990). *Critical accounts: Reorientating accounting research.* London: McMillan.

De Fuentes Barberá, C., Gandía Cabedo, J. L., & García Benau, M. A. (1994). Hacia un modelo ideal de Universidad: concepción teórica y análisis descriptivo. *Comunicación presentada al VI Encuentro de Profesores Universitarios de Contabilidad.* 26–28 de mayo, Madrid.

De Fuentes, C., & Pucheta, C. (2003). Audit quality and security prices analysis: A study of the Enron event within the agency theory framework. *EAA Congress,* Abril, Seville.

Donoso Anes, J. A. (1991). El porqué del fracaso universitario. *Comunicación presentada al IV Encuentro de Profesores Universitarios de Contabilidad.* Junio, Santander.

Flint, D., & Shaw, J. C. (1981). Accounting research from the perspective of practice. In: M. Bromwich & A. Hopwood (Eds), *Essays in British Accounting Research* (pp. 134–154). London: Pitman.

García-Ayuso Covarsí, M., & Sierra Molina, G. (1994). La relación entre investigación y práctica en Contabilidad. *Revista Española de Financiación y Contabilidad, XXIII*, Enero-Marzo, 234–287.

García Benau, M. A., Gandía Cabedo, J. L., & Vico Martínez, A. (1996). *Relación entre teoría y práctica contable: un análisis de la situación en España.* Serie Estudios Empíricos. Madrid: Asociación Española de Contabilidad y Administración de Empresas.

García Benau, M. A., Gandía Cabedo, J. L., & De Fuentes Barberá, C. (1997). Grado de satisfacción de los profesores universitarios de contabilidad con la carrera académica. *Revista Española de Financiación y Contabilidad, XXVI*(91), 541–575.

García Benau, M. A., & Giner Inchausti, B. (2000). Perspectiva de investigación de la contabilidad financiera en el ámbito internacional. *IX Encuentro de Profesores Universitarios de Contabilidad,* Las Palmas de Gran Canarias.

Gonzalo Angulo, J. A. (1999). La tesis doctoral (planificación y ejecución de un trabajo de investigación en contabilidad o finanzas). *Revista Española de Financiación y Contabilidad, 12*(100), 219–290.

Hopwood, A. G. (1987). The archaeology of accounting systems. *Accounting, Organizations and Society, 12*(3), 207–234.

Jones, M. J., Brinn, T., & Pendlebury, T. (1996). Judging the quality of research in business schools: a comment from accounting. *Omega, 24*(5), 597–602.

Laínez Gadea, J. A., & Martínez García, J. (2002). La información contable y la auditoría ante los cambios derivados del nuevo escenario internacional. *X Encuentro de Profesores Universitarios de Contabilidad*. Santiago de Compostela.

Larrán, M., Piñero, J., & Ruiz, E. (1996). Estudio de experiencias realizadas en la docencia de Análisis Contable: Objetivos y Métodos Didácticos. *Revista Española de Financiación y Contabilidad, XXV*(88), 715–742.

Larrinaga González, C. (1999). Perspectivas alternativas de investigación en contabilidad: una revisión. *Revista de Contabilidad, 2*(3), 103–131.

Laughlin, R. C. (1981). On the nature of accounting methodology. *Journal of Business, Finance and Accounting, 8*(3), 329–351.

Ley Orgánica 25 de Agosto de 1983. Ley de Reforma Universitaria (LRU).

Ley Orgánica de 24 de Diciembre de 2001. Ley Orgánica de Universidades (LOU).

Loft, A. (1986). Towards a critical understanding of accounting: The case of cost accounting in the U.K. 1914–1925. *Accounting, Organizations and Society, 11*(2), 137–170.

Loft, A., Jorissen, A., & Walton, P. (2002). From newsletter to academic journal: creating the European Accounting Review. *European Accounting Review, 11*(1), 43–76.

Martínez Churiaque, J. I. (1992). La educación contable universitaria: Presente y futuro" en *Contabilidad en España*. Madrid, Instituto de Contabilidad y Auditoría de Cuentas, Ministerio de Economía y Hacienda (pp. 477–494).

McRae, T. W. (1974). Citational analysis of the accounting information network. *Journal of Accounting Research, 12* (Spring), 80–92.

Monterrey Mayoral, J. (1996). Un recorrido por la contabilidad positiva. Ponencia presentada en La investigación Empírica en Contabilidad Financiera, Research Workshop, Universidad de Cádiz.

Ruíz Barbadillo, E. (1996). Un análisis de las fases de conflicto en el entorno de la auditoría en España. *Revista Española de Financiación y Contabilidad, XXV*(89), 785–820.

Ryan, B., Scapens, R., & Theobald, M. (2002). *Research method and methodology in finance and accounting*. London: Thomson.

Sanchez Segura, A. (1994). La rentabilidad económica y financiera de la gran empresa española. Análisis de los factores determinantes. *Revista Española de Financiación y Contabilidad, XXII*(78), 159–179.

Smith, G., & Krogstal, G. (1991). Sources and uses of auditing: A Journal of Practice and Theory's literature: The first decade. *Auditing: A Journal of Practice and Theory, 10* (Fall), 84–97.

Tinker, T. (1985). *Paper prophets*. New York, NY: Praeger Publishers Co.

Tinker, T., & Puxty, T. (1995). *Policing accounting knowledge*. London: Paul Chapman.

Tinker, A. M., Merino, B. D., & Neimark, M. (1982). The normative origins of positive theories: Ideology and accounting thought. *Accounting, Organizations and Society, 7*(2), 167–200.

Vico Martínez, A. (1997). Expectativas ante la auditoría: la independencia del auditor. Tesis Doctoral, Universitat Jaime I de Castellón.

Vico Martínez, A., & Pucheta Martínez, M. C. (2001). Un estudio empírico acerca de la relevancia del informe de auditoría entre los analistas de riesgos de las entidades de crédito. *Comunicación presentada en el XI Congreso de AECA* (Septiembre) Madrid.

Watts, R. L., & Zimmerman, J. L. (1978). Towards a positive theory of the determination of accounting standard. *The Accounting Review, LIII* (January), 112–134.

Watts, R. L., & Zimmerman, J. L. (1990). Positive accounting theory: A ten year perspective. *The Accounting Review, LXV* (January), 131–156.

Whittington, G. (1986). Financial accounting theory: An overview. *British Accounting Review, 18*(4), 4–41.

Whittington, G. (1987). Positive accounting research a review article. *Accounting and Business Research, 68* (Autumn), 327–336.

Whittington, G. (1993). The 1992 research assessment exercise. *British Accounting Review, 25*(4), 383–395.

Yin, R. K. (1984). *Case studies research, design and methods.* Beverly Hills, CA: Sage.

Zeff, S. A. (1978). The rise of economic consequences. *Journal of Accountancy, 146* (December), 56–63.

Zeff, S. A. (1996). A study of academic research journals in accounting. *Accounting Horizons, 10*(3), 158–177.

Chapter 6

'Nice Work': Writing a Ph.D. Thesis in Accounting

Anne Loft

> I read your article in *Accounting, Organizations and Society* on the history
> of cost accounting: I thought you would be taller (Japanese academic to
> Anne Loft in the lift at the IAAER Congress in Kyoto 1987).

Introduction

This is the tale of the writing of a thesis. The thesis was entitled: "Understanding
Accounting in its Social and Historical Context: The Case of Cost Accounting in the
U.K. 1914–1925". Written between 1981 and 1986 while I was at the London Business
School, and with Professor Anthony Hopwood as supervisor, it was published in book
form by Garland Press in 1988. It represented one of the first attempts to use the ideas
of Michel Foucault to understand the development of accounting, examining the
increasing prominence of cost accounting as a disciplinary technology in factories
during the period 1914–1925. Inspired by Foucault's concept of genealogical history, it
drew on a wide range of archival material not just about accounting, but more generally
about the society of the period: from governmental legislation to engineering
magazines, newspaper articles, and interviews with elderly members of the cost
accounting profession. While most previous histories of cost accounting had been about
cost accounting in its factory context, its focus was on cost accounting in its wider social
context. One aspect of this explored in the thesis being how the actions of the State
affect cost accounting in enterprises. For example, how regulations introduced in the
First World War to control prices of goods on the basis of what they cost to make,
actually forced many manufacturers to develop cost accounting systems for the first
time.

  The thesis had been started with a completely different aim however, which was to
study if the way in which research and development (R&D) was accounting for affected
what R&D was done. I hoped to do this at the Liberal Studies in Science Department

The Real Life Guide to Accounting Research: A Behind-the-Scenes View of Using Qualitative
Research Methods
Copyright © 2004 by Elsevier Ltd.
All rights of reproduction in any form reserved.
ISBN: 0-08-043972-1

at Manchester University. The research proposal was only a page long, and contained little on either the theoretical perspective or the method to be used to study it. This 'real life' article is written with the aim of describing the convoluted trail that lay between the brief proposal of 1981 and the finished thesis of 1986, a year when I also had an article published in *Accounting, Organizations and Society* (Loft 1986). An article which would in the coming years meet with some success in the 'small world' of accounting academia,[1] and would form the basis for my future career as an accounting academic.

In the process of writing 'the thesis writer's tale', as Chaucer might have described it, I found four different types of stories emerging, all of which are present in this account. The *first* of these stories was a history of ideas – what academic fields and ideas were drawn on, what books made an impression, all explained quite neatly in terms of their relation to my thesis. This would be the most academic and impressive of the histories where 'I' was replaced by a kind of universal third person whose work moves continually forward. The myth of progress embodied in the writing of a thesis. The *second* was a very different story, one of where I came from, why I did it, and of the ensuing pains and pleasures of writing. This would be a tale of mental agonies: of time 'wasted', opportunities 'lost', even of bodily agonies: the painful bleeding eczema on my writing hand. On the other, of the pleasures: of working in the Round Reading Room at the British Library, the excitement of discovery, and of reading so intensely into things of the early twentieth century, that the present seemed dizzily strange. A *third* story was of the communal things, a tale of networks: of seminars, meetings, conferences, pubs and curry houses. One of discussions with Anthony Hopwood my Ph.D. supervisor, and with my fellow Ph.D. students, of courses and seminars and of how the feedback I got from others altered my ideas and set the course for my thesis. Last, but not least, was a *fourth* history, which was how I learnt from the 'elders' of the academic world to become a more or less fully-fledged academic versed in the complex rituals of academia. Not only the techniques of citation, of reference and of acknowledgement, but also the ways and means of the world of accounting academe.

There is one important proviso to this history, it is an account written in 2002 and not in 1986, I have relied on memory and the story inevitably ends up by being shaped by later events, large and small, for example my reading of David Lodge's book *Nice Work* published in 1988.[2] It is surely not the story I would have written sitting in my office in Copenhagen in the winter of 1986, trying to learn Danish, but that story cannot be written now.

The idea of writing this is to give a 'real life' account of the process of writing a thesis, to bring out the 'human' side, a side that, for good or bad, is difficult to separate from the academic process. Hopefully it will help to breakdown the myth that you start the first day with a research proposal and progress in a linear and orderly way through a literature review, theory and methodology on to do the actual research, completing the

---

[1] It was ranked as an accounting 'classic' in an international study of influential articles in accounting (world rank no. 24) (Brown 1996).

[2] David Lodge's books have either sharpened (or maybe clouded) my view of academia. *Nice Work* (1988) is particularly evocative for me, as it is a tale of a factory and a university in Rummidge (Birmingham). See also *Changing Places* (1975), *Small World* (1984) and *Thinks* (2001).

thesis with results and conclusions ready to deliver, and well before the due date! It is not that simple for most people, especially those who want to make an original contribution to the literature — and why otherwise write a thesis? I enjoyed writing my thesis, and I hope that this article will encourage others to write one too.

First I will start with putting the thesis in my personal context. The years I had already spent studying, and my period working as an auditor were important to way in which the thesis developed. I did not start at the London Business School as a blank piece of paper on 1st September 1981, although it almost felt like that!

From University to Auditing: 1955–1981 — Somewhat Autobiographical

I came from the semi-detached suburbs of Birmingham, from a family where no one had been to university. Born in 1955, from the age of eleven I went to Bartley Green Girls' Grammar School, a non-descript school perched on a hill near where we lived. The teachers were a mixed bunch, but a physics teacher who introduced teaching methods heavily based on experiments inspired me to want to do science,[3] and I decided to do geology at Manchester University, but at the last minute I swapped to physics. I completed first year physics, where surprisingly my best subject was advanced mathematics, but decided to specialise in 'Liberal Studies in Science', which I had taken as an option in the first year. The degree was about looking at the relationship between science and technology in society, and I was really fascinated by it, especially the whole question of to what extent scientific knowledge was socially determined. In 1974–1976 when I was there, this department was one of the pioneers in an area which was to produce a lot of innovative and fascinating work in the 1980s (for examples, Latour & Woolgar 1986; Latour 1987). I got good marks for my degree, but I did not make it to a 'first'. However, the two projects I had done had turned out well, and the head of department, Professor Michael Gibbons, suggested to my parents (!) after the degree ceremony that I should think about doing a Ph.D. I had other plans though, I was moving back to Birmingham to be with my fiancé who was reading law. I had applied to several of the 'Big 8' firms, and had got a position as a graduate trainee with Touche Ross (now part of the Big 4 firm, Deloitte and Touche). I thought it must be a useful qualification, and imagined that I could get a job as an accountant in an interesting organisation like Oxfam afterwards.

In retrospect, working for Touche Ross in Birmingham was a wonderful experience, although it did not always seem so at the time. We zoomed up and down the motorways clocking up 'mileage' driving to audits in the industrial West Midlands. Being a trainee accountant gave a unique insight into life in factories and offices. I was sent on the audit of firms engaged in the traditional engineering and metal trades, like Wolverhampton Die Castings and the GEC Stafford and Rugby divisions. Many of the firms were in the 'Black Country', an area to the west of Birmingham, which was one of the 'cradles' of

---

[3] Mrs Fremlin had been a member of the left-wing 'Science in Society' group at Cambridge in the 1930s; but this I only discovered much later.

the Industrial Revolution in England. It was known for metalworking and engineering, originally based on using the local coal supplies. The name 'Black Country' came from the pollution caused by these industries. Michael Power writes in the Preface to the *Audit Society* that "[a]s auditors we would huddle on winter evenings in the worst part of the client premises" (1997: xi). As the auditors of factories in the West Midlands we were lucky not to have to huddle in the very worst parts of the client premises, for the offices were fairly civilised compared to the shop floor of a foundry![4] Some of these factories were enormous, stretching over acres and acres, some were quite ramshackle, and others showed the remains of camouflage paint from the Second World War. Not surprisingly, one of the most common points in the audit papers was that the fixed assets were fully depreciated many years ago.

Huge areas of what must have originally been scenic countryside were covered by the remnants of various ages of industrial production. It reminded me of scenes in a book I had read repeatedly since my teenage years — the dark and ruined landscape of Mordor in J. R. R. Tolkien's the *Lord of the Rings* (1954/1955),[5] although this was not something that I mentioned to my auditing colleagues! Over a pint of 'real ale' at lunchtime (most women in the audit team adopted the same drinking habits as the men) I would occasionally reflect on some of the literature from my technology and society course at Manchester.

During my second and third years at Touche Ross (about 1978) we introduced a new audit system called 'TRAP' (Touche Ross Audit Process). So instead of doing much the same as the previous year we began to reconsider the process at each client, starting with making flow-charts of systems. Basically we had to flow-chart the whole recording system of the company in so far as the records in question affected the financial accounts. Many hours went trying to fathom out systems that were not always wholly logical, and it seemed to be an immensely difficult task that had to be carried out in very little time.[6] It often transpired that many of the clerks processing documents had no idea at all what they were doing or why, and referred to, for example, 'goods received notes' as 'greens'. This involved visits to the shop floor, examining grubby production sheets and other documents held in grimy offices deep in the factory. It really brought me into thinking about issues concerning the relations between the 'flows' of paper and the 'flows' of material items and the control of production (which I later found that Braverman (1974) had written very eloquently about). Many clients still used accounting machines, and it was the records produced by them that were the basis for the systems we audited. Only the very largest clients had a computer, which would be housed by itself in a special air-conditioned room, run using mountains of punched cards and producing thick unwieldy files of printout.

Audit work was interspersed with periods of intense study for professional examinations in a whirlwind of activity. However, my life changed drastically when my

---

[4] David Lodge gives a good description of life in such a factory in the West Midlands in the novel *Nice Work* (Lodge 1988).

[5] This is perhaps not surprising as J.R.R. Tolkein spent most of his childhood in Birmingham, and the Black Country is believed by commentators to have provided an important source of inspiration for Mordor.

[6] No one would do an audit like this now, as it would cost too much in terms of hours of work.

fiancé left me, and I did not become the accountant-wife of a solicitor. I bought a terraced house near Birmingham University, found new friends, and decided I wanted to do a Ph.D. I decided that by combining my theoretical knowledge in the field of liberal studies in science with my theoretical and practical knowledge of accounting, I could make an interesting and useful research project. I formulated a project proposal arguing that it was necessary to investigate how the way in which R&D was accounted for would affect what kind of R&D was done. I contacted the head of Liberal Studies in Science, Professor Mike Gibbons, who was positive about it, and I went to Birmingham University library to look for more ideas. Looking at the current journals rack I saw a journal called *Accounting, Organizations and Society* (*AOS*). Opening it up I found the very first article was one entitled "The Roles of Accountancy in Organizations and Society" (Burchell *et al.* 1980). This was an important discovery; the article seemed very relevant to my proposed project. It enabled me to connect in a more meaningful way my two 'worlds', the liberal studies in science world and the accounting world. I began to see my project on accounting and R&D as being about the accounting, technology and society relationship. Amongst the authors I discovered a Professor Anthony Hopwood[7] at the London Business School, I sent him my proposal, which he liked, and when someone dropped out of the doctoral programme at the LBS he called me down to London and offered me a place. I had to choose between Manchester and London on the spot! After considering the matter for about 2 seconds I decided on LBS, a decision I did not regret.

I started at LBS in the autumn of 1981, I rented my terraced house in Selly Oak out to students, and I got a residential room at the School itself. My thesis work began with my first visit to the library the week before the formal start of the programme — I had decided it was important to get going as soon as possible, and I started tracing the references in my well thumbed copy of the article "The Role of Accounting in Organizations and Society" which was my 'bible' at the time.

Despite this early start it still took me until March 1986 to finish the thesis, in other words, $4\frac{1}{2}$ years. Here I have decided to divide the discussion of writing the thesis, into 3 periods of $1\frac{1}{2}$ years; the honeymoon period (when it seems as though I had a long time to write the thesis), the middle period (until the grant ran out) and the 'extra time', the period when I actually got down to finishing it.

Joining the LBS: The first year and a half: September 1981–March 1983

LBS occupied a curved white building with distinctive oriental towers facing Regent's Park. Designed by the famous architect John Nash, it stood in its own grounds on the outer circle of the park. I got a residential room in the main building, and a shared office in the Victorian terraces, and with a grant for three years there was very little excuse for not writing. I made some good friends amongst the Ph.D. students who 'lived in', and there was always a contingent ready to go to the local pub in the late evening. There were also a couple of postdoctoral students in residence, one of whom was Ted

---

[7] For a review of the Anthony Hopwood's career, see Loft (2001) and Power (1999).

O'Leary,[8] another was the ebullient 'Archie' Pitts a mathematician doing a second Ph.D. in finance.

I often think of Elizabeth Gaskell's novel *North and South* (1973, originally 1854/1855) when I think of my move to LBS. I moved from visiting dirty old factories like Wolverhampton Die Castings, to one of London's most elegant buildings facing a beautiful park. From a 'northern' (well, West Midlands) manufacturing district I had moved to the wealthy south. The mainstay of LBS at this time, the two year Master's course,[9] seemed to me to be a kind of 'finishing school' for members of the genteel classes whose Oxbridge education had not quite equipped them for a career in business. Most considered Birmingham was a city best not viewed from any closer than Spaghetti Junction and the M6 *en route* to Scotland. I used to joke that they got an education which showed them how, from their offices in London, they could make the decision to close down businesses in the Black Country. Indeed, many of these businesses, including Wolverhampton Die Castings, did disappear when the hard economic 'medicine' of Margaret Thatcher took effect in Britain in the 1980s. My Birmingham accent did not help me fit in (or maybe this is my imagination), and one lecturer at the LBS with distinctly upper-class connections referred to me as a 'working-class girl made good', which was one way of looking at things!

The development of the London Business School had been inspired by the American model, in particular the Harvard Business School. Thus one of the important elements of the doctoral programme was taking courses, this made it quite unlike most other programmes in the U.K. at this time. I took several courses including 'How to write a Ph.D.', run by Professor Derek Pugh, who masterminded the famous Aston Studies (for example, Pugh *et al.* 1968) and it was interesting to hear him talk about how these studies were carried out. Among the things we had to do was to select a completed Ph.D. from the LBS library and to present and discuss it. I managed to select one which was actually rather poor — but I learnt something about bread production, and it had the positive effect of showing that a thesis did not have to be a masterpiece of prose, or as long as Wai Fong Chua's, which sat in an impressively large pile on Anthony Hopwood's filing cabinet.[10] Derek Pugh had many prescriptions for success, like "don't take a job before you have finished your thesis" which some students found rather wearing and towards the end there was only myself and another student called Sue Bates left, and we agreed that we were then obliged to attend to the bitter end. Actually, I enjoyed the course, and in retrospect it was very useful.

I took a course in finance run by Professor Dick Brealey (well I started it), and one in strategic management organised by the dynamic Professor Kenneth Simmonds, whose academic jet-setter life-style with homes in several different countries begged belief. I attended Anthony Hopwood's lectures on management accounting for the

---

[8] Later to get together with Peter Miller to write papers such as Miller & O'Leary (1987)

[9] There were no undergraduate courses at the LBS; most of the students were on the Master's Programme, which was arguably the best in the U.K. and well respected abroad. There were other shorter programmes for executives.

[10] Anthony Hopwood was external examiner for Wai Fong Chua's impressive thesis; Chua (1986) is directly based on the empirical research reported in the thesis.

Masters students, and his small study group for his own Ph.D. students. We were only around two/three persons[11] and held meetings in his office. We were really too few to make for good discussions, and I do not think we reached any new intellectual heights in our analysis of amongst other classics, Beaver's *Accounting Revolution* (1981), but it was useful to have made acquaintance with them. There were only a few people in accounting at LBS, I actually only remember Jeremy Dent and Professor Walter Reid. While two of Anthony Hopwood's research team from Oxford, Stuart Burchell and Colin Clubb were still around; the project was nearing its end and I saw little of them. However they were still writing articles based on that work, notably Burchell *et al.* (1985).

On Friday lunchtime research seminars were organised for staff and Ph.D. students, and often there were presentations from visitors. Sandwiches and beer were provided, and the seminars were very popular with the Ph.D. students, not least because of the 'free lunch' effect. Thus although there were only a couple of Ph.D. students in accounting, there was generally a good research environment, and I found I had much in common with the organizational behaviour and strategy people, among the staff in this area being John Roberts,[12] Professor Denis Pym and Rob Goffee.

I began to read all kinds of things but generally did not make a lot of progress with my thesis. For reasons I cannot now remember, I dropped the accounting and R&D project, and began to work on something more general on accounting for assets. I made a new research proposal but I do not think Anthony Hopwood was very impressed — I could clearly see his 'thought bubble'. I remember walking through a rainy Regent's Park at the beginning of the autumn term a year after I had started my thesis being very unsure what to do and very depressed about it all. This was the lowest point of my career as a Ph.D. student.

Anthony Hopwood suggested that I might find inspiration in Michel Foucault's *Discipline and Punish* (1977a).[13] I found it hard going, but I carried it around in my bag all the time, and read and reread bits of it. I ended up underlining all the important bits — a large proportion of the book! The book opens in the seventeenth century with the violent public death of a prisoner who is bodily punished in the most gruesome way. This is contrasted starkly with the later development of a carefully administered penitentiary regime, where the focus is on reforming the individual prisoner, on altering his soul, and not on revenge on the body. Foucault uses Jeremy Bentham's *Panopticon* in his illustrations of the general principle of this new form of power. A form of building 'invented' in 1796, it was a circular building so contrived that the inmates (for example, prisoners) could be observed all the time from guards in a central tower. It enabled

---

[11] The others were Salwa Hameed from Sudan who completed a thesis on auditing in 1985 and Clem Ladrido from the Philippines who was writing about radical record companies, he vanished while working on the final draft of his thesis in 1986, and has not been seen or heard of since — at least in accounting circles.

[12] John Roberts has written several articles on accounting, see for instance Roberts & Scapens (1985) and Roberts (1991).

[13] Two of Anthony Hopwood's best known papers were inspired to some extent by the works of Foucault: the joint paper with Stuart Burchell and Colin Clubb entitled 'Accounting in its Social Context: Towards a History of Value Added in the United Kingdom' (Burchell *et al.* 1985) and the 'Archaeology of Accounting Systems' (Hopwood 1986).

guards to see all the motions of the inmates, but not *vice versa*, and was a powerful symbol of a new form of power which functions "like a piece of machinery" a power which "constantly supervises" but "functions permanently and largely in silence" (Foucault 1977a: 177).[14]

I decided that the way in which Foucault (following Bentham) looked at the architecture of the *Panopticon* had its parallel in the way in which bookkeeping and accounting acted to discipline activity in the factory. All the time I had in my mind the images from the factories I had visited as an auditor. They were often arranged in such a way that production was made visible to supervisors and managers, who had offices in the factory with glass windows and doors. Production was seen and controlled by those in charge. However, more importantly to my thesis was the fact that in these factories records were being continually created which in a sense enabled inspection through time, in that they represented a particular reproduction of the physical processes on record cards or lists. Following Braverman (1974) I imagined the flows of paper mirroring the flows of production. Reflecting on Foucault, I considered how records, particularly records of costs, could provide a basis for the exercise of discipline at another point in time and another place to that where production occurred. This brought a time dimension in.

I was very excited to find out that Bentham actually wrote about bookkeeping as a way of controlling in institutions in the same way he wrote about the *Panopticon* as a disciplinary system. I got really interested in Bentham and went to study Bentham's original material in the Bentham library at University College in London (gaining inspiration from his embalmed body — or something which resembled it — in the display case in the entrance!). I went quickly through Bentham's collected works to find out where he wrote about this, which was mostly in connection with his grand plans for the reform of the Poor Law. Bentham imagined that it was possible to deal with the problem of what to do about the pauper population in England in the late eighteenth century by building 250 poor-*panopticons* round the country, each with 2000 inhabitants. Bookkeeping was crucial to his system of managing these *panopticons*, but in Bentham's terms bookkeeping was about much more than costs, everything possible being recorded. He wrote that "bookkeeping is one instrument in the hand of economy, architecture another" (Bentham 1843, Vol. VIII, p. 392). Looking at it theoretically, I saw how this could link Foucault's ideas in *Discipline and Punish* to the development of cost accounting. I could use Bentham's ideas about bookkeeping in my work on accounting as a discipline in the way in which Foucault used the penitentiary *Panopticon*.

This was really exciting stuff, and I began to try to read Bentham's original manuscripts. However, it was very difficult to make head or tail of them, because Bentham's handwriting was hard to read, and he always started a new sheet of paper with a new sentence, which meant the order was not always clear. I got very involved

---

[14] During the following decades Foucault's discussion of Bentham's *Panopticon* has inspired many writers, just one interesting example is David Lyon's discussion *The Surveillance Society* (Lyon 1994).

in the world of Bentham,[15] but when Anthony asked me if I was going to do my thesis on Bentham, I went away and thought . . . maybe not! I think one of the reasons was that I had realised what a bizarre following Bentham had, it seemed that people got fascinated by his ideas and that the world of scholarship in this area consisted of good academics who were 'merely' fascinated by Bentham, and amateurs who were fascinated by his ideas and who really would like to see his ideas brought to fruition in the modern world! I vaguely recall now reading that 'The Bentham Society' held annual meetings where his preserved body, normally parked in the entrance to University College, was wheeled in to 'observe' the debate. I felt I needed to 'escape' from Bentham. While I ended up including something on this in my thesis (Loft 1988: 30–33), it was very little compared to the work I did. Additionally, I never really pulled this theoretical insight through my work as much as I wanted to, because I ended up with a different kind of empirical material — but I will return to this later.

I decided I needed to know more about Foucault's work and looked for an evening class to study at. I found a course on post-structuralism and registered for it; I went to a number of the sessions. I found it interesting but hard to relate to the concerns of my thesis. In October 1982 I took over teaching a course on 'accounting, organisations and society' that Stuart Burchell had taught at a college near Reading. It was part of a degree in organisational behaviour. This was interesting and useful both for the experience of teaching and because I myself had to get an overview of the literature in order to choose what to teach.

I had finished my courses at the LBS in the first year of my studies, but a new possibility came up in 1982/1983, and that was that Anthony Hopwood arranged for there to be held doctoral seminars on methodology — with Peter Miller as the teacher. Peter was at the time working on finishing his Ph.D. in sociology, and was a central member of the 'Ideology and Consciousness' group. There was quite a lot of discussion of French theorists, especially the works of Foucault.[16] The participants on the course included Ted O'Leary, and a number of researchers in the organisational behaviour area. This was very useful for putting Foucault in a theoretical context.

Besides the Ph.D. courses Anthony Hopwood arranged 'accounting, organisations and society' seminars at the LBS about once a month; these provided the high points of

---

[15] My dedication to Bentham may have saved my life! I was feeling tired one day and my mother suggested over the phone that I should relax in Regent's Park the next day. I remember thinking that this was a good idea, and that I had never been to one of the concerts held just across the lake from LBS. However, I did not go to Regent's Park, I felt I had to make progress with Bentham and spent all day in the Bentham Library struggling away with his texts. When I got back in the early evening I found that the whole area around Regent's Park was cordoned off — the IRA had blown up the bandstand in the Park and killed about 14 people. The blast was so powerful it blew out windows at LBS.

[16] The works of Michel Foucault were attracting interest in the UK at the time, and a group of British scholars interested in Foucault established an 'Ideology and Consciousness' group, and published a journal known as *I&C*. Stuart Burchell's brother Graham was a central member of this group. *I&C* ceased publication in 1981 but several of those involved continued to write articles and books together in the following years, for example, *The Foucault Effect: Studies in Governmentality*, edited by Graham Burchell, Colin Gordon & Peter Miller (1991). Yves Gendron & Richard Baker (2002) have written about the way in which Foucault became introduced into the accounting literature.

academic life at the School, at least for me! I will write more about these in the next section.

By this stage I had moved from *Discipline and Punish* to reading Foucault's other works, but it remained the most important to me, together with the book *Knowledge/ Power* (1980). I began to look at how Foucault wrote about the past, and to look at my project in terms of making a genealogy (or rather a partial genealogy) of cost and management accounting. Genealogy involves giving a "meticulous and patiently documented" (Foucault 1977b) account of the complex ways in which accounting techniques for 'knowing' and disciplining organisations emerged. It would involve "making a detailed examination of the complex interplay between knowledge, techniques, institutions and occupational claims" (Loft 1986: 167). Following discussions with Anthony Hopwood I decided to take four different periods of time and to do case studies to examine the changes over time. As I recall, today these were as follows: the first would be at the close of the eighteenth century, where industrialists like James Watt and Josiah Wedgwood began to get interested in costs; the second the Great Depression in the latter part of the nineteenth century (traditionally considered the period where cost accounting emerged); third, the period from 1912 to 1925 when costing seemed to become more important, and became linked with scientific management and the 1950s–1960s with the development of modern management accounting.

The Middle Period: March 1983–September 1984

By the autumn of 1982 new Ph.D. offices had been created in one of the Victorian terraces the other side of the LBS quadrangle. As head of the Doctoral Programme Anthony Hopwood had an office there, as did his secretary, Mary Scott-Fleming. She administered the Ph.D. programme and dealt with the problems of the doctoral students (which were many). It was a friendly and pleasant place to work.

I had already collected some material on the early period on James Watt and Josiah Wedgwood, and I was much influenced by the work of Hobsbawm (for example 1975). Steve Butters, a friend from Birmingham now working in London on a research project introduced me to the work of Pollard (for example 1968), which I found useful. I also decided to get into the *zeitgeist* of the period by reading the so-called 'industrial novels'. I ended up reading quite a few novels (in bed at night, and not in 'work time'!). The two I found particularly relevant were Elizabeth Gaskell's *North and South* and Charles Dickens' *Hard Times*, and the pictures that they gave of factory life in the mid-nineteenth century, were 'plotted in' with the images I had from my time as an auditor in the twentieth century. I plodded along looking at this period for a while, but then I decided to move on to the period around the First World War, which looked more interesting.

By April 1983 I had got far enough to present some ideas at a doctoral session at the Sixth European Accounting Association Congress in Glasgow. It was a start. This was the first time I presented at a conference, but after this I went on to present quite a few times, and this process of agreeing to present a paper, and then being forced to write up some of my material for that paper ended up being my salvation. Ultimately I could assemble this material into something that resembled chapters of a thesis and then work further on this to produce the actual thesis.

An enthusiastic amateur when it came to historical research,[17] I started off working in a rather haphazard way, looking at a variety of secondary literature and a wide variety of primary sources. However, there was some method in it all, in that in a particular topic I tended to circle outwards from the known, which was basically the existing accounting history (for examples, Chatfield 1977; Garner 1954; Stacey 1954). Then I went to look at the professional and technical journals where cost accounting or the cost accounting profession was written about, in particular *The Accountant* and *The Cost Accountant*. At this period meetings were often reported verbatim, and even contained comments on the audiences' reaction, such as 'laughter' or 'cheers'. I studied accounting textbooks in detail, especially the different editions of Garcke & Fells (1887–) and Elbourne (1914–). From these 'homely' accounting sources I branched out to *The Engineer*, *Engineering* and *System* and even *Efficiency Magazine*, although articles on cost accounting and 'systems' were buried amongst oceans of pages on more technical engineering issues and most did not have indexes, which made searching for material a painstaking matter. I also read a variety of contemporary writers, for example Fabian tracts by the socialist Webbs, and Alfred Williams' book, *Life in a Railway Factory* (1915)[18] and Vera Brittain's autobiography (1933). I went through histories of the First World War, in particular I read and reread the work of A. J. P. Taylor, an over opinionated but brilliant historian (for example 1970). I read about the industrialists of the time, and about the factories they created, Lord Leverhulme was one person I read about in detail, as he was interested in cost accounting. I checked out *Hansard* (the Parliamentary record) and the newspaper *The Times*, which was kept on microfiche rolls which had to be read in small darkened rooms which made you feel that you were literally 'mining' for information. Amongst other magazines I read other secondary sources, such as the *History Workshop Journal* and otherwise kept an eye open for interesting things, like for instance *Efficiency Magazine*, whose remit ranged from improving efficiency in the home to the office and the factory and in the fighting of the war. Sometimes just browsing revealed interesting things, for example one of the few copies of the limited edition history of the *Ministry of Munitions*, which was never actually published, was kept on an open shelf in the basement of the LSE library.

I thus followed one lead and then the other in an exciting journey from the British Library at the British Museum, to the Newspaper Library at Colindale, to the BLPES library at the London School of Economics, to London University's Senate House Library and the library at Birkbeck College. However, the British Library became my favourite haunt. The famous domed Round Reading Room situated in the middle of the British Museum in Bloomsbury was a wonderful and invocative place to work. It was

---

[17] Something I shared (and share) with nearly all other researchers in accounting history.
[18] This is a fascinating book, by a man called the 'Hammerman Poet'. See http://www.swindonweb.com/guid/peopwill0.htm for more details of his life.

a *panopticon* itself, a fact which I often reflected on whilst sitting there. First the reader (as users are known) had to find the book in the catalogues, most of which were to be found on circular shelves in the centre of the building. The reader then ordered the book from a counter on a raised dais in the centre of the building, by noting on a small slip of paper their name, their seat number and the details of the book. Books were delivered to readers at their desks when obtained from the stacks (some were at a distant location and often I had to wait to the next day). The desks, which were identified by letters and numbers, spread out in rays from the centre such that the occupants could be observed from the central point. 'Guards' walked round looking for 'offenders' who might be stealing material. Every so often visitors to the British Museum were allowed to peek in at the room and at the scholars scratching away with their pencils (like Bentham envisioned that visitors to his penitentiary *Panopticon* would act as an extra discipline). The system allowed the librarians to know where every book was at any point in time. It was fantastic to be able to order every edition of Garcke and Fell's textbook on cost accounting (1887–) and compare them.[19]

It was hard not to get lost in all the fascinating historical materials, sitting in the British Library's newspaper library at Colindale, I folded out a inset in one of the large engineering magazines finding a beautiful engineering drawing of the Titanic, and an article describing exactly why and how it was the world's most advanced ship. I felt curiously shocked by this, and seeing the ship written about in this way brought tears to my eyes! Looking at *The Times* I was continuously distracted by 'irrelevant' articles, it was odd to see the major events such as the sinking of the Lusitania,[20] reported side by side with advertisements for fur coats and whalebone corsets. The dreadful grisly reality and major losses of trench warfare, which we associate with the First World War, seemed under-represented. After long days at the libraries (sometimes I left Colindale at 5 p.m. when it closed and then went to the British Library, which closed at 9 p.m., on the way home) it was almost hard to come back to 1984. It was a kind of total immersion.

Often I would walk from the London Business School to the British Museum, which took around 45 minutes, arriving at about 11.00 am and leaving sometime between 6.00 p.m. and 9.00 p.m. when it closed for the evening, having left only briefly to eat a few snacks and drinks. I always intended to make it for opening time one day in order to be able to sit in the seat in which Karl Marx sat when he wrote *Das Kapital* (its number was printed in the guide to the library). However I never managed to get up so early. It was a long and rather boring walk, so on the way I used to look at my favourite poems, T. S. Eliot's *Four Quartets* (1943) memorising some of my favourite lines (like "At the still point of the turning world.") as I walked along. My understanding of the poems was improved by the fact that one day I arrived at the British Library and ordered several Commentaries on T. S. Eliot instead of my usual material on cost accounting!

---

[19] A. S. Byatt's wonderful novel *Possession* (1990), contains a description of life in the British library.
[20] The Lusitania was a British passenger liner sunk by a German U-boat off the coast of Ireland in May 1915 with the loss of 1201 lives (see http://www.lusitania.net).

The poems dealt a lot with perceptions of time, which interested me, and I tried to draw them into my thesis (see also, Loft 1995a).

I had regular meetings with Anthony Hopwood concerning the thesis. He gave hints and useful tips, but at the same time was of the opinion that one of the important things about doing a Ph.D. was that the students themselves found out what they wanted to do. As I dug deeper and deeper into the material covering the First World War period I vaguely remember him mentioning the other three periods that I was supposed to be working on! However, the early period was difficult, as the raw material to write it was more difficult to access and it was of a different type. The later periods I simply did not reach! Gradually it transpired that my thesis was going to focus on the period 1914–1925.

At the beginning of 1984 I started work on a paper for the Doctoral Colloquium at the 7th Annual EAA Conference, to be held in St Gallen, Switzerland in April of that year. In a paper entitled "Cost Accounting, Work Control and the Development of Cost Accounting in Britain 1914–1925" (Crawford 1984), I presented my Foucauldian approach to looking at accounting as a discipline, and discussed the way in which cost accounting became important during the First World War and what happened in the immediate post-war period. It was forty-five pages long, and basically represented my work to that point in time. The presentation at the Congress was a veritable baptism of fire, as the arrangement was that important professors were engaged to critique doctoral students' work — but anyone at the Congress should go. I remember my session: the room was not large but packed to bursting point. Gary Sundem was given the job of commenting on my work, and it became, not surprisingly, to a certain extent a general critique of the *AOS* approach. I somehow got through this, it helped that Anthony Hopwood warned me about what could happen. However, it was later decided that in future the EAA doctoral colloquium would be held separate from the main event — a good idea!

At this time I decided to teach myself to touch-type, as I was clearly not going to be able to afford to have my thesis typed professionally. This is something I recommend to all budding academics (including men). It was painfully slow to start with, and the fumes from the large quantities of 'tippex' I used to cover up mistakes made me feel dizzy, but I ultimately succeeded.

We had some good seminars with Jeremy Dent and John Roberts from LBS, Peter Miller, Alaister Preston from Bath (who had just completed his Ph.D. (see Preston 1986), and others when they were visiting. These included Ted O'Leary (who was back in Cork by now), Hugh Willmott from Aston and Eamonn Walsh from the LSE. David Cooper was an important participant; he was associate editor of *AOS* at the time[21] and quite often in London for meetings with Anthony. He was at East Anglia but got a professorship at UMIST in Manchester about 1985. He had a 'foot' both in the MBS camp and the LBS camp. There were a couple of other external Ph.D. students of Anthony's who joined the meetings around 1984/1985, including Phil Bougen from

---

[21] He was Associate Editor of *AOS* until 1990, when (from his new base in Alberta) he started *Critical Perspectives on Accounting* with another expatriate who had been at MBS, namely Tony Tinker.

Leeds[22] and Brendan McSweeney. These were good discussions, but ultimately writing a PhD is a lonely task, and those I felt I had most in common with were the other suffering 'souls' on the Ph.D. corridor at the LBS.

At a national level at this time there were basically two groups in the U.K. who were doing critical work on accounting, although there were others working more or less individually. The 'Northern' group, around Professor Tony Lowe in Sheffield, and connected also with Manchester Business School (MBS) and also loosely with the 'management control' group, whose members included Trevor Hopper and Tony Puxty. The 'Southern' group was that around Anthony Hopwood at LBS. I had attended several meetings of the 'management control group'. The meetings were held at different institutions, and at one point they held a meeting at LBS where I presented my work. One commentator (I think it was Trevor Hopper) said, what I already knew in a kind of way but could not face thinking, that if I wanted to explore my ideas about Foucault, control and discipline in the factory I really needed empirical material concerning the use of cost accounting. This was an important point! However I did not have this and I did not seem to be able to find any easy way of getting it. How could I, at this stage in my thesis, start looking at the archives of a twentieth century factory? I left this point 'hanging' and kept my work focused on the idea that I was doing 'genealogy'.

Towards the end of this period (when I should have been finishing my thesis) I became particularly interested in the growth of a profession for cost accountants. I spent many days at the London headquarters of what is now known as CIMA (Chartered Institute of Management Accountants) at 63 Portland Place, which was in walking distance of LBS. In the 1980s when I was there it was known as the ICMA (Institute of Cost and Management Accountants) although it had begun life in 1919 as a professional body for cost accountants, the ICWA (Institute of Cost and Works Accountants). I started off going through what they had in the library, and a picture of me actually appeared in some of their publicity material where the reader is supposed to assume I am studying for their examinations (real students seemed rarely seemed to visit the library, they were too busy working). The librarian, Soot Ng Hong, was very helpful, and I got access to their archives.

CIMA's archives were a collection of dusty boxes in the basement of the building. They were not sorted or catalogued, and I carried everything up to the room in the attic that they had designated for me to work in. It had not been used for many years and everything was grey with dust.[23] Luckily I did not have to freeze as they found an (very) old electric fire for me to use. When the dust was cleared it was actually quite a cosy and pleasant place to work, with a view of rooftops from the window and the deafening sound of pigeons cooing and mating at the beginning of the nesting season. I extracted the material dealing with the early years and organised it in a systematic way, giving

---

[22] Phil Bougen wrote an interesting thesis on the relationship of accounting and industrial relations during the first half of the twentieth century using the case of the Renolds Company. The essence of it was ultimately published in an article in *AOS* (Bougen 1989).

[23] This room had an interesting history. It was part of the flat earlier inhabited by the Secretary of the Institute, Derek du Pré. It had a double floor to protect those working at the Institute from the sound of his daughter, Jacqueline du Pré, practising the cello. It was recently portrayed (inaccurately) in the film of the book about her life and death 'Genius in the Family'.

items file labels and numbers. There was not a lot, but the Minute books were detailed and together with the Institute journal (*The Cost Accountant*) I gradually put the picture together. I used to arrive in the morning, get cups of coffee from the vending machine, eat lunch with the staff and leave in the late afternoon. In other words I began to behave almost like a staff member there at the time I should have been writing up my thesis! I read the literature on the sociology of the professions, discussed it with Rob Goffee, who was in the OB department at LBS, and generally acted as though I was starting a new thesis on the professionalisation project of cost accountants in the U.K. in the period after the First World War. I was especially inspired by Margali Sarfatti Larson's book *The Rise of Professionalism: A Sociological Analysis* (1977).

I had read the journal 'History Workshop' with great interest. The focus of this journal, and the movement which it represented, was on the history of ordinary people, and I was inspired to want to do some oral history of cost accounting. I obtained some funding from the ICMA to interview their oldest members, and I began in the spring of 1984. I was only interested in those who were at work around 1920, so by the nature of things they were all over 80 years old, and my 'sample' was not random but selected by its ability to survive to old age! It was a race against time, and one man, who had worked as 'scientific manager and cost accountant' died a week or so before I was going to interview him. Interviewing them was a fascinating, and a curiously moving experience, as most saw my visit more or less as an opportunity to sum up their life and career for posterity, I think I can understand this now in which I did not at the time. I could talk to them about people, cost accounting systems and office machinery, which no one else had talked to them about for decades. I was delighted to discover that the first woman member of the ICWA was still alive, I went on a long journey to visit her in hospital, only to discover she was completely senile and kept in a large ward in the depths of the hospital with many other women in the same condition. It was a ghastly experience, as I had just read her spirited comments at an ICWA meeting in a report in *The Cost Accountant*. This was depressing, other events were more bizarre; my discussion with one old man went on so long that it was dark when we finished; on the way out he said to me that because of his eyes he was not supposed to drive in the dark. He insisted on driving me to the station, which luckily was not far, as his sight was too poor for anything so sophisticated as 'lane discipline' and I spent the whole journey imagining a head-on collision.

Generally the interviews were really useful as they gave insights and mental pictures of how it was to work as a cost accountant that archive material never could. One thing, which came out of this for me was a sense of personal histories overlapping with the histories of accounting techniques. It joined the past to the present for me, and I suddenly appreciated how the story of their careers, and what they did at work was also a story of cost accounting. For instance Thomas Badgery, born in 1900, was employed as a cost clerk at Dunlop's in 1920, where he sat at a sloping desk putting figures from time cards for the men onto 16 column sheets and adding them up. At the other extreme, he told me that in the 1960s towards the end of his career he was involved in installing computers at Raleigh (Loft 1990: 122–125). The old systems were thus sedimented in the new in a personal as well as technical sense. Unfortunately, for reasons I will outline below, these results of these interviews never got explicitly worked into my thesis, however they were included in the history which was later published by CIMA (Loft 1990).

Extra Time: September 1984–March 1986

I should have finished in September 1984, when my three-year grant ran out. In July 1984 I got married, changing my name to 'Loft', but leaving my new husband alone in our flat in Copenhagen, I existed on the money I got from having sold my terraced house in Selly Oak in Birmingham to my brother, Robert. I had already received a vague promise of a job at the Copenhagen Business School, where I already had contacts, including Jan Mouritsen, who had been working on the Coal Board project with Tony Lowe, David Cooper and others (Hopper *et al.* 1986). The future looked bright, but the present not quite so good, as my thesis was not at all finished by September 1984. I will never forget Tony Lowe standing in the bar at the LBS telling me about my marital responsibility to follow my husband (it did not help, and did not endear me to Tony Lowe!). However, following the advice of Derek Pugh I was determined not to take another job until I had finished my thesis.

The pressure was on . . . About this time I wrote a long and detailed chapter dealing with studies of management accounting, but chatting about it over coffee one day, one of my colleagues, Jackie Ord, asked me how it fitted in with the rest of my thesis. I realised in one awful moment I was wasting my time! I felt sick as I put it away in a file and tried to find something more relevant to write about (but see Loft 1995b). Instead I tackled the process of formation and establishment of ICWA after the War as a 'project' of professionalisation' (Larson 1977). Here I focused 'inwards' upon the ICWA's attempt to establish themselves as a professional accounting association, and the related process of definition of the role of the cost accountant by the Association. This moved on into a discussion of the relationship between cost accounting and the social organisation of the practitioners, and the turbulent social context of Britain in the 1920s.

I moved on to write about the division of labour in the office and the accompanying rationalisation of office work, looking at the appearance of 'office' professionals such as cost accountants in the context of the associated occupations such as 'clerk'. I was inspired by photographs and descriptions of offices from magazines such as *Engineering*, and by my time as an auditor flow-charting accounting systems at places like the Turbines division at GEC Stafford. The experiences from my years as an auditor had given me a picture of the organisation of work in factory offices in the 1970s in the U.K.; a bureaucratic form of organisation that seemed to originate from the period immediately following the First World War. This was an idea that was confirmed by my examination of how office occupations were dealt with in successive censuses.[24] Thus I was now seeing accounting as a disciplinary technology (in Foucault's sense) based on information about the production of men and machines recorded on work tickets, clock cards and so on. Information that was analysed by a growing bureaucracy of clerks and

---

[24] For later exploration of this idea see Kirkham & Loft (1993, 1999).

managers in the works office, the 'centre of calculation' (Latour 1987) which created management 'knowledge' like cost accounting which could be used for disciplinary purposes.

I presented my work on the professionalisation of cost accounting at the EAA Doctoral Colloquium held in Brussels in March 1985.[25] Following this Anthony Hopwood encouraged me to write up what was basically my EAA 1984 paper for *AOS* (Crawford 1984, to become Loft 1986); probably thinking it would get me going writing instead of doing more research, and because people were already beginning to quote it. Writing it all up was a tough process, especially revising it again and again. I decided to present an early draft of the *AOS* article at the first Interdisciplinary Perspectives on Accounting (IPA) conference at Manchester in July 1985. This was a baptism of fire, the room was packed, and a couple of members of the audience attacked my work rather aggressively. I cannot remember the precise critique, but I think it had to do with the fact that I was examining the developments in the control of workers (and managers) in factories through techniques of cost accounting, but not in a Marxist or neo-Marxist framework. Basing my work on Foucault I was effectively denying the presence of the capitalist at the top of the hierarchy of control in the factory (see Foucault 1980), which was a kind of 'red rag to a bull' for Marxists.[26] One person asked who my external examiner was going to be in a tone that suggested that this could surely not be approved! David Cooper 'owned up' to being the proposed external examiner; I cannot remember if this helped or not! It was all rather unpleasant.

I wrote my work by hand, and then took it to the computer room in the basement at the London Business School to type. The idea was really that it was the doctoral students' data that got processed there, but these students began to use if for writing their theses too, and no one seemed to object. I had no data of the kind that required a computer to process, but I went down there too. It was a very primitive programme, but it enabled correction without the use of tippex! Footnotes were a nightmare though, there was no automatic updating, and I had hundreds of them that I had to keep renumbering every time I moved text round. There was only a few places at the terminals in the computer room, and I used to get there when they opened, and type all day with only short breaks (just enough to eat baked-beans on toast) so that I could justify keeping my place at the machine. It was not really just typing; I wrote and rewrote the thesis down there in the harsh neon light of this claustrophobic windowless basement of the London Business School.[27]

In the autumn of 1985, Anthony Hopwood moved to a professorship in international accounting at the London School of Economics (LSE), where together with Michael Bromwich, he planned to re-establish it as the leading Department in the country.[28] I

---

[25] This was where I met Ann Jorissen with whom I later became joint editor of the new journal *European Accounting Review*, and several other people who would later be involved (see Loft *et al.* 2002).

[26] I should add here that Anthony Hopwood was on one of his summer visits to Penn State University in the U.S., and was not at the conference.

[27] At this time (1985) personal computers were just beginning to replace electronic typewriters in ordinary offices. LBS secretaries were all issued with them, and I remember inspecting with awe Mary Scott-Flemming's model under its dust cover in the corner of the office.

[28] A project that succeeded.

remained at the LBS, with the seminars and many of the interesting visitors gone, it became a less attractive place. Not least as my husband rang me each evening to ask how I was getting on with finishing the monster! I began to get bad eczema on my hands; it bled and was so painful that there were a couple of days I could not even write. My doctor told me it was stress, although later it turned out to be at least partly due to allergy to the strong cleaning fluid supplied to our kitchen at the LBS.

The worst part was Chapter 2, the chapter that laid out the theoretical frame of reference. In the autumn of 1985 I got the flu really badly and went home to Birmingham, I let my mother administer the kind of care I had not had since I was a child, and as I recovered, tried again to write it. I arranged and rearranged the paragraphs, rubbing out text, adding new text, and chopping it up into pieces with scissors and reassembling it with tape. I ended up with typed bits from earlier intertwined with smudgy new contributions, some bits with several layers of tape holding them together.

I knew why it was difficult, I had taken theoretical insights from a range of sources: there was a basis mixture which was the *AOS* literature, and to this had been added a large dollop of Foucault, and a slightly lesser one of the recent sociology of the professions; there were smaller dollops of 'history workshop', organisation theory, history of the professions and Marxist labour process — in particular Braverman. Doing my genealogical history had taken me away from the factory and cost accounting as a discipline, and I had found myself examining the influence of the State in the momentous developments associated with the First World War. It had also taken me to the development of the occupation and would-be profession of 'cost accountant', and to argue for the effect of this on the development of the techniques of cost accounting. I felt I needed to knit the different theories into some kind of coherent chapter that could then provide a kind of frame on which my wide variety of empirical material could hang.

Anthony Hopwood patiently wrote comments on each draft of this chapter, and it went into at least four drafts. I remember meeting him in the LBS bar (he no longer had an office at LBS) in the early evening when it was fairly empty and going through one of the drafts. I felt tired and depressed after my flu and asked him if it was not possible for me to do the doctorate in the form of two or three papers, one of which would be based on the 'cost accounting as discipline' theme, the other on the attempts to make a profession for cost accountants, and possibly a third on cost accounting in the First World War. I am glad in retrospect that he did not consider this a good idea, as eventually I got the chapter done, more or less coherently, by presenting the Foucauldian approach, and then discussing its limitations and bringing in the other aspects. I quote here what I eventually wrote:

> Thus whilst maintaining the Foucauldian position advanced earlier: that cost and management accounting is a disciplinary technique which is powerful because of the way in which it creates 'knowledge' about the activity of work; this will be extended and developed from the viewpoint that the questions of who puts into practice disciplinary technologies, and from where in society they come, are important ones. Influencing not

only the extent and intensity with which disciplinary techniques are used,
but the very nature of those techniques themselves (Loft 1988: 56).

That paragraph cost me a lot of 'brainwork,' as Sydney and Beatrice Webb so
picturesquely describe it (1917)! From this position I could go on to discuss the
development of specialist practitioners, and the process of professionalisation and thus
link it altogether.

The other chapters were relatively easier, although I often found underway that I had
to go back to the libraries to fill in some background or details I was missing. For each
chapter I had assembled all the paragraphs I had already written about the topic in a file,
and I started off working from that. Chapter 3, which was the historical introduction,
was also difficult though. I wanted to write genealogy, but I had to start somewhere, and
to make that introduction I had no option but to use a variety of secondary sources. This
rather went against the genealogical 'grain'. The chapter following this, the one on the
First World War was the one I had done most work on earlier, so this went fairly quickly.
The aim of the chapter being to tell the complex and fascinating story of how cost
accounting came to be seen as a crucial tool in the war effort. The fifth chapter, which
dealt with the period just after the War ('Reconstruction and Reality'), flowed on from
the chapter on the War and I enjoyed this one.[29]

Then I came to writing chapter 6, which was about the 'project' of professionalisation
(Larson 1977) which the early ICWA engaged in, and the way in which they aimed to
be like professional chartered accountants who worked from professional offices. This
flowed into the following Chapter 7, which broadened the discussion to look at the
complex relationship between the development of cost accounting techniques and the
emergence of a professional body in the social and political context of Britain in the
1920s. Here in these two chapters I had meant to include various 'gems' from my
interviews with retired cost accountants, which had by this point been transcribed. The
problem was I had no time left, and I dashed on to write a draft of the last chapter, the
conclusion, which was an absolute necessity. I did not do such a good job of finishing
the thesis as I wanted to, and I had mixed feelings about it. I did not think it included
half of the fascinating material I had collected or ideas I had had. I thought that I pushed
through the genealogy perspective as well as I could in the circumstances, but I was not
100% happy with how Chapter 7 on the formation of the ICWA really quite fitted in, and
the same applied to some of Chapter 8.

In March 1986 I finally delivered the thesis; having it bound by the university
publishers in the required blue cover with gold letters. I moved to Denmark, returning
for the examination a month or so later which would be at the LSE. As I nervously
approached, I met David Cooper on the traffic island outside the entrance, who as I
recall it was putting on his tie while he waited for the lights to change (but he may only
have been adjusting it). An action which was both everyday and symbolic in the
situation – this was a formal occasion and not an ordinary kind of seminar. I had found
it difficult to imagine how to prepare for such an examination, and although I had flicked
through the thesis the day before I was not really prepared for David's questions. I do

---

[29] These two chapters later provided the basis for Loft (1994).

not recall them precisely, but only that they were difficult — the kind of 'big' questions: 'life, the universe and accounting' to paraphrase a book popular at the time (Adams 1982). I think I had difficulty putting my thesis in context so soon after I had finished it. I could see Anthony looking more and more disconcerted, and I felt more and more miserable, feeling I had let him down in front of David Cooper. Instead of being one of the best days of my life, it became one of the less good days, and I went back to the LBS and wept! However, a couple of days later I organised a party for everyone I knew from the LBS, it went much better than the examination (!). The food included a number of Danish cheeses which I had imported for the occasion, including an 'old Ole' which was a very stinky old well matured type. I am not sure anyone ate any, but it was a talking point and I was finished!

Postscript: Some (Possibly) Good Advice . . .

Every Ph.D. is different, but if I should give advice I would say be ambitious, try to be innovative and get a supervisor who is interested in your topic. Remember though, that you are unlikely to be able to produce a whole new theory of accounting and finishing is important! The traditional structure of a thesis: introduction, literature review, theory, method, empirical material, analysis, conclusion and future perspectives may seem dull but it can help in structuring your life and time. Do continuous 'reality' checks by thinking about where and what you might publish afterwards and find other Ph.D. students to drown your sorrows with. Don't ever think about writing more than three hundred and fifty pages, whatever your topic or research method, not even your parents will want to read it. Besides, you will need something to work at afterwards!

References

Adams, D. (1982). *Life, the universe and everything*. Harmony Books.

Armstrong, P. (1987). The rise of accounting controls in British capitalist enterprises. *Accounting, Organizations and Society, 12*(5), 415–436.

Beaver, W. H. (1981). *Financial reporting: An accounting revolution*. Englewood Cliffs: Prentice Hall.

Bentham, J. (1843). *Works of Jeremy Bentham* (Ed.). Bowring, Edinburgh: William Tait.

Bougen, P. (1989). The emergence, roles and consequences of an accounting-industrial relations interaction. *Accounting, Organizations and Society, 14*(3), 203–234.

Braverman, H. (1974). *Labour and monopoly capital*. London: Monthly Review Press.

Brittain, V. (1933). *Testament of youth*. Victor Gollancz.

Brown, L. D. (1996). Influential accounting articles, individuals, Ph.D. granting institutions and faculties: a citational analysis. *Accounting, Organizations and Society, 21*(7/8), 723–754.

Burchell, S., Clubb, C., Hopwood, A. and Nahapiet, J. (1980). The roles of accounting in organizations and society. *Accounting, Organizations and Society, 5*(1), 5–27.

Burchell, S., Clubb, C., & Hopwood, A. G. (1985). Accounting in its social context: towards a history of value added in the United Kingdom. *Accounting, Organizations and Society, 10*(4), 381–413.

Burchell, G., Gordon, C., & Miller, P. (Eds) (1991). *The Foucault effect: Studies in Governmentality with two lectures by and an interview with Michel Foucault*. Chicago: University of Chicago Press.

Byatt, A. S. (1990). *Possession: A romance*. London: Chatto and Windus.

Chatfield, M. (1977). *A history of accounting thought*. New York: Robert E. Krieger.

Chua, W. F. (1986). Theoretical constructions of and by the real. *Accounting, Organizations and Society, 11*(6), 583–598.

Crawford, A. (1984). Cost accounting, work control and the development of cost accounting in Britain 1914–1925. Unpublished paper presented at *European Accounting Association Conference,* St Gallen, Switzerland.

Dickens, C. (1979). *Hard times*. London: J. M. Dent.

Elbourne, E. T. (1914). *Factory administration and accounts*. London: Longmans.

Eliot, T. S. (1943). *Four quartets*. London: Faber and Faber.

Foucault, M. (1977a). *Discipline and punish: The birth of the prison*. Harmondsworth: Penguin.

Foucault, M. (1977b). *Language, counter-memory, practice*. Ithaca, NY: Cornell University Press.

Foucault, M. (1980). *Power/knowledge*. Brighton: Harvester Press.

Garcke, E., & Fells, J. M. (1887–1922). *Factory accounts*. London, Crosby: Lockwood.

Garner, S. P. (1954). *Evolution of cost accounting to 1925*. Alabama, AL: University of Alabama Press.

Gaskell, E. (1973). *North and south*. Oxford: Oxford University Press.

Gendron, Y., & Baker, R. C. (2002). On interdisciplinary movements: The translation of Foucaltian perspectives into accounting research. Working Paper available from the authors: yves.gendron@ualberta.ca

Hobsbawm, E. J. (1975). *The age of capital, 1848–1875*. London: Cardinal.

Hopper, T., Cooper, D., Capps, T., Lowe, E. A., & Mouritsen, J. (1986). Financial control in the labour process: managerial strategies and worker resistance in the National Coal Board. In: H. Willmott & D. Knights (Eds), *Managing the labour process* (pp. 109–141). Aldershot: Gower.

Hopwood, A. G. (1987). The archaeology of accounting systems. *Accounting, Organizations and Society, 12*(3), 207–234.

Kirkham, L. M., & Loft, A. (1993). Gender and the construction of the professional accountant. *Accounting, Organizations and Society, 18*(6), 507–558.

Kirkham, L. M., & Loft A. (1999). Census reports and the construction of the professional accountant. Working Paper, Copenhagen Business School, Department of Accounting and Auditing (3–1999).

Larson, M. S. (1977). *The rise of professionalism: A sociological analysis*. Berkeley: University of California Press.

Latour, B. (1987). *Science in action*. Milton Keynes: Open University Press.

Latour, B., & Woolgar, S. (1986). *Laboratory life: The construction of scientific facts*. Princeton, N.J: Princeton University Life.

Lodge, D. (1975). *Changing places*. London: Secker and Warburg.

Lodge, D. (1984). *Small world*. London: Secker and Warburg.

Lodge, D. (1988). *Nice work*. New York: Viking Press.

Lodge, D. (2001). *Thinks*. London: Secker and Warburg.

Loft, A. (1986). Towards a critical understanding of accounting: the case of cost accounting in the U.K. 1914–1925. *Accounting, Organizations and Society, 11*(2), 137–169.

Loft, A. (1988). *Understanding accounting in its social and historical context: The case of cost accounting in the U.K. 1914–1925*. New York: Garland Press. (This is the published version of Ph.D. thesis, London Business School 1986).

Loft, A. (1990). *Coming into the light: A study of the development of a professional association for cost accountants in Britain in the wake of the First World War*. London: CIMA.

Loft, A. (1992). Accountancy and the gendered division of labour: a review essay. *Accounting, Organizations and Society, 17*(3/4), 367–378.

Loft, A. (1994). Accountancy and the first world war. In: A. G. Hopwood & P. Miller (Eds), *Accounting as social and institutional practice* (pp. 116–137). Cambridge: Cambridge University Press.

Loft, A. (1994a). Accounting and visibility: A discussion of the link between cost accounting and control in the history of the factory. In: K. Artsberg, A. Loft & S. Yard (Eds), *Accounting Research in Lund*. Lund: Lund University Press.

Loft, A. (1995a). Time is money. *Studies in Cultures, Organizations and Society, 1*, 127–145.

Loft, A. (1995b). The history of management accounting: relevance found. In: D. Ashton, T. Hopper & R. Scapens (Eds), *Issues in management accounting* 2/E. Englewood Cliffs: Prentice Hall.

Loft, A. (2001). Hopwood, Anthony. In: M. Warner (Ed.), *The IEBM Handbook of Management Thinking*. London: International Thomson Business Press.

Loft, A., Jorisson, A., & Walton, P. (2002). From newsletter to academic journal: Creating the European Accounting Review. *European Accounting Review, 11*(1), 43–75.

Lyon, D. (1994). *The electronic eye: The rise of surveillance society*. Minneapolis: University of Minnesota Press.

Miller, P., & O'Leary, T. (1987). Accounting and the construction of the governable person. *Accounting, Organizations and Society, 12*(3), 235–265.

Miller, P., Hopper, T., & Laughlin, R. (1991). The new accounting history: An introduction. *Accounting, Organizations and Society, 16*(5/6), 395–403.

Preston, A. (1986). Interactions and arrangements in the process of informing. *Accounting, Organizations and Society, 11*(6), 521–540.

Pollard, S. (1968). *The genesis of modern management*. Harmondsworth: Penguin.

Power, M. (1997). *The audit society*. Oxford: Oxford University Press.

Power, M. (1999). Eulogy to 1998 BAA Distinguished Academic — Prof Anthony Hopwood: 1998 BAA Distinguished Academic. *British Accounting Review, 31*(1), 31–34.

Pugh, D. S., Hickson, D. J., Hinings, C. R., & Turner, C. (1968). Dimensions of organizational structure. *Administrative Science Quarterly, 13*, 65–105.

Roberts, J. (1991). The possibilities of accountability. *Accounting, Organizations and Society, 16*(4), 355–368.

Roberts, J., & Scapens, R. (1985). Accounting systems and systems of accountability: Understanding accounting practices in their organizational contexts. *Accounting Organizations and Society, 10*(4), 443–456.

Stacey, N. H. A., (1954). *English accountancy, a study in social and economic history 1800–1954*. London: Gee.

Taylor, A. J. P. (1970). *English history 1914–1945*. Harmondsworth: Pelican.

Tolkien, J. R. (1954/1955). *The Lord of the Rings*. London: George Allen and Unwin.

Webb, B., & Webb, S. (1917). What is to be learnt from the professional associations of brainworkers as to the sphere of control by vocational organizations? Fabian Report published in the *New Statesman* as additional pages: 21 April 1917: pp. 1–24; 28 April 1917: pp. 25–48.
Williams, O. A. (1915). *Life in a railway factory*. London: Duckworth.

Chapter 7

Learning to Balance: The Experience of an Overseas Ph.D. student in the U.K.

Naoko Komori

Introduction

"Crap!" When I heard my supervisor use this word to categorise my work, I was initially very shocked and wondered whether I had come to the right place to study. However, it was from this moment that I really began to realise what studying for a Ph.D. was all about and how my attitude as a student and my approach to research needed to change. This chapter is a biographical account of what I feel I have learned during my time as a Ph.D. student in Sheffield, England. I came to Sheffield University to study for a Ph.D. on the subject of gender and accounting with particular reference to the Japanese context. Subsequently, I began to work as an accounting academic in a Japanese University. However, I have yet to finish my Ph.D. — during the latter stages of my fieldwork in Japan, I had a serious car accident and was hospitalised for more than 8 months. I am now recovering and hope to finish my thesis in the next 12–18 months. This chapter has been written partly to aid my process of rehabilitation before I return to complete my Ph.D. The account is thus incomplete in the sense that I cannot report all that I have gained from my doctoral studies. Nevertheless, my experiences have made me think a lot about the nature of research and its personal significance. In this chapter, I have tried to reflect on the process of undertaking a Ph.D. and to show how the experience of conducting such research across cultures has changed my ways of thinking and my general approach to life. I also consider what I have learned from my experiences and what advice I would pass on to overseas students seeking to do a Ph.D. in an English speaking country such as the U.K.

This chapter describes the process by which my thesis came into shape. By so doing, I intend to explore how my life as a female research student from Japan studying in the U.K. played a significant role in developing my research. There has existed a dialectical interaction between the research project and my life. My experience of life in the U.K. changed my views and attitudes towards work and research, and subsequently the

The Real Life Guide to Accounting Research: A Behind-the-Scenes View of Using Qualitative Research Methods research influenced and changed my ways of thinking about life. The chapter has four main sections. The first section explains how I ended up taking a Ph.D. in the U.K. The second section focuses on the way in which my Ph.D. research developed and how I came to terms with living in the U.K. The third section demonstrates how the content and issues raised by my research began to influence (and make me re-think) my approach to life. Finally, I consider how changes in my life and the impact of my accident have influenced the nature of my research and my approach to research. I also reflect on what research has brought to my life after such a traumatic event.

Deciding to do a Ph.D. at Sheffield

Searching for Freedom

There were many factors, including quite a bit of luck, which led me to take Ph.D. at Sheffield. One of the main reasons that led me to take a Ph.D. in accounting is the fact that I really wanted to build my life free from the control of my father and the constraints at home. My father saw it as his obligation to make sure that his children obtained a good school record and would pursue this obligation very strictly. If I were not doing well at school, he would not let me eat proper food for a period of time. Since I liked eating, this policy was very tough. In the short term, I had to sneak food when he was asleep but soon decided that I needed to work harder to get better marks. My school performance enabled me to enter the Department of Business Administration at Kobe University, one of the best in Japan. I chose to study business as I really wanted to pursue a different pattern of life to the normal Japanese woman — female students in Kobe represented about 10% of the faculty's cohort. Generally, women in Japan are expected to be good housewives and mothers rather than pursuing a long-term career, but it always seemed natural for me to pursue a working career. A business education seemed to be a good basis for this.

Another reason that led me to Sheffield is that I had always had a strong motivation to study abroad. I had lived in the USA for two years from the age of ten. Although I knew little English at the beginning, I really enjoyed the stay. Even though I was very young, I remember that I felt free to express myself there. In Japan, it was important to follow what other people did, even if you did not understand why or did not really want to do so. In fact, it was difficult to adjust to the Japanese society when I came back from the USA. I was often criticised at school for being too different, too opinionated and too persistent. I often asked questions but realized such an attitude was not welcome. Feeling different, I became interested more in how Japanese society works and the differences with other countries. I entered many English speech contests and essay competitions to express my opinions and ended up winning awards, which further enhanced my motivation to study abroad. I gradually learned to adapt to others without expressing my opinions and made friends, although I never felt completely comfortable having to suppress my views. Boyfriends seemed a way out from School but most of them never understood when I said I really wanted to study abroad. They would often say to me, "Japan is such a nice country. It is well-off, safe, rich in nice foods and nice people, above all you can use Japanese! Why do you want to go abroad so much?" This only further enhanced my motivation to study abroad and to try and ensure that I was in a different position from other women (and men) in Japanese society.

Accounting — A Knowledge to be Free

When I progressed to university, I majored in accounting — I had decided that I wanted to be an accounting professional. Although Japanese companies generally provided lifetime employment, normally this was limited to men. After having children, women were not expected to work in career positions in Japanese companies. As an accounting professional, I would have more independence and more say over the length of my working life. I also saw accountancy as basic literacy and knowledge that I needed to live properly. Since I really wanted to be free and independent from my father's control, I wanted to learn how to understand real life. To understand about life, I needed to understand about money. To understand about money, I needed to understand about accounting. However, university classes disappointed me. Far from my impression that accounting was a way to learn about real lives, the accounting that I learned at university was nothing different from schoolwork. I had to cram information into my head and to learn answers in a parrot-like fashion. Although bored, I made an effort to be diligent and ended up with top-grades — but I was still looking for something different.

The Road to Sheffield

After my undergraduate degree, I chose to pursue an academic accounting career, taking a master's degree and planning to do a Ph.D. at Kobe University, while most of my colleagues found jobs in companies. I wanted to study accounting from different perspectives, not just from the technical perspective dominant during my undergraduate course. I still held the view that accounting was concerned with real lives and provided a significant perspective with which to understand the nature of Japanese society, a basic concern of my life. With this in mind, I entered an essay competition held by the Nikkei newspaper for all Japanese university students on the post-war U.S.-Japan relationship. My essay, which I wrote from the perspective of accounting, was awarded a prize and I received a trip to the USA to debate the issue with university students there. Unfortunately, I could not make the trip, as it was the same day as my entrance examination for my master's course — but the event still motivated me to pursue an academic career in accounting.

However, my master's course was disappointing, as I had to study many things that I found to be of little interest. I questioned myself many times on why I had taken the course. Only one class really interested me — a course on "social analysis in accounting". The course leader seemed quite original. He introduced new theoretical frameworks in accounting from the U.K. and Australia and explored qualitative methodologies — accounting research in this area seemed very different and very interesting. I chose this area as my major area of study and subsequently progressed to the Ph.D. course at Kobe with plans to study the social significance of the accounting profession (involving at least some comparative work and the chance to study abroad).

In the first summer of my Ph.D. course at Kobe, I met a visiting accounting professor from Sheffield University and managed to talk to him about my research. Understanding my background and standpoints, he spoke of the possibility of me doing a Ph.D. in Sheffield. By now I had started to consider the position of women in Japan, and particularly in the Japanese accounting profession where more and more women were taking the CPA examination. He told me that gender issues in accounting were increasing and suggested that I may be able to make a contribution from a Japanese perspective. This struck me as a really good opportunity and I can remember that my excitement was such that I found it really difficult to sleep at night. I enjoyed spending time with my future supervisor and his partner, showing them around Kobe and Osaka, and this gave me sufficient confidence to go to Sheffield.

Walking Down a Road Stuck with Barriers and Removing Them

I came to Sheffield and started my Ph.D. course. Living a life as a Ph.D. student in Sheffield, I encountered various changes in my life. These changes affected my working style and my ways of thinking about work.

Getting Rid of the Barrier between Work and Life

The first big shock I had after coming to Sheffield was the different mode of relationship with my supervisor. The student-supervisor relationship is much closer than it is in Japan. I had chances to see many different perspectives and ways of thinking and to discuss my thesis in an informal way. I could be more honest about my feelings and opinions. Normally the relationship between a supervisor and a student in Japan is based on hierarchy. Students are expected to follow what the supervisor says, although it does not necessarily mean that the student respects everything about the supervisor. In work, I tried to be a good student, obedient and diligent, listening intently to what my Japanese supervisor was saying. But outside work, I had my own life that I could never share with my supervisor, setting myself free and behaving more honestly to my own feelings. In Japan, as long as I was behaving obediently, everything went smoothly. I tried to accept and follow what he expected me to do without thinking critically about my own opinion. As long as I did this, it was OK and I could get good marks. However, the relationship with my supervisor in Sheffield was too close to hide myself. It was the first time in my life that my personal views and emotions entered the sphere of work.

Gradually, I came to understand why it is so significant to have a close relationship with a supervisor. Getting close to the supervisor mixes the mentality of work and life. In a sense, I needed to reconstruct my frame of reference concerning my life — I was really searching for my life and in doing so I started to change my perspective towards work, which in turn further changed my perspective on life. In Japan, when work and life is separated and when personal views and feelings are left outside of work, I only needed to solve questions that already had answers or could be easily answered with a bit more work. However, once I started to mix work and life, the research questions became more complicated, with either many, or possibly no, answers. The close relationship with one's supervisor was academically good but also very difficult since it was forcing me to view my life more critically than I had ever done in Japan.

The Student has to Act, Not Sit and Receive

The close relationship with the supervisor began to influence my working style. Losing the hierarchical relationship that I had been used to made me very unstable. In Japan, what is mostly expected in academic work was to read loyally what is written and accumulate knowledge in the existing research frame. When I produced my first major piece of work (outlining what I was going to do in my thesis) in the same manner that I had been accustomed to in Japan, I got the reaction from my supervisor mentioned at the start of the chapter — with him adding: "I don't believe this is what you want to do".

This gave me an opportunity to think about my attitude to work. I recognized that I had been protected by the hierarchical supervisory relationship in Japan. Assuming this hierarchy was in place in the U.K., I had effectively taken for granted that it was the duty of the supervisor to respect the work of his/her students. However, such ways of thinking did not apply to my supervisor. He was very busy and there was a lot of competition with people to see him. I often waited outside his office for hours for him to come back, but when he returned, he ended up seeing people who had waited less time than me (either because they had more urgent matters or were just more pushy than me). When I finally managed to show him my work, I was very shocked to see his reaction and how often reading it seemed to make him sleepy! This was the hardest reaction that I had ever received in my life. I could endure much criticism but it was very hard to see that my work was capable of making someone fall asleep. If this message was from a distant supervisor who did not understand me, I would have been able to distance myself from such a reaction. However, this message was from someone that I liked, who understood me well, and whom I wanted to understand. So this reaction struck directly to my heart. I felt badly about giving him what seemed to be poor quality work and I really sought to change my attitude as his student. I could not just sit and wait for his supervision like an obligated student. My work needed to improve and I needed a strategy to attract his interest, to wake him up and see my work and to survive the competition for his time.

An Empty Heart

In the early stages of my structuring my Ph.D. project, I tried hard to understand why my supervisor did not find my ideas more interesting. He often challenged me for not being specific enough or for not viewing literature more critically. He would often say that "Naoko Komori always wants to talk about the world" in response to my reflections on the general role of woman and men in society. When I made comments about the role of accounting in Japan and the role of women in relation to accounting, he seemed to show more interest. I started to understand that I needed to be more focused and to make sure that I understood fully the existing Western literature on gender in accounting. However, it also worried me that I did not have anything really specific to argue about women and accounting based on my own experiences and observations. All I could ask was very general and something that is discussed everywhere — are women discriminated against? There was nothing particularly strong coming from my heart. This was hard to face in the U.K. It had been easy in Japan as my feelings were largely divorced from my work. In the U.K., academics seemed more emotionally involved in their work and I wanted to be so but all my reference points were coming from books and literature and this seemed too impersonal and less persuasive. If I got personal, my supervisor would tell me it was too general as I was not focusing on women and accounting (my intended thesis) but worrying more about women in general in society. I felt an additional starting point had to be to consider my life as a woman both in Japan and in U.K. and to draw on this in shaping my understanding of the relationship between women and accounting. This enhanced my sense of significance and in the early days of my studies led to me getting involved more with friends and people and the life in Sheffield rather than just sitting and reading in front of the computer isolated from the outside world. I included pubs and nightclubs as the places for my research. Indeed, they became my significant fieldwork sites to understand more about women and gender. The relationship with accounting was something that I had to try and draw from the literature, prior to my planned fieldwork back in Japan.

Reading is Writing. Writing is Thinking — Doing Three Things at the Same Time

I started to explore a wide range of academic literature to develop my perspective on the relationship between women and accounting. I looked at studies in different areas apart from accounting such as sociological studies on gender, Japanese women and society, as well as studies on Japanese business and management. However, this process created big problems. One was the difficulty of identifying key themes. I kept reading books and papers but I could not find any clear way of structuring things. There were mountains of material and I was getting lost. Seeing this, my supervisor emphasized, after quite a long period of reading, that 'the golden rule is to write something'. It was very difficult to start writing the first sentence, but writing made me think more thematically. I learned that writing while reading helps one think more clearly.

In writing about each key theme, however, I hit further problems as each theme started to become too big and complicated the more articles and books I read. For instance, in analysing the Japanese context and its significance to woman and accounting, I ended up with far too much on the Japanese context and not very much on women and accounting in Japan. I knew it was getting unmanageable and half expected my supervisor's comment that I was again 'talking about the world'. A great help here was the ability to consult with my second supervisor. He liked me talking about the world and so we had a good starting point. The discussions with him helped me to understand what had been argued in the gender literature in the West and this really helped me to cut through a lot of material and clarify my own perspective and research directions. In specific terms, it made me concentrate more specifically on organizational contexts and the way in which social traditions are played out in organizations and the effect that this can have on the role of women in the workforce. We found it more difficult to agree about the role of women in the household and their attitudes towards accounting and the relationship between Japanese husbands and wives — but this was something I had to put to one side at this stage (although as I will explain later it was an issue that would turn out to be a great help to me in developing my thesis).

The Significance of Context

The difficulty with my research was the different way in which people in the U.K. generally viewed the position of Japanese women. It was generally perceived that women are located in the lower hierarchy in society, which may derive from the clichéd view of Japanese women being 'three steps behind men'. Almost everybody concerned with my work — except my supervisor and some professors who had experienced life in Japan — started discussions with the assumption that Japanese women were treated rather like second-class citizens. However, this did not fit comfortably with my observation and experience of everyday life in Japan. It was true when talking about the position of women in the workplace, where it is far more difficult for women than men to climb the career ladder. However, I seldom met a woman who complained about such a state of affairs. Indeed, it was rather the opposite. Many male colleagues and friends were insisting, without being ironic, that the life of women is far more comfortable than their lives. "As a woman, you do not have to go to drink with your seniors and listen to their boring stories every night until one to two o'clock in the morning. You can just say you are feeling ill when you want to finish work and go home early. You can even say that you have to go back early to cook for your husband. No male seniors question you and kindly let you go home. They would tell you to go home to prepare for your husband. That is more important. Then they tell the men to do your work even if it means staying late. Women also do not need to pay money for dating. Men pay for meals, dresses and jewellery for women — and after doing all there is no guarantee for the man that a woman would marry him. How can you say women are discriminated against?" Since most of my friends in Japan were men, I could see their viewpoints. Outside of the workplace, women are very strong in Japan.

My life in Sheffield also made me think critically about the general assumption in studies on the social position of women that women in the West have more freedom and control over their lives compared to women in Japan. I soon realized that it is difficult to have a social life without a boyfriend. I became more conscious about being a woman — in everyday scenes of life like greetings, seeing my supervisors or any men related to my work, going to restaurants with male colleagues and friends, I kept seeing sexual distinctions and became very conscious that I am a woman, a feeling I had never had in

Japan. Many close expressions were used in everyday life like kisses and hugs that I only used in sexual contexts in Japan. I have to confess I was practicing how to kiss and hug naturally as well as to receive such things nicely because I was so tense! I could easily go to a restaurant alone in Japan while I did not 'dare' to go alone to restaurants in Sheffield. It was funny to find people thinking that I was a lesbian when I was always with the same female friend. Even here, a sexual significance was attributed to an acknowledged relationship with a person, rather than it being accepted as just a friendship. In this respect, Japan is less gender-conscious than the West, even though it is often argued that Japan is a male-dominated country.

This gap between my observations and the general perception I was encountering in the U.K. caused me to ensure that I studied the relationship between women and accounting by taking account of differences in context. For example, considering the significance of the family and the household, the significance of a private-public distinction, the meaning of power, and the nature of control. Contextual differences were to become a very important part of my thesis. Also seeing the gap between my understanding and the assumption of some arguments, I started to change my reading style. Whenever I read literature, I questioned its assumptions and critically considered its implications rather than keeping on reading mountains of material without questioning. Critical thinking was becoming a significant core skill for developing my research.

To Listen is to Understand, Not to Accept

Cross-cultural research had always interested me but I never understood how difficult it is until I actually lived my life in different contexts. The experience of living in different cultural contexts made me see how listening is significant for understanding different ways of thinking. In Sheffield, I became very conscious about being a Japanese person. In Japan, I had not been conscious of being a Japanese person since most people I see in everyday life are Japanese. However, in the U.K., like it or not, I was seen Japanese, before being understood as a person. I also found myself arguing like a representative of Japan when people made negative comments about Japan without having actually been there. It made me realize how difficult it is to understand people from different cultures and contexts. When the opinions were too prejudiced and negative, I tended to get upset. Being Japanese, I naively took these opinions as criticism of me. My supervisor advised me to ask "why?", telling me that it is necessary to understand their views and perspectives to understand the country rather than getting upset and rejecting different opinions. In fact, my arguments with them helped me to consider their views and perspectives and this came to be very important in the later stages of my research.

I learned how to listen and how to make an argument for the first time in my life. I had tended to consider that listening was 'accepting' and that making an argument was 'rejecting'. Since I was not ready to accept other opinions, I did not have enough patience to listen. But I learned that listening is not accepting, but understanding. When you listen to a different opinion, it is important to have your own opinion and to think how they relate to each other. Making an argument is also not rejection but understanding too. To consider the significance of listening and how to make an argument became very significant knowledge for the task of conducting interviews, something that is discussed in the next section.

Accounting Research gives a Different Picture of Life

When I finished my literature review, I went back to Japan and made a presentation of my findings at the *Asian Pacific Interdisciplinary Research in Accounting Conference* at Osaka in 1998. The reaction to my research was motivating. However, I found that Western theory for explaining the relationship between accounting and women was not easily transferable to the Japanese context. This made me realize an issue that I needed to overcome — to explain contextual differences more concretely. In Japan, I also started to conduct my fieldwork, interviewing women accounting professionals from different backgrounds about their working experiences and comparing their experiences with reported experiences of women accountants in the West. I also wanted to develop the area of household accounting and started to plan appropriate fieldwork. Going back and forth between Japan and Sheffield, my work started to influence my life and my viewpoints on life.

Understanding and Communicating — The Most Significant Knowledge in the Interview

Constructing interview questions requires thorough preparation. In order to compare the experience of my respondents in Japan with women accounting professionals in the West, my interviews sought to explore their experiences and viewpoints about work and life. However, with such a degree of vagueness and generality, I really had no clue where to start. My supervisor advised me to ask questions that invited them to talk about their life, which was very helpful. I made questions as simple as possible and not too specific, leaving them room to construct their stories and reflections. It was also necessary to prepare questions in way that encouraged clear and direct answers. There were some terms that can be taken for granted in a particular context, yet which represent how people construct their reality. For example, I needed to find what the term 'women' signified to each interviewee. But the question "what does the term 'woman' mean to you?" may have been too obscure. I asked them about experiences that made them conscious of being a woman. This made it easier for them to answer the interview questions.

In the course of an interview, you may find that the assumption of interview questions does not necessarily reflect how interviewees construct their views. Before I conducted an interview, I had assumed that women accounting professionals in Japan had experienced many difficulties similar to those reported in gender research in Anglo-Saxon countries and that it would be easy for them to talk about such experiences. As soon as I began my interviews, however, I found such an assumption was wrong. Many of them said they have never experienced any difficulties through being a woman. So I changed my question to "have you ever felt like quitting the profession?", which enabled me to understand how they viewed their work in the accounting profession, the role of women, and themselves more specifically.

The interview requires good communication not just with the interviewee but also with your inner-self. In the course of an interview, the reaction and response from interviewees may challenge your research and your ways of thinking. In my case, the response of interviewees challenged my approach to life. Many older senior women accounting professionals were initially reluctant to answer some key questions in the interview, as if they were saying "how can this little girl understand me?". Their reaction made me think critically about myself and to use such critical reflection to convince them to continue with the interview. In order to open their hearts, I tried to demonstrate that I had similarities in my background to them. I introduced myself as a researcher from Sheffield but also holding a position at a Japanese university. However, while this usually helped with the older interviewees, this was ineffective with some younger interviewees. They showed obvious hostility to me, aggressively asking many questions about how I managed to get a chance to study in the U.K. instead of answering my interview questions. I realized that the key point to gaining the trust of interviewees and to make them feel comfortable about talking about their experiences to a stranger was not to explain my position but to open up myself to them. Subsequently, I started to explain my background, why I was interested in this research, the problems that I have in my work at university, and the difficulty of studying abroad. I even talked about problems I had in my relationships and my views on the most preferable form of relationship, including marriage. Then they seemed to be very interested and the interviews became very long and lively. Interviewees became willing to talk about themselves and I even ended up going out to dinner and to bars with some interviewees and talking over many topics, including their plans to work in U.S. accounting firms, their future business plans and even their problems with their boyfriends!

After I finished fieldwork, interviewing more than 50 Japanese women CPA's and trainees, I was very surprised to see how much I did not really understand myself, the people and the phenomenon as I assumed that I did. My view of life gradually started to change. First, my way of thinking changed. I had been strong and opinionated, judging everything in either black or white. I had assumed that it was correct behaviour for the researcher to have an independent point of view and to give a response to each question according to that point of view. However, in the course of meeting many people through my fieldwork, I came to see to how difficult it was to acquire a deep understanding of events and people, which enhanced the sense of necessity to listen and to learn different ways of thinking before judging whether I found particular statements to be acceptable or not. I had previously categorized people in simple ways but now started to take more complex stances, understanding the significance of context in shaping personal nature. The major change was that I was understanding myself better. I was starting to have a clearer idea about my research, my attitudes and how to relate myself to society both through my work and life. The interview process gave me a chance to communicate not only with the interviewee but with myself which consequently enhanced my self-trust.

Managing to be both Persistent and Flexible

I also wanted to study the relationship between accounting and women at home in Japan as I felt this was a crucial dimension in understanding the contextual position of Japanese women accounting professionals — particularly given that women traditionally had played a significant role in the maintenance and development of household accounting. However, as there was little information available on this topic, this was not an easy task. After a long process of research through the internet and other investigation work, I found information on a governmental institution that had held an annual prize scheme for household accounting practices and which had regularly published articles on the experiences of prize-winning households. This provided me with a valuable database from which to study household accounting in Japan.

While persistence is significant for developing the research, it is also important to be flexible and to change research plans accordingly. When I was conducting my research, it was noticeable that the interest of other researchers in household accounting in the U.K. was increasing. *Accounting, Auditing and Accountability Journal* then made a formal call for papers for a special issue on accounting at home. My supervisor suggested that this would be a valuable opportunity to develop my ideas and thinking on household accounting and its significance in terms of enhancing understanding of the relationship between Japanese women and accounting and between Japanese women accounting professionals and the Japanese accounting firms/profession. My initial experience here helped me to realise the importance of balancing two personal qualities, namely the need to be persistent to endure the long research process but also to be flexible to accept unexpected changes and opportunities. My contact with household accounting, however, was to have a bigger impact on my research and my life.

Accounting Research Reflects Your Position and Life

One of the biggest difficulties of my research was that I had to switch between two different codes of life and cultural contexts. What I increasingly started to notice was how much of this was reflected in my position as a woman in each context. In Sheffield, I was experiencing life as a 'beginner' — a woman becoming accustomed to different social situations and sexual distinctions. When I went back to Japan, I was viewed as a strange woman who was devoting her life to strange work. Some colleagues referred to me as 'Miss Gender'. This was reflective of a Japanese tradition of using 'Anglo-expressions' to describe somebody who seems to be overly accepting of Western culture and disrespectful of Japanese culture. For example, in the late nineteenth century when the concept of democracy was imported in Japan, many magazines used the word 'democracy' improperly to make fun of people who thought that Western culture was fashionable. My name 'Miss Gender' was used in a similar context. Many of my male colleagues and friends in Japan backed away as if I were a dangerous creature. I felt increasingly isolated, as if half of me was in Japan and the other half in Sheffield and I really belonged nowhere.

It was my work with household accounting that enabled me to end this growing sense of isolation. I began to understand that my feelings derived from the diverse roles of women in the two societies and the way in which social expectations and norms helped to shape respective lifestyles and the ways of thinking. I could now see accounting as having a crucial role in such processes. It not only reflected gender relationships, but the long association of Japanese women with household accounting had contributed to the creation and sustaining of a certain social role and lifestyle. The mode of accounting practiced at home and by the profession shapes women's experiences in each realm. As modes of accounting practice could vary, so could women's attitudes to accounting and broader processes of social control. The attitude and ways of thinking of women accounting professionals could be seen to differ across different generations and often contradicted with women from similar generations engaging only in accounting at home. All in all, the relationship between women and accounting started to appear far more complicated than the gender accounting research to date has tended to suggest. I also began to gain in confidence as I realised that gender accounting research had as much to do with accounting practice as any other form of 'accounting research'. In particular, I started to see clear links with studies on issues of accounting and accountability in Japan, particularly with respect to concerns being raised over the transparency and reliability of Japanese corporate financial reporting. Studies in this arena have spoken of a Japanese preference for responsibility over accountability or of a lesser degree of belief in notions of (professional) independence and a cultural preference for dependent forms of (business) relationships. However, such claims have all been made with no reference to issues of gender and the respective role and influence of men and women.

Historically, financial modes of control have been operated by women in the Japanese home but women have not been influential in the public realm where men work. Applying a gender perspective potentially offers much value in re-framing traditional (westernised) depictions of Japanese accounting and organisational/social control. The currently changing role and position of women in Japan may well reshape accountability and control processes and the particular social significance of the accounting profession and processes of accountability.

Accounting Research Questions and Changes Your Life

My doctoral research to date has not only reflected my life but has also questioned and changed it. It made me question whether I was in the right domestic relationship. My relationship had been an important support for my work, particularly as research is a lonely job. I went out with Japanese boyfriends both in Japan and in Sheffield. Assuming that trust and stability were the most important elements, my relationship was based on like a very close family ties with me acting a role of a mother. However, as the research progressed, this role as a mother became so frustrating. Though I was always fighting with my research like a soldier and feeling tired and sometimes upset, after work I had to be a calm, nice and generous mother and cherish my boyfriend. Through themes in my research, I began to see such a contradiction very clearly and eventually the relationship I had in Sheffield with a Japanese boyfriend finished.

My research helped me understand what is really significant for me in life. When I did not have an enjoyable time in my private life after breaking up with my boyfriend, I felt quite comfortable as my research progressed very well. Studying the relationship between women and accounting, I had an opportunity to broaden my view of notions of independence and trust. I wanted to be respected for what I was doing in my work. I also wanted to be respected as a woman but not to be treated as a (prospective) 'mother' who is expected to adapt her behaviour to accommodate the needs of her 'sons'. I also began to realise that the mode of love can take quite different forms depending on a social context.

The Research Process is a Process of Understanding Life

By the year 2000, I had finished my literature review and the major part of my interviews and fieldwork. I had also made an analysis of the household accounting practice in Japan with my supervisor and published a paper in *Accounting, Auditing and Accountability Journal (AAAJ)*. After completing the analysis of women and accounting at home in Japan, I changed the structure of my thesis and came to the final, writing-up stage. I went back to Japan to fill in missing parts of the fieldwork analysis and a couple of areas where recent developments meant that I needed to update my literature review. However, while I was working on writing up the thesis, I had a very serious car accident. I was left in a coma hovering between life and death. Fortunately, I was alive but seriously injured, with many broken bones and major damage to my vocal chords. I had to make a huge effort to fight back to recover to something like normality and I am still in the process of recuperating. In this section, I consider the problems I faced in the writing up stage, how I feel I have overcome them and how the task of research has helped me to recover from the accident.

Restructuring and Writing Up the Thesis

The analysis of the women and household accounting really helped the structure and content of my thesis as it gave me the opportunity to clarify relations between gender and accounting issues and to position better the experiences and standpoints of professional women accountants working in the public sphere. Working on the *AAAJ* piece with my supervisor was particularly useful as it drove home to me the importance of showing your written work to your supervisor and gave me good insights into how to go about revising written work. It also made me see weaknesses in my writing style, especially in terms of the importance of structure and flow of argument. I learned that writing is directly related to how you structure the logic to reach to your conclusion and it is necessary always to think critically why and what your findings imply. Writing in English also requires a different attitude from writing in Japanese. In English, the most important information generally comes first (or early on in an article — for instance, highlighted in the introduction), while in Japanese, generally the important information comes last. This difference in writing style requires different attitudes. Having to know what is the most significant information and putting it up front, pressured me to be in full command of what I wanted to write. Writing in Japanese, I would have more redundancy in the text as I worked my way through to the key elements of the argument. I began to understand that if I was having difficulty in writing in English, it was not just because of language but also because of a lack of sound analysis and clarity of ideas.

The Researcher is not only an Observer, but also a Participant

My working experience in a Japanese university also played a significant role in my research. My changing position from a student to a staff member of the university gave me many experiences that I have never encountered before in Japan — experiences similar to those of my interviewees in accounting firms. Furthermore, having lived in Sheffield for a few years, the everyday customs in Japan that I had taken for granted before were now things that I started to question.

The developing nature of my research made me change my views on life and my style of working. I analysed my everyday experience more critically and reconsidered the analysis of my fieldwork research in light of my day-to-day experiences. Comparing interviewees' experiences with mine gave me opportunities to re-consider the reasons behind their reported actions. My teaching also gave me the opportunity to explore various thoughts and ideas — drawing on my research and related work in an attempt to explain to students the significance and role of accounting in shaping the lifestyles of the men and women that construct corporate society in Japan.

As a result of such experiences, I came to see that the role of a researcher is not to sit back and observe phenomenon from the outside. For me, the role of the researcher is to experience the phenomenon as an inside participant but analyse its experience with the eyes of an outside observer. However, it is also important to keep some distance between life and research and not to be overwhelmed by problems in either sphere. I found it motivating to set a target number of pages to write everyday — it helped me to see progress and ensured that I wasn't just reading for reading's sake. Checking my progress in this way also helped to build my confidence that I could overcome pressure, which is essential for completing a doctoral thesis.

The Significance of the Environment for the Accounting Research

The social environment at the university workplace where a researcher is based is particularly important qualitative accounting research. To have a good relationship, and to spend time, with your supervisor is crucial. It is very important that your supervisor understands not only your research but also yourself as a person since much of the research develops on the basis of the personal qualities of the researcher. It is necessary to have someone who can make you see the qualities you have and help you to develop research that integrates these qualities. A good supervisor will not tell you what to do but will be a guide and suggest how to do things based on an understanding not only of your research but also your personal nature. It is the doctoral student's responsibility to make sure your supervisor understands you and what you are trying to do.

Travelling between Sheffield and Japan really drove home to me the importance of one's working environment. In Japan, I found it more difficult to express freely my views and to discuss research issues with colleagues. My opinions and perspectives seemed to be getting too different. The type of critical thinking that I had been encouraged to do at Sheffield was more difficult in Japan — in my subject area it seemed to be taken more as a rejection of Japanese social life rather than just an opinion.

Research is a Process, not a Goal

During my studies I also changed my way of thinking about research. Initially, I had seen the award of a Ph.D. as the major research goal. Clearly, in academic work it is essential to accumulate knowledge, to learn about existing analytical frameworks, etc. However, it is also important to understand that research is a process of constructing knowledge. It is not about learning answers to pre-set questions or even learning answers that already existed but rather a process of searching for the answers to questions that have not been answered and may even have no answer. In searching for answers, the most important issue is to set appropriate research questions and to identify appropriate ways of trying to answer, or at least debate, such questions. From this perspective, critical thinking becomes very important as it opens up the scope for considering and constructing different viewpoints and not being overly accepting of things.

Research questions and research goals can change as you progress with your work. My research questions essentially shifted from using the example of Japan to challenge claims made by gender research in accounting in the West to an attempt to understand how accounting in Japan depends significantly on gender relations and social contexts — in short, moving from comparing differences to understanding how differences are constructed. Changes in questions can change the structure of the thesis and, all in all, you soon realise that research is not an easy process. It is not a form of work where you can sit from 9:00 a.m. to 5:00 p.m. to complete the tasks that you are asked to do. The amount of time you work does not necessarily reflect progress in writing. At times, I found what I had produced signified nothing, deleted all the work that I produced and started writing again from scratch. I often had to re-read literature that I had reviewed a long time ago, since shifts in perspective can generate shifts in the significance of particular material. Above all, I realised that the research process was not only significant for work but also very valuable for life.

Reaching a Balance in Life – Guided by your Research

In the long process of recovering from my accident, I found my Ph.D. work to be a critical element of support. In terms of recovering, the most difficult thing to overcome was not physical injury (even though my injuries were severe) but rather the emotional injury caused by the accident. I was totally unable to control myself, feeling fearful, angry, depressed and a real need to cling on to something that gave me security. I needed something that would give me an understanding of the significance of this uncontrollable event in my life and would help me understand how to react to it.

The drafts of my Ph.D. thesis gave me one answer. Reading them after the accident, I started to remember the long process by which my research had taken shape, how I had changed my views, balanced different contexts, emotions and experiences. It made me see that the life is also a process of change and a process where conflicting tensions interact to make balance. It told me that the life is not necessarily oriented to secured certainty with absolute answers. I recalled the emotions that I had experienced in my research process; from enthusiasm and a keenness to discuss and argue, to difficulties in making progress and agony in not making good progress, from optimism and over-ambitious targets to depression and a feeling of struggling to write anything, and from a fear of rejection to a sense of fulfilment at finding ways of overcoming problems and tough questions. I saw clear parallels in my emotions associated with the research process with those associated with my process of recovering from the accident. I realised that the depression and traumatic emotion after the accident was not different from my research-related emotions and I decided it was more important to react positively to this traumatic experience rather than being occupied with negative thoughts. The view that life is a process of change and the realisation that you have to pursue a sense of balance gave me direction and really made it possible for me to overcome the trauma of the accident.

Conclusion — The Dialectical Relationship between Life and Research

The experience of taking (and still seeking to complete) a Ph.D. in U.K. has helped me to understand a number of significant points for conducting qualitative research in accounting. One is the significance of critical thinking. Every time you read literature, you need to consider critically the implication and position of the literature before accepting without questioning. Contradictions should not be seen as a problem, rather they can help you to develop new perspectives. Secondly, you need to build up your personal strength. As your research goals change (indeed, often it is difficult to see a clear goal), you may find that you need to be even stronger in your devotion to work and willingness to keep an open mind. You have to be patient as well as progressive and flexible to find a real sense of direction. You also need to remain motivated as at some stage you are going to get lost and lose direction. Thirdly, you have to push yourself to progress your arguments — you have to listen to advice but also know when to stand up and fight your corner. You also need to retain a sense of clarity, especially when writing up the thesis in English, knowing what you want to say. Fourthly, it is also important to learn to control yourself and to be able to handle pressure. Finally, it is important to view everyday life in a critical fashion as this can really help in sharpening your analytical skills and thinking about the broader significance of your research. Living as an overseas student is a good opportunity to find contradictions in your research assumptions and arguments. The ability to contrast living experiences in different countries can help you to challenge particular research frameworks and continually assess the significance of your research. You may lose certain reference points and experience periods of imbalance but this is all part of the learning process.

In my experience, qualitative research in accounting really does influence your life as a researcher. In the course of my research, I have not only learned more about myself but also changed my frames of reference on life. The development of research reflects life, enhances your understanding of it and, ultimately, changes your life. In this sense, I have found the interaction between research and my life to be a dialectical process with one reflecting and changing the other in various (anticipated and unanticipated) ways. I really feel that to secure good progress in research, it is essential to commit your life to the research process (at least until your thesis is finished!), rather than isolating research from the rest of your life. From my experience, your research will come to support and guide you when you are lost in your life. How much such a 'partner' can support you in life is up to you — it depends on how much you want to commit yourself to building up, and relying on, such a partnership.

Section Two: Managing the Research Process

Once an area for investigation has been chosen and academics are engaged in research, an important part of their everyday life will be the management of that project. The project may be an individual one — such as a Ph.D. — or it may be a major, externally funded, project involving a whole team of researchers. Each project will involve not only the application of ideas to explain the phenomenon that is being researched, but also a whole set of relationships with people that the researchers have to meet with on a more or less frequent basis. These different parties will include providers of research funds, respondents, research partners from other institutions, other staff holding subordinate or more senior positions. The different interests of the various parties will have to be respected and relationships with them will have to be managed if the research objectives are not to be compromised. An important aspect of qualitative research that contrasts markedly with quantitative research is that while the latter will often require the investigator to handle databases of impersonal, statistical information, qualitative methods will generally necessitate that the researcher has face-to-face relationships with respondents. It is important that the researchers do not simply exploit the respondents for their own ends, or allow the respondents to do the opposite. The six chapters in this section are of two types. Chapters eight to eleven are about managing research. Chapters twelve and thirteen include considerations about the independence of the researcher and the ethical decisions that may be encountered in the course of a research project.

In deciding from whom to commission chapters about a research project, we were sensitive to a range of factors capable of impacting on the everyday experience of researchers, including the source of funding that supports a project, the position of the person in a research team and the ease with which fieldwork access for the researchers can be secured and maintained. We have chosen authors who have particular forms of insight into the project management role and can provide comment on one or more of these issues. In chapter eight, Frank Birkin — who has played a key role in a number of European Union research initiatives — discusses the management of resulting, large-scale research projects. As Frank points out, European Union research initiatives are both numerous and frequently policy-oriented, meaning that academics interested in securing EU funding may have to do a considerable amount of sifting through information to find one that complements their research interests and will need to obtain partners from other European countries in order to be able to proceed. Frank's chapter addresses these issues and considers how to submit a research proposal and manage a project through to fruition once a grant has been obtained. In chapter nine, Jane

Broadbent and Richard Laughlin — who have extensive experience of leading projects — discuss how the theory and concepts that guide their research, planning of a project, employment of particular methods and the resolution of a range of practical issues can really help to contribute to the success of a project. In chapter ten, John Burns writes about his experiences as a research assistant employed on major research projects led by other academics. John explores many of the issues that research assistants have to deal with on a day-to-day basis. These include the organisation of travel, the management of conflicting demands on a research assistant's time, balancing a range of academic commitments of staff on the project, maintaining respondents' interests, supervision by others and the management of teams and trying to complete a PhD being undertaken at the same time as working as a research assistant. John also makes a number of practical recommendations as to how best to manage such a complex state of affairs. In chapter eleven, Irvine Lapsley discusses the management of a doctoral student where not all of the related project's objectives were met. The study entailed the employment of participant observation to investigate investment appraisal methods in a National Health Service context. The chapter documents a range of problems that were encountered in gaining access to the research site and highlights the difficulties of executing a research strategy when an investigation is not supported by key organizational respondents.

In commissioning chapters about the ethical dilemmas confronted by qualitative researchers, we have secured contributions that address quite different dimensions of the choices and stances that researchers have to make in the course of their work. Chapter twelve is written by two Canadian researchers, Jean Bédard and Yves Gendron. After explaining the pressures to publish in North America and the difficulties of publishing qualitative research, Jean and Yves discuss the issue of remaining sensitive to respondents' interests in the context of how they had to manage their research into the role of audit committees in Canada. Their chapter discusses the problems of gaining research access, something common to qualitative researchers across a number of countries, and also outlines the complex regulations that research funding bodies and institutions are demanding increasingly to protect respondents' interests. This includes the need for respondents to sign forms indicating their informed consent. Jean and Yves outline how they handled this when interviewing their respondents, the benefits that arose when sending transcripts back to respondents to check as another provision under the "informed consent" regulations and some of the constraints that such procedures are placing on researchers. In chapter thirteen, Brendan McSweeney addresses the real life dilemmas that researchers face when their independence is being challenged. Defining independence as the ability to take into account the views of all parties involved significantly in the research and to constantly interrogate one's own views and conclusions, Brendan explains his role as an academic advisor to a local trade union who were faced by a series of organizational change proposals from senior management at a company in Ireland and how he sought to maintain independence while helping to reach a conclusion that did not prejudge management's claims of the imperative for change. Brendan's chapter also considers the translation of events at the company into academic research articles that remained consistent with his ideas of independence.

Chapter 8

Starting and Managing a European Union Funded Research Project

Frank Birkin

Introduction

In this chapter, some of the practicalities of obtaining and managing European Union (EU) research projects are related. This information is based on personal experience of participating on several of such projects both as a partner and a manager. This is not intended to be a formal procedural guide since this kind of document is readily available from several European or national information sources. It is also not intended to review or comment upon the EU research work programmes. These are many, varied and changing and you need to refer to the websites identified later in this chapter for such information.

There is a skill to obtaining and managing European Union funded research projects so that benefits are maximised and pains minimised. It is of course related to the skills needed to run any team research project but it also differs in significant ways. Whilst relating encounters with EU projects, this chapter also provides tips on how to obtain points for good style, some tricks of the trade and a little direct advice, not so much about how to solve the problems that arise with these projects, but rather on how to avoid such problems in the first place. The rest of the chapter is organised to reflect the sequence of tasks to be performed when applying for and managing a EU project and these are: identifying a relevant programme; finding partners; submitting a proposal; and managing a project. A reflective final section provides a few thoughts as an after-the-event evaluation of a project.

Identifying a Relevant Programme

Naturally, you start with an idea. The idea has to be of interest to you and an appropriate research community. This idea can be made substantial by state-of-the-art knowledge of an area of research together with an imaginative view of possible developments.

The Real Life Guide to Accounting Research: A Behind-the-Scenes View of Using Qualitative Research Methods
© 2004 Published by Elsevier Ltd.
ISBN: 0-08-043972-1

Eventually a set of objectives needs to be written down and they have to be worth committing the considerable time and expense that even submitting a project proposal demands. But the objectives of the project are not to be only the property of the project team. Since you require EU funding, it is necessary to develop project aims that are of interest to you and your team but which are also irresistible to the project proposal evaluators assembled by the European Commission (EC).

For example, the Sustainable Tourism Environmental Protection System for islands (STEPS for islands) was a research concept I developed out of my own interests but it was focused on the requirements of an EU Environment and Climate Research programme. STEPS was based on the idea that in order to sustain wealth creation, business needs healthy social and ecological systems. On tourism islands, this need is emphasised by the nature of the tourism product. Experiences and memories gained by tourists are all embracing. This link between community, environment and business is the key to solving island environmental problems. In place of a burden of imposed environmental costs and legislation, there can be the businesses that integrate economic and environmental objectives within day-to-day practice. When sustainable development brings clear benefits to businesses and the community, small and medium-sized enterprises (SMEs) can become self-motivating agents of change.

Periodically, the EC develops a set of research aims and specifies work programmes to achieve these aims. These work programmes are provided in sufficient detail to focus a project proposal and enable you to prepare an almost day-to-day specification of the workload over the whole of a typical two or three-year period. When your proposal is evaluated, it will be scrutinized by experts to this level of detail.

STEPS was developed to comply with the objectives of the Environment and Climate 1994–1998 Work programme, theme 4, areas 4.2, 4.3 and 4.4. This was achieved identifying the following prime objectives.

- To research the guiding principles, approaches and format of a management and policy tool that will maximise island tourism SME sustainable wealth generation and to use the tool to:

  (1) reduce SME proposers' total materials and overhead costs by 5% to 20%;
  (2) increase the value added and expanding markets leading to income increases of 5% to 10% of revenue earned by SME proposers; and
  (3) prepare sustainable business development plans in agreement with island resource capacities and key sustainable development initiatives.

- To use the tool with each island's association of SME and other stakeholders to:

  (1) reduce costs and generate income in a group of three other SME's per island;
  (2) identify inter-trading opportunities within islands to stimulate local economic activity and reducing total island resource imports by an initial 2% to 4%;
  (3) target information provision and awareness raising among the island community;
  (4) integrate business development with island ecological carrying capacity;
  (5) identify the opportunities for one to three permanent jobs per island; and
  (6) prepare island sustainable development plans;

- To externally validate the tool by reporting to and surveying the responses of:

  (1) each SME partner's island community;
  (2) each SME partner's island tourists;
  (3) thirty mainland travel agents and tour operators; and
  (4) ten key policy oriented institutions (for example, including departments with responsibilities for tourism development in Greek, Italian and United Kingdom governments and the European Commission DGXIII, United Nations Environment Programme and World Wide Fund for Nature).

Whilst the EC evaluators will assess a proposal's scientific merits such as aims, literature survey and methodology, they will also need to satisfy themselves that the proposal does indeed offer to complete some part or parts of an appropriate work programme. If your proposal falls short of achieving this end, or specifies some very desirable aims and objectives that the EC *ought* to be funding, then failure is imminent. To apply for EU funding is to participate in a competitive bidding process among some very experienced and skilful researchers across Europe. If your proposal does not possess excellent scientific merit as well as precisely satisfying the needs of an EC work programme, then it is likely that some other proposal will.

EU work programmes are enormously varied and comprehensive. Each work programme is integrated around a particular theme with overriding requirements such as sustainable development and a European dimension. The work programmes also differ in the way they are administered. For example, some funds make use of a two-stage proposal process or offer an initial vetoing service. Small and medium sized enterprises, for example, can submit an outline project proposal after which, upon successfully completing this first stage, a full proposal may be prepared and submitted with the added confidence of a one in two chance of success in the second round.

STEPS for islands was submitted to the EU's CRAFT programme in an application for funding to enable a detailed proposal to be prepared. This first stage proposal filled some six pages. The bid was successful and the funding enabled the SMEs on the project to do preliminary research, partner searches and administration for preparation of a bid to another EU work programme for a project funding of around half a million ECU. The search for appropriate sources of funds is made more difficult by the interdisciplinary nature of many subjects. For example, the STEPS proposal could have found appropriate funds in EC research work programmes ranging from telematics to environment, socio-economic aspects, transport, waste management, water management, power generation or, of course, tourism itself.

Such diversity increases uncertainty and it is sensible to approach the EC officer responsible for a particular fund with a request either for comments on a brief project outline or an interview to discuss a proposal. It is of course necessary to have a draft proposal completed for all-important aspects since the officer is unlikely to be prepared to help in the writing. But if it is possible, an officer can help enormously by indicating any significant gaps or misconceptions in a proposal. An industrial survey, for example, seemed comprehensive in one proposal of mine with 80% of firms in the sector covered. But this 80% consisted of large companies only with no SMEs and it needed a EU officer to point out that this proposal could well be rejected for not being representative.

The officer may also be prepared to express the Commission's concerns about work programmes such as a lack of applications coming from southern Europe or about funds that are under-subscribed, as was the case with some funds earmarked for the former eastern block states a few years ago.

Identifying appropriate EU funds for a project is difficult but it is a process for which there exists considerable assistance at national and international levels. If you work in a university with a research office, then this should be your first contact. For U.K. universities, there is a Brussels based information service. There are many EU research funds all of which are described in detail on the Community Research and Development Information Service (CORDIS) website[1] along with the provision of considerable amounts of information such as descriptions of all EU funded research programmes, project and partner-search databases, guidance and background links and a variety of interactive services including an online forum. Fund application forms are also provided on the CORDIS website. Unfortunately, the amount and complexity of information mean that this is not an easy website to use.

A EU work programme is a large and comprehensive statement and not all of it may be offered to the research community at one time. The Commission may approve only selections from these programmes depending on their priorities and projects previously approved and underway. These selections are published as "calls". National contact points for the work programmes are often very helpful in advising about the likely contents of calls and the timing of deadlines. Another source of information is 'Cordis Focus', a community research and development information service.[2] This newsletter contains information about calls and tenders, programme implementation, publications and events as well as research and development news. For European researchers, it is well worth regular scrutiny. The publications section contains the booklets and reports that are the output of research projects and there may even be requests for participation in such as workshops to prepare project applications. As a result of an article published in Cordis Focus, we made an application to a research team based in Madrid to attend an Information Technology Society workshop that was assembling a team to submit a tourism-telematics proposal. However, finding an appropriate programme to fund a project is difficult. It is necessary to listen to the advice given by as many informed sources as possible. A first source should be the research or European offices of your own institution.

Finding Partners

Joining a partnership to apply for EU project funding can be beguilingly easy. The effort required being little more than responding to a fax, making a few phones calls, reading a ten-page research proposal and signing on the dotted line. But even in cases such as

---

[1] http://www.cordis.lu/en/home.html
[2] A hard copy of the newsletter may be obtained by sending a request together with your addresses to innovation@cec.eu.int. The newsletter is based on information taken from Cordis News at http://www.cordis.lu/news.

these, the eventual partnership will be more substantial that a casual introduction might suggest.

The first EU project I worked on was called PREMISE (Preventative Environmental Management in Small Enterprises) by the Danish and Austrian scientists who wrote the proposal. PREMISE began for me with a fax sent to U.K. academic departments with some interest in environmental accounting. This was at that time in the early 1990s when environmental accounting and management were developing and were small enough in terms of membership and content to fall almost entirely within a single person's remit. I applied to join PREMISE and arranged my credentials around two themes:

- Knowledge of environmental issues based on a first degree in science, years of dedication to outdoor pursuits and of environmental accounting from the summer schools at the University of Dundee; and
- Experience of management systems from management accountancy practice and of environmental management systems having attended several BS7750 (the British environmental management system standard) conferences and workshops.

However casual or fortuitous the partner selection procedures appeared to be from an outside perspective, there was nothing unprofessional about the (other) Europeans. First of all, the other partners were already well known to each other. They had been meeting regularly on the International Standards Organisation's (ISO) environmental management committees and working groups. Hence, they were familiar with each other's work and personalities and had some indication of the kind of contribution each might bring to PREMISE. The two proponents of PREMISE were their respective national representatives during the development and writing of the initial ISO 14000 environmental managements systems standard. A third member of the initial team was also well known to the other two as a result of other EU funded activities. I then was the outsider. Three of the partners had worked together in some capacity prior to submitting the proposal. Between them, they had identified a need for a fourth partner in a fourth country. The selection of the U.K. made sense since this country had been the first to establish an environmental management system standard and it was also taking the initiative with regard to environmental reporting and accounting. Hence, the seemingly casual recruitment to the PREMISE project was in fact supported by the well-informed analysis, extensive collaboration and relevant experience of the other partners. I was the risky outsider.

If you are not fortunate enough to be asked to participate on someone else's proposal, then you will have to recruit your own partners. There is usually a minimum requirement that partners are drawn from at least two different EU countries. If you have good working relationships with colleagues across Europe and these colleagues are willing and able to make distinctive and necessary contributions to a project, then it is sensible to use these colleagues to create a core group for that extra degree of familiarity just might drive a project through difficult times. But do not write a proposal to satisfy a group of colleagues since it is with the EU work programme that you must ultimately comply. Whilst there are sometimes opportunities to improve probabilities of success by including partners from relevant nation states, it is important that these partners are clear contributions to the proposed project's work plan and that they are not mere cosmetic additions. For example, an officer of the EU might report that a particular fund is oversubscribed by researchers from northern European nations and it may seem that a Portuguese partner may significantly increase chances of success. But if that Portuguese partner does not have a clear and necessary contribution to make to the project's research, chances of success will be reduced by a weakly structured proposal. Always be well aware that the Commission is not short of applications and that any weakness in a proposal provides a valid reason for rejection.

A group of familiar colleagues might be regarded as sufficient for a strictly technical project where the work and output are perceived to be tightly defined and, as a result of previous work, the 'property' of the group, but even in this case there are good arguments for introducing a new partner or partners. For projects that fall within social sciences (such as management and accounting), the other perspectives, values and attitudes that new partners could bring are perhaps *de rigour*. The arguments for introducing new partners to an established group are to take the opportunity to enlarge the scope and applicability of the project; to introduce new skills and experiences that will refresh and sharpen the established group; to comply better with European Union needs; and to better motivate the group with the prospect of new intellectual territory and to restructure and refresh group dynamics. Suitable new partners are perhaps most easily found at international gatherings that are focussed on an area of interest closely related to that of the proposed project. Conferences, workshops and seminars bring together like minds and enable a brief evaluation of an individual's personal suitability. After all, project work is teamwork and no matter how well qualified and suitable an individual might be, a difficult personality will not help a project to run smoothly. It was at an environmental accounting workshop in Holland that the research partnership for my STEPS project was formed.

Another source of possible partners is the partner search facility to be found among the databases on the Cordis website. So, in theory, if you need a partner whose skills are to be water infrastructure investment decision analysis in Romania or international portfolio theory comparisons, then this website is worth trying. This service did provide an excellent group of willing and suitable partners who were to perform stakeholder analysis in southern Africa for another proposal of mine that was unfortunately rejected.[3]

Submitting a Proposal

Once the project's outline task, methodology, novelty and European dimensions have been established, the next task is the completion of the application forms and that is a job that should be taken very seriously. A few years ago, I was informed by an officer of the EC that a typical research proposal submitted to the then "Environment and Climate" work programme took an average of six person-months and twenty thousand

---

[3] Whilst this project was judged to be "urgently needed", the general Southern African experience of the team was considered insufficiently focused for this specifically Swaziland project and the proposal was rejected.

pounds to complete. Such a task can easily be equivalent to writing a paper or two for an academic journal. The application forms and supporting information provided by the Commission are very thorough. The technical content of the proposal is outlined with section and subsection headings provided together with maximum page lengths for each section. The forms are available from the detailed work programmes on the Cordis website. There is no reason to deviate from this outline layout provided. The team of experts assembled to assess proposals come from across Europe and for many of them English will not be their first language so clarity and simplicity are essential. Furthermore, whilst the experts are selected approximately according to disciplines, it may be that the details of particular topics of a proposal are not well known to all of the assessors. A U.K. seismological expert, for example, may be an expert called in by the Commission to assess environmental research proposals and this person, as part of a team, could be required to assess a proposal about environmental management in the leather industries of Portugal when their knowledge of environmental management is minimal. This in fact does happen and once, on Eurostar en route to Brussels, I did meet with and discuss environmental management with exactly such an expert recruited by the Commission for its 'Environment and Climate' assessments.

These assessment teams typically have a large number of proposals to assess in too few days. To stand out and make an impact on such teams, the format of a proposal cannot afford to be subtle, convoluted or divergent from the EC's schematic content. A proposal needs to be to the point and easily accessible. Imagine being in a Brussels office or hotel room with forty twenty-page and densely written proposals to read and assess in three days. Then think how best to write a proposal to be accurate, stimulating and kind to the assessors. Ideally, a proposal should be prepared with contributions from all the research team. As we know, consultation and participation lead to greater commitment. But with a research team spread across Europe that possesses different backgrounds and priorities, care must be taken not to anticipate too much about the contributions that others will make. Whilst it is also important for future working relationships that the proposal is not the property of one person and, hence, country. EU funded projects are lucrative and it is not too difficult to obtain signatures on proposals from universities across Europe. If the full commitment of partners is not made to the work involved, and not only the money, then project deadlines may be threatened when partner's 'other commitments' become too pressing.

Ideally, each researcher should complete the sections about aims, objectives and work plans with regard to their responsibilities on the proposed project. But it is perhaps a part of human nature, especially an overworked human nature, to put off doing things until the last minute. Even if you start early with a proposal and ask your partners to submit their sections well in advance, you may still find yourself chasing documents at the last minute. One answer, if the money and time is available, is to obtain agreement and contributions for the proposal during a few away-days held for the whole team. It is, unfortunately, often much easier for one individual to complete the whole proposal.

Whilst preparing the STEPS proposal, the research partners to the project were responsive and helpful but it was predominately my idea. There is a limit to how much you might expect from other researchers in other countries when detailing a project that is based on the ideas of a single person. Apart from the potential for misunderstandings and extrapolations of the idea to different circumstances, it is not reasonable to expect a group of people across Europe to work almost alone and produce a combined result that fits together into a seamless and coherent whole. A proposal needs a leader to run with, develop and express an idea in the details needed by the EC. The other partners on the proposal can contribute but it has been my experience that such contributions need comprehensive guidance and strict limits if the integrity and simplicity of a proposal is to be achieved in a short time.

Lack of time to complete a proposal may result in the cutting of corners. Some types of funding opportunities are on open call and may be submitted at any time, but most of the major research funds are subject to strictly enforced submission deadlines. Some work programmes will have a schedule of submission deadlines on their CORDIS web pages. However even with deadlines declared, the relevant parts of the work programme that will be 'on call' for any particular deadline may not be known. Sometimes whole programmes may not be published on the forecast date when, for example, approval across nation states has not been achieved. Whilst such delays consume time and may result in the Commission falling behind on its own deadlines, the existing deadlines for final submission of project proposals are frequently not changed leaving the research community with even less time.

Managing a Project

Once successful, the detailed contract negotiations completed and the initial payment has been made by the EC, it can seem as if the major work has been done. However, the clock is now ticking and the management that underlies the achieving of the detailed workload needs to be approached with much thought and caution. Whilst many tasks, the management structure and the milestones of the project have already been specified in the proposal, the project is a long way from running itself. As with any team, the key issue is human relationships. Time needs to be allowed for familiarisation and this is of course more difficult to achieve when a team is dispersed across Europe.

Team meetings will typically last for a day or two and much work is usually performed in this time. These meetings also provide the opportunity for planning and agreeing individual goals for the following period. However, away from such meetings, other non-project activities will inevitably intervene and communicating with European team members can be very difficult. Even if people responded quickly to emails or were available whenever you telephoned, there are disabling limits to the effectiveness of this kind of link. Project strategic issues and the resolution of problems relating to revisions of roles are very difficult to settle in anything other than face-to-face discussions. Video conferencing has not been available on the terminals of most of my European colleagues. In theory, monitoring and co-ordinating project work can be performed by the project coordinator according to a strict daily or weekly schedule. However, in a team of four or more individuals, it is unlikely that someone will not fall behind and, usually for good reasons, seek to postpone their contribution, typically until a few days prior to a team meeting. The danger of proceeding without all contributions is, since all contributions are vital, that developments, decisions and activities may take place that are inappropriate or inconsistent with the overall aims. Small divergences can, if left to follow their own logic, produce major problems.

The preparation of a manual for management, for example, that is based on project results could easily be specified in a few words of a project work package. But 'manuals for management' differ between countries. One country's manuals may lend themselves to a strictly systematic, prescriptive and impersonal approach whilst those of another country may be more aware of the needs to motivate, involve and sell themselves to management. When a 'write manual' task has been completed and all parts are assembled during the final days of a project, it is disheartening to discover such a major discrepancy in national styles that do not fit well in a single document. So even though individuals have performed their tasks as described in the project's work packages, there is always scope for significant cultural differences on EU projects. The project coordinator might spot these problems if material is made available to that person in time but it may also go overlooked until all parts are brought together. Even if the coordinator does recognise the problem for what it is, the task of removing one particular culturally determined view from an individual and replacing it with another from a different country may be impossible over a telephone or via emails and the final resolution may have to wait for another face-to-face meeting.

In spite of these difficulties, EU research projects are completed, though not all of them. After submitting the final reports and statements, the question arises was it worthwhile? Well your work could become international rather than national and attract the attention of the relevant international agencies. For EU funded research, there is a requirement for it to be at least European. The impact of tourism, for example, crosses all of Europe. The results of the STEPS project, completed at the time of writing this chapter, were presented at a conference co-hosted by project partners in Venice. Among the institutions agreeing to speak at this conference were the EC, United Nations Environment Programme, WWF International, the World Tourism Organisation and ANPA, the Italian state environmental agency. You will also make many new friends in many nations.

Care needs to be taken if the European research is being considered for the more personal purposes of advancing a career in U.K. universities. As already pointed out, preparing a proposal alone is very time consuming and can easily be equivalent to writing a paper or two. Add to this the resources consumed when actually running the project and an ultimate high number of papers derived directly from project research are needed for justification on these grounds alone. Once, the ability to attract very large sums of research funding was in itself considered noteworthy. Some universities however no longer consider this achievement in the promotion stakes since they argue that the true measure of research is academic papers, not finance. With a well-conceived and timely project, the academic output should be achieved even allowing for the veiled 'commercial potential' inherent in many, if not all, EU work programmes. So, whilst it may take a little longer to publish than to simple claim funding levels achieved, your career prospects should be improved by a EU project. But, there are many other personal benefits to be enjoyed including the funding for presenting results at prestigious conferences or hosting your own; exposure to new ideas and practices; establishing and promoting international benchmarks for your work; and extensive, expenses paid travel.

Chapter 9

Management of a Research Team

Jane Broadbent and Richard Laughlin

Introduction

In considering how one might achieve effective management of a research team this chapter will draw upon our particular experience of working together and with a variety of other people over the last 12 years. Before moving on to the detailed discussion it is perhaps fair to first of all say a little about the notion of 'management' in relation to research of the type that we engage in. In many ways the term 'management' seems to be a strange one in relation to our notion of a research team. It is, however, an aspect that is covered in mainstream texts on 'how to do research' and hence we retain the link to this term, rather than ignore it. Our view is that the issues to be managed directly are the processes of undertaking the research, such as the timing of activities to ensure that outputs are delivered on time, especially where external funders are concerned. Hence, rather than think of 'management' we would prefer to speak about the notion of planning and monitoring the process and outputs. Thus, the team working together must negotiate mutually agreed strategies as to what must be done — and when — in order to achieve the desired outputs. Thus the process is one that relies on the reflexive professionalism and commitment of the team members, rather than being one of driving their activity. This will be discussed in more detail later in the chapter, but is an important precursor to the overall discussion.

In order to develop the relevant themes the chapter will be structured in the following fashion. First, our particular research approach will be discussed as the particular methodological approach undoubtedly provides the background for the sort of methods applied. This is not meant to imply that this is how everyone should do research, but to illustrate how the approach taken impacts upon the decisions as to how to proceed. We will then deal with some priors that need to be considered in the planning of the research in Section Two. The methods themselves will then be dealt with in more detail in the third section and here the implications of the methods for managing the research will be discussed. This in turn sets the context in which the team will be constituted and managed. The fourth section will look at the practical aspects of working in a research team and the final section will therefore provide an overall reflection upon 'doing

The Real Life Guide to Accounting Research: A Behind-the-Scenes View of Using Qualitative Research Methods
© 2004 Published by Elsevier Ltd.
ISBN: 0-08-043972-1

research'. In essence the chapter will start with more abstract issues about how the choice of approach affects the management of the team and the project. It will then move on to a discussion of some of the practical issues that 'real life' entails. Throughout the chapter we will keep returning to the theme that the approach to management of a research team is to some extent dependent on the mode of research itself.

Our Approach to Research

This first substantive section, as noted above, outlines our own approach to research in order to provide the foundation for our discussion and to give an illustration of how we think about approaching our work. Laughlin (1995) argues that in undertaking empirical research, choices must be made as to the theoretical and methodological approach to be adopted, noting that all empirical work will be partial and incomplete. In his paper the argument is made as to why one might choose to use an approach called 'middle-range thinking' (MRT), again noting that this is a personal preference and not 'the answer' or indeed the necessary choice of every researcher. Broadbent & Laughlin (1997) developed the theme showing how this approach was operationalised in a particular research project and Laughlin (forthcoming) sought to clarify the thinking more cogently in the light of debate and critique of the approach (Lowe, forthcoming). More detailed discussion of middle range thinking is therefore available from these sources and this chapter will therefore provide only the broad outline of the salient aspects of MRT that is needed to illustrate how we develop our research.

MRT is an approach that seeks to use theory: however, it adopts a theoretical framework not as a means by which to test or predict the outcomes in the social world but to provide a language for exploring that world. As such it is different from a positivist approach that uses theory with the assumption that there are regularities and patterns in human behaviour that can be tested and predicted. Equally, it does not seek to build theory from the ground upwards with empirics providing the base for this, eschewing the idea that this can be done as if the researcher is a *tabula rasa* with no preconceptions. MRT is based upon a belief that we must always bring our taken for granted frames of reference with us and seeks to make these explicit, yet use them critically and reflectively. Thus, theory is used as a framework that provides a language with which to explore the empirical situation and equally the empirical situation provides the possibility for development of the theoretical framework. It follows that empirical research is central to what we do and thus research that engages with organisations and their members is a necessary part of the approach that we adopt. Past projects have therefore seen us engaging with schools, GP Practices and National Health Service Trusts. Our focus is upon these organisations and the people who work in them. Although we do not focus immediately on the industry or sectoral macro-level we explore the societal institutions that control these organisations (in the cases above the Departments of Education and Health respectively) and their impact. This is to enable us to understand the organisational context better.

The specific theoretical framework that we have used is one that is based on the contributions of Jurgen Habermas and is concerned with processes of change and structures and processes of control and regulation. Our methodology emerges from the same source. We explore both of these aspects briefly below. First Habermas' work provides, as noted above, the theoretical framework that becomes the base of our interest. We are interested in processes of 'steering' (control) in both organisational and societal level and we are concerned with the use of accounting and management control in this process. Habermas' model of social evolution sees that, as the world becomes more complex, there is a differentiation of purpose of structural elements within it, i.e. different elements are formed to take on diverse roles. Thus *steering media* develop to guide societal *systems* in ways that are commensurate with the societal *lifeworld*. By the societal lifeworld, Habermas refers to the taken for granted assumptions and values that guide our behaviour. He suggested steering media might be institutions associated with law or money. Arguably, the accounting and management processes we have studied can be seen as technologies to operationalise the use of the steering medium of money. Societal systems are the entities that carry out the different operations that comprise society. The ones we have studied are entities such as the National Health Service (NHS) or the education system in the U.K., but could equally be other organisations such as commercial firms. Our interest is in how systems of societal 'steering' — the laws that are created — affect these organisations, as well as how the internal processes of organisational steering (the management control systems such as accounting) are developed and operated.

One attraction of this Habermasian model is that it provides a view of the social world that recognises both structure and subjectivity. Hence the research we do is structured by recognition of the importance of both the subjective and the material conditions of our society. This societal model is one that we have also adapted for use at an organisational level (Broadbent, Laughlin & Read 1991; Laughlin 1991) arguing that the different elements of lifeworld, steering media and systems also exist within organisations. At the organisational level these are labelled interpretive schemes, design archetypes and sub-systems and can be seen as the organisational culture, systems such as the accounting control systems and the operational arena of the organisation. In this schema, we have institutions, set up for that function which carry out the process of societal steering. Because they are institutions, they also develop their particular interpretive schemes, design archetypes and sub-systems. It follows that there is the possibility of contradiction developing between the institutional steering media, and the organisational systems they steer. For example, the Department of Health may seek to 'steer' the NHS in ways that are not amenable to the members of the NHS.

Thus, the first implication of using the Habermasian framework is that it implies we are interested in both the structural aspects of steering and the subjective taken-for-granted values that inform those steering processes. This means that the research approach must be one that explores and identifies the structures of control such as the relationships between the Department of Education and the Schools. It must research the processes used to control these relationships, the laws and their implementation. Finally it must explore the lifeworlds and interpretive schemes by developing understanding of the taken for granted assumptions and values of the people in these organisations. Thus the research process must be geared towards achieving this. Whilst we use an abstract model of the social world, it nevertheless provides a language that allows us to discuss the empirical situation and guides us to the elements we are seeking to explore. As such the theoretical understandings will frame our initial exploration of the empirics. Equally important, the empirics should also be used to reflect upon the theory and suggest necessary changes. Hence there is reflexivity in the use of the framework.

The second implication of using a Habermasian approach is the embeddedness of the belief in the centrality of discourse. Discourse is not only central to an understanding of society and organisations, but guides the discovery processes and the methods used. It therefore has implications for the way in which the research is designed and managed. The key issue is that the lifeworld is considered to be discursively produced and hence it is always likely to be dynamic and changeful. Equally, because it is intangible it is something that can be discovered both by considering its expression in the more tangible aspects like the steering media themselves and also through the use of rigorous and analytical qualitative approaches that are themselves discursively based. These approaches are ones that again define the way in which the research is undertaken, (see Laughlin (1987) and Broadbent & Laughlin (1997) for more details).

Adopting this research framework has allowed us to explore the extent to which the Government has used its institutional machinery, the Department of Health and the Department of Education, for example, to impose change upon GP Practices and Schools. Our work with GPs and Schools has shown how in these organisations the changes have been resisted because they are not seen to be sensible in the context of the interpretive schemes held by members of the organisation. We have shown how 'absorbing groups' have been set up to ensure that the changes imposed have not impacted too much upon the day-to-day operation of the organisations in question. Thus, although some changes have been imposed these are ones of a 'first-order'. They do not change the way that the organisations think in the deepest sense and the obligations imposed are simply seen as something that has to be 'managed'. So, for example, in GP Practices the changes that were brought about to try to introduce more health promotion impacted only in that nurses were brought in to provide these services. The work of GPs themselves was not, at the time we studied them, changed at all (see Broadbent & Laughlin (1998) for more details).

Approaching the Research Project

In turning to a consideration of the development of the project we assume that the project has been defined and planned and that the outputs expected have been considered. Clearly the choice of theoretical approach (be it a priori theorising, emergent theorising or MRT) is an important element that is part of the planning process. Whilst not wishing to repeat the discussion on planning we have discussed the issue of theory choice in some depth because it is so central to our work and has a particular impact on the methods adopted.

Another aspect of the planning process that also has a particular impact because of the nature of our approach is the issue of access. Because of the type of research that we undertake we need to have a research site, thus access to organisations and their members and other relevant sources of information, such as archives is particularly important. Access to organisations can be difficult to achieve and often may be found as much through serendipitous means as by planning. However, the issue of obtaining access is so central that consideration must be given to acquiring this type of skill within the team. It may well be that access is needed to develop a successful research proposal and hence it is a foundation of being able to undertake funded research. 'Cold-calling' is difficult and can lead to instant rebuttal; it is helpful to have some links, formal or informal, that will enhance your legitimacy. Introductions to organisations may be achieved through existing contacts; friends or associates often can help to introduce researchers into organisations. Sometimes organisations may contact universities directly for help with particular problems providing the opportunity for interaction and it is helpful to be alert to these areas or to let relevant people in your University know about your areas of interest. At other times it may be necessary to work with networks to meet the relevant people and introduce your ideas in an informal setting — we have attended seminars on particular topics (PFI for example) as a means of building networks that will help us to get a hearing. Some of these have been commercial conferences others have been run by the Accountancy professional bodies. Liaison with professional bodies in relevant areas is useful more generally in achieving legitimacy. We have worked with the professional accounting bodies and also Local Medical Committees to gain their support for our work in this respect.

In order to ensure external financing it is important that the objectives and timetable of the project are carefully clarified before the project starts.[1] It is helpful to do this as the clarity will also be useful in obtaining access to organisations — often people will need to have a clear view of what they are committing themselves to if they engage in research projects. In qualitative research the commitment is often considerable. For example, in the project that involved the Schools we attended many meetings and hence, for those in the organisation there was always another person to invite and another set of papers to duplicate. There were interviews with people at all levels and so their time had to be given over to this as well. In gaining access, polite persistence is important it is not always possible to get easily to the people who can make the decisions. Gaining the co-operation or support of gatekeepers such as secretaries can be helpful here and the occasional box of chocolates on relevant occasions is appreciated and signifies the gratitude felt! It is also important to try to be able to offer people some practical return for the time and energy that they are likely to support you with. This could be to undertake a particular task on their behalf, often in our experience, this might be something like explaining a particular aspect of accounting. It may simply be to act as a sounding board for them. We have often found that head-teachers and GPs undertaking new activities are grateful to have someone to talk to about the things that they are doing for the first time.

---

[1] Bearing in mind that these need to be constantly reviewed and updated.

Engagement with the organisation could in some methodological approaches be seen as problematic particularly where the role of the researcher is perceived to be objective, and thus seen as distant and 'outside' the situation. Our approach instead recognises the involvement of the researcher and involves the organisational members explicitly in the research (as will be discussed in detail in the section on methods).

Prior planning also needs to ensure the required skill mix is achieved within the research team; again we should recognise that what this is depends upon the approach that is to be adopted. It will not be the same for all projects. Using the framework that we have outlined in the proceeding section, we need to seek information about three elements. First, we need to define the extent of the systems that are being studied — the organisations that form the basis of the enquiry. For example in our studies of Schools we were interested in the way in which education is delivered to the pupils. Our main focus was, therefore, the Schools themselves and not directly on the other aspects of the system such as the Local Education Authority or the Department for Education. Second we need information about the steering media that guide the systems: the formal rules and procedures, the legislative framework and the structure of these. In the Schools project we were particularly concerned with the content of the Education Reform Act 1988 and the statutory instruments and management directives that accompanied this. Finally, we need to explore the lifeworlds of the participants as reflected both in the nature of internal steering media and their reactions to and perceptions of any externally imposed steering media. In the Schools research project, for example, we were concerned to know about the values of teachers and the things that they found important. Exploring the more tangible steering media as well as understanding the history of the situation can discern the nature of the lifeworld. The content of the controls that are imposed give a clue for the values behind them. Equally, current contextual information such as evidence about the nature of the surroundings or the way in which the organisation is ordered and the behaviour and treatment of its members or customers and clients, provides information about the taken-for-granted views of the organisational members. When visiting schools it was relevant to look at the nature of the decoration — the extent to which pupils work was displayed for example, as well as the way that pupils and teachers interacted as they moved through the school. Finally the espoused views can be obtained through discussion and interviews with organisational members.

In order to find about all these elements we need to collect a range of evidence and information. This requires the adoption of a number of approaches and the use of a range of skills. The information required is obtained by interviewing those involved inside and outside the organisation; from the documentation describing the processes; and from the observation of what was happening in reality. Thus a project requires that the team have access to library or archival skills, interviewing skills and the ability to be an observer or participant observer. Thus the members of the research team have to understand this wide range of sources of information and need to have the skills required to be able to tap all these elements.

It should finally be recognised that in choosing the team it is necessary to ensure that those who are joining are comfortable with the chosen methodological approach if, as the principal researcher you are committed to a particular approach, either through promises to funding bodies or intellectual preference. In our case, where two of us are committed to our particular approach and have used it for some time, it is particularly necessary to ensure that new team members can feel comfortable with the basic approach. We always spend some time directly discussing the issue with potential co-researchers.

Methods

The approach that we take requires discursive skills, not only in the context of the collection of interview data but also in the implementation of the three stage approach that seeks to empower the organisation in the longer term. The first stage of the process (formally called the formation of critical theorems) is researcher led. In this stage the concern is to gather the data and for the researchers to develop their own analysis. In the second stage (the process of enlightenment) then the understandings of the researchers are taken back to the organisational members to gather their perceptions of the insights gained and to update and enrich the understandings by the inclusion of their views. In the third stage (the selection of strategies) the members themselves are the leaders of the process using these jointly generated insights for the on-going development of their understanding of their own organisation and the development of solutions to problems (Laughlin 1991; Broadbent & Laughlin 1997). The second and third stage illustrate that the 'team' using this approach does not just include the academic researchers, but the organisational members in the situations studied. The third stage also registers that the aim of the research is to move beyond understanding to consideration of any actions that should follow them.

The operationalisation of our approach rests upon the use of a process that is based upon the Habermasian notion of the *Ideal Speech Situation*. This is a focused method of discussion. It provides a process in which research understandings are discussed at all three stages and in which the analysis is developed. The aim of the process is to seek to clarify understandings of the situation researched and then to move beyond the clarification towards analysis and possibly change. The process is based on the application of an ideal speech situation in which there is a commitment to achieving common understandings (this does not necessarily mean consensus formation — we may agree to disagree). The ideal speech situation is based on 'speech acts' that are dialogical contributions from all the participants. These will be, themselves, rooted in the lifeworld understandings of the participants. Thus they are more than the words that are being said and recognise and reflect that there is an existing context of shared understandings. As well as being rooted in and constituted by the lifeworld, the discursive processes of the ideal speech situation, like any process of discourse, are also constitutive of the lifeworld. This means that we should not take for granted the claims that are made, but should interrogate them to 'check' our interpretations. As noted earlier, for this process to be successful there has to be a commitment from all members to engage in a communication process geared to understanding. There has to be equality of opportunity both to contribute to the discourse and also to challenge contributions — hence hierarchies in roles and relationships must be suspended. In this sense the process is one that is overtly seeking to be democratic.

In summary, discourse is a process in which participants come together to mutually question their basic assumptions and commitments in the context of the information gathered. In the context of the research team this means that everyone must have the opportunity to make contributions on an equal basis and it is through this process that understanding and analysis is generated.

The extent to which the team that was involved in the research in Schools and GP practices could really be said to be able to engage in this 'ideal type' process was challenged by others in the context of our presenting papers on the work. Of course this is not necessarily easy, but there is an ideal to work to and we tried hard to achieve this. Our team consisted two women (one lecturer and one researcher) and one male professor. The question was raised at to whether it was really possible, given the hierarchical position of the one professorial man, for there to be equality of access to the two women colleagues. Clearly this was a reasonable question, but one that surprised us at first, as we had never felt any hierarchy in the team. Perhaps the fact that the research team had been formed before the 'elevation' of our male colleague from the ranks of lecturers to a chair was an element; alternatively perhaps the two women were simply not overawed by 'status'. However, none of us found this was ever an issue. Perhaps we are just misguided but the issue is that whether the ideal is achieved or not it should provide the template that is the aim. In discussing issues such as this, the hope is that an explicit consideration will provide some guard against a lack of openness.

When we are explicitly engaged in a project we try to have a weekly discussion session based on the work that has been undertaken over the previous week. This discussion is based upon the presentation of information from members of the team which might include interview notes, details of documentation or legislation, descriptions of the research site and its context and history or any other relevant information. Our approach is for one person to lead the session having provided brief written notes beforehand. The lead person will present the information and then will seek to pull out the evidence that substantiates claims as to the nature of the lifeworld or the steering media. For example, to try to give a 'flavour' for how the process unfolds, consider the type of information we discussed in relation to GP practices. Here we were seeking to understand the lifeworlds of GP practices in the context of the Government seeking to make them change their operation through the application of a new contract (an externally imposed steering medium) in relation to the nature and payment for their work in the NHS. Following a visit to one doctors' surgery our researcher described a waiting room with a small window that was opened by the receptionist when a patient entered and was closed as any exchange finished. The waiting area was two rows of hard chairs and the walls were filled with notices about missed appointments. The argument was put (on the basis of this and other comments from the interview with the practice manager) that the practice in question was not one that was patient oriented. The reception staff was oriented to the support of the doctor and not to the needs of the patients. The rest of us were then able to challenge any aspects of the interpretation (although in this case there was perceived to be little to challenge) using other evidence from the interview notes. The aim was to achieve some indication of the lifeworld of the members of the practice. The implications of this in the context of the approaches to steering were also discussed. This discussion was extended in light of information (provided by our analysis of the administrative structures in the Practice) that the main administrative systems were under the control of the GP and not managed by a practice manager. This suggested that there was little change in the structures despite the implementation of the new contract (most practices had appointed a practice manager to this task). Having discussed the practice in particular we would then proceed to a comparison of the site with the other practices that we had visited, seeking to highlight differences and similarities. At the end of the process we would have a set of our own views of the issues that we would then go back to the practice members to discuss. Again these could be challenged by the practice members and would be developed in light of their insights.

The meetings were informal yet intensive and the person leading would alternate. Each person was allowed to have his or her say and the aim was not to privilege any one member of the team. It should be noted that the use of the discursive approach has the benefit of ensuring that the team meet regularly and must talk to each other. It means that the understandings that are generated are ones that are truly joint. The process is an important element in building the team because of the extent of the interaction that is engendered.

It should also be recognised that the participants of the process must be open to changing their interpretations. If someone has a very deep-rooted view about the nature of a particular issue (for example, all doctors are great and cannot do wrong) then to open up a debate about the nature of their practice will be difficult. The greater danger is when participants do not realise they are in some ways deeply biased in a given respect. This can be countered if team members are open to the processes of discourse, but equally the team as a whole might become embedded in their own set of biases. The presentation of ideas in conferences is perhaps some sort of challenge to this, but it is something that must always be kept at the front of one's mind.

The benefit of working closely with a particular person over a long time is that there is no sense of hierarchy and a strong sense of what we are trying to do and how. It should also be remembered in this situation, new team members might feel it difficult to give their own contribution and could feel 'out of place'. This again is a problem that has no easy resolution other than ensuring that the issue is always at the front of our minds and is perhaps discussed explicitly yet sensitively. Sensitivity and openness must always be at the forefront in these processes of analysis. This approach is also important in the context of the research process itself.

Clearly in the context of using this main method of analysis we are dependent not just on the quality of the processes of discourse, but also on the quality of the evidence presented for discussion. Thus members of the team must have a range of skills that are used to collect that evidence. This must include the archival skills to collate legislation and to build historic and contextual profiles of the organisations, as well as broad qualitative research skills to allow engagement with organisational members. The latter includes the sensitivity to undertake open-ended and semi-structured interviews.

Whilst the issues and the skills needed in other approaches may differ, the first issue that any research team must address is the nature of the approach they take, to ensure they have the relevant skills required. The nature of the research that is undertaken and the types of skills and activities that are used will in turn have implications for the manner in which the team operates and is organised.

Practicalities

In some ways the preceding discussion has been somewhat abstract and impersonal, it is however an important element of planning how a team should be constructed and how a project can operate. In moving to consider practicalities we move onto the more personal and anecdotal elements of what it is like to undertake research.

Having decided on the skill mix required the next stage must be to recruit and build the team. Recruitment is not easy and could involve either research assistance bought in or working with colleagues either within or outside the organisation. If it is the former then it should be recognised that finding someone with the requisite skills who is willing to work for a low salary on a temporary contract is not easy.[2] Sometimes it is a good role for a person who is completing studies of some sort, perhaps a Masters course or a Ph.D. Sometimes someone who is looking to return to a university research after a career-break, or perhaps having been working abroad might be interested in the role. There are some dedicated people who are willing to take the uncertainty that contract research produces. Sometimes it may be easier to take on a couple of different people with diverse skills. It may sometimes be easier to recruit part-time help from someone who is downsizing on their career due to other commitments (family or retirement or simply wishing to expand into other interests).

Working with colleagues is the other alternative and one benefit of this approach is that you are likely to have a better understanding of the skills they have. You will also know if you like them! This is helpful in the context of the type of research that we are involved in as the extent of the interaction means that it is helpful if you get along well. It can be easier to talk through issues with a friend and you are likely to know about their approach to research and recognise the extent of the compatibility of your approaches to research. This said it should also be recognised that sometimes it can be more difficult to address problems with someone you know well for fear of hurting their feelings and thus this reiterates the need for open and honest interaction from the start. Another advantage of working with an academic colleague is the fact that they are in an established post and the worry of finding follow-on funding is not so great.

It is important to realise the implications of the fact that with a 'bought-in' research associate, although you are members of the team, you are in a sort of employment relationship. In an open and honest and democratic relationship this may not be something that really occurs to the fully tenured investigators on a day to day level, everyone is just part of the team. However, this can have pressures, as there is a sense of responsibility to someone whose livelihood rests with your capacity to gain renewed funding. The sense of needing to gain grant income to re-engage your RA can be quite onerous and it is important to be open and honest about the tenuous nature of research

---

[2] It should be noted that this is the result of the funding regimes for U.K. research rather than a desire on our part to employ people on such terms!

funding. Don't make promises you cannot keep simply to try and encourage a good researcher to join you!

Implicit in much of the discussion above is the point that working in a team, especially a small team, requires for some personal rapport between the members, whether you have a previous acquaintance or not, i.e. it helps if you get on well together. You will also need to be tolerant as well. For example, the issue of skill mix is something that has been emphasised earlier. However, it should be recognised that not everyone needs to have all the skills required within the project; indeed, it is unlikely that any one person will have them all! This mix of skills in different people has positive and negative aspects. On the positive side one person may be better at dealing with particular issues. For example, consider access — when working with GPs in the NHS we found that Doctors' Receptionists were more likely to pass a call from a man with a doctoral title to the GPs than a call from either of the two women team members! However, another person might well be better in other aspects of the work, the technical aspects for example, or archival research. People's various strengths should be used to the full without exploiting someone who is particularly good at more difficult or mundane tasks. A mix of skills can also be a point of tension if it means that one member has to take on all the less desirable tasks whilst someone else does all the interesting bits. This may well mean some element of sharing. One point of working in a team should be to celebrate and enjoy differences and not be irritated by the fact that someone cannot do something as well as you might or be jealous of their talent.

If you are a principal researcher and the instigator of a project it is also important to remember a project that is your 'baby' may not hold quite the same fascination for everyone else. (As joint researchers working with others this is a particular issue for us to remember). You may wish to spend all your waking moments thinking about the project and carrying out your research, but colleagues might have other commitments as well. This requires some tolerance and an ability to recognise that commitment levels are different and this is completely natural. What matters is that people do what they say they will and this means that some negotiation about contribution needs to be undertaken before embarking on a project. It also means that all concerned need to remind themselves of the commitments made from time to time and ensure they meet them. (For those of us who work together over time (and indeed live together) the converse is also true and it is also important not to let the research intrude too heavily. Some time is needed to refresh our batteries as well as deal with the weekly shopping and cleaning!) It is in this respect that the development of a research plan with a timetable can be of huge importance. The research plan will need to be updated in line with the on-going situation, but nevertheless it can provide some framework to guide the expectations of different people in the team. This of course assumes that there is ownership of the plan in the first case, and so the plan itself should be the result of open discussion that itself follows the spirit of the ideal speech situation.

Whilst commitment may be high from all, it is also important to recognise that there may also be differences in the way that people approach tasks. Some people can write a near final draft first time round having thought out structures and ideas in their heads. Others of us need to write and re-draft on the screen or on paper perhaps several times. Some people work to a well-ordered timescale others find the adrenalin of the last minute the best way to achieve. People have differences in the times that they work, seen as either owls and larks, one set working late or all night the others being early risers. These are all differences with which we have had to deal with! Working with the same research team means that these issues become well known and managing the differences is taken for granted. This is not true for new research partners. The way to ensure that these issues do not lead to difficulties is to discuss the parameters of the approach and the organisation of the research process at an early stage. This is particularly important when new projects introduce new members to the team. As noted earlier if some members of a team have worked together for a long time, it can be easy to forget that things that are taken for granted by the existing group will not be necessarily apparent to all others. This can be difficult if it leads to a situation where there is an inner and outer circle of team members either intentionally or unintentionally. This is an issue that the team must constantly review.

This leads to consideration and reflection on one final practical issue, the question of the effect of working together with a close collaborator over a long time, something that has been referred to implicitly throughout our chapter. Our joint research career, like all long-term collaborations brings both advantages and disadvantages. The advantages relate to the easiness that arises from knowing well how someone else functions and knowing how to deal with that. There is a sense in which it is practically easy as the problems that may arise relate to how to do the particular research project rather than how to deal with each other. There is ease in knowing how each other thinks and is likely to react to particular situations. There is a huge level of moral support, rarely are both of us 'down' at the same time and this is important in the context of getting research 'done'. The danger is not switching off and always being 'on-the-job'. Also, there is a need to ensure that you are not in a rut and hence it is useful to have others to work with as this provides a lever by which the 'taken-for-granteds' are questioned. No matter how self-reflexive you try to be the questioning of another person is always helpful. This can be achieved by ensuring a healthy conference circuit attendance but can also be helped by working with others. To ensure this freshness of outlook it can also be helpful to work apart and with others on individual projects as well as working with each other. It should be recognised that what works for one set of people may not work for others, nevertheless working in a close team can provide huge moral support for what is sometimes a difficult task, that of undertaking research and getting it published.

Finally

In summary: research is a process of discovery both of the subject of the project itself, but also it is a process of self-discovery. This means that anyone undertaking research will always be to some extent at the mercy of the situation and whilst lessons from others may be helpful they will not give all the answers. Some things can be suggested: in this chapter we have stressed the need to be sure about the nature of the research approach to be adopted as we have argued that this has important implications for the way in which the team is constructed, developed and managed. Infused into the approach that we advocate is a need for teams to be open honest and democratic. We are aware of a constant need for self-reflexivity in the context of both the research findings and also the way in which the discursive processes are undertaken. Clearly there will be times when the ideal is not achieved and indeed it is likely that the process is more often flawed than not. It is nevertheless important to continue to remember what we are trying to work towards.

It should be remembered that research should be something that is enjoyed. Working in a team is a good way to ensure that this is the case. Often there can be knock-backs, access may not be coming through as you hoped or the paper you are drafting is not working through. Working in a team provides the possibility that there is someone who can help out. Rarely is everyone 'down' at once. Managing a research team in this sense is about planning and co-ordinating activity. The process of discourse provides the vehicle for these processes as much as for the analysis of the material. In this sense the research reflects an approach to life rather than a separate 'work' activity.

References

Broadbent, J., & Laughlin, R. (1997). Developing empirical research in accounting: an example informed by a Habermasian approach. *Accounting, Auditing and Accountability Journal, 10*(5), 622–648.

Broadbent, J., & Laughlin, R. (1998). The 'New Public Management' reforms in schools and GP Practices: professional resistance and the role of absorption and absorbing Groups. *Accounting, Auditing and Accountability Journal, 11*(4), 339–361.

Broadbent, J., Laughlin, R., & Read, S. (1991). Recent financial and administrative Changes in the NHS: a critical theory analysis. *Critical Perspectives on Accounting, 2*(1), 1–29.

Laughlin, R. (1987). Accounting in organisational contexts: a case for critical theory. *Accounting, Organizations and Society, 12*(5), 479–502.

Laughlin, R. (1991). Environmental disturbances and organisational transition and transformations: some alternative models. *Organization Studies, 12*(2), 209–232.

Laughlin, R. (1995). Empirical research in accounting: alternative approaches and a case for middle range thinking. *Accounting, Auditing and Accountability Journal, 8*(1), 63–87.

Laughlin, R. (forthcoming). Putting the record straight: A commentary on Methodological choices and the construction of facts: some implications from the Sociology of Knowledge. *Critical Perspectives on Accounting.*

Lowe, A. (forthcoming). Methodological choices and the construction of facts: Some implications from the Sociology of Knowledge. *Critical Perspectives on Accounting.*

Chapter 10

Confessions of a Research Assistant

John Burns[1]

Introduction

Eleven years ago, I stumbled into accounting academia as a failed practising accountant. Although I had always intended to eventually pursue an academic career, my original plan was to go down this path *with*, rather than without, a professional qualification, thinking (then) that such a qualification would be important for my progress in academia. However, after being relinquished of my duties at Ernst and Young, in 1992, due to disappointing exams results, my plan was put into action much sooner than I had originally envisaged.

I engaged in a Masters degree at the University of Manchester, studying economics. And, nearing its end, while most of my contemporaries were scanning the newspapers for lucrative positions in the City, I was looking for something in the circles of academia. I was hauled in by an advertisement for a research assistant, at the School of Accounting and Finance, literally across the road from where I was studying for my Masters.

Fortunately, I got the job (*and* my Masters degree), with an official start date of September 1st 1993. I would assist Professors Scapens and Turley on a research project entitled "Financial reporting and management decisions — a study of their interrelationships in U.K. companies" (hereafter referred to as Project One). It was one of the many research projects that evolved from the claims in Johnson & Kaplan's book (1987) *Relevance Lost*.

At that time, I had neither heard of Johnson and Kaplan, nor did I have any background in accounting research. I even failed management accounting in my first sit of stage-one professional exams. If I were to be honest, marriage between myself and the research assistantship also had considerable undertones of desperation — a real marriage was taking place later that year (to Nichola) and I needed a payroll number to

[1] I wish to thank my colleagues on these projects, for their guidance and friendship; and CIMA and ESRC for financial support.

legitimate myself to my future father-in-law. Nevertheless, I did have a modicum of business experience as one inevitably and very quickly gains when embracing the life of a junior auditor, a solid background in economics, and an enthusiasm for 'research' (only as far as I knew what it was!).

So much for how I stumbled into accounting academia — the rest, as they say, is history. Project One was completed, after which I immediately began as a research assistant on another (larger-scale) project, alongside Professors Ezzamel and Scapens (hereafter Project Two). Broadly speaking, Project Two (lasting from 1995 through to 1998) explored the changing nature of U.K. management accounting practices. The following presents personal reflections on my days as a research assistant on both research projects. There is little by way of scientific input, but rather an honest tale of the life and times for one particular research assistant. While I would not claim that the following is necessarily generalisable material, I do intend to draw out some lessons learned (both positive and negative) from which other research assistants might learn (and from which I am still learning).

The chapter is structured as follows: the next section provides additional background to both research projects, in particular their respective subject matter, the research teams and the work undertaken. After which, I then outline certain issues/problems encountered during my time as a research assistant, and reflections on how I dealt (or failed to deal) with them, namely: (1) the travelling; (2) the heavy and, at times, complicated work schedules; (3) tensions between multiple duties; (4) research contacts' waning interest; (5) supervision issues; and (6) management of research teams. These are by no means the only issues that I could have highlighted but, on reflection, they seem important.

The Research Projects

Project One[2] comprised a questionnaire to 1000 CIMA members, fifteen follow-up interviews, and three case studies (each lasting around 18 months). The team comprised six people — one professor, two senior lecturers, two lecturers and myself. The (two) fund holders, a professor and a senior lecturer, each adopted one of the case studies. The third case study was adopted by the other senior lecturer, while the two lecturers respectively assisted with (statistical) analysis of the questionnaire data and the follow-up interviews. However, as research assistant, I was involved in all parts of the research project and thus had five different individuals to work with at any point in time.

There was nothing outstanding or surprising about our results, at least in terms of what we unravelled about the relationship between external financial reporting and management decision-making. Indeed, probably the most telling result from Project One was the direction it gave for Project Two. More to the point, although the results confirmed our initial suspicion that financial reporting requirements did not dominate management decisions (nor, by implication, management accounting), the latter

---

[2] Kindly sponsored by CIMA. Publications from this project include: Joseph *et al.* (1996); Scapens *et al.* (1996); Burns *et al.* (1996); and Burns *et al.* (1997).

nevertheless appeared very slow in changing, despite significant broader (technological, global competitive, organisational and managerial) changes to have taken place during the 1980s and 1990s. Thus, our purpose (for Project Two) was to ask *why* there was such slow pace of change in management accounting practices.

Project Two, 'Resistance to accounting change,[3] was a much bigger affair than its predecessor. It comprised a questionnaire (again, to 1000 CIMA members), twelve follow-up interviews, and eight longitudinal case studies (ranging from one to five years in duration).[4] The research team had four members, namely: two professors; myself; and, for one year, an additional research assistant. Both professors adopted two case studies each. As research assistant, I was involved in all of these case studies, and led on four.

Travelling and the Interviews

The normal schedule, especially for Project Two, comprised two/three days each week frequenting U.K. motorways, travelling to and from case study interviews. Three of the case studies, selected because they promised (and gave) very interesting case stories, were located 200 miles from Manchester. Such that, on occasions, a whole day's travelling by car could be made for just a single interview. In hindsight, this was utterly illogical; however, sometimes, one interview was all that can be arranged. Alternatively, plans were made for additional interviews, but these had been cancelled by the time of arrival. This is an extremely frustrating part of case study research, yet one that we usually swallow. Moreover, it is my belief that the researcher should, unless there are very good reasons (illness, etc.), avoid cancelling interviews, even when only one interview has been arranged — there is too much to lose in terms of your contact's goodwill.

When a researcher seeks access to an organisation, he/she is somewhat at the beck and call of interviewees, and quite often this can mean compromising with sub-optimal appointment times. Your interview subjects are busy individuals, and your interview usually constitutes no more than goodwill on their part — so, you must be prepared to fall in with the interviewee's schedule. On numerous occasions, I would be driving south, down the M6 motorway, from 5.00 a.m., and returning home at about 9.00 p.m. This can be stressful and, as I discovered to my cost, can involve dangerous liaisons (i.e. with other cars) if one is not ultra-careful. Illogical work schedules can work only to a degree. Thus, my recommendation for others, and what I usually do myself now, is try to arrange a half/full day of interviews at a single case study site, travelling down the night before and stopping over at one of the many good-value hotel lodgings available nowadays. Being fresh and un-rushed in the morning undoubtedly makes for clearer focus in interviews that day. Of course, another alternative would be to gain access for research at an organisation on your doorstep.

---

[3] Kindly sponsored, jointly, by CIMA and ESRC. Publications from this project include: Burns *et al.* (1999); Burns & Scapens (2000); Burns (2000), Scapens *et al.* (2000); Burns & Vaivio (2001), Burns & Yazdifar (2001); Burns *et al.* (2002); and Scapens *et al.* (2002).

[4] Two of the case studies were, as planned, a continuation from Project One.

One benefit of the travel-by-car, most definitely, was the expenses. Research assistants are not usually paid great amounts, so any supplementary income is most welcome. Although, of course, these benefits should be set against, for instance, depreciation of your car, and the stress and dangers associated with such travel. Another benefit was gained particularly from the journeys when I had the company of a senior academic colleague(s), which was nearly always the case in my first year as research assistant. The conversations we had during the journeys helped me to quickly learn about university life, academia — as well as certain academics! This prepared me well for later years. I would recommend to any aspiring research assistant who has intentions to eventually step further up the academic ladder to find out as much as they can, at an early stage, about universities and academia — it is a complex world.

Finally, for what it is worth, I can offer some tips about conducting the interviews, several of which pertain to common sense. First, do not be late for an interview, no matter how well you think that you know your contact. Nowadays, of course, and not really in my days as an assistant, there is always the mobile phone to fall back on if timings start to go belly-up. However, I still maintain that this is a very poor substitute to over-compensating in your journey time, thus arriving early, parking up and reading through your notes before you enter the premises. Second, always dress smartly. First impressions count and you are much more likely to gain respect this way rather than if you emulate the stereotype academic (please — no blazers with corduroy patches). Third, be sure to obtain clear directions to the case study site in ample time. Fourth, always accept, and request if necessary, to have a site tour — even if you do not really want to. I am reminded of touring a chemicals manufacturing site with Professor Scapens in 1993. We donned hard-hats, overalls, protective spectacles and heavy-duty gloves; and we experienced the most atrocious smells and fumes that one could imagine. But, importantly, that particular tour provided insight and background to the organisational processes that made subsequent interviewing so much easier than I suspect they would otherwise have been — we quickly related to references made to 'vessels', 'drums', 'utilities' and other organisation-specific terms. Finally, in all interviews, but particularly when meeting someone for the first time, following a (brief) introduction to the research project, it is sensible to begin an interview by asking the interviewee for their background. From my experience, most people like talking about themselves; so, this is a useful tactic for breaking-the-ice, putting the interviewee at ease, and instilling the necessary (initial) interest.

I've Got Three Jobs

So, what else was in my remit, besides the travelling and interviewing? I had always presented myself to family and close friends as having three jobs. That is, in addition to being a research assistant; I was writing a Ph.D. (this being a stipulation of Project One); and, I taught for roughly 7 hours per week. So, how did I manage my time?

First, I disciplined myself rigidly through a 'rolling' diary — updating at least twice a week and forever making plans by it. This rolling diary is still used (and 'rolled') to this day. Any tool for personal time management would suffice — the important thing is routinising its use. Second, there was undoubtedly personal sacrifice during this period. Make no mistake, doing a Ph.D. at the same time as acting as research assistant is hard graft. I would regularly be working on my Ph.D. (i.e. September 1993 to April 1996) from early evening until the small hours of the next morning — then, occasionally, re-starting before light that same morning. I was burning the candle at both ends, *and* in the middle — countered by developing a knack to 'power-nap', and through regular bursts at the gym.

Most of all, I guess that I had a strong personal drive — something which, I believe, every research assistant/Ph.D. student must have. It is a hard slog over a few years, but the potential rewards of moving into full-time academia, particularly in a leading research-led institution in your field of research, usually fuels sufficient motivation. Having said that, I would urge any new research assistants to be careful not to compromise their Ph.D. for the sake of other duties (including those in connection with servicing the research project). The split between respective duties (never entirely linear, week-by-week) should be as clear as possible to both fund-holder(s) and research assistant at the outset; and, importantly, it should be kept to as far as (reasonably) possible. Keep a record of the hours that you have worked. Just because it has taken longer for you to do something than you and/or your seniors expected, this does not necessarily mean that you performed in a sub-standard fashion. It may indicate that the time originally set for the task was unrealistic.

Looking back, there were also certain aspects of my various roles that *enabled* me to manage the heavy schedule — aspects which I would recommend researchers in similar demanding situations to consider. First, during my early years at Manchester University, I was not expected to convene, or lecture, on any courses. Thus, from 1993 to 1995, my teaching involved fairly routine (textbook-based) tutorials and workshops for which I had ample guidelines/answers. Teaching duties for a research assistant, if taken, represent excellent experience, and will look good on your curriculum vitae when/if you apply for a permanent academic post in future years. However, it is important that such teaching does not become a burden in terms of consuming your time. For similar reasons, it was a great help that my early teaching responsibilities (including my first lecturing roles from 1995 to 1998) were pitched at familiar topics. At that time, for me, this meant auditing and financial reporting — in contrast to what I later pursued in my research. Auditing and financial reporting was my 'best' option because I felt some comfort in being able to fall back on recent experiences at Ernst and Young. Conversely, at the time, I would have felt far less equipped to deliver more technically-oriented accounting courses with emphasis on calculation and method — unless I had spent considerable additional time in preparation (my academic background was traditional economics). So, in summary, tailor (negotiate) your teaching responsibilities around topic areas that offer minimal time consumption (in preparation, etc.). If this happens also to be your research area (i.e. the research project and/or your Ph.D.), that is fine; but, in my experience, the two do not necessarily have to be the same.

Economies in my Ph.D. also enabled me to maintain the heavy schedule. In a nutshell, I allowed for the research question of Project One to shape the research question in my PhD, although I do not recall admitting such things to my external examiner. To not do so would have meant having *four* jobs, because I would have had to undertake additional interviews that focused specifically on my (Ph.D.) research question. The subject of Project One, it will be recalled, was the extent to which external financial reporting requirements dominated management decisions (and, by implication, management accounting). I (broadly) adopted the same research question for my PhD. In my mind, given an already-extensive workload, to pursue an entirely independent PhD would have been to stretch things too far.

Tensions and Compromise

So, how did I separate my (Ph.D.) research from that of the project, and what would be my specific contribution to the literature? First, CIMA's formal requirements for Project One included an article in *Management Accounting* (now *Financial Management*) and a monograph report — both of which were geared primarily towards practitioners rather than academics. So, here was my opening. While focused on the same overall research question, respective practitioner and academic-geared research will usually highlight different (albeit usually overlapping) aspects. I envisaged little problem in teasing out different angles to the case studies for my Ph.D. research — it is a matter of wearing different lenses and making good use of theories (see below). However, admittedly, this is easier when there is a clear distinction between practitioner and academic-geared research outputs. On the other hand, when the primary/sole objectives and responsibilities of a research team are academic papers, there will likely be a need for the research assistant and his/her supervisor to carefully plan out the respective research and PhD outputs at an early stage. Do not compromise too much — as well as completing your PhD (from which, in my view, you should attempt to develop at least one sole-author working paper in time for pending job interviews) it is not unreasonable to expect to be a co-author of several subsequent academic papers, the writing of which you have been involved with (see later also).

An important dimension to my Ph.D. was its theoretical contribution. I had been reading multiple articles and books in the area of institutional economics, a relatively untouched theoretical approach within the accounting literature. My initial tampering with such literature emerged while doing my economics masters' degree, especially after attending a seminar given by Professor Geoffrey Hodgson (then, of the Judge Institute, Cambridge). It was my intention to develop an institutional framework of accounting for my thesis and, in so doing, originality in my theoretical contribution (I think) more than outweighed any potential lack of originality in the empirical work. It is important to offer some degree of originality in your Ph.D. — so, careful thought and forward planning is needed when your research evidence derives from someone else's project on which you are working and gathering evidence.

As Project One came to its end in September 1995, I began to consider my duties for Project Two. I was about to become involved in an extremely topical and interesting research project, alongside two reputable academics, and earning a reasonable income. But, there were costs also, which needed setting against the benefits. For instance, I agreed with the new fund-holders to finish my Ph.D. as soon as possible. I managed to successfully defend the thesis in April 1996 (two and a half years in total); however, in hindsight, I wish that I had spent an additional 6 months developing particular areas of this work.

The decision over when to submit my Ph.D. thesis for examination was partly driven by the schedules and responsibilities of my new role, and partly by my personal income stream aspirations. Project One's salary ran for two years, so the financial lure of Project Two was significant. Given the opportunity to re-visit this, I would probably have tried to negotiate a delay to the start of the new project, for a few months, subject to hopefully securing available funding (by no means a certainty), and worked on the Ph.D. for that little bit longer. There were certain chapters, in particular the research methods chapter which, with the benefit of hindsight and more experience, were under-developed. And, analysis of the case studies, infused with institutional theory, could have been stretched much further than it was.

The disappointment goes further, because due to my involvement in a new research project so soon after the first, it meant that I also failed to get as much out of my Ph.D. as I ought in terms of publishable articles. In fact, my Ph.D. remains relatively untouched, to this day, in respect of publications, although some chapters eventually became feeders to later publications — for example, Burns & Scapens (2000) was an adaptation of my Ph.D. theoretical framework chapter, and Burns (2000) extended analysis of one of the case studies undertaken during my PhD. Nevertheless, in general, once left, a Ph.D. becomes very difficult to find time to return to. As a summary note, I would advise research assistants to think carefully about taking on one/two-year posts if, at the same time, you intend to begin a PhD. If available, elect for studentships that last for at least three years, thereby allowing sufficient time (and funding) to do justice to your Ph.D. and working papers.

Waning Interests

A significant and ongoing issue, as a research assistant, was maintaining the interests of business contacts in my/our research. As mentioned already, these people are extremely busy and, for most, I expect that an hour or so spent with an academic researcher is usually non-value-adding activity. Interestingly, I sensed that having CIMA affiliated to both research projects helped, at least in terms of establishing a foot-in-the-door. Several interviewees would comment on their willingness to 'do their bit' for the accounting profession.

Another (hardly surprising) observation from both research projects was that some of the most interesting and fruitful (in terms of publications) case studies, with reliable access and continuing cooperation, came in organisations where a member of our research team had a personal contact. This contact would be just one of numerous potential interviewees, thus there was never really any compromise of independence between researcher and the research subject. More importantly, the personal contact remained key to accessibility — it is much easier and safer to impose yourself, and be a nuisance, to somebody who you already know well.

Peer pressure appeared to hold weight. For instance, twice, when in conversation with an interviewee, a more senior colleague approached the person and asked who I was, in my presence. And, on learning my identity (on both occasions, with a courteous but rather false hand-shake) both seniors demanded that time devoted to the interview should be kept to a minimum. With these comments being made in my presence, it was rather embarrassing. However, as stated above, I did sympathise — in my capacity as researcher on these projects, I was not really adding value to the business.

In my experience of U.K. accounting academia, research output generally commands low regard amongst business managers and accounting practitioners compared, say, to our Scandinavian colleagues who especially enjoy much closer partnerships in research with national industry. This, I suggest, is a cultural thing rather than reflection of differences in the quality of respective research. To this day, I know of only a handful of contacts in industry and/or the accounting profession who actually read academic accounting publications. Most would not know *Accounting, Organizations and Society* if it hit them in the face. Thus, in my case studies, I was generally taken on as a measure of goodwill rather than as someone who might actually offer some value-adding advice.

If researchers rank amongst the 'lepers' of the business world, what are we to do? We are second, probably, only to the external auditors — except that, in practice, an organisation can say "no" to us and refuse access. Initial goodwill can soon fade. So, it is important to keep business contacts happy even when, in so doing, there can be temporary conflict with the academic plan. Admittedly, for the sake of the duration of a case study that produces enough material for a possible academic paper, keeping your contacts happy might merely involve manipulating your contacts' perceptions rather than necessarily having to compromise your original research objectives. However, my personal view is that, in today's 'add value or perish' business world, it is naïve to expect open doors to a research site without some form of payback for the organisation. This might include a consulting report and/or training sessions provided to staff.

There are precedents. Numerous accounting scholars, particularly in Scandinavian and Nordic countries (for examples, Jonsson 1996; 1998a, b; Gronhaug & Olson 1999) have successfully struck a balance between working in/for organisations; and, at the same time, producing excellent, insightful academic output. Some have seconded themselves to the day-to-day accounting and management routines of a business, while others offer payback via a project report on a more consulting-type basis. Organisations for their part would, at a minimum, commit to assisting with access to interviewees, and provide some (financial) support. There is still much to be learnt about the shape 'consulting' accounting research might take — possibly drawing insight from other academic disciplines where academic-practitioner partnerships are more common-place.

My final remarks in respect of managing your contacts' goodwill would be that you can never do too much cajoling. While the number of visits should not be burdensome, there are other tactics which might be considered in between visits. For instance, practices which I maintain, include: (1) sending thank-you letters after each visit, to *all* those people interviewed; (2) sending Christmas cards every year, at least while your research in that organisation is still active; (3) sending main contacts final copies of reports (for example, CIMA monographs); (4) sending invitations to attend School-hosted conferences and/or workshops; and, in some cases, (5) inviting contacts to become members of School advisory committees. To date, I would say that such tactics have been successful. I maintain many research contacts which were established back in the 1990s, several continue to offer research access (in one case, recently, one contact reversed the process and has invited me to become involved in a major change project — as an observer, not a consultant as such), and several have also since kindly agreed access for colleagues and/or Ph.D. students.

Supervision

For both research projects I had two supervisors, to whom I owe much, particularly my long-time research colleague, Robert Scapens, who was a fund holder on both projects. The three supervisors (i.e. Scapens, Turley and Ezzamel) are very different characters,[5] respected for their works in different areas, and adopting different research styles. As such, there were occasions when I found myself trying to balance, sometimes wrestle with, these differences — for example, there would be differences in opinion as to how much time I should devote to non-research activities such as teaching, article reviews, academic/business networking, and so on. Nevertheless, as a research assistant who was learning his trade, exposure to such differences in opinion tended to be enlightening rather than necessarily a burden — I usually made my own decisions in the end.

I was also fortunate that my senior colleagues continually supported my attendance at, and approved necessary funding for, numerous workshops, conferences and doctoral summer schools. I recommend that other research assistants attend, and present at, as many of these events as possible in the early stages of their careers — it is a critical part of your development. I say this despite being on the receiving end of some extremely negative remarks from Anthony Hopwood against a paper I presented at an EIASM seminar in 1995. It was most certainly a blow to my efforts, and immediately sparked some searching questions as to what it was all about. On reflection, such experiences too infuse into the learning curve, as did the words of encouragement from other scholars who approached me afterwards to let me know that 'Anthony was wrong' (thanks Luca).

However, in addition to learning from senior colleagues in case study methods, it is equally important for novice researchers to gain as much front-line experience as possible, and as soon as possible. I personally have little difficulty in conversing with business people on one-to-one or group situations — my brief spell as an auditor may have helped in this. My main problem, however, in the early months as a research assistant, was a lack of understanding of the issues that were being investigated. My limited background knowledge of (real-world) accounting and management practice, and research, meant that I could be anonymous in discussions between senior management and the lead project researchers. This considerably embarrassed and frustrated me. Sitting amongst (frequently high-level) discussants without making any real contribution can be demoralising for anyone.

---

[5] They support Liverpool, Manchester City and Leeds, respectively — need I say more.

Moreover, my confidence in such situations was further undermined by the amount of time I spent, during interviews, checking whether or not the tape recorder was working properly. Silly, but true. All (case study-based) research projects should employ the best available recorder, tapes and (always new) batteries. Nowadays, there are several digital recording machines available which hopefully will make recording much easier (and more reliable) than in the past. For Project Two, we employed what we believed at the time to be the best available recording equipment; however, I still felt the need to check (and re-check) the tape machine during interviews — probably much to the annoyance of my interviewees. I put this down to a hangover from poor equipment (and, as a result, some poor transcripts) during Project One.

However, as my knowledge and understanding of the project issues grew, I began to have much more to say and ask during subsequent interviews. And, it is at this stage that a research assistant should ensure he/she has opportunity to develop in this way rather than merely be an onlooker to interviews that are dominated by more senior research colleagues. In the main, my colleagues were sensitive to this; but, for Project Two, I specifically requested that I personally take on some of the case studies and, through these, was able to experiment and develop in my own research skills. Such experience, from as early as possible, is an important part of a research assistant's development (you, and your supervisor, usually have a fair idea when you think you are ready for this).

One final remark can be made about supervisors and senior colleagues. People inevitably move on to new jobs, including research assistants, and new assistants/Ph.D. students come along. As such, your (regular) research time and interaction with particular senior, experienced colleagues can be short-lived. Thus, make sure that you get the most out of your time working with these people; and, if you feel this is not happening, (politely) say so. As mentioned above, it is not unreasonable, as a research assistant, to be a co-author on most publications to emerge from a project, and I imagine that most academics would abide by this. However, it is important that you try to establish a role in the writing-up of such publications rather than relying on your senior colleagues to undertake the entire writing-up process. As a junior researcher, there is likely much still to be learned in terms of writing-up your results — but good supervisors will help you along with this and will involve you.

Team Management

Large research teams have the advantage of pooling together a multitude of skills and intellect. But, in my experience, this can also create significant logistic and administrative problems, which usually affect the research assistant the most. For instance, during Project One, it was particularly difficult to arrange meetings for the research team and, for that reason, we actually had very few team meetings. As mentioned above, different elements of the research project were delegated amongst six team members. I would attempt to meet my colleagues in work, usually on days that complemented their teaching schedules — i.e. on the days when I could guarantee they would be at work. At times, if I were honest, I felt like a frustrated secretary rather than an aspiring researcher. Case study visits (which I organised) would also be driven primarily by the availability of my senior colleagues, tallying up with interviewees' availability on a certain day. In so doing, it was essential to make such arrangements at least two months in advance — in my experience, having more available dates to work with outweighs any potential vulnerability towards late cancellations.

The considerable time spent on team logistics (including arranging interview dates) had a knock on effect for the time available to devote to other project-related responsibilities. Because I also had several other non-project-related responsibilities (including my Ph.D. and teaching), it meant that certain tasks (which might have benefited the projects) were not undertaken to their fullest — for instance, prior background research into an organisation before the inaugural visit, ongoing review of transcripts, and writing up the case study as our research progressed. That said, I did scan previous transcripts, and prepared notes and questions, before every new interview. This was usually done in a motorway café, en route to a particular research site. I would also spend some of the journey time playing tapes from previous interviews in my car[6] — how sad is that? However, (seriously) writing-up a case study only usually occurred as a research project neared its end.

On reflection, I would nowadays argue that large research projects must have a designated administrator(s), besides its senior and junior researchers. This could be a (part-time) role for a Masters'/Ph.D. student, who broadly understands the research issues being investigated, and who welcomes the supplementary income and research/ work experience. For a reasonable fee, these assistants could help, for example, in organising suitable dates for interviews and meetings, arranging for tapes to be transcribed,[7] searching for and photocopying essential papers, and other routine jobs which can consume a considerable amount of the research assistant's time. However, importantly, this administrator should be designated entirely to the research project, and not shared with other local (School/Departmental) administrative functions — hence, my suggestion that it might be a student. Otherwise, from my experience, in busy administrative periods in the department, a research project will lose out, and it is usually the research assistant who suffers the most.

Concluding Remarks

That concludes a brief and personal insight into life as a research assistant. I have no doubt made mistakes along the way, and my peers have probably made mistakes too. But, I have since taken these experiences into full academia, and continue to (re-)apply the cumulative knowledge in new research projects. Such learning, however, never ceases.

The constraints upon, and expectations of, a research assistantship can be both significant and frustrating. Yet, at the same time, I do look back at those years in a

[6] Always make copies of your tapes prior to despatch to the transcriber.
[7] Voice-to-word processor technology may soon make this easier, and to the extent that transcribing becomes a relatively easy role for the student assistant.

positive manner — for one thing, a research assistantship presents an excellent platform for a full academic career, which I personally aimed for, and particularly where it coincides with doing a Ph.D. Your time spent as a research assistant develops skills that you will need, and will further augment, throughout your academic career — not just the years spent servicing the project.

References

Burns, J. (2000). The dynamics of accounting change: inter-play of new practices, routines, institutions, power and politics. *Accounting, Auditing and Accountability Journal, 13*(5), 566–596.

Burns, J., & Scapens, R. (2000). Conceptualising management accounting change: an institutional framework. *Management Accounting Research, 11*(1), 1–19.

Burns, J., & Vaivio, J. (2001). Management accounting change. *Management Accounting Research, 12*(4), 389–402.

Burns, J., & Yazdifar, H. (2001). Trick or treats. *Financial Management, March*, 32–34.

Burns, J., Ezzamel, M., & Scapens, R. (1999). Management accounting change in the UK. *Management Accounting, 77*(March), 28–30.

Burns, J., Ezzamel, M., & Scapens, R. (2002). *The challenge of management accounting change: Behavioural and cultural aspects of change management.* London: CIMA Publishing.

Burns, J., Scapens, R., & Turley, S. (1996). Some further thoughts on the changing practice of management accounting. *Management Accounting, 74*(October), 58–60.

Burns, J., Scapens, R., & Turley, S. (1997). The crunch for numbers. *Accountancy, 119*(May), 112–113.

Gronhaug, K., & Olson, O. (1999). Action research and knowledge creation: merits and challenges. *Qualitative Market Research.*

Johnson, H., & Kaplan, R. (1987). *Relevance lost.* Boston, Mass: Harvard Business School Press.

Jonsson, S. (1996). *Accounting for improvement.* London: Pergamon.

Jonsson, S. (1998a). Relate management accounting research to managerial work! *Accounting, Organizations and Society, 23*(4), 411–434.

Jonsson, S. (1998b). Action research in management accounting studies. Working paper presented at *The EIASM workshop on New Directions in Management Accounting: Innovations in Research and Practice*, 10–12 December, Brussels.

Joseph. N., Turley, S., Burns, J., Scapens, R., Lewis, L., & Southworth, A. (1996). External financial reporting and management information: a survey of U.K. management accountants. *Management Accounting Research, 7*(1), 73–93.

Scapens, R., Ezzamel, M., Baldvinsdottir, G., & Burns, J. (2002). *The future direction of U.K. management accounting practice.* London: CIMA Publishing.

Scapens, R., Jazayeri, M., & Scapens, J. (1998). SAP: Integrated information systems and the implications for management accountants. *Management Accounting, 76*(September), 46–48.

Scapens, R., Turley, S., Burns, J., Joseph, N., Lewis, L., & Southworth, A. (1996). *External reporting and management decisions: A study of their interrelationship in U.K. companies.* London: CIMA Publishing.

Chapter 11

Making Sense of Interactions in an Investigation of Organisational Practices and Processes

Irvine Lapsley

> "But Mousie, thou art no thy lane,
> In proving foresight may be vain,
> The best-laid schemes o'mice an' men
> Gang aft agley[1]" (Burns, 1785)

Introduction

This chapter is based on research methods used in a study of investment decisions in a not-for-profit context. As the 18th century Scots poet cited in the preamble suggests, planning, foresight and cause and effect may provide daunting challenges for creatures and mankind. This observation applies to the practice of investment appraisal itself and to the investigation of investment appraisal practices by researchers.

This chapter is an example of complexity of *research approach*, specifically the use of combined research strategies to investigate complex decisions. There is an established literature (see Smith 1975; Denzin 1978; Brewer & Hunter 1989) on the use of combined methods of research investigation — a literature with which the present writer has a great deal of empathy. The essence of the combined approach is simple. Basically, advocates of multiple or combined methods of research are sceptical about the validity of research results where a single method (for example, survey, model-building, observation or archival searches) is used. Instead they advocate more than one

---

[1] This quotation is from a poem by Robert Burns, Scotland's most celebrated poet who was famed for his ability to observe and comment upon life. As he ploughed his field, he disturbed a mouse's nest and commented on its inability to plan with precision ('gang aft agley' — translation — often goes wrong).

The Real Life Guide to Accounting Research: A Behind-the-Scenes View of Using Qualitative Research Methods
© 2004 Published by Elsevier Ltd.
ISBN: 0-08-043972-1

method to corroborate findings. The combined research approach is most relevant to field studies or case study settings. This advocacy of combined methods of research investigation is an explicit recognition of the need to study complex processes in organisations on a broad front. This chapter is an exemplification of the merits and difficulties of this approach.

Indeed, as this chapter shows, the reality of investigating organisational practices and processes is not straightforward. Once researchers leave behind their desks and offices and step into organisations, they can expect to find messiness and untidy situations from which recommended research methods abstract themselves. A major part of this messiness revolves around the need to make sense of interactions with key actors in organisations. There is a temptation to take all interactions at face value. This study cautions against this. The deeper inside the organisations which researchers penetrate, the greater the need to be sensitive to the interpretation of 'facts' and 'events' in the study settings.

Framing an Investigation of Investment Decisions

The specific not-for-profit context in which this chapter reports on is a study into investment decisions in health care — the U.K.'s National Health Service (NHS). In framing this investigation, the traditional theoretical model building approach of cost-benefit analysis was rejected. Analysis of published cost-benefit analyses reveals technical difficulties (for example, inadequate operational measures of intangibles) of the rational economic approach (see, for example, Drummond 1981; Drummond *et al.* 1986) and this has resulted in variants or re-labelling of this approach to embrace cost effectiveness analysis (no explicit valuations of benefits) and cost-utility analysis (with quality adjusted life years or health status measures as proxies for benefits). However, these approaches emphasise technique at the expense of context.

In particular, the rationalistic view of the traditional (or its variants) economist's approach ignores emerging theories of complex organisations in which: (a) the existence of subcultures and corporate cultures are significant factors in organisational life and writ large within the NHS; and (b) there is sensitivity to the ambiguities attaching to information and the contexts in which it is used to undermine the rationalistic, deterministic, interpretation of events. Indeed, health economists specialising in NHS investment appraisal have expressed puzzlement at the existence of such complexity in the NHS and the absence of a well-ordered, well-defined stable situation (Henderson & Mooney 1986). However, the recognition of the constraints on *a priori* model building of investment appraisal poses particular challenges to researchers investigating investment decisions. The manner of combined research strategies to study capital expenditure decisions is taken up, next.

The study of investment appraisal practices has been an active area of research by management accountants for many years. In general, such practices are investigated by the use of surveys, and mainly by postal survey. There are numerous examples of this approach being adopted in the literature. See for example, Pike (1982), Klammer *et al.*'s

(1991) U.S. study and Lapsley's (1986) survey of U.K. not-for-profit organisations. However, it is suggested here that such approaches to the study of one of the most important decisions of any organisation are limited both in their scope and their design. The survey approach to the investigation of investment decisions in organisations suffers from the same difficulties as the *a priori* model-building approach of rational economic theory. Neither of these approaches captures the ambiguities and complexities in the use of accounting information in organisations. Therefore, in this study, a combined approach was selected for the investigation of investment appraisal practices in the NHS.

Investigating Investment Appraisal Practices: A Combined Approach

These complexities of both: (a) the practicalities of what is the most appropriate theoretical model for investment appraisals; and (b) the context in which formal guidance to NHS managers and accountants on how to implement such ideas is acted upon, suggests that an incomplete and superficial picture will be obtained by the conventional technique of surveying the producers of such appraisals. Therefore, the present chapter explores the use of a triangulation of methods and data sources (Denzin 1970) to address this issue of complexity.

The whole process and organisational context should be looked at to help in understanding any decision made, as the decision process will be of more importance to the outcome than the actual techniques used. The need to study social, and in particular accounting, problems within the context and organisation in which they exist is now well recognised. This interpretation of events identifies the problem of the methodology of social science research, in particular the traditional, 'scientific', statistical methods of investigating practice may not be appropriate. The particular problems of using the scientific approach lie in the difficulties of achieving reliability and validity.

Various authors have suggested ways of attempting to achieve validity in research concerned with social areas. Stacey (1969) uses the description 'combined operations' while Denzin (1970) refers to 'triangulation' and Douglas (1976) suggests 'mixed strategies'. The common factor which these authors stress is that a combination of various techniques and approaches can give different insights into the social area being investigated and as such could provide independent confirmatory evidence. The need for such confirmation arises due to the often subjective nature of the evidence gathering and analysis processes. For example, the need for interpretations and perceptions of behaviour are common features of social sciences research. Therefore, observation can be supported by interview, or case studies by interviewing the people involved. The more the points of 'triangulation' then the greater the likelihood of obtaining valid, reliable information.

The focus here is on investment appraisals within the NHS. Different dimensions of this process were examined by: (a) interviews with personnel undertaking appraisals; (b) gathering examples of completed investment appraisals; and (c) participant observation of the activities of project appraisal teams decisions (Ferguson & Lapsley 1988; Ferguson 1989a, b). Within (a) the particular focus of the study was on: (i) the origins of project proposals; (ii) the techniques of appraisal utilised; and (iii) the existence or otherwise of post-completion reviews. In (b) examples of completed investment appraisals were gathered to reinforce interview evidence on techniques utilised. Data was collected successfully for the first two strands of this triangulation, with interviews being held with personnel conducting investment appraisals and examples of investment appraisal exercises being collected. The third strand of this triangulation proved to be problematic. This approach to investment decisions was confounded by the messiness of processes and the actions of key informants. The difficulties of undertaking participant observation as a means of examining organisational processes is therefore a major focus of this chapter.

Participant Observation: Characteristics

There is an established literature on this method of research (see Whyte 1984; Jorgensen 1989). The technique of participant observation (PO) originated from sociological and anthropological research. This original research and further work led to the refinement of the technique and the realisation of its potential as a method of investigating social processes with the possibility of minimising the subjects' reactions to the PO as 'research instrument' unlike direct interview and experiment. These early attempts at participant observation, as in anthropological studies of remote communities were of a particular type i.e. *overt* participant observations (Jorgensen 1989: 46; White 1984: 30), in which the identity and role of the observer is known to all. This is the type of participant observation discussed here.

The alternative approach — *covert* observation — presumes it is possible for the participant to be assimilated within the group. This is most likely when the researcher is also already a member of the group targeted for study. Where the researcher does not have this entrée, the covert style of participant observation depends crucially on the creation of an identity or role which will remain undetected or the research will be jeopardised. In study settings such as those discussed in this chapter, where other members of the group might detect the cover story for a covert PO, there is limited option but an overt participation.

The PO facilitates the study of the process of making decisions, however, studying *process* is complex. In studying the process of operation within a group or study setting, there are numerous aspects of group behaviour of which the observer needs to be aware. In observing the evaluation of alternative courses of action, there may be difficulty in getting behind stances adopted to detect the stimuli for particular positions taken, especially where there may be complex situations (for example, implicit sanctions). There is also the possibility of informal interaction between key actors outside the formal study setting and the apparent unanimity of the group being examined which

Table 1: Main phases of participant observation (after Freidrichs & Ludtke 1975).

| Stage | As Viewed By | | |
	Subject	Others	Self
1. Application	Interloper	Voyeur	Salesman
2. Orientation	Novice	Insider Informant	Stranger
3. Initiation	Probationer	Psuedo Professional	Initiate
4. Assimilation	Limbo member	Public Defender	True Believer
5. Cessation	Deserter	Expert	Worker who has completed his task

may mask subdivisions or splinter groups. This may be revealed, for example, by divergences in commitment to organisational goals by members of the group being studied. It may require 'out of committee' meetings, discussions to detect such nuances of behaviour.

The PO is also dynamic and interactive, as the observation goes through different phases (see Table 1). These phases are not in themselves discrete but are expected to be perceived differently by the different people involved in the PO. During each of these phases the role of the observer may be viewed differently by those involved. Therefore, it was anticipated that different approaches might be required of the researcher. So, for instance, during stage one, it was considered important to dispel fears or misconceptions over the researchers role then, during stage two, it was anticipated that it would be necessary to adopt a "learning" attitude rather than claiming to be an expert. However, as the story of this investigation unfolds, it is clear that the PO in this study did not get beyond being regarded as a 'Voyeur' or 'Insider Informant', with adverse consequences for this part of the study.

From this it can be seen that it is vital for research validity that the observer is *accepted* and his role is in agreement with the given norms of role which the group see him in. This can be achieved by ensuring that during stages one and two the observer does not try to present an 'expert' facade. Instead the observer should behave like an initiate into the group and only gradually be seen to take on full group membership. The assimilation of the participant observer within specific study settings is often depicted as being most easily achieved with permission from people in authority in organisations (Jorgensen 1989: 45), but in this study this accepted wisdom was counter-productive and led to the PO being regarded as an 'insider informant'.

Prima facie, the problem of acceptance of the observer in these groups is not as great as in a social grouping, because the capital development teams are task orientated and work related, and it might be considered that personal characteristics are less important. We formed the view that this acceptance should be achieved if the researcher was patient and realised his/her privileged position, ensuring at the outset that this role and position are clearly explained. However, the dynamics and sensitivity of the tasks being observed attenuated this strategy, as discussed further, below.

In planning this PO, the researchers also gave careful consideration to data collection, which, in observational studies are usually recorded in notes. These notes fulfil two major functions. The first is to provide a record of data. The second is to control threats to validity and reliability as well as minimising observer bias. The observer has to be sensitive to the effect of his/her presence on the decision process, as more 'sophisticated' techniques are likely to be used if decision makers are being observed. The second function is aided by adopting a note-taking schema that forces the separation of data collection and data analysis. One such schema is advocated by McKinnon (1988) where notes are recorded under one of the following headings: observational notes, which are detailed, verbatim facts; theoretical notes, which are the researchers developing ideas; and methodological notes which describe the research strategies adopted in the collection and analysis of data and what the research plans to do next. A variant of this approach was developed for this study.

The PO methodology is appropriate to the investigation of the capital investment decision process. The approach of being present during the decision process gives the investigator access to data that no other technique can provide. There is intimacy associated with this means of data collection that offers the potential for a wider range of information to be gathered which is relevant to the focus of the study. However, in planning this study, the researchers were sensitive to potential obstacles to the realisation of a PO study: the successful negotiation of entry into the study settings, the reactions of other members of the committees to the presence of the PO, the potential for the PO to obtain a 'partial' picture of events because of his particular expertise and background and also because of the potential for informal meetings by members of the committees outside the view of the observer. The research team was sensitive to these potential drawbacks and set up a series of debriefing meetings after each period of observation to examine these various dimensions of the PO experience.

However, despite such potential difficulties, the benefit for this particular study of NHS investment appraisal lay in obtaining an insight into the decision process, and in obtaining a third 'triangulation' point to complement: (1) the personal interviews with finance experts undertaking investment appraisals; and (2) the analysis of completed investment appraisal reports. This chapter examines an attempt to perform a participant observation with three different Capital Development Teams (CDTs). These were the groups charged with the progression of different capital projects in three different health areas. To bring this third dimension of this research investigation to fruition, refinement of initial planning was necessary for means of data collection and in negotiating access to study sites. We discuss this experience of participant observation, first, before telling the story of the experiences of the study sites. The experience of attempting to gain access to these teams is described, as are the problems encountered in carrying out a PO. An analysis of the eventual failure and the lessons to be learned from it are also given.

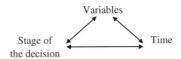

Figure 1: Diagrammatic representation of investigative framework.

Experience of Attempting a Participant Observation: (1) Refining Plans for Data Collection

The method of data collection had to be planned carefully to ensure it was accurate and comprehensive. This data collection had to be designed to fit into an analysis framework. Such a framework has to be flexible enough to allow unforeseen categories and concepts to arise, while at the same time providing some basis for aggregation and analysis. The first step was to design a framework from which the data collection method could be drawn. A three dimensional framework was generated using the following dimensions: 1. Stage of the decision; 2. Variables; and 3. Time. This can be represented as shown in Figure 1.

Each of the dimensions were broken down to give more detail. This detail is given in Table 2. This framework draws on the approach adopted by Glaser & Strauss (1968) in their development of 'grounded theory' and on guidance issued by Departments of Health on the conduct of investment appraisals (see for example, SHHD 1986).

The advantage of this detailed framework was that in an ordered way it offered the potential for a comparison to be made between different capital development teams and different decisions. Having decided on the framework for analysis, the method for data collection was further developed. This was done by drawing up a structured note pad (see McKinnon 1988) which analysed the identified variables into yet more detail. A generalised decision process was used which on later analysis could be aggregated to allow analysis of the variables. The ordering used within the note pad is given in Table 3.

Table 2: Detailed dimensions of framework.

Stage of Decision	Variables	Time
Initiation	Understanding	Months
Objectives	Discussion	Formal meetings
Screening of options generated	Information required	
Identification of costs and benefits	Techniques used	
Discounting and sensitivity analysis	Decisions made	
Elimination of options by participants		
Decision reached		

Table 3: Ordering of note pad.

---

1. *Issues to be discussed: Initiation*:
Split into how this was decided, who decided it and what choices were raised.

2. *The objective of the discussion*:
The dimensions investigated here were: (a) clarity of objective; (b) how easily this was understood by the Capital Development Team; and (c) the discussion which arose on the objectives.

3. *Alternatives generated*:
What was the alternative generated, what was minuted, who raised them and how many alternatives were actually generated?

4. *Information used: techniques, identification of costs and benefits*:
Notes were to be taken on the form of the information used, who supplied it, was it sufficient, was it accepted or rejected?

5. *People involved in the discussion of options*:
Analysed into who they were, what information they supplied and their formal, organisational authority in making a decision.

6. *Decisions reached*:
How the decision was reached, for example, whether by bargaining, railroading or persuasion. How long it took to arrive at a decision; whether there were any delays or delaying tactics.

It was intended to use the structured note pad to achieve two added benefits. Firstly, as copious note taking could be avoided the researcher would be able to concentrate on what was happening within the meeting. Secondly, by avoiding the impression of writing everything down, it was envisaged that the researcher would be seen as less of a threat by group members. It was intended that fuller notes would be written up after the meeting, using the note pad as an *aide-memoire*.

Experience of Attempting a Participant Observation: (2) Accessing Study Sites

After careful planning of the methods of data collection to be used, the research team was ready. One member of the research team (not the present writer) was designated as the observer in this PO exercise. The author of this chapter was the most experienced member in this team and he maintained regular contact throughout the process of data collection, with discussions of obstacles and difficulties at every stage. Three different health areas were approached via the officers interviewed during the personal interview phase of a research project on NHS investment decisions. These officers were asked if one of the research team could join a designated CDT (Capital Development Team) at the beginning of a project and follow the project through to the disbanding of the CDT. None of the officers was able to give a reply to this request, instead it was passed to the Chief Executive of the health areas for his decision. In all three cases, access was granted. This response accords with the recommended approach to negotiating access (see Jorgensen 1989).

The next stage was, in discussion with the capital officers, to decide which projects would be suitable. The capital plan in each of the three health areas was scrutinised to find suitable projects. Suitability was judged by the timing of the project, the size and hence time commitment required and the general representativeness of the project considered in relation to specific health area capital programmes. It should be noted that CDTs were ad hoc and were multi disciplinary teams commissioned for one specific project before being disbanded. The representativeness of the project was felt to be important. It was hoped to join a type of appraisal that had been performed before and was not a one-off unusual evaluation. It was anticipated that this would reduce some of the problems of generalisation when the case studies were written up.

(1) Participant Observation: Rebutted Once, Rebutted Twice

Rebutted once: in one health area an imminent investment appraisal was identified. The capital officer was uncertain about when this area review of a service was to commence. He also appeared to be less than completely enthusiastic about the POs involvement with the appraisal. However, having raised his objections, he then promised to inform the PO when the appraisal began. The appraisal began and was virtually completed before the PO was informed. In fact, the participant observer only discovered this outcome by phoning the officer concerned to enquire about the commencement date. As there were no other investment appraisals on the planning horizon it was reluctantly agreed with the officer's conclusion that further research involvement would be pointless. This was a story of a complete failure to connect with the study setting: the PO was never accepted in this study setting.

It was interesting to note that this health area had produced an investment appraisal that appeared, *prima facie* to be technically sophisticated in its use of benefit ranking. The analysis of this completed investment appraisal showed that the sophistication was overstated. The personal interviews with the capital officer involved also gave the impression of a high degree of sophistication which it later emerged had never been used on an actual project. Given these findings it could be suggested that this organisation was keen to promote an image of innovation and co-operation. This image appeared to be in contrast to the reality of their appraisal techniques; where no discounting was used and projects were often just costed. The officer's approach of appearing to be willing and then blocking the POs entry achieved the outcome of presenting an innovative and co-operative image while still allowing the reality to be hidden.

Rebutted twice: the situation in the second health area was very different. In this case, there were many projects on the planning horizon, however these projects had either started, were due to take longer than the research project, or were not due to start in the immediate future. It may be overstating the case to suggest that this health area deliberately blocked access to the PO, but the fact remains that the officer concerned could not identify a suitable project from the many that they were planning. Again, reluctantly, no further involvement was possible.

(2) Participant Observation: The Runaround

The third health area's capital officer suggested a suitable project that was about to commence and which appeared to be suitable for all the parties involved. The project selected was the redevelopment of an acute hospital to provide only geriatric and outpatient services. The context of this redevelopment was that the acute hospital had been closed but then, due to "intense political pressure" (as described by the building services manager), the hospital was reopened but only to provide a local service for geriatrics and outpatient treatment. The aim of the CDT was to initiate and implement this redevelopment. The CDT consisted of: the local manager (who also provided the clinical input, as he was a part-time consultant), the unit administrator, the unit finance officer, the unit/area building services manager, the unit works officer, the unit nursing officer, and an architect commissioned from a practice outside the NHS.

The research contact with the CDT was designated as the building services manager as it was through his supervisor that access had been obtained. This building services manager was told by his superior to keep the PO informed of any meetings. No information was forthcoming from this manager and quite by chance and, through another route, the PO discovered the time of the first meeting of the CDT. The building services manager was surprised at the POs attendance at the meeting. No one had been informed of the POs involvement, though this manager was supposed to have informed the CDT of the commitment to assisting with this study.

The first meeting went smoothly and the structured note pad worked well. Despite an initially cautious welcome by the CDT members, by the end of the meeting most members had been reassured that the research would not be used against them and would hopefully provide positive benefits. The date for the next meeting could not be agreed until certain costings were made by the finance officer. The administrator was to contact all members of the date of the next meeting. The building services manager told the administrator that he would contact the PO so there was no need for the administrator to do this.

Given the unreliable start shown by the building services manager it was decided to contact directly the administrator after several weeks had passed and no contact had been made. The administrator said that two meetings had subsequently taken place and the members had been surprised at the PO's non-attendance. The building services manager had thought that the meetings would have been of no interest to the research project. On being contacted he apologised and offered instead involvement with another project. It transpired that this second project had reached the building stage and was therefore not suitable.

He then stated that he felt that the participant observer should not be involved in the first project and should have a further discussion with his superior on a replacement project. This was done and his supervisor, the capital officer, said that the participant observer should either continue to be involved in the original project or become involved in an alternative project; a maternity review. The suggestion was made for involvement in both to ensure that some involvement was achieved. This was agreed and unfortunately the same building services manager was to be the official contact in both projects. Despite numerous phone calls from the participant observer and a phone call from his superior, no contact was made by the building services manager. Due to time pressures eventually no further contact was attempted. No reply was ever received. Despite seeking to reassure members of the group that the participant observer was a bona fide, independent researcher, the tensions in this study setting meant that the observer was never accepted as this.

(3) Participant Observation: Making Sense of Interactions

The difficulties of conducting a participant observation of capital project teams in action can be seen on a number of levels. One dimension is the logistics of identifying and tracking specific project proposals. For example, in the two health areas in which there were 'no' suitable projects can be seen as highlighting the problem of attempting research within a predefined time limit. The long time periods involved in and between capital projects could result in severe difficulties for a PO approach. Future research should be planned to coincide with such projects. It was unrealistic in this research project to expect to find capital projects which would fit neatly into the time available. Therefore, despite careful planning, it could be agreed that certain logistical difficulties impeded the progress of the proposed participant observation. However, the reality is the behaviour of key actors who could have co-operated with this study, but did not, and who were more critical in this project not coming to fruition, as discussed below.

In negotiating access, we followed the recommended approach in gaining the support of senior management for the proposed project (see, for example, Jorgensen 1989), but this did not prove to be enough to achieve co-operation. As regards the negotiation of access it would appear that problems at high levels of the NHS are not insurmountable. The chief executives were convinced of the utility of this research and were willing to co-operate. The motivation for their acceptance may have been two-fold. Firstly, they may have had a genuine interest in allowing researchers to see how well certain capital practices were performed within their health area. Secondly, they may have regarded the research as a means of achieving an insight into parts of the organisation from which they were excluded. The guarantees of anonymity given regarding the health area concerned meant the chief executives had no fear of being identified in this process.

The advocacy of access to an organisation based on the support and recommendation of senior management may work in a unitary organisation with clearly designated responsibilities and a hierarchical structure. However, the NHS is a more complex kind of organisation. *Prima facie*, very bureaucratic, but this is a simplistic notion of the health service which is multi-layered, with different strata of professional cadres who influence and shape organisational life and none more so than the medical profession. This multi-disciplinary aspect of health care was also a feature of the capital development teams that were the focus of the study. Also, in such a large complex organisation, there may be considerable agency affects at work, in which subordinates may have, or may assume, delegated powers that may or may not be exercised directly in line with management aspirations.

In a research exercise such as this the researchers may be exposed to the micro-politics of the organisation being studied. For example, one interpretation of the motives of the capital officer in the third health area was that the capital officer may have been keen for the research to proceed knowing that it could expose the weaknesses of his subordinate as well as putting that subordinate (the building services manager) under the pressure of knowing that his work was being 'evaluated' by an outsider. The experience of attempting a PO suggests that it is very difficult to ensure that potential participants have an incentive to participate. As an overt, rather than a covert participation, the actual participant observation proved impossible to conduct in the face of an opposition that was sustained, but never explicitly hostile. This experience shows that subordinates have the ability to thwart the PO merely by: (a) ignoring it; or (b) by slowing down the process and not being helpful. It is interesting that in no case did the subordinate behave in an openly unhelpful way. Each appeared to be willing to help.

The response of the subordinate in this particular study setting highlights the problem of gatekeepers within an organisation that is accentuated in an overt participant observation. Such individuals can choose not to co-operate and the researcher has little influence to exert if the gatekeeper decides on non-cooperation. There were no incentives for this gatekeeper in the third health area to become involved. It appeared that this person felt able to ignore his superior's directives without direct sanction. It was learned later from another source that the capital officer had previously been promoted to his post in preference to the building services manager and that there existed an open hostility between the two men. This is an example of researchers being caught up innocently in organisational micro-politics.

It is difficult to give a prescriptive solution to such a situation. One potential way would have been to be patient and persistent and continue pressing for involvement until this was achieved, either at this or other study settings. However, this abstracts from a problem of this set of failed attempts at participation observation that was not evident until after the project was completed. This problem relates to the non-assimilation of the participant observer into the study settings. The participant observer never got beyond being regarded as an interloper or an intruder. He was not accepted as a member of the group.

There was a set of influences which may have initiated against his acceptance and which could explain the response of the officials with whom he had to deal. The support of senior management becomes a two-edged sword — the researcher is seen as an agent of senior management rather than an independent researcher. The specific techniques being utilised were novel to the target study groups which may have made the members of these groups feel that the participant observer was evaluating their expertise, on behalf of senior management. The bona fides of the researcher in these study settings were also suspected by other members of the groups. These officials had been subject to considerable organisational change, often led by external management consultants. In this case the participant observer was seen as being too close to such expertise because of his manner, behaviour and dress ('sharp suit, cool car') and the health care professionals' perception of the researcher was that he was an intruder to whom they did not immediately relate. Here, the issues for intending researchers are the identification of cues — codes of behaviour and dress, the corporate culture — that will facilitate the assimilation of the researcher into the study context. Crucially, this is about blending in and not sticking out as 'different' in the study setting.

Conclusion

This chapter has discussed a combined strategy to investigate the capital investment decisions in the NHS, with particular focus on one aspect — participant observation. Earlier parts of this investigation had been completed successfully: completed examples of investment appraisals were collected and interviews were held with specialists in NHS capital expenditure. Both the gathering of examples and the interviews with specialists yielded interesting insights into investment decisions in the NHS. In this sense, the project had fulfilled its purpose: there was substantive-enough output not to make the participation observation critical to the overall success of the project. Nevertheless, it was hoped that the participation observation (PO) would have added depth to our understanding of investment decisions. Indeed, although this chapter has highlighted many of the problems of performing a PO, it is this researchers opinion that the technique is valid and can add significantly to an investigation of a decision process. Even attending only the one meeting of the Capital Development Team gave the PO a rich insight into the subtlety of a capital investment decision. The major lesson learned from attempting a PO was that the costs of involvement are very high but so were the potential benefits. The costs consisted of the amount of forward planning, the logistics of meetings and the necessity of being available at short notice.

The fact that the capital officers blocked and thwarted access could be seen as confirming the findings of the personal interviews and the analysis of completed capital investment reports. If the new guidance, the new forms of investment appraisal are merely the old techniques of appraisal but under a different name, then the capital officers may wish to conceal this fact from their sponsoring department. What may be important to the officers is that a report is produced which appears to conform with central government directives. The actual techniques and approaches adopted may be secondary to the image presented. That is, decisions are made outside the rational — logical framework of investment appraisal, and the investment appraisal framework is then used to justify the choice of the preferred option. An exercise in legitimation (Richardson 1987). The benefits of these findings have been enduring factors in subsequent studies of accounting's role in complex organisations.

As a method of investigation, the PO approach has much to commend it. Even in the context of the present study, the limited nature of the participant observation undertaken provided additional insights into the specific area of investigation. This pointed to the conduct of these studies in a manner consistent with 'sagacious conformity' (Meyer &

Rowan 1977) with rules and procedures. A more extensive observation should provide an even greater depth of understanding of the specific focus of the research.

However the choice of the overt approach to PO poses particular difficulties, with defensive obstruction possible by key actors in the field of study. The conventional recommendation of gaining support from senior management may exacerbate these difficulties in organisations that do not have rigid, hierarchical management relationships. The rationale for the presence of a PO in a situation in which other key actors are apprehensive about being 'evaluated', where the other participants misunderstand, or are fearful of the stated aims of the project, proved extremely difficult in this case. There are particular issues of assimilation into groups targeted for research: researchers may have to consider organisational norms, codes of behaviour and access to facilitate a successful PO.

A covert PO in which the observer is known to members of the group, has a contribution to make and is perceived as non-threatening by the group is more likely to lead to a successful PO project on the basis of this experience. There are those (for example, Beattie *et al.* 2002) who advocate an open, transparent exchange with study settings on the grounds that this is the most ethically appropriate behaviour. However, in observation studies the classic research of the Hawthorne experiment demonstrated how such open observation impacts on behaviour: the presence of the researcher is not neutral. In other words, an 'ethically appropriate' (in Beattie *et al.*'s (*op cit.*) terms) behaviour will undermine the intended research.

The results of an attempt to act this way, as set out in this chapter, confirm the classic interpretation of what happens in observational studies. But should we consider covert participant observation to be unethical? The standard approach to ethical issues in health care research is that such issues arise in the context of the impact on the subject of the study: can anyone or an organisation be harmed by a covert observation? If not, this would not be deemed unethical. Here, the critical issue is one of confidentiality and the non-attributable nature of results.

Researchers seeking to enter complex organisations in which they are not known, and where it is intended to investigate sensitive decision making processes, should regard PO alone as a high risk research strategy, but one with immense potential if connections are made successfully with the study setting.

References

Beattie, R. S., Kellock Hay, G., Munro, P., & Livingston, R. (2002). The methodological and ethical issues of conducting management research in the voluntary sector. *Public Management Review 2002, 4*(1), 119–127.

Brewer, J., & Hunter, A. (1989). *Multimethod research — A synthesis of styles*. London: Sage.

Burns, R. (1785). To a mouse: on turning her up in her nest with the plough, pp. 152–154, reprinted in W. E. Henley, & T. F. Henderson (Eds), *The poetry of Robert Burns*, Vol. 1, Surrey: The Caxton Publishing Co 1896.

Denzin, N. K. (1970). *The research act*. Chicago: Aldine.

Douglas, J. (1976). *Investigative social research*. Beverly Hills, California: Sage.

Drummond, M. F. (1981). *Studies in economic appraisal in health care.* Oxford: Oxford University Press.

Drummond, M. F., Ludbrook, A., Lowson, K., & Steele, A. (1986). *Appraisal in health care.* Oxford: Oxford University Press.

Ferguson, K. (1989a). Participant observation of investment appraisal. Discussion Paper No.11, University of Stirling Institute of Public Sector Accounting Research.

Ferguson, K. (1989b). An analysis of completed investment appraisals in the Scottish NHS. Discussion Paper No 12, University of Stirling Institute of Public Sector Accounting Research.

Ferguson, K., & Lapsley, I. (1988). Investment appraisal in the National Health Service. Discussion Paper No. 4, University of Stirling Institute of Public Sector Accounting Research.

Friedrichs, J., & Ludtke, H. (1975). *Participant observation.* Farnborough, Hants: Saxon House.

Glaser, B. G., & Strauss, A. C. (1968). *The discovery of grounded theory of qualitative research.* London: Weidenfeld and Nicolson.

Henderson, J., & Mooney, G. (1986). Option appraisal in the U.K. National Health Service. *Financial Accountability and Management, 2*(3), 181–202.

Jorgensen, D. L. (1989). *Participant observation: A methodology for human studies.* London: Sage.

Klammer, T., Koch, B., & Wilner, N. (1991). Capital budgeting practices — a survey of corporate use. *Journal of Management Accounting Research, 3*(Fall), 113–130.

Lapsley, I. (1986). Investment appraisal in U.K. non-trading organisations. *Financial Accountability and Management, 2*(2), 135–151.

McKinnon, J. (1988). Reliability and validity in field research: Some strategies and tactics. *Accounting, Auditing and Accountability Journal, 1*(1), 34–54.

Meyer, J., & Rowan, B. (1977). Institutional organisations: formal structures as myth and ceremony. *American Journal of Sociology, 83*(2), 340–363.

Pike, R. (1982). *Capital budgeting in the 1980s.* London: CIMA.

Richardson, A. (1987). Accounting as a legitimating institution. *Accounting, Organizations and Society, 12*(4), 341–355.

SHHD (1986). *Health building procurement approval in principle, conduct of options appraisals.* DGM(86).

Smith, H. W. (1975). *Strategies of social research — The methodological imagination.* London: Prentice-Hall.

Stacey, M. (1969). *Methods of social research.* Oxford: Pergamon.

Whyte, W. F. (1984). *Learning from the field: A guide from experience.* London: Sage.

Chapter 12

Qualitative Research on Accounting: Some Thoughts on What Occurs Behind the Scene[1]

Jean Bédard and Yves Gendron

Introduction

The undertaking of any research project involves substantial activity that is not visible in published papers. Such papers typically present research as a sequential and rational activity, the research question being first formulated from an exhaustive review of literature, the research methods next being specified, and the findings finally being presented in a persuasive way through the use of tables, figures and/or interview quotes. However, as argued by Latour (1987), the sequential scientific process that one finds when reading published papers is far removed from the realities of scientific practice. Papers do not reflect several types of activities (such as getting research funding) that are critical in successfully carrying out research. In this chapter, we draw on our experiences as researchers to make visible some of the key activities that occur behind the scene in conducting qualitative research projects. We rely mainly on an ongoing research project on audit committees that we initiated in 1998.

Jean is an audit researcher at a large French Canadian university who has conducted both quantitative and qualitative projects — specifically on auditors' decision-making, professional self-regulation, and audit committees. Yves is a qualitative audit researcher employed at a large English Canadian university. In addition to being involved with Jean on the research on audit committees, Yves has carried out qualitative research on auditors' client-acceptance decision, the WebTrust seal of assurance, and state auditing.

Though we deal with every stage of the qualitative research process, we pay particular attention to behind the scene activities that surround the undertaking of research interviews — which constitute a crucial stage in qualitative work since field data often is derived mainly from interviews. We also seek to make visible the multiplicity of

---

[1] The authors thank Joane Martel for helpful comments.

ethical and institutional constraints that one has to deal with daily as a qualitative researcher.

Setting the Stage of Qualitative Research

Significant time and energy are devoted behind the scene by qualitative researchers in setting the stage for their research, before any data collection takes place. This section aims to provide insights on these 'out of sight' activities. We especially pay attention to the problems and constraints that qualitative researchers have to deal with before fieldwork begins.

Being Pressured to Publish

Academics in several parts of the world are subject to institutional pressures to publish. For accounting researchers in North America, institutional pressures to publish in accounting journals that are viewed generally as top-quality journals (i.e. *Accounting Review, Journal of Accounting Research, Journal of Accounting & Economics, Contemporary Accounting Research* and, to some extent, *Accounting, Organizations and Society*) are significant. For example, at the University of Alberta, annual wage increases, promotions and tenure decisions are based largely on performance with regard to publication — especially in prestigious journals. Institutional pressures are less strong at Université Laval because of the rank salary structure whereby a faculty, no matter her/his performance, has a fixed salary increase every year. Furthermore, the weight given to research productivity in promoting academics is lower (Bédard & Dodds 1994: 101). These weaker institutional pressures to 'publish in the main journals or perish' were determinant in allowing Jean to embrace qualitative research. It should be noted that except for Jean's research, qualitative inquiry in accounting is almost non-existent in Québec. This may be surprising given the degree of influence exerted by French intellectuals (for example, Michel Foucault, Bruno Latour) on qualitative accounting research (Gendron & Baker 2001). However, most accounting researchers in Québec completed their doctoral studies either in the United States or Canada, where positivistic accounting research is considerably influential.

Thus, to maximize their wage increases and/or avoid being laid off by the end of their tenure clock, it is to the advantage of a large number of North American accounting academics to publish in top journals. Even in academic settings that do not rely significantly on institutional incentives to manage research productivity, publishing in top journals constitutes an obligatory passage point (Latour 1987) in establishing one's reputation in North America. However, publications in such journals are a significant challenge for qualitative researchers since, apart from *Accounting, Organizations and Society*, these journals publish qualitative papers only occasionally. For example, a recurring comment that Yves received from the reviewers of a qualitative paper (Gendron 2001) recently published in *Contemporary Accounting Research* was to substantially shorten the text — a challenge for qualitative papers. There were also some concerns regarding some of the terms used in the original text which were seen as obstacles to reading the paper — for example one reviewer objected to using the verb 'to problematise' due to its vagueness. In spite of such difficulties, it is worth noting that competition to publish quantitative research in top accounting journals is very strong, thereby giving some advantages to qualitative researchers in terms of submitting original research.

The institutional environment therefore exerts pressure on North American accounting researchers to consistently carry out research projects and publish in peer-review journals (preferably in 'top-quality' ones) — though there is variability in the degree of pressure to which one is exposed. Whether or not such institutional pressures benefit society (or a significant part of society) is an open question.

Starting the Project

In the mid-1990s there was growing interest in North American and British business communities towards audit committees (for examples, Cadbury report 1992; Dey report 1994). Audit committees were seen as a means of strengthening auditor independence and improving the quality of financial statements. A few academic papers on audit committees were published in the same period in North American accounting journals (for example, Kalbers & Fogarty 1993). Our interest in undertaking research on audit committees emerged from our curiosity to better understand the way in which committees operate in practice, and from our belief that journal editors would be interested in the matter, thereby potentially increasing the likelihood of publication.

Our examination of audit committee literature convinced us of the appropriateness of undertaking a qualitative research project on the matter. We found that prior research mainly examined the antecedents and consequents of various structural attributes of audit committees (Bédard & Marrakchi Chtourou 1998; Bédard *et al.* forthcoming). While these studies show an association between some of the variables examined, they nonetheless provide little information as to how audit committees operate in practice. We wanted to open the black box, and study the dynamics occurring in audit committees. One of our main objectives was to better understand the activities that audit committee members carry out in action, and how these activities are perceived by managers, auditors, and audit committee members themselves. To us, the most relevant method to conduct the investigation consisted of in-depth interviews with all of the main categories of stakeholders involved with the audit committees of a small number of public corporations (i.e. managers, auditors, and audit committee members). We initially planned to conduct the study in four organizations. Our project therefore began with a very broad objective in mind — which is quite typical of qualitative research projects (for example, Glaser & Strauss 1967). It is by collecting and analysing data that we were able to formulate a more precise research question.

Funding the Project

Doing qualitative research is costly. The researcher needs to invest time and resources in developing her/his own database. Travel expenses often have to be incurred to interview informants, and when the researcher tapes the interviews (as we did), s/he also needs to pay for transcriptions. With regard to our audit committee project, we expected to travel frequently all over the country to conduct about thirty interviews. Our funding needs therefore were significant. In October 1998, we submitted a research proposal to the Social Sciences and Humanities Research Council of Canada (SSHRC), which is one of the main providers of funds for accounting research in Canada. However, getting this institution to fund qualitative research is not easy. SSHRC's evaluation committees for accounting projects generally are composed of mainstream accounting or finance academics, whose expertise and receptivity towards small-sample and inductive studies are often relatively low. Not surprisingly, SSHRC assessors felt uncomfortable with our proposal, as indicated in the following excerpts from the reviews that were sent to us:

> "The committee considers that the proposed methodology, although appropriate, is ambiguous. Furthermore, the project lacks clarity with regard to the proposed interviews." (Committee formal comments, our translation)

> "An exploratory study of activities carried out by some audit committees will only generate a few details whose potential for generalization is very low." (Assessor #1, our translation)

Although we received a relatively low score for the quality of our project, our score on the second evaluative dimension used by SSHRC, that is to say the quality of the profile of the researchers, was better and the project was accepted in June 1999 and funded for three years. This suggests that the researcher's track record is of prime importance for funding qualitative research proposals from quasi-governmental institutions such as SSHRC. Quantitative research proposals are easier to evaluate since they generally explicitly describe the theory under which the study is predicated, as well as its hypotheses, design, sample, variables, and statistical analysis model. It is almost impossible in a qualitative proposal to be as explicit on these items due to the inductive nature of qualitative research. Furthermore, mainstream assessors generally are uncomfortable with some of the vocabulary and procedures used by qualitative researchers in their proposals, such as 'theoretical sampling', 'theory building', and the 'continuous revision' of the research questions. The profile of the qualitative researcher (especially her/his publication record) therefore is crucial for her/him to be trusted by funding institutions.

Getting Access to Field Data

In qualitative research, collecting data does not depend on the researcher's capacity to buy the latest dataset on a CD, but on her/his ability to access the field. Our field investigation was predicated on interviewing the main actors involved with each participating organization's audit committee. It was thus necessary to negotiate access with target organizations. It may be relatively difficult, though, to convince organizations to participate in field research — particularly when contact individuals consider the project as a threat to their organization's legitimacy, when interviewees are of higher rank, and when information about actual processes is likely to be disclosed by the researcher (Gendron 2000). Getting access to organizations also was difficult for our audit committee project, even though the audit committee is generally recognised as a crucial mechanism in ensuring high-quality financial disclosures (for example, BRC report 1999).

Before contacting target organizations for participation, we prepared a summary of the research project to allow contact individuals to become easily acquainted with our research. The document stated the objective of the research (i.e. to better understand what audit committees do in practice), specified some key aspects of our data-gathering procedures (for example, target interviewees, duration of the interview — about one hour), and highlighted that we were willing to present at the organization's headquarters a summary of the research findings. The document ended by underlining that we were committed to follow SSHRC's ethics guidelines.

Seventeen public companies were approached at the end of 1999 and during the year 2000 for participation in the research. Ten of these companies never answered our numerous attempts to contact them. Four others answered negatively in terms such as: "Thanks for your interest in [Corporation]. We are not interested in participating at this time".

Various reasons may explain this lack of support. Time constraints may have prevented practitioners from participating in our project. It is indeed widely recognised that key workers such as top managers and directors tend to be increasingly overwhelmed with working tasks (for example, Bron & Gaulejac 1995), thereby making them hesitant, perhaps even reluctant, to being involved in additional activities. Alternatively, top managers may have perceived our project as threatening (Gendron & Bédard 2001), in that it could make visible some aspects of their audit committee that are inconsistent with social expectations held by regulators and shareholders. Indeed, one of the firms declined participation because it was a newly listed company, and its corporate governance practices were still "needing improvement". This apprehension may have been exacerbated by the fact that both of us are not known to companies as consultants or authors in business journals. No matter the nature of the reasons for rejection, the difficulties that we had in finding corporations willing to participate bluntly illustrate that the undertaking of qualitative research is constrained significantly by practitioners' powers to supply research data.

However, although 'mountains' often stand between qualitative researchers and field data (Sikka *et al.* 1995), there are likely to be some 'passes' to get to the latter (Gendron 2000: 190). No matter how difficult it may be to get access to the field, chances are that some organizations will eventually accept to provide data to qualitative researchers. However, accounting academics (and would-be academics) who consider conducting qualitative research should expect to devote considerable time and energies to find participating organizations. As a result of our efforts, three public corporations (out of the seventeen initially contacted) agreed to participate in our project.

Of course, given the high number of organizations that typically refuse to provide field data, qualitative research is subject to the criticism of representativeness. In the context of our field study, the question is whether audit committee procedures in the fourteen target corporations that did not participate are different than those of the three participating organizations. The way we use to address this criticism is to highlight it in the limitations of the study. Convenience sampling is a generally accepted qualitative procedure (Glaser & Strauss 1967), and as long as its limits are recognised in the paper, reviewers do not tend to be significantly concerned about it.

Over the years, our experience in conducting qualitative research also showed us that individuals tend to agree to participate more easily in research projects than organizations. For example, in two other research projects in which Yves is involved almost all contacted individuals agreed to participate.[2] It therefore seems that gate-keeping forces are considerably more active at the level of the organization than at that of the individual. Thus, depending on the study's unit of analysis, it may be to the advantage of qualitative researchers to contact potential interviewees directly, and to bypass organizational approval and screening procedures. This strategy may also prevent the qualitative researcher from being subjected to the representativeness criticism.

Obtaining Ethics Approval

Before starting fieldwork, we had to go through another layer of gatekeepers: our respective university's ethics committee. Both Laval and Alberta require researchers to submit to ethical scrutiny projects involving human subjects. As a matter of fact, researchers funded by SSHRC (and their institutions) have to follow the ethical principles stated in SSHRC's *Ethical Conduct for Research Involving Humans Policy* (SSHRC 2000). Both of our universities have established bureaucratized procedures to make sure that funded projects comply with these principles. A few months after the project was accepted by SSHRC, Jean received an e-mail from Laval's administration requesting that he completes a statement indicating whether the project involved human subjects. The grant's funds could not be used until Laval's *Comité d'éthique de la recherche* approved the project. To obtain the approval, we needed to submit a document that described the interview procedures as well as the informed consent form that both interviewer and interviewee would have to sign at the onset of the interview. The objective of this form is to ensure that the interviewee is "given the opportunity to give free and informed consent about participation" (SSHRC 2000). We developed the form (in French) by drawing on a form that Jean used in another study. In particular, the form specified the interviewee's right to stop the interview at any time, and that anonymity would be provided to her/him and to her/his organization. We finally received our certificate of compliance from Laval in June 2000.

By that time, the University of Alberta's School of Business had established a new ethics committee from which Yves also needed to secure approval. The new ethics committee is made up of eight members; five of them are employed at the School and three are external members — two of the latter being lawyers. Lawyers' involvement is

---

[2] The first project investigates accountants' attempt to establish their presence in the electronic-commerce domain through the WebTrust seal of assurance (Gendron & Barrett 2002). The second project examines the points of view of Chartered Accountants on the notion of professional commitment.

indicative of the mindset upon which projects are assessed (for example, the consent form is conceived of as a legal "contract" between the researcher and the interviewee), and of potential consequences for researchers for not obtaining the committee's approval before carrying out empirical studies with human subjects. For example, one member of the committee told Yves that the School intends to support researchers in the event that they are prosecuted in relation to research activities only when the ethics committee initially approved these activities.

To meet Alberta's requirements, we translated the French consent form and modified it by drawing especially from the exhaustive form used by Martel (1999) in her prison study with human subjects. In particular, we added to the French form that interviewees have the right to refuse the interview being taped, and that they would have the opportunity to verify the accuracy of the transcript and add changes that they felt might be needed to make them comfortable with what they said during the interview. We have reproduced the form in the appendix — so that interested readers could easily refer to it.

Meeting the requirements of ethics committees therefore requires time and is often difficult. Indeed, one member of the committee at the University of Alberta stressed that it is often more difficult to convince the School's new committee that a project is ethically appropriate than it is to persuade the editor of an academic journal to publish a paper.

Conducting and Analysing Interviews

Interviews often constitute a very effective means of collecting data when the qualitative researcher seeks to better understand organizational and group processes (Patton 1990). Generally speaking, three sources of data may be used in qualitative research, namely, observation, documentation and interviews. With regard to our audit committee project, we rejected direct observation since we thought that it would be almost impossible to secure permission to attend audit committee meetings of public companies. We also thought that exclusive reliance on official documentation (for example, audit committee charter, minutes of audit committee meetings) would provide a very incomplete picture of audit committee activities since processes officially described in writing are typically much different than processes in action (Mintzberg 1979). Consequently, to carry out our investigation, we relied mainly on interviews — which were conducted by either one of us.[3]

Prior to fieldwork, we developed a semi-structured interview instrument that specified certain themes to discuss while being flexible enough to explore emerging paths during the interview. The instrument was designed based on our research questions, previous research, as well as our own experiences and intuitions. Each of us had the latitude to ask the questions in our own words and to sequence them differently, and to ask probes and follow-up questions when necessary. After a long discussion, we also decided that

---

[3] Readers interested in learning more about the qualitative procedures that we followed to collect and analyse data in our research on audit committees may refer to Gendron & Bédard (2002).

it would be preferable to tape the interviews and to have full transcripts, in spite of the risk that the tape-recorder might prevent interviewees from disclosing some data.[4] Although no interviewee objected to the presence of the tape-recorder, in a few instances they manifested reluctance to provide information. For example, in one instance an audit committee member refused to provide detailed information about a specific difficult situation described earlier by another willing interviewee. The member merely indicated that the situation was an accounting problem. To get a more detailed answer, Jean underlined that another committee member had already discussed the situation with him — to no avail. The interviewee just acknowledged that such situations were normal. Jean then asked the interviewee whether s/he would be willing to answer specific questions about the situation. The member refused and indicated that we should ask these questions to the committee chairperson, which we had done previously. Jean gave up and moved to another topic.

During the first few minutes of each interview, we sought to reduce the risk of response bias and make the interviewee more willing to freely answer to questions — which was critical in the context of our research due to the sensitive nature of some of the themes under study. The importance of being trustworthy in the eyes of interviewees should not be downplayed since the validity of the data depends on it. Accordingly, at the beginning of each interview, we first sought to establish a good relationship with the interviewee by discussing a matter unrelated to the research. Then, after having thanked the interviewee for participating to the study, we introduced the informed consent form, which we presented as a university requirement aimed at ensuring the researchers' ethical behaviour *vis-à-vis* interviewees. We especially used the form to describe the broad objective of the research, to ask for permission to tape the interview, to specify the interviewee's right to refuse to answer any question, and to describe the procedures to ensure anonymity. We also emphasised that the participant would have the opportunity to verify subsequently the accuracy of the interview transcript and add changes s/he feels might be needed to make her/him comfortable with what s/he said during the interview. The participant was then asked to sign the form. Interviewees (who consisted of board directors, high-ranking auditors and top managers) did not manifest any concern when signing the form, nor asked any question — perhaps as a result of the trustworthiness emerging from our comprehensive and official ethical procedures.

Using our semi-structured instrument, we then went through the main part of the interview. We made sure that the first questions asked to the interviewee were not related to potentially sensitive issues — again in order to make the interviewee more comfortable at providing information. It is worth emphasising that questioning is very demanding to the qualitative researcher. S/he needs to simultaneously listen to the interviewee's answer, be attentive to the interviewee's non-verbal cues, encourage her/him to provide information (such as nodding from time to time when the interviewee is talking), think about the next question to ask, and take field notes. The notes that we took generally consisted of what we perceived as significant information provided by the interviewee as well as reminders of follow-up questions to ask later during the

---

[4] Rubin & Rubin (1995: 125–128) provide a useful discussion of the factors to consider in deciding how to keep a record of the interview.

interview. These notes were useful to slow down the interviewee, check the extent to which her/his response made sense, and, in one case, recollect the interviewee's answers due to a tape-recording failure.

It is worth noting that it generally took us only a few questions to have a good idea of the extent to which the interview would produce relevant data. For example, the interim CEO recently appointed at the head of one of the participant corporations mentioned that s/he did not always attend audit committee meetings. However, even in such a case, we nonetheless asked questions to the CEO because we thought that the impression that we would make on her/him could be important in securing other interviews in the corporation. Being diplomatic is another skill that is often useful to the qualitative researcher.

We also systematically made sure to end the recorded part of the interview with a broad question, asking whether we omitted to discuss anything important in relation to the corporation's audit committee. This question allowed several interviewees to summarise their previous answers, and to disclose a few additional pieces of information. We also needed to remain fully concentrated when the tape recorder was turned off because oftentimes the interviewee continued to provide information — which we rapidly took into note once we were outside of the corporation's premises. Finally, before leaving the interviewee's office we mentioned that we might contact her/him later to clarify some answers, and thanked her/him for the information provided. Leaving a favourable impression was important since we did not want to compromise the subsequent interviews that were scheduled in the interviewee's participating corporation. Also, after each interview, we modified our semi-structured instrument in accordance with our perception of the 'effectiveness' of the questions, and noted any idea that emerged and that might later be useful in making sense of the data.

It is worth emphasising that being tolerant of uncertainty is part of the fundamental skills of the qualitative researcher. S/he needs especially to tolerate the uncertainty and frustration of not controlling the data collection process. For example, in spite of important efforts to schedule and coordinate interviews with actors involved with the participating organizations' audit committee, problems occurred when collecting data. One scheduled meeting was cancelled less than 24 hours before the appointed time and had to be rescheduled. As well, Jean went out of town to conduct an interview to find out that there was an error in the interviewee's agenda — the interview being planned for the subsequent week. As a result, Jean had to travel again the following week. Finally, we noticed a few hours after another interview that our tape-recorder failed to tape the entire discussion. We needed to rely on the notes taken during the interview to write a detailed recollection of the interview.

Once the interviews were transcribed, one of us validated the transcripts, being especially attentive to acronyms since transcribers tend not to write them correctly. We then sent the corresponding transcript to each participant, asking her/him to verify its accuracy and allowing her/him to modify it so that s/he would be comfortable with what s/he had said during the interview. Though it can be argued that providing each interviewee with the possibility of changing her/his transcript may alter significantly the data, less than half of the interviewees sent us a modified transcript, and the modifications to a large extent did not alter in any significant way what was originally said during the interview. As a matter of fact, most modifications consisted of grammar improvements or complements of information on the matters originally discussed during the interview. One interviewee whose original transcript was basically useless because of excessive rambling even provided us with a fully modified and understandable document.

Though some analysis took place during fieldwork, most of the analytical procedures occurred subsequently. To analyse the data, we coded the transcripts using a coding scheme that we developed while reading interviews to enhance data sensitivity. Afterwards, for each corporation, a conceptual matrix was prepared to summarise the main themes discussed by the interviewees. To ensure the validity of the interviews, we especially made sure that interviewees' answers within the same corporation were converging, that it to say that they were 'triangulating' (Yin 1989). We then had a discussion in which we evaluated the main findings.

Our specific research question emerged when we analysed the transcripts. Our fieldwork indicated that in each participating organization effectiveness of the organization's audit committee appeared to be a strongly held perception among interviewees. In contrast, prior field research on audit committees has brought to light auditors' and managers' concerns about the lack of effectiveness of many audit committees (for example, Spira 1999). We therefore thought that we were uniquely positioned to make a significant contribution to the literature. Given the generally held perceptions of audit committee effectiveness in our participating organizations, we decided that our research question would be: how is the perception that a given corporation's audit committee is effective socially constructed?

As readers can see, collecting and analysing interview data is not only labour intensive but also requires a high level of domain and research knowledge and abilities. Contrary to quantitative research where a good research assistant can collect data and carry out statistical analysis, with regard to qualitative research the researcher needs to be intensely involved in data collection and analysis. Furthermore, the specific objective of the study is not always determined *a priori*, but often 'emerges' from fieldwork.

The richness of the data that one finds when going in the field, and the excitement in trying to make sense of the data, however, largely compensate for these "costs". For example, when analysing our data on audit committees, we found that private meetings held at the end of each regular audit committee meeting with auditors without management being present are considerably more than ceremonial rituals aimed at signalling that the audit committee follows practices congruent with social expectations (Gendron & Bédard 2002). During these private meetings, audit committee members indeed regularly question both external and internal auditors on whether difficult issues came up during the course of their audits, and whether they had unrestricted access to information. The stakes for the auditors during private meetings are considerably high, as indicated in the following interview excerpt:

> "With the external auditor, we sit them down and look them in the eye, and say is there anything that is going on that you want to tell us about that you wouldn't say in front of anybody else. And are you getting the cooperation, are you getting everything you need? [. . .] So unless they

want to lie to us, which they can do, but if they are going to lie once they are going to lie six times a year, because we are going to ask them every time. And eventually if we find out [that they lied], of course they are gone" (Audit committee member).

These findings led us to argue that private meetings may be conceived of as confessional settings — in which auditors submit claims of truthfulness to referees —, and that the powers inherent to this avowal process are likely to be significant. As maintained by Foucault (1988), the auditor then becomes tied to the intentions and thoughts avowed in the confession, thereby inciting her/him to change her/his attitudes and behaviours, with the guidance provided by the categories and languages used by the audit committee members (Covaleski *et al.* 1998: 298). It is very unlikely that a quantitative researcher would have been able to develop such conclusions without getting immersed in field data.

Finally, we would like to underline that the difficulties that we have had over the years in finding interviewees in a number of our research projects have been paradoxically beneficial to us. That is, we came to be extremely respectful of individuals who take some of their time to share their thoughts on matters in which they have been involved over several years or decades. We believe that this attitude helps us in our ongoing research projects in establishing trust relationships with interviewees — thereby allowing them to answer questions more freely, and to discuss topics and issues not covered in interviewing grids.

Writing Qualitative Papers

Writing the first draft of a qualitative paper is challenging. As argued by Yin (1989), in contrast with quantitative research where most researchers tend to write papers by relying on the same compositional structure, there is no generally recognised structure for qualitative papers — and probably never will be due to the holistic nature of qualitative research. Writing the first draft of a qualitative paper therefore is very dependent on the specific nature of the investigation and the compositional style of the researcher.[5]

The way we wrote the preliminary draft of the first paper derived from our research on audit committees (Gendron & Bédard 2002) illustrates the challenge inherent in putting into words the process and outcomes of a qualitative inquiry. Once all the interview data were coded and summarized in conceptual matrices, Yves took a few minutes daily for a few weeks to think about a potential compositional structure — which he outlined on pieces of paper. He began to write the paper once he became sufficiently comfortable with the structure. Of course, throughout writing, Yves continuously went back and forth between his computer screen, the structure outline, conceptual matrices and coded transcripts; analysis therefore extended to the writing

---

[5] Of course, we have target journals in mind when writing qualitative papers. The selection of our targets is not unconstrained, though. Our choice is influenced to a large extent by the North American academic institutional context described above.

process. In particular, Yves was attentive during the interrelated process of analysis and writing to integrate in the paper interview quotes that are representative of the main findings while being likely to arouse the interest of potential readers. Although time consuming, writing the preliminary draft of a qualitative paper is a rewarding experience, in the sense that it challenges our intellectual capacities.

Conclusion

Qualitative research often is the most effective method to conduct empirical investigations aimed at better understanding phenomena occurring in their natural context. This chapter aimed to provide readers with an understanding of the numerous 'behind-the-scene' activities that take place in conducting qualitative research projects. We especially underlined some of the constraints to the undertaking of qualitative research and showed how these constraints may be addressed.

As we illustrated in the context of our audit committee research project, one of the constraints that hinders significantly the undertaking of qualitative research consists of the difficulties of finding participating organizations. Participation proposals indeed are subject to the scrutiny of organizational gatekeepers. One of the most probable consequences of this scrutiny is self-selection of participating organizations, in the sense that organizations are less likely to participate when gatekeepers view their organization's processes as ineffective or not in accordance with widely accepted cultural values. Society may be negatively affected by this self-selection — in that it is harder to improve regulation and other large-scale control mechanisms when knowledge is scant about ineffective processes. We argue that qualitative researchers in accounting should not remain passive in the face of organizational gatekeeping. For example, academics could write papers aimed at shedding light on the ways in which organizations police the development of knowledge (for example, Gendron 2000). Such publications should not be limited to academic journals — business press should also be targeted. Accounting academics could also do a better job at making business students aware of the significance of research, in the hope that when students will occupy positions of power in organizations they will be more inclined to sustain research projects.

Finally, we also hope that this chapter will arouse the interest of accounting academics and Ph.D. students in North America towards qualitative research. Most accounting academics in North America are not exposed in any significant way during their graduate studies to qualitative research. Normal science (Kuhn 1970) is assumed to be quantitative and predicated on theoretical frameworks derived from economics or, to some extent, from psychology. Typically, qualitative research is discussed briefly during methodology courses, or totally ignored. However, given the methodological strengths of qualitative research in investigating real-world phenomena, we suggest that North American accounting academics and graduate students broaden their horizons to qualitative research in order to avoid being trapped in unequivocal views of the world in which only quantitative data are seen as legitimate. This can be done in a variety of ways — for example by following a qualitative methodology course or by discussing informally with qualitative researchers. The 'real life' of qualitative researchers in North America would be improved if the research environment were more supportive of field research.

References

Bédard, J., & Dodds, C. (1994). The university accounting professoriate in Canada. *Contemporary Accounting Research*, Special educational research issue, 75–109.

Bédard, J., & Marrakchi Chtourou, S. (1998). Gouverne d'entreprise et fiabilité des informations financières: une évaluation. *Gestion, 23*(3), 30–36.

Bédard, J., Marrakchi Chtourou, S., & Courteau, L. (forthcoming). The effect of audit committee expertise, independence, and activity on aggressive earnings. *Auditing: A Journal of Practice & Theory*.

Blue Ribbon Committee on Improving the Effectiveness of Corporate Audit Committees (BRC report) (1999). *Report and recommendations of the Blue Ribbon Committee on improving the effectiveness of corporate audit committee*. New York: New York Stock Exchange/National Association of Securities Dealers.

Bron, A., & Gaulejac de, V. (1995). *La gourmandise du tapir*. Paris: Desclée De Brouwer.

Cadbury Committee (1992). *Report of the committee on the financial aspects of corporate governance*. London: Gee.

Covaleski, M. A., Dirsmith, M. W., Heian, J. B., & Samuel S. (1998). The calculated and the avowed: techniques of discipline and struggles over identity in Big Six public accounting firms. *Administrative Science Quarterly, 43*(2), 298–327.

Dey Report (1994). *Where were the directors? Guidelines for improved corporate governance in Canada*. Report of the Toronto Stock Exchange Committee on Corporate Governance in Canada.

Foucault, M. (1988). Technologies of the self. In: L. Martin, H. Gutman, & P. Hutton (Eds), *A Seminar with Michel Foucault* (pp. 16–49). Amherst: University of Massachusetts Press.

Gendron, Y. (2000). Openness to context-based research: the gulf between the claims and actions of Big Six firms in the USA. *Accounting, Auditing & Accountability Journal, 13*(2), 175–196.

Gendron, Y. (2001). The difficult client-acceptance decision in Canadian audit firms: a field investigation. *Contemporary Accounting Research, 18*(2), 283–310.

Gendron, Y., & Baker, C. R. (2001). Par-delà les frontières disciplinaires et linguistiques: l'influence des penseurs français sur la recherche en comptabilité. *Comptabilité — Contrôle — Audit, 7*(2), 5–23.

Gendron, Y., & Barrett, M. (2002). Professionalization in action: accountants' attempt at building a network of support for the WebTrust E-Commerce seal of assurance. Working paper, University of Alberta.

Gendron, Y., & Bédard, J. (2001). Academic auditing research: an exploratory investigation into its usefulness. *Critical Perspectives on Accounting, 12*(3), 339–368.

Gendron, Y., & Bédard, J. (2002). The construction of audit committee effectiveness within public corporations: a perceptual analysis. Working paper, University of Alberta.

Glaser, B. G., & Strauss, A. L. (1967). *The discovery of grounded theory*. Hawthorne, New York: Aldine de Gruyter.

Kalbers, L. P., & Fogarty, T. J. (1993). Audit committee effectiveness: an empirical investigation of the contribution of power. *Auditing: A Journal of Practice & Theory, 12*(1), 24–50.

Kuhn, T. S. (1970). *The structure of scientific revolutions*. Chicago: The University of Chicago Press.

Latour, B. (1987). *Science in action*. Cambridge, Massachusetts: Harvard University Press.

Martel, J. (1999). *Solitude in cold storage: Women's journeys of endurance in segregation*. Edmonton, Alberta: ACI Communication.

Mintzberg, H. (1979). *The structuring of organization*. Englewood Cliffs, New Jersey: Prentice-Hall.

Patton, M. Q. (1990). *Qualitative evaluation and research methods* (2nd ed.). Newbury Park, California: Sage Publications.

Rubin, J., & Rubin, I. S. (1995). *Qualitative interviewing: The art of hearing data*. Thousand Oaks: Sage Publications.

Sikka, P., Willmott, H., & Puxty, T. (1995). The mountains are still there: accounting academics and the bearings of intellectuals. *Accounting, Auditing & Accountability Journal, 8*(3), 113–140.

Spira, L. F. (1999). Ceremonies of governance: perspectives on the role of the audit committee. *Journal of Management and Governance, 3*(3), 231–260.

Social Sciences and Humanities Research Council of Canada (SSHRC) (2000). Tri-council policy statement: ethical conduct for research involving humans. Policy disclosed on the following web site: http://www.nserc.ca/programs/ethics/english/policy.htm.

Yin, R. K. (1989). *Case study research: Design and methods* (Rev. ed). Newbury Park, California: Sage Publications.

Appendix

INFORMED CONSENT FORM

I the undersigned, ..., certify that I freely participate to the research project "The Role of Audit Committees in the Governance of Canadian Public Corporations". The nature of the research project is as follows:

(1) The project aims to better understand the role played by audit committees in Canadian public corporations.
(2) Data will be gathered through interviews from members of audit committees, managers of public corporations, and internal/external auditors. Each interview is expected to last between 60 and 90 minutes. With the interviewee's consent, we would like to tape the interview.
(3) Each interview will focus on the following themes:

- Background information on the interviewee, such as the length of time for which s/he has been member of the audit committee, the process by which s/he has been recruited, and her/his expertise and experience in the financial domain.

- Information on the tasks performed by the audit committee, such as the nature of the information provided to audit committee members, the average duration of the audit committee meetings, and the interviewee's perception of the role and effectiveness of the corporation's audit committee.

(4) The interviewee has the right to refuse to answer any question, and may stop the interview at any time, without having to provide any justification.
(5) There will be no risks to the participants of the study. Anonymity will be provided to protect participants.
(6) The following steps will be taken with regard to anonymity and confidentiality of information:

- In papers the identity of the corporation / audit firm / interviewee will be kept anonymous. An alphabetical code will be used to refer to specific corporations / audit firms / interviewees. As well, evidence that could be used by a reader to identify the corporation / audit firm will be avoided (e.g. sentences like "the corporation is the biggest in Canada").

- No other member of the corporation / audit firm will have access to the information disclosed during the interview.

- Only the active members of the research team will have access to the tapes/ transcripts of the interview.

- Once the interview is transcribed, and if the interviewee requests it, we will send her/him a copy of the transcript. The interviewee will then verify the accuracy of the transcript and have the opportunity to add changes s/he feels might be needed to make her/him comfortable with what s/he said during the interview. Each interviewee will be given six weeks to communicate to the researchers any concern or modification. Once the six-week period is over, the researchers will assume that the interviewee agrees with the transcript.

- When a draft of a research paper is produced, and if the interviewee requests it, we will send her/him a copy of the research paper. The interviewee will then review the document.

- The original tapes will be destroyed one year after the interview.

- The final anonymous transcripts will be kept in a locked file for twenty years after the project is completed.

(7) Research papers / presentations / teaching materials will be written from the data gathered, and eventually published in academic and/or practitioner journals.
(8) A summary of the research will be sent to participants who ask for it.
(9) The research project is under the responsibility of Dr. Jean Bédard (Université Laval), to whom any complaint can be addressed. Complaints can also be addressed to Dr. Yves Gendron (University of Alberta), and to the Research Ethics Board of the School of Business, University of Alberta.

Read and approved on ....
                                                              Participant's signature
                                                              ....
                                                              Researcher's signature

Chapter 13

Critical Independence

Brendan McSweeney

Introduction

Scholarship requires of its practitioners a vital minimum of independence: the capacity to achieve some distance from ones prejudices; the ability to enter into and engage with rival views; the integrity to discard interpretations that do not pass tests of evidence; and an unwillingness to be pressurised into reaching hasty or partisan results. The independence of organizational research faces challenges from self and others.

Self: there are two such threats. One is excessive *a priorism*. Acceptance that there can be no atheoretical basis for analysing an organization — no 'view from nowhere' — does not negate our responsibility to seek to understand the specifics of the organization being researched and to seek to question and test our findings. Merely imposing what is presupposed is cognitive over-dependence, not independence. Sufficiently situated and adequately validated analysis cannot be produced by a 'subsuming' approach (McSweeney 1995) — by a universal, acontingent, explanation drawn from some grand social theory, the pronouncements of a management 'guru', a normative textbook, or wherever. Invariably the empirical data 'found' through such analysis serves only to legitimate the researcher's pre-existing 'knowledge'.

The second potential threat to independence from self is to suppose that there is just one valid rationality — usually profit maximization or shareholder value. Such an approach overly warps the analytical framework. It encourages researchers to avoid, ignore, or define as irrational or misguided the alternative views, values, and influence of many vital to, and knowledgeable about, richness and diversity within organizations.

Others: even when advice is not formally part of the research design, organizational actors — or research sponsors — may seek to shape the process. Researchers may be selectively informed, steered away from particular information, discouraged from obtaining the views of certain groups within an organization, asked to make specific recommendations, reveal information or report views acquired elsewhere within the

The Real Life Guide to Accounting Research: A Behind-the-Scenes View of Using Qualitative Research Methods
© 2004 Published by Elsevier Ltd.
ISBN: 0-08-043972-1

organization. If the researcher succumbs to these pressures, critical independence is jeopardised. This is a challenge for all research in organizations, whether or not it seeks to be action-orientated[1]

The responsibility of academics undertaking organizational analysis is to do so in a manner that is not institutionally, or cognitively, over-dependent. If we fail in this respect, we are nothing more than poorly paid consultants. I define independence of research in organizations as the willingness and ability to analyze in the round and to 'ongoingly test' ones 'findings'. 'In the round' analysis requires the researcher to take reasonable steps to take into account views and circumstances of all significant parties who fall within the ambit of the research. 'Ongoingly test' imposes a duty on the researcher to seek to discern where possible the specifics of the area of investigation and routinely check, and interrogate his/her views and conclusions. The independent research attitude is not to seek to confirm, but rather to continuously ask: 'How can I be sure?' 'Is there counter-evidence?'. If research is to be genuinely academic, the researcher must always proceed with doubt. Neither 'in the round' nor 'ongoingly test' is fully achievable, but failure to strive for these objectives leads to excessive partiality and *a priorism* (McSweeney 2002).

In this chapter, I consider some challenges to the achievement of independent research through a discussion of how I sought to interpret, apply, and protect my independence during one of my field studies and throughout the analysis of that work (McSweeney 1995).

Getting Involved

My involvement in the field, in Waterford Crystal Ltd. (WCL)[2] — a leading Irish based manufacturing firm — did not start as academic research. The main trade union (the Union) at the company asked me to be their honorary advisor about their members' newly acquired shares in the company. All employees had been given such shares as part of an unprecedented three-year pay and conditions agreement and anticipated being offered more in future negotiations. The role of an advisor would be, the Union said, in effect to be an 'interpreter': to answer questions about 'jargon and so forth'.

The Union were suspicious of all information provided to them by the company's management seeing it as either constructed to 'fool them' or unwittingly failing to

---

[1] For discussion of varieties of action-orientated research: 'action research'; 'action inquiry'; 'action science'; 'interventionist research'; and so forth, see special issues of *Human Relations* (Vol. 46, No. 1 1993); *Journal of Applied Behavioral Science* (Vol. 32), and *Management Learning* (Vol. 30, No. 2 1999). See also McSweeney (2000).

[2] WCL produced 'handmade' (hand-drawn, mouth-blown, hand-cut) full-lead crystal glass items — such as stemware. It was ranked in the top 20 of Irish based companies in terms of turnover and in the top 10 for employment. Although most of its costs were in Irish púnts, more than 80% of its sales of were U.S. dollar based. Production was undertaken exclusively in, or near, the City of Waterford in Ireland. There were about 3,000 employees, but production had many characteristics of a craft industry with lengthy training and sharp work/skill demarcations. Average wages were significantly higher than average industrial earnings. The great majority of employees were members of the Union. (The past tense is used here is to describe company characteristics at the time of the fieldwork. WCL still exists.)

appreciate the 'full-story'. The Union wanted my advice not only for my assumed expertise but also because they regarded me as someone 'sympathetic to the trade union movement', that is, someone who considered their interests to be legitimate and who was willing to demystify or challenge 'whatever management claimed'.

Their belief in my trustworthiness was primarily based on an analysis I had undertaken for the Union at the same company some years previously. At that time management at the company had claimed 'inability to pay' a wage increase which had been nationally agreed between employee and employer representatives and government. In the event of such a claim, the National Wage Agreement (the Agreement) allowed the appointment of an 'independent assessor'. I was then an official of the Irish Congress of Trade Unions (ICTU).[3] Although its General Secretary wanted the Union to appoint as the assessor a 'consultant' from a tripartite organization, of which he was a non-executive director — the Irish Productivity Committee — the Union representatives at WCL insisted on my appointment. A number of shop stewards from the company had earlier attended a course on financial analysis I had run on behalf of the ICTU. Although hostile to such local choices, the General Secretary was unable to overrule their decision as the Agreement had given the power of appointment to workplace union members. The national union's full-time official in Waterford (the city), supported by the General Secretary, privately urged me to approve Management's claim on the grounds that the employees were 'already very well paid'. This I refused to do insisting on my role as an independent assessor of WCL's financial position.

It was not difficult for me to demonstrate that Management's calculations were bogus. Forecasted revenue was from sales of crystal only, whilst the expenses included many costs from the wider multi-industry group unrelated to the crystal business. The employees got their pay increase and yet the following year, the company reported record profits. Over time, recollections of my achievement grew ever more heroic: "I believe you stuffed the annual report down the managing director's throat" (the Convenor).[4]

I anticipated that my renewed contact with the Union at WCL would make minimal demands on my time, as on this occasion I was to undertake a much less challenging role. I was also attracted by the prospects of renewing contact with an active trade union. I hoped that engaging with Union representatives and members would be a part antidote to various biases I was unhappy with at Warwick Business School (WBS) where I had obtained my first academic appointment. The Conservative Party had formed its third consecutive government since 1979 and hostility to critical views had intensified. This 'climate', reinforced by the School's growing dependence on fee-paying MBA students uninterested in public policy issues and perspectives other than that of shareholders and top management, was beginning to generate intellectual self-censorship within WBS. Maximization of shareholders' benefits ('returns'; 'value' — Rappaport 1986) was increasingly being nationally institutionalized as the uncontestable stated aim of business and within WBS overt commitment to that orientation was becoming, despite the unease of many faculty members, the dominant teaching evaluation criterion. In

---

[3] Similar to the British Trades Union Congress or the U.S. ALF-CIO.
[4] The 'Convenor' was the senior shop steward and chaired all Union meetings at WCL.

contrast, government policy in Ireland was not driven by New Right nostrums, tri-partite bodies flourished, and trade union rights had not been weakened.[5] I therefore agreed to the Union representative's request. In performing the role of 'interpreter' I anticipated only a limited demand on my time as I thought that I could readily draw on standard accounting/finance knowledge in answering their questions.

Over the following few months I only had to respond to a few telephone calls and letters from the Union and I had just one meeting with their representatives. My advisory role did not directly contribute to my academic research and there were no challenges to my independence. But then the relationship with the Union changed.

Into the Conflict

After many years of unbroken improvements in employees' pay and conditions, Management[6] now claimed that: "severely worsening financial circumstances and prospects urgently require the immediate introduction of extensive work practice changes". Unlike in most companies, Union approval of such changes was required. That power was as a consequence of being a monopoly supplier of an essential and non-substitutable asset. Both Management and the Union believed[7] that for purchasers it was essential that the crystal items were: (i) handmade; and (ii) made in Ireland. This precluded: (a) substitution of technology for labour; (b) transferring any production outside of Ireland; and (c) introduction of cheaper labour — as the skills of blowing and cutting skills took years to acquire and substitute labour with such skills was unobtainable in any significant numbers from elsewhere in Ireland.

In the past the Union had only agreed piecemeal changes and negotiated improvements in pay and/or conditions for each agreed change. From the perspective of almost every accounting and management textbook the Union's refusal to accept corporate profit maximization as the determining action criterion was irrational. But their insistence on occasional and 'compensated' changes had been perfectly rational as they had been confident that this policy would not jeopardize the company's prospects and thereby not their own: "[i]t's like having a bank account. Every now and then we decide to take money out of it" (Convenor). But now Management had challenged the assumption that there was no conflict between refusal to approve major work practice changes and the continuity of the firm. They were claiming that without large-scale uncompensated changes there would be severe adverse consequences for everyone. The Union did not accept or reject Management's claim — but they took it seriously — and so they wanted someone they trusted to assess it. This they asked me to do.

---

[5] And per capita income was rising much more rapidly than in the U.K.

[6] 'Management' refers to the top management in the company. The leading Management representatives were the Assistant General Manager (who was also an accountant, General Manager — Operations, and a member of the board of Waterford Glass Group plc, the holding company) and the General Manager-Personnel.

[7] Quite some time after the research period of this paper, WCL discovered that its key U.S. customers did not associate the brand 'Waterford' with the place Waterford. Outsourced products now account for about 40% of WCL's sales revenue by value.

The Union's new request came when I was trying to establish myself as an academic and under pressure to complete a demanding doctorate at the LSE. Furthermore during my previous intense involvement with the company the General Secretary of the ICTU, displeased that I had rejected Management's claims, had made conditions at work intolerable for me. In effect I was 'constructively dismissed'. My commitment to independent research had been costly. I momentarily wondered whether analysis of yet more gloomy claims from WCL's management would destroy another one of my careers. However, having earlier agreed to act as the Union's advisor, I felt obliged to assist them.

Insisting on Independence

The relationship between Management and the Union at WCL, as in most companies, was not based on extensive data analysis. Changes were agreed, or not, through power-based negotiations as was the amount of 'compensation' paid to employees for any implemented changes. Financial estimates of the possible effects of changes were neither sought by the Union nor disclosed by Management. Neither party therefore had any experience of jointly discussing accounting data. I anticipated that unless I took pre-emptive action, the discussions about the firm's prospects would take the form of negotiations and that each side would rapidly try to get me to side with them. I did not, nor do I, object to assisting one side in a dispute, if I am sympathetic to their aims. But 'answers' not based on adequate analysis are not independent and may indeed be counterproductive for the party one wishes to assist.

My determination not to reach, or be pressurized into reaching, narrow or hurried conclusions was strongly shaped by my experience as a trade union advisor in the U.K. Since arriving in the U.K., I had, for some years, undertaken analysis of accounting data to assist numerous trade unions in their responses to management claims of corporate financial crisis. But I had become very dissatisfied with the restrictions on that analysis and, as a consequence, had ceased to do it. None of the trade union officials who had sought my assistance seemed interested in deeper analysis which might suggest longer-term remedial actions. They merely sought quick arguments from me that would allow them to claim that profits were understated or losses overstated. It was often quite easy to challenge the accuracy/adequacy of the financial statements presented to the unions — usually by questioning the accounting policy choices. But such analysis cannot, of itself, determine whether or not a company is likely to fail nor generate remedies, if required. The predictive capability of analysis of the mere accounting numbers is also very limited, notwithstanding the exaggerated claims in many textbooks on financial analysis and capital budgeting (McSweeney 2002; Bower 1972). Richer data cannot eliminate uncertainty, but it may improve predictions (Makridakis 1990; McCloskey 1988).

Whether the management of the individual companies would have been willing to engage with the trade unions on discussions of strategies and prospects is another matter. Certainly the notion that the relationship between trade unions and management was a zero-sum was widespread in both management and trade union circles. During that period I had also attended many meetings of the Accounting Standards Committee (now Accounting Standards Board) where I had observed some of its members — purportedly independent — single-mindedly and unashamedly advocate changes in ASC standards solely in the interests of shareholders — sometimes to the clear detriment of employees.

Had the Union at WCL merely wanted me to provide them with negotiation ammunition rather than undertake an independent analysis I would not have continued. The future was too open and my knowledge of the specifics of WCL was dated. Without completing such an analysis I could not reasonably say, nor could the Union, whether or not the changes sought by Management were required to ensure the continuation of WCL. Were any, changes necessary to ensure the company's survival or would agreed changes just boost profits? I did not know, the Union did not know, indeed Management, despite its claims, quite possibly did not know. However, in contrast with negotiation contexts into which I had previously been drawn by trade unions in the U.K., the Union wanted to base their discussions and ultimately their negotiations with Management on an assessment of the company's prospects. They had suspended their usual assumption that their actions would not endanger the company's future — in the sense of continuity. Their willingness to seek such an analysis was reinforced by their long-term perspective on the company: "many of their [union members] fathers worked here and every man expects to get a job here for at least one or more of his sons".

Nonetheless, I still set out in writing the terms on which I was prepared to undertake the analysis. The key conditions were that: (i) I would be an assessor, not an advocate; and (ii) all information or reports I requested would be provided to me. Despite initial objections by the Union, it was agreed that Management could debar Union access to some information provided to me. The revised terms were signed by all.

Although I had been 'invited in' by the Union, Management also regarded me as capable and impartial. At my first joint meeting with the Union and Management, the leader of the Management side — the Assistant General Manager — who was also an accountant — recalled reading a number of my articles in *Accountancy Age* that, prior to becoming an academic, I had prolifically produced. He also mentioned my earlier involvement and praised the 'meticulous' way I had unpacked Management's financial assertions, and claimed that he — then a more junior manager — had disagreed with senior management's declarations about WCL's financial position and prospects. Of course, these comments may have merely been intended to flatter me, to generate a more trusting attitude to Management's claims. But as Management knew of my prior trade union involvement, they would not have agreed to give me unlimited access to information — including 'price sensitive' information — had they believed that I would be overly partisan in my approach.

Effects of Formal Arrangements

I insisted that, Union representatives should also attend every meeting I had with Management. The explicit purposes for their participation were to enable them: (a) to comment on Management's statements — drawing on their shop-floor knowledge; and (b) to be able to up-date the Union members with the progress of my investigations.

The formal tripartite process allowed me to emphasise explicitness and clarity. After each round of my analysis I sent Management a list of additional information I required and insisted that the answers be provided in writing. Previously I had found that obtaining quantitative data aurally from a company's management was very unsatisfactory — it was difficult to accurately record the information and it encouraged the presenter to be evasive and polemical. The procedures adopted at WCL were also usually an efficient way of getting information. Notice of each tripartite meeting set a deadline for Management to provide the information I had requested.

An unintended effect of this arrangement was to reinforce my independence from Management as they could not offer me some inducements or otherwise try to pressurize me into favouring their arguments — even had they wished to do so. In contrast with someone hired by Management I was able to include the interests of WCL employees into my analysis, for example, I could ask detailed questions about possible consequences for employees and not be obliged to treat increased profits as a self-evident good. As I was not being paid (save reimbursement of expenses), I was not financially dependent on either party.

However, ironically the formal arrangements for information disclosure and discussion also weakened my independence in the sense of reducing my ability to obtain potentially significant information. Although I had extensive access to written data — both prepared by and for Management — I could not access informal, tacit, undocumented, information which Management might have, indeed I believe would have, been willing to reveal.

Pressure to Leak Information

As I came to the meetings accompanied by Union representatives, I felt it necessary each time to 'signal' to both parties in various ways — where I sat, what I said, and so forth — that the meetings were investigatory not negotiatory. However, on some occasions I met the Union representatives alone. As the Union had invited me 'in', they felt obliged to act as my hosts/minders — meeting me at the airport, escorting me to lunch, and so forth. This lead to some challenges to my independence.

As I had been guaranteed unrestricted access to information, some of the data I requested and was given was deemed by Management to be "[share] price sensitive" and so I was prohibited from giving it to the Union. I informed the Union of the *type* of information which I was debarred from disclosing to them, but I did not give them the information itself. Unrestricted data was handed to me at the tripartite meetings; restricted information was usually posted or faxed to me. Management's desire to disclose some documents only to me was heightened further when, during the study period, the 'plc' (Waterford Glass Group) was seeking to acquire Wedgwood plc. and to raise $40 million through a share issue in the USA.

On a few occasions the senior Union representatives mentioned that they would like to 'have a quick look at' the 'confidential' data, but did not press the point. Later, however, they asked for a copy of one of the restricted documents — a very detailed capital expenditure report and budget — as it contained a lot of very specific information and costings about proposed work practice changes the Union believed would that it would help them plan their bargaining.

Based in part on my own prior experience as a trade union negotiator, I had no doubt about the tactical advantage the report would give the Union. Furthermore, I was sceptical about Management's claims of the price sensitivity of that document as the reason for withholding it from the Union. Management had already given the Union information which I considered to be much more price sensitive — such as three year forecast profit and loss accounts. There was also a danger that if I refused to give the document to the Union representatives they would interpret my action as mistrust of them and as evidence of less impartiality than they had hitherto believed.

The timing of release of the capital expenditure budget to me was also problematic. I sometimes held 'informal meetings' over lunch with Union representatives in pubs — a common practice in Ireland — where most pubs are multi-generational, mixed social-class places. I rarely stayed overnight in Waterford — I flew in and flew out the same day. On this occasion I was staying overnight and was invited to a hotel pub frequented by many WCL employees. Rather than spending the evening examining yet another batch of information I had requested and obtained from Management, I justified to myself that going to the pub would allow me to get the views of employees additional to that of the Union activists. Later in the evening in the relaxed pub atmosphere, the Convenor and the Deputy Convenor pressed me to give them a copy of the report. I told them that such action might damage my continuing access to information from Management and be in breach of the conditions upon which it was disclosed. Their response was to dilute their request to just be allowed read the report in my presence. I could trust them, they said, nobody else would know. They would use the information but never reveal that they had got it from the capital expenditure budget. I had no doubt but that the information would help their short-term negotiations, but I had made a commitment — which the Union had approved — not to release restricted information.

My desire to remain independent was reinforced by a more pragmatic belief that were the Union to use any of the information the source would be obvious to Management. I would have strongly supported Union access to the report after the conclusion of my analysis but to disclose it immediately would probably destroy my ability to complete the analysis as Management would most likely refuse to give me continuing access to vital data. Fortunately, I was reasonably sober. I told the Union why I could not give nor show them the document. However I pointed out to them that now that they knew of its existence they could use their undoubted power to demand a copy from Management. The Union representatives were however well aware that they could get the report directly from Management — now that they knew of its existence — but obtaining it in that manner had disadvantages for them. It would create expectations that they directly engage with Management about its contents — a process in which Management would have the analytical advantage. If, however, they covertly knew what was in the report they could selectively use the data in a manner that suited them and without having to acknowledge that they had read the report.

As I was unwilling even to let the representatives read the document, they diluted their request further. They said they would be satisfied if they could see the costings of just two key changes Management had already proposed. This was information which I believed should have been readily available to the Union, but responsibility for its disclosure was not mine. Closure was not achieved by a final, absolute refusal, but by a diversion. A dinner-dance had just finished in the hotel. From where we sat, we could see many young unmarried couples booking rooms at the hotel reception. This was certainly a change from the very puritanical, 'priest-ridden' Ireland I had grown-up in. I turned the conversation towards discussing the declining influence of the Catholic Church. At that stage it was early morning and we eventually went our separate ways having parted on friendly terms. The Union representatives were disappointed that I would not reveal to them the information they wanted, but they acknowledged my desire not to compromise my independence. Fortunately, in advance of my next and only other overnight-stay, Management invited me to a joint dinner with their two most senior managers and the two leading Union representatives. The conversation was largely about national politics (about which I knew a lot); the performance of the local football team (about which I knew very little); and the experience of being Irish in England compared with the USA. The condition and prospects of the company and the progress of my investigation were not discussed.

Getting and Trying to Get Data

I hoped that Management's gloomy forecasts were demonstrably flawed so that I could quickly satisfy the Union and extract myself from increasingly complex relationships. I initially focused on analyzing the accounting information which I had requested: audited accounts, budgets, and so forth — subjecting them to a battery of tests (McSweeney 1995). A review of the scale and timing of foreign currency hedging and a challenge to the validity of one expense item of IR£1.2 million — a criticism accepted by Management — weakened, but did not fundamentally undermine, Management's gloomy forecasts. A very large proportion of costs were gross labour costs (about 77%). As the Union had recently agreed a three-year pay deal, which included a commitment to no redundancies, the annual increase in those costs was predictable. I sought and obtained information on all other cost items in Management's budgets focusing especially on significant items which were predicted to change. In parallel I sought to understand the underlying dynamic of the company, by talking to all the main parties, touring the shop-floor, examining the manufacturing process, speaking to pre-selected, and some randomly met, managers and employees, meeting some key customers, and obtaining copies of the views of external commentators including investment analysts. Through this process, I came to understand most specifically: the source of the Union's unusual power (above); their rationality for resistance to change; and the reasons for the variable quality of the products. Having largely completed my analysis of expense records and forecasts (assuming no work practice changes), I informed the Union (and Management) that these seemed to be quite reasonable.

I then focused on the revenue forecasts — those assuming, and those not assuming, work practice changes. The aim of those sought by Management was primarily to increase sales by removing bottlenecks (mainly caused as the Union's Convenor privately acknowledged to me — by demarcation disputes between different groups of Union members) and improving product consistency (which my discussions with buyers in a number of London and New York stores[8] satisfied me was a problem). Management's growth approach was a welcome change from an inward-looking focus on cost reductions. I had frequently observed this fatalistic perspective in many other companies which, like WCL, had claimed to be financially challenged. Unfortunately I was pessimistic about the feasibility of Management's 'strategy of growth'. Having commenced hoping to conclude that Management's claim was unfounded, or exaggerated, it now seemed to me that the revenue forecasts were over-optimistic. Two factors seemed vital — the U.S. dollar/Irish Punt exchange rate and the drivers of volume sales.

In excess of 80% of sales were in dollars so that the revenues were very exposed to a weakening of the Dollar which had remained strong for an unusually long period. Predicting exchange rates is highly problematic. The best I could do was compare Management's exchange rate assumptions with that of others. They were broadly consistent.

My initial analysis also suggested that sales volume also seemed vulnerable to changes, including declining attractiveness of crystal products in the important 'bridal gift market', and changing priorities of some of it key U.S. retail outlets. I had formed that view, in part, on the basis of reading a range of trade and consumer magazines and market research reports that I had requested from Management. Getting data from Management to evaluate its sales volume forecasts was problematic. Most of the marketing data I requested had to be obtained from WCL's U.S. office. As the USA was WCL's main market it was not surprising that most of the market research and data compilation was undertaken there. What was worrying about the management of the company and the plausibility of Management's forecasts was that much of that information had not prior to my request been sent to, and therefore not read by, Management at WCL's head office in Waterford.

The sales volume and income forecasts upon which Management's claims of impending financial crisis were based seemed to be largely founded on hunches and on some overall estimates sent from WCL in the USA. This form of 'emergent strategy' (using instinct plus some local knowledge) would perhaps meet the approval of popular anti-strategic planning writers such as Henry Mintzberg (1983, 1994). Indeed, I was not unsympathetic to such an approach to strategy *formation*. But it was not acceptable to me as a *justification* for Management's claim. Of course forecasts cannot be proved to be true in an objectivist sense. They are estimations about the fundamentally unknowable future, but it is possible to access the reasonableness of their construction. How do they differ from past performance and why? What assumptions have been made about key future influences? How plausible are those assumptions? And so forth. This I was seeking to do. My evidence standard at WCL was 'on the balance of probabilities'.

---

[8] I had visited New York to attend an academic conference, but used the opportunity to make this enquiry.

Some time later an academic colleague argued that it was Management's responsibility to prove its claims 'beyond all reasonable doubt' and that my employment of the weaker standard compromised my independence. However, in my view, it is impossible to effectively apply the latter test to longer-term corporate forecasts and to have attempted to do so at WCL would have irresponsibly risked the futures of all the parties. My task was not to 'grade' Management's forecasts, but to form a judgement about the corporation's prospects — with and without the proposed changes. My evaluation of Management's forecasts was merely a means of achieving that, not an end in itself.

I sought a range of data and reports for my analysis of WCL's revenue forecasts. A substantial amount was provided quite quickly to me. But I had not acquired much of what I considered to be the most crucial data including: breakdown of sales volume per product item; historic price-volume relations; details of stocks held in U.S. warehouses; and various information on competitors: "this will take weeks as I have to get them from the USA." (General Manager-Operations). The absence of such data at the centre of WCL — I was convinced that Management were not merely delaying — and its apparent dispersion (at best) within the U.S. part of the organization, increased further my doubts about the adequacy of the WCL's revenue forecasting procedures. However, before I had received sufficient data to allow me to complete my evaluation of Management's sales income forecasts, both the Union and Management began to press me for a conclusion.

Pressure to Conclude

Management had already decided that extensive change was required and were anxious to get Union agreement to those changes. The Union were now seeking a final report: "the lads [Union members] are pressing" (Convenor). Three events or circumstances intensified their desire for what I regarded to be premature closure.

First, the introduction of Management's largely accounting data depicted claims and the Union's willingness to have these examined had largely silenced the Union. The level (aggregate) and type (monetary) of data of the claim prevented the Union from engaging with the specifics of Management's forecasts. There was no point, no aspect, which allowed the Union to use its detailed — but non-accounting — knowledge of the workplace to engage with Management's financially aggregated claim. The contrast between their usual fluency about the workplace and their virtual silence when confronted with Management's accounting articulated forecasts was striking. They were acting "as if they were suddenly dispossessed of their own language" (Bourdieu 1992: 52). The Union was anxious to be free of this 'gagging'.

Secondly, an unintended outcome of the analysis, which I had so far completed, was to strengthen the Union's belief that Management's overall claim was correct. The Union's primary evaluation criterion was honesty, not competence: "Are they telling the truth? Are they trying to pull the wool over our eyes? Are they fooling us?" (Various shop stewards). Although I too was concerned to form an opinion on whether management's claims had been made in good faith, my primary criterion was reasonableness of those claims regardless of whether they were made in good or bad faith. My initial acceptance of Management's depiction of historic and estimated *expenses*, I later came to realise, was interpreted by the Union to mean that Management were being 'straight' in *all* they had claimed. The Union did not, it seems, doubt Management's ability to predict, only whether they had been attempting to 'fool' the Union. Having decided on the basis of my analysis of expenses that Management was acting in good faith, the Union drew the conclusion that Management's pessimism was justified, "if the company is heading for trouble we must act as quickly as possible or things could get worse" (Convenor).

Thirdly, the 'market' issues on which I wished to obtain further information: branding; characteristics of buyers and distributors; threats from substitutes; and so forth, meant very little to them. Not because they were unintelligent — they were very bright — but because their awareness of these issues was necessarily limited in WCL. In a different company with different products/markets Union representatives might have been more aware of the significance of these matters. But WCL products were not part of the employees' domestic lives. The typical purchaser of Waterford Crystal was an American who "lives with her husband, an upper management executive or entrepreneur, in a large suburban home . . . with 10 times the national average income required to qualify for an American Express gold card" (from a WCL market research report). Understandably Union members were unfamiliar with the shopping values and behaviours of such consumers and the attractiveness to them of the products' intangible attributes (high status and so forth). Their impression of a crystal item was primarily that it was something physical produced by them. So the significance of the market information (possible changes in major sales outlets; indications of declining attractiveness of traditional designs, threats from substitute products, and so forth) that I required if I was to evaluate Management's sales volume forecasts, largely eluded them.

Asking the Impossible

The issue for the Union was now not whether change was required, but how much change and which changes. They wanted to ensure that that they did not agree to changes in excess of what was required; that some of the 'savings' be paid back to members; that they controlled the implementation of the agreed changes; and that these did not intensify demarcation disputes amongst Union members.

My analysis of historic accounting data — especially of expenses — had unintentionally resulted in the Union's acceptance of the broad accuracy of Management's claims about the future. Now the Union believed that accounting data combined with their knowledge of the workplace would allow me to indicate with precision the particular work practices that needed to change. To their surprise, I stated that neither I, nor indeed Management, could accurately forecast the financial effects (on costs or revenues) of the proposed changes.

There were a number of reasons why I chose not to attempt the financial estimates sought by the Union. The costing system at WCL was quite basic and detailed costings of individual changes had not underpinned Management's proposals. In any event, I believed that even a 'sophisticated' accounting system could not overcome the internal and external uncertainties about the micro-effects of specific changes. My view was reinforced by events outside WCL. The idea that detailed identification of multiple cost 'drivers' and their financial consequences was readily achievable had then become fashionable through its assertive promotion by Robert Kaplan, the Chartered Institute of Management Accountants, and others. In contrast, a focus of some of my research was to problematize the notions of calculative transparency and reductive notions of readily identifiable causality. Furthermore, evaluation of the possible impact of specific changes would have involved me too closely in Management-Union negotiations and in work demarcation disputes between different sections of the Union. I was not prepared to rely on the presumption that underlies most business textbooks and courses: that more profit is better — so that the changes proposed by Management should be regarded as desirable regardless of how financially robust the company was. Nor could I get comfort from another *a priori* position: a romanticized view of labour whose interests are always the opposite of those of management.

Being Independent and Making Them Happy

My commitment to analytical independence meant that I would not finalize my judgement of Management's claim until I had obtained and evaluated all of the market information I had requested. But the context had changed. The Union had now accepted that significant changes were required and wanted to commence negotiations with Management about the details of change.

I could have 'saved face' and announced my conclusion on Management's claim. On the basis of the extensive information I had already obtained and analyzed I could readily have concocted a credible report that either supported or rejected Management's claims. I could avoid blame whichever conclusion I announced. I was confident that if I recommended rejection, the company would not have collapsed for at least two years. I was of the opinion that WCL faced severe long-term problems, but not an immediate crisis.[9] Although it was a high profile company about which financial and other journalists frequently commented, if it were ultimately to fail, my involvement would have been long forgotten and in any event I could attribute blame to events that occurred after my association. But a recommendation to reject the proposed changes would not have been analysis-based and it might effectively have caused the eventual closure of the company. Alternatively I could have recommended acceptance. But it too would not have been based on a completed analysis. If the changes turned out to be in excess of what was necessary for longer-term survival and the 'surplus' was not reinvested, WCL's major shareholders exclusively would benefit.[10]

A recommendation to reject or accept the proposed changes could not reasonably be based on my analysis — as this was as yet incomplete. I was not prepared to give advice that compromised my independence. So what was I to do?

---

[9] WCL made losses in each of five successive years after the period in which the field research was undertaken.

[10] It has of course been argued that maximizing the interests of shareholders fortuitously also maximizes the interests of others (for example, Copeland *et al.* 2000). The empirical evidence upon which such claims have been made can politely be described as partial.

There I was at the centre of a meeting with about 80 representatives of over 3,000 employees who were seeking a recommendation from me. I stated I could not advise the Union on the scale of change they should agree and that I was unsure whether the slow and still very incomplete delivery of market information to me was a deliberate delaying tactic of Management or difficulties in obtaining the requested data. But I could not disengage using the conclusion to many academic articles: 'further research is required'. I was being asked to prescribe a course of treatment, as it were, that might kill the 'patient' i.e. lead ultimately to the failure of the company, or be excessively expensive for the Union. I needed a recommendation that would avoid both outcomes.

Accounting came to the 'rescue'. I proposed that the major changes which would enhance or maintain sales should be agreed. The results would be examined annually for the next few years through a review of the audited final accounts — adjusted if necessary for any inappropriate accounting policy changes. If the agreed changes appeared to be excessive, a monetary 'compensation' would be paid to the employees. At WCL the Union would be able to enforce such an agreement. If on the other hand, the agreed changes appeared to have been insufficient, the Union would discuss the possibility of approving further changes. This proposal was accepted by the Union and shortly afterwards by Management.

Bringing Theories In

What theories did I use or reject whilst in WCL and in my subsequent academic analysis? One reason I had become an academic was to find a way beyond reductive and wholly structural notions such as 'capital' and 'class', which had intellectually dominated my former Marxist and trade union background. The labour process approach, which had a significant following in academia, was not satisfying. In my view it was essentially the obverse version of aggressive managerialism. Instead of eulogizing management, it demonized it and over-romanticized an abstract notion of labour. Both apparently opposite views were united in effectively reducing workplace relations to a zero-sum 'game' between 'labour' and 'capital'. True there were conflicts between the interests of the Union and Management (and the major Shareholders) at WCL, but there were commonalties also, not least in the survival of the firm. The labour process view, and its managerialist twin, were also too deterministic for me. I did not accept the view that ideas, discourses, theories, stories, narratives were mere 'superstructures' — dependent outcomes or relays of underlying "structural" forces. It seemed to me that the actors in WCL — Union and Management — were capable of standing back to some extent from their usual relationships and could consciously construct strategies for change (or not).

When I began the WCL field work I was intensely reading various textual, contextualised, coherence, notions of knowledge — what might loosely be called post-modernism — for instance the work of Richard Rorty. But whilst rejection in that literature of objective uncontested certitude appealed to me, its indifference to action and failure to adequately specify criteria of evidence was disappointing. The challenge to analyze the specifics of WCL reinforced my dissatisfaction with the authors' apparent detachment and evasion or opaqueness about validity. I looked for satisfactory synthesis or reconciliations of structure and agency. Whilst these may exist, those that I read during that period — for example the attempts of Richard Bernstein and Anthony Giddens — were, for me, inadequate. Giddens' work was becoming increasingly popular. His notion of 'structuration' seemed to some to have transcended the subject-object dualism and thus the apparently never-ending antagonism between subjectivist and objectivist analysis. But having read a number of his books, I concluded that he failed to transcend the divide. 'Structuration' is essentially the *problem* of transcendence rephrased as a *solution*, thus making it ineffective for the analysis of local interactive situations such as that at WCL.

During the fieldwork I was encouraged by Hacking's less ambitious, more pragmatic, view of analysis as an 'intervention' (1983) which avoided the two extremes of a utopian search for absolute truth and an unending condemnation of that search. My trade union background — both as an official and as an activist — had reinforced my awareness of the validity of rationalities additional to Management's. Indeed, I had seen many instances where a too powerful and short-term orientated management had squeezed out vital investment, training, and workforce commitment. The presupposition in most strategy literature that it is management who chooses successful strategies is not universally true. There are instances of 'union failure': where trade unions have blocked crucial actions, but there are also instances where unions have imposed successful strategies on management.[11] My knowledge of accounting policies — developed especially during my period as a drafter of accounting standards — helped me interrogate Management about the implicit assumptions upon which its financial statements were built. Working in a business school and directing a senior management programme had increased my familiarity with 'disciplines' additional to accounting. Most useful were marketing and strategy. Whilst that literature is — in the main — overassertive, anecdotal, functional, partial, and greatly exaggerates predictive capability, it provided me with some broad frameworks and checklists to focus my questioning of Management's claims.

Publication

Whilst the various parties at WCL had, of course, been very interested in my analysis, why should anyone else be? What significance, if any, did my fieldwork have for accounting theory, management theory or social theory more widely (Humphrey & Scapens 1996)?

I had already completed a paper on the representational properties of accounting numbers — arguing through textual analysis that judgement cannot be eliminated from such calculations. More unusually it also suggested that although absolute truth was impossible it could still validly act as a "regulative ideal" (McSweeney 1997). In a new paper, I used the WCL data to develop this argument. As the first paper was under review by *Accounting, Organizations and Society* I decided to send the second to another journal. I consciously chose one based in the USA: *Accounting, Management*

---

[11] For a discussion of the imposition of good strategy by the managed see Sinchcombe (2000) and Thomas (1994).

and Information Technology[12] (*AMIT*) as: I thought that an article with data from an Irish company well known in America would not be the object of the bias against non-American data in U.S. journals. Furthermore, I thought *AMIT*'s editor would find my reflexive arguments of interest. The reviews were extraordinarily positive and helpful. But they were also very demanding. In brief they argued that the potential contribution to accounting/social theory of the fieldwork was underdeveloped. It did not sufficiently answer the 'so what?' question. What is the wider relevance of a local event? This challenge forced me to read or re-read studies of accounting in action. As I did not teach management accounting and the WCL study was only loosely related to my other research I was not fully familiar with that literature.

My literature search identified some fine 'situated' (McSweeney 1995), genuinely exploratory field studies. But the great majority of papers, which purported to explain events in a specific organization did so wholly on the basis of what the authors had clearly decided prior to their fieldwork, was a universal answer. Often pretentious paraphrasing of one of the 'great' social theorists was combined with highly selective use of data from the field. It seemed to me that these studies lacked intellectual independence. Instead of genuinely exploring the specifics of the field and testing, interrogating, their general notions, the authors 'found' what they already 'knew'. Too much fieldwork allegedly inspired by Foucault, Habermas, or Marx, for instance, at the level of grand theory has been carried out on a one sided positivistic way on the ground.

A description that is over-determined by presuppositions whatever their source (organizational parties, a favourite theory, or whatever) is not independent and thus cannot do justice to, provide useful insights into, the situation it purports to represent. Some of the field studies made claims consistent with the chosen interpretation of the favoured social theory and yet had clearly ignored readily available data that contradicted their 'findings'. The exercise of independence in qualitative field-research does not always require an extensive search for counterfactuals, as that process, though ideal, may be impractical. But research in which doubt is not exercised is not independent.

Having admired the field studies that demonstrated the author's intellectual independence and being, frankly angered by the excessive *a priorism*, the singularity of the confirmatory process, which underlay some other studies, I reflected again on my work in WCL. It seemed to me that the intellectual openness I sought, even if imperfectly achieved, is a necessary quality of that which is genuinely academic. Independence is not a guarantee of truth (however we define it), no observations can finally arbitrate between interpretative differences, but an unwillingness to have largely pre-interpreted what is to be interpreted is a necessary characteristic of processes which obtain valid results. Rethinking validity does not mean its rejection. To be critical — epistemologically — is to be independent.

I rewrote my WCL study around the notion of contingency and openness. What seemed distinctive about accounting at WCL was that technically unchanged accounting had nonetheless been significant in the constitution of particular *organizational* change

---

[12] Now renamed as: *Information and Organization*.

— but not in an acontextual, consistent, or predictable manner. I sought to explain longitudinally accounting's significance in the Union's move from veto of extensive work practice changes to acceptance. It was located within and contributed to a critique of characterization of deterministic and predictable effects of accounting in organizations. The outcome at WCL was neither predetermined nor predictable but ultimately depended on the actors' — and in particular the Union's — interpretation of the situation. In theorizing this I contrasted notions of 'power-of' and 'power-with' drawing on, for example, Mary Parker Follet's 'power over' and 'power with' (in Boland 1979) and Michel Callon's ideas of 'diffusion' and 'translation' (1986). The former view is that entities, such as accounting, have inherent capabilities. The alternative view is that there are no acontexual effects so that whilst accounting may sometimes be a necessary condition for particular consequences, it is never sufficient, hence the label: 'power-with'. The paper then subdivided 'power-with' theories into 'subsuming explanations' and 'situated explanations'. I used the WCL study to critique the former and support the latter arguing that that there were local contingencies at WCL *and* that they mattered in enabling and being able to explain accounting's involvement in the action processes.

Whilst the paper accepted the impossibility of a 'neutral' research in the sense of wholly transparent relationship between 'reality'' and its representations, and thus the acknowledgement of the fallibility of observation and experience, it also argued against the abandonment of a desire for intellectual/empirical openness and the responsibility to be ongoingly critical of our own analysis as it unfolds. In brief, to be self-critically reflexive. In conducting the research and writing it up, I sought by explication of my criteria of justification for my findings to find a way that avoided the extremes of foundationalism, coherentism or epistemic tribalism. As James states: "when . . . we give up the doctrine of objective certitude, we do not thereby [necessarily] give up the quest or hope of truth itself" (1956: 17). The paper was accepted.

Some Reflections and Lessons

The Journal

In retrospect my choice of journal was probably a mistake. Although the refereeing was extensive, useful, and encouraging, the journal was not widely read by accounting academics — probably because of its interdisciplinary character. In my paper I believe I exposed fundamental flaws in a widely cited accounting field study. And yet, that study — published in an exclusively accounting journal — continues to be uncritically cited whilst my article has disappeared into academic 'limbo'. I might have avoided that fate by sending photocopies of my paper with a suitable accompanying letter to key accounting academics many of whom I knew, and I could readily have identified others. But my attitude then was that those who are intellectually curious would discover and read my paper. I underestimated the distracting effect of the huge increase in the number of articles published and the inaccessibility of the journal for many because of the unwillingness of many U.K. university libraries to subscribe to it because of restrictions on their budgets.

Evidence

The existence of many, too many, published field studies in which data is used to merely confirm theoretically derived assertions is evidence that over-determination is not necessarily a barrier to publication. Each field worker must decide what their aim is: another line on a CV or analysis driven by real curiosity. I believe that we have not, and can not, learn anything genuinely insightful from those studies which derive and report field data to confirm, to empirically legitimate, that which was effectively pre-decided.

The Theme

Fieldwork is usually undertaken to address a specific research question. But the WCL study did not commence in that way. Whilst I agree with Hacking's rejection of the idea that an: 'experiment' or field-work can only be significant for theory if it has been pre-designed to 'test' a theory about the phenomena under scrutiny (1983), it is a lot easier to write research if it is preceded by a well defined research question. From WCL I acquired huge quantities of data, but using it for academic purposes was much more problematic than it would have been had I entered the field with specific academic aims. The circumstances of my access/involvement in WCL precluded that approach, but it made later academic analysis more difficult. Fortunately I participated in WCL at a time of disruption of the everyday, which allowed me to observe and record revealing events and processes. I took detailed notes of meetings and other matters which in retrospect functioned as field notes. Undertaking research without a clear research aim frequently leads to failure. True, there is occasionally a unique contribution. But it's a very risky approach.

Formal Arrangements

The circumstances of my intervention into WCL; the unusually powerful position of the Union; and importance for both sides of the results of my analysis; my strong desire to avoid becoming involved in negotiations resulted in quite formal arrangements for information disclosure. These arrangements had advantages, but possible benefits of less formal links, such as the willingness of Management to be more open in the absence of Union were lost.

Setting out the terms on which one will analyze/research from the outset can be valuable. In WCL's case it allowed me to reflect on what I was going to do and how I was going to do it. It achieved acceptance from both Management and the Union of the idea of an independent assessor, something they had little prior experience of. And later, when my independence was threatened I was able to refer back to the jointly agreed terms of reference. But my awareness of the Union's trust of me and of their everyday negotiating practice should perhaps have made me avoid overly informal contact with Union representatives. That is not to suggest that such informality is always inappropriate, indeed, considerable amounts may be essential for 'thick' descriptions.

But for action-research, where the outcome might possibly have adverse or uneven consequences for diverse organizational parties, I suggest that in the initial exploratory stage relations are best kept formal — to help the researcher avoid circumstances in which they can be overly pressurized to reach predetermined results or to employ prescribed frameworks.

Expectations

Organisational actors often over-estimate the analytical and remedial capability of research. The popularity of the instant cures promised by management 'gurus', and others, suggests widescale belief in the quick 'cure-all' (Collins 2000). At WCL both sides unrealistically assumed that I could readily pronounce with certainty about the company's prospects. Yet even if all the information I had requested had been provided in time I would have merely made a judgement based on my assessment of the probability of a world that did not then exist: the future. Research should not offer what cannot be provided. That I did not do, but I was pressurized to do so. Researchers need to be aware of the often unrealizable expectations of those in the field. The compromise arrangement I reached disentangled me and preserved my commitment to intellectual independence, but such principled escapes are not always possible.

References

Bourdieu, P. (1992). *Language and symbolic power*. Cambridge: Polity Press.

Bower, J. L. (1972). *Managing the resource allocation process*. Homewood: Irwin.

Callon, M. (1986). Struggles and negotiations to define what is problematic and what is not: domestication of the scallops and the fishermen of S. Brieuc Bay. In: J. Law (Ed.), *Power, action and belief: A new sociology of knowledge* (pp. 196–233). London: Routledge and Kegan Paul.

Collins, D. (2000). *Management fads and buzzwords: Critical-practical perspectives*. London: Routledge.

Copeland, T., Koller, T., & Murrin, T. (2000). *Valuation: Measuring and managing the value of companies* (3rd ed.). New York: John Wiley and Sons.

Hacking, I. (1983). *Representing and intervening*. Cambridge: Cambridge University Press.

Humphrey C., & Scapens, R. W. (1996). Theories and case studies of organizational accounting practices: limitation or liberation? *Accounting, Auditing & Accountability Journal*, 9(4), 86–106.

James, W. (1956). *The will to believe*. New York: Dover Publications.

Mintzberg, H. (1983). *Power in and around organizations*. New York: Free Press.

Mintzberg, H. (1994). *The rise and fall of strategic planning*. New York: Free Press.

McCloskey, D. N. (1988). The limits of expertise: if you're so smart, why ain't you rich? *The American Scholar*, 57(3), 393–406.

McSweeney, B. (1995). Accounting in organizational action: a subsuming explanation or situated explanations? *Accounting, Management and Information Technologies*, 5(3/4), 245–282.

McSweeney, B. (1997). The unbearable ambiguity of accounting. *Accounting, Organizations and Society*, 22(7,) 691–712.

McSweeney, B. (2000). Action research: mission impossible? *Accounting Forum, 24*(4), 379–390.

McSweeney, B. (2002). Hofstede's model of national cultural differences and their consequences: a triumph of faith — a failure of analysis. *Human Relations, 55*(1), 89–118.

Makridakis, S. (1990). *Forecasting, planning and strategy for the 21st century.* New York: Free Press.

Rappaport, A. (1986). *Creating shareholder value: The new standard for business performance.* New York: Free Press.

Sinchcombe, A. L. (2000). Unions and coin tossing: a reply to Oliver and Henderson. In: J. A. C. Baum, & F. Dobbin (Eds), *Economics Meets Sociology in Strategic Management* (pp. 303–305).

Thomas, R. J. (1994). *What machines can't do: Politics and technology in the industrial enterprise.* Berkeley: University of California Press.

Section Three: Collecting and Analysing Data

The collection and analysis of data are crucial parts of any research project. It is perhaps not surprising, therefore, that this section is the longest in the book and contains ten chapters. When commissioning chapters, we have focused on the different stages and decisions involved in data collection and analysis, rather than opting for a large number of chapters on all of the different methods that are available to collect and analyse data. Thus, there are two chapters concerned with research design, another on defining research questions, two that relate to issues of access for research, two on data collection, another on recording research data and two others on data analysis.

Case studies often figure prominently in qualitative research. They are sometimes presented simply as a collection of research methods. However, they are also a way of framing a research problem with all of the related epistemological, ontological, methodological and theoretical issues that that entails. Similarly, they are also a way of dividing up the population, with the resulting demand for statements explaining and/or justifying the significance of the research findings from a 'singular' case. They are, therefore, important in the design of research projects. In selecting authors to discuss the value of case studies, we have deliberately invited people who have assisted the development and application of case studies in accounting research. Tony Berry and David Otley have not only employed case studies, but have also written about them widely. In chapter fourteen, Tony and David discuss all of these different dimensions of case study research and provide a review of the range of case-based projects that have been conducted in accounting. Chapter fifteen is written by Bob Scapens, who in his role as editor-in-chief of *Management Accounting Research*, has sought actively to promote case-based research. Bob outlines the uses to which case studies may be put and the different types of objectives that they can help to realise. He also describes the problems and process of selection involved in picking suitable cases, the variety of relationships that the researcher may adopt towards the respondents and the main steps in gathering, analysing and presenting the findings of a case study. Both his and Tony and David's chapter suggest that it is important for the researcher to understand clearly how they want to use case studies when framing their research questions.

This is often far more difficult than it may appear, as different theories may contain heavily culturally-based assumptions. It is, thus, not only important for researchers to adopt a critically reflexive approach to their theories and methods, but it is important to attempt to step outside of their own culture if they want to generate research questions that have broad relevance. It is for this reason that we have included chapter sixteen by

Masaya Fujita and Yoshiaki Jinnai, two Japanese scholars. Their chapter provides a dialogue around differences between what are perceived as important issues for research in Japan and those that are considered important by Anglo-American scholars. Their paper helps to highlight how theories that vary in either their substance or interpretation between Japan and the West inform — and draw from — the study of accounting in quite different ways. As Masaya and Yoshi indicate, their chapter could help Western scholars understand studies of accounting in Japan and may also assist others whose first language is not English to appreciate the difficulties of getting their research understood better by English-speaking audiences.

Once a research question has been defined and respondents targeted, an initial issue that researchers will have to address will be access into the field. Although access is often an issue that is glossed over, gaining, maintaining and even limiting access are issues that can affect the success of a project. The two chapters that we have commissioned address access and the related issues from almost polar opposite sets of experience. In chapter seventeen, Thomas Ahrens looks at conventional forms of access into organisations where it is often difficult to obtain commitment from respondents. Thomas argues against viewing access in dichotomous terms of either being gained or not being gained. Instead, he discusses the idea of access as a process and puts his own perspective on a range of issues and strategies relating to access and ensuring that meaningful data is obtained from the research process. In chapter eighteen, Alan Sangster and David Tyrrall highlight the difficulties of access of a different type wherein the introduction of the internet has created the problem of data overload. Alan and David emphasise the importance of limiting the type of data for which access is sought on any particular topic. Their discussion of their own web-based research helps to highlight the importance of not relying wholly on the web to define a population for study, the ease with which it is possible to refine a search if it proves either too limited or broad in its scope, the importance of strategies for strictly focusing the scope of material generated and the impact that this can have on the research process.

Once issues of access are resolved, the suitability of methods becomes important. As indicated above, there are a range of methods for collecting qualitative data, from the most intrusive, such as participant-observation, through to interviewing and questionnaires of different types (with varying degrees of intrusion), to those such as the analysis of documentary evidence that may entail no real intrusion on organizational actors. We only have the space to include chapters on the method that tends to be employed most frequently in accounting research, namely interviews. In chapter nineteen, David Marginson locates the use of interviewing in the broader use of an organizational case study. While recognising that interviews are only one of a number of sources of data that can be used in a case study, David explores a range of practical issues involved in interviewing. In particular, he considers the relationship between theory and the conduct of an interview, practical questions of the value of data collected in an interview, the intertwined relationship of qualitative data collection and analysis and problems of presenting interview data in published papers. In chapter twenty, Joanne Horton, Richard Macve and Geert Struyven also consider issues involved in interviewing. They draw on their research into changes in insurance accounting and reporting in the U.K. and the E.U. to illustrate the merits of semi-structured interviews, the patterns of formulating and refining an interview schedule and associated implications for the selection of respondents, the conduct of interviews and any subsequent analysis. An important issue when conducting interviews is how to record the information. For example, whether or not to audio-tape the interview exchange. In chapter twenty-one, Treasa Hayes and Ruth Mattimoe contrast a study where tape-recording was used with one where interviews were recorded in written form and not tape-recorded. They consider the merits and drawbacks of different methods of recording and provide a range of practical tips on how to manage different recording processes.

When research data has been collected, there are decisions about how it should be analysed in order to identify key patterns, explain actions, events and reported opinions and seek to determine any particular contributions to existing knowledge and theoretical perspectives. In selecting chapters about this stage of research, we have chosen authors who provide new and detailed insights into the analysis of interview data. There is now a range of computerised packages to help in analysing data. Fiona Anderson-Gough has been involved in a number of qualitative projects that have used such tools. In chapter twenty-two, she describes the decisions that have to be taken when using computerised packages for analysing interview data and the strengths and weaknesses of such an option. In chapter twenty-three, Brendan O'Dwyer presents a seemingly contrasting approach in that he did not exploit computerised techniques, but chose to rely on an intuitive analytical method, relaying on repeated reading and re-reading of his interview data in pursuit of rigorous analytical codes. The commitment to detailed analysis in both Fiona's and Brendan's chapters and the evident use of judgement in each raises a number of interesting questions regarding the supposedly different nature of computerised and non-computerised methods of data analysis.

Chapter 14

Case-Based Research in Accounting

Anthony J. Berry and David T. Otley

Introduction

This chapter reflects our long commitment to case based research in accounting, a commitment based upon its richness in addressing the task of understanding and theorising the content, processes and context of the practice of accounting. We have included reflections on our own case research and of the problems we have found, especially research design and theoretical development. We hope that this chapter will give the reader some ideas on how to think about, construct, design and interpret case-based research in accounting, especially to understand how accounting case-based research has moved on from positivist methods to include constructivist and subjectivist approaches.

In the chapter we set out an epistemological and ontological framework which enables us to suggest how our own and others' case-based research may be placed, to acknowledge and understand the differences between various approaches and the problems we have had with both methods and the development of accounting theory. Our intention is to give full value to the wide variety of case-based approaches in the hope that this inclusivity will encourage future development of both case-based research and understanding among accounting researchers. We also hope that fellow researchers and new researchers will find the experiences, ideas and discussion to be helpful in formulating case-based research in accounting. In particular we seek to redress a problem that Lukka & Granlund (2002) noted which was that the researchers representing different approaches do not frequently meet each other. Here we hope that such meetings are possible by attending to a wide range of approaches in the same chapter.

The use of case studies in accounting research has been the subject of considerable development and debate, a debate that owes much to the questioning of the tradition of positivism and indeed empiricism and instrumentalism in economics, in finance and in accounting (Hagg & Hedlund 1979; Laughlin 1995; Humphrey & Scapens 1996; Jonsson & Macintosh 1997; Humphrey 2001). The methodological underpinnings of accounting research are an important starting point for consideration of case-based

The Real Life Guide to Accounting Research: A Behind-the-Scenes View of Using Qualitative Research Methods
© 2004 Published by Elsevier Ltd.
ISBN: 0-08-043972-1

research, for here we can see how such research has expanded from a positivist and functional base to include a wide array of approaches including ethnographic, constructionist, and critical approaches. Hence this chapter begins with a brief review of these issues before considering case study methods. A selection of the methods that have been used in accounting research are then set out, followed by a review of some issues and compromises involved in research design, and in conducting case-based fieldwork. We have some misgivings about the range and depth of theoretical development that has been achieved so far, even if we do believe that there is much promise in the case-based method. These sections are complemented by a review of the skills needed to undertake case-based research and some consideration of the ethical issues that can arise. The final section of the chapter considers the contributions and limitations of case-based research in accounting.

Approaches to Accounting Research

There has been a considerable debate about the nature of accounting research and its purpose. Definitions range from the idea of basic research which is about the pursuit of knowledge for its own sake, applied research which is about solving some practical problem, to action research which is about solving some ill defined problem which goes beyond present knowledge and has as its output both a 'solved' problem and a contribution to theory.

The traditions of research in finance and in accounting were largely based upon those of economics (Ryan *et al.* 1992, 2002). These authors trace the evolution of such research through the English empiricism of Bacon, Hume, Locke and Berkeley and its contrast with rationalism. They note the debates of idealism (knowledge is created by the perceiving mind) and realism (that there exists a mind-independent reality which can form the basis of our experience) is still current in the literature of finance and accounting. Ryan *et al.* suggest that the dominant approaches in finance and accounting have been strongly rationalist, realist and positivist. However the more relativist position in research is taken by hermeneutic and critical theoretic approaches, which are based upon an argument that "any interpretation of reality is so strongly conditioned by subjective, theoretical and cultural factors that appeals to reality to test particular theories are quite meaningless" (Ryan *et al.* 1992: 9).

The positivism implicit and explicit in much research in accounting is a continuation of the empiricist tradition. From this standpoint all other kinds of statements are meaningless. Yet, as with all constructions of knowledge, positivism has its problems, problems that are rather discarded by the instrumentalism that simply says that the basis of theory is not important as long as the predictions are useful. Popper (1959) took this issue further by suggesting that the possibility of falsifiability (rather than verification) was the distinctive characteristic of a scientific theory: through falsifiability the possibility of refutation was established. A problem arises here as to the nature of any observation which can be made; for it is arguable that observations can never be theory free, indeed it is suggested by Kuhn and Lakatos that all observation is theory-laden and hence there can be no determining refutation in Popper's sense. Ryan *et al.* argue somewhat heroically that this assertion of theory laden-ness renders what they regard as science to be impossible and flies in the face of their and others experience of the physical sciences. Yet while their position of weak-form realism together with coherence and social consensus is serviceable and provides them with the possibility of reliability (in principle replicability), it is not necessarily the case that it can apply to social phenomena. This latter point only matters if you regard accounting as a social phenomena, in much the same way as Ryan *et al.* see scientific endeavour as a social phenomena.

It is sometimes asserted that the methods of the physical sciences are the only effective or indeed the only legitimate means of doing accounting research. However, it should be clear from the above arguments that such a conclusion is not sustainable and that constructionist and relativist methods are justifiable in their own right. It can be argued that the nature of knowledge is different in the social sciences from that in the physical sciences. For example, a physicist generally assumes that the behaviour of the phenomenon that is being studied is invariant in space and time. That is, it is irrelevant when it is studied and where it is studied, and that general laws of behaviour can be formulated. Such a statement is usually false where social phenomena are concerned. The behaviour of managers operating a management control system is likely to change over time, given the introduction of new techniques (and regardless of whether these are real improvements or merely management fads); the outcomes of a given behaviour are also likely to be different in different locations and organizational and national cultures. The difficulty for the empirical researcher lies in attempting to differentiate between those aspects of behaviour that are potentially generalizable, and those that are context-specific. This is the issue that Laughlin (1995) tackles when drawing the distinction between the generalized 'skeleton' and the empirical 'flesh' in middle range theories.

There is, however, a different positioning of qualitative research in the nature of the results that it produces. At the more objectivist end of the spectrum, one main role of positivist qualitative research is exploratory. That is, it seeks to develop theory in areas where little existed before, and the output of the work may be to suggest hypotheses that are worth testing in subsequent studies. Towards the more subjectivist and relativist position, qualitative research has a more central role in developing particular explanations and understanding of phenomena that have been observed. From such a perspective it is not intended that research produces theories with the same type of predictive ability that is the hallmark of the physical sciences. Thus, the appropriate use of qualitative methods is determined both by the nature of the phenomena studied, the ideology of the researchers and the philosophical underpinnings of the theoretical approach being adopted.

In case-based research, as in other research, there is a distinction to be made between theory (what this research is about), ontology (the assumptions made about the nature of reality), epistemology (how knowledge is to be understood) and method (how research is to be conducted). In the positivist tradition these elements are more clearly separate, but from the more phenomenological or relativist stance they are interconnected. Johnson & Duberley (2000: 180) provide a simple mapping of four quadrants derived from subjectivist and objectivist stances on ontology and epistemology. These authors note that conventionalism in management and, we note, in accounting research

Table 1: Epistemology and ontology of different theoretical approaches.[1]

	Ontology		
Epistemology	Objectivist Realist	Critical realism	Subjectivist Idealist
Objectivist	Positivism Neo-positivist		Incoherence
Relativist Constructionist		Critical Theory	
Subjectivist	Pragmatism		Post modernism

[1] We discuss positivist approaches in the next main section and constructionist, critical and subjectivist approaches in the main section after that.

may span both the objectivist and subjectivist ontology. It has been a common mistake to distinguish the positivist tradition as being quantitative and the other approaches as qualitative, but as we shall note this means that there are many varieties of qualitative case-based research. From their framework we derive a slightly extended version (see above). We have explicitly included critical realist ontology and a constructionist epistemology (although these separations are not precise).

These issues are of great significance to us as case-based researchers, though it is fair to say that David has worked more than Tony in the positivist arena, as he has had a consistent intent to aid the practice of accounting and management. But we see that the epistemological and ontological assumptions of various case-based approaches is important because it will enable us to acknowledge and respect differences and prevent us from engaging in somewhat familiar critiques of one approach from the stance of another. It also enables us to see why case-based research is potentially difficult to accumulate (that is, building from one case to another) and why there is such engaging variety in the literature. But it also reminds us to be clear about our methodological starting points.

We acknowledge that our values lead us to choose both research problems and research approaches, but this does not mean that we cannot work in a variety of traditions. As the bibliography shows we have both undertaken case studies from several standpoints and we feel that it is important to avoid becoming locked in one tradition, becoming boring to ourselves! Besides our own interest we have to flexible to work with the different approaches of our other co-researchers and research students.

Yin (1994: 13) working from a positivist stance defines a case study as "an empirical inquiry that investigates a contemporary phenomena within its real life context, especially when the boundaries between the phenomena and context are not clearly evident". In contrast Stake (1995: xi) from the relativist stance noted "we study a case when it is of very special interest. We look for the detail of interaction within its contexts. Case study is the study of the particularity and complexity of a single case, coming to understand its activity within important circumstances". And "I develop a view of case studies that draws from naturalistic, holistic, ethnographic, phenomeno-logical and biographic research methods". So it is clear that Yin and Stake differ in respect of their understanding of the object of enquiry, the epistemological stance and the methods to be used. We will explore these issues in relation to accounting research.

Case-based Research Design

No case-based research design is likely to be fixed and unchanging but is certain to have embedded in it the ontological and epistemological stances of the researchers. The very nature of case-based research requires an openness to the possibility of discovery so that precisely-specified design is to be avoided. There is though a need to have some research intent around a question in order to provide a framework for the data collection plans. Clearly such designs are compromises of many kinds, and given the limitations of researcher time and attentiveness, there is a trade off between depth and breadth of both data and insight, both of which limit possible analysis in different ways. We may only have had accidental access to a site for a limited amount of time; there might be the possibility of studying in depth what has been noted, from a prior broader study, to be a typical case. Or it might be that there is the possibility of exploring what promises to be a case, which could lead to a significant disconfirmation of a current theory. A case-based design might be like a snowball, with one case leading to another, gaining complexity and subtlety of insight as they build. Yet again a case could be chosen because it has political significance both as to what is discovered and to the theoretical development. For researchers attempting to minimise the possibility of failure there is always the consideration of potential richness, so that a less than successful or perhaps an aborted study still leads to some research output. For further discussion of case-based research in accounting see Scapens (1990), Llewellyn (1992), Otley & Berry (1994) and Humphrey (2001). From the published research, it is clear that there are many different kinds of case studies in accounting research; among them are cases of description, illustration, experiment, exploration and explanation. Further case methods may be quantitative, qualitative or a variety of methods drawn from both approaches.

We take the view that researchers should clarify their research approach at the start of the research observations; to specify the theoretical and methodological lenses through which they intend to conduct their investigations and the major questions they wish to pursue without restriction as to the development of these questions and other questions as the project progresses; (see the discussion in Otley & Berry 1994). We have found that it is difficult, if not impossible, (as case-based researchers) to give a full account of the data so we recognise that it is difficult for others to form independent understandings. Hence it is incumbent upon us to delineate endpoints, so that others may understand the movement of the project from its initial position to the final theoretical formulations, together with an ability to understand the evidence that lead to such changes (see Berry *et al.* 1991). It can be argued that the output of this type of inductive research is the development of new theory, or at least, the elaboration of existing theory. Thus, its contribution is measured by the difference between the theoretical perspectives adopted at the start of the research process, and those which come to be adopted by its conclusion.

We continue the chapter by examining positivist methods in the next section; and constructionist, critical and subjectivist methods in the section after that. In both sections we encounter problems of Case-based Research Design and Theory Building. These are discussed subsequently, followed by reflections on fieldwork and the researcher skills needed. We then turn to the important and ever present issue of ethics and close by considering the value of the respective approaches, the credibility of researchers and some of the practical limitations and strengths of case research.

Positivist Case Methods

The single most referenced author in this area is Yin (1994) who has provided a useful monograph to guide social science researchers in the appropriate uses of case-based methods. However, Yin's training was as an experimental psychologist, and he tends towards favouring quasi-experimental methods and multiple case designs. This is not a problem where such methods are practicable, but it needs to be recognised that much work in accounting is necessarily characterised by single case studies of complex phenomena. However, Yin (1994) usefully sets out four criteria by which the quality of research design in a social science setting may be evaluated. These are:

- *Construct validity*: establishing an appropriate measurement of the concepts being studied;
- *Internal validity*: distinguishing between causal relationships and spurious relationships (only for explanatory studies, not descriptive or exploratory studies);
- *External validity*: establishing the domain within which the findings can be generalised;
- *Reliability*: demonstrating that a study can be replicated with similar results.

All of these criteria are potentially problematic in case research. The constructs may well be developed out of the data that is being collected (for example, the development of the 'style of budget use' measure in Hopwood's (1974) seminal study, which although not presented as a case study, is in fact an analysis of a single organization and its control techniques. Internal validity is demonstrated only weakly unless a time series of observations is involved, and then only if plausible alternative explanations are proposed and rejected. External validity essentially requires the use of some form of replication, and reliability is often unverifiable as access constraints preclude repetition. Indeed the phenomena being studied are not necessarily stable over time. Yet some form of conclusions may be developed through a series of unconnected case studies over time. For example, the use of the 'controllability principle' in management accounting has been called into doubt in at least two independent case studies (Otley 1990). Given the strongly established place of this principle in management accounting 'theory', it would seem that even two well-documented counter-examples provide a basis for seriously re-examining the supposed universality of this 'principle'.

This is not to say that research design is unimportant, but rather to recognise that in many accounting studies the constraints are such that many of the above criteria will be violated. In particular, we have found that research access is often opportunistic and precludes proper advance design. Perhaps the most realistic advice that we can offer is to consider the impact of breaching the above principles, and attempting to design and redesign a study that will provide some useful outputs despite the constraints under which it is conducted. This was the case with the project of a Ph.D. student (now graduated) studying the role of cost management in an Egyptian organisation. The study discovered that there had been little attention to cost management, that the managers were very reactive in orientation. Hence the focus shifted to consider explanations for the lack of change, a shift that necessitated a theoretical extension based upon new institutional theory.

A second important issue discussed by Yin is that of analysing the evidence that is amassed during case study research. This is a well-recognized problem, and we have had (and many authors describe) the experience of 'drowning in data'. Yin suggests that data analysis is one of the least developed and most difficult aspects of conducting case study research. His only bright note is that he argues that this gives the experienced researcher no great advantage over the novice at the analytic stage! However, more important than any particular approach is to have a general analytic strategy. The ultimate goal is to treat evidence fairly, to produce compelling analytical conclusions, and to rule out alternative explanations. He suggests two possible general strategies for achieving these ends.

First, is to follow the theoretical propositions that led to the case study, and to use the research questions that were originally developed. Having collected evidence, it may also become evident that other theoretical approaches to those originally discussed, may also have relevance, and the data can be interpreted in the light of such additional theory. General causal questions can be analysed: what appears to have caused a particular behaviour to have occurred; and what do its consequences appear to be? Second, a different strategy is to develop a descriptive framework for organising the case evidence. The case study may have more than a descriptive aim, but description may provide the basis for higher-level analysis. Basically, the researcher is looking for patterns, and then attempting to construct plausible explanations for the regularities that have been observed. If there are multiple cases, then this may be extended across cases as well as within cases.

These processes can be observed within the RIF case study, conducted by ourselves and another colleague (Berry *et al.* 1991). This was an 'accidental' case where access was achieved by personal contacts, and where extension to further organizational units, although sought, was not permitted. Two main findings stand out. The first concerns the use of an odd accounting procedure. Here, we had managers describing to us a method of constructing a branch profitability statement that disregarded a number of fundamental accounting principles (for example, it failed to match income and expenditure). So odd did this appear, we initially did not believe that the explanations the managers were giving were correct — we believed that the managers had misunderstood what was going on. Only by repeated questioning at various management levels, and with regional accountants, did we accept that the evidence we were being given was true. Perhaps our own biases as to what constituted appropriate accounting practice got in the way of our seeing clear evidence. However, only when we had accepted the existence of the phenomenon could we go on to develop explanations for its existence. In the end, we concluded that, despite its theoretical shortcomings, it appeared to be a useful heuristic that helped managers cope with their situation with few apparent dysfunctional side effects. The second result started by one of the research team noticing that senior staff appeared to visit local offices far more frequently than those located at a distance. It occurred to us that patterns of control might vary because of geographical distance. Once this thought had occurred, it was a relatively simple matter to look for patterns based on distance, although the small sample precluded too much being read into this. Nevertheless, it appears that patterns of control differ significantly in organizations characterised by single sites and those characterised by geographically separate units.

In this RIF case, we were concerned to discover where the organisation held the predictive models that were used to establish the organisational expectations, as a basis for control. Quite accidentally we came across them, or rather, the model, in the hands of a staff officer. His predictions were accepted to be more accurate than the aggregated predictions of the various levels of managers and were used to change the targets of each of these managers. So one predictive model was used to dominate all of the other managers' predictive models, none of which were as well formulated (or as simple) as the staff officer's model.

Although there is now software available to enable the easier handling of qualitative data, there is still no substitute for the researcher painstakingly coding the data collected according to theoretical categories. These will include those expected in advance, but also those developed out of the evidence itself. Once data is coded, patterns can be sought. Finally, it may be appropriate to test these tentative conclusions by the collection of further data from other similar situations. Ultimately, it is incumbent upon the researcher to provide theoretical conclusions, difficult though that might be.

In the positivist tradition theory precedes the case data collection, but even so matters do not always follow so simply. When greater variety of materials cannot be ignored then a new problem of theorising arises. Eisenhardt (1989) provides an account of how theory may be built from case studies. She notes (from a rather positivist standpoint) that such theory would be novel, testable and empirically valid and offers support to the idea that this kind of theory building is particularly suited to new areas of research and hence complementary to 'normal science'.

Without wishing to over-categorise the work of fellow academics we will suggest some examples of case studies from a positivist standpoint which include: Berry (1976); Berry *et al.* (1991); Malmi (1997); Bartolomeo *et al.* (2000); Chaston & Mangels

(2001); Larrinaga-Gonzalez *et al.* (2001); Haw *et al.* (2001); Granlund (2001); Bernstein (2001); and Norris (2002).

Constructionist and Subjectivist "Qualitative" Case-based Methods

In our introduction we noted that case studies were especially suited to understanding the content, processes and contexts of the practice of accounting. The sheer complexity and richness of content, processes and context precludes a reductionist stance and leads us towards a case-based method. This informed Tony's choice of a case to study the control of capital investment, a study that extended over 30 months (see Berry 1976). In addition to complexity issues we suggest that explaining how accounting practice is established and developed also requires constructionist and critical studies in the traditions of social science.

Patton (1990) argues that qualitative research can be every bit as difficult and demanding as traditional 'scientific' methods and moreover there are three distinct but related inquiry elements:

(1) Rigorous technique and methods for gathering high quality data that is carefully analysed, with attentions to issues of validity, reliability and triangulation;

(2) The credibility of the researcher, which is dependent upon training, experience, track record, status, the presentation of self; and

(3) Philosophical belief in the phenomenological paradigm, that is, a fundamental appreciation of naturalistic inquiry, qualitative methods, inductive analysis and holistic thinking.

These three issues demonstrate that these methods are not merely a second best solution to difficult problems but are demanding criteria against which any research study may be assessed. Clearly, however, the researcher, far from being a rational designer of experiments, is now a centre stage actor, both in the design and conduct of the research programme, but more importantly in the way in which significance and meanings is derived from the research. Equally there are no claims to 'objectivity' here, nor is there an insistence upon the distinction of the subjective and objective. It is interesting to note that for Patton the acceptance of the approach is a matter of belief rather than argument, a point, which was discussed earlier in this paper where it was argued that there is no basis for a positivist 'scientist' to dismiss any other approaches to knowledge.

In the traditional way of presenting and understanding scientific inquiry we have to give attention to the issue of validity, by which is meant that the theoretical statements or hypotheses under examination are logically derived from some more general theory such that the examination of a particular hypothesis is, in some sense, also a test of the more general theory. In the qualitative approach this separation of data and theory development is not maintained. In the qualitative or grounded approaches (Glaser & Strauss 1967; Strauss & Corbin 1990) "generating theory from data means that most hypotheses and concepts not only come from the data, but are systemically worked out in relation to the data during the course of the research" (Strauss & Corbin 1990: 5–6).

Varieties of Case-based Approaches

There are a number of different approaches to constructionist and subjectivist case-based research in the social sciences. In this sub-section we will briefly outline several of the more common, and tentatively suggest some examples of them.

Phenomenological inquiry has its roots in philosophy and is concerned with the structure and essence of experience of the phenomena, for example, the use of an accounting system by managers in an organisation. Lowe & Shaw's (1968) study of bias in budgeting is an early example, as are Hopwood (1974) and Otley (1978) studies of the uses of accounting. Both of these latter studies, although presented as analyses of questionnaire responses, rely very heavily on interview-based understandings of how managers actually used accounting and budgetary information in two, rather different, large organizations.

Naturalistic inquiry is a label often given to phenomenological studies, for the task is to study phenomena in their setting, without attempting to isolate them from other events, indeed the connectedness of phenomena is an important aspect of this approach (see Berry *et al.* 1985; Bakar 1993). A current piece of work of Berry & Collier (2002) is such a study of how managers and accountants conceive of risk and how these conceptions are implicated in budgeting. We found that the personal and organisational issues were important aspects of the four cases.

Ethnographic studies are representational, interpretive and rhetorical (Jonsson & McIntosh 1997); these authors set out to make the case for ethnographic accounting research and provide an entertaining examination of rational (positivist), ethnographic and critical case approaches in relation to their intentions and in relation to each others knowledge claims. An example of a cognitive ethnographic study is given by Dent (1991) in his analysis of how accounting evolved in British Rail. Further examples are Jonsson's (1982) examination of budgetary behaviour in a local government, Berry *et al.*'s (1985) studies of accounting in the U.K. coal industry and Llewellyn's (1998) research on generating or exploring narrative as a case method. The hermeneutic processes of understanding the conditions under which human acts and phenomena occur; providing interpretations of the meanings which actors can give to their experience and, further, for the researcher to give interpretations (which could be meanings for the actors and for the researcher) is central to these approaches (Llewellyn 1993). Some of the sheer excitement of such case-based research came home to Tony in the National Coal Board (NCB) study. For after the case research began the industry was subject to a deep and bitter labour dispute. One of the case-based papers was thrown across the despatch box in the House of Commons; an interesting use of theoretical ammunition!

Ethnomethodology (from origins in Sociology) leads towards studies of how managers and staff make senses and meanings of their experience of accounting and financial management in their day-to-day experience. Tomkins & Groves (1983) is a nice example here (but also see the comment by Willmott 1983).

Symbolic interactionism could lead to studies of how the symbols of accounting are given common understandings and emerge to give meanings to people's interactions — for example, how a management team make use of Profit as a symbol of success or of masculinity, especially when set in the context of other symbols of the social group, for example, harmony, equality, fair pay, employment protection, etc. (Boland & Pondy 1986; Czarniawska-Joerges & Jacobsson 1989).

Social construction begins from the stance that meanings are in a process of construction and reconstruction in the domain. An example is Richardson *et al.* (1996). Abdul-Rahman & Goddard (1998) claim to have used grounded theory in an interpretative inquiry of accounting practices in religious organisations (also see Parker & Roffey 1987). Quattrone & Hopper (2001) move to a constructivist stance to consider organisational change and implications for accounting studies, an approach also taken by Pettersen (2001) in relating organisational learning, management accounting and change.

The critical approaches take an explicit view of the nature of power and its distribution in organisations. Such studies are concerned with the way in which accounting data and practices act as a means of maintaining positions of power, which might also reflect wider societal considerations, and be concerned also how such issues of power lead to modifications in accounting practices. Humphrey (2001: 92) commented that: "Critical case studies duly came to be dominated by this desire to apply social theories to the discipline of accounting-with cases illustrating the work of social theorists such as Foucault, Habermas, Giddens etc." Earlier Owen *et al.* (1997) had invited or challenged these case writers to be involved in practice. Examples here include Knights & Collinson (1987); Tinker & Neimark (1987); Knights & Willmott (1993); Broadbent *et al.* (1994); and Bakar & Bettner (1997).

Jonsson & McIntosh (1997: 375) argued that many critical accounting researchers "aim to demonstrate how accounting systems are part of the control apparatuses of an exploitive and coercive social order" with cases being used as illustrations of a theory rather than as a contribution to a critical engagement with the originating theory. However, it may be observed that critical theorists, like new institutional theorists, seek to demonstrate how organisations are the theatres within which may be observed the play of values, beliefs and modes of order. And further, critical theorists seek to show how these institutional values and beliefs are in need of radical consideration and change (see Merino & Mayper 2001; Tinker 2001).

Recently Neu *et al.* (2001), perhaps responding to criticism of the critical case traditions were concerned to explore how intellectuals could intervene in organisations to enable the actors to work with critical theoretical notions. In some ways this follows the idea that critical research should be empirically sound, plausible, and critically pitched and ethically insightful; which sounds compelling but is a counsel of perfection.

Of special interest is the series of case research by Laughlin *et al.* following a Habermasian approach (Laughlin 1987; Power & Laughlin in Alvesson & Willmott 1992). The ethics of the relationship between accounting researchers and their research field has been engaged with by Laughlin and Broadbent who have built case studies in a constructionist epistemology and a critical realist ontology, including in their work an action orientation similar to Critical Action Inquiry (for example, see Broadbent *et al.* 1994). This enables both the actors in the field and the researchers to share control over the research process and the evolution of theory (also see Llewellyn 1996).

Post-modern accounting case studies are rare; we sought out examples but failed in our Anglo-centred literature to find any. But perhaps it is only possible for the actors to write their own case studies and for researchers to write critical reflexive accounts of their own experience of being case researchers. But the work of Lowe (2000) and Miller & O'Leary (1987) leads towards post-modern cases.

The above is a brief review of a wide range of approaches, methods and their associated philosophical roots. There are a number of sources of fuller description, (for example, see Van Maanen 1983; Patton 1990; Miles & Huberman 1994; Cassell & Symon (Eds) 1995; Johnson & Duberley 2000; Ryan *et al.* 2002). Having reviewed some of the constructionist, critical and subjective approaches and noted some examples we turn to two important and vexing questions, namely, case study research design in practice and the issue of theory building.

This issue involves both attention to methods and to the theoretical stance of the researcher. Baxter & Chua (2003) provide a rich account of what they term alternative management accounting research, by which they appear to mean non- positivist. They discuss research from non-rational, naturalistic, institutional theory and critical and radical stances following from both Foucault and Latour. Much of the research they cite is case-based, including historical cases. They argue that these approaches have been fertile and have "demonstrated the different rationalities of practice; the variety of ways in which management accounting practice is enacted and given meaning; the potency of management accounting technologies; the unpredictable, non linear and socially embedded nature of management accounting change; and the ways in which management accounting practice is both constrained and enabled by the bodily habitudes of its exponents" (Baxter & Chua 2003: 112).

Research Design and Theory Building

Research Design

We have found that qualitative case research can be research by wandering around (for 30 months in a study of capital investment) but while accidental encounters do provide opportunities, almost all such projects are (should be?) subject to a considerable design effort in order to ensure that the data collection effort bears a strong relationship to the research questions. In what Patton (1990) calls the pure form of qualitative research, the design would be based upon naturalistic modes of inquiry, producing qualitative data which would be analysed via forms of content and other textual analysis. Yet it is quite possible for qualitative research projects to have some hybrid characteristics and combine a naturalistic inquiry with some quantitative data and some statistical analysis; there is no need to exclude useful data collection and analysis for the sake of purity of approach. But this is also to note that the distinctions marked above between varieties of qualitative methods are, in practice, not necessarily held apart, except by epistemological purists.

One of the key compromises in qualitative case research occurs around the problem of access to study domains. From our reading of the research literature it seems that many studies are the products of the access that can be obtained to the field, with research design following possibility. Qualitative case research sometimes takes place around accidents, for example, the studies of the reports of Inspectors appointed to examine particular cases of public concern such as the Pergamon affair (for example, Tinker 1985; Cahill 1989). These studies have some elements in common with critical incident analysis, where a particular event has so much richness of data and apparent significance that it becomes an exemplar of phenomena of interest. A review of the internal audit practices at Barings Bank when financial disaster struck or of the Enron Corporation would have this character. However these kinds of incidents are so sensitive and embroiled in the courts that organizational research access is almost impossible. The compromise here is to work from secondary data such as reports of inspectors or commissions of enquiry.

Design and conduct of enquiries are also compromised when an action research project based around a current managerial or organisational issue/problem or perhaps a consulting assignment of redesigning some part of the accounting system. In such studies, researchers can gain some tantalising glimpses of possibility but have to be content with limited data and with a realisation that understanding is compromised. However research so conducted appears to be done at a number of levels, that of the issue or problem, that of the organisational participants understanding and that of the researchers.

It seems necessary to accept these compromises for it is through the continuing experience of researchers in a range of research opportunities that they are able to build the interpretive and theoretical knowledge that transcends the particular piece of work. While this may appear to be akin to archaeological exploration of a field site (Hopwood 1987), it is/has been the only way to undertake projects. Of course this has become a slow process, measured in decades, rather slower than seems proper for managerial attention, but is perhaps a suitable time horizon for insightful theory development. And in truth the design of the written and published case may emerge out of the process of sense making that accompanies the production of case notes, discussion notes, working papers and conference papers. So published cases are often extracts from wider materials, constructions of the authors in their contexts that make some particular contribution. Hence the theorising may be *ex ante*, but is as likely to be read into the writing process, reshaping the significance of the evidence.

Theory Building

The output of qualitative case research is essentially theoretical and particular which may have face validity and which may be of very limited generalisability to other settings. Such studies may then be followed by both further qualitative and also by more quantitative and generalisable approaches, which may seek to establish the bounds within which the generalisations might hold. It is possible that some predictive ability may emerge, where patterns emerge and such phenomena are observed to have some fundamental similarities of behaviour in certain settings. More usually, it will produce particular insights and understandings, which are indicative of underlying social processes which can only provide a very general level of understanding of such processes in other settings.

The task of theory building cannot be understood apart from the methodological discussion earlier for this shapes the nature of the theory that is developed. There are a series of traps for researchers, especially the allure of functional frameworks, which offer such an apparently elegant tidying up of so much jumble and ambiguity, and that of theoretical preconception being buried or repressed in the data collection, only to emerge in a covert manner as the theory is spun from the cotton ball of data; a case of TITO. (theory in and theory out}. Avoiding these traps is not easy. It is important for researchers to be wary of simple linear cause and effect conjectures. Almost always social interactions are in spirals of progression and regression (Weick 1979). An example of such spirals was observed in a study (recently undertaken by one of us) of the adoption of annualised hours budgeting in a hospital, where the managers and the staff were locked in a regressive spiral such that the meanings given to the exercise were almost absurdly different. The path of speculation and interpretation has to be trodden with delicacy and care with a reflexive focus upon the rigour within which alternative conjectures are critically examined. In one sense the task for theory is to create a new description of the field and phenomena; at another level the task is to produce conjectures and/or hypotheses about the particular phenomena observed. Whether these are explanations is a matter of epistemology, not a matter of fact. See Stake (*op cit*) for a further discussion.

The question of interpretation arises as a significant problem in case-based research in accounting as in any study domain. Interpretation is not so much the logical transformation from one language to another, allowing for the expression of meanings (see also Stake, *op cit*). It is rather the giving of new meanings by interpreting events and data through (or perhaps into) a theoretical frame, which provides insight to the actors in the field as well as to the researchers. This issue of interpretation is subject to some rather difficult issues of integrity for self-delusion can easily occur and it is rather easy to claim to be interpretative while actually shoving phenomena through a well-used ideological mincer. One way past this problem is to engage in the hermeneutic processes of relating emerging theory with the texts and modifying the theory until some closure of the process has been obtained (Llewellyn 1993).

Theory building from a number of qualitative case research studies is potentially difficult because the researchers have worked from different methodological stances and hence their research findings may complement rather than build on each other (Otley & Berry 1994). This would be an unhappy state of affairs, which could only be remedied by a more consistent set of case research studies.[1] McPhee (1990) suggested three approaches to integrating across a set of studies: subsuming different data under the same theoretical model, which requires assurance that the data was similar; different kinds of explanations of the same basic type of phenomena, which also requires some means of recognising the phenomena; and recognising that the studies involve different incommensurable, but comparable types of phenomena.

---

[1] The set of cases from the Management Control Association — RIF; Rumenco; Pensco; and NCB were an attempt at this. See Otley & Berry (1994) for a discussion.

Such questions require some attention to the issue of whether findings from case research can be in any sense cumulative. One possible approach (see Laughlin 1995) suggests the use of "middle range" theories. Here it is suggested that there may be possibilities of theoretical development through the construction of outline frameworks or 'skeletons', which can be helpful in understanding new observations and situations. But this approach clearly recognises the need to put different 'flesh' on these skeletons in any specific circumstances. Thus the results of research may be limited to the development of appropriate processes that can be used to arrive at a better understanding of any specific situation. More attention needs to be given to the nature of research results for case approaches to accounting research and connections made with concomitant developments in the social sciences more generally (see Baxter & Chua 2003 for a recent, interesting perspective on this issue).

The problem of theory building of the content, processes and contexts of accounting practice is clearly open to a variety of stances of knowledge as the above discussion and the published case research demonstrates. We admit to a sense of uncertainty and puzzlement about what has been achieved to date, so much so that we have begun a critical review project to examine this problem in greater depth.

Doing Fieldwork through Case-Based Research

The fieldwork to be undertaken in much case research is derived from that of the social scientist and anthropologist. These methods of observation, whether using field notes, interviews, film, video, audio tape recordings, questionnaires, subject self reports in a variety of modes, recording of archive material, documents of organisational record, personal documents and so on require great care in their execution especially in recording of the field workers' notes and commentary that accompanies the building of the database. No two persons are likely to have exactly the same insight or attentiveness to the great complexity of phenomena which are to be observed. Indeed some methodological extremist of the theory laden observation persuasion could claim that it is impossible for two researchers to make the same field notes. This interesting idea might be enriched by adding a third person and arranging for them to develop a dialogue about the varied observations — something that we are aware that Broadbent & Laughlin have followed in their fieldwork (in conversation 2003).

It is the task of the researcher to build up a record or archive of the project. From this raw data there may be constructed a case record which is the beginning steps of analysis whereby a holistic and comprehensive picture might be developed and from which a case study, perhaps chronological and/or thematic, could be constructed (Patton, *op cit*). Content analysis provides a careful and detailed method (Cahill 1989), requiring complex and multiple coding of elements around typologies, which themselves emerge from theoretical preconceptions and from exploring in the data itself. It is important to keep the subjects of the research involved in these emerging (mis)understandings, for the organisational memory held in particular persons can be jogged to reveal more layers of data and meaning, as well as providing correction to mis-recording of data and a dialogue of meanings. In the Berry *et al.* (1985) study in the NCB the researchers took their emerging insights to the managers concerned and were surprised by the commentary which a senior manager, trained as an historian, was able to provide. Laughlin and Broadbent also sought, as do the critical action researchers, a dialogue with the actors as to the nature and substance of the research observations and conclusions. It is also possible to use questionnaire methods to check whether insights from case-based work have a more general applicability.

There are protocols for the analysis of qualitative case research field data, the protocols being devised to ensure that the internal intellectual processes of the analyst are formally held in order to ensure that conclusions are not jumped to, that the whole field is explored and that conjectures are held contingent and subject to rigorous cross checking. There is room in this chapter to make only a passing reference to the subtlety of these processes. For example Moustakos (1988) refers to the processes of heuristic inquiry as consisting of the phases of immersion in the data, incubation of ideas (contemplation, awareness, tacit and intuitive insights) illumination of expanding awareness; explication (the experience of the project is delineated and depicted) and creative synthesis as a bringing together all of the insights. This process is similar to that of Dent's study at British Rail and Lowe & Shaw's (1968) study of biasing in budgeting. For further useful contributions to discussions on field methods, the work of a number of accounting researchers is recommended (for example, Ahrens & Dent 1988; Baxter & Chua 1988; Llewellyn 1993; 1999; Lapsley & Llewellyn 1995; Laughlin 1995; Atkinson & Shaffir 1998).

Researcher Roles and Skills in Case-Based Research

Stake (1995) provides a useful list of case researcher roles; he notes them to be teacher, advocate of a particular interpretation, as evaluator of the phenomena in the domain of study, as biographer of the domain actors, as interpreter in a particular theoretical rather than universal sense, as constructor of meanings and as an actor in the domain, imbued with relativism.

The range of case-based research and the issues discussed above may appear to place the task of doing case-based research in accounting as a task for research paragons. It is perhaps that accounting scholars are not trained as social scientists but are rather brought up in a more instrumental positivist tradition, which would render them unused to the non-objective nature of qualitative research. The essential skills are those of research design with the methodological presuppositions clearly in mind, data gathering skills, especially triangulation of all kinds, data, method and analysis, critical inquiring and open mindeness, the capacity to explore in ambiguity and indeterminacy and the capacity to create rival conjectures and subject them to rigorous analysis. It is also necessary to have the humility to see each study as contributing to a wider project, that of understanding accounting in its social contexts. The person also needs to work with integrity, to acknowledge the bias in backgrounds, the possible biases in evaluation and to be able to be critically reflexive of theory, ontology, epistemology and methods.

One important idea in fieldwork is that of honesty of observation from trained and experienced researchers. Given that the worker is often the only instrument of observation it is imperative that the worker can at least reflexively address prejudice and theoretical presuppositions about how he/she is undertaking the work. To this end it is important to take as many bearings as possible upon what come to be seen as important bits of data. In all such research there cannot be a separation of field worker and analyst, for it is in the very immersion in the data that sensitises the researcher to the task of analysis. But as Humphrey (2001) noted if you have no ideas then it is going to be a dull case; so try to tell an interesting story.

Ethical Issues in Case-Based Research

One of us knew an Australian anthropologist who was asked by a subject of his research: "What do you get out of this?" The academic answer was followed by another question: "What do I and us get out of this?" As there was no satisfactory answer the anthropologist gave up the study and research and found another life. In a similar vein Frost and Stablein (1992) raise three ethical questions

(1) Will this study harm any person or group of persons directly or indirectly?
(2) Who benefits and who does not benefit from this study?
(3) Does this study serve as a basis for empowering people and, if so, who benefits and who does not?

In case-based methods the researcher may well be made privy to organisational secrets, which may be cases of considerable injustice to individuals as in the use of malformed data for performance appraisal where success may be accidental or manipulated. In the conduct of case studies we have, as we know others have, come across data in the field which for reasons of embarrassment, commercial confidentiality, internal politics or for reasons of care for individual persons cannot be brought into the public domain and cannot be brought at all into the research project itself — a limitation which has a material impact upon any analysis where suppression leads to some incorrect conjectures and explanations. These processes of exclusion appear to be the necessary costs of doing such research. This might be regarded as a necessary hypocrisy of case-based methods.

The problem with the three questions asked by Frost and Stablein (*op cit.*) is that they are not definitively answerable prior to the study being undertaken. They may, however, give reasons to stop a study, except that perceptive managers might then be able to pick up the issues and make use of them to the disadvantage of others.

A further ethical compromise arises from the wish of the researchers not to objectify the subjects and isolate them from the learning process (see Reason & Rowan 1981; Reason 1988; and Reason 1994). Accordingly, studies can get designed and conducted so that the research project and the lessons drawn from it are both the continuing property of the research organisation as well as being available for wider dissemination. There are dangers in this approach in that the researchers may lose their independence of thought and critical reflection.

Discussion

From the range of literature reviewed, we claim that case-based research in addressing the content, processes and contexts of accounting practices has been useful and fruitful in many different modes. Accounts have been given of practices in a variety of settings and from many theoretical standpoints. If there has been no contribution greater than illustrating how accounting is implicated in and affects organisational behaviour, managerial practices and policy discussions then it has been very valuable for it has justified the study of the problems and the methods of research. But it has done more because it has begun to affect the way in which accounting is both researched, taught and studied and has made more evident the limitations of a narrow technical approach to research in accounting.

The literature that we have cited demonstrates that there is much energy, much good case research in both of the main traditions of positivism and constructivism. But we need to be clear that there are important differences in these approaches; as positivists seek predictability and public and inter-subjective testability as an essential element in their scientific schema, they argue that functionalism is not scientific because it is vague in its definitions, incapable of prediction, is unable to explain changes and is somewhat tautological. Further positivists argue that the constructivists and subjective approaches to knowledge are irrelevant to the scientific study of social phenomena. In its turn, positivism tends to overemphasise experimental technique, an approach that is often inapplicable to social phenomena. Further as positivism is addicted to measurement and quantification, it does not pay attention to establishing the meanings actors construct for their experiences. From a functionalist and holist perspective, positivists proceed by a process of reductionism and fragmentation to variables and conjectured relationships, which effectively render the social system unavailable for examination and analysis. From the standpoint of critical and hermeneutic approaches, the functionalist approach is so rooted in its analytical tautologies that it is incapable of explaining change and worse than that it actually tends to sustain and justify the present state of the system of social relations without examining the issues of ideology and power which maintain inequality and the current purposes of accounting in an organisation.

These critiques are familiar enough in the accounting literature (see Lowe & Puxty 1989; Jonsson & McIntosh 1997). What is more problematic is that there is no meta-epistemological stance from which the matter may be decided in favour of one (or none) of them. There are quite different approaches to knowledge, with different rules and so on, which may well relate to different ideological presuppositions of their adherents. So they cannot be used to dismiss each other, merely to illuminate differences. Hence there is no sense in which it may be that positivistic, 'quantitative' case research is superior to constructionist or subjectivist research for they come from different traditions of knowledge. The relevance and interest of a particular research approach is itself a matter of subjective judgement.

The credibility of the researchers, both in terms of their professional knowledge and their personal integrity, is of central importance in ethnographic constructivist research whereas it is generally dismissed as a side issue in the physical sciences. This arises because of the central role of replication in physical science, which is seldom, if ever, possible in the social sciences. If work can be replicated, issues other than accurate reporting to enable replication are not of central importance; here work which fails to be replicated does not stand up. But the nature of many investigations in social science is such that replication is impossible, except where it is argued that that the behaviour of the subjects of the study is in some way universal. Most studies of organisations cannot be repeated except in the broadest sense, their results cannot be used for prediction, and the value of the study lies in the insightful nature of descriptions and explanations offered. Thus a much greater degree of reliance is placed on the skills and integrity of the investigators whose influence can never be removed from the results presented. So researchers and their subjects should be able to evaluate the contribution of case-based projects in a perceptive and insightful manner. It is weakness that this is not often the case, though Reason (1994) and his collaborators demonstrate the value and the difficulty of doing it.

There is also the issue of who should conduct case studies; in particular, are they suitable for Ph.D. students. Our own position on this issue is that, despite the issues involved, it is essential that research training is offered in these methods. These issues involve gaining and maintaining access, observing in organizations, interviewing (where two people are better than one), and critically analysing the empirical evidence once it is gathered. It is possible to minimise some of these risks, but the greatest risk is that case-based research is inevitably 'back-end loaded'; that is the most difficult part occurs at the end. By contrast, traditional hypothesis testing work is mainly 'front-end loaded', with the most difficult part being the construction of the research proposal; once designed, it is downhill all the way! Thus the nature of supervision and support may need to be adapted to cope with this issue. The supervision of students using case research methods can be very demanding for it is important that the supervisor works closely at all stages of the emerging project. Especially in the constructivist tradition it is necessary to encourage a continuing dialogue between the emerging case notes and theoretical conjectures, to ensure that the project does not get "lost" and that the student does not come to premature closure of debate or slip into unexplored conclusions. Further the analysis and writing-up stages are much more demanding here than in the positivist tradition, for the success of the research project is often established late in the day (or in years!).

A major practical limitation of case research is one of time and cost; for the projects require considerable depth of access and hence organisational cost as well as researcher time. The analysis of such projects is also lengthy. However, the strength of case-based methods is that they ground theoretical speculation in the empirical observation of real-world phenomena. Despite the wide variety of perspectives used in gathering and interpreting their data, case-based researchers all seek to maintain a strong link between evidence and argument in ways that are appropriate to their subject matter. An excessive pre-occupation with rigour in research methods has led to signs of 'rigor mortis' in the development of the discipline of accounting. Case-based research methods, although not a panacea, provide one avenue for avoiding such sterility. It is almost impossible for a serious case investigation not to uncover many items of interest to those interested in understanding and explaining the role of accounting content, processes and contexts in the functioning of organizations and the societies in which they are set. Yet, as

Humphrey (2001) has suggested, we seem to be falling in to presenting the results of our case investigations in a routine and stilted manner that reflects the standardised approach becoming normal in quantitative and positivist research; it may well be appropriate for us to use a much wider variety of styles in such presentations.

Case-based work has become respectable, in that it is now able to be published in a wide variety of outlets. We should avoid making it boring by demanding that it conform to an inappropriate set of standardised templates. The respectability exists because of the importance of the problem posed which is to seek understandings of the content, processes and contexts of accounting practice, recognising that these interact. It is difficult to see how a reductionist approach could begin to grapple with this complexity, but it is, as we have noted, difficult to come to a definite conclusion about the quality of theoretical work. But that does not mean that the range of studies in the bibliography have not made important contributions.

This chapter has been informed by the work of our varied encounters with our own work and that of accounting scholars with case research methods. It is contended that case methods in accounting are making a considerable contribution to the understanding of accounting and of accounting in its social and organisational context. In this chapter we have set out to consider the broad array of case approaches and have drawn attention to the problems. We claim that much progress has been made, as witnessed by the variety and depth of studies which are now in the literature. In noting the problems as well we trust that greater co-operation of academic researchers, practitioners and the profession can be brought to bear upon the necessary tasks of more cumulative projects in theory building.

Conclusions

The strengths of case-based approaches to accounting research are that they study the operation of accounting, both content and processes, in its organisational, social and societal contexts, demonstrating a fuller understanding of accounting processes that can be offered to both the subjects of the research and to a wider public.

Accounting case-based research has developed from its positive roots and opened up the social and organisational constitutional and constitutive nature of accounting for intensive study and new avenues for research. It has set out to deal with great complexity and interconnectedness, stimulated a continuing and hotly contested debate about ideology, methodology and methods, has begun to become more sensitive to the actors in the field and has produced a growing volume of research output. There are reservations about the degree to which this academic effort has been located in hermetically sealed academic camps with their own journals; the degree of impact upon professional and organisational practice; the degree to which accounting theory has been developed; the degree of cumulative nature of the research output; and the degree of cross fertilisation of the various camps. Nevertheless it has provided an important means of resisting the sterility that has tended to hinder some forms of accounting research as it has 'developed' over the past two decades. Case-based methods are not perfect, but we would argue that they provide a valuable mechanism to help us orient our work to addressing important issues relevant to our organizations and societies.

But given the internationalisation of accounting and commerce it is odd and sad that there are so few cross-national let alone cross-cultural cases in the literature (although, it could be that there are many and we have missed them all in our U.K. and English language based literature search — see Ahrens 1999; Bartolomeo *et al.* 2001). There is also a need for more case studies to reflect the rapidly changing economic, technological, social and religious context of accounting and control.

There is a need for a critical take on the development of accounting theory that has been produced by case study research. There is a suspicion that such research has been more productive in examining contexts and processes than it has been in developing accounting theory; a potential case of relevance lost?

Finally, we add a rather personal view. We both have undertaken case studies, continue to have case-based projects and believe that for some of the problems we face this is the only way of doing research with the potential to match the rich complexity of the field. But we still find it difficult and demanding, frustrating and elusive. We thought some twenty five years ago that case-based research would make more progress than it has, but that speaks to the difficulty of the enterprise and is in no sense critical of the efforts of friends and colleagues whose work we have read with pleasure and profit. To all of them we wish to express our gratitude and we hope that you the reader will be similarly grateful.

References

Abernathy, M. A., Chua, W. F., Luckett, P. F., & Sella, F. A. (1990). Research in management accounting; learning from others experience. *Accounting and Finance, 39*(1), 1–27.

Abdul-Rahman, A. R., & Goddard, A. (1998). An interpretive inquiry of accounting practices in religious organisations. *Financial Accountability and Management, 14*(2), 183–201.

Ahrens, T., & Dent, J. (1988). Accounting and organisations: realising the richness of field research. *Journal of Management Accounting Research, 10.* 1–40.

Ahrens, T. (1997). Talking of accounting: an ethnography of accounting knowledge in British and German Brewers. *Accounting Organizations and Society, 22*(7), 617–638.

Ahrens, T. (1999). *Contrasting involvements: A study of management accounting practices in Britain and Germany.* Amsterdam: Harwood Academic Press.

Alvesson, M., & Willmott, H. (1992). *Critical management studies.* London: Sage.

Anderson, S. W. (1997). ABC in General Motors from 1986 to 1993. *Journal of Management Accounting Research, 7,* 1–51.

Atkinson, A. A., & Shaffir, W. (1998). Standards for field research in management accounting. *Journal of Management Accounting Research, 10,* 41–68.

Bakar, A. (1991). Control in a TV company. Unpublished PhD thesis. Victoria, University of Manchester.

Bakar, C. R., & Bettner, M. S. (1997). Interpretive and critical research in accounting; a comment on its absence from mainstream accounting research. *Critical Perspectives in Accounting, 8*(4), 293–310.

Bartolomeo, M., Bennett, M., Bourna, J. J., Heydkamp, P., & James, P. (2000). Environmental management accounting in Europe: current practice and potential. *European Accounting Review, 9*(1), 31–52.

Baxter, J. A., & Chua, W. F. (1998). Doing field research: practice and meta theory in counterpoint. *Journal of Management Accounting Research, 10*, 69–88.

Baxter, J. A, & Chua, W. F. (2003). Alternative management accounting research-whence and whither. *Accounting, Organizations and Society, 28*(2–3), 97–126.

Bernstein, D. J. (2001). Local government measurement use to focus on performance and results. *Evaluation and Programme Planning, 24*(1), 95–101.

Berry, A. J. (1976). Control of capital investment. Unpublished Ph.D. Thesis. Victoria University of Manchester.

Berry, A. J., Capps, T., Cooper, D., Ferguson, P., Hopper, T., & Lowe, E. A. (1985). Management control in an area of the NCB: rationales of accounting in a public enterprise. *Accounting, Organizations and Society, 10*(1), 3–28.

Berry, A. J., Laughton, E., & Otley, D. T. (1991). Control in a financial service company (RIF): a case study. *Management Accounting Research, 2*(2), 109–130.

Boland, R. J., & Pondy, L. R. (1986). The micro-dynamics of a budget cutting process: modes, models and structure. *Accounting, Organizations and Society, 11*(4–5), 403–422.

Broadbent, J. M., Laughlin, R., & Willig-Atherton, G. (1994). Financial controls and schools: accounting in 'public' and 'private' spheres. *The British Accounting Review, 26*(3), 255–279.

Cahill, E. (1989). Accounting disclosure. Unpublished Ph.D. Thesis. Trinity College, Dublin.

Cassell, C., & Symon, G. (Eds) (1994). *Qualitative methods in organisational research*. London: Sage.

Chaston, I., & Mangels, T. (2001). E-commerce and small U.K. accounting firms: influence of marketing style orientation. *The Services Industries Journal, 21*(4), 83–99.

Christansen, J. K., & Skaerbaek, P. (1997). Implementing budgetary control in the performing arts; games in the organisational theatre. *Management Accounting Research, 8*(4), 405–438.

Chua, W. F. (1988). Interpretive sociology and management accounting research — a critical review. *Accounting, Auditing and Accountability Journal, 1*(2), 59–79.

Collier, P., & Berry, A. J. (2002). Risk in the process of budgeting. *Management Accounting Research, 13*(3), 273–298.

Covalevski, M. A., & Dirsmith, M. W. (1983). Budgeting as a means of control and loose coupling. *Accounting, Organizations and Society, 8*(4), 323–340.

Czarniawska-Joerges, B., & Jacobsson, B. (1989). Budget in a cold climate. *Accounting, Organizations and Society, 14*(1), 29–39.

Dent, J. F. (1991). Accounting and organisational cultures: a field study of the emergence of a new organisational rationality. *Accounting, Organizations and Society, 16*(8), 705–732.

Eisenhardt, K. M. (1989). Building theories from case study research. *The Academy of Management Review, 14*(4), 532–551.

Frost, P., & Stablein, R. (1992). *Doing exemplary research*. London: Sage.

Glaser, B. G., & Strauss, A. L. (1967). *The discovery of grounded theory. Strategies for qualitative research*. New York: Aldine de Gruyter.

Granlund, M. (2001). Towards explaining stability in and around management accounting systems. *Management Accounting Research, 12*(2), 141–166.

Hagg, I., & Hedlund, G. (1979). Case studies in accounting research. *Accounting, Organizations and Society, 4*(1–2), 135–143.

Haw, I. M, Qi, D., & Wu, W. (2001). The nature of information in accruals and cash flows in an emerging capital market: the case of China. *The International Journal of Accounting, 36*(4), 391–406.

Hopwood, A. G. (1974). *Accounting and human behaviour*. London: Haymarket Publishing.

Hopwood, A. G. (1987). The archaeology of accounting systems. *Accounting Organizations and Society*, *12*(3), 207–234.

Humphrey, C. (2001). Paper prophets and the continuing case for thinking differently about accounting research. *British Accounting Review*, *33*(1), 91–103.

Humphrey, C., & Scapens, R. W. (1996). Theories and case studies of organisational accounting practices: limitation or liberation? *Accountability, Auditing and Accountability Journal*, *9*(4), 86–103.

Johnson, P., & Duberley, J. (2000): *Understanding management research*. London: Sage.

Jonsson, S. (1982). Budgetary behaviour in local government — A case study over three years. *Accounting Organizations and Society*, *7*(3), 287–304.

Jonsson, S., & Macintosh, N. (1997). CATS, RATS and EARS: making the case for ethnographic accounting research. *Accounting Organizations and Society*, *22*(3/4), 367–386.

Kaplan, R. S. (1998). Innovative accounting research. *Journal of Management Accounting Research*, *10*, 89–118.

Knights, D., & Collinson, D. (1987). Disciplining the shopfloor: A comparison of the disciplinary effects of managerial psychology and financial accounting. *Accounting Organizations and Society*, *12*(5), 457–478.

Knights, D., & Willmott, H. (1993). It's a very foreign discipline: the genesis of expense control in a mutual life insurance company (Pensco). *British Journal of Management*, *4*(1), 1–18.

Lapsley, I., & Llewellyn, S. (1995). Real life constructs: the exploration of organisational processes in case studies. *Management Accounting Research*, *6*(3), 223–235.

Larringa-Gonzalez, C., Carrasco-Fenech, F., Caro-Gonzalez, F. J., Correa-Ruiz, C., & Páez-Sandubete, J. M. (2001). The role of environmental accounting in organisation change — an exploration of Spanish companies. *Accounting, Auditing and Accountability Journal*, *14*(2), 213–239.

Laughlin, R. (1987). Accounting systems in organisational contexts: a case for critical theory. *Accounting, Organizations and Society*, *12*(5), 479–502.

Laughlin, R. (1995). Empirical research in accounting: alternative approaches and a case for middle range thinking. *Accounting Auditing and Accountability Journal*, *8*(1), 63–87.

Llewellyn, S. (1992). The role of case study methods in management accounting and research: a comment. *British Accounting Review*, *24*(1), 17–32.

Llewellyn, S. (1993). Working in hermeneutic circles in management accounting research: some implications and applications. *Management Accounting Research*, *4*(3), 231–250.

Llewellyn, S. (1996). Theories for theorists or theories for practice? liberating academic accounting research? *Accounting Auditing and Accountability Journal*, *9*(4), 112–118.

Llewellyn, S. (1999). Narratives in accounting and management research. *Accounting, Auditing and Accountability Journal*, *12*(2), 220–236.

Lowe, A. (2000). After ANT: An illustrative discussion of the implications for qualitative accounting case research. *Accounting, Auditing and Accountability Journal*, *14*(3), 327–351.

Lowe, E. A., & Puxty, A. (1989). The problem of a paradigm: a critique of the prevailing orthodoxy in management control. In: W. F. Chua, E. A. Lowe, & A. Puxty (Eds), *Critical perspectives in management control* (Chapter 2, pp. 9–26). London: MacMillan.

Lowe, E. A., & Shaw, R. W. (1968). An analysis of managerial biasing: evidence from a company's budgeting process. *Journal of Management Studies*, *5*(6), 304–315.

Lukka, K., & Granlund, M. (2002). The fragmented communication structure within the accounting academy; the case of activity based costing research. *Accounting, Organizations and Society*, *27*(1), 165–190.

Malmi, T. (1997). Towards explaining activity based costing failure; accounting and control in a decentralised organisation. *Management Accounting Research, 8*(4), 459–480.

McLean, T. (1996). Bureaucratic and craft administration of the production process; the form of accounting and non accounting control arrangements. *Management Accounting Research, 7*(1), 119–134.

McPhee, R. D. (1990). Alternate approaches to integrating longitudinal case studies. *Organisation Science, 1*(4), 393.

McSweeney, B. (1997). The unbearable ambiguity of accounting. *Accounting Organizations and Society, 22*(7), 691–712.

Merino, B. D., & Mayper, A. G. (2001). Securities legislation and the accounting profession in the 1930s: the rhetoric and reality of the American dream. *Critical Perspectives on Accounting, 12*(4), 501–526.

Miles, M. B., & Huberman, A. M. (1994). *Qualitative data analysis.* London: Sage.

Mouritsen, J. (1996). Five aspects of accounting departments' work. *Management Accounting Research, 7*(3), 283–302.

Moustakos, C. (1988). *Phenomenology, science and psychotherapy.* Canada: Family Life Institute.

Neu, D., Cooper, D. J., & Everett, J. (2001). Critical accounting interventions. *Critical Perspectives on Accounting, 12*(6), 735–762.

Norris, G. (2002). Chalk and cheese; grounded theory case studies of the introduction and usage of activity based information in two British banks. *British Accounting Review, 34*(3), 223–256.

Otley, D. T. (1978). Budget use and managerial performance. *Journal of Accounting Research, 16*(1), 122–149.

Otley, D. T. (1990). Issues in accountability and control: Some observations from a study of colliery accountability in the British Coal Corporation. *Management Accounting Research, 1*(2), 91–165.

Otley, D. T. (2001). Extending the boundaries of management accounting research: developing systems for performance management. *British Accounting Review, 33*(3), 243–261.

Otley, D. T., & Berry, A. J. (1994). Case study research in management accounting and control. *Management Accounting Research, 5*(1), 289–299.

Otley, D. T., Berry, A. J., & Laughton, E. (1991). Retail and industrial finance. *Management Accounting Research, 2*(1), 109–139.

Owen, D., Gray, R., & Bebbington, J. (1997). Green accounting, cosmetic irrelevance or radical agenda for change. *Asia Pacific Journal of Accounting, 4*(2), 175–198.

Parker, L. D., & Roffey, B. H. (1997). Back to the drawing board: revisiting grounded theory and the everyday accountant. *Accounting, Auditing and Accountability Journal, 10*(2), pp. 212–247.

Patton, M. Q. (1990). *Qualitative research and evaluation methods.* London: Sage. (Also 3rd ed. 2002, London: Sage.)

Petterson, I. J. (2001). Implementing management accounting reforms in the public sector: the difficult journey from intentions to effects. *European Accounting Review, 10*(3), 561–581.

Popper, K. (1959). *The logic of scientific discovery.* London: Hutchinson.

Quattrone, P., & Hopper, T. (2001). What does organisational change mean? speculations on a taken for granted category. *Management Accounting Research. 12*(4), 403–430.

Reason, P., & Rowan, J. (1981). *Human inquiry. A sourcebook of new paradigm research.* London: Wiley.

Reason, P. (Ed.) (1988). *Human inquiry in action.* London: Sage.

Reason, P. (1994). *Participation in human inquiry.* London: Sage.

Richardson, S., Cullen, J., & Richardson, W. (1996). The story of a schizoid organisation: how accounting and the accountant are implicated in its creation. *Accounting, Auditing and Accountability Journal, 9*(1), 8–30.

Ryan, B., Scapens, R. W., & Theobald, M. (1992). *Research method and methodology in finance and accounting.* London: Academic Press. (Also 2nd ed. 2002, London: Thompson Learning.)

Scapens, R. W. (1990). Researching management accounting practice: The role of case study methods. *British Accounting Review, 22*(3), 259–281.

Scapens, R. W., & Roberts, J. (1993). Accounting and control; a case study of resistance to accounting change. *Management Accounting Research, 4*(1), 1–32.

Sinclair, A. (1995). The chameleon of accountability: forms and discourses. *Accounting Organizations and Society, 20*(2–3), 219–237.

Stake, R. (1995). *The art of case study research.* London: Sage.

Strauss, A., & Corbin, L. (1990). *Basics of qualitative research; Grounded theory procedures and techniques.* Newbury Park: Sage.

Tayles, M., & Walley, P. (1997). Integrating manufacturing and management accounting strategy: case insights. *International Journal of Production Economics, 53*(1), 43–55.

Tinker, T. (1985). *Paper prophets: A social critique of accounting.* New York: Praeger Publishers Co.

Tinker, T. (2001). Paper prophets: an autocritique. *The British Accounting Review, 33*(1), 77–89.

Tinker, A., & Neimark, M. (1987). The role of annual reports in gender and class contradictions at General Motors. *Accounting, Organizations and Society, 12*(5), 71–78.

Tomkins, C., & Groves, R. (1983). The everyday accountant and researching his reality. *Accounting, Organizations and Society, 8*(4), 361–374.

Van Maanen, J. (Ed.) (1983). *Qualitative Methodology.* Beverly Hills, CA: Sage.

Watson, T. J. (1994). Managing, crafting and researching; words, skill and imagination in shaping management research. *British Journal of Management, 5* (Special Issue), 77–87.

Weick, K. E. (1979). *The social psychology of organising* (2nd ed.). New York: Random House.

Willmott, H. (1983). Paradigms for accounting research: critical reflections on Tomkins and Groves. *Accounting, Organizations and Society, 8*(4), 389–405.

Yin, R. K. (1994). *Case study research.* London: Sage.

Young, J., & Preston, A. (1996). Are accounting researchers under the tyranny of single theory perspectives. *Accounting, Auditing and Accountability Journal, 9*(4), 107–111.

Chapter 15

Doing Case Study Research

Robert W. Scapens

Introduction

In recent years, case studies have become a popular method in accounting research, and accounting case studies are now to be found in a wide range of research journals. As editor-in-chief of *Management Accounting Research* I have encouraged the use of case studies and in the journal's first ten years (1990–1999) 24% of the papers used case study research methods, and a further 13% used field studies (see Scapens & Bromwich 2001). Nevertheless, case studies remain a controversial subject and various questions, both methodological and practical, need to be raised about their use in accounting research. In this chapter I will explore some of the practical questions that need to be addressed by case study researchers.[1]

Case studies are sometimes thought to be the easier alternative when compared to quantitative accounting research, which requires mathematical expertise and knowledge of statistics. However, having taught research methodology to graduate students for many years, and having undertaken both quantitative research and case study research in my career, I can certainly agree with Yin (1984: 26) that: "Case study research is remarkably hard, even though case studies have traditionally been considered to be 'soft' research. Paradoxically, the 'softer' a research technique, the harder it is to do." Considerable thought needs to be given to the design of case study research and to the practicalities of conducting a case study. In this chapter I will draw on my own experience in doing case studies and in supervising doctoral students conducting their own case studies. Specifically, I will explore various practical issues that need to be

---

[1] This chapter will draw on material that appears in the chapter on "Methods of case study research" which I wrote for Ryan *et al.* (2002). Here I will focus on the practical issues and add illustrations drawn from my own case study research. Readers interested in the methodological issues surrounding case study research are urged to read Chapter 8 in Ryan *et al.* (2002).

addressed by case study researchers. But first it may be helpful to explain how I came to start using case study research methods.

In the 1980s management accounting researchers began to explore the gap between management accounting theory and practice (see Scapens 1984, 1985). Previously it had been assumed by researchers that once practitioners understood the 'theory' (largely based on quantitative techniques informed by neo-classical economic theory — see Arnold & Scapens 1986) they would change their practices. However, it was increasingly recognised in the 1980s that despite exposure to the new management accounting theory, practices were not changing. Furthermore, researchers understood little about the nature and determinants of management accounting practices, other than a general awareness that they did not conform to the prevailing management accounting theory. Some researchers responded by undertaking surveys of management accounting practices — to establish the nature of those practices — and others began conducting case studies (see Cooper *et al.* 1983 and Scapens *et al.* 1987).

Initially, my response was to adapt the economics-based mathematical modelling approach, which I used in the 1970s to study financial accounting issues (see Scapens 1978). I had already adapted this modelling approach to study the nature of residual income in divisionalised organisations (see Scapens 1979). In the early 1980s I drew on this model to provide the theoretical underpinnings for survey-based research, aimed at explaining the management accounting practices of divisionalised companies in the U.S. and the U.K. However, despite a large sample of both U.S. and U.K. companies, and the use of some of the more sophisticated mathematical and statistical techniques available at the time, I was unable to find any of the predicted relationships. The only really significant finding was the lack of any significant correlations (see Scapens & Sale 1985). It was the failure of this quantitative study to explain management accounting practices that led me to look for other ways of understanding management accounting practices, and thus I started to use case study research methods. Nevertheless, the objectives of my research remained the same — to explain management accounting practices — although the theoretical approaches which underpinned the research also changed. Initially, I used Giddens' structuration theory (see Roberts & Scapens 1985, and Macintosh & Scapens 1990), and more recently institutional theory (see Burns & Scapens 2000). Over the years I have continued to use case study research methods, but the focus of the research has shifted to understanding the processes of management accounting change.

My experience in conducting case research certainly confirms Yin's view that case study research is remarkably hard. It is not just a matter of going to visit companies and writing up the results, as some critics seem to believe. Case study research requires clear research questions, a thorough understanding of the existing literature, a well-formulated research design with sound theoretical underpinnings, and above all excellent language skills. Whereas quantitative researchers use mathematical skills in their research, language skills are essential for case study researchers. They must be able to communicate with both the subjects of the research and the readers of their research reports and papers. They must also be able to synthesise large amounts of quite diverse data, such as interview notes and transcripts, documents, observations of meetings and so on, and from all this data produce theoretically informed and convincingly argued conclusions.

In this chapter, I will begin by identifying some of the different types of case studies and then discuss the issues to be considered in selecting suitable cases. I will continue by setting out the main steps in a case study. The chapter will be completed with a discussion of writing up case study research and getting it published.

Types of Accounting Case Study

It is important to start by recognising that case studies can be used in a variety of different ways in accounting research. The following are some of the types of accounting case studies. However, the list is intended to be neither definitive nor exhaustive. It merely seeks to indicate some of the different ways in which case studies can be used.

Descriptive case studies: these describe accounting systems, techniques and procedures used in practice. A number of companies may be selected as cases to describe different accounting practices or the similarity of practices in different companies. Descriptive case studies were particularly useful in the 1980s as researchers attempted to provide descriptions of management accounting practice (see Scapens *et al.* 1987). Then and subsequently such studies have often been funded by professional accounting bodies because they appear to offer the possibility of determining 'best' practice — sometimes conceived as the most common practice and sometimes as the practice adopted by 'successful' companies. However, such studies beg the crucial question of what constitutes 'best' practice and 'successful' companies. Nevertheless, such case studies are useful in providing information concerning the nature of contemporary accounting practices.

Illustrative case studies: in management accounting research (especially in North America), case studies have been used to illustrate new and possibly innovative practices developed by particular companies. For example, Kaplan (1986, 1998) has argued that accounting researchers can learn a lot from studying the practices of innovative companies. Such case studies provide an illustration of what has been achieved in practice. However, there is an implied assumption that the practices of these 'innovative' companies are, in some sense, superior to the practices of other companies. An illustrative case study cannot provide a justification for, nor can it test the validity of, this assumption.

Case studies can also be illustrative in the sense of providing a Weberian 'ideal-type'. These are case studies which provide empirical exemplars of the embodiment of particular theories. They are not intended to illustrate practices that are necessarily superior to others. Instead, they provide illustrations of the way in which particular theoretical categorisations can be observed in practice.

Experimental case studies: accounting researchers frequently develop new accounting procedures and techniques that are intended to be helpful to accounting practitioners. Sometimes, however, it can be difficult to implement the researchers' recommendations. An experimental case study could be used to examine implementation problems and to evaluate the potential benefits. Such cases would have been very helpful in the 1970s when researchers were developing sophisticated management accounting techniques — few of which were ever used in practice. Experimental case studies would have indicated the difficulties of implementing the proposed techniques. More recently, however, researchers have been conducting case studies to explore the implementation and use of new techniques — for example, de Haas & Algera (2002) used an experimental case study of a Dutch Steel Company to examine how new techniques can be used to stimulate goal congruent behaviour.

Exploratory case studies: the critics of case study research sometimes argue that, although case studies can be useful in exploratory research, larger scale studies are needed to generalise the findings. Such critics seem to have in mind exploratory case studies, which are used to explore the possible reasons for particular accounting practices and to enable the researcher to generate hypotheses that can be tested subsequently using survey methods and quantitative techniques. As such, an exploratory case study represents a preliminary investigation, which is intended to generate ideas and hypotheses for rigorous empirical testing at a later stage. The objective of the subsequent research being to produce generalisations about accounting practices. From this perspective, exploratory case studies are only the first step in the research — the important hypothesis-testing phase of the research comes later. Case studies of this type frequently contain an 'apology' that the research is only exploratory and cannot be generalised, as the case represents only a small sample.

Explanatory case studies: it is when we come to these case studies, which are the type that I use in my own research, that we see the real potential of case study research. Explanatory case studies attempt to explain the reasons for observed accounting practices. The focus of the research is on the specific case. Theory is used in order to understand and explain the specifics, rather than to produce generalisations. Theory is useful insofar as it enables the researcher to provide convincing explanations of the observed practices. If available theories do not provide satisfactory explanations, it will be necessary to modify them or to develop new theories, which can then be used in other case studies. The objective of the research is to generate theory that provides good explanations of the case.

The distinctions between these different types of case studies are not necessarily clear-cut. For example, it may not be clear which practices should be considered as innovative and the subject matter of illustrative case studies, and which should be regarded as existing procedures and the basis for descriptive case studies. Ultimately, it is the intention of the researcher that determines the classification. Furthermore, the distinction between exploration and explanation is rather ambiguous. An exploratory study, for instance, may be concerned with generating initial ideas that will form the basis of subsequent explanations of accounting practices. Despite such ambiguities, the above list gives an indication of the range of uses of case studies and the different emphases that researchers give to their work.

There is one distinction, however, which needs to be made clear, as it is important for the following sections of this chapter: that is the distinction between positive and interpretive case studies.[2] Traditional accounting research has utilised a positive empirical methodology, which relies to a great extent on the methods and theories of neo-classical economics. Such research sees the world as essentially objective and external to the researcher, uses deductive reasoning and hypothesis testing, and sees the role of accounting as assisting economic decision-making. It is from such a methodological perspective that case studies are seen as largely exploratory, and used to generate hypotheses for later testing through large-scale surveys and statistical generalisation.

An alternative methodological perspective views the world as socially constructed and subjective. In researching such a world the researcher cannot step outside the social processes, and must seek to interpret accounting within its organisational, economic and social contexts. Here we see the importance of explanatory case studies, which seek to provide deep and rich understandings of the social nature of accounting practices. It is this type of case study, the interpretive case study, which I have used in my own research. Such case studies require an in-depth understanding of the company or organisation being studied. Furthermore, as my most recent research has focussed on processes of management accounting change, my co-researchers and I have undertaken longitudinal studies in which we have conducted interpretive case studies over longer periods of time — sometimes as much as five years. In the following sections of this chapter I will be referring to interpretive case studies, unless it is indicated otherwise.

The particular uses made of case study research methods will depend on the methodological choices of the researcher and the nature of the research; specifically, the research questions to be addressed. I will return later to the importance of clearly specifying the research questions, when I discuss the main steps in a case study. But in the meantime, some comments are needed on the selection of suitable cases.

Selecting Suitable Cases

Researchers, who approach case studies from a positive methodological perspective may fall into what Yin (1984: 39) calls "the trap of trying to select a 'representative' case or set of cases". Such researchers, being concerned with generalising their findings, view case studies as a sample that, if correctly selected, may be used to generalise to a larger population. However, in such research it is not always clear what the selected cases are representative of — what aspect(s) of the population is the case supposed to represent? It may not be possible to answer this question until the research has been completed, particularly in exploratory case research. This can create problems for the selection of 'representative' cases.

Interpretative case studies, on the other hand, are used to develop and extend theory. Thus, the selection of cases should reflect the needs of theory development, rather than generalisation to some larger population.[3] Cases should be selected so that the

---

[2] For an extended discussion of the distinction between positive and interpretive case studies see the chapters on *Alternative philosophies of accounting research* and *Methods of case study research* in Ryan *et al.* 2002 (Chapters. 2 & 8). Only a brief summary can be provided here.
[3] Issues of generalisation (or transferability) in case research are discussed later.

researcher can focus on the questions to be addressed in the research. The research question(s), together with the theoretical framework that underpins the research, will define the characteristics of the cases to be studied, and the researcher should try to select cases that display those characteristics. Whereas the positive case researcher may be seeking representative cases, the interpretive case researcher may actually find it helpful to look for 'critical' or 'extreme' cases.

Where there is a well-formulated theory and the major research issues are clearly defined, it may be helpful to select a 'critical case' — i.e. a case in which the issues addressed in the research are brought into focus by some critical event which raises those issues to the surface in the organisation being studied. For example, in studying the nature of management accounting practices, I found it helpful to study organisations in which an event, such as a take-over or the appointment of a new chief executive, had caused management accounting systems to be re-examined. This was how my interest in management accounting change emerged. Initially, my interest was in the nature of management accounting practices *per se*, but I found it useful to study critical cases where management accounting practices were being scrutinised within particular companies — i.e. where management accounting change was taking place.

In situations where the researcher wants to extend a theory to cover a wider range of circumstances, it may be appropriate to select an 'extreme case'. For example, such a case might involve studying as very large or a very small company, or a company that is in a totally different industrial setting. Such a case study would indicate the extent to which the existing theory can be extended to provide explanations in widely differing circumstances, and may identify the extent to which the theory needs to be modified if it is to be applied to a much wider set of instances. For example, although my research on management accounting change has focussed on large, usually multinational companies, it would be of interest to broaden the research to study management accounting change in public sector organisations that are in the process of being privatised, or to study management accounting change in very small companies. Such studies would involve extreme cases for the theoretical insights that I have developed in my case studies of large private companies.

This line of argument can be extended to situations where there is little available theory. Here an 'exploratory case' could be used to begin the process of theory development.[4] The selection of the particular case for study may be relatively unimportant. What is needed is a relevant case that will enable the researcher to begin the process of theory development. Possibly, the case should be 'simple', in the sense that it avoids as far as possible complex issues, so that the study can focus on key issues — although it may actually be difficult to specify what these should be, before the study is undertaken. Nevertheless, when such 'exploratory cases' have been undertaken the initial theory can then be refined and extended as additional cases are studied by the researcher, or by other researchers. This brings us to the issue of multiple case studies.

---

[4] Here I'm talking about an exploratory case that will begin the process of explanation. In a sense, it is still an explanatory case, as the objective of the research is to explain the case, albeit in a tentative way. This is quite different to the exploratory cases of positive researchers.

In a programme of case study research multiple case studies can be used for two purposes — replication and theory development. A number of similar cases might be selected to replicate the theoretical explanations. Alternatively, dissimilar cases may be selected to draw out implications from their comparison and/or to extend the theory to a wider set of circumstances. The differences between the individual cases will be determined by the direction in which theoretical extension is desired. The objective of such multiple cases is to develop a rich theoretical framework, capable of explaining a wide range of circumstances. It is important to recognise the difference between multiple case studies and field studies. Although some researchers refer to the latter as a series of case studies,[5] their explanations are usually based on cross-sectional analysis of the entire set of organisations studied. In the former, however, each case is analysed separately and the explanations derived from the particular circumstances of the case; the theory is then extended to encompass all the cases.

Ideally, the selection of cases to be studied should follow a clear specification of the research questions and the theoretical framework for the research. The researcher can then use the points raised above in selecting suitable cases. However, in practice other problems may emerge, especially in research undertaken for a Ph.D., where the time and resources are severely constrained. The researcher may have to make use of easily accessible cases, and this may require some modification of the research questions and/ or the theoretical framework. Furthermore, as the research progresses issues may emerge which were not anticipated at the outset. This could represent a problem as the researcher may not be able to address the intended research question(s), or it could be an opportunity as new, and potentially more interesting, issues can be addressed. In either case, the researcher should be prepared to modify the research questions as the research progresses and to refine and develop the theoretical framework. As will be pointed out later, case research does not follow a simple linear process — defining research questions, selecting a theoretical framework and then conducting the case research. It is often much more 'messy', with the researcher having to adapt as the case progresses.

The Role of the Researcher

In selecting a case study it is important to consider the role of the researcher vis-à-vis the subject(s) of the research. There is a range of possibilities with the researcher more or less involved in the case — it is only where the researcher is an 'outsider' that he/she has no direct involvement in the case. In all the other possibilities the researcher has the potential to influence the case. Concerns are sometimes expressed about 'action research', as the researcher is part of the process being studied and not independent of the case. But to varying degrees this criticism applies all types of case study research. Before discussing this issue further I will list some of the possible roles of the researcher.

---

[5] Or 'mini case studies'.

Outsider: here the researcher relies on readily available evidence, such as published reports and other such secondary sources. The researcher does not have any contact with and cannot therefore influence the participants in the case. But even here, the resulting case study is still subjective — the researcher selects and interprets the evidence. As with all other types of case study, the output is the interpretation of the researcher. Historical case research is often the best example of the researcher as an outsider. With contemporary organisations the case researcher will normally make at least some 'site' visits, which bring us to the next possibility.

Visitor: this is probably the most common image of the case researcher — someone who visits the case site, and interviews the subjects of the research. Although the researcher is not directly involved in the issues being researched, the act of asking questions about these issues can have an impact upon those who are the subject of the research. It is this role that I have tended to adopt in my case research, and I am conscious of the impact which discussing issues can have on individuals in the case. In one case, we interviewed the managing director and chief accountant who explained their reasons for not implementing ABC. But several months later, ABC was being more widely discussed in the company. Was this the influence of the research process? Quite possibly!

Facilitator: in this next role the researcher is closely involved in the case site, explicitly raising issues, giving advice and opening up options for the subjects of the research to evaluate. However, the researcher does not provide solutions, rather he/she enables the subjects of the research to recognise the nature of their problems and helps them to find their own solutions. For example, a few years ago a group of Scandinavian researchers worked with a number of small to medium sized companies studying the process of developing and implementing new management information systems.

Participant: a classical approach in sociological studies was for the researcher to actually work in the organisation being studied — for examples, see Gouldner (1954) and Dalton (1959). Working as a participant allows the researcher to obtain insights into the everyday workings of the company. In some of these early studies the researchers did not disclose the research agenda to those with whom they were working. They were simply employees of the company — but they maintained detailed records of their experiences. However, there are now strict ethical codes which place limits on this type of research.

Actor: in action research the researcher is a key player in the subject matter of the research — possibly introducing a new technique or procedure. As such, the researcher intervenes in the case and is an active participant in the issues being researched. A group of accounting researchers in Finland have been using such an approach to study the implementation of modern management accounting techniques — see Lukka (2000) and Kasanen et al. (1993), who term their research method the 'constructive approach'.

When the researcher is an actor and intentionally intervenes in the case it is very clear that the research process influences the case study. But even when the researcher has a different role, he/she cannot be said to be independent of the case. The research process always has the potential to influence the case, except where the researcher is an outsider, and in all types of case study the output represents the interpretation of the researcher and is therefore inevitably subjective. Thus, it is important for such researchers to be aware that case research cannot be a neutral and objective process. The concerns sometimes expressed about action research (i.e. about the involvement of the researcher) apply in varying degrees to all case research and the researcher must keep this in mind when undertaking the case study and writing up the results.

Main Steps in a Case Study

In this section I will describe the main steps in a case study, assuming that a suitable case has been selected and access arranged. Although the steps will be listed in what might appear to be a logical sequence, it has to be emphasised that case study research is complex and interactive, and cannot be characterised by a simple linear process. In the course of a case study, the researcher may have to iterate through these steps several times, possibly in different orders and with different interactions between the individual steps. Nevertheless, it is useful to list the various steps so that the main elements of a case study can be discussed.

Preparation

The first step in any research, and particularly in case research, is to specify as clearly as possible the research question(s) to be addressed. This will usually be done in conjunction with a review of the existing research literature. The research question(s) will then shape the research design, including the research methods and even the methodology. The question(s) should be sufficiently focussed to provide a feasible research plan, given the available resources, especially time. This is particularly important where the research is undertaken for a research degree, as the time frame may be constrained and other resources limited. Given a specification of the research question(s), it will then be possible to select the appropriate type of (case) research method, and to decide on the researcher's role in the case — see above.

Now, assuming the research question(s) has(ve) been specified, and the nature of the case and the involvement of the researcher decided, the available theories relevant to the case should be reviewed in order to draw up a checklist of things to look for in the study. This review of prior theory will determine the way in which the researcher approaches the case. It is sometimes suggested that the researcher should begin a case study totally unencumbered by prior theory. This is quite impossible. Every researcher will be influenced by his/her past experience, previous research, papers read and so on. Thus, in any (every) case study there will be prior theory, although much of it will be implicit. To make the research meaningful to others, the researcher should make explicit, and as comprehensive as possible, the theory that shapes the case study. In addition to a preparatory review of prior theory, additional theory may be introduced as the case proceeds and new theories are developed. The researcher should be sufficiently flexible to allow such developments to take place.

Collecting Evidence

The preparatory review of theory will give an initial indication of the types of evidence that should be looked for in the case study. It may be helpful to consider each research question, possibly each element of each research question in turn, and identify the evidence that is needed in each instance. Mason (2002)[6] provides a useful layout for a chart linking research questions to sources of evidence, and other research issues, including ethical issues — see Figure 1 below. Such a chart should be completed when the research is being designed. But as the case study progresses, the researcher should be constantly alert for any evidence that appears to be important in explaining the case, and should be prepared to allow issues and theories to emerge out of the case, rather than being imposed on it. In most cases it will be necessary to use multiple sources of evidence. These could include the following:

Artefacts: these are any tangible items, such as formal reports and statements, minutes of meetings, informal records, and personal notes and memos made during meetings.

Questionnaires: these can be useful, even in case studies, to obtain evidence from a large number of people. They can also be used to gather information in a consistent and comparable manner. They could be mailed, or more likely completed during meetings with the researcher. Such meetings provide the opportunity for issues raised by the questionnaire to be discussed and any ambiguities to be resolved.

Interviews: this is the type of evidence most usually associated with case research. Interviews can take different forms, but probably the most important issue to consider is the extent to which they should be structured, semi-structured or unstructured. Structured interviews ensure that similar questions are asked of different people and that comparable information is obtained. But this requires the researcher to have a clear idea

Figure 1: Layout of chart for linking research questions, methods, practicalities and ethics.

Research Questions	Data Sources and Methods (i.e. evidence)	Justification (how evidence will be used?)	Practicalities (e.g. resources, access, skills)	Ethical Issues (such as confidentiality)

Source: Mason (2002: 30) — Adapted.

[6] Jennifer Mason's book on *Qualitative Researching* is very useful for anyone planning to do qualitative research, including case study research. Although it does not focus on accounting research, I have recommended it to all my research students since the first edition appeared in 1996.

of the type of information to be generated. Unstructured interviews, which is the way I tend to do my research, allow the researcher the flexibility to pursue new issues and ideas as they arise and thereby to explore emerging lines of enquiry. With semi-structured interviews the researcher has a broad framework for the questioning, which means that similar issues are discussed with a number of different people, but there remains sufficient flexibility to explore the issues in depth, and to follow up the responses that are given by the interviewee.

Observing actions and meetings: attending meetings can be an important source of evidence for accounting researchers. Clearly, it is better to attend meetings than to rely on the recollections of others who were present. Personally, I have found it difficult to obtain permission to attend important meetings. However, it can be easier to gain such permission when the researcher is actively involved as, say, a facilitator or actor — see above.

Assessing (measuring) the outcomes of actions: where actions have been taken at the case site, either by the researcher, or the subjects being studied, evidence of the outcomes is likely to be very important. Evidence collected by the researcher is clearly desirable, but it may be necessary to rely on the organisation's own information systems.

All evidence collected by the researcher should be recorded in an ordered and coherent manner for subsequent analysis and reflection, and where possible interviews and meetings should be tape recorded, or notes taken at the time. Where neither tape recording nor note taking is feasible, a record of what was said should be made in writing (or on tape recorder or word processor) as soon as possible thereafter. Memories can fade very quickly. Even where notes are made at the time, these should be converted into a more formal record as soon as possible. It is some times suggested that this should always be done before the end of the day — sleep dulls the memory! Thus, in arranging interviews, etc., it is important that, if several are to be held on the same day, time is allowed for writing up notes.

While formally collecting evidence, it is also important to be aware of informal evidence. For example, when interviewing a manager about the use of an accounting system, clues may be obtained about, say, the relationship between production and accounting staff through casual comments, tone of answers, physical gestures, etc. The researcher should be prepared to follow up such informal clues in any appropriate way; for example, by asking additional questions, interviewing other managers, observing meetings, and so on. Apart from suggesting new issues to explore, informal evidence may also give indications about the credibility of different information sources. All such informal evidence should be noted. For example, where an interview is tape recorded, if interesting non-verbal signals are obtained, the researcher could append suitable notes at the end of the tape.

When travelling to a case site to conduct an interview, I always allow plenty of time so that there is an opportunity before the interview to record at the start of the tape such issues as: the purposes of the interview, how it relates to previous interviews, what is expected, and how the interview is to be conducted. When there are two or more researchers attending the interview we usually stop (frequently at motorway services) to discuss these issues over coffee. We record these pre-interview discussions at the start of the tape, and comparable post-interview discussions are recorded in a similar way after the interview. These post-interview discussions review the informal information not on the tape — such as non-verbal signals, whether we felt the interviewee was open or guarded in his/her responses, and so on. We also discuss interesting issues which had been raised, especially where they might need following up elsewhere, how the interview related to other evidence, and finally how the evidence which is emerging relates to our theoretical ideas.

When there is only one researcher such pre- and post-interview thoughts could be dictated onto the tape, or if a tape recorder is not used the information could be noted on paper, preferably in a bound book. All the records, notes and other evidence collected by the researcher should be retained, as these comprise the 'field notes' from which the case analysis will be produced. Care should be taken to ensure that the field notes are as comprehensive and coherent as possible. They represent the case researcher's database.

Assessing Evidence

In conducting quantitative empirical research researchers are concerned with the reliability and validity of their evidence (see Ryan *et al*. 2002, Chapter 6). Reliability is the extent to which evidence is independent of the person using it, and validity is the extent to which the data are in some sense a 'true' reflection of the real world. But in case research, such notions of reliability and validity are unlikely to be appropriate. Reliability implies an independent, impersonal investigator, and validity implies an objective reality — both of which are meaningless in much case study research. As will be discussed below, the interpretations of the researcher and his/her relation to the subject matter are essential elements of any case study. Thus, alternatives to the criteria of reliability and validity are needed for case study research.

Whereas in quantitative research reliability requires an independent and neutral observer, in case study research it is important to know that the researcher has adopted appropriate and reliable research methods and procedures. This is known as *procedural reliability*. The research should have a good design that addresses clearly specified research questions; there should be a comprehensive research plan; all evidence should be recorded in coherent and comprehensive field notes; and the case analysis should be fully documented. In this way the researcher can demonstrate that the case study findings are reliable, and another person could in principle, at least, examine what has been done. In accounting terms, this might be described as an audit trail.

In discussing questions of validity it is usual to distinguish internal and external validity (see Ryan *et al*. 2002, Chapter 6). Whereas internal validity relates to the use of appropriate controls within the study, external validity concerns the extent to which its findings can be generalised to other settings. However, statistical generalisations are clearly problematic in case study research, especially in case studies where the objective is to develop theoretically informed explanations of the observed phenomena. The researcher will come to the case with knowledge of existing theories, and will examine whether the observations accord to this existing theory, and if not, the theory will have to be modified. But if the theory does explain the observations, other researchers may want to replicate the study, both in similar conditions and in different contexts. Consequently, theories are developed and modified through case study research, and they are retained so long as they continue to explain contemporary observations.

Thus, it is more appropriate to apply the logic of replication and extension, rather than a sampling logic, to case study research. This means viewing case studies as a method by which theories are used to explain observations. The theories that provide convincing explanations are retained and used in other case studies, whereas theories that do not explain will be modified or rejected. The objective of individual case studies is to explain the particular circumstances of the case, whereas the objective of a research programme based on these case studies is to generate theories capable of explaining all the observations made. As case studies seek to apply theories in new contexts, the theory is likely to be refined and/or modified, and through this process the theory is generalised. Such a process could be described as theoretical generalisation.[7] However, the potential confusion over different forms of generalisation has led some case study researchers to avoid the term altogether. According to Lincoln & Guba (1985) "the only generalisation is: there is no generalisation" (title of Chapter 5: 110–128). Instead, they talk about the *transferability* of the findings from one context to another and 'fittingness' as to the degree of comparability of different contexts (1985: 124 — see also Flick 1998: 234).

Turning now to internal validity, in case study research this criterion is replaced by the notion of *contextual validity*, which indicates the credibility of the case study evidence and the resulting conclusions drawn. This can entail several different elements.

First, the validity of each piece of evidence should be assessed by comparing it with other kinds of evidence on the same issue. Other subjects might be interviewed, records checked or observations made. This process of collecting multiple sources of evidence on a particular issue is known as triangulation — specifically data triangulation.

Second, the validity of particular sources of evidence should be assessed by collecting other evidence about those sources. If characteristic distortions emerge about a particular source the researcher will be able to assess the validity of evidence from that source. In addition, evidence might be collected using different research methods — for example, using a mixture of questionnaires to collect information from a large number of people, together with a combination of structured and unstructured interviews, and observation of meetings. This could be described as method triangulation.

Third, researchers should also assess the validity of their own interpretations of the evidence. Feeding evidence and interpretations to the subjects of the study can be helpful in confirming the researcher's own interpretation. But, as I have found, this may not always be possible, especially where an assurance of confidentiality has been given to individual informants. Personally, I like to work in research teams in order to avoid the bias that I, as an individual researcher, might bring to the study. By using a number of researchers, sometimes with different academic backgrounds, areas of interest, research experience, and so on, it should be possible to arrive at an agreed interpretation

---

[7] See Lukka & Kasanen (1995) for a discussion of different forms of generalization.

of the case, rather than one biased by the personal characteristics of the individual researchers. This could be described as researcher triangulation.

Finally, alternative theories, or even alternative methodologies, could be used to study a specific case. This might open up a diverse range of insights to be considered in interpreting the case. However, whereas an individual researcher might draw on alternative theories — using theory triangulation — it might be more difficult for an individual researcher to adopt alternative methodological positions. However, if different researchers approach the same issues using alternative methodologies, it might be possible for them to at least discuss their respective findings. Some might argue that such an approach would be unfruitful because of the incommensurability of different methodologies. But if a pluralistic attitude is taken and the alternative findings approached in an open-minded way, it may be possible to derive richer understandings through such methodological triangulation. However, I have to admit that I have not found a good example of this really working!

To summarise, whereas traditionally, empirical and especially quantitative researchers talk about reliability, validity and generalisability, in case study research we should think in terms of procedural reliability, contextual validity and transferability.

Identifying and Explaining Patterns

As the case study progresses a great deal of data will be amassed: notes and/or transcripts of interviews, documents and other reports, records of meeting, and also informal information. The researcher needs to go though all this data, possibly repeatedly, in order to identify themes and patterns. This can be very time consuming and there are no short cuts. Personally, I like to work though the transcripts of interviews (the main source of my data), highlighting relevant sections and noting interesting issues. I transfer these issues to separate sheets, cross-referenced to the transcripts, and then seek to build up a picture of the case. It is sometimes helpful to prepare diagrams or charts that attempt to link the various themes and issues so that patterns can emerge. But before illustrating such a chart, some other points need to be made.

There are now various types of computer software for handling qualitative data and for developing and arranging theoretical constructs; for example, Ethnograph and QSR NUD*IST. Personally, I have not found any them helpful for my research. But I understand that others do find them very helpful. They seem most appropriate when similar questions and issues are covered in a number of different interviews — for example, when structured interviews are used. But in my case research I normally use unstructured interviews and work with the word-processed transcripts.

I usually have all interviews transcribed professionally. I can do this because I normally have the necessary research funding. However, transcribing interviews is a very time consuming (and accordingly expensive) activity. I recognise that most Ph.D. students do not have the resources to have their interviews transcribed professionally and so have to do their own transcriptions. This can take a considerable amount of time. I sometimes tell Ph.D. students to be selective in what they transcribe. Initially, I suggest listening to the tapes and noting interesting sections and relevant issues on index cards.

Using a tape recorder with a number counter, or better still a modern digital recorder, it is possible to cross-reference these cards to the positions on the original recording — so that they can be easily located again. As a picture of the case begins to emerge, the more important tapes and relevant sections of other tapes can be transcribed as necessary.

Now returning to charts and diagrams, they can be helpful to give a picture of relationships between the issues which are emerging in the case. In this way missing connections, inconsistencies, etc., can be located and avenues identified for further investigation. As more evidence is collected, it may be possible to expand the diagrams and charts, adding new connections, and even reinterpreting the evidence collected earlier. The emerging patterns identified by the researchers will serve both to describe and explain the case.

In analysing the case of Omega, see Scapens & Roberts (1993), we were faced with a vast amount of data in the form of transcripts of interviews with various people who had been involved in the implementation of a new production control system, known as the Production Cost Control Project (PCCP), at one of the sites which was piloting the new system. However, the implementation had been unsuccessful and we wanted to explain why PCCP was resisted at this pilot site. A wide range of issues were identified in the interviews, ranging from the company's history as a monopoly supplier up until the 1970s, when it became subject to increasing competition. Within this context a

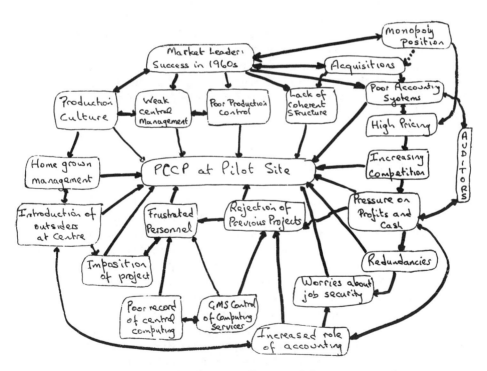

Figure 2: Example of pattern diagram of Omega case study.

production culture had emerged in the company, but this culture came into conflict with the increasing role of accounting due to pressure on cash flows and profits. Other issues were also involved, such as concerns about redundancies, poor experiences with centrally designed computer systems, the appointment of people from outside the company to senior management positions, and so on. To try to make sense of all these issues and the interconnections, we produced the chart shown in Figure 2 (see previous page).

When we write a case study we have to write in a linear fashion, with one sentence/ paragraph following another, and with one idea following another. We tend to think in such a linear fashion as well. However, in a case study the events and issues are much more complex, with many interconnections and reciprocal relationships — it is generally far from linear. Nevertheless, we have to translate this complexity into a structure through which we can tell the 'story'. The chart shown in Figure 2 enabled us to see the broader picture, to understand the interconnections between issues and events, and thereby to develop a structure for writing up the case. For instance, the lower part of the chart links the increased role of accounting with pressure on profits and cash, and the introduction of outsiders to central management. This interacted with redundancies, worries about job security, rejection of previous projects, frustrated personnel and so on, to create a situation in which the new production cost control system, introduced by the accountants, was perceived as a threat by many people at the pilot site.

We also produced another chart, see Figure 3 opposite, to help us see the connection between the various literatures that were used to interpret this and other case studies — these ranged from social theory, in particular Giddens' structuration theory, to organisation theory, and to the information systems and management control literatures. There is nothing fundamental in the nature of these particular diagrams, they simply provided a convenient with a way of making sense of a wide range of issues and literatures, and thereby they made it easier for us to begin the difficult task of writing up the case.

Writing-up Case Study Research

The time and effort involved in writing up case study research should not be under-estimated. It can be a very time consuming process. A useful rule-of-thumb in case study research is that it takes one third of the time to set up the study, one third to do the fieldwork and one third to write it up. However, case study research is all about writing — writing is not confined to the final writing-up stage. Planning a case study involves writing proposals, research plans, preparing interview schedules, etc.

During the fieldwork there will be considerable writing of notes and possibly reports to be fed back to the subjects of the research and so on. Finally, the writing up stage involves the production of a detailed case analysis and an interpretation of the case, which together form the basis for research papers and possibly a dissertation. Thus, case study researchers need to have good language skills, as this is the basis of the research method; in the same way that quantitative researchers need numerical skills.

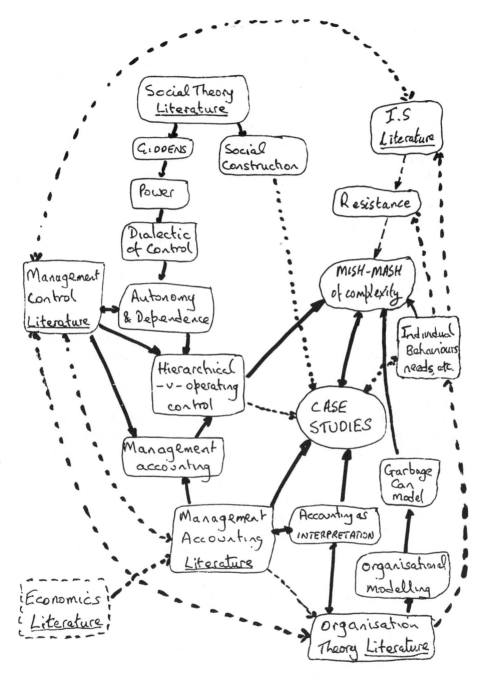

Figure 3: Example of pattern diagram of literature review.

The writing up stage involves the construction of the case study from what is likely to be a mountain of data, field notes, reports, etc. which have been collected during the fieldwork. This is a creative and literary act and, as such, the case researcher is the author-writer of the case study. In this writing the researcher has to produce a convincing text — that is a text that convinces the reader. But the first stage in convincing a reader is convincing oneself as a researcher. First, the researcher should feel he/she fully understands what is happening in the case. There should be no loose ends or outstanding issues — all issues considered relevant should have been explored and explained. Second the research must have a high level of procedural reliability, contextual validity, and transferability. Finally, and most importantly, the researcher must be convinced that selective plausibility has been avoided. Selective plausibility occurs when evidence is selected simply because it fits the researcher's own theory, while other evidence is ignored because it does not fit that theory. One way to avoid selective plausibility is build into the research design a recognition of, and an explicit search for, the types of evidence which would contradict the researcher's theory.

Once the researcher has convinced himself or herself, the task of writing a text to convince others can begin. Golden-Biddle & Locke (1993) suggest that convincing texts have authenticity, plausibility and criticality.

Authenticity is achieved by demonstrating that the researcher's interpretations are grounded in the case. The text should give the reader a clear sense of the author having been there. This can be achieved by providing rich details of the case and by explaining the extent of the researcher's relationship with the case. For example, details of the people interviewed, meetings attended, etc., should all be provided in sufficient detail for the reader to see how deeply the researcher has become immersed in the case. Authenticity will also be enhanced by the use of appropriate data to support the arguments being advanced. I try to use the interviewees' own words, and include many quotes in my case studies. But when quotes are used, it is important to ensure that they relate clearly to the points being made.

Plausibility will be enhanced if the text make sense to the reader and displays a high level of knowledge on the part of the author. A coherently written and well-structured case study will also increase the plausibility of the text. The issues raised by the case should be linked to the existing literature and recognise relationships with other cases and theories, including other disciplines, where relevant. However, it can be difficult to include a comprehensive literature review in a case study paper for a research journal — due to length restrictions. Nevertheless, it is important to show the reader the theoretical grounding of the case study and how it fits with broader literatures, but as concisely as possible.

The criticality of the text relates to the possibilities it provokes. The case may raise new ideas and/or add to theory. Further, it may have implications, both at the level of the case itself and more generally; for example, by drawing out theoretical insights which can be taken to other case studies. This relates directly to the issues of transferability discussed earlier.

Although these three criteria can be met in a variety of ways, a text which has authenticity, plausibility and criticality is likely to be convincing, and, as such, to be a good case study. And if you have produced a good case study, you are likely to want to get it published

Getting It Published

Clearly, to be published, a case study must be well written and thus authenticity, plausibility and criticality are very important. Also important is a good research design, with clearly developed research questions, which are explicitly addressed through the case study. The study must be theoretically well informed, with explicit theoretical underpinnings and consistent use of theory. It must also make appropriate use of evidence, which has been carefully collected and properly triangulated. In short, the study must have given appropriate consideration to the issues raised in this chapter. However, I would make some additional points, based on my experience as an editor of *Management Accounting Research*.

For a case study to be publishable it must make a contribution to the existing knowledge of the subject. In other words, it must contain some originality. This will normally be found in the implications of the research, which may be either theoretical or practical. But for publication in an international research journal some theoretical contribution is probably necessary. However, identifying suitable contributions in individual research papers can be quite difficult, especially when the research has been done as part of a research degree. Such a study will have been written up in the form of a dissertation and the researcher may then want to divide it up into two or more separate papers for submission to research journals. Here it is important to identify the specific 'message' that each paper is seeking to convey — i.e. its contribution. Sometimes, it is tempting for a doctoral researcher simply to summarise the entire research in one paper. In such cases, I usually find that there is no clear message, and as such the paper fails to make a sufficient contribution to justify publication. Rather than starting from a summary of the research, it is better to start by establishing the messages that each paper is to convey, and then asking whether there is sufficient originality to justify publication. It is always important expose such papers to wider audiences at conferences and workshops before submitting them to journals. Contribution to knowledge can be a subjective matter and can be difficult for the individual researcher (especially the inexperienced researcher) to recognise.

In translating a large-scale study into a series of research papers, it is important to ensure that each paper makes its own contribution. As such, although references can be made to other papers, each individual paper must stand on its own. Thus, there must be a clear research question or questions which are addressed in the paper, and which have specific implications. However, it is not normally necessary to repeat the development of the theoretical framework in each paper — cross-referencing to other papers is usually sufficient. This brings me to the use of theory in case study based research papers. There is a tendency to produce papers which could be described as 'thick sandwiches', which contain some initial theory, followed by a detailed description of the case, and then some (usually brief) theoretical discussion. In such papers, there is little or no evident theory in the case description. However, if the case study is theoretically informed, one would expect to see the case description penetrated by theory. It may not be necessary to keep referring to theoretical ideas and concepts in the case description, but the structure of the case description should have a clear theoretical underpinning. It may be as simple as using sub-sections and sub-headings derived from the theoretical framework to organise the case material.

Finally, it is important to recognise that the case studies published in different journals may have different styles. For example, in some journals there are extensive case descriptions, while only limited descriptions are provided in others; in some extensive quotes are used, whereas in others there are few, if any, quotes. Thus, it is important to be familiar with the style of papers in the intended journal, and more generally always to write with a specific journal and audience in mind. Furthermore, if that journal does not accept the paper, it should be revised before it is submitted to a new journal. When a paper has been rejected it is not normally a good idea to send it unchanged to another journal. Apart from differences in journal styles and audience, it could be sent to the same reviewer. In such an event, if the reviewer's previous comments have not been incorporated into a rewritten version, the reviewer is likely to be very negative about the paper, even if it is now submitted to a 'less prestigious' journal (whatever that may mean!). I have been asked to review an unchanged version of paper I had previously reviewed for another journal on several occasions in my career. Finally, when reviewing a paper for a specific journal it is always worrying to see a bibliography that contains no (or very few) references to that journal, when you know it has already published various papers in the area.

Concluding Reflections

As I said at the beginning of this chapter, case studies are not the easy option — even the initial stages of negotiating access to suitable case sites can be much more problematic than obtaining data tapes or sending out questionnaires. But in addition, case study research requires very sound methodological as well as theoretical understandings. The research must also have clear research questions, and the researcher must be very well organised, both when collecting evidence and in synthesising the results. But most importantly, the researcher needs excellent language skills to be able to convince the reader that his/her interpretation of the case provides real insights into the subject matter of the research.

As case studies have become a more established method of (management) accounting research, expectations concerning the level of methodological and theoretical sophistication have increased. When case studies were relatively new in accounting research, reviewers and journal editors were sometimes prepared to accept papers with largely descriptive case studies, especially if they were in an area that had not previously been researched. Similar comments could also be made about case studies in research dissertations. However, nowadays case study researchers are expected to have given appropriate consideration to the methodological and theoretical underpinnings of their research design, and to have used/developed theoretical understandings of the subject matter of their study. As such it could be said that doing case studies is becoming harder!

In a review of the first decade of *Management Accounting Research*, which I undertook with my co-editor, Professor Michael Bromwich, we categorised a significant number of papers (40% in 1990–1994 and 29% in 1995–1999) as 'applied' research — that is, they had no explicit, or clearly discernible implicit, theoretical framework (see Scapens & Bromwich 2001). These papers were usually either case studies or surveys. However, we emphasised that papers which are not explicit about their theoretical underpinnings are less likely to be published in the future (Scapens & Bromwich 2001: 249).

Nevertheless, despite the difficulties, case study research can be very rewarding. At a personal level, having undertaken case studies myself and supervised others conducting case studies over a period of approaching twenty years, I now feel that I have some understanding of why management accounting practice takes the form that we observe in contemporary organisations, and I am now beginning to make sense of the processes of management accounting change. The case studies that I undertook with John Roberts in the early 1980s helped shape my understanding of the role of management accounting in organisations. This research drew on Giddens' structuration theory and focussed on the role accounting in the signification, legitimation and domination of organisational activities (see Roberts & Scapens 1985), and led to my interest in researching resistance to management accounting change (see Scapens & Roberts 1993). This later research was extended through case studies with John Burns in the 1990s, which used institutional theory to study management accounting change. These case studies have emphasised the importance of exploring the 'taken-for-granted' assumptions that underpin organisational activity when seeking to implement new management accounting systems and techniques (Burns *et al.* 2003).

But this does not mean that I now understand everything about management accounting, much still remains to be done. Nevertheless, I believe that I now have much richer insights and a more theoretically informed understanding of management accounting practice in contemporary organisations, than I could have obtained had I continued using survey-based research, irrespective of the sophistication of the quantitative techniques used to analyse it. For me, case studies are essential for understanding the nature of management accounting practices in contemporary organisations. I hope my comments in this chapter will encourage other researchers to use (and to continue using) case studies in their own fields of accounting research.

References

Arnold, J. A., & Scapens, R. W. (1986). Economics and management accounting research. In: M. Bromwich, & A. Hopwood (Eds), *Research and current issues in management accounting* (pp. 78–102). London: Pitman.

Burns, J., & Scapens, R. W. (2000). Conceptualising management accounting change: An institutional framework. *Management Accounting Research*, *10*(1), 3–25.

Burns, J., Ezzamel, M., & Scapens, R. W. (2003). *The challenge of management accounting change: Behavioural and cultural aspects of change management*. Oxford: Elsevier/CIMA Publishing.

Cooper, D., Scapens, R., & Arnold, J. (1983). *Management accounting research and practice*. London: Chartered Institute of Management Accountants.

Dalton, M. (1959). *Men who manage*. London: Wiley.

Flick, U. (1998). *An introduction to qualitative research*. New York: Sage.

Golden-Biddle, K., & Locke, K. (1993). Appealing works: an investigation of how ethnographic texts convince. *Organization Science*, *4*(4), 595–616.

Gouldner, A. W. (1954). *Patterns of industrial democracy*. New York: Free Press.

de Haas, M., & Algera, J. A. (2002). Demonstrating the effect of the strategic dialogue: participation in designing the management control system. *Management Accounting Research*, *13*(1), 41–70

Kaplan, R. S. (1986). The role of empirical research in management accounting. *Accounting, Organizations and Society*, *11*(4/5), 429–452.

Kaplan, R. S. (1998). Innovation action research: creating new management theory and practice. *Journal of Management Accounting Research*, *10*, 89–118.

Kasanen, E., Lukka, K., & Siitonen, A. (1993). The constructive approach in management accounting research. *Journal of Management Accounting Research*, *5*, 243–264.

Lincoln, Y. S., & Guba, E. G. (1985). *Naturalistic inquiry*. Beverly Hills, CA: Sage

Lukka, K. (2000). The key issues of applying the constructive approach to field research. In: T. Repneu (Ed.), *Management expertise for the new millennium* (pp. 1–16). Turku, Finland: Turku School of Economics and Business Administration, A-1.

Lukka, K., & Kasanen, E. (1995). The problem of generalizability: anecdotes and evidence in accounting research. *Accounting, Auditing and Accountability Journal*, *8*(5), 71–90.

Macintosh, N., & Scapens, R. (1990). Structuration theory in management accounting. *Accounting Organizations and Society*, *15*(5), 455–477.

Mason, J. (2002). *Qualitative researching* (2nd ed.). London: Sage Publications.

Roberts, J., & Scapens, R. W. (1985). Accounting systems and systems of accountability — understanding accounting practices in their organizational contexts. *Accounting, Organizations and Society*, *10*(4), 443–456.

Ryan, R., Scapens, R., & Theobald, M. (2002). *Research methods and methodology in accounting and finance* (2nd ed.). London: Thomson.

Scapens, R. W. (1978). A neoclassical measure of profit. *The Accounting Review*, *LIII*(2), 448–469.

Scapens, R. W. (1979). Profit measurement in divisionalised companies. *Journal of Business Finance and Accounting*, *6*(3), 281–305.

Scapens, R. W. (1984). Management accounting — A survey paper. In: R. W. Scapens, D. T. Otley, & R. J. Lister (Eds), *Management accounting, organisation theory and capital budgeting — three surveys* (pp. 1–95). London: Macmillan/ESRC.

Scapens, R. W. (1985). *Management accounting: A review of recent developments*. London: Macmillan.

Scapens, R. W., & Bromwich, M. (2001). Management accounting research: the first decade. *Management Accounting Research*, *12*(2), 245–254.

Scapens, R. W., & Roberts, J. (1993). Accounting and control: a case study of resistance to accounting and change. *Management Accounting Research*, *4*(1), 1–32.

Scapens, R. W., & Sale, J. T. (1985). An international study of accounting practices in divisionalised companies and their associations with organizational variables. *The Accounting Review*, *LX*(2), 231–247.

Scapens, R., Cooper, D., & Arnold, J. (1987). *Management accounting: British case studies.* London: Chartered Institute of Management Accountants.

Yin, R. K. (1984). *Case study research, design and methods.* Beverley Hills, CA: Sage Publications.

Chapter 16

What is the Object of Accounting?
A Dialogue

Masaya Fujita and Yoshiaki Jinnai

Introduction

This dialogue has two principal aims: one is to present a radical way of questioning or
problem-setting as the starting point of qualitative accounting research providing root-
oriented insights into the ways in which the researchers' way of thinking, analysing and
theorising are fundamentally determined. The other is to provide tips to academics who
are seeking to publish qualitative accounting research in English speaking journals when
English is not their first language.

In their inquiries into accounting the authors have benefited a great deal from a series
of methodological and epistemological problems that have been raised by Japanese
critical accounting theory, which originated in the early 1930s. It is not an overstatement
to say that the foundations of academic inquiry into accounting in Japan were first laid
by critical accounting research. This archetype of Japanese critical accounting research
is generally called the 'capital movement approach', which has roots in Marxist theory
and is constructed on a general hypothesis that the method of accounting is more or less
a reflected form of the movement of capital employed in a business enterprise. In the
1950s the 'socio-political superstructure approach', another type of Japanese critical
theory of accounting, was elaborated in an attempt to criticise and then overcome the
limitations in the scope and methodology of the 'capital movement approach' based on
a general hypothesis that accounting exists only when it does not reflect the actual
movement of capital employed in a business enterprise. This approach has roots in
Marxist theory, too.

A qualitative approach was often applied by the pioneers of these two different
critical accounting approaches to their analysis of the methods and institutions of the
capitalist mode of accounting. These pioneers criticised the then mainstream

The Real Life Guide to Accounting Research: A Behind-the-Scenes View of Using Qualitative
Research Methods
Copyright © 2004 by Elsevier Ltd.
All rights of reproduction in any form reserved.
ISBN: 0-08-043972-1

explanation of accounting not only by clarifying the actual capitalist functions of accounting in practice but also by examining the mainstream use of words, way of thinking, problem-setting, and personal values. The works of the critical accounting scholars, in turn, have provided a rich source of ideas for critical and qualitative accounting research. The authors are familiar with the real life insights into the formation of theory in the research process of the Japanese pioneers of critical accounting, which are virtually unknown to Western scholars to date.[1] In addition, the authors have experiences of visiting departments of accounting of universities in the U.K., of presenting papers at international conferences where English was the only official language, and of publishing research in English speaking journals.[2]

In our experience, there is a considerable gap in the way of problem-setting as well as in the use of key words such as 'object', 'function', 'accounting', and 'accountability' between Anglo-American and Japanese critical researchers. It is our opinion that this gap as such can be an object of qualitative and comparative research in accounting, and that to notice this gap will help researchers whose first language is not English to make their research accepted by English speaking journals.

Anglo-American critical accounting research has developed since the mid-1970s, and has contributed mainly to theorising about the organisational and social functions of the institutions, policies, and professions of accounting. However, there remains an unquestioned theoretical issue: "What is the object of accounting research"? This question is closely related to another fundamental question "What is the object of accounting?" This latter question, in turn, is closely related to a more fundamental question "What is accounting?" These questions should be in one's mind at the very beginning of his/her qualitative research in accounting.

Concentrating principally on the question "what is the object of accounting", the dialogue that follows consists of nine parts: Two types of accounting theory, the object of accounting, profit as the ultimate object of accounting, the method of accounting, the capital movement approach, the socio-political superstructure approach, the relationship between the object of accounting and the method of accounting, accounting institutions, and language and accounting theory.

Among these nine issues, the capital movement approach has provided a series of radical insights into fundamental concepts of accounting such as the object of accounting and the method of accounting. By contrast, the socio-political superstructure approach is more functional and shares research interest with the Anglo-American critical accounting school; both of these focus on the accounting institutions by which the function of control is structurised within contemporary society. The last part of the dialogue provides tips to researchers whose first language is not English and who are seeking to publish qualitative research in English.

---

[1] Tanaka (ed.) (1990) is an epoch-making work of qualitative research into the formation of accounting theory in Japan. The authors were involved in some of the interviews, in which they asked each of interviewees about the foundation and formation of his intellect: how he came to be interested in accounting, with what knowledge he started research into accounting, what problems he set at the start of his research, why he employed his method of research, and how he applied the method to his elaboration of accounting theory.
[2] Some of the authors' works in English are: Fujita (2002); Jinnai (1990); and Jinnai (forthcoming).

Dialogue

Two Types of Accounting Theory

A: One of the most important questions when starting accounting research is what are the key problems in accounting research, isn't it?

B: Yes, it is. But what are the key problems depends on which type of accounting theory the researcher would pursue.

A: Generally, there have been two types of accounting theories: the 'proposal' or 'normative' type and the 'descriptive' or 'positive' type. The former takes a form in which the researcher proposes some alternative way of accounting: an alternative method of assets valuation by the market value and/or the present value (discounted expected cash flows), for example. A proposal of accounting by the fair value not by the historical cost, for financial instruments from the viewpoint of the usefulness of accounting information for the decision-making of the users of financial statements falls within this type of theory. By contrast, the latter type of accounting theory takes a form in which the researcher analyses and describes the existing mode of accounting. For example, the actual functions and social significance of the present-day accounting systems.

B: Further more, the latter type of accounting theory could vary depending on what objective the researcher has in his/her mind.

A: In the former type of theory, the objective of the researcher usually is to prepare a better way of accounting: for instance, an alternative way of financial disclosure which provides more suitable information than that provided by the present way for the decision-making of the users of financial statements. What about the latter type?

B: The latter type of accounting theory is often called 'theoretical' or 'scientific', and the fundamental attitude of the researchers who pursue this type of research usually is to examine how accounting exists and functions within our society.

A: Generally, of these two types, which, do you think, should a researcher pursue? Or, shouldn't we determine which is more valuable or adequate? Is there any convincing criterion on which the validity of an accounting theory can be measured?

B: This is a very difficult question. It will be justifiable to say that, for both the 'proposal' and the 'descriptive' types of theory, the most important subject is to grasp the existing state of accounting properly. The former type usually aims at bridging the gap between the information provided by the existing system of accounting and the information needed by the users of accounting through improvements to the existing system. Hence, the starting point of this type of theory is to affirm the existing needs of the users of accounting information. By contrast, the latter type of theory aims at clarifying the actual meaning of the existing accounting system including the information provided by it and the needs of the users for accounting information.

The Object of Accounting

A: Then, is there any general standard on which the researcher would choose one that he/she should pursue? Or, is the choice simply a matter of one's taste?

B: Now, let's have a look at the theoretical issues from the standpoint of the latter type of accounting research. What is most important in accounting research? I would say that the most important is the 'object' of accounting, that is the thing to which the recognition and measurement activity in accounting is directed. The object of accounting is important because the object of accounting fundamentally determines the 'method' of accounting, i.e., the way by which the object is recognised and measured. What is disclosed by the existing system of accounting is the information provided by the existing method of accounting.

A: What is the object of accounting, then? It is generally supposed that, in the case of business accounting, the object of accounting is business activities, or the economic events and economic resources of a business enterprise. However, can we say that the object of accounting is simply 'business activities' of a business enterprise? Rather, isn't it more appropriate to say that the object of accounting is the enterprise's 'capital movement', which concept is obtained through an abstraction of business activities?

B: If one regards business activities as the object of accounting, then to what aspect of the business activities is accounting directed? Or, is accounting directed to all sorts of activities of the enterprise?

A: It can't be. Accounting is directed to only a part of the business activities.

B: What sort of part, then? It will not be very difficult for one to admit that the object of accounting is business activities. At the same time, accounting is sometimes directed to events that occur outside the business activities in order to gather information required for evaluating assets and liabilities: their market values, for example.

A: Then, conversely, isn't accounting directed to business activities?

B: Yes. We have to say that accounting is indeed directed to business activities. And in this understanding, we should examine the meaning of the 'object of accounting' more carefully and strictly.

Profit: The Ultimate Object of Accounting

A: Can you say more about the strict understanding of the object of accounting?

B: Let me say plainly. The ultimate object of recognition in accounting is profit. Profit as such can neither be seized nor be touched.

A: Is it so? Can't we seize or touch profit by looking at an increment or decrement of assets?

B: We can recognise an increment or decrement of assets only by comparing two different amounts of assets at two different points in time, or more precisely, by subtracting the basic amount of value or physical quantity of the stocks of assets at a given point in time from the amount of value or physical quantity of the stocks of assets at another and latter point in time. The former amount serves as the base of comparison. This sort of activity as such is accounting calculation irrespective of the form of calculation.

A: To do mental arithmetic is a form of such calculation, isn't it?

B: Of course, it is. Therefore, profit is made recognisable indirectly only by the mediation of accounting calculation: subtraction of a number (the amount of costs) from another (the amount of revenue), and the remainder of which appears to be profit. Accounting, therefore, is like a mirror, which makes something invisible visible.

In accounting, the information about the numbers for this subtraction, i.e. the minuend, or, the number from which another is to be subtracted, and the subtrahend, or, the number to be subtracted, are obtained from business activities. The proposition that the object of accounting is business activities does mean that the source of the information about the numbers for accounting subtraction is within the business activities. Accordingly, accounting is neither directed to all of the business activities, nor aims at picturing the whole of the activities. This also means that accounting does not gather information from all aspects of the business activities. And conversely, it does not mean that accounting does not obtain information from outside the business activities. When it is required for calculation, information sometimes is gathered from the markets outside the entity,

The Method of Accounting

A: Now, I understand that the question of "what is the object of accounting?" is important for an accounting theory. How is the problem of the object of accounting related to other problems of accounting?

B: As we will discuss later, the problem of the object of accounting has been related to the theoretical issues that Japanese critical accounting has raised and Anglo-American critical accounting has seldom discussed to date: an example of the issues is the relationship between the object of accounting and the method of accounting.

A: Does this mean that the problem of the method of accounting is important for accounting research?

B: We may say that one of the objects of accounting research is the method of accounting. And this object will be important even when one positively denies the significance of it as an object of research in accounting.

A: What do you mean by 'the method of accounting'?

B: The method of accounting may include the technique of bookkeeping, which is composed of the double-entry system and/or the single-entry system.

A: Does the term 'method of accounting' correspond solely to the mere technical aspects of bookkeeping such as debtor and creditor?

B: Your usage of 'the mere technical aspects of bookkeeping' may connote an underrating of the importance of the object. I would claim that the very 'technique' of bookkeeping is extremely important. And the technique or method of accounting is closely linked with the economic and legal forms of enterprise: partnership and stock corporation, for example. The method of accounting of a partnership, for example, has its peculiar structure, just as that of a stock corporation has a structure of its own. The peculiarity of the method of accounting should be uppermost in accounting researchers' minds.

A: In corporate accounting, there are several accepted standards of accounting for various kinds of allowances, deferred assets, and assets valuation, for example, and a corporation often tries to make the most of the plurality and flexibility of these accepted accounting standards in calculating its annual profit. Are these also included in the method of accounting?

B: Of course, they are.

A: It is sometimes said that the object of accounting research is not the method of accounting but the actual practice of accounting, isn't it?

B: I know that. The claim that the object of accounting research is the actual practice of accounting seems to be persuasive. But, is it really feasible for one to see accounting practice? We have never heard that those who insist that the object of accounting research is the actual practice of accounting have ever seen the actual practice.

A: If we accept the hypothesis that the object of accounting research is the method of accounting, then what is the adequate approach to the method of accounting?

B: It is not an easy question. And this brings us back to the starting point of questioning. I have pointed out that the method of accounting includes the double-entry bookkeeping system. Accounting scholars tend to be impressed by the beauty of the mathematical consistency of the double-entry bookkeeping system. And they tend to be in doubt as to how they should analyse the double-entry system theoretically. In case one decided to pursue the 'descriptive' type of theory, it is not very easy for him/her to describe the double-entry system as something historical or, something with capitalist connotations, because its mathematical consistency itself is ahistorical.

A: But it is of no use to praise the beauty or consistency of the double-entry system.

B: Yes, indeed. And a typical interpretation of the double-entry system is the functionalist's one; in which it is claimed that the double-entry bookkeeping system does have a mathematical completeness and is pure from any blemish, and the fault, if any, lies with the person who uses the system and not with the system as such.

A: We have frequently seen such an approach. What sorts of problems are there in this approach?

B: While the object of accounting research may include the double-entry system as a kind of accounting method, this approach focuses not on the method of accounting but on the fault of the person who uses it. In other words, it is generally insisted in this approach that the management as the representative of the spirit of capitalism utilises the method of accounting for the pursuit of profit, and sometimes manipulates accounting numbers in order to deceive people in the markets. In this respect, it should be noted that there is a kind of substitution of logic in this approach. Of course, one can insist that the object of his/her research is not the existing method of accounting but the contemporary mode of capitalism, and, therefore, the contemporary mode of accounting can only be looked at as a phenomenon of contemporary capitalism. This type of functionalist approach would result in the neglect of the method of accounting, which underlies any mode of accounting.

The Capital Movement Approach to Accounting

A: What, do you think, is the significance of the 'capital movement approach' that originated in the 1930s as an archetype of Japanese critical theory of accounting?

B: The capital movement approach aims at clarifying the method of accounting referring to the movement or circulation of capital of a business enterprise. This approach can be described as 'reductionism', to use the terminology widely recognised by Western theorists. This approach starts from the hypothesis that the object of accounting research is the method of accounting, and that the object of accounting is the capital movement or circulation of individual business enterprise. By adopting the supposition that the bookkeeping method reflects the capital movement of the business enterprise, this approach has tried to clarify that the bookkeeping method, which seemingly is of ahistorical characters, is in fact of capitalist, hence historical and specific characters. This is the reason why it is important for a researcher to question "what is the object of accounting?" and "what does accounting try to represent?"

A: Do you think that the capital movement approach to accounting has been successful?

B: The evaluation of this approach may vary as Japanese critical theory has split into several streams. A crucial question is to what extent the existing method of accounting can be explained in terms of the movement or circulation of capital in an enterprise. Do you think that the existing method of accounting for allowances, for example, can be fully clarified from the viewpoint of capital circulation?

A: This task doesn't seem very easy. More generally, not only allowances but also many other items on the credit side of the balance sheet cannot be fully understood from the viewpoint of capital circulation because many of these items cannot be conceptualised as a form of capital employed in a business enterprise.

B: From the viewpoint of capital circulation, an accrual of cost is explained as a transfer of value to the product. In this approach, there exists the transfer of value as a movement of capital first, and then basing on it, the recognition of cost is explained. However, in the case of allowances, neither the corresponding cost nor the transfer of value has been actually accrued yet. Nevertheless, allowances are calculated and reported in accounting practice. Allowances cannot be clarified on the basis of the transfer of value. In this sense, it can be said that the capital movement approach to accounting has not been very successful.

The Socio-political Superstructure Approach to Accounting

A: The above sort of doubt about the effectiveness of the capital movement approach resulted in the emergence and development of the 'socio-political superstructure approach', another type of Japanese critical theory of accounting, didn't it?

B: Yes, it did. The socio-political superstructure approach can be described as 'voluntarism' in that it aims at clarifying the class, or subjective characteristics of capitalist accounting. This approach regards capitalist accounting as a historical product created by the economic 'base' for its reinforcement and development. It is said in this approach that, while management accounting serves to acquire the monopolist 'maximum' profit, financial accounting serves to conceal or justify the profit by providing others with false accounting information that does not reflect the actual economic phenomena.

A: Returning to the problem of the object of accounting, what is supposed as the object of accounting in this approach?

B: If one seriously pursues the object of accounting, one tends to run into the capital movement approach or the like. The socio-political superstructure approach has been escaping from, or taking no account of, this type of consideration and discussion. As a result, the socio-political superstructure approach has been inclined towards function-alism without questioning the structure of accounting and the nature of the information produced by accounting. This provides us with a historical lesson on the importance of setting the problem: "What is the object of accounting?"

The Relationship between the Object of Accounting and the Method of Accounting

A: You said that the object of accounting, or, more precisely, the object of accounting recognition, is 'profit'. What, do you think, is the relationship between the object of accounting recognition and the method of accounting?

B: This problem is how to understand the relationship of the method of accounting to the object of accounting. In the traditional way of thinking of the capital movement approach, a typical understanding of the relationship between the two is a reflection: the understanding that the method of accounting has developed in order to reflect the capital movement of a business enterprise. This understanding has been more or less shared not only by critical accounting scholars but also by researchers who regard accounting as something reflecting business activities, or regard the method of accounting as that which was made up to reflect the business activities.

A: If accounting can be regarded as a reflected or represented 'form' of business activities, a set of business activities that is reflected or represented in accounting is the "content" of accounting. This relationship between accounting and business activities seems to be very similar to that between words that represent objects and the objects that are represented by words in a language.

B: Yes, it does. As previously mentioned, I think that the object of accounting is 'profit', and that the calculation of profit consists of two elements: a 'minuend', or a number from which another is to be subtracted, and a 'subtrahend', or a number to be subtracted. In my understanding, accounting may be characterised as a method that calculates profit by classifying the elements into two groups: minuends and subtrahends. Therefore, the object of accounting can be described as profit, or something invisible and untouchable, and the method of accounting may be explained as the means by which the profit is made visible as if it does actually exist. The relationship between the method of accounting and profit, therefore, can be regarded as the relationship between 'signifier' and 'signified', the terms used in linguistics. As you know, the signifier, to put it simply, is the word, and the signified is the thing or idea the word represents. It should be noted that the relationship between these two could be considered not accidental but necessary. Likewise, the relationship between accounting method and profit can be considered necessary as long as no method of profit calculation other than accounting calculation has been elaborated to date.

A: You said that the object of accounting is profit. But isn't it inappropriate to insist that the object of accounting for not-for-profit organisations/public sector bodies is also profit?

B: It's a good question. Profit calculation is not the only purpose of accounting. In addition to profit calculation, accounting is used for various purposes: to show the financial condition of an entity and to control the stocks of assets on hand, for example. Nevertheless, the method of accounting, or the system of double-entry bookkeeping, was originally formed to calculate profit: not to show the financial condition of an entity nor to control the stocks of assets. When the double-entry bookkeeping system is adopted in not-for-profit organisations/public sector bodies, there arises an accounting notion of profit or surplus. The purpose of the adoption of the double-entry system by not-for-profit organisations/public sector bodies seems to be the efficient administration of the organisation by the accounting recognition of profit or surplus.

Accounting Institutions

A: The Anglo-American schools of critical accounting have focused on the accounting institutions and analysed the contemporary structure of control within the society through the accounting institutions. How do you theorise about the accounting institutions?

B: Management accounting can indeed be analysed in the scheme of the conflict between capital and labour, and the controlling power or functions of management accounting can be clarified by applying the research results of theories of organisation. By contrast in Japan, partly because critical accounting research has developed in the field of financial accounting, it is not very easy to discuss the capitalist characteristics of accounting directly in the scheme of the conflict between capital and labour. As a result, it has been specifically insisted that the accounting institutions belong to the socio-political superstructure of the society, and serve the economic base of the society as a lever by which capital accumulation is promoted and accelerated. In this case, however, the researchers unintentionally ran into functionalism.

A: What are the negative aspects of functionalism?

B: Functionalism in accounting research tends to focus on an aspect of accounting that is used as the means for a certain objective: the objective of concealing the profit from the public, or of appropriating monopolistic profit, for example. While accounting research should have its own object distinct from that in economic research, in the above approach accounting is regarded as a means for an objective, and the target object of accounting research is not the means as such but the objective and use of accounting. Hence, perpetual analysis in this approach is not directed to accounting as such but to something that renders accounting to have an objective or a purpose: instances of such things are business enterprises and the monopolistic system of economy. In other words, in such research the stress is not on accounting as institutions, and the analysis results in a description of two elements: accounting as the means and the institutions (such as business enterprises and monopolist capitalism) by which the objective of accounting is set up.

A: You mean that accounting itself as an institution should be analysed in accounting research, don't you?

B: Yes, I do. An analysis of accounting as an institution should not be a mere combination of a description of accounting as the means for the institution and an analysis of the institution as the accounting's purpose-setter, but should rather be an analysis of the accounting institutions as such, i.e., an analysis of the characteristics of the 'institutionalised mode of accounting' in its totality.

Language and Accounting Theory

A: In this dialogue we have used the term 'object' frequently. The term 'object' is widely used in Japanese academic writing: not only in philosophy but also in natural and social sciences including accounting. The 'object of recognition' and the 'object of observation', for example, are terms widely accepted in philosophical and scientific papers, and it is not difficult for Japanese researchers to understand the meaning of these terms. By contrast in the U.K., it seems that a majority of researchers find the term 'object' indistinct or incomprehensible. Haven't you found any difficulty in making the audience fully understand what you think and what you say at a research seminar at a university in the U.K.?

B: Yes, I have. I have found that there is a considerable gap in terminology between Anglo-American and Japanese accounting researchers. The term 'object of accounting' seldom appears in papers written by Anglo-American researchers.

A: I have the same sort of experience at universities in the U.K.: the experience that the exact meaning and significance of the term 'object' in our talks and papers have seldom been fully understood by the colleagues at the universities. A colleague said to me that terms such as 'objective' and 'focus' are much more natural and suitable to 'accounting'.

B: But this communication gap was not caused by an inadequate usage of the term, was it?

A: It wasn't at all. In English translations of German philosophies the term 'object' has been used in its exact sense, as is shown in 'the object of recognition', for example. The difficulty to understand, therefore, was not caused by the usage of language but by the researchers' ways of thinking, problem-setting, reasoning, theorising, and so on.

B: There seems to be a difference in the use of the term 'accounting' between Anglo-American and Japanese researchers. There has been a general tendency for Anglo-American accounting researchers to regard accounting simply as published accounts, or financial statements. By contrast in Japan, many accounting researchers regard accounting fundamentally as the method by which economic transactions and events are recorded and calculated. Published accounts are regarded as a result or product of the method.

A: I think that the difference in the conceptualisation of accounting results in the difference in the problem setting and the methodology adopted in accounting research. Anglo-American researchers tend to focus directly on the impact of financial statements on the social and organisational behaviour of people, while Japanese researchers tend to focus principally on the method of accounting that underlies the total process of accounting from which financial statements are derived.

B: I think so, too. And this difference, in turn, results in the difference in the whole style of research. Some Japanese researchers can spend almost all their career studying an accounting concept such as depreciation and goodwill as their lifework and seldom undertake empirical research work. By contrast, Anglo-American researchers can accept depreciation and goodwill as a concept that can be taught in a one hour introductory accounting lecture, and some researchers employ approaches where they talk more about the impact of accounting on organisational behaviour etc. and seldom discuss ways of improving the form and content of accounting measurement systems and accounting concepts.

A: Generally speaking, Anglo-American researchers tend to accept an accounting concept taking it for granted, while Japanese researchers tend to problematise the concept itself first. To problematise a concept itself can be a source of ideas from which a series of fruitful problem-setting may be derived for a qualitative research into accounting: problem-setting concerning the components of the concept, historical changes in the content of the concept, and the relationship of the researcher's personal values to his/her interpretation of the concept, for example.

B: Don't you have any experiences in which you succeeded in publishing in English and in making presentations to English-speaking academics by problematising a concept?

A: Yes, I have some. I have argued that some of the fundamental concepts of accounting and/or accounting theory that are taken for granted by Anglo-American accounting researchers can be, and should be, questioned. The concepts of 'accounting', 'accountability', the 'function of accounting', as well as the 'object of accounting' are examples of such concepts. My discussion on the function of accounting had a number of positive responses by English speaking researchers when it was presented at international conferences both in the U.K. and the U.S. The point of my discussion was that the function of accounting should be conceptually distinguished from the profession of accounting or the specialised works of accountants. I think that this kind of problematisation of an existing concept will provide a useful theoretical framework for qualitative accounting research for considering both the personal and interpersonal or social formation of, and the historical transformation of, such a concept, especially in Anglo-American countries where the professionalisation of accountants has been fully accomplished and hence the related concepts of accounting have generally been taken for granted.

B: It seems to me that one of the reasons why I have succeeded in publishing a paper on the concept of accounting profit in an English-speaking journal was that my discussion contributed to the problematisation and reconceptualisation of both the accounting calculation of profit and the object of accounting. These concepts have seldom been questioned and/or analysed by Anglo-American accounting researchers.

A: More fundamentally, what motivated you to publish in English journals?

B: The motivation was that I wanted to provide Anglo-American accounting researchers with an alternative way of constructing an accounting theory that can clarify the characteristics of the mode of accounting: the object of accounting, the method of accounting, the institutions of accounting, and the functions of accounting.

A: Your way of thinking must be new to Anglo-American accounting academics. Do you mean that you aimed at criticising the general trend of Anglo-American critical accounting theories?

B: Yes, I do. I think that to show an alternative mode of radical theory of accounting would be a great contribution to Anglo-American accounting academics who are much more oriented towards functionalism than Japanese accounting academics. How about you? Have you learned much from your experience of publishing research in English journals?

A: Yes. I have learned especially from the editorial process about the respective Western-Japanese understandings of accounting and accounting theory. One of the most important findings is the problem of translation: Literal translations of words and/or sentences quoted from Japanese and German articles or books were sometimes too difficult for reviewers of English journals to understand. There certainly is a barrier for researchers when English is not their first language and their background knowledge is different from that possessed by the average Anglo-American academic. There is an established standard of academic English for English speaking journals, on the one hand. And there is a limitation in Anglo-American reviewers' knowledge, problem setting, and way of thinking, on the other hand. Both of these construct "the" standard of English journals. Hence, academics who would like to publish in English journals should examine carefully the quality and the understandability of their English translation of quotations from the originals written in a language other than English.

B: I hope the historical lessons of Japanese critical theories especially on the fundamental questions of "what is the object of accounting?" as well as our personal experience in presenting and publishing research in English will help 'qualitative', 'radical' and 'critical' research in accounting to develop in a more inclusive way.

References

Fujita, M. (2002). Genesis of accounting profit: a dialectical approach. *Critical Perspectives on Accounting*, *13*(4), 463–476.

Jinnai, Y. (1990). The Function of Accounting: a Japanese Perspective. *Accounting, Auditing & Accountability Journal*, *3*(2), 8–23,

Jinnai, Y. (forthcoming). Towards a dialectical interpretation of the contemporary mode of capitalist accounting. *Critical Perspectives on Accounting*.

Tanaka, A. (Ed.) (1990). *The development of accounting research in Japan: Interviews with twelve pioneers* (in Japanese). Tokyo: Dobunkan.

Chapter 17

Refining Research Questions in the Course of Negotiating Access for Fieldwork[1]

Thomas Ahrens

Introduction

All too often, the negotiation of access for qualitative accounting fieldwork is thought of as an important obstacle to research — and not without reason. Preparing the approach to an organisation is often time consuming and may be ultimately unsuccessful. Much is to be learned, however, from considering the negotiation of access as an ongoing process that accompanies the fieldwork and may even extend into the publication of results. Fieldworkers come into contact with many organisational members, all of whom may need to be persuaded differently to contribute to the research. By making comparisons between them and paying attention to the ways in which the negotiations for access shed light on the organisational members' interrelationships, the researcher may unearth some important organisational character-istics, which may themselves be suggestive of further developing the original research questions. This chapter suggests some possibilities for learning from the process of access negotiation with illustrations from an ongoing fieldwork project in a German retail bank.[2] It distinguishes the 'binary' understanding of access from the 'relationship' view of access. Rather than ask ourselves "Am I in or am I out?" we should reflect on the ways in which we develop relationships with different organisational gatekeepers and the nature of the organisation that enables those relationships.

This chapter is organised as follows. The next section explains why the task of gaining research access is best regarded as a process of ongoing persuasion and not a

[1] I would like to thank Rihab Khalifa and Andrea Mennicken for their comments. Thanks are also due the managers at RB for their continuing support of this study.
[2] The aim of the fieldwork was to develop a case study of an integrated performance measurement system in practice. I was particularly interested in the ways in which organisational members would trade off financial and non-financial performance measures. Rather than conduct a longitudinal single case study, the idea was to develop a series of shorter cases to gain comparative insights. Those other cases are still to be researched.

task that can be accomplished at the beginning of a research project. The following section explains the implications of this point for the ways in which the research agenda is likely to develop in the field. The chapter then turns to a specific case study of a retail bank to further explore the relationship between access and conceptual development. The first section on the bank describes the initial approach to the organisation and the posture that I adopted. It is followed by a description of the first contacts with the gatekeeper whom I was asked to contact. The third section on the bank reflects on the motivations of organisational members. Why do they volunteer some kinds of information and withhold others? What may this tell the researcher about the nature of the organisation and its uses of accounting and performance information? This is followed by a section on the relationships between types of access and styles of management observed in the bank. The section after that discusses a recurring obstacle of qualitative fieldwork, which stems from the widespread belief amongst managers that observation of their work is not necessary because they feel that they can competently describe it to the researcher in interviews. Following this, I offer some reflections on the specific research questions that arose at the different stages of gaining access to the bank and in which direction the research could be further developed. The chapter concludes with a summary of the lessons on how to develop access.

Ongoing Persuasion

Many researchers have experienced just how time consuming the negotiation of organisational access for interviews and observation can be. It requires subtlety and luck (Buchanan 1988). From the point of view of those who are going to be researched this should not come as a surprise. Many organisational members see themselves engaged in complex and important tasks. They protect their own work time and the social relationships at work through which they hope to achieve their goals. Opening their social network to outsiders may compromise their ability to do so.

This can make it harder for fieldworkers to obtain access, but it also affords an important research opportunity. Where the granting of access to an outsider is taken very seriously, we can expect organisational members to exercise great care to avoid giving too much, or the wrong kind of access. Their negotiations with the fieldworker become practical examples of organisational logics-in-use from which much may be learned about the organisation. Negotiations for access may, for example, shed light on the hierarchical and collegial relationships between organisational members, the organisa-tion's self image in relation to different environments, and — particularly where access for academic research is concerned — the perceived relationships between internal and external sources of organisational expertise.

The key to learning about these and other organisational characteristics lies in avoiding a 'binary' understanding of access, thinking that you either do or do not have access. There are of course situations in which an approach has been rejected and the gatekeepers just will not be persuaded to grant access in the future. But where careful preparation or luck has resulted in some approval for research activities the situation is rarely so clear-cut.

Initial interviews may be obtained from just one organisational member who may have a predominantly personal interest in discussing certain topics with a researcher. A 'successful' initial interview may result in repeat conversations, in person or over the telephone, mail or email exchanges of information, recommendations to other colleagues in the organisation, or in other organisations if the researcher is interested in a wider organisational field. A few weeks into the fieldwork, the researcher may be known to various people in and around an organisation, access may be very informal and consist of a mix of unstructured interviews, quick telephone calls, and lunch time meetings. Without formal permissions, access of some sort has been obtained. In this kind of situation access is clearly not binary.

But also where much more formal access is pursued and granted, for example, as part of a long-term research project sponsored by senior management, the processual nature of access can make it difficult to predict what forms such access may take. There are different reasons for this.

- Senior management may offer support, but junior managers will often still need persuasion that they, too, ought to devote time to the researcher.
- Gatekeepers tend not to be familiar with the concepts and practices of qualitative research. After, for example, agreeing to some 'shadowing'. organisational members may subsequently reject the concrete actions suggested by the researcher.
- The course of research may lead across different organisational divisions and functions into areas where the original sponsor has little formal authority, or, worse, is regarded as a competitor for power and influence.
- Particularly in exploratory fieldwork the exact course of research depends on the development of more specific research questions after some initial time in the field.

This means that negotiations for access cannot be dealt with in stage one of your research project. Negotiations for access are usually a permanent feature of the research process.

Those ongoing negotiations — explicit and implicit — are conducted with various organisational members. They can take the shape of formally weighing costs and benefits for the organisation. They may involve secret hopes of illegitimate gains, and obtuse references to the wishes of distant senior managers. They also depend on the personal chemistry between researcher and organisational member. No matter how much pre-planning goes into the field research, the precise forms that access will take emerge only gradually in the course of the research itself.

Research Objectives in Fieldwork

This has important implications for the research objectives. The emerging nature of fieldwork access may mean that the researcher becomes effectively barred from pursuing the original research agenda. At the same time, however, the vagaries of negotiating access can suggest new, more fruitful research questions. Where fieldworkers do not rely strongly on preconceived theoretical constructs, it could scarcely be otherwise. Exploratory interpretive accounting research sets out to learn from the field in ways that go beyond mere confirmation of abstract constructs (Ahrens & Dent 1998). Organisational members are often unconcerned with academic distinctions between managerial concepts. The ways in which they put them to specific organisational uses are often suggestive of practical interrelationships between concepts that are left unexplored in the literature (Ahrens & Chapman 2000). Understanding the idiosyncratic assemblages of concepts that may have gone through multiple processes of translation and adaptation (Miller & O'Leary 1994) is an important general objective of fieldwork. For accounting research, the importance of documenting specific modes of concept adaptation through fieldwork is very valuable because adopters of management accounting concepts and techniques are mostly unconcerned with conceptual purity.

The fieldworker's ability to shed light on conceptual assemblages and the particular meaningful practices of which they can become part depends on her location in the field, the specific ways in which she interacts with different groups of organisational members and encounters certain organisational perspectives. Since her location in the field depends on ongoing negotiations for access, the possible contribution from fieldwork-based research also depends on those negotiations. Fieldworkers with access to more diverse field sites within an organisation (or a wider organisational field) can develop more comprehensive understandings of the field. Both in the field and when they publish their findings, they can engage in more complex discussions of management accounting practices. Whilst still in the field, they can better use preliminary insights and ideas to negotiate further access. With this in mind, there are no exact rules for how to develop an exploratory accounting field study like the one I am about to describe. Depending on your location in the field you can or cannot see how people's actions and ideas relate to academic debates. Once you spot a possible connection you can try to pursue it if it fits with your general interests (Ahrens & Dent 1998).

To give some examples of how ongoing negotiations for access may yield insights into important organisational characteristics and how research questions may develop hand in hand with observations in different parts of an organisation, the remainder of this chapter will describe some episodes from an ongoing research project in a German retail bank.

Approaching Retail Bank

Retail Bank (RB) is a medium sized German bank with branches in most regions of Germany. It caught my attention as a potential research site because a relative who worked there as a manager had told me earlier that RB was using non-financial performance measures as part of a company-wide quality management programme. At the time, I wanted to conduct an exploratory study of the uses of integrated performance measurement systems. I have used family, friends and acquaintances to help with access in the past and I also know of colleagues who established initial contacts in this way. It can be a very useful starting point to avoid cold calling (Buchanan 1988).

The relative's advice on access reflected his experience of the importance that organisational members attached to the formal hierarchy. He said that the board director in charge of the quality management programme was the 'natural' point of entry to the organisation. In a phone call from the relative, the board director, described as not unresponsive to academic discussions around quality management and performance measurement, signalled initial interest. Now I was to write a letter seeking the bank's cooperation for the research project. During previous studies in British and German companies I had noticed management interest in comparative information about other organisations in the same industry. My letter asked for research access for a case study as part of a wider research project on the uses of integrated performance measurement systems in British and German banks. I promised anonymised feedback and said that my research costs would be covered by research funds.

Rightly or wrongly, I opted for an authoritative posture. The letter outlined my interest in integrated performance measurement systems and, particularly, the difficulties of establishing causal relationship between lead and lag indicators of financial performance and related it to rising competitive pressures in the banking industry. To support my authority, I included a biographical fact sheet, half a page long and written in German on my headed paper.[3] I asked the relative to check my letter and biographical fact sheet for appropriateness, specifically the use of technical English language terms, and was assured that over the last couple of years RB's senior management had begun to use just the same kind of English language management speak.

Dr H is Friendly but Unenthusiastic

The overall impression of formal decorum was confirmed when, some weeks later, I received a letter from Dr H, the head of human resources reporting directly to the board director, informing me that the director had asked him to support me in any way he can in my research endeavours. Dr H was not easily reached by telephone and could not be relied on to return calls. By fax I outlined my research interests in the uses of integrated performance measurement systems to him and hinted that I would like to speak to the heads of different operating divisions and some of the technical staff involved in running the integrated performance measurement system during 2 or 3 visits of perhaps 3 days each. If he could suggest whom I might talk to . . .? When I finally got hold of Dr H on the telephone, he appeared not to have understood the fax. In my experience, managers never simply understand research rationales outlined in letters or faxes addressed to them. They always seem to require some additional talking through, and if one requests any assistance in establishing contact to colleagues, one needs to see them in person. I ended up flying to Munich just for one day to talk only to Dr H.

He was happy enough to outline RB's general approach to quality management in principle and explain some of the key measures, but he had scheduled another appointment 90 minutes after our meeting began. I flew to Munich for another day to

---

[3] This is not to privilege the authoritative access strategy over other options. As a doctoral student my default access strategy was that of a helpless student seeking support, which worked well. The vast majority of senior management accountants and managers in Germany have studied business economics. They are familiar with academic project and thesis requirements and accept a certain responsibility to contribute to the education of new generations of business economists without expecting tangible benefits in return.

see him a second time and resolve some open questions. After agreeing that RB operated a very impressive quality management system, and listening to some brief examples of how it changed organisational members' ways of working, I insisted that I needed to see how it operated in practice and how financial and non-financial performance measures were traded off. Dr H agreed to put me in touch with Herr S, the head of the service division, and find me the documentation of a quality improvement project, small enough to understand for an outsider, but complex enough to illustrate the diverse pressures and trade-offs that could be made in quality management. In the end he did neither. After some reminders I gave up on the project documentation and contacted Herr S myself. Other organisational members later confirmed that Dr H was not known to go out of his way to support other people's projects.

What the Fieldworker May See (and Why)

The initial contacts emphasised the difference between obtaining formal permission for access and being able to study an organisation. My request was approved by the director ultimately responsible for the quality management programme. But it was by no means clear what kind of access the board director had approved. My research was clearly not a priority. The director was too busy to talk to me personally and his involvement was purely formal. His motives remained elusive. Access may have been granted to appear interested. Or was it out of politeness to my relative? Dr H, to whom I was delegated, made no efforts at all to assist my specific research questions on the uses of performance measurement. His behaviour signalled that he was not convinced that the benefits of studying performance measurement in action outweighed the costs of referring me to colleagues for further interviews. Had he been told to stall the research from the beginning? Did he lack the imagination to see why I wanted to widen and deepen access? He may also have considered it wise to control my moves in the organisation. It later transpired that his handling of the quality management programme was not regarded as an unqualified success by all. It turned out that his quality manager, whom he had never suggested as an interview partner, was about to leave the bank over disagreements over the development of the quality management programme. Perhaps I was not to find out too much about the different viewpoints on quality management?

Having conduced more research in RB since then, it would appear that the difficulties of winning Dr H's support were furthermore related to more general problems of quality management and integrated performance measurement in a divisional organisation. Central staff functions like Dr H's were charged with pursuing the quality agenda and developing management tools. Operating divisions that faced very different competitive conditions were measured by the new non-financial performance indicators. Unlike the information on achievement of cost and revenue budgets, which was kept secret between departmental heads and divisional heads, non-financial performance measures were publicised throughout the bank. They had considerable reputation effects. Line managers were keen to ensure that their units 'looked good'. For Dr H, perceptions of how his department handled the non-financial performance measures were critical. A researcher who could wander about and spread uncomfortable questions or simply other divisions' perceptions between key line managers without giving Dr H an opportunity for effective control, may well have looked like presenting a potential downside without any real upsides. My initial contacts with RB were thus suggestive of paying greater attention to the political character of integrated performance measurement.

That said, personal or political motivations were perhaps not even the biggest obstacle to studying the uses of management accounting or performance measurement systems. Dr H's descriptions of how performance measurement worked at RB were also indicative of a rational prejudice that I have frequently encountered elsewhere. He seemed to see himself as a rational manager who could understand his and other managers' arguments for adopting various positions with regards to quality management and integrated performance measurement systems. He also seemed to regard his complex insights into the functioning of RB's systems as fully sufficient for the sort of inquiry that an academic might want to pursue. The rational prejudice takes for granted that managers can understand the functioning of complex organisations and that such conscious knowledge of the organisation is all that accounting researchers may want to study.

Within the limitations imagined by Dr H, I could only have researched material for yet another study of how different managers talk differently about different aspects of financial and non-financial management. But that was not what I had set out to study. I wanted to observe how managers refer to or are influenced by performance measurement systems in day-to-day work in order to gauge its effects on practice. To improve my access I needed to discard the possibility that Dr H might make introductions to other managers. I contacted them myself. The head of the management accounting department was happy to give an interview but did not want to explain how his costing systems functioned in detail. He was very critical of how RB's non-financial performance measures could be, and were, manipulated by canny divisional managers. He also claimed that for competitive reasons he could not possibly tell me how exactly RB's costing systems worked. Having exhausted the interview possibilities with the two main staff managers in charge of the actual performance measures of RB's systems I turned to the divisional manager with the greatest success in the non-financial performance measures with a request for an interview.

Mindful of Dr H's role as my supposedly main contact in the organisation I have always kept him informed by email of my approaches to other managers. Even though he was not supportive of how I wanted to develop the research, he also did, to my knowledge, not seek to dissuade other managers from being in contact with me or otherwise obstruct the fieldwork. An important characteristic of 'access' to RB has been managers' willingness to speak with me when I mentioned the approval of the board director. Nebulous though this approval may have been, it suggested that one should at least formally comply with the director's wishes and grant me an interview.

Who Gives What Kind of Access?

Herr S, head of the service division, was no exception to this. In contrast to the two managers I had encountered previously, he seemed keen to use my presence as an occasion to get the managers in his own division to reflect on their uses of the quality management system. At this point I had widened my declared research interest to 'quality management and the uses of financial and non-financial performance measures'. Dr H had told me earlier that the service division had persistently shown the highest employee satisfaction of all the bank's divisions despite considerable restructuring and lay-offs over the past couple of years. Senior management of the service division had bought into the principles of quality management early on, in order to achieve the efficiency gains and service level improvements that the board of directors had demanded from them.

Establishing contact with the service division was easy. One telephone call to Herr S was enough to agree a group discussion with some of Herr S's departmental managers. On a personal note, if someone offers you a group interview, accept it! Interviews with one person can become a bit staid and may need the perspectives from other interviews to reframe and open up further the issues discussed in them. In good group interviews those other perspectives are right there in the room, intervening by themselves when they feel challenged and taking the conversation very quickly to the kinds of argumentative positions that organisational members habitually use to frame key issues.

This is not to say that group interviews are always interesting or that one can only learn from interesting group interviews. For instance, in the management accounting department I conducted a very boring group interview in which the subordinate of the head of management accounting supported her boss' every argument, including why they could not possibly tell me how exactly their costing systems worked. It did not do much for my understanding of how integrated performance measurement might function in practice but it gave a good insight into how, in the words of a manager from a different division, "this bank's management accounting department avoids answering any questions that we really want answered by them". What irritates you as a researcher about certain managers, probably also irritates other people in the organisation.

The senior managers in the service division were very different from the two senior management accountants. The departmental managers of the service division showed none of the subservience of the subordinate manager in the management accounting department. Differences of opinion that extended to key policy issues were exchanged openly. The discussion was spontaneous. Criticism was offered quickly and was easily qualified or retracted without loss of face when the others disagreed. Despite different points of view, the managers held each other in high regard; they had worked together in the service division for many years. They openly praised each other's work but also told me in private who they thought tended to be too 'riotous' or too 'bureaucratic'.

During our first group interview they gave me an overview of how they used different financial and non-financial performance measures. I could also confront the participants with different theoretical arguments on quality management and integrated performance measurement with which they were not familiar as concepts but for which they had practical answers. I promised feedback and prepared a list of 14 questions, partly for clarification of simple facts, partly regarding their understandings of concepts, which I sent by email. I had expected that they might reply individually but I had not reckoned with the iron law that says that managers will never read, reflect, and act upon any written communication. Even the access-friendliest manager will only ever read what you send them. For responses, you will have to coax them through some personal communication on the telephone or in an interview or a meeting.

Overcoming the Rational Prejudice

We therefore arranged a second group discussion. Its most valuable outcome was to obtain agreement to observe one of the managers at work for a few days. Obtaining this agreement seemed a matter of luck at the time, but with hindsight it is clear that I had unwittingly 'pressed the right buttons'. Responding to my question of why in our first group interview the service division managers had not mentioned the concept of continuous improvement to describe their quality management activities (even though they had made reference to so many other management concepts) one departmental head replied that of course they also aimed for continuous improvement. But one cannot mention *all* the concepts that are bandied about, and, anyhow, the crux of quality management lies in how it is done and not how one talked about it. To me this presented an unforeseen opportunity! For the first time in my research career, a manager had suggested to *me* a justification for why I would need to observe them, why interviewing was just no good. By unwittingly straining the assumption of the rational prejudice (that management practice is rational and can fully be conceptualised by practitioners) I had made a manager admit that concepts are not very useful to understand quality management practices, thereby legitimising my request for observation. I intend to use this gambit for future research situations.

The power of the rational prejudice is, however, not to be underestimated. When, some weeks later I showed up at his office, scheduled to 'shadow' him for three days he needed reminding of why I really needed to be with him all day. Discussing what we should do for the coming three days, I mentioned that the key to understanding performance measurement practices lay in observation. "In Britain, this is known as 'shadowing'." "Ah, 'shadowing'? Hmmmm, we don't do that around here . . .". Fortunately he gave up his objections out of his own accord later during the day. After trying out the reactions of colleagues who came to his office to consult him, whilst I was sitting at the meeting table section that connected to his desk surface, busy making notes and pretending that this was all very normal, he later did not mention his objection again and just told me to come along when we went to meetings in other managers' offices.

Reflections on Access and the Refinement of Research Questions

The contours of this research project are, at this stage, still somewhat hazy. This is not something to worry about. Up to now, I have only conducted a couple of interviews and some observation in one bank. I will hopefully return to RB and undertake fieldwork in other banks. After initial agreement from the board director each subsequent research contact needed to be persuaded individually to give time and information. My requests for access were not met with uniform enthusiasm. If, as I suggested in the introduction to this chapter, my ongoing negotiations with the organisational members were practical examples of RB's different logics-in-use, then what exactly have I learned from them about the organisation and about performance measurement more generally?

Throughout my negotiations for access in RB I have been struck by the importance of hierarchy. Initial access was obtained through the board director even though his involvement was ceremonial. Subsequently it was useful to be able to make reference to his official approval. My impression was that it assured managers that talking to me was part of their duties, whether they personally thought it useful (or enjoyable) or not. In the service division, when discussing how to further develop the research with one of Herr S's heads of department, he was careful to suggest that I approach Herr S himself with those ideas. The head of department also thought it best not mention the discussion I had with him to Herr S. Even though the working relationship of the senior managers in the service division was characterised by openness and frank criticism, it was usually very clear who was boss. Discussion and criticism were considered necessary to arrive at the best solution and to maintain a climate of participation. However, when agreement could not be reached, the boss decided and the subordinate managers fell in line. The character of hierarchy in the service division was not deferential, but it was understood as functional. To get certain jobs done one needed to obtain agreement at the right hierarchical level. Only then would all the resources needed become available. The right level for developing my research project within the service division was Herr S. Hence there was not much point making detailed research plans with his heads of departments beforehand.

A second important principle of RB's organisation was the divisional structure. When asking Dr H or Herr S about how their performance measurement practices compared to those in other divisions of RB they tended to know only about the general principles of performance measurement in other divisions but not the everyday uses of it. Research on those questions was always talked about as "extending the research to division X", which would have entailed access negotiations with the head of that division. Despite this I was able to find out about some of other divisions' practices through observing the inter-divisional contacts of one of the departmental heads in the service division. Whilst managers thought of RB as strictly divisionalised, in practice they had lateral contacts in the other divisions. They were regularly in touch — not only with old buddies with whom they had worked together in different parts of RB — but with contacts whose respective functional work was related to theirs. Even though some of those relationships were characterised by overt derision ("Your division never gets anything done on time") they met to coordinate cross-divisional workflows for approval by their respective division heads. Access to the service division allowed me to study other divisions 'laterally' in the same 'informal' manner in which cross-divisional cooperation took place.

In RB, trying to negotiate access for observation was, with the exception of the manager who admitted that management cannot be explained, only practiced, as difficult as ever. The service division's managers had very complex notions of management and the management process and they did not feel threatened by an outsider. It transpired that their division had been subject to several studies for contracting out (but no cheaper or better alternatives were found in the market). They displayed none of the insecurity that is often left behind after such studies. Instead they were serious about remaining a market leader in banking services. At the same time they were happy to admit that they could not really articulate exactly how and why their division was successful. The weakening of their rational prejudice became visible in how they thought about research access.

The contrasts between the group interviews in the central management accounting staff function and in the service division illuminated different notions of organisational expertise and the management process. The management accounting department was used to severe criticism from other departments and RB's board of directors. Their reports were often regarded as crude and untimely. They had no inclination to discuss the technical side of their financial reports with me and presented a united front. The senior managers of the service division, by contrast, were used to supportive feedback from their own staff and from other divisions. They welcomed the opportunity to discuss with one another about their management methods and uses of performance measurement. They were happy to explain them in detail and illustrate with examples to obtain feedback from an outsider. They accepted that their work had weaknesses but they regarded them as normal shortcomings that were successively tackled. New problems would then arise from unforeseen consequences of their corrective action or from changed circumstances. The quality of access to their internal discussions that they granted me reflected a particular understanding of management expertise and the management process, and a fair degree of self-confidence.

Once an additional level of access was granted it often lead to new suggestions for research themes. From an original concern with integrated performance measurement, the interviews with Dr H and, particularly, the group discussions in the service division led me to think of performance measurement in the more general context of quality management. Quality was the banner under which the board of directors had introduced non-financial performance measures and designed the integrated performance measurement system. To date, the literature is surprisingly quiet on the relationship between integrated performance measurement and quality management.

Different ideas came out of the observations of one departmental head in the service division. Observing this manager's interaction with colleagues, subordinates, and bosses, and talking to him about his ideas for further developing his section of the service division, especially the possibility of offering his services to competing financial institutions, gave the impression that he was not managing a support group for the 'real banking' business, but that his department itself was the bank's new business. I learned that the contracting out of banking support services is now known as 'transaction banking' and that dedicated transaction banks are about to be established in Germany. As a consequence, I have begun to read about 'networked' organisations. The idea is that sections of organisations are no longer conceived as parts of a larger bureaucratic whole, but loosely coupled modules that are controlled by a mix of financial and quality measures. Some modules find a place inside the organisation, others exist as outside contractors. I also learned in the field that the contracting out of traditional service departments has become possible because of changes in German banking supervision. This suggested I devote some attention to the relationship between regulatory conceptions of organisation and risk, and commercial management.

Concluding Comments: How to Develop Research Access as Part of Finding Things Out

Fieldwork needs a good deal of opportunism because fieldworkers need to be responsive in order to learn from the field (Buchanan 1988; Ahrens & Dent 1998). However, in exploratory research of this kind there is a risk of engaging with too many topics (performance measurement systems, quality management, network organisations, regulation) at the same time and losing focus. Even though the insights from engaging with different existing literatures simultaneously can be considerable, interdisciplinary work is often hard to focus and explain (and therefore to publish). Make sure to take stock ever so often and reflect on why you are pursuing different lines of enquiry. Try out your ideas on colleagues over lunch. Find out which of your findings generate most interest. Be sure that you are researching something that can be related to the existing literature in a way that adds to existing knowledge, be it by way of extension, refinement, or refutation.

Enthusiasm for pursuing a bundle of different research topics in one project can be a great motivator for what is often a drawn out and quite lonely activity. It allows you to privilege the data over abstract theoretical reasoning and pursue what you personally, for whatever reasons, find interesting. The period of the fieldwork is probably the only time when you are allowed to do this. Remember, there are no dull organisations, only dull researchers. Engaging with fieldwork material can be fun, but, more instrumentally, it also keeps you alert to the subtleties of the field material. This is important because it lies at the heart of why you do fieldwork in the first place, developing an 'experience near' (Geertz 1993: 58) understanding of a complex context. This is what makes your fieldwork valuable. It is therefore good advice to avoid premature theoretical closure.

The importance of letting yourself be guided by the evolving field research has important implications for how you should manage access. Access should be carefully planned as far as possible, but be prepared to change your plans opportunistically. You never know where you will end up. It therefore can pay off to be polite to the various gatekeepers and organisational members with whom you get into contact, even when you think they cannot be of help, or you feel that you have 'done' that particular part or aspect of the organisation. Remember to remain professional as a researcher. If, for instance, it appears that you cannot get access to certain parts of the organisation, do not let your disappointment show. Argue your point, accept (temporary) defeat. Keep digging from different directions, you just might develop access in different ways, for example, through lateral contacts from other divisions. It is important to remain credible for the organisational members whom you might encounter again.

As you encounter different people, note the differences in their positions. How they negotiate access is most likely related to how they manage their operations. This can give useful clues on your research topic. And with time, as you find out what others think about them, you can usually learn more precisely why they responded to you in their particular ways.

To make use of these recommendations you need to think of access as a long, drawn out process that evolves in parallel with the development of your research questions.

Access if hardly ever a binary 'on/off' switching. This means equally that your management of access can in practice not remain separated from the other research tasks in the field, such as data collection and data analysis. Whilst it can be useful to distinguish between those tasks in order to reflect on the different demands that they make on you, once you are in the field you need to pay attention to their interconnections. What interviewees say, what they hide, and what they reveal all reflect the structure of your field access.

And lastly, keep questioning the linkages between the gradual development of access and your emergent findings. Use your theoretical insights to obtain wider and deeper access. Most organisational members who are willing to grant you access want to know what you think. It is likely that they are flattered to be research subjects. I have often made the mistake of holding back insights that I thought would be 'too academic' for my contacts. But many of them had considerable tolerance for new and divergent perspectives. More often than not, they have had similar thoughts, phrased differently. To let selected contacts into your emerging views can deepen your relationship. It can also encourage the contacts to suggest further avenues of inquiry, other contacts, or archival material that you had not considered important. Use your contacts to improve your research and let them benefit from the outsider perspective that you can offer.

References

Ahrens, T., & Chapman, C. (2000). Occupational identity of management accountants in Britain and Germany. *European Accounting Review, 9*(4), 477–498.

Ahrens, T., & Dent, J. F. (1998). Accounting and organizations: realizing the richness of field research. *Journal of Management Accounting Research, 10,* 1–39.

Buchanan, D., Boddy, D., & McCalman, J. (1988). Getting in, getting on, getting out and getting back. In: A. Bryman (Ed.), *Doing research in organizations* (pp. 77–89). London: Routledge.

Geertz, C. (1993). From the native's point of view: on the nature of anthropological understanding. In: C. Geertz, *Local knowledge*. London: Fontana Press.

Miller, P., & O'Leary, T. (1994). Accounting, "economic citizenship" and the spatial reordering of manufacture. *Accounting, Organization and Society, 19*(1), 15–43.

Chapter 18

Insights from Internet-Based Research: Realising a Qualitative Understanding from a Quantitative Search Process

Alan Sangster and David E. Tyrrall

Introduction

This chapter relates the experiences of two researchers who conducted qualitative research using the *World Wide Web* (the web) as a main data source rather than following the more traditional fieldwork approach of gathering and analysing interview data. The aim is to illustrate the practical opportunities and the potential pitfalls inherent in such research.

The web came into existence in 1991 and developed from virtually nothing (130 websites in June 1993) to a position where, in January 1997, there were an estimated 650,000 websites (Gray 1996). By June 2001, this had risen to 8.4 million websites (Online Computer Library Corporation 2003). From a situation in 1997 where organisations were just beginning to recognise the Internet as a significant resource, it is now all-pervasive. Large organisations without a website are now very much in a minority (Fry *et al.* 2001).

Clearly, without the web, electronic commerce and the Amazon.coms of this world would not exist. This repackaging of traditional activities typifies the manner in which the existence of the web has changed the ways in which individuals view their work roles, private lives and interactions with other people and organisations. Information that previously would have either been impossible to obtain or, at the very least, difficult to find can now be obtained at the click of a mouse. Even at the simplest level, questions, such as, where can I get 'x', are now asked routinely through web search engines where previously they might have been considered virtually unanswerable.

At more sophisticated levels, researchers have grasped this opportunity to utilise the web to conduct literature searches, examine the way in which companies report their performance, analyse the availability of products and services, and even to access interim findings arising from the work of others in their field. For qualitative

The Real Life Guide to Accounting Research: A Behind-the-Scenes View of Using Qualitative Research Methods
© 2004 Published by Elsevier Ltd.
ISBN: 0-08-043972-1

researchers, the web offers an apparently impersonal collection of artefacts (for examples, text, multimedia, streaming audio, streaming video, workstations, servers, software, web cameras) concerning business and interpersonal processes and inter-actions. These artefacts provide a rich source of previously non-existent insights capable of providing a different, and perhaps deeper, understanding of a wider range of phenomena than was previously possible. Further, the widespread availability and amount of data on the web has led to researchers asking new questions, developing new research ideas and theories, to reach a different and potentially richer understanding of phenomena than was possible in any given time frame even as recently as 10 years ago.

In this chapter, we report on two qualitative research projects in which the web played a central role, how our experiences helped inform our understanding of key issues relating to our chosen subject areas and enabled us to learn a number of important lessons on how to approach the web and web-based research. We argue that in web-based research, the generation of research ideas and collection of data are integrated and interdependent activities, perhaps even more than in other forms of research. Clearly, however, the difference in the two case study topics reported in this chapter — educational services and small breweries — gives only a small indication of the span in subject matter available on the web, which extends to all disciplines, industries, nations and demographic groups and beyond.

The first researcher, Alan Sangster, conducted research into web-based accounting education in 1997, when use of the web in education was still in its infancy. The second, David Tyrrall, researched the use of the web by small independent breweries some four years later, in 2001, by which time the World Wide Web had developed dramatically and its use by small and medium sized businesses appeared to have become relatively commonplace. In both cases, we adopted a perspectival approach to the research undertaken. That is, we both acted in the role of participative observers interacting with the object of research rather than as detached observers of independent phenomena.

We present the two projects below, not as they would traditionally be presented in an academic paper (introduction, hypotheses, analysis, conclusions), but rather as stylised and intertwined narratives. They are presented in this way, not to sanitise them (indeed rather the opposite), but to highlight lessons or 'morals' from our experience. Both researchers undertook their research as part of research teams to whom we are both very grateful,[1] but again for purely stylistic reasons we have recounted our research activities in the first person.

This chapter proceeds by first reviewing the motivation behind the studies. It explains how they started. It describes how the research process circulated through iterative stages of investigation, refinement, refocusing, back to investigation and so on. Lessons learnt concerning the conduct of web-based research are drawn at each stage. The outcomes from each study are discussed, and the research methods reviewed. Finally,

[1] Alan Sangster would like to acknowledge Christina Mulligan and Andy Lymer for their contributions to the work reported here and David Tyrrall would like to acknowledge and thank his co-researchers, Jackie Fry, G. Pugh and J. Wyld for their contributions.

the publishability of research of this kind is discussed in the context of the outputs from the studies.

Motivation

The Accounting Education Study

This study was motivated by a number of articles that forecast the start of a new educational era based upon the web. Its focus was an investigation of how the web was being used in education especially in relation to its use in accounting and finance education. On the basis of this literature and given that the web had developed from virtually nothing (130 websites in June 1993) to a position where, in January 1997, there were an estimated 650,000 websites (Gray 1996), it was felt likely that a number of pioneer academics would have already integrated the technology into their courses. The initial focus of the research was to find out whether there were simply a handful of web adopters or whether a vibrant community had already developed, and what early adopters were doing on their websites.

I did not come to this topic uninformed. I had been accessing the web since 1993, using it in courses since 1994, and had developed the first full-scale U.K. accounting department website. I had published research on the use of the web in education (Sangster 1995), on the use of the web in research (Sangster *et al.* 1997) and on the integration of the web into an accounting systems module (Sangster & Mulligan 1997). Hence, I felt well-equipped to empathise with the educators who were using the web in their teaching and to understand what I found. Both of these I felt to be prerequisites for being able to interpret what was observed.

The Small Breweries Study

At first sight this was not an obvious topic for me, as an accounting academic, to get involved in, so it is worth explaining what motivated the research. My colleagues and I had been approached by the pressure group CAMRA (Campaign for Real Ale) to analyse and develop an economic case for them to present to HM Treasury in support of tax concessions for small brewers. We concluded that since the distribution channels in the industry were dominated by the major breweries that they did have a case. We published a paper (Pugh *et al.* 2001) based on this work and eventually CAMRA won the concessions from HM Treasury in 2002.

The success of the first paper aroused our interest in the small brewery sector. We knew that difficulties in identifying the population are an acknowledged problem for small business research (Watson & Everett 1999; Nucci 1999) but, serendipitously, in looking at small breweries we had found a small business sector where it was possible to identify and survey the entire population (it is in CAMRA's annually updated *Good Beer Guide*).

During coffee table discussions we speculated on whether websites could provide small breweries with a means of circumventing the distribution channels dominated by the brewing majors. We also knew that it was U.K. government policy to make the U.K. the "best environment in the world for e-commerce" (Cabinet Office 1999: 1), with special emphasis on the development of e-commerce among small and medium sized enterprises (SMEs).

The initial idea was simply to survey how many small breweries had websites and what they had on the sites. We felt we could do the survey via the Internet. This approach could solve a number of problems that typically bedevil small business research. It would avoid the problem of traditionally low response rates to questionnaire surveys and the expense in terms of both time and money of a telephone survey. The issues and medium were topical; the population was available; it would be fun to do; and the work seemed comfortingly (to an accountant) quantitative.

Lessons:

(1) Both of us had thought in advance about whether the research was likely to generate publishable results before we even got started. Putting it differently, was the outcome likely to pass the 'so what?' test? Although this moral is clearly applicable to all research, we feel it is easier to forget this when setting off on web based research. It is all too easy to dive into the web, seduced by the ease with which mounds of data can be accessed. Indeed to some extent, David fell into this trap. Alan clearly knew more about his topic than David did about his, but both knowledge and ignorance had their advantages and disadvantages as we shall see, especially since neither study turned out the way it had been expected to turn out.

(2) More specifically, if you are interested in surveying a population or a sample of a population via the web, it is clearly useful to have some independent (in this case, non-web-based) way of enumerating it as a starting point. We both had such lists that did this; Alan, a list of universities, and David, a list of independent breweries.

Getting Started — A Toe in the Water

The Accounting Education Study

I was initially interested in how much accounting course material was available on the web. In a way, my initial question, like David's was a purely quantitative one — 'how many?' In one sense, such a web search in those days (1997) was not nearly as easy as it is now (2002). I was very familiar with the capabilities of search engines. In 1997 search engine algorithms were fairly crude — you could not simply type in the phrase, 'accounting courses' and expect a helpful result. My initial search using *Lycos* produced 2,173 URLs, and took 2 minutes (Sangster 1995). In just a few minutes of searching I found that, even with the more limited capabilities of the web and search engines at that time compared to today, using search engines was going to result in information overload. Given that I was initially trying to find out how much there was out there on the web — the short answer was 'too much', or at least too much to look at in any reasonable time scale. As a result, I dropped the idea of using search engines to trawl the web for relevant sites.

Of course, the problem of overload is much greater now. To demonstrate how things have changed and are continuing to change, a search on 'accounting courses' using the *Google* search engine in April 2002 produced approximately 18,600 URLs in under 2 seconds. An identical search in October 2002 produced approximately 23,300 URLs in 0.36 seconds. A search in October 2002 for the word 'accounting' found approximately 9.64 million URLs in 0.22 seconds. Using *Lycos*, over 4.8 million URLs were found in less than 2 seconds.

The Small Breweries Study

Alan did not know in advance how much he was going to find. Our problem was somewhat different. At least we knew the maximum number of websites we had to find was around 450, if every independent brewery had one, which we felt was very unlikely.

We started trying to find the brewery websites by searching on key words or phrases using *AltaVista*, but soon found that millions of URLs were displayed — far too many to investigate other than on a blind sample basis. For example, the following key phrases generated the number of URLs shown:

- Beer   2,600,025
- Beer U.K.   12,207,184
- Breweries   14,201
- U.K. breweries   7,158,405
- Real ale   789,545
- U.K. real ale   12,510,780

The peculiar result that 'beer U.K.' generated more hits than 'beer' was due to *AltaVista* finding pages that had either 'beer' or 'U.K.' present. Evidently it was too big a haystack for too few needles. An important lesson was learnt at that point: use precise search strings so as to significantly reduce the number of hits generated. But, in this case, doing so still resulted in too many URLs being found. Nevertheless, this preliminary result gave us the germ of an idea.

Lessons:

These are obvious. The web is big and growing. If you have not limited your search area enough beforehand, you will find that there is too much to look at. If you have delimited your search area, you may still find that you cannot locate what you want. Either way, the comforting aspects are that:

(1) this initial kind of search is easy to do; and
(2) when it fails you will still have plenty of time to set about refining the search.

Refining the Search

The Accounting Education Study

I had to find some way to reduce the volume of material selected for investigation. After some consideration of what was available, I adopted three approaches:

(1) I knew of a meta-site called *World Lecture Hall* (http://www.utexas.edu/world/lecture) which I had first heard about through an email discussion list. I had used it previously when directing students to worthwhile sources of alternative course material, and had submitted one of my own courses for inclusion in its database. The site was first launched in 1994 and by April 1997 it contained links to material from over 1,350 course modules, including 30 on accounting, 10 on finance, 25 on business administration, and 21 on management. Using that resource, I accessed the accounting and finance websites listed there and then drilled down looking for links they offered to other course websites.
(2) I searched the *Yahoo!* database for anything relating to education and investigated the sites it listed for any evidence of accounting and finance course material. Using *Yahoo!* was a way of limiting the search because, I understood that site holders at that time had to register their sites with *Yahoo!* so only the websites of those with sufficient motivation to register them were listed. Also it was then, and is still now (searchenginewatch.com, August 2002) one of the most popular search engines, so anyone who really wanted people to find their accounting courses would place them on *Yahoo!*
(3) I also searched all the existing U.K. university accounting and finance department websites (not all had websites at that time). Many of the department URLs were available on a metalist I had used previously. Others were accessed by drilling down from their university's home page to see if there was a website for an accounting and/or finance department.

Of these three strategies, the third proved both mind-numbingly tedious and very unsuccessful. There was very little course material at U.K. accounting and finance departments in 1997 but, having presented a number of conference papers about the use of the web, I had expected this result. Arguably this confirmation of the lack of adoption of the web among U.K. accounting and finance departments was, in itself, something worth reporting — but it was clearly insufficient to merit a full-length paper.

The *Yahoo!* searches were rather more successful. They yielded many educational web sites extolling the virtues of the use of the web in education and some excellent examples of how it could be done. However, I found very few accounting and finance department websites in *Yahoo!*, and even fewer with course materials. It seemed that

U.K. accounting and finance departments were no more or less dilatory in introducing websites than their colleagues elsewhere. It was another interesting finding but still insufficient for a paper.

In contrast, the *World Lecture Hall* was a success in providing accounting and finance course material URLs. However, these were a self-selecting sample of course materials since only sites that informed World Lecture Hall of their existence would be present on it. Quantifying what was out there was fading as an option.

The Small Breweries Study

The initial difficulties we had encountered in locating the websites gave us the idea of gauging the first time accessibility of the websites to potential customers. Accessibility is critical if product or company information is to influence customers' decisions (Thelwall 2000a, b). As accessibility is obviously going to be easier for someone skilled in how to find information on the web, we decided to look at the accessibility of brewery websites from the perspective of the individuals who would be most likely to want to visit them, many of whom would be relative novices in the use of the web. In short, we took an ethnographic approach. To that end, the search methods we adopted were those we expected most people interested in finding independent brewery websites to adopt. These were (Ernst & Young 2000; Thelwall 2000a):

 (i) typing in a known address,
 (ii) following a link from a search engine,
(iii) using online shopping malls.

We started by using search engines, selecting *AltaVista* and *Yahoo!* because of their popularity (*Search Engine Watch* 2000), rather than because they were necessarily 'the best' search engines to use. But clearly, there was no guarantee that *AltaVista* and *Yahoo!* provided a complete listing of all independent breweries' URLs.

For those breweries the websites of which were not located using these sources, we typed in intuitive URLs (after Pirchegger & Wagenhofer 1999) for each brewery based on its name (as provided in the *Good Beer Guide*, CAMRA 2000) to see if a website existed. For example, Arkell's Brewery was entered as www.arkells.co.uk, www.arkellsbrewery.co.uk and www.arkells-brewery.co.uk.

We also tried looking at shopping malls, as our preliminary equivalent of Alan's meta-site. We swiftly found that, as we expected, they were useless. However, early on during our URL search we had found a number of very useful meta-sites with links to a large number (indeed a majority) of brewery websites.

We knew that simply finding out how many independent breweries had web sites would not suffice for a paper, so while locating, listing and book-marking the sites, we also recorded details of what facilities the breweries presented on, or how they used, their websites. Modes of use are typically presented as some form of progressive adoption ladder (DTI 2000a), as stages in e-business development (Ernst & Young 2000) or as rankings (Cockburn & Wilson 1996; Thelwall 2000a). In fact, all methods display strong similarities. However, in order to take account of the specifics of the brewing industry, we had to make qualitative decisions on classification and scoring.

In effect, we were replicating Alan's strategy — but where he was using these approaches to focus his study downwards, we were using them to find what we had already decided to focus upon. For us therefore, it made sense to start gathering data very early on in our survey, something that Alan did not really get into until the next stage.

Lessons:

(1) Researching on the web inevitably revolves around the use of multiple data collection strategies, such as the methods described above — typing in both known and intuitive addresses, use of search engines, and use of meta-sites. In addition, you could now use a domain name registration service such as *Simply Names* (http://www.simply.com/) to search all extensions of an intuitive name at once. However, this would only confirm the registration of a domain name. You would still have had to check whether or not a website actually existed. In addition, you would still fail to uncover websites with non-obvious names for their URL. For example, if you had looked for the (alas, no longer independent) Wolverhampton and Dudley brewery, you would have failed. They used the completely non-obvious www.fullpint.co.uk as their URL.

(2) If you know (more or less) what you are looking for in web sites, it will save time if you start collecting such data as you find the sites. If you are less clear — don't bother — as the chances are high you will spend time collecting data you do not use. At this stage David was collecting (mostly) directly usable data, while Alan was collecting data (department URLs) the usefulness of which was not yet known in respect of the research question (they may or may not include links to course material). To some degree, you may simply have to resign yourself to collecting data that you do not use.

(3) In either case, if you are using the web to collect survey-type data (as we both were), data collection will almost certainly have to be done reasonably quickly. If you miss any tricks during the data collection phase, you may not be able to simply retrace your steps and fill-in-the-blanks later. The web will have moved on, and you cannot backtrack the web to reinstate the earlier position. It is not the same as obtaining data through interviews — you cannot simply go back and interview the web a second time or seek clarification by telephone! This can mean that a wrong step or a misunderstanding of the robustness of the method or findings can lead to an entire study having to be repeated. Even more critically, flaws of this nature in web-based research may only come to light at the review stage of a paper, thereby making the entire paper and many months work relatively worthless.

Because of these three problems, you are likely to have to persevere through several stages of reconsidering the research project.

Reconsidering the Research Project

The Accounting Education Study

The main purpose of conducting this research was to show colleagues in accounting and finance what other accounting and finance academics were doing, in the hope that they would appreciate the benefits to both them and their students in embracing the technology. Change is much more likely to come about if there are obvious similarities in background between those being encouraged to change and those who have already changed. And, more directly to the point, research is far more likely to be published if editors can see the relevance to the discipline of the work being reported.

Given that overall quantification of relevant websites had proved impossible, how could the research study be refocused in order to produce something worthwhile? I considered focusing on the use of the web in education in general and using the *Yahoo!* registered sites. However, that would have meant changing the focus of the research so much that, while the results would undoubtedly have been of interest to an accounting and finance audience, they would not have been directly applicable to the discipline, and so might not have been acceptable to the editors of the leading accounting and finance journals. I had to maintain an accounting and finance focus if I were to stand a realistic chance of having the research findings published in my target journal.

I decided I had sufficient data to demonstrate the range of accounting and finance course material being offered on websites, but that I needed to ensure that: (a) I did not understate what was available; and (b) the picture I presented of what was being presented was not demonstrably skewed as a result of omitting additional and easy to obtain data.

I decided to re-examine the nature of the websites I had found and spent a couple of days looking at them gaining a picture of the sort of information they contained. It became clear that some of those placing their course material on the web had extensive links from their web pages to other people's course material. This seemed to be a way in which to avoid missing very many relevant websites. As a result, I decided to investigate the websites of the most web-aware accounting and finance academics (as defined by the inclusion of their course material at the *World Lecture Hall*) and use them as the main source for finding other relevant websites.

Any websites found in this way would, by definition, be accounting and finance focused, fulfilling the original aim of the research. However, by doing so, I acknowledged that only a self-selecting sample would result, potentially limiting the generalisability of the findings. However, that did not prevent the findings being generalised across the websites that had been found. David had to be able to generalise across his population of small breweries, but for me being able to generalise across a population was not necessarily relevant. What was relevant was that I could demonstrate that the findings were relevant to: (a) the source of those findings (the accounting and finance websites that had been identified); and (b) demonstrably of interest to a wider community (accounting and finance academics).

Bearing in mind the need for speed, spending 12–15 hours a day over each of the next seven days, 86 potentially relevant course URLs (30 accounting, 10 finance, 25 business administration, and 21 management) were examined and those with accounting and finance material were bookmarked. In each case, the relevant department website was also examined to see if any other accounting and finance modules had made course material available on the web.

From this point, I switched to looking in detail at the material in each site to see if there were any links to other course materials provided elsewhere. It was during this phase that I found a meta-site of accounting course material as one of the resources on offer at a course website. The meta-site was called '*Accounting Academia*' (http://www.taxsites.com/academia.html). It listed 65 accounting module websites and led to another site maintained by the same person that listed 43 tax module websites. Then, while continuing my survey of finance course URLs, I found yet another meta-site '*Finance Courses on the Web*' (http://fisher.osu.edu/fin/resources_education/edcourse.htm) that held 128 module URLs. Just as David had found, these much more specific meta-sites proved to be the turning point in the research.

Again, it was time to redefine the research. At the last revision, I felt that it would be too difficult to find a good cross-section of websites and a switch in focus had been made towards looking mainly at the ones recorded at the *World Lecture Hall*. Now, everything had changed and many more websites were available than had been expected — too many, in fact, to enable the content of them all to be analysed. I decided to focus on the 65 accounting modules linked from *Accounting Academia*.

Lessons:

(1) Alan's problem had been finding some way of narrowing focus. David's problem had been finding an unknown quantity (but not more than 450!) of needles in a haystack. In both cases meta-sites had been very significant, indeed essential to success. A key technique in refining, and hence expediting, any search is to locate any meta-sites that deal with the field of interest. It is highly likely that someone (public-spirited) has been there before you.
(2) Methodologically however, it will be necessary to consider if it matters whether you can locate the population you seek or whether useful results may be obtained from the sample you happen to uncover. Putting it differently, the critical aspect is to decide what it is you are seeking and be able to justify the search method selected, while being aware that
(3) What you seek is likely to be conditioned by what you can find. However, at least you are well down the pathway of funnel and focus.

Funnel and Focus

The Small Breweries Study

We had never ruled out quantification — indeed it was our goal, and we seemed to be almost there. We circulated our brewery URL listings on an informal basis to the people running meta-sites, and they confirmed that, so far as they were aware, our list was complete. The URL identification procedure we used may have omitted some breweries, but it is likely that only a small minority of the population of independent brewery websites were missing by the time we had compiled our list. Indeed, our own view was, and still is, that we found the lot — but academic caveats do not permit such bold assertions, so we settled on the formulation in the previous sentence for our journal submission! At the same time, we had also collected a lot of data on the facilities present on the web sites. The problem now was what to do with all this data. We were down the funnel, but what was the focus? Putting it differently, what question, if any, did we have the answer to?

The Accounting Education Study

In contrast, I already had a focus. Adopting an ethnographic approach, I was investigating what was happening on all these 65 websites, reflecting on what I found through the lens of my own experiences in doing the same thing. But this meant I had not really started down the funnel of collecting data, something that David had almost completed by this stage.

I started by creating an initial list of features to look for in course websites. As the basis for this list, I used the range of things I had established at my own course website — notes, spreadsheets, links to other resources, past exam papers, assignments, email contact to faculty, electronic class discussion list, timetable, course glossary. As I visited the first few websites, other features were added to the list, including additional notes, objective tests, class lists, and password protected access. Each time a new feature was added, previously visited websites were swiftly revisited and reclassified where appropriate.

After I had examined 20 or so sites I realised that some of these features needed to be split, so lecture notes were split into ASCII text, word-processed documents, adobe acrobat files, and PowerPoint notes. Further refinements were made to the list as more sites were visited, including overhead transparency availability and the availability of soundbites. Again, each time a feature was split, such as occurred with overhead transparencies (when the feature was split into word-processed, HTML, and PowerPoint) each of the sites where the original feature had been found was revisited and reclassified. The process of observing the content of the sixty-five websites took two weeks, working twelve to fifteen hours a day every day. Ironically, both Sundays — the best day at that time to do this type of work — were lost due to the transatlantic line into the Janet network going down — something so rare nowadays that it would seldom matter but, in 1996, this was not an infrequent occurrence.

During the following six weeks, the sites were all revisited to see if there had been any significant changes. A behaviour change across the sites was apparent, even in such a short period. One site moved from free access to student work and grades to password protected access, some of the sites that provided resource links updated their lists, one did so dynamically every time something of interest was found by the lecturer. Some added overhead transparencies and lectures as each week passed. Others removed material as its relevance passed. Those that included discussion lists and FAQs changed frequently.

It was a very dynamic and changing environment and, at that time, it did look as if free access was likely to grow although restricted access to some materials, even then, was beginning to become noticeable. None of the sites charged for materials. However, in the course of the research a link was found to a website offering a pay-for-use on-line CPE-credit-bearing auditing course.

In two cases, I attempted on-line sample objective tests. In another site I tried an early attempt at a graphical demo that involved entering data and then seeing the effect on a graph. I could have sent messages to some of the discussion lists, but did not. However, I did review and monitor the communication in the discussion lists over the six-week monitoring period. While this was undoubtedly participative observation (as I was doing what many of the student users were doing in accessing the course material) at no time did I let any of the academics whose courses I was monitoring know I was doing this and they will all have been totally unaware of my having been observing them.

Lessons:

Both studies encountered a theory issue. The tentative theories with which we both started were used as springboards to get started. After that the nature of the data we uncovered began to dictate a research approach. Participative observation was adopted in Alan's case. In David's, there was no benefit to the research in doing so. The key is to be open to the opportunities presented and to adjust research method accordingly, but that leads to a problem in theorising the results.

Theorising the Results

The Small Breweries Study

Our initial hypothesis that independent breweries might use the Internet as a means of bypassing the distribution channels dominated by the major breweries was clearly wrong. Indeed, we formed the view that the majority of brewery websites were not very accessible to anyone looking for them, and on reflection, realised that this was our most striking finding. In other words, the breweries had created low visibility web-sites. Why would they do this? Or, putting it differently, what had we discovered?

We explored the possibility of relating our results to the major models of business decision-making, the rational or classical model (Ansoff 1965), the emergent model (Mintzberg 1987) and even the garbage can model (Cohen *et al.* 1972), but our existing work did not enable us to make more than preliminary judgements. It would require extensive and careful interview and survey-based research to uncover the issues.

We had already looked at other surveys (for example, DTI 2000a), and were getting very similar results for the proportion of micro-businesses with websites, despite having markedly different research strategies. This meant we were not barking up the wrong tree — but that we still needed a way of presenting our major result. We knew that attempts had been made in the literature to measure the accessibility of web sites — but none that balanced the results of a range of search techniques. So we decided to devise one ourselves.

Each website was awarded points according to various aspects of its accessibility: links to the brewery meta-sites, appearing in the 'top 20 hits' of an *AltaVista* search, having a *Yahoo!* directory listing and having a URL that we rated as 'easy' to guess. From this we were able to generate a frequency distribution showing that the breweries scored badly on our accessibility rating. This was in line with our expectations and other research (Thelwall 2000a), but we were troubled by this result because it gave a heavy weighting to a presence on the meta-sites. We experimented with two different weighting systems to overcome this. Both reduced the effective weightings on meta-sites. In one case the heavy weightings were transferred to registrations with search engines. Predictably, this made the breweries' accessibilities appear even worse. The other weighting placed more emphasis on an easy URL, which equally predictably improved all the ratings. In the end, we decided that it would be best to stick with the simple accessibility rating. Of course this had the curious result that an overtly quantitative frequency distribution was actually underpinned by a series of qualitative decisions.

It is still a bit too early to judge how much of a success or failure this project was. At the theoretical level, we had found an anomalous result in need of a theoretical explanation — a limited contribution (at best). But arguably that had never been our intention. Instead, we wrote it up into a paper that focused on the business and policy implications of our findings. We had found a lower uptake of the higher steps on the adoption ladder among small breweries than the DTI (2000a) had found among its sample of small businesses in general. Indeed most were still at level zero (no website). Furthermore, it appeared likely that many of those with web sites could enhance their web site usage by a variety of comparatively simple and non-technical steps. Yet U.K. government advice on business use of the Internet tends to focus on the technical aspects of the Internet rather than on the business aspects (DTI 2000b). Hence the appropriateness of the advice on offer was probably meaningless to all but a minority of the independent breweries, and by extension, to many small businesses. Our paper was considered of sufficient merit to be accepted for a respectable refereed conference, and it appeared in the proceedings (Fry *et al.* 2001). It has now been accepted by a leading journal after taking referees' suggestions to focus even more closely on the business and policy aspects.

The Accounting Education Study

By the end of this period of participative observation, I had built up a picture of how the web was being used in accounting education and had formed a view concerning trends in availability and in restriction of access. A number of case studies on the use of the web in education had been found. Reference back to the educational material found near the start of the research found evidence to support the view that the trends in web usage noticed in respect of accounting courses were also happening in university education in general.

The entire research exercise took about three months. It generated a number of case studies describing innovative ways people were using the web in accounting and finance education from various institutions around the world. In particular, it was able to present views on educational use of the technology, pointers to a range of web-related developments, and indications of the wealth of support available on the *Internet* for integrating *World Wide Web* into the curriculum. Despite its ethnographic, non-positivist focus, it resulted in three refereed conference papers, a seminar paper, and a paper published (Sangster & Lymer 1998) in the American Accounting Association journal, *Issues in Accounting Education.*

Lessons:

We both encountered problems in developing theoretical implications of our findings, which we resolved in different ways.

(1) Alan did not attempt to find an explanation for what was found, but he did develop a model to classify and characterise the websites identified. Once he had developed the model and completed his classification, he then utilised the strengths of the vehicle of investigation (the web browser) to play the role of a participant observer in order to identify trends in behaviour and provision that appeared to be emerging. Despite the adoption of a qualitative approach to the research, the research resulted in findings that were of sufficient interest to be published in a leading accounting journal.

(2) David found some surprising evidence that indicated that independent breweries did not appear to be using their websites in a manner that would make them commercially worthwhile developing, but found it impossible to explain what had been found. Another project would be needed to find such explanations — but that is the most commonly observed result of any research! On the other hand it did generate practical business and policy implications relevant to small business — which was the original intent.

Conclusion

In this chapter, we have reported on two studies conducted four years apart, both of which focused on the existence of information on the web. The first investigated the availability of accounting course materials on the web and the second investigated the existence of independent brewery websites and their accessibility to real ale enthusiasts.

One major issue confronted in both studies was that the web is in a constant state of flux. Organisations and individuals remain a long way from deciding how best to use the medium. What is here today may be gone tomorrow (Katz 2000). As a result, academic theory and research practice have lagged behind developments in the adoption of web technology. This means that there is either a pressing need for research that can capture and explain rapidly changing phenomena, or that we may be attempting to deal with ephemera. Observation studies, such as the one carried out by Alan once he had identified where to look, may be the key to identifying trends in this area. Indeed, David, in reworking his paper to meet the referees' recommendations, took the opportunity to revisit the web sites as a form of observation study. However, for web-based research more generally, there remain the problems inherent in actually identifying where to look in the first place.

Consequently, it is in the nature of web-focused research that the primary need was, and still is to find out what is being done before attempting to explain it. Essentially our approaches were, as in Poon & Swatman (1999: 10) 'exploratory' and we did not commence 'with any specific set of hypotheses'. Any research conducted that focuses on the web as the object of research needs to be flexible and reactive to change. While a tentative hypothesis existed at the start of each of our studies, in reality, they both progressed through the development and continual refining of research questions.

More prosaically, we learned some practical lessons about web-based research, in addition to those already mentioned earlier. In David's case, he dived into this one blind. He knew comparatively little about company websites or web technology. Rather he was seduced by the possibilities of surveying a population rather than a sample, and of building on his previous work. In David's case, it might have been a good idea to get someone with specific knowledge of our areas of ignorance into the team. On the other hand, having a defined population also defined the research target — the methods changed and so, therefore, did the result but the target was fixed all along. But if David had known more, he might never have done it, which would have been a pity, because there is clearly an opportunity for more research in this field. Alan was much more informed before he started out but even he was surprised by the amount of material out there and had to change his research target and focus as he learned more.

Despite neither project adopting a positivist perspective, both proved of interest to the research community. In doing so, they demonstrate that web-focused qualitative research is both a viable and challenging activity and one that lends itself more to grounded theory and participative observation than might naturally be assumed to be the case. We would both recommend it as a research mode - and we will both do it again!

References

Ansoff, I. (1965). *Corporate strategy.* U.K.: McGraw-Hill.
Cabinet Office (1999). E-commerce@its.best.uk. Performance and Innovation Unit Report. http://www.cabinet-office.gov.uk/innovation/1999/ecommerce/index.htm.

CAMRA (1999). *The Good Beer Guide 2000*. St. Albans: CAMRA.

CAMRA (2000). *The Good Beer Guide 2001*. St. Albans: CAMRA.

Cockburn, C., & Wilson. T. (1996). Business use of the world wide web. *International Journal of Information Management*, *16*(2), 83–102.

Cohen, M., March, J., & Olsen, J. (1972). A garbage can model of organizational choice. *Administrative Science Quarterly*, *17*(1), 1–25.

DTI (2000a). *Business in the information age: International benchmarking study 2000*. http://www.ukonlineforbusiness.gov.uk.

DTI (2000b). *E-commerce: How trading on-line can work for you*. http://www.ukonlineforbusiness.gov.uk/.

Ernst and Young (2000). *Global online retailing*, (Ernst and Young Special Report), EandY. http://www.ey.com/global/gcr.nsf/international/global_online_retailing_-_RCP.

Fry, J., Pugh, G. T., Tyrrall, D., & Wyld, J. (2001). The use of the world wide web by U.K. independent breweries: global reach or global invisibility? Proceedings of the International Academy of Business Conference, April 6–7, Manchester, U.K.

Gray, M. (1996). *Web growth summary*, http://www.mit.edu/people/mkgray/net/web-growth-summary.html.

Katz, J. (2000). This changes everything? Implications of e-commerce for entrepreneurship research. Keynote address to the 2000 Small Business and Enterprise Development Conference, April 10th–11th, University of Manchester, Manchester, England.

Mintzberg, H. (1987). Crafting strategy. *Harvard Business Review*, July–August, 65–75.

Nucci, A. (1999). The demography of business closings. *Small Business Economics*, *12*(1), 25–39.

Online Computer Library Corporation (2003). http://wcp.oclc.org/

Pirchegger, B., & Wagenhofer, A. (1999). Financial information on the internet. *European Accounting Review*, *8*(2), 383–395.

Poon, S., & Swatman, P. (1999). An exploratory study of small business internet commerce issues. *Information and Management*, *35*(1), 9–18.

Pugh, G. T., Tyrrall, D., & Wyld, J. (2001). Will progressive beer duty really help U.K. small breweries? A case study in profit appropriation. *Journal of Small Business and Enterprise Development*, *8*(4), 311–337.

Sangster, A. (1995). World wide web — what can it do for education? *Active Learning*, *1*(2, July), 3–8.

Sangster, A., & Mulligan, C. (1997). Integrating the world wide web into an accounting systems course. *Accounting Education: An International Journal*, *6*(1), 53–62.

Sangster, A., & Lymer, A. M. (1998). How to survive a new educational era. *Issues in Accounting Education (AAA)*, *13*(4), 1095–1109.

Sangster, A., Baldwin, A., & Lymer, A. M. (1997). Using the world wide web in accounting research: A huge step forward or a new constraint? *British Accounting Review*, *29*(4), 395–407.

Search Engine Watch (2000). The major search engines. http://searchenginewatch.com/links/Major_Search_Engines/The_Major_Search_Engines/index.html Accessed September 2000 and August 2002.

Thelwall, M. (2000a). Effective websites for small and medium-sized enterprises. *Journal of Small Business and Enterprise Development*, *7*(2), 149–159.

Thelwall, M. (2000b). Commercial websites: lost in cyberspace? *Internet Research: Electronic Networking Applications and Policy*, *10*(2), 150–159.

Watson, T., & Everett, J. (1999). Small business failure rates. *International Small Business Journal*, *17*(2), 31–45.

Chapter 19

The Case Study, The Interview and The Issues: A Personal Reflection

David E. W. Marginson

Introduction

Management control systems (MCS) have long been viewed as integral to the strategy process (Anthony 1965); they are generally regarded as 'tools of strategy implementation' (Simons 1994). At the same time, however, surprisingly little is known about the nature and extent of the MCS-strategy interplay, especially at levels below the apex of the firm (Simons 1995). Yet, the issue of strategy and its control is of growing importance to firms, not least because of their increasing dependency on the creativity and innovations of middle-level managers (Bartlett & Ghoshal 1993; Simons 1995, 1999). In these circumstances, understanding how (and why) firms might seek to control managers' 'grass-roots' activity, while also seeking to understand the effects that MCS have on the strategy process, is crucial if firms are to devise more effective means of achieving desired strategic objectives. To that end, I set out to explore the nature and extent of the relationship between MCS and the strategy process by conducting an in-depth, longitudinal case study of Telco, plc, a major U.K. based organization, which operates in what it describes as the 'global communications and infotainment business'. This company provided a valuable research site, not least because it relies heavily on the creativity and innovations of middle-level managers in order to maintain its leading position in a fast-changing and highly uncertain business environment.

Standard procedures for exploratory case study research were applied, which meant that, while multiple sources of data were used during the course of the investigation, the interview was the predominant data collection vehicle (Yin 1983, 1993). Given this, the nature and 'quality' of the interviewing process holds non-trivial implications for the robustness of the case study project, and it is perhaps for this reason that interviewing has been the subject of much discussion in the social science literature, particularly in regard to the conduct of interviews and the role of the interviewer (Ackroyd & Hughes 1992). In other respects, however, the literature on interviews and their role in case study research remains remarkably under-developed. To date, for example, there has been little discussion about the role of theory in semi-directional interviews.

Researchers in accounting are encouraged to adopt multiple theoretical perspectives (see for example, Otley & Berry 1994), but there has been little discussion about the potential and problems of doing so within the case study in general, and the interview in particular. Virtually nothing has been said about how one might reconcile the iterative nature of most case research with the idea of complying with a pre-determined interview protocol. But, it was precisely these issues that I encountered during the study of Telco plc, and my aim here is to reflect on their nature and report on how I sought to deal with each in my own research. In so doing, I seek to bring attention to issues that arise in the process of case studies. The overall objective is to offer a forum for debate among seasoned researchers, while also offering comment and reflection that the less experienced researcher may find useful. In short, I seek to address in this paper some of the things 'one only really learns about through experience'.

The section that follows discusses the role of *a priori* theory in case study research in general, and the interview in particular. Section three examines issues relating to data collection, section four considers the iterative nature of data analysis in case research, and reflects on how developing interview questions as the study proceeds may conflict with the notion of interview protocols. The final section concludes the discussion.

Theory and Interviewing

It is generally accepted within the accounting literature that the case study method of empirical enquiry is best deployed inductively in order to develop, modify and extend existing ideas and theories in the light of emerging evidence (Berry *et al.* 1991); the researcher may even unearth some previously undocumented technique, process, behaviour or cause-effect relationship. But, inductively based research begs an important question: what role should *a priori* theory play in the study in general, and the interview in particular? I begin by exploring this question.

Social science researchers employing qualitative research methods espouse an approach in which theory and research are interwoven. The delineation of theoretical ideas is viewed as a phase that occurs during the end of a study, rather than being a precursor to it. The prior specification of theory is discouraged because of the likelihood of introducing bias and premature closure on the matter to be investigated, as well as the possibility of theory departing greatly from the views of the participants in whatever setting. A number of writers (for examples, Bryman 1988; Ackroyd & Hughes 1992; May 1993) consider the case study to be synonymous with qualitative research and, as such, should adopt a similar approach to the issue of theory. That is, the researcher should begin each study with a 'blank sheet of paper'. However, whatever the nature of case research (that is, whether quantitative, qualitative, or both), it has also been recognised (Kaplan 1986; Berry *et al.* 1991) that such an idealistic position is impossible to attain. Besides the personal baggage (for example, beliefs, values) that the researcher brings to any investigation, preparatory reading on the subject will unavoidably imbue him or her with prior conceptual and theoretical perspectives.

As a counter to this difficulty, it is suggested that the researcher in management accounting and control forearm him or herself with an understanding and appreciation of, not one, but a number of theoretical perspectives which can then be revised in the light of emerging evidence (Berry *et al.* 1991). The main argument for being pluralistic in perspective is to avoid 'theory-in-theory-out', i.e. to avoid interpreting a real-world situation from a single theoretical standpoint, which may serve only to reinforce the initial theoretical position (Otley & Berry 1994). Moreover, the researcher(s) should use *a priori* theoretical perspectives as 'guiding perspectives rather than firm theoretical frameworks', and should thereby remain open to alternative explanations of observations made (Marginson 1999). I sought to apply these principles in my own investigation. Four 'guiding perspectives were adopted at the outset: a management control perspective, a cybernetic perspective, an organizational theory perspective, and finally a contingency perspective — see Marginson (1999) for an elaboration of each. However, the intellectual and emotional implications of adopting such an open, pluralistic approach are non-trivial. For me, the most demanding issue was thinking of appropriate follow-up questions 'on the spot' to the responses given by interviewees. The notion of a semi-structured interview, which is seemingly so liked by accounting researchers, implies the use of further questions to explore issues in more depth. For me, however, the problem was keeping in mind each theoretical perspective whilst responding to the interviewee's response! This might simply expose my own intellectual limitations, but applying multiple perspectives during the interview seems to require not inconsiderable concentration and understanding on the part of the researcher. Obviously, interviews can be tape-recorded. But, *ex post* transcription cannot retrieve a lost opportunity to ask meaningful and pertinent follow-up questions at the time of the interview.

On reflection, it is, perhaps, imperative for the researcher to be fully immersed in the literature in order that s/he is better able to appreciate when in an interview to pursue particular points and observations that appear to contradict or at least fit awkwardly with existing theories and concepts. A strong understanding of extant theory, including the silenced assumptions on which a particular concept or idea is based, is imperative if the potential significance of the interviewee's responses is to be acknowledged. In my own case, for example, an understanding that the budgeting literature is based on the (largely implicit) view that budgets, of themselves, have little motivational impact, allowed me to pursue initial insights which suggested otherwise. For reasons that are elaborated elsewhere (see Marginson 1999, 2002), the case study company operated a budgetary system that was devoid of formal accountability and reward systems (cost centre managers were not held formally responsible for their budget performance, nor were they rewarded for meeting the budget). However, interviews revealed considerable 'behavioural inflexibility'; many managers insisted on budgetary targets being met, even though there was little formal incentive to do so, and even though initial targets could be exceeded for 'strategic reasons'. These revelations appeared to contradict extant ideas and arguments about how budgetary control can and should be exercised within the firm. At the time, however, evidence was emerging during the (initial) interviews which presented a 'real-time' dilemma: how to follow up on these seemingly important insights in order to identify and explore possible reason(s) for managers' unexpected behaviour. To this end, I personally found it useful to build in a little more 'thinking time' into the interview in order to develop ideas in relation to extant theory. I did so by adopting five basic tactics as outlined by Manzoni (1994).

The first tactic is about making it clear to respondents that the researcher(s) does not have a specific theory to prove or disprove, and thus interviewees are not meant to provide the 'right answer'. A brief statement to this effect can be made at the start of an interview. This statement can also be expanded to include a comment to the effect that the researcher's own background is immaterial to the discussion. This is to help reduce the response effect that is argued to occur when interviewees become aware of the interviewer's area of interest or 'expertise'. For example, knowledge that an interviewer is interested in accounting may colour the responses provided by the interviewee according to his or her understanding, opinions, etc., of accountants!

A second tactic is to ask respondents to illustrate the behaviour or issue s/he was describing ("that's interesting, could you provide an example or elaborate a little more"). In addition, answers/illustrations can be probed a little deeper where managers appear to feel particularly troubled by an issue. The issue of managers' inflexibility towards budgetary performance illustrates this point. It became evident during interviews that some managers were 'bothered' by the degree of uncertainty and ambiguity that prevailed throughout the organization; they were experiencing role ambiguity (Kahn *et al.* 1964). It was also becoming evident that many of these managers adopted an inflexible attitude towards the issue of budgetary performance; targets had to be met. This apparent association between the experience of ambiguity and budget style was explored further through a third tactic.

This third tactic is about asking the respondent to explain how they know what they are saying to be 'true'. The prototype question is "what leads you to believe (this)?", a question which can be used to get the respondent to provide data supporting his or her position and/or to articulate the reasoning underlying it. In the present example, I was able to glean from respondents that they saw the budgetary system as providing much needed structure and clarity to the role; "At least I know where I stand with the budget", as one interviewee commented.

A fourth tactic which may be used to flesh out one's understanding of emerging issues is to inquire into comments that appear to be puzzling and/or inconsistent with prior remarks (made earlier in the interview or made in a previous interview). This should be done in a way that seeks to communicate the absence of value judgement on behalf of the researcher, and may be accomplished by stating the puzzle, explaining why the comment is puzzling, and asking the interviewee to "help the researcher understand the point better". For example, in terms of the use of the budget as a source of clarity and structure, it was still unclear to me as to how this translated into 'behavioural inflexibility' towards budgetary performance. To that end, I asked for help in my understanding of this point. For example, I would make a comment along the following lines: "I'm puzzled by what appears to be a strong commitment to the budget around here, even though there seems to be little formal incentive to meet budgetary targets. I wonder if I may labour this point a little further in order that I may understand why this is? Why are you keen on seeing budgetary targets being met?"

As a fifth tactic, I would seek to re-phrase interviewee's remarks in a bid to test the accuracy of my understandings. There are several ways to craft this re-phrasing, such as: "So let me re-phrase the way I understand this and please tell me if that's correct", or "let me tell you how I understand this in my own words and you tell me whether that's a fair representation of what you are saying". Employing this approach in the present example enabled me to glean that some managers were using the budget as a 'coping mechanism' against the experience of uncertainty and ambiguity. However, the budget could only be used in this manner so long as initial targets were met. It was the meeting of the target that provided the 'certainty', and thus behavioural inflexibility ensued despite the absence of traditional motivational factors, such as accountability and rewards.

Useful as it is in teasing out subtle and sometimes 'hidden' intricacies and relationships, this interviewing approach has three potential drawbacks (Manzoni 1994). At a practical or operational level, interviews are likely to last longer when respondents are probed for illustrations or explanations than when they are not. This may be particularly troublesome given the time pressures most managers are under. However, re-interviews and later telephone conversations may provide opportunities to clarify puzzling comments. Adopting the tactics described above also requires the interviewer to adapt continuously to the respondent's answers, which makes it difficult to ensure that all the issues of interest receive an equivalent amount of time with each individual. This may impact on the researcher's ability to follow prescribed and pre-planned interview protocols (Yin 1983). Finally, one could be accused of badgering the interviewee, particularly if s/he is reluctant to illustrate his or her answers and is unable to reflect on the theories governing his or her inferences and beliefs about colleagues' behaviour. Interviewees' reluctance or inability to explain his or her attitude towards the budget was a feature of the present study. Understandably, some managers felt uncomfortable discussing how they were 'bothered' by uncertainty and ambiguity within the role, and to that extent, qualitative insights concerning a potential association between role ambiguity and style of budget use were pursued further through a questionnaire survey involving a broad cross-section of the company's managers. The issue of using both qualitative and quantitative data within a case study is returned to later in the chapter.

Collecting Data

Interviewing is obviously one means of collecting data in case study research. Indeed, to Yin (1993) the interview is the cornerstone of case study research. At the same time, it is also recognised that the ability to collect data from several sources, including interviews, archival records, documents, non-participant observation and so on, is a major strength of the case study, not least because it allows for 'triangulation' (Scapens 1990). Triangulation, in turn, is seen as a way of enhancing construct validity as each source of evidence may be 'tested' against each other source of evidence. For example, with regard to, say the issue of strategy implementation and the role of management control systems within this process, one could triangulate the suggestion that management meetings are a crucial route through which strategy is implemented by observing several or more of these meetings. But, what if this evidence contradicts comments made by managers in interviews? Does one reject these comments in favour of some alternative explanation? Or should more evidence be collected from each source? What if this 'new' evidence contradicts the 'old'? What if there is then contradiction and corroboration? Questions such as these give rise to more substantive questions about data analysis and interpretation, and in the next section I discuss some of my own experiences in this regard. Before then, I wish to reflect further on the issue of data collection.

There are, perhaps, three general questions one may ask about the practice of data collection in case study research: what to collect, how much to collect, and how to ensure the accuracy of what is collected. In my own experience, it is not the first of these questions, but the latter two that can be most problematic when doing the research. The issue of what to collect is largely addressed by the research question and I found it reasonably straightforward to devise an initial list of interview questions around the topic of interest: the nature and extent of the relationship between management control systems and the strategy process. My agenda was informed by Robert Simons' (1994, 1995) conceptualisations. Simons argues that top management may use several 'levers of control' to influence and support both the formation and implementation of strategy. To that extent, interviews were broadly based, and included questions relating to the use of belief systems, administrative processes such as management-by-objective schemes, the budgetary system and performance metrics in directing and controlling strategic activity within the firm. Initial interviews also comprised questions about accountability, given that performance evaluation is deemed to be the cornerstone of management control (Otley 1987). Consistent with a grounded approach, questions for subsequent interviews were driven largely by initial findings (see Glaser & Strauss 1967, 1970).

In contrast to the issue of what to collect, questions about how much to collect and how to ensure the accuracy of what is collected seem anything but straightforward. The question of how much is, perhaps, best considered in terms of how little. Perhaps my experiences were unique, but I faced the problem of 'where to draw the line' in terms of data collection. There are several dimensions to this issue. One is the interview, or more precisely, how to get interviewees to stop talking! Once a rapport had been established, it was difficult to draw the interview to a close. On many occasions I was only saved from mental exhaustion (given what was discussed earlier) and/or running out of tape by a telephone call (although most managers' telephones were surprisingly quiet, given this was a telecommunications company) or the interruption of the secretary informing the manager that s/he had another meeting scheduled that day. Indeed, my experiences in this regard makes me think that case study researchers probably do not give sufficient weight to the potential social value of their research, in that people are generally pleased when someone takes an interest in what they are doing.

Another 'line-drawing' problem arose in regard to how many interviews to conduct. The 'numbers game' is difficult to judge, and my own approach was, not to chose a number and then seek to arrange that many interviews, but to seek to cover as many of the company's business units and management levels as possible and see how many interviews that would take. The resulting number of interviews was not insubstantial, but it may be that you are offered the possibility of conducting more interviews than originally scheduled. Do you take this opportunity? Will it disrupt the initial schedule? What if these 'extra' interviews provide conflicting evidence? Not only were interviewees willing to 'proffer' their colleagues and subordinates for interview, but I received offers of 'help' through the questionnaire survey that I conducted as part of the case study. My response was to grab the opportunity when it arose, primarily because, with the best will in the world, it is probably only possible to interview a fraction of a company's workforce, particularly if you are researching a medium to large size organization. My personal objective was to interview at least 5% of Telco's managerial workforce.

This is all very well, but it raises a serious point about data overload; basically, when should the researcher stop collecting the data? 'Theory' suggests that this is when the researcher has achieved 'saturation'. In other words, the researcher should apply the diminishing returns argument and bring closure to data collection when theoretical saturation is reached; when incremental learning is minimal because the researcher is observing phenomena seen before. Moreover, 'theory' also suggests that the iteration process between theory and data will reach saturation point when incremental improvement to theory is also minimal (Dent 1991). However, besides the fact that the amount of data collected is more likely to be driven by financial and time constraints, these arguments imply a degree of homogeneity to the data which appears unrealistic in the context of human endeavour. So, what if you collect a range of opinions and views about a particular issue or issues? What if there is little homogeneity in the data? A picture was emerging from my research, but it was one of diversity rather than homogeneity. I shall return to this issue in the next section.

The third point that must be addressed when collecting case study data is how to ensure the validity and reliability of these data, and to a large extent we have already covered ways of so doing. My attempts to build in cognitive time into the interview using Manzoni's (1994) approach served a dual purpose in helping to address some of the issues of interviewing that can undermine the validity of interview data. For example, by asking for details and illustrations one is, arguably, in a better position to detect 'demand effects' (in which the interviewee acts in a way s/he believes the researcher requires in order to help the researcher) and to counter 'researcher expectancy effects' (whereby the evidence gathered is influenced by the expectations of the researcher). Triangulation, which as also been mentioned, is way of addressing both contextual and construct validity of the data. Contextual validity refers to the extent to which the study captures all the relevant evidence, while construct validity may be defined broadly as the extent to which whatever one uses to measure something actually measures the concept it is supposed to measure (Pinto & Pinder 1972). The interview question, for example, should be framed in such a way that it reflects the issue under consideration. It is 'merely' a matter of 'asking the right questions'! During investigations at Telco, I was particularly keen on attending management meetings and 'shadowing' those managers who would agree to it as a means of improving the accuracy and validity of interview comments. The main objective of these exercises was to guard against possibilities that interviewees were proffering espoused theories rather than theories-in-use (Argyris *et al.* 1985). I found little evidence that what managers said they did contradicted what they appeared to do.

Analysis and Interpretation

So you have established an important research question, established the initial theoretical perspectives, contemplated their role in semi-directional interviews, and have begun collecting the data. Now comes analysis and interpretation, followed by the write-up. The general opinion, particularly among social scientists, is that analysis should follow data collection; that is, after all data have been collected — you are supposed to suspend judgement until then (Bryman 1988). However, experience suggests that collection and analysis are inexorably intertwined, even within an individual interview. After all, is not the idea of interpreting interviewees' responses in the light of initial theoretical perspectives a form of analysis and interpretation? Moreover, given the inevitable staggering of interviews, and in view of the fact that academics are meant to possess considerable intellectual curiosity, iteration in terms of data collection and analysis appears unavoidable. Indeed, there is a cogent argument which suggests that the researcher should seek to develop an empathy with the data, particularly interview data, in order, for example, to interpret what these data tell of participants' realities and the processes through which they unfold.

This process may require the collection of further data if deviations from patterns emerge, or if alternative explanations are possible. Ideally, interpretations would be constantly up-dated until the 'optimal' explanation emerges. At the same time, however, the sheer richness and variety of case study data can undermine such a task. As noted above, case study research is based on a great wealth and variety of empirical data. This variety appears as much in the diversity of data as in their treatment. Sources of data often include official documents, interviewees'/informants' remarks, news reports, and so on. The case thus considers data of different origins, which are produced by different types of knowledge. Interviewees' comments express a direct type of knowledge, whereas news reports and official documents involve a more elaborate form of knowledge (although this characterisation is not meant to denigrate the personal knowledge revealed by what interviewees say).

The analysis of all these data poses problems, which are analogous to the kinds of incompatibilities that exist between documents produced in different computer systems, i.e. the data are in a different code, making analysis potentially problematic. I applied a 'weighting' approach in response. That is, statements of 'fact' which could be challenged through other data sources were given greater attention than secondary data sources (such as newspaper reports) which already contain interpretation and opinion. The aim was to reduce the extent to which I might have been influenced by the views of others. The aim was 'original' interpretation, but the process of interpreting proved even more problematic, not least because of the diversity of behaviour and opinion that became evident during the course of the study. I responded to this by trying to identify the origin(s) of such diversity, particularly as it contradicts notions of alignment that underpin traditional management control theory. This involved more data collection (through further meetings with those managers willing to give of their time) and analysing further both interview and questionnaire data.

The conclusions reached were that diversity was a natural part of management control in situations where there is a need to balance tensions between the need for innovation and learning on the one hand, and predictable goal achievement on the other. It was the aggregate effect that was important; 'balance' was achieved because of diversity not despite of it! The reasons for this diversity were several, and included the notion of group effects; localised solutions were being applied to global problems. But, finding this did not necessarily help, as it introduced additional perspectives (for example, social psychology) into the study. Indeed, one of the most striking aspects of the present case was the richness of both the data and their interpretation; there may be a considerable intellectual downside from being 'too open' in one's approach to case study research!

Two other issues stand out from my experiences of trying to follow case study protocol as reported in the literature in the context of analysis and interpretation. First, the notion of applying interview protocols contradicts the idea of iteration and grounded research, and second, how does one deal with the ideas and interpretations one develops from the 'ether', from one's intuition, rather than from the actual data?

In terms of interviewing, 'theory' demands that one asks the same set of questions of all interviewees in order to enhance construct validity (Yin 1983). However, iteration is, in part, about developing ideas for further analysis as important new insights 'emerge'. In practical terms, these insights should be followed-up during the next interview, and so on. This is especially the case if it is not possible to arrange another set of interviews to address questions emerging from the first interview phase. But, such on-going iteration conflicts with the notion of an interview protocol because, in essence, more questions will have been added to the initial list. Yet, not to follow-up on emerging issues also appears misguided. What should you do? I chose to ask the questions, both in interviews and through a questionnaire survey, which I hoped would help to enhance understanding and interpretation. In other words, I was not seeking to use the quantitative data for rigorous hypothesis testing; rather, I sought to use these data as further triangulation. The questionnaire was used also to explore ideas and inter-pretations that I was developing from just 'being around' the organization.

Crucially, several questions were devised in a bid to capture the trade-offs that I felt were being made during the course of strategy implementation. For example, tensions were evident within the budgetary system, given pressure on managers to be creative in the context of 'tight' budgetary goals. My questions sought to capture these tensions and the trade-offs, for example, between long-term performance and short-term performance that managers appeared to encounter regularly. This approach proved extremely useful in confirming the degree of diversity that appeared to exist within the firm, particularly in relation to the issue of budgetary performance. Questionnaire results showed that some managers took an inflexible approach while others expected their subordinates to miss initial budgetary targets for reasons related to unfolding events and innovative opportunities. In essence, the combination of interviews and questionnaire helped me to gain new insight into how accounting and budgets may be used within the firm. Yet, the notion of using one's intuition (to whatever extent) as a basis for questionnaire design does cut against the principle that questions asked, whether through interviews or through questionnaire surveys, should derive from 'something tangible' (either extant literature and/or from the prior evidence). Moreover, both this approach and the action of combining qualitative and quantitative evidence in the same study produced non-trivial 'knock-on' effects when I sought to write up the case study in the form of academic papers. The issue of write-up is the last to be discussed in this chapter.

Writing Up

Case studies can (and do!) produce large quantities of data. Pettigrew (1988: 98) succinctly describes the problem concerning the copious amounts of data collected during most case studies when writing, "there is an ever present danger of death by data asphyxiation". Yin (1993) suggests that narrative accounts should be organised around the substantive topic of the case study and not the individual interview or specific meeting. Yin also advises the integration of evidence, i.e. assembling together qualitative and quantitative data that address the same topic and integrating interview segments from different respondents that also address the same topic. Glaser & Strauss (1967) also contend that grounded theory can be applied to quantitative data, which means, for example, developing theory on the basis of correlations that emerge from an exploratory analysis of such data. I drew on these arguments in response to accounting reviewers who seemed to take exception to the integration of qualitative and quantitative data within the same paper. The view that evidence of a quantitative nature should be preceded with hypotheses while qualitative evidence should form part of a descriptive analysis of the case appears to endure within the field of accounting; under no circumstances should the two sets of data be mixed.

My experiences in this respect might explain the current dearth of publications that have attempted to integrate qualitative and quantitative data. Alternatively, they may yet again simply expose the limits of my intellectual abilities. Admittedly, there are papers that contain both types of data, but generally the qualitative precedes the quantitative; the inductive comes before the deductive. Little attempt has been made to heed either Glaser and Strauss's or Yin's advice to assemble together qualitative and quantitative data. Yet, paradoxically, it is the use of multiple data sources and data gathering techniques that really distinguishes case study research (Scapens 1990; Yin 1993).

However one addresses the above issue, it is something of an inevitability that most case study reports will form a lengthy narrative which follows no predictable structure, making it hard to write and even harder to read. There is also the danger that a chasm may develop, separating data from conclusions. Miles & Huberman (1984: 35) comment on this very problem, writing: "One cannot ordinarily follow how a researcher got from 3,600 pages of field notes to the final conclusions, sprinkled with vivid quotes though they may be." Such difficulty in following the lines of logic stems largely from the presence of information asymmetry. Only the person(s) conducting the research possess all pertinent data from which interpretations are drawn. This may render any evaluative exercise somewhat superficial, a non-trivial point in academe. Aside from attempting to replicate the investigation themselves, the assessors of case studies have little scope for confirming the accuracy of the analysis and interpretation of the evidence. Ultimately, perhaps, it may be that, as with all other methods of empirical investigation, the only purposeful way of trying to maximise a sense of 'truth' and minimise 'manipulation' is to ensure that people set out with 'good' intentions and methods. *A priori* instruction and training in the potential and problems of case study research, especially the task of interviewing, may help in this regard for, as this chapter has tried to demonstrate, issues and problems may arise when one seeks to operationalise suggested 'good practice' (Yin 1983; Spicer 1992).

Summary and Conclusions

Despite the impression that I may have portrayed above, I got a lot out of my own case study. It gave me a chance to 'get out there' and to discuss matters of management control with managers and senior managers alike. It provided a 'reality check', and, more importantly, the knowledge gained has helped me to develop what it is I tell my students. I must have enjoyed it for, at the time of writing, I am yet again involved in a case study of considerable size and depth. Nonetheless, 'doing' case research is not unproblematic, and in the discussion above I have attempted to convey some of my experiences, particularly in regard to interviewing. In seeking to follow case study protocol, I encountered several issues for which there is probably no specific answer. Addressing the role of *a priori* theory in semi-directional interviews and 'coping' with multiple perspectives proved to be particularly troublesome, not least because of the intellectual and emotional demands they place on the researcher. Indeed, if we accept that case studies are essentially qualitative, seeking not only to observe and describe phenomena or issues but also to explain them in as plausible way as possible, then considerable dependency is laid upon three key qualities of the researcher: the accuracy and honesty of observation, the sensitivities and perceptions of the observer, and the imaginative interpretation of observations. The practicalities of case research are a direct consequence of the nature of these three particular requirements. The quality of a study's findings is dependent on both the soundness of the data collected and the interpretation placed on such data. Indeed, the importance of such issues is further highlighted by the difficulty in evaluating the findings of a study, primarily because of the information asymmetry that exists between the researcher and the reader.

But that is not to say that these are the only issues one must consider. On the contrary, there are many that have not been discussed in this chapter. These include, for example, ethical issues, issues relating to the boundaries of case study research, the 'slowness' of case study research in relation to the production of papers, and the question about how many case studies to undertake at any one time and by how many persons. These issues were not covered, not because they are any less important, but largely because, in my own case, the main intellectual challenges lay with the ones that have been discussed.

In conclusion, if the case study is to gain the recognition it deserves, and become more widely accepted as a rigorous methodological tool within the research community, it is important not only to appreciate the method's value but at the same time to recognise the practical difficulties which might arise. To get the most out of the method, it should be shown as much respect in terms of the 'doing' as is normally reserved for the more quantitative methods of research that still predominate in the field of accounting. The 'rewards' may then be considerable. In my own case, I managed to tease out several interesting and potentially important findings. One concerns the apparent multi-dimensional nature of the relationship between MCS and strategy (Marginson, 1997), another relates to the effects that MCS may have on the formation of strategy (Marginson 2002), yet another is a previously undocumented approach to budgetary control (Marginson 1999), while the final one to mention here concerns the nature of the relationship between experienced role ambiguity and style of budget use (Marginson 2003). Of the study's contribution to the literature, it is, perhaps, this particular finding that exemplifies the value of exploratory case research, for it was something that emerged from the interviews, rather than it being a topic of initial research interest.

References

Ackroyd, S., & Hughes, J. (1992). *Data collection in context*. London: Longman.

Anthony, R. N. (1965). *Planning and control systems: A framework for analysis*. Boston: Harvard University Press.

Argyris, C., Putman, R., & McLain Smith, D. (1985). *Action science: Concepts, methods and skills for research and intervention*. New York: Jossey Bass.

Bartlett, C. A., & Ghoshal, S. (1993). Beyond the m-form organization: towards a managerial theory of the firm. *Strategic Management Journal, 4*(Winter, Special Issue), 23–46.

Berry, A., Loughton, E., & Otley, D. (1991). Control in a financial services company (RIF): A case study. *Management Accounting Research, 2*(1), 109–139.

Bryman, A. (1988). *Quality and quantity in social research*. London: Unwin Hyman.

Dent, J. F. (1991). Accounting and organisation cultures. *Accounting, Organizations and Society, 14*(7), 705–716.

Glaser, B. G., & Strauss, A. L. (1967). *The discovery of grounded theory*. Hawthorne, NY: Aldine de Gruyter.

Glaser, B. G., & Strauss, A. L. (1970). Discovery of substantive theory: a basic strategy underlying qualitative research. In: W. Filstead (Ed.), *Qualitative methodology* (pp. 288–297). Chicago, Il: Rand McNally.

Kahn, R. L., Wolfe, D., Quinn, R., Snoek, J. D., & Rosenthal, R. (1964). *Organizational stress: Studies in role conflict and ambiguity*. New York: Wiley.

Kaplan, R. S. (1986). The role for empirical research in management accounting. *Accounting, Organizations and Society, 11*(4/5), 429–452.

Manzoni, J-F. (1994). Use of quantitative feedback by superiors of manufacturing cost center managers: a field study. Unpublished Working Paper. Boulevard de Constance, Fontainebleau Cedex, France.

Marginson, D. E. W. (1997). Investigating the relationship between an organization's strategy and its management control systems. Unpublished Ph.D. Thesis. Lancaster University.

Marginson, D. E. W. (1999). Beyond the budgetary control system: towards a two-tiered process of management control. *Management Accounting Research, 10*(3), 203–230.

Marginson, D. E. W. (2002). Management control systems and their effects on strategy formation at middle-management levels: evidence from a U.K. organization. *Strategic Management Journal, 23*(11), 1019–1031.

Marginson, D. E. W. (2003). Coping with role ambiguity through the budget. Departmental working paper. Manchester School of Management, UMIST, Manchester, England.

May, T. (1993). *Social research: Issues, methods and process*. Milton Keynes: Open University Press.

Miles, M. B., & Huberman, A. M. (1984). *Qualitative data analysis: A sourcebook of new methods*. London: Sage Publications.

Otley, D. (1980). The contingency theory of management accounting: achievements and prognosis. *Accounting, Organizations and Society, 5*(4), 413–428.

Otley, D. (1987). *Accounting controls and organizational behaviour.* London: Heinemann, published in association with CIMA.

Otley, D. T., & Berry, A. J. (1994). Case study research in management accounting and control. *Management Accounting Research, 5*(1), 45–65.

Pettigrew, A. M. (1988) *Competitiveness and the management process*. Oxford: Blackwell.

Pinto, P. R., & Pinder, C. C. (1972). A cluster analytic approach to the study of organizations. *Organizational Behaviour and Human Performance, 8*(3), 408–422.

Scapens, R. W. (1990). Researching management accounting practice: the role of case study methods. *British Accounting Review, 22*(3), 259–281.

Simons, R. (1994). How new top managers use control systems as levers of strategic renewal. *Strategic Management Journal, 15*(3), 169–189.

Simons, R. (1995). *Levers of control*. Boston, MA: Harvard Business School Press.

Simons, R. (1999). *Performance measurement and control systems for implementing strategy.* Englewood Cliffs, NJ: Prentice-Hall.

Spicer, B. H. (1992). The resurgence of cost and management accounting: a review of some recent developments in practice, theories and case research methods. *Management Accounting Research, 3*(2), 1–37.

Yin, R (1983). *Case study research: Design and methods*. London: Sage.

Yin, R. (1993). *A review of case study research: Design and methods*. London: Sage.

Chapter 20

Qualitative Research: Experiences in Using Semi-Structured Interviews[1]

Joanne Horton, Richard Macve and Geert Struyven

Introduction

The aim of this chapter is to set out some 'real-life' experiences in using semi-structured interviews in studies by Horton and Macve and Macve and Struyven respectively. The studies were both related to the major changes in insurance accounting and reporting that have been taking place from 1990 onwards, both in the U.K. and more widely in the EU (see Horton & Macve 1995, 1997, 1998; Macve & Struyven 1995; Struyven 1995).

In the U.K. study semi-structured interviews with interested parties were employed, whilst the debate was still in its infancy, in order to gain a fuller understanding of the motives for, and consequences of, the emerging changes in accounting policies. In the EU study the focus was on gaining insight into the historical background and factors that had led to the adoption of the EU Insurance Accounts Directive (IAD) in 1991 and the likely consequences of its implementation. At that time we all found, when initially designing the qualitative research, that there was in fact very little documented information, either in academic articles or published books, about the procedures for implementation of interview-based research and in particular about how to make the actual interview process work successfully (cf. Walker 1985).

In the following sections we cover the reasons for using semi-structured interviews, the design and development of the questionnaires used, the process of interviewing and choice of interviewees, and some of the problems encountered and overcome. We first cover the U.K. study and then draw some contrasts from the EU study.

[1] Funding for elements of this research was provided by the ICAEW Research Board, KPMG and the University of Wales, Aberystwyth Research Fund.

The U.K. Study

Why Use Semi-structured Interviews?

We had initially considered whether to use structured questionnaires in a postal survey. However, given the novelty of the issues being discussed (so that it was not even clear initially what would be the most important questions to ask) and the need to ensure that the views of the most important protagonists were obtained, the flexibility of semi-structured interviews greatly outweighed the limitations on statistical analysis that would result. In fact flexibility both in designing and refining the interview guides and in actually conducting the interviews is probably the most important key to success in using this technique. This kind of interviewing also allowed us (Horton and Macve) to weigh up the credibility of the responses for ourselves and explore some of the underlying motives more directly. So semi-structured interviews were chosen in order to allow the interviewees a degree of freedom to explain their thoughts and to highlight areas of particular interest and expertise that they felt they had,[2] as well as to enable certain responses to be questioned in greater depth, and in particular to bring out and resolve apparent contradictions. For example, in some areas interviewees did hold what appeared to be contradictory views — for example, in relation to whether the market is efficient or not, there was often a tension between believing that all that was needed was better information, and believing that a 'bottom line' accounting profit would make a difference. For example, a number of interviewees expressed the view that the market was relatively efficient and consequently insurance firms were not underpriced as suggested, but that they reflected a 'correct price'. But at the same time they also believed that the new accounting method proposed would help with the valuation process because it would enable companies to produce a bottom line number which in their view would encapsulate the firms' overall profitability (such as an earnings-per-share). This form of interviewing also revealed certain issues that we had not previously identified and which could be followed up in further questioning as well as in later interviews and/or could be investigated empirically.

However, in order to control the subjectiveness of this process various techniques were employed to enhance the credibility of the information obtained and its interpretation — in particular the design and conduct of the interviews and the subsequent analysis by both of us together (cf. a 'good cop'/'bad cop' set up! — with respect to the conduct of the interviewees rather than the any subsequent analysis). In both studies other information sources and research techniques were also employed to complement the interviews.

Designing and Developing the Questionnaires

Prior to the U.K. interviews taking place we felt it necessary to clarify our own thinking and theoretical priors (for example, by reviewing the literature on reasons for accounting

---

[2] See, for examples, Cottle (1977: 27) and Jones (1985).

changes), to design the types of questions that would need to be asked in order to explore the reasons for this major accounting change. The initial questions were constructed after reviewing the accounting policy proposals and other relevant articles (for example, *Financial Times* commentary, professional comments) and coming up with our own unanswered questions. For example, why the sudden need to change the accounting method now? What will it achieve? This preparatory 'brainstorming' was originally done by one of us and then independently reviewed and added to by the other. The resulting questions were then found to fall naturally into a few main headings.

The first interviewees were selected from the major instigators of the new accounting method and the questionnaires were then sent to them. This was done initially in response to a request by one of the interviewees who wanted to assess the types of questions he would be required to answer. However, we felt it would also be useful for all interviewees to be sent a copy in advance so this procedure was adopted throughout. This proved to be very productive since many of the participants not only filled in the questionnaire but also asked, and in some cases conscripted, colleagues from different departments to fill in the questionnaire. It also helped to establish our own credibility in so far as having sufficient expertise and understanding of the technically complex accounting issues and the strategic factors involved in the debate so that senior executives were then prepared to devote time to the interviews themselves.

After the first couple of interviews the questionnaire was reassessed and this resulted in two changes being made. Firstly, we found both that some of the questions tended to be repetitive, since the issues were generally addressed in the responses to previous questions, and that some of the questions encompassed more than one issue. Hence a number of the questions were redefined and split into more than one question and the repetitive questions were erased. Also during the first interviews a number of additional issues came to light that we had no previous knowledge about, so questions involving these new areas were then designed. The overall impact of these changes resulted in more than doubling the number of questions from the original questionnaire.

Secondly, we felt that given the different types of expertise each interviewee had (for example actuaries compared to analysts etc.) the detail of the questionnaire should reflect these differences and this resulted in three types of questionnaires being designed (based on the original questionnaire but with different emphases), one for each of: investment analysts and fund managers; company managers; actuaries and accountants. (The questionnaire for actuaries/accountants is attached at Appendix A).

Whom should we Interview?

The key parties for this research were senior professionals who would have some significant contact with the new accounting numbers, for example through auditing or analysing the figures, as major investors, or through being involved in committees responsible for developing the proposals or for giving professional commentary and/or guidance on the proposals. This resulted in thirty-six people being interviewed, representing twenty-five different organisations. In gaining initial access to the first interviewees it may have been important that one of us was at the time a Council member of the ICAEW. However as the research progressed gaining access to other interested parties was helped by the fact that (a) the debate being investigated was extremely topical at the time and (b) the interviewees thought it extremely important to be a part of that debate. It may also be noted that previous interviewees also suggested certain people to talk to who would be of interest (in some cases because the interviewee knew that the suggested person held very different views to theirs — in some instances the interviewee primed these potential interviewees prior to our visit). The community of insurance 'experts' is relatively small and close-knit. Individuals to interview were identified in many cases by asking earlier interviewees to suggest names of those whom they would recommend as able to speak with authority on the issues or who held views that they themselves were particularly opposed to. In several cases interviewees were aware of whom we had already spoken to, or had appointments to speak to, and suggested particular lines of enquiry that would 'draw out' significant views.[3] Indeed in some cases interviewees had already been contacted by other people we had interviewed to ask if they had been 'Horton and Macve'd' yet!

Conducting the Interviews

The interviews were conducted on the basis that opinions would not be attributed to specific individuals or organisations without their permission, or except insofar as the views had been stated in published material, and that the interviews could go 'off the record' at any stage. This approach was employed in the case of 'company managers' in particular, and to some extent in the other categories, since the respondents were often at pains to emphasise that their view was not necessarily the 'official' view of their employer organisation.

There was one insurance company manager who refused see us, but generally the responses were extremely favourable although we sometimes had to be very flexible about finding times convenient to the interviewees. Some managers initially bounded their time commitment by having another meeting scheduled for an hour or so (in some cases half an hour) later. However, as they generally became interested in the discussion and more respectful of our objectives and credentials, these appointments often evaporated!

To ensure accuracy interviews were taped whenever circumstances allowed but in some cases interviewees did not wish to be taped, or the meeting place (for example, over lunch or while the interviewee was getting dressed up ready to go out to the opera!) did not allow efficient use of a tape-recorder. All the tapes were transcribed (although sometimes the noise of the office air conditioning in the background made this task difficult!) and sent back to the interviewee(s) in order to ensure accuracy and in some case to add further comments they had not noted during the interview. In a few cases interviewees actually removed certain comments made since they felt they may be

---

[3] There also appeared to be traces of an 'interviewees' curse' in that three of the most outspoken people we interviewed were made redundant or changed careers to a different area shortly afterwards!

sensitive: further confirmation that in the interviews themselves they had expressed themselves freely.

Both of us were present at all the interviews which lasted anywhere from 45 minutes to an hour and a half (so again it was important to allow flexibility when arranging interview times). We found that having both of us present was extremely valuable since one of us would be assigned, prior to the interview, with picking up on any contradictions, or areas in which the interviewee felt uncomfortable. This could not have been achieved as efficiently if there had only been one interviewer given it is very difficult for one person to note the comments, whilst also thinking of additional questions and at the same time watching the body language of the interviewee. Some of the participants were interviewed twice following new information found post-interview. For example, after carrying out empirical testing on a number of the assertions made the results were taken back to the relevant interviewees for further comments. In some organisations only one interviewee was present but often there were two (for example, a senior officer and his or her deputy — although in one case the deputy's attention frequently wandered and he was taken by surprise when the occasional question was referred to him!). In one situation, at a firm of consulting actuaries, several partners were present and the discussion took on the character of an academic seminar with points of argument being hotly debated between the participants themselves. Under these conditions we found it extremely important that we were flexible in our interview approach so that issues and arguments could be fully discussed and aired. However, it should be noted that under these conditions we had to make sure the discussions between these multiple interviewees did not digress too far from the issues in question and having the semi-structured questionnaires in front of us helped bring the debate back to these issues.

We did not feel that any particular topic or issues could not be addressed although due to our different interview styles some questions poised were subtler than others. For example one of us suggested to a company director that some additional information disclosed by their company in their annual reports was merely done in order to cover up the company's poor results. This rather direct question resulted in a kick under the table by the other interviewer due to its lack of subtlety, however it may be noted the company director did attempt to answer the question.

When the senior officer and his or her deputy was also present we did find at times that issues the deputy considered more important were not able to be covered in as much detail. We therefore suggested to the senior officer that it would be useful to go over any day-to-day detail with their deputy on a one-to-one basis. This resulted in a number of interviews with deputies by themselves and some useful insights into practical issues any new accounting method would have for the company.

Writing up the Interviews

We were both involved with the writing up of the interviews in order to enhance validity and allow a more objective assessment to be made of the significance of interviewees' comments and remarks. A form of content analysis (Janckowicz 1991) was employed which was considered appropriate to the circumstances and objectives of the research. The method adopted was for one researcher to write up an overview of the issues aired and differing points of view expressed, and then for the other researcher to check this against the detailed transcripts, adding suitably illuminating original quotations where appropriate, and, in several instances, challenging and revising the interpretations of the first researcher. After further discussion a 'consensus' rendering was agreed. Given our own prior expertise in relation to the specialist areas being investigated and the open and conversational character of much of the interviewing this seemed likely to be more satisfactory and productive than employing a research assistant to attempt a formalised 'coding' of the transcripts (cf. Walker 1985). Given the presumed personal nature of the responses and the inherent difficulty of categorising interviewees' roles no attempt was made to analyse the responses statistically (for example to attempt to correlate arguments with particular vested interests). However, some summarising of the responses in tabulated form was attempted, but this was often less than satisfactory as it was necessary to make dichotomous classifications of answers which, in context, were not 'black or white' but expressed subtle 'tones of grey'. The tabular results would therefore only have any meaning when interpreted within the particular textual context.

'Beneath' or 'Alongside' the Numbers?

The interviews were conducted as one part of a study that also embraced statistical market-based research into the impact of the proposed accounting change (Horton & Macve 1998). While the two kinds of study were complementary and the results provided a rich all-round perspective on the developments, in our opinion the interviews were, on balance, the more valuable part of the research precisely because they did allow us to explore 'beneath the numbers' in order to understand the views and interests driving the debate over the proposed accounting change and its significance in the eyes of its proponents and adversaries, as well as of those remaining on the sidelines. We were attempting to meet here Lev's (1989) challenge to researchers to try and understand why managers choose different accounting methods rather than simply investigate, say, the impact upon earnings and stock returns (see Horton & Macve 1997, Chapter 4). As Frankfurter & McGoun (1993: 8) have argued:

> "Event studies are routinely used to verify that indeed signalling took place, yet there is never the slightest effort at an alternative or parallel verification through the simple expedient of asking at least some of the parties involved about signalling."

What Did We Learn?

The currency of the debate enabled the interviewing almost to take on aspects of a 'participant observation'[4] of the process of change, whereby some interviewees commented that the discipline of answering questions helped them clarify their own

---

[4] See, for example, Walker (1985: 6).

thinking about the issues and indeed about what were the issues. We were both pleasantly surprised by the willingness and in some cases eagerness of participants identified as possible interviewees. In some cases a number of interested parties contacted us after being notified of the study, since they felt that they had particular arguments for or against the proposal, which may not have been noted by past interviewees.[5] As to whether we actually changed interviewees' opinions (which was not the point of the study) or indeed the debate as a whole is questionable and would be difficult to ascertain.

In many cases interviewees' responses indicated a considerable — indeed surprising — depth of feeling about the issues that had arisen in the debate. For example, some interviewees appeared to treat this opportunity of expressing their views as itself a 'round' in the 'contest' in which they were seeking to advance their own position or attack the well known views of others whom we had already interviewed or would be interviewing. Indeed, some interviewees tried to use us as unofficial spokespersons to forward their arguments and concerns on to other participants in the debate in order to make sure they knew how each other felt and to try, in some instances, to change each other's views. This in itself was also helpful to us since a number of remarks made by the interviewees such as "he would say that wouldn't he . . ." enabled us to put these comments into context which we would not have otherwise been able to do.

A major issue that concerned us was whether interviewees' comments should be taken at face value or as representing self-justification for their own perceived interests, made in order to protect or advance their own positions. Our response was, first that, as in any debate involving the vested interests of different parties, it is important to obtain the range of arguments (or 'excuses'[6]) that are likely to be deployed in the course of developing an accounting standard. Second, we believed that, as interviews were conducted on a non-attributable basis, in a mainly conversational mode as between equals, and given the (sometimes surprising) intellectual quality of the arguments used, we are justified in interpreting the responses, in general, as being not 'special pleading' but genuinely held beliefs.

Moreover, as noted above, the interviewing was in parallel to a statistical study of market behaviour. Nevertheless, even without that complementary study (which in some instances confirmed but in others contradicted interviewees' views) we believe that these interviews enabled us to form a valid understanding of protagonists' behaviour and beliefs and of how these have shaped the debate.

The European Study: Additional Problems in Interviewing Abroad

The Insurance Accounts Directive (IAD) was issued in December 1991, requiring translation into the laws of Member States by 31 December 1993, so as to be effective for accounting periods beginning on or after 1 January 1995. Many of the requirements

---

[5] A researcher conducting a related study (Edwards 1993) also contacted the researchers in order to conduct one of his own series of interviews with authorities on life insurance accounting.
[6] Watts & Zimmerman (1978).

of the proposed Directive were controversial, and a large number of Member State and company options remained in the final version.

The purpose of the research by Macve and Struyven was to explore the process of EU harmonisation by focusing on a particular industry and investigating the attitudes to, and impacts of, the IAD in three major countries, France, Germany and the U.K.

To this end the evidence examined included previous published work of researchers, various official EU documents and publications, and the annual accounts of various insurance companies in the three countries investigated. More importantly, major sources of information consisted of personal interviews and internal, sometimes 'confidential' and 'private', documents. The interviews provided some important empirical evidence about the perceptions, interests and views of those involved in the development of the IAD, in respect of some controversial issues, which had not previously been available in the public domain.

With regard to the semi-structured interviews, much of the process was similar to the experience described in the study discussed above, so here we just aim to bring out the major contrasts and in particular the additional factors arising from conducting interviews in continental Europe.

The interviews were informal and of considerable depth and lasted from one and a half hours to over three hours (i.e. generally longer than the U.K. interviews). Once again, before each interview the confidentiality of the conversation was discussed and it was agreed with the interviewees neither to quote them, nor to attribute particular criticisms, controversial ideas or comments to them individually or to their organisation. In this way, we (Macve and Struyven) were able to probe more freely, for example, into how accounting actually operates in practice, as compared with how it is supposed to operate under the legislation, and to obtain a closer understanding of the different accounting philosophies in the three countries.

For the purposes of this research, where the primary objective was to understand differences between the three major countries as to their existing accounting methods and their approach to the development of the Directive and its implementation, it was considered that just one form of questionnaire could be utilised, but that with certain interviewees fuller responses on some areas would be expected than on others. (The questionnaire is attached at Appendix B.)

A number of interviewees were chosen from each of the three Member States examined. In many cases they were once again suggested by other interviewees. Interviewees included insurance accounting experts in France, Germany and the U.K., including the regulatory authorities and the European Commission and its advisers,[7] resulting in 25 interviews with 17 different organisations.

Problems Encountered

Unfortunately, not all the people contacted were available, or willing, to agree to a meeting, so compared to the experience of Horton and Macve described above, we had

---

[7] i.e. the Fédération des Experts Comptables Européens (FEE).

greater difficulty in obtaining co-operation, particularly from companies in France and Germany. Even though major companies in those countries issue 'international' accounts, in English, it was sometimes difficult to find a relevant officer who would agree to be interviewed. The reasons for this may include:

(a) relative unfamiliarity with the experience of being interviewed by academic researchers given that (at least at that time) accounting research of this kind appeared to be less common in France and Germany. This may also explain the phenomenon that, while access was somewhat more difficult in France and Germany than in the U.K., nevertheless company interviewees there tended to be more generous with their time than in the U.K., so that interviews could last a whole morning or afternoon;

(b) suspicion of our credentials, even though these were made as clear as possible in the introductory letters of request;

(c) the fact that this research was not externally sponsored;[8] so that, for example, the ICAEW's (or ESRC's) support could not be cited;

(d) fears about discussing complex technical issues in English. To this end interviewees were made aware that one of us was competent in French and German,[9] and indeed in one case the only person available for interview in one of the German companies insisted that the interview be in German. A German version of the questionnaire was therefore prepared. In the event the interview was very successful as the interviewee took pains to answer in extremely clear German, so that both of us could follow the line of argument at the time, and he was in fact also happy to accept extemporised questions in English (which he answered in German!). (The interview tape was also later translated into English.)

Similar procedures as to confidentiality, taping of interviews, writing up etc. were followed as with the other study discussed above.

The Value of the Interview Process

The interviews were particularly valuable for revealing insights into the actual process of development and implementation of an EU accounting Directive. (Previous research, for example by Diggle & Nobes (1994) had relied primarily on public documentation.) The interviews were also valuable in creating a network of contacts in the U.K. and continental Europe which will be of benefit for future research on the way in which individual States and companies further develop their insurance accounting following the Directive's implementation, as they adapt to new pressures for accounting change.

Once again, interviews of this kind may be criticised on the grounds that interviewees will give, either openly or subtly disguised (or even unconsciously), the views that they wish the interviewers to have and report rather than their true beliefs and opinions.

---

[8] Funding for this research was provided by the Aberystwyth Research Fund.
[9] The other researcher also has limited understanding of French and German. Both are stronger in French than in German.

There is little that can be done directly to eliminate this possibility. However, the context within which the interviews were conducted, in particular the assurances about confidentiality already described, provided the most informal situation possible within which people could be encouraged to be open about their opinions. Moreover, given that the outcome of the negotiations over the Directive was complete, it is unlikely that the parties would have perceived these interviews as an opportunity to continue to try to press their own interests. In addition, we would respect, in general, the sincerity with which interviewees expressed what they often described to be their own personal (rather than 'official') views. Finally, the validity of responses is to some extent confirmed by their consistency among different interviewees, which enabled a reasonably coherent overall picture to be developed.

Other Information Sources Used

Moreover, although the interviews were an important part of the information obtained, they were not the only, or main, source of primary information. We were also able to obtain a large number of official and other documents, which were not publicly available. These included:

- minutes of all the meetings of the FEE Insurance Working Party established at the request of the Commission to develop the Draft Directive. These minutes provided us with inside information which had never been studied before;
- the files of the ICAEW Insurance Committee. These files contained not only all official documentation on the IAD, but also private correspondence between the ICAEW and its various member firms etc. These were treated as highly confidential, and we agreed not to attribute any comments or ideas to the various individuals or the firms that they were representing. The files also included, *inter alia*, official responses to the ICAEW/DTI/ABI questionnaires and proposals; responses to the draft proposals of the IAD and CEA comments; as well as correspondence between the EC Commission and the main accounting firms, regulatory authorities and insurance companies in the various Member States. It is impossible to know how far access to these files may have been facilitated by the senior status of one of us who was at the time a Council member of the ICAEW.

The combination of these various sources provided us with valuable new information that allowed them to gain new insights into the overall process of accounting harmonisation.

Concluding Comments

The use of semi-structured interviews, with their open format, provides a valuable means to allow researchers to explore how far their own theoretical priors are reflected in the behaviour and perceptions of significant actors in the arena of accounting changes, and to enable new 'grounded' theorising to be formulated.

> "Without allowing people to speak freely we will never know what their
> real intentions are, and what the true meaning of their words might be."
> (Cottle 1977: 27).

With respect to our studies above and the type of arena we were all working in, we found the following desirable in order to allow a valuable dialogue to emerge, *ceteris paribus*.

  (i) one of the interviewers to be a senior academic;
 (ii) interviewees to have sight of the questionnaire in advance;
(iii) two interviewers to be present and interviews to be taped;[10]
 (iv) maximum use to be made of the open nature of the questionnaire so that a conversation develops which brings out the nuances of meaning and avoids false 'yes/no' dichotomies;
  (v) the content analysis of the interviews, whether by formal coding or more intuitive interpretation of the material, to be validated by both of us;
 (vi) while the material may be in some cases be amenable to statistical analysis, in many cases its role is primarily interpretative of perceptions and interests, many of which may be contradictory (even in the case of one individual). Tabular presentations are likely to need to be interpreted within a textual context which emphasises that classifications may not be mutually exclusive. The use of direct quotations can be valuable in highlighting the way in which interviewees themselves approach the issues.

Finally, it goes without saying that any confidentiality negotiated must be strictly observed in any published material derived from the interviews.

References

Cottle, T. J. (1977). *Private lives and public accounts*. New York: New Viewpoints.

Diggle, G., & Nobes, C. (1994). European rule-making in accounting: the seventh directive as a case study. *Accounting and business research*. 24(96), 319–333.

Edwards, C. R. (1993). Life assurance financial reporting and life profit recognition. MBA dissertation, University of Loughborough, October.

Frankfurter, G. M., & McGoun, E. (1993). The event study: an industrial strength method. *International Review of Financial Analysis*, 2(2), 121–141.

Horton, J., & Macve, R. (1995). *Accounting principles for life insurance: A true and fair view?* London: Institute of Chartered Accountants in England and Wales.

Horton, J., & Macve, R. (1997). *U.K. life insurance: Accounting for business performance*. London: Financial Times.

Horton, J., & Macve, R. (1998). Planned changes in accounting principles for life insurance companies: a preliminary investigation of stock market impact. *Journal of Business Finance and Accounting*, 25(1/2), 69–102.

Janckowicz, A. D. (1991). *Business research projects for students* (1st ed.). London: Chapman and Hall.

---

[10] It is also vital to ensure the tape recorder is working properly, batteries charged etc!

Jones, S. (1985). Depth interviewing. In: R. Walker (Ed.), *op cit.* (pp. 56–70).

Lev, B. (1989). On the usefulness of earnings and earnings research: lessons and directions from two decades of empirical research. *Journal of Accounting Research,* 27(Supplementary), 153–168.

Macve, R., & Struyven, G. (1995). Influences on the EC insurance accounts directive and its implementation in the U.K., France and Germany. Presented at the Ernst and Young International Accounting Symposium, Aberystwyth, October 1995.

Struyven, G. (1995). EU accounting harmonisation: an analysis of the development, shaping and impact of the insurance accounts directive in the U.K., France and Germany. Ph.D. dissertation, University of Wales, Aberystwyth.

Walker, R. (Ed.) (1985). *Applied qualitative research.* Aldershot: Gower.

Watts, R., & Zimmerman, J. (1978). Towards a positive theory of the determination of accounting standards. *Accounting Review, LIII,* 112–134.

APPENDICES A and B: SEMI-STRUCTURED QUESTIONNAIRES

Note: The appendices reproduce the content but not the precise format of the research instruments, which in the original allowed much more space between questions for interviewees to make written responses or preparatory notes for the interview meeting.

Appendix A: Semi-Structured Questionnaire For Accountants/Actuaries

I. Pressures for change:

(1) Why do you think such a debate has arisen now?

(2) What are your views regarding the Pearl takeover, in particular do you believe the shares were purchased cheaply by AMP?

(3) Is the threat of takeovers still an important factor in prompting accounting changes and how else are U.K. companies defending themselves and their current policyholders' and shareholders' interests?

(4) What do you believe affects the price of shares on the stock market?
(a) generally
(b) in particular, life company shares

(5) Do you believe the sector is under/over-valued?

(6) Are individual companies under/overvalued?

(7) What do you believe are the major reasons for and likely effect of the introduction of a new accounting method?

(8) Has the level of debate on the new method affected share prices?

II. Responses

(1) Why have some companies chosen to publish the embedded value?

(2) How did you interpret the 10.8% price movement of Legal and General following their disclosure of the embedded value, and its impact upon the rest of the sector?

(3) Would it be useful for companies generally to disclose an embedded value?

(4) How accurate are external estimates of embedded values?

(5) Why have some companies decided to publish an appraisal value?

(6) Would it be useful for companies generally to disclose an appraisal value?

(7) How accurate are external estimates of appraisal values?

(8) How far is information already available, e.g. in DTI Returns, to enable a realistic estimate of shareholders' value to be made?

(9) What further information will become available as a result of the EC Directive?

(10) What additional information is needed to enable a realistic valuation to be made?

III. Accruals method

(1) What information is provided by the accruals method that is not already provided by established methods, such as embedded value?

(2) *External consequences of adoption*

    (i) Do you believe it will increase the share prices of insurance companies?

    (ii) Do you believe it will alter the allocation of profits between shareholders and policyholders?

    (iii) Do you believe it will affect the level of dividend distribution?

    (iv) Do you anticipate any tax effects?

    (v) Do you anticipate any gearing effects?

(3) *Internal consequences of adoption*

    (i) How are managers usually evaluated?

    (ii) Do you think it will affect the way in which managers' performance is evaluated?

    (iii) Will the type of product offered be affected?

IV. Implementation of proposals

(1) Which major issues of concern to the actuarial\accounting professions are still outstanding?

    (a) coverage of policyholder accounting and mutuals

    (b) compatibility with the EC Directive

    (c) degree of flexibility

    (d) pattern of profit emergence

        – prudence about Day 1 profit
        – volatility
        – concepts of "risk" and "work done"
        – treatment of acquisition costs
        – investment gains and losses

(2) How much data is available on the likely patterns of profit emergence under different methods?

(3) How accurate are external estimates of accruals results?

(4) Why have the actuarial/accounting arguments in favour of alternative approaches e.g. Realistic Provisions, "Australian" method not been followed up by the ABI?

(5) How do your professional concerns relate to those of the other professional bodies? (e.g. accountants/actuaries)

(6) What differences remain about views of what is needed to meet the "true and fair" reporting requirement in relation to e.g.
provisions and reserves,
earning of income,
wording of audit report.

(7) Is the planned experimentation now the most appropriate way forward?

(8) How widespread do you expect adoption of the accruals method to be by different types of insurance companies?

(9) How important is it that the ABI gets a franked SORP?

(10) Would you expect there to be differing impacts depending on where the new values/results are published i.e. in the balance sheet and profit and loss, or in notes to the accounts, or as unaudited supplementary information?

(11) What are the respective roles of ABI, ASB and the accounting and actuarial professions in developing guidance on reporting?

V. Preparation for change

(1) What are the costs of implementing such a proposal?

(2) How much preparation time is needed?

(3) Are interim as well as annual results feasible?

(4) What are the respective roles of accountants and actuaries in relation to the final accounts and are their responsibilities changing?

VI. Other

(1) Who else do you believe we should talk to for more details?

Appendix B: IAD Interview Questionnaire

I. Insurance business

What are the distinctive features of insurance business in your country?

In Germany, what has been the impact of unification on the insurance market?

Does the nature of the insurance products in your country, or the kind of investments held by insurance companies, make it appropriate to have a different kind of accounting from companies in other Member States (for example, U.K., France, Germany)?

Is this changing?

Have you been involved in cross-border take-overs?

What difficulties do you face in

(a) interpreting
(b) consolidating

the accounts of insurance companies in different Member States?

What mechanisms do you have to limit the threat of take-overs from other companies, in your own or other countries?

II. The harmonisation program

Which are the regulatory authorities in charge of implementing the Directive into national law?

When do you expect it to be introduced, and when will the accounts of insurance companies have to comply with the new regulation?

Has the regulatory authority taken the ideas/ wishes of the industry into account when implementing the Directive — and how have they (if at all) consulted the industry and the accounting profession?

What have been the main driving forces behind the Directive — who has had the biggest influence and why?

What compromises have had to be made to obtain agreement on the Directive?

Do you think the Directive will be effective for harmonisation purposes — Do you think the annual accounts of insurance companies will be really comparable or will the same layout not necessarily mean that the figures which look alike, actually mean the same thing

(a) within your country
(b) within the EC?

What do you expect to be the major effects of the Directive?

What do you think are the major advantages of the Directive?

What are in your opinion the major criticisms of the Directive?

What do you consider as being the biggest difference in practice between

(a) different companies
(b) member states?

What do you think are the major obstacles for further harmonisation?

What other harmonisation programs do you think still need to be completed/undertaken to create a single EC market in insurance?

III. True and fair

What does the true and fair requirement mean

(a) to you
(b) to the general audience here?

Will the introduction of the requirement change anything for insurance accounts in this country?

What do you regard as the main objective(s) of accounting reports of insurance companies in your country? How are these changing?

Who are the primary users of accounting reports in your country?

What do you think is the influence of the stock exchange on accounting principles and practices for insurance companies? Is this changing?

What is the influence of regulatory requirements on your accounting?

What is the influence of taxation rules on your accounting?

IV. Investments valuation

Which are the different categories which are disclosed separately?

Which are the different valuation methods which are allowed for:

* listed securities   (a) equities   (b) fixed interest
* unlisted securities   (a) equities   (b) fixed interest
* properties
* mortgages and loans

Will the introduction of the requirement to disclose the current values of the investments change accounting practice

(a) in the balance sheet
(b) in the notes?

When and how will it be implemented?

Will the current value disclosed be the current market value or some prudent estimate of value?

Investment income

Is the investment income generally taken to the Profit and Loss or is it taken to a "technical account"?

Does the investment income have to be disclosed as a separate item? Into what categories is it analysed?

What are the different valuation rules allowed?

How will the Directive change current practice?

Investment gains

What is the difference in treatment between the realised and unrealised gains?

Is there a general tendency to disclose unrealised gains?

Are you in favour of the current approach?

Are you happy with the requirement of the Directive that all realised gains/losses should pass through life technical account and/or Profit and Loss?

How will the Directive change the treatment of unrealised gains and losses?

V. Deferred acquisition costs

What may these include and how are they calculated?

Are they disclosed and where?

Are you happy with the current legislation/Directive in this matter?

How will the implementation of the Directive change current practice?

VI. Discounting

How far is 'implicit' discounting currently used?

Is 'explicit' discounting used for any items?

What may these include and how are they calculated?

Are they disclosed and where?

Are you happy with the current legislation/Directive in this matter?

How will the implementation of the Directive change current practice?

VII. Equalisation reserves

In which ways do you think insurance companies can most easily smooth their profits?

Can they continue to do so under the Directive?

What may equalisation reserves include and how are they calculated?

Are they disclosed and where?

Are you happy with the current legislation/Directive in this matter?

How will the implementation of the Directive change current practice?

Will you utilise the option for a "fund for future appropriations"?

VIII. Tax

Will the Directive change anything for the reported profits?

Which accounting rules or options do you see as having been included in the Directive as the result of the German principle of the *"Maßgeblichkeitsprinzip"*?

IX. General

Do you have any specific comments?

Do you think we have omitted an important or interesting aspect of the Directive?

Who else do you think we should talk to?

Chapter 21

To Tape or Not to Tape: Reflections on Methods of Data Collection

Treasa Hayes and Ruth Mattimoe

Introduction

A pivotal part of the qualitative research process is dependent on the collection of large quantities of interview data. Some insights into this part of the qualitative research task are presented here, based on our personal experiences in two separate studies. One of us (Ruth) chose the audio-tape route to gather her data, while the other (Treasa) opted for manual recording of interview material. We now share some of the lessons gleaned in the course of these respective research journeys.

In order to provide some context for the discussion, we provide an overview of the two studies (Mattimoe 2002; Hayes 1996) for which the data were gathered. While both studies were interpretivist, Study A, undertaken by Ruth, took the 'tape' route during interviews conducted for this research, whereas manual recording was the route chosen for data collection in Study B, which was undertaken by Treasa. Next, various aspects of the debate surrounding the question: 'To tape or not to tape?' are addressed. The discussion finishes with some final reflections that may be of use to other researchers.

The Studies

Study A: Overview

This study centred on an in-depth investigation into the complex processes of room rate pricing in the Irish hotel industry, which is a key sector in the Irish economy. In the research, I (Ruth) sought to identify the rich panoply of influences at both macro and micro level that shape the setting of the room-rate. For example, I needed to explore developments in training and education in the hotel sector. Also, accounting and marketing perspectives on the micro processes of room-rate pricing had to be factored

The Real Life Guide to Accounting Research: A Behind-the-Scenes View of Using Qualitative Research Methods
© 2004 Published by Elsevier Ltd.
ISBN: 0-08-043972-1

into the enquiry. There was little previous research into pricing in the Irish hotel industry, so there was a medium to high uncertainty attached to my topic. I was also the first academic trained as a chartered accountant to research this industry.

Because of the uncertainty surrounding the project, I decided that a qualitative approach would be most conducive. I needed to probe the hotel manager's understanding of room rate pricing in his/her particular hotel, as well as to grasp the constraints provided by the macro environment of hotel operations. To capture all of this, my empirical research centred on two main areas: (1) an investigation into the structure of the industry, of government and EU incentives; and (2) micro-level case studies in two hotels. To address the first question, I decided to focus on a select group of people who could provide informative insights into the key influences on the development of tourism and hotels as an industry from the 1960s to the present. On the recommendations of some academic colleagues with knowledge of the industry, I decided to interview the CEO of the Irish Hotel Federation, and a government advisor, who was one of the architects of the aid package (lower access fares by air and sea, tax relief, EU grants for staff training and capital/product improvement etc.) which revived the industry since the recession of the 1980s, spurring a trebling of visitor numbers and a huge growth in room stock. Other interviewees included: a training manager from the State Hotel Training Agency; an academic who was head of one of the biggest centres for hospitality management degrees in Ireland; a tour operator; a conference organiser and a partner in a chartered accountancy firm with many hotel clients. A series of in-depth interviews with these (seven) informants was carried out and this helped to inform the choice of strikingly contrasting case sites. My study was thus processual (in its inquiry at the micro level) and historical (in tracing influences over time on the macro environment).

Having captured the broad range of influences impacting on room rate pricing, I augmented the data by undertaking two major case studies set in two contrasting types of accommodation. One was a 3* hotel in the west of Ireland while the other was a third level facility which offered large-scale budget type accommodation in Dublin, during the summer months.

My main research consisted of conducting a series of unstructured interviews with the manager at each case site. I augmented these by holding interviews with other key actors such as the accountant and the marketing manager at both locations. The overall data gathering process involved undertaking a total of eighteen interviews at the two sites, with an input of about fifty hours interviewing time. The seven interviews with key informants, mentioned above, took an additional twenty hours. I taped all the interviews for this study.

Study B: Overview

The research for Study B focused on an exploratory study of management, control and accountability in Irish voluntary organisations. The main fieldwork for the research was qualitative in nature and I (Treasa) undertook individual interviews without using a tape recorder. Much literature was available on management, control and accountability in general, so my work was to develop this literature for the voluntary sector. The uncertainty inherent in the research topic was low to medium. The core of this empirical research centred on a sample of ten Irish voluntary organisations. I interviewed four respondents in each of the ten organisations — the CEO, the accountant, a Board member and a volunteer — yielding a final total of forty in-depth interviews.

In preparations for the interview process, I drew up an interview schedule in order to ensure that I gathered the required information in relation to three broad areas:

- General background information on each organisation in terms of age, service, clients, staffing, income, together with profiles of the respondents;
- Detailed information relating to control;
- Approaches to accountability.

This research instrument was used as a guide for all of the forty interviews undertaken, each of which lasted about two hours. The schedule of open-ended questions permitted a free flow of responses while also providing a common framework for each interview. With such a large number of interviews, this approach was deemed necessary in order to ensure that the same 'territory' was covered in each individual encounter, thus providing overall comparability in the data collected. All of my interviews for Study B were recorded manually.

Having provided brief background sketches of our two pieces of research, we now move on to consider the central issue which relates to taping or manually recording interview data.

To Tape or Not to Tape?

As outlined above, we used two contrasting methods of capturing interview data in the course of our respective research journeys. As we both managed to achieve our ultimate goal of a completed research project, this confirms that, in practice, both the route of taping interviews and that of manual recording of data can be effective in the craft of qualitative research, suggesting that there is no 'one-best-way' to tackle the task of data collection. The decision to tape or not to tape is influenced by a number of key determinants. These include: (a) the nature of the research topic; (b) the willingness of the interviewee to be taped; (c) the interviewer's preference and competence with either technique; and (d) the benefits and drawbacks of the techniques themselves. Each of these aspects of the decision is now considered in some detail.

The Research Topic

The less structured the nature of the topic under investigation, the more exploratory the research. This can suggest a preference for taking the taping route to record data, because of the need to probe for insights into the broad area under review, adding or discarding some questions and refining or changing the course of the research during individual interviews. Thus, in cases where the overall research issue is not well defined, it is not possible to have a detailed, pre-determined list of questions. Rather, the researcher works from a list of broad topics that need to be explored. Adopting this approach gives the interviewee the opportunity to talk freely. This type of interaction is often labelled an informant interview, since it is the interviewee's perceptions that guide the conduct of the interview (Easterby-Smith *et al.* 1991). A lot of probing and discovery is required and much data may be garnered as 'guidance' rather than as raw data. The interview task represents a type of navigation of the research 'river' which inevitably involves a lot of meandering and wrong turns, before the destination can be reached.

Study A is an example of this type of research topic where I (Ruth) had little by way of guidance from previous research and initially my topic was very wide. Therefore I had to be very flexible during the data gathering process, using broad topics as a guide for conducting my interviews. Given this scenario, it would have been very difficult to record the interviews manually. Realising this, I opted for the taping route at the outset of my work. In contrast when the research topic is more structured and the researcher is reasonably clear about what is to be asked during the interview, it is easier to use the manual method of recording data. For example, in Study B, the open-ended questions were pre-determined, requiring less adjustment during the interview.

The structure of the overall study, in terms of the number of case sites, is another aspect that has to be taken into consideration. As Study B was spread over ten case sites and forty in-depth interviews, Treasa needed the guidance of a reasonably detailed interview schedule in order to ensure that the same issues were explored during each of her forty interviews. Otherwise there was a danger that she would end up with patchy interview data. In contrast, Ruth's study centred on a detailed investigation, confined to two case sites. Therefore the need for consistency over a larger number of case sites did not arise.

Resistance to Taping

Resistance to taping on the part of the interviewee can be an issue. In fact, sometimes the possibility of such resistance may be anticipated, leading the researcher to opt for manual recording of the interview. This was the situation I (Treasa) encountered in Study B. Given the context of the voluntary sector, where many respondents might not have been accustomed to the use of a tape, I anticipated that some of them might be unhappy, if not altogether unwilling, to have the interview material taped. My research supervisor, who had extensive experience in this sector, agreed with this assessment. Due to the possible risks associated with using a tape, in terms of causing unease for respondents which could have a negative impact on the quality of the data gathered (Saunders, Thornhill & Lewis 1997), opting for manual recording seemed to be a safer option.

In cases where the interviewer takes the decision to tape interviews but meets with resistance in a particular encounter, it has to be addressed. The reasons for the resistance must be probed. It may arise simply from a lack of self-confidence or unfamiliarity with the technique, similar to the reluctance of some to speak to voicemail/telephone answering machines. First of all, one must simply inquire if the interviewee would feel confident speaking to a tape or is it a wider issue that might require some discussion and re-assurance. If opposition to the tape is obvious, then take the manual route. The interviewee may, however, indicate that they are reluctant to be taped, simply because they are unsure about how the data are to be used. If the answer seems to indicate a lack of trust on the part of the interviewee in the research process or a lack of faith in the interviewer's competence/expertise, then it may still be possible to overcome these and continue the taping route. Some pathways to overcome these obstacles are now discussed.

Lack of trust by the interviewee in the research process (i.e. what will be done with the data, where will findings be published, will the quotes be traceable back to him/her etc) is a delicate problem and requires sensitivity and imagination to resolve it. Competence and trust issues may in fact be intertwined and feed off each other, so both need to be dealt with. Interviewer and interviewee bias may arise in the process of data collection (Robson 1993). The lack of trust created (say due to unease with taping) and/ or any lack of competence manifested by the interviewer, may bias his/her interpretation of responses. Interviewee bias can arise in the form of more stilted responses, perhaps caused by the interaction with, and his/her perceptions about, the interviewer. Therefore, these issues must be dealt with at the outset and kept in mind throughout the interview process.

The opening minutes of conversation can have a significant impact on the overall outcome of the interview. Bearing in mind that the respondent has demonstrated some interest in the project by agreeing to be interviewed, the researcher must try to build this interest into a positive relationship. In principle, the interviewee is willing to participate, but is sensitive to in-depth exploration on sensitive topics, which s/he does not wish or is not empowered to disclose. The interviewer must explain why a tape is being used. Very often, the real reasons for any reluctance may be the respondent's lack of clarity about what data is required, how it will be used and the precise purpose of the research. From the outset, the researcher must try to win the confidence of the respondent, by allaying his/her uncertainties about providing information and by giving an assurance of confidentiality. Throughout the interview process, it is necessary to watch out for areas where lack of trust might arise in relation to sensitive issues and be appropriately tactful to keep the relationship positive. If the respondent is promised the interview transcript and told that s/he can edit or clarify any part of it and if quotes being used by the researcher are marked on it with highlighter pen, then this 'look-back control' may overcome any final resistance. In the case of a once-off interview where all these efforts do not bear fruit, in terms of countering the initial resistance to taping, the researcher must respect the wishes of the respondent and resort to manual recording. However, if the study is a longitudinal one, involving a number of visits, the build up of trust and rapport over time may overcome the initial resistance to taping.

In Study A, I (Ruth) took some precautionary steps at the outset of each interview with a view to countering any resistance to taping that might be encountered. For instance, before commencing each interview, I undertook a number of steps in order to 'set-the-scene' for a positive outcome. While these are process issues and do not yield data, they are very important to ensuring that the interview is successful. In each case,

I commenced the encounter by explaining the purpose of the research and affording each respondent an opportunity to raise any points that might need clarification. I asked whether a tape could be used and tried to assuage any doubts or unease of the respondent, but I was always prepared for switching to manual recording if necessary.

I made it clear at the outset of each interview that all the material would be treated in confidence and that individuals would not be identified in the subsequent report of the research. Pseudonyms would be used to protect their anonymity. I promised that when each interview had been transcribed, the record would be returned to that respondent for their comments and amendment. This process seemed to re-assure each interviewee and led to a rapport that negated any concerns that could have arisen regarding taping of material.

I also prepared in advance for interviews so demonstrating that I was technically competent and knowledgeable. By demonstrating competence, the researcher conveys a professional image and boosts his/her credibility in the eyes of the respondent. Taping an interview is a mechanistic task, requiring technical competence. The other type of competence that must be displayed by the interviewer is analytical/knowledge competence. Before the first interview with anyone, thorough advance research on the case sites, on the key informants and on the background and debates about pricing in the hotel industry is recommended. The research focus should be clarified and the researcher should practice explaining what are the issues at the heart of his/her research. This is part of "rehearsing one's act", but is only one aspect of the required knowledge/ analytical aspects of interviewer competence. Other aspects of the latter (for example, active listening, reflection and analysis during the interview) require ongoing attention and have to be honed over many hours of interviewing. This entails the ability to grasp and analyse the salient points of any interview and to engage in an informed manner with any interviewee. If there is a lack of empathy, knowledge or analytical ability, the interviewee may sense this, get irritated, cut short the interview or complain about time being wasted, regardless of whether you taped or manually recorded the interview. The practical aspects of how taping as opposed to the manual method can assist with active listening, reflection and analysis are discussed in the next section on interviewer competence.

Interviewer Competence — Taping

Another factor that determines whether or not to tape is the preference, familiarity and technical competence of the interviewer with either method. Turning first to taping, these are a few tips, which I (Ruth) found useful when using this method. While taping of interviews is much more than just a mechanical exercise, nonetheless the researcher must have technical competence in taping. The equipment must be in perfect working order. It is essential that the interviewer is familiar with the tape machine being used. The best way to avoid any technical pitfalls is to buy high quality state-of-the-art equipment and then practise beforehand by undertaking a 'dry run', which will highlight any difficulties. I got a full demonstration and the manufacturer's instruction manual from the shop assistant, who sold me the equipment. It is also necessary to be prepared for physical difficulties in connecting the tape machine, by always bringing an adaptor and a long extension lead to the interview. I encountered a problem in this area. On one occasion when my extension lead was too short, I got side-tracked temporarily into some furniture re-arranging before the interview could commence. Bringing batteries is advisable as another precaution.

Having mastered the technical aspects of the taping process, the next step is to conduct the interview itself. Minor interruptions can distract both the interviewer and the respondent. For instance, I found out that it is not a good idea to conduct an interview in a hotel lobby area, even if the armchairs and the ambience are particularly inviting! The background noise and the fact that the hotel manager was highly visible led to interruptions. A proper choice of location, as well as technical efficiency, will facilitate the smooth flow of the interview and make the respondent less aware of the tape.

A few additional points are worth sharing here in relation to keeping the interview on course. Even though the tape acts as a 'dumb assistant' in terms of recording what has been said, this does not permit the interviewer to operate in passive mode throughout the interview. Rather in my case, I noticed it was important to listen, grasping relevant points that arose in the interview, in order to follow up on them. This was my way of displaying analytical competence and maintaining my credibility in the eyes of the respondent. As an inexperienced doctoral student, it is tempting to feel that once the tapes are in the bag, the analysis can wait until the transcripts are typed up and you have the money to pay for them!

While the tape allowed me to defer actual transcription, I did not let it allow me defer reflection and analysis which were ongoing, both throughout the interview process and immediately afterwards when I listened to the tape. If this is not done, when you get to read the transcripts, you can see key themes that should have been discussed, but the opportunity has passed, unless another interview is granted. Also, there can be issues which need re-checking or which should be cross-checked with other interviewees. I found that sometimes an interviewee had assumed a lot of knowledge on my part and explained complex areas quickly. The tape, when re-played, was a great 'bailout strategy' for me. I could request clarification the next day and even re-play the tape in front of the interviewee and query points made.

As part of actively reflecting on the interview content, I found that if the material was particularly intricate, making it challenging to grasp, it was helpful to make notes or ask the interviewee to draw a diagram or give me documentary evidence. For example, when the hotel manager at the West of Ireland site gave graphic descriptions of the room rate calculations, I asked him if we could stop so that he could write them down for me. Note-taking was done sporadically during interviews at my own discretion and was of enormous benefit in clarifying particular points, identifying themes for follow-up with the same interviewee at the next session or with other respondents. It kept me in active listening mode and proved a valuable additional control in the case of long-winded interviewees, which is discussed shortly.

The tape also assisted me by capturing everything that was said on a real-time basis. My comprehension of difficult sections of the interview, could be checked (the bailout strategy) by replaying the tape in the evening and listing points for re-iteration and follow-up. This is not so difficult when staying in a nice hotel room overnight at a reduced rate, because you have arranged another interview for the next day! In particular, it facilitated the accurate capture of data in the case of someone who spoke very rapidly, since it proceeded at the pace of the interviewee's speech. This may rate as an advantage over the manual method, where you would have to ask a rapid talker to slow down, while you take notes. This can be a bit daunting, if the interviewee is, for example, a noted government advisor and you only have an hour of his precious time. The tape obviates this. Provided you do the active listening and the follow-up, the tape becomes more than a "dumb assistant", but in fact an intelligent one. It is not just a separate mechanical recording device, but is a vital and integral part of doing the research. If used properly, it helps the analytical competence of the researcher. However, some obstacles do arise in the taping process.

To use a metaphor, some respondents are natural ramblers (as opposed to precise hill-walkers who use maps and stick to the path) and wander off into anecdotes and irrelevancies. This common problem means you can end up with pages of 'junk' in the transcript. To avoid this heartache, positive and negative ways of overcoming this problem, exist. A positive effort is to intervene during the interview. You can encourage the rambling respondent back onto the trail, by actively controlling the interview. This involves interjecting and re-focusing with a new question. This intervention is extremely important if time is short and only one interview has been granted with the particular respondent. When I was doing a longer interview and time was not restricted, I learned to interject and re-focus, but also tried another trick. During long interviews, I often suggested a relaxing coffee break (and paid for a nice bun as well) and explained the need for concise answering before re-commencing. Negative ways include judiciously stopping the tape and re-starting it when something more relevant is being said. These actions may be noticed by the interviewee and lessen rapport. There is a chance that the interviewee may retort by reminding you that you have not paid for his/her time.

Problems of focus can arise due to external factors at the case site. For instance, one manager that I interviewed tended to operate in the 'interrupt mode' and was often unfocused in his answering due to him dealing with suppliers, employees, guests and phone calls during the interview process. A final factor to note is the necessity for researchers to develop perception to see whether or not some game-playing is going on. This may materialise when important information is being requested from the respondent. I found this to be a tricky problem to overcome. Diplomacy was required because, as my line of questioning became deeper, the manager was more likely to get up and answer an outside query or request that the in-depth questions be deferred until the next visit. When I noticed some game-playing, I defused the situation by suggesting that we break for coffee. Another tactic I found useful was to re-phrase the questions in a less threatening way.

In the conduct of a series of interviews with one person, human factors should never be forgotten. On the positive side, the need for the 'preliminaries' associated with the first interview such as building rapport and trust and displaying competence and credibility, were no longer necessary. Subsequent interviews tended to flow more smoothly. Respondents were more forthcoming and less guarded in their responses. At one of the later interviews with the manager of the budget accommodation site in

Dublin, I found that when the tape was switched off and I thought the interview had ended, he began to talk about a very relevant topic related to pricing. I began to make notes and when it became obvious that he intended to continue speaking for some time, I asked him if I could turn the tape back on, which proved no problem. Indeed, during this interview, he quipped that when he was negotiating the room rate face-to-face with one language school, that he knew he was trusted by them if he was given coffee in a cracked coffee mug, since he felt that this mug was given only to their inner circle of business associates! Intuitively, I then felt that the rapport had been secured in our own interview, with this helpful and amusing anecdote.

On the negative side when conducting a series of interviews with one person, a certain *ennui* may set in. A series of interviews with the same person can be more difficult to handle than just one with a key informant or a series of non-sequential interviews with a number of different people. At one case site, I interviewed the hotel manager, then moved to the marketing manager and then to the accountant, before returning for a second interview with the hotel manager. I found that this was a good ploy to stave off boredom on either side and to keep the rapport alive.

Sorting and transcribing tapes: Once the interviews have been taped, the next task is to have the data transcribed. In Study A, as individual interviews lasted between one and three hours, this meant that a number of tapes had to be used for each session. Therefore, in order to avoid confusion down the line, tapes were labelled beforehand, noting date, name of respondent and tape 1,2,3 etc of total X. Then, I tied together the bundle of tapes for each interview. This prevented a confused jumble of tapes and the possible need to play many to locate the one I required. Good 'housekeeping' has enormous benefit in the overall research process, even though it tends to be ignored in much of the scholarly literature.

Getting the information in order was the first step. Then it had to be transcribed to facilitate its usage at the analysis stage. It has to be acknowledged that transcription of tapes is a tedious process, at best. Yet it has to be done. If you do not undertake the work yourself, you need to pay someone who has a reasonable understanding of the content. Otherwise it will be very difficult for the transcriber to make sense of the taped material and you may end up with inaccurate or incomprehensible data. To assist the person who transcribed my tapes, I spent some time explaining the project to her. Also I provided her with a copy of the topic outline I had used during each interview and this gave her some idea of what to expect, rather than having to tackle the transcription task 'cold'.

A potential downside of contracting out the transcription of tapes is that you get a record back with everything that was said in the course of the interview. As mentioned above, some respondents have a tendency to ramble. An outside transcriber will type both salient material and irrelevant data (for example, long-winded anecdotes and colloquialisms). If one does the transcription oneself, one can simply omit to transcribe the parts where the interviewee has rambled. Therefore, if you are undertaking small-scale research and have only a few interviews to transcribe, it may be better to do this task yourself.

As the information from individual interviews has to be analysed eventually, giving some thought to the layout of the transcription before it is typed up can pay dividends later. I arranged to have it set out clearly in question/topic order, in accordance with the actual course of the interview, with clear delineation of the transition between topics. Then I inserted replies to any questions that were asked informally (and recorded manually) when the tape had been turned off, into the relevant section of the interview transcript. I also carefully kept any hand-written notes (which I took at my own discretion even though the tape was running), and attached them to the back of the relevant transcripts. I cross-referenced by inserting a mark on those parts of the transcript where the hand-written material applied.

Collecting documentary evidence: In addition, when I collected documentary evidence to support comments made during the interview, I noted this on the transcript with a coded number for each item collected. I took copies of relevant internal performance and other reports on forward bookings as well as the annual accounts. These were very useful to me later in making sense of the pricing routines and associated profitability.

Interviewer Competence — Manual Recording of Interviews

As previously mentioned, the tape records all of the interview as it unfolds at whatever speed is dictated by the respondent. In contrast, manual recording involves the need to listen, think, assess, edit and then write down the comments, practically all at the same time. This is very demanding of the interviewer who must be active, alert and conscious of the need to identify and write down the salient points and quotes, while conducting the interview. One needs training to listen, edit and write, without disturbing the natural flow of the interview.

A word or two about the actual interview schedule used with the manual method of recording, may be apposite here as it is important to get it right in terms of physical layout, (as well as content). The actual interview schedule, which I (Treasa) used in Study B for all forty interviews, was quite long and detailed. It was informed by the literature and preliminary fieldwork. It was set out very clearly in main topics and sub-topics, as I considered that it was necessary at this stage to have some clarity regarding the areas I wanted to cover in the course of the interviews.

In the physical layout of this document, plenty of space was left between each topic, enabling me to record individual responses in the appropriate 'slot'. This 'spacing' issue is very important. When I had set out each topic on a separate page, it made both the manual recording of the interview and the subsequent analysis of the data, easier. If the initial manual recording of the interview data is all cramped together, it makes the analysis task immeasurably more difficult. I learned this lesson about 'spacing' the hard way. When the interview schedule for my first few interviews did not have sufficient space in which to record responses in the appropriate slot, I had to re-write all the notes from these interviews. Once I became aware of my error, I amended the layout and had no further difficulty.

When interviews are recorded manually, an annotated version of the interview is written down, based on the researcher's judgement of what is important. This happens because, unlike taping which captures everything that has been said, every word of an interview cannot possibly be recorded manually. Thus it is suggested that the manual method should be chosen only by a researcher with considerable prior experience in undertaking and manually recording long, open-ended interviews. Such a person can edit as the interview progresses, making judgements about what is important to record.

At the beginning of each interview, I (Treasa) focused on getting the 'climate' right. As mentioned in relation to Study A, this contributes to the success of the core interview. Therefore it cannot be ignored. Accordingly, before embarking on the actual data collection, I talked for a short while to each respondent about my interest and previous experience in the voluntary sector, which had motivated me to undertake the research. This helped to establish a good initial rapport. Then I outlined the aims of the study and explained about the interview schedule. I gave an assurance of confidentiality and anonymity, as suggested by Taylor & Bogdan (1984), regarding information disclosed in the course of each interview as I felt that this would contribute to putting the respondent at ease. At this stage also I checked if it was all right to make some notes as the interview progressed.

While this preliminary stage of the interview takes time, it helps build up trust before entering into the core of the interview. If you do not get the interviewee 'on side' at the outset, the subsequent interview will be less than satisfactory in terms of data collected. Therefore my advice is to give it as much time as it takes in order to 'get it right'. When each respondent seemed at ease, I then proceeded with the main part of the interview, using the interview schedule to keep it on track.

Once I had clarified at the outset the need to record data, note taking during the interview itself did not pose any problems. Regarding the actual notation of the interview material, while I had no formal training in taking shorthand, over the years I had developed my own version of the art, which proved adequate for the job in hand.

I found that each respondent, as s/he saw me writing, seemed to understand that I needed brief pauses to jot down points as they arose and made this time available to me, without me having to ask specifically for it. Maintaining eye contact as much as possible right through the interview kept the momentum going. Also I found it useful to make brief comments such as: 'That's interesting'/'I see what you mean' etc., in order to avoid any long silences as I wrote, which might break the flow of the conversation.

The overall process involved a delicate balancing act between asking questions and note-taking, with eye contact acting as the 'glue' to keep it all running smoothly. The fact that I had an interview schedule that identified the topics I wished to cover, provided a reasonable structure for each interview while also allowing ample scope for comment and elaboration on individual issues. In fact it was very useful in preventing the interview from going 'off track'.

At the conclusion of each interview, I had my data. However, as it was manually recorded, the record was not as comprehensive as if I had taped every word. Therefore, it was really important to make the most of what I had gleaned by going back over my record immediately afterwards. Accordingly, in order to ensure accuracy and comprehension of my interview data, on return to my car after each interview, I read over the relevant interview notes, fleshing out my inevitable abbreviations and deciphering my scribbles. This enabled me to 'unscramble' unclear writing while the interview encounter was still fresh in my mind. In contrast, it will stubbornly remain a blur if you defer the 'de-coding' to a later time.

Due to the challenges associated with accurate manual recording, many novice researchers may prefer to rely on the 'dumb assistant' so as to allow greater focus on the content and conduct of the interview. Indeed many unstructured interviews are 'guided conversations' (Lofland 1971) where the interviewer joins in, interjects and seeks clarification of meaning, requiring the respondent to repeat explanations, so the tape is the obvious choice. Most student researchers should be advised to tape the interview because the ability to transcribe quotes etc. required for the manual method demands well-honed skills.

Taping: Benefits and Drawbacks

Finally, the relative advantages and disadvantages of taping or manual recording need to be assessed, once the other three factors discussed above have been considered. Undoubtedly, taping an interview ensures a full, unedited record of the ground covered in the course of the discussion and this is available to the researcher who can replay it afterwards. However, in order to analyse the data post-interview, all the material gathered on tape must be transcribed and edited. This can be a costly exercise if contracted to a secretary. Ruth was fortunate enough to get a grant from the Research Committee in the university to fund this work. So a tip here for other researchers is to explore ways of getting financial assistance for research tasks such as transcription which can be off-loaded.

If the research coffers are empty, the time consuming transcription has to be done by the researcher. Robson (1993) warns that a one-hour recording may take up to ten hours to transcribe. So, think of the time required to type up fifty hours of interviewing, particularly if you are not a trained secretary with good typing speeds. Then, the process of distilling and editing the transcript has to be completed as it provides a permanent, vouchable record of the interview from which direct quotes may be extracted.

In contrast, the manual method of recording data makes an edited record available immediately after the interview. As it eliminates the considerable cost of transcription (in terms of either money or time) and greatly reduces the post-interview editing task, this makes it much easier to handle the data. In fact, in Study B, once I had completed my forty interviews and had read over them, clarifying my 'shorthand', I was ready to analyse the data. The time saved here, when compared to the input required to transcribe and edit tapes, helped to shorten the overall research process. This can be a significant consideration in any research project that has to be completed within a fixed time frame.

Making the Decision

Mindful of the advantages of each method, it is up to the researcher to discern which approach — tape or manual — is apposite in a particular research encounter and to take action accordingly. The choice is not dichotomous as, in practice, many researchers make notes while the tape records. If the interviewee objects to taping or even seems uncomfortable with it and efforts to allay these concerns are unsuccessful, it may be prudent to settle for the manual route.

Probably a good general guiding principle here centres on the issue of establishing rapport. As it is a vital component of engaging in an open and frank discussion, which allows the capture of the required data for qualitative research, the method selected should serve to nurture this rapport. In practice, this calls for matching the method to this requirement in each case. The reality is that the respondent's wishes must be respected. As has been shown in our two studies, both methods worked equally well for us, given their different contents and contexts.

Final Reflections

It should be evident that the decision to tape or not to tape is somewhat more complex than is suggested in some standard textbooks. Some of the important 'ingredients' that need to be factored into the ultimate decision include: the nature of the topic being researched; the sectoral setting of the study; the preferences of individual respondents and the preference and competencies of the researcher. This suggests there is no 'one best way' to capture data in qualitative research, but the best method of recording is dependent on the context of the specific research being undertaken. Even within one study, variations in the approach to data gathering may be necessary. If a particular respondent does not wish to have an interview taped, do you, the researcher, try to 'convert' him/her to acquiesce? Even if you succeed this far and turn on the tape, what effect does this initial reluctance to be taped have on the ensuing interview? Does it reduce the level of rapport? As a result, does this impact negatively on the quality of the data collected? Would the interview have proceeded more smoothly if you had abandoned efforts at 'conversion', resorting to manual recording when faced with the initial reluctance to taping? How would this later decision affect the quantity of data collected?

All of this suggests the need for flexibility on the part of the researcher during the data-gathering journey. At the start of a study, you may plan to tape all interviews. However, this pre-determined strategy might have to be modified, if tape-shy respondents appear in your study cohort. As they are the providers of the information you seek, you must be prepared to play the game their way, adapting your initial strategy accordingly. Conversely, if you set out to record interviews manually, some respondent may seem impatient with this slower recording process. In such a case, having a tape recorder on hand could address the demand for speeding up the process. The broad guideline for the researcher is to make every effort to facilitate the wishes of the respondent, while aiming to gather good quality data.

In conclusion it has to be said that the research journey is not straightforward. Rather it tends to throw up challenges along the way. Be clear about mapping out your route, in terms of the information you are seeking. Gather it either by taping or manual recording, depending on its appropriateness in the particular situation. On completion of this task, you are ready to analyse your findings in order to reach your final destination of a well-executed study. It's not a totally smooth passage, but with practice, flexibility and patience you should meet with success and satisfaction at the finishing line. We hope that some of the tips we have shared with you will be helpful in completing the research circuit.

References

Easterby-Smith, M., Thorp, R., & Lowe, A. (1991). *Management research: An introduction.* London: Sage.

Hayes, T. (1996). *Management, control and accountability in nonprofit/voluntary organizations.* Aldershot: Ashgate Publishing.

Lofland, J. (1971). *Analysing social settings* (2nd ed.). Belmont, CA: Wadsworth.

Mattimoe, R. (2002). An institutional study of room rate pricing in the Irish hotel industry. Unpublished Ph.D., Manchester School of Accounting and Finance.

Robson, C. (1993). *Real world research.* Oxford: Blackwell.

Saunders, M., Thornhill, A., & Lewis, P. (1997). *Research methods for business students.* London: Financial Times/Pitman.

Taylor, S. J., & Bogdan, R. (1984). *Introduction to qualitative research methods* (2nd ed.). New York: Wiley.

Chapter 22

Using Computer Assisted Qualitative Data Analysis Software: Respecting Voices Within Data Management and Analysis[1]

Fiona Anderson-Gough

Introduction

Qualitative research has been a growing focus of interest within the accounting and finance disciplines over recent years. This is particularly so for those academics concerned with undertaking 'critical' research which aims to disrupt the status quo by revealing its conditions of possibility. Indeed the increasing recognition of the value of 'behavioural finance' signifies the current recognition of this methodological under-pinning and its assumptions for these disciplines. Part of the process of undertaking qualitative research requires taking a position on issues around data management and analysis that will involve decisions about IT use and data coding. In deciding whether to use computer packages and how elaborate and formal to make the coding process key research questions and assumptions are raised and explored. These issues are at the heart of the research process whether or not one is using IT.

I have no particular desire to try and convert all qualitative researchers in our field into Computer Assisted Qualitative Data Analysis Software (CAQDAS) users. However I am certain that throughout my research career so far CAQDAS has been a most useful and welcome part of my research life, and in that respect I do regard myself as a bit of an advocate. The aim of this chapter is to bring the use of CAQDAS to life a little more for non-users, and to raise some points about data management and analysis that can be addressed through CAQDAS use. I also hope to show that deciding to use, or not to use, CAQDAS and managing the process of using it is much more than a 'technical' issue. I begin by focusing on the details of CAQDAS use within one particular research project that I have worked on. The following sections of the chapter offer some thoughts on the

[1] I would like to thank Keith Hoskin, Martin Gough and Keith Robson for their comments.

broader issues involved in becoming someone who uses coding and IT as part of their research process based on my experience across my career to date.

The Ethnograph

I have worked with two CAQDAS packages. One of these was a bespoke package designed to code and quantify the attributions made in interviews and was a central resource in my work as a researcher within Psychology. The other is *The Ethnograph*, a generally available program, which I learnt to use in 1993–1994 within my role as researcher on the ESRC funded project on water privatisation supervised by Stuart Ogden and Peter Moizer. I have continued to use this program to date (although not in its Windows version), across all the research projects I have undertaken since 1994 in the area of professional identity and accountancy education and training. In this section I elaborate on using *The Ethnograph* within the first accountancy socialisation project I was involved with. Supervised by Chris Grey and Keith Robson, this ICAEW funded research was undertaken between November 1995 and February 1997 (for example, Anderson-Gough, Grey & Robson 1998a).

At the time that project began there was little academic work on what happens inside accountancy firms (Hanlon 1994 and Coffey 1993 were notable exceptions) but there was much concern about the growth of these firms as large managerial organisations, and their relation to notions of 'professional'. The role of the research then, very broadly, was to continue developing understandings of how professional and organisational identity were developed in large firms and as part of that elucidate the 'content' of that identity more. So, the research questions (hypotheses) were built around that perceived need for more enquiry generally and were informed by other socialisation studies on professional identity (beyond accountancy):

(1) Socialisation processes focus not only upon examination performance, but presentation to clients and ability to integrate with the social norms of peers, managers and partners.
(2) The socialisation of audit trainees is into organisational culture first and professional culture second.
(3) Socialisation processes vary between divisions and give rise to differing conceptions of the role of the professional accountant.

In order to explore these assumptions and to flesh out the detail of what was happening we developed a semi-structured interview schedule and conducted interviews in two international firms (i.e. one regional office of each in England). Each interview lasted for about one hour, it was tape-recorded, and there were 77 of these interviews. The length of each interview and number of interviews in total were part of our ideal design and so from the beginning of the fieldwork we knew we were hopefully going to be faced with the challenge of figuring out how to go about analysing hours of interview material across a team of researchers (located in two geographically separate institutions). Although they had not used the software before, Keith and Chris (the supervisors) were keen to see what the benefits might be, and so quite early on in the project we decided we would use *The Ethnograph* to assist in data management and therefore facilitate the analysis process accordingly. As stated in the manual for Version 4 of the program (Seidel, Friese & Leonard 1995: 1):

"THE ETHNOGRAPH facilitates the processes of

- noticing interesting things in your data
- marking those things with code words
- retrieving those things for further analysis."

This is precisely what it does.[2] Version 4 was an MS-DOS version, that is it was not a Windows program (there is now a Windows version which became available in 1998 I believe). It requires the taped interviews to be transcribed, the transcripts to be saved as text files with the initials of the speaker prefacing each paragraph and separated from the text by a colon. These text files are then processed by the program in order to number each line (down the right hand side). The numbers are then used to identify which lines certain codes are deemed to be relevant to. The generation of the codes and the 'deeming relevant' are entirely the work of the researchers.

So, when using this program the codes are generated by the researchers and the coding is done by the researchers. Coding is the central activity underpinning the use of the program and therefore adopting this software assumes that the researchers have decided they do value coding as part of the data management and analysis process, or at least wish to determine how useful it is by trying the process out. Within all the projects that I have used 'coding' the codes have been a mix of things that the researchers are interested in prior to actually starting the interviews and things that become salient as the interviews are undertaken and the transcripts read. Using these sources for generating the codes is standard practice (for example, Ryan & Bernard 2000) and therefore the fact that a certain amount of interpretation of the data has already happened in generating and agreeing on such a list led to Miles & Huberman (1994: 56) stating "Coding is analysis".

Already in this profile of coding, however, there are features mentioned, relating to the nature of coding which may be subscribed to rather differently across individuals. Some researchers may wish to concentrate on generating codes that may be described as content 'labels' which are developed around the perceived content of the data and

[2] One fear of people considering the use of CAQDAS is the over-determining quality of the program on the analysis, that is that the doing of the analysis is taken over by the software. As things stand it is fair to say that the software does not do the theory-building rather it facilitates it (for example, Weitzman & Miles, 1995). Of course it is not the case that the programme is somehow some 'neutral' technical device as the program authors will have their own assumptions somehow reflected in the design. As things develop the use of artificial intelligence may impact on the role of the software and theory development but providing sufficient pre-purchase research is done this should not impact negatively on the researcher who does not want such assistance (Weitzman, 2000). A serious engagement with the types of package available, for example Text Retrievers, Textbase Managers, Code-and-Retrieve Programs, Code-Based Theory Builders and Conceptual Network Builders (for example, Weitzman, 2000) compared with the type of data analysis you wish to undertake, for example Free Lists, Pile Sorts, Frame Substitution, Componential Analysis, Taxonomies, Mental Maps, Key-Words-In-Context, Word Counts, Structural Analysis and Semantic Networks, Cognitive Maps, Grounded Theory, Schema Analysis, Content Analysis, Decision Models etc. (Ryan & Barnard, 2000) should enable a good choice of program.

serve to capture the main elements of the transcript or notes. However, claiming a focus on description as opposed to conceptual interpretation becomes a claim needing, and often leading to, discussion when one accepts that codes will already often have some conceptual underpinnings even at this level. As Weaver & Atkinson (1994: 66) note "codes are not inherent in the data; rather they are inherent to the interpretation of the data". For example, in a project I am currently working on (for example, Anderson-Gough *et al.* 2003) detailed codes around different aspects of accountancy expertise, learning, and knowledge(s) are being developed, and the discussions around the nature of these concepts are proving fruitful beyond simply finalising a list of codes. These discussions insist on elaborating for each of us what is seemingly straightforward and what is troublesome within our research problematic. For example, *Performance* and *Competence* may be seen as codes that have a simple relationship — with the *Performance* simply being a demonstration of the *Competence*. Or the *Performance* may be seen as something obliquely linked to something that might be called a *Competence* (Anderson-Gough *et al.* 2003). It is essential to have these discussions as the codes are generated rather than assuming that they mean the same thing to everybody, or to assume your slightly different interpretation does not matter overall and that silence on the issue is the most useful response.

In the process of turning talk into text even the level of detail captured in a transcript will vary according to the type of analysis performed. For example, conversation analysis requires detail around lengths of pauses, non-word sounds, and 'interruptions' such as agreements that are not meant to interject but are vocalisations of support or encouragement. On the whole, none of the latter details were flagged up as important to the person undertaking the transcription work on the socialisation project under discussion here, and so they were not made visible in the transcripts we generated within that work.

So, as already noted, my experience has been one of producing lists that are a mix of content 'labels' and codes already informed by a conceptual framing. Developing the coding framework (list of codes) has always been seen as an iterative process in the teams I have worked in. In the socialisation project we developed a list of codes after the first handful of interviews had been done, transcribed and circulated for reading. Each person would look at the sample of transcripts and generate a list of codes that they felt captured their theoretical interests and the themes that were being discussed in the interviews. We discussed our ideas for codes that we each felt should be included, decided on a list to pilot, and then all coded the same interview. We then met up and discussed our coding of this interview in order to see how we were all interpreting the codes and the content of the transcript, as well as looking to see if there were any aspects of the interviews that the codes were not capturing. This process led to some revision of the coding list and for the first few interviews that were coded we kept in close contact as a team discussing how we were coding and how satisfied we felt with the codes. We all put a good deal of effort into this activity and all three of us commented at the time, and at the end of the project, that the discussions triggered by the process of generating the coding framework were immensely helpful. This experience of the very productive nature of this process is something that has been common across all the projects I have worked on, and other team members have expressed similar sentiments across all those projects likewise.

The codes were linguistic, abbreviations of the summary term(s) that we chose to represent the core area of interest to be pulled together under that code. We developed a detailed definitional list, a paragraph of explanation next to each code, and a summary sheet as follows:

Codes used for the Socialisation Project (from Anderson-Gough *et al.* 1998a)

- RECSEL: Recruitment and selection processes
- EARLYEXP: Early experience of firm/profession
- CAREER: Career (plans, expectations etc.)
- SOCIALTIME: Socializing and time or time-keeping issues
- COOPCOMP: Co-operation and competition within and between firms
- TRPROF: Professional training including external tutoring
- TRMODE: Training mode (full time, link, split-intensive, end-loaded)
- TRINHOUSE: In-house training
- TRMENTOR: Mentors and mentoring
- TRGEN: Training — general/other
- APPFORM: Formal appraisal procedures
- APPINFORM: Informal appraisal
- APPGEN: Appraisal — general/other
- PERSON: References to inter-personal relations and personality (own or others including clashes of personality)
- ATROCITY: Atrocity stories (organizational narratives or experiences, not necessarily bad; cf. Silverman 1993)
- HIERCON: Hierarchy and control processes within firms
- RESIST: Resistance to forms of organizational control
- EMP: Empathy (for example, between staff)
- LUCK: Luck (for example, role in career)
- GENDER: References to perceived gender roles, discrimination in work and study
- SUCFAIL: Accounts of or references to organizational or career success and failure
- REWARDS: Reward systems within firms: formal/informal
- PROF: References to profession and professional
- PROFKNOW: Professional knowledge and expertise
- CLIENTS: Clients of firms
- OTHERDIVS: Perceptions of other divisions
- OTHERFIRM: Comments about or attitudes expressed towards other accountancy firms
- SELFIMAGE: Self-image of interviewee
- CULORGID: Culture (organizationally specific practices or identities)
- CULFITIN: Processes of adjustment; Fitting in to an organization's culture
- CULLANG: Culturally specific language or discourses

- CULOBSDRS: Culture (Objects and Dress)
- EXPGOOD: Good experience
- EXPBAD: Bad experience
- PROGRESS: Reference to changes over time
- GOLD: Very interesting or important comment; could be about anything

In terms of *The Ethnograph* Version 4 each line of the transcript can be assigned up to twelve codes. Generally blocks of text, rather than single lines, were coded using as many codes as we felt appropriate subject to the previous limitation and also the fact that a maximum of seven overlaps is possible between blocks of text within this program. This extract, for example, has one overlap, where a discussion of time and fees is introduced to explain the hierarchical distribution of some work:

#-HIERCON

TR: No, it's understood in a sense.	712 -#
They don't shove everything down to	713 |
you, like just because they are a	714 |
Senior doesn't mean they don't do any	715 |
photo-copying. They probably do half	716 |
the photo-copying or whatever. They	717 |
don't actually just push it down.	718 |
	|
	|
I: So it's not like, if it's photo-	721 |
copying it goes to	722 |
	|
	|

$-SOCIALTIME

TR: No, It's only like "I'm really	725 |-$
busy, I can't do it" or "You haven't	726 ||
got anything to do" or it's a long job	727 ||
and money wise Seniors at £100 plus an	728 ||
hour and the Assistant's £35 logistics	729 ||
wise it's, that kind of work	730 ||
particularly if it's unbillable work,	731 ||
money wise it should go to the	732 ||
Assistant.	733 -#|

TR = Trainee and I = Interviewer

Version 4, as mentioned above, was an MS-DOS version and involved the line numbers at the beginning of the section and the end of the section being manually entered into the program, along with the codes to be attached also being typed in. In practice it was agreed that I, as research fellow on the project, would enter all of the coding (and send disks to other team members so they could update the directory with the data in on their computers) and that this would serve as a continual reliability check over usage of the codes across team members. This meant that in order to code the rest of the team needed to have a paper print-out of the transcript and that they needed to write the codes onto the paper at the right hand side of the transcript with a line at the beginning of the section following the text down to the designated section end. They would then pass this manually coded version back to me for entering onto the computer. This also had the benefit of not only allowing the coding to be done away from the computer (and perhaps therefore in more comfortable or convenient environments) but also meant that the coder was able to read in a manner more akin to 'normal', i.e. non IT screen, reading. That is, for those who find scrolling up and down computer screens less easy than flicking back and forwards through paper sheets, this reading process feels more 'comfortable'. This is perhaps more likely to result in a more complex interpretation process than would take place if one feels more like treating each screen as a separate entity. I am currently working in a team where one of the researchers is learning how to use NVivo, as this is the institutionally supported package. I have yet to learn how to use it but am informed by the team member in question that my preference for coding firstly on paper may change once I have engaged with NVivo which, more akin to word-processing screens, makes reading and then coding straight onto screen easier.

By chunking the data and attaching codes to help us identify sections according to the above themes/areas we were then able to address our research questions by pulling out, through performing a 'search' across interview files, what was said about key aspects of those questions. With the facility to attach Face Sheets with demographic information to each interview the search outputs could be easily grouped together and differentiated in terms of the different firms, years, divisions, and sexes. So, we were able to 'ask' the data the following sorts of questions by performing different searches, and pulling out paragraphs from the transcripts that had been coded with codes relating to the question or issue in mind. For example, how was success and failure in these firms experienced and signalled (for example, SUCFAIL, APPFORM, APPINFORM, REWARDS)? How was success and failure experienced in terms of the examination experience and beyond (for example, SUCFAIL and TRPROF)? How were other divisions seen in contrast to one's own (OTHERDIVS, SELFIMAGE, PROFKNOW) and what meaning and importance did 'professional' have in relation to these schemas of 'success' (PROF)?

Through having codes that allowed a sense of whether the interviewee was offering the comment as something they approved or disapproved of (EXPGOOD and EXPBAD) we were also easily able to pull together those things that were problematic for interviewees and those things that were valued by the trainee accountants we were talking to. As noted above whilst some of the codes can be seen as more (i.e. relatively) straightforward 'labels' referring to types of events, institutions and themes (for example, those beginning with TR for Training or APP for Appraisal) there were other codes that reflected our conceptual framings of issues we wanted to explore (for example, HIERCON), which required more interpretation on the part of the coder in that the interviewee would not generally be talking in the same sort of language as that framing the code. Or indeed there were codes that had a more discursive focus in that the way the interviewee was using language was indeed the focus of the code (for example, CULLANG). Other codes allowed an openness, particularly GOLD, in that we could mark aspects as generally requiring further attention (as well as being excellent examples of a certain code).

This first stage analysis, via the software, allowed us to engage with our research questions feeling confident that we were all sufficiently familiar with the detail of the interviews. For those of the team who had not conducted the interviews, having coded a proportion of them gave enough familiarity to know whether comments from other team members in respect of findings fitted in with what they had read. A search on certain codes relating to the points in question would allow further reassurance, and the availability of all the files to either read on screen or to print out allowed for less segmented reading if that was felt necessary. Given that the transcripts were on average around 2000 numbered lines in length (approximately 30 pages of text for each interview) and the research project as a whole therefore generated around 160,000 lines of transcription this feeling of some level of mastery over the content seems a significant achievement.

This ability to gain some mastery over all of that data is, to me, where one of the key benefits of using IT can be most clearly seen. Packages like *The Ethnograph* only claim to be data management packages, they help the researcher store data in a way that maximises the possibility of using it (all). If the other alternative is stacks and stacks of paper it is likely that interviews, or part of, could be lost and their loss not noticed. This is certainly likely over long periods of time, which may involve office and institution moves, or at the very least office clear-outs or various stages of the evolution of the sedimentation of layers of documents. Also the sheer enormity of rummaging through piles of paper it seems to me is far more off-putting and less likely to lead to thorough analysis procedures than being able to scroll around on screen, and at the push of one or two buttons produce 'packages' of output relevant to the analysis being undertaken. Of course word processing makes the storage problem less of an issue but it does not solve the problem of wading through numerous files looking for particular instances of something. IT storage and coding, whilst requiring a good deal of time to be invested in the early stages, enables the data to be easily available across time and space, across dispersed teams, well into the future when the original research project has ended, within a framework that at least allows for joint analysis work on the basis of some shared understandings and experiences of the data. So what CAQDAS facilitates is the real possibility of a thorough analysis through the insistence of a detailed reading of each interview and the permanent marking of issues of interest. This marking allows easy retrieval across vast amounts of data and is therefore likely to reduce the temptation to 'cherry-pick' certain aspects of the data as findings as a result of trying to manage such unwieldy amounts of data manually.

As mentioned above, the decision to adopt a formal coding scheme and coding process has, across all the projects I have worked on, engendered key discussions about the research questions and the purposes and direction of analysis during the data gathering process as a result of needing to talk about codes. Even if one were not fully to utilise the (potential) output of the software, the discussions around coding are, I would argue, of significant value in drawing out assumptions, and early working hypotheses, held by the researcher(s) in a timely fashion.

The initial research report was only one published output from this project. As we became more familiar with our material and our codes we moved beyond our initial research questions and were able to explore issues that were salient because of the way they cut across codes, or because of the way codes inter-related. It is certainly the case that we could have gone back to coded interviews and broken down some codes into smaller sub-codes, but once the project funding had ended and writing was a key priority it was difficult for any one of us to find the time to re-code, although it is certainly a possibility within the design of the program. For example, we discovered that the SOCIALTIME code generated a huge amount of output. Indeed in coding the later interviews we separated the coding into SOCIAL and TIME to make this part of the analysis more focused and manageable. This in itself was significant to us. The trainees were finding that time demands and time discipline were aspects of life in the firm that they had not realistically anticipated. The new engagement with time was one of the key aspects of socialisation. Likewise their experience of the notion of 'the client' was cutting across many codes. It was present within recruitment criteria, the way work plans were set and justified, how people were evaluated, and the reason why home life was (allowed to be) made secondary and almost invisible. Self-presentation was at the heart of 'being professional' and this linked to concerns over time and the client, success and failure. Within the PROF category public duty was rarely mentioned and the ICAEW was simply the hurdle-setter, the guardian of membership of the elite. So, across this relatively short list of codes we were able to profile the dynamic of organisational socialisation and the particular impact this was having in producing professionals who were faced with succeeding simultaneously as students and workers in a system that segregated both experiences, and, through its 'in at the deep end' quality, brought the commercial reality of pleasing the client and presenting the appropriate self to various audiences to the forefront of socialisation. These findings were explored in now published papers (for example, Anderson-Gough *et al.* 1998b, 2000), and they still inform my work today on professional identity and accountancy education and training (for example, Hoskin & Anderson-Gough, forthcoming; Anderson-Gough *et al.* 2003).

It is difficult at one level for me to say if we could have engaged with our data at this level without *The Ethnograph* and without coding, because we did not try to analyse the data without this process. Indeed I have always used software as part of my data management and analysis work. However, given that we have developed this work beyond the original funded time span of the project and still have that data at our fingertips with records of how we coded it I am certainly of the opinion that these later, continued, investigations of the data would have been less likely to happen, or to be undertaken with the thoroughness and familiarity that characterise first analyses which take place shortly after the interviews happen, without the software. In support of this view I do know that others (for example, Keith Robson) who have analysed data without CAQDAS are most definitely of the opinion that it is a most valuable exercise because the coding is an intense process and leads to one reflecting on the content of the interviews more, and remembering more of that content as a result.

CAQDAS and Respect for the Subject

In turning talk (or action) into text, and then chunking that text into more or less interesting fragments the issue of respect for the subject needs to be considered. The subject of the ethics of qualitative research and use of CAQDAS is worthy of more attention than I can give within this chapter. However, I wish to raise the issue and offer a few practical suggestions which not only protect the identity of people who have taken part in in-depth studies, where this is requested, but which also try to do justice to the complexities of their life and thus produce good quality research which respects the subject.

At an initial level, independently of the application of CAQDAS, I begin each interview by introducing myself, explaining how the interview (or observation) material will be used, what sort of places the findings would be published, how the findings will be reported in a general manner and anonymised, and who else is taking part in the research as researchers, and at a very general level with regard to who else is being researched. I leave my card so they can contact me with any queries or concerns. I adopt a coding system for the identities of the participants. This usually involves a letter or number to represent the organisation they belong to, the first three letters of their first name and first letter of their second name plus the date. Once the interview has been taped I write only this code on the tape box so unless they mention their own name in the interview even the transcriber does not know the identity of the individual. I keep the master list which allows a check on which interview is who, but the facility for Face Sheet Codes (for demographic type information) in *The Ethnograph* permits sufficient detail to be given to team members so that they can situate the person in a little more detail without needing this master list. These code names become the file names on the software. During the checking of the returned transcript, or at the point of including extracts as examples in reports and papers, other names or things mentioned which could identify someone are changed. In publications individuals are either given a false name or known by their 'position' (for example, Manager of Water Company A, or Third Year Audit Trainee).

Beyond protecting participants/subjects through such procedures, we may feel that we have a duty to make sure we do not report findings that are wrong nor, perhaps more pertinently, 'selective', as evidenced by alternative and sometimes competing inter-pretations of the data by a team of researchers. We may look to the post-structuralist critical framework as explanatory of this phenomenon of competing interpretations, since it emphasises precisely not the fallibility of the personal memory of the researcher reporting on the interview that they conducted and so 'co-authored'.[3] Rather it emphasises the public nature of meaning by which we are permitted to reinterpret individual intentions.[4] This framework opens up the question of who is to say whether or not something is wrong or too selective. I would argue that whether one understands oneself as the traditional researcher aiming to tell an overarching narrative of 'how it is'

---

[3] C.f., the New Criticism's point about the fallibility of authors' reports about their own intentions as argued by Beardsley & Wimsatt (1954).

[4] As explored in Barthes (1977), and (re)interpreted by various authors (for example, Gough 1997).

in a paper or report, or whether one refuses to take this stance and rather acknowledge and work with the possibility of multiple readings by presenting data without the explicit explanation of the traditional researcher, engaging with the data beyond a first stage re-reading of outputs generated by a number of 'searches' is necessary to avoid the fragmentation that concerns some people. That is, the coding and the search outputs can be seen as products of the "urge to divide data into discrete fragments" (Mello 2002: 235), which will lead to situations where those segmented aspects of the text will be isolated from the text as a whole and this therefore "has the potential for divorcing the original story from its human environment" (Mello 2002: 235). Mello (2002: 241) adopts the term 'Collocation Data Analysis' to describe the process of ". . . combining, juxtaposing, and examining narrative date in terms of its several organic operations . . .". I would hold that certain principles of good research, set out for example by Seale (1999) [see following paragraph], generally enable this broader engagement with the data and are certainly made possible by using software packages. This requires the researcher to plan to do this as the software to date does not, as far as I am aware, reflect the necessity of such 'collocation' in contemporary software designs. It needs to be reiterated perhaps at this point however that the need to engage intensely with the data, as a result of the coding, limits the chances of fragmented selection of findings. Therefore this aspect of attaining a thorough and un-fragmented understanding of the data is facilitated by the design aspect of the software in that the possibility of successful data management across vast amounts of data is inherent in CAQDAS packages such as *The Ethnograph*. It is also the case that most of these packages offer the choice of how much text is reproduced for each segment, which enables some discretion over the degree to which selected aspects of the text are prefixed and suffixed by surrounding text.

Re-reading (some of) the interviews after a first-stage analysis is especially important in the presenting of data involving a number of subjects. Here we are not seeking to represent the meaning conveyed by each individual in turn so much as to provide a conclusion as regards a wider group. By definition, then, what is true about the group is not necessarily what is true of any one member and so no disrespect to them will arise: rather, the more investigation into interpretative patterns arising out of the data, the richer, even perhaps more 'objective', will the findings be. In this way if we take the practices of 'accounting for contradiction' and 'using numbers' (see Seale 1999, Chapters 6 and 9 respectively) we can produce a rich account of a rich data source. Actively counting instances of events can reduce 'anecdotalism' (for example, Bryman 1988; Seale 1999) or looking for counter-claims or contradictions within texts and sets of texts can, if judged to be appropriate, improve the quality of qualitative research. Rather than regarding such practices as inappropriate hang-ups relating to positivistic methodologies Seale's review of work illustrates the value of such practices very cogently. I would suggest that these considerations and activities should be an important part of research that utilises code-and-retrieve packages (whilst noting that the possibility of such engagement is, however, also shaped by the time demands of the funding and other work situations). There are of course problematic issues that still face qualitative researchers. One key issue, related to the notion of reducing anecdotalism, is how does one write a paper in a way that shows one has used this software without simply pandering to particular notions of what counts as good social science, replicability, and associated audit trails?

Managing CAQDAS and the Ethics of Research Project Management

I mentioned at the outset of the chapter that I see decisions around CAQDAS use as much more than 'technical'. Deciding whether to use CAQDAS, what programs to use, and how to manage the process and what codes to use all involve issues of identity and resourcing. Given the issues of staffing projects with temporary researchers, with constraints on start dates and researchers having no history of engagement with the project, it is often going to be the case that the decision to work with software and the familiarisation of the researchers with the software is not going to fall neatly into some pre-data-gathering phase of an ideal research timetable. If the investment of money and time required to become competent in using the software is seen as something with long-term benefits this should not matter. If the researchers are able to use the skills in future projects, and indeed to enhance their 'marketability' through having acquired this skill, then it would seem to be a good investment. Likewise, if the data is then available for years to come so it can be thoroughly explored and written about beyond the shorter-term research funding body end of grant report, then it would seem to be a good investment. However, if the time constraints of doing a pre-specified amount of fieldwork, and of literature reviews being needed to help academics stay up-to-date despite the vast demands on their time as a result of ever-burgeoning roles, mean that the researchers need to be deployed elsewhere then it may be that the rigour, quality, self-development and long-term value of such an investment may need to be sacrificed due to short-term frameworks and targets and the general context of academic life, and the current process of generating research funding and corresponding reputations. As I write, now as a lecturer with a project management role, I am facing precisely that dilemma with a view to (myself and our researchers) using/learning NVivo the program of choice of my institution (i.e. the only program which will get support from the IT staff). These are very real choices and it is important not just to trivialise such choices by simply regarding them as whether to bother with IT packages or not.

If the decision to use such a package, or even to code data (without CAQDAS), is made, people's concerns over using the software need to be allowed to be aired. Some people may enjoy finding the hidden 'techie' part of their self (mentioning no names!), others may wish to resist that association for numerous reasons (again, mentioning no names!). Also, in pulling together new teams, people's ways of engaging with coding will differ. Individual disciplinary backgrounds will influence not only researchers' choices of theoretically derived codes but also how they frame key 'content' issues in the text. Consequently the process of merging lists and agreeing terms and definitions of codes reflects these different backgrounds. Indeed the whole process of negotiation reflects these differences, and the outcome reflects whether one view is in the minority or not and, possibly, relative seniority within the team. In my own case in the first accountancy projects I undertook I was a psychologist in the land of sociologists. I had to learn not only how to look at the text with a sociological eye but also relate to a different way of writing the codes and using them. I was originally trained in using codes that were numerical (although representing linguistic categories), and indeed using vast numbers of codes to make sure the whole data set was translated into these codes, such that a very detailed understanding of a set of attributions could be gleaned from looking at the huge set of numbers describing it. For both the above accounting-related projects we used non-numerical codes, and a relatively small list of them. My initial instinct was, and actually still is, to produce long lists of detailed codes. I also automatically code most of the interview so that I can trawl for counter-instances of findings within and across interviews, and profile the standard repetitive issues for each interviewee. However, that is not necessarily standard practice. Some coders prefer to code much more selectively and being able to interpret their implicit rule for inclusion for coding can be a source of doubt and disagreement that will remain at the final analysis phase if not addressed. In my experience the latter has not affected the reliability of findings in projects I have undertaken as the process of reading the texts beyond the fragmented outputs has been undertaken by all the members of the research team.

Practical Points

Over and above my reflections on the broad practice of using CAQDAS and the various technical and ethical issues referred to above, or perhaps in summing up those reflections, there are a few rather mundane but useful pointers to bear in mind when planning a project that will use such software.

Timing

Unrealistic ideal timeframes in relation to all of the stages of CAQDAS use can be a source of frustration and tension. The decision phase, purchasing, installation, learning to use the software, and developing a coding framework that suits everybody, tend to take a rather unpredictable amount of time. This is due to practical issues such as finding out about options, time taken to process purchase orders, time taken to learn how to use the software etc. It also refers to the way in which using IT packages affects the way we do our research and discuss our research as discussed above, and therefore the way we see ourselves as researchers and managers of research and other people's career experiences and opportunities. Building in flexibility of timing is therefore a key aspect at the level of practical planning and the mindset brought to the whole process. So, ideally the decision to use CAQDAS, and which package to use, needs to be made early in the life of a research project. However, the pressures for an earlyish decision must not allow the experience and underpinning research assumptions and beliefs of the researchers making up the team, which may well differ in fundamental ways, to be pushed to one side in the haste to make a decision.

Once the coding framework itself is agreed the pressure to get transcripts coded so analysis can begin as soon as possible can be immense. Therefore, it is essential to make realistic estimates of how long you expect yourself and others to spend using the software each day. After the initial novelty of new software and/or new data wears off after even ten minutes of entering codes the process can become very tedious. I always wanted to get it over and done with as soon as possible. Typing in the number of the start line and end line of a section that is having codes attached to it, in this tired and bored state, may lead to mistyped lines. (These will be spotted in outputs as the section will not relate to the code or will be too short or too long, but it helps with the broader notion of building confidence in the process if there are as few errors as possible for correction). In addition, if the coding has originally been done on a hard copy then flicking one's eyes from paper to screen making sure lines and numbers are correct can actually have a slightly deleterious effect on well-being as, without wishing to be too graphic, I often used to end up feeling nauseous after inputting the codes for longer than twenty minutes and so a realistic schedule that allows short bursts of inputting now and again would always be my preferred way of working.[5]

Funding for research provides many opportunities but it also brings with it reporting timeframes as part of the accountability system that accompanies the funding. Indeed the increasing pressure to produce x amount of publications within a number of years also adds to the time management pressure facing researchers regardless of funding status. If researchers are employed on fixed term contracts the management of their ultimately limited time is also a key issue for supervisors. Consequently the time management of the coding and analysis phases is a crucial aspect of undertaking research in that rushing and cutting corners, even though one has initially invested a lot of time in the early stages of using CAQDAS, might be a temptation. To get the most from using such packages researchers need to be vigilant in setting up their activities so that the need for, or temptation of, cutting corners is minimised.

Networks of Expertise and Discussion

In the process of an initial purchase, finding out how other people have used different programs is essential. Reading reviews and talking to people in your institution or conferences etc. about their experiences of programs helps bring the strengths and weaknesses of programs to light, and forces you to begin to think through, or begin to articulate clearly, what it is you envisage as your analysis and data management needs. Demonstration copies of the software are often available and it is worth trying these if possible. I found the few email communications I had with Seidel *et al.* (the program authors of *The Ethnograph*) at the purchase stage very friendly and helpful, and the instruction manual easy to work through — a good sign in any first-stage engagements with software.

The same imperative, to feel there is a support network to some degree, also applies to the coding process. Discussing the coding process as much as possible to make

---

[5] The latest version of *The Ethnograph* (Version 5.0) utilises Windows progamming as opposed to the MS-DOS version with which I am most familiar. Version 5.0 therefore enables the text to be highlighted by the mouse and this automatically adds the line numbers to the coding instruction box, I believe.

differences and assumptions that are underpinning the (pre-)analysis work explicit sooner rather than later yields benefits for the entire research process. The iterative process of generating the coding framework needs to be tied into a developing sense of inquiry that is reflected in the interview, or general data-gathering, process. Developing a 'good' coding framework in a timely way requires reflecting on issues that are coming through the early interviews. This in turn enables changes to the data gathering process as a consequence of any new and unexpected areas of interest that are being raised, or indeed of addressing a seeming paucity of information around issues that the original research design had as central concerns. It would be possible to use a coding framework that does not grow out of an engagement with the data, and it would be possible to be 'lazy' and wait until the end of the process and see what comes out of the data set as a whole before engaging with the research questions and findings. As ever CAQDAS cannot prevent bad research practice entirely, but used well the practical pressures to get the process moving can be a force for the good when researchers are willing and able to make the most of the reflective (as well as data management) opportunities provided at all stages of CAQDAS use.

Conclusion

CAQDAS can be a supremely helpful aid to analysis but such success does not follow from just using the software as set out in the instruction manuals, it requires the same good research practice that should underpin any project. Using the software is likely to make such considerations of the nature of good research practice salient and for that reason alone can be a good discipline for researchers. Having masses of coded data easily available is a great resource in terms of enabling a thorough analysis process. As mentioned above it allows an efficient long-term engagement with the content which enables analyses at their fullest to take place. This wealth of rich data in a permanently available form can, according to some, bring with it temptations to over-analyse in the sense of losing sight of the key issues that underpin the data set, or of 'forgetting' the fact that the data was gathered at certain times and places. However, I used the data set of the socialisation project as the main detail of my Ph.D. thesis (Anderson-Gough 2002), which I completed six years after the data were collected. As part of my continuing engagement with the nature of expertise and identity I re-analysed the data using Foucauldian and Post-Foucauldian frameworks to unpick the lived experience of the knowledge-power relation further. However, the work on the thesis was taking part at the same time as I was undertaking new fieldwork in similar sites, and I was much better acquainted with the organisational and institutional context of the large accountancy firms than when I first set out doing those interviews back in 1996. I was, therefore, able to reflect on whether it seemed that any aspects of the original findings may no longer hold true. It turned out that it was more a case of the same issues of fragmentation of professionalism and an under-utilised sense of the ethicality of technical expertise being just as true today and even more troublesome in the eyes of many than in the early/mid-1990s. I believe a reflective awareness of the timeframe of the data collection and analysis can therefore make this temporally more distant (from the data collection) analysis useful and valid.

In this chapter I have tried to raise issues that are perhaps more practical or technical but I have also tried to reflect on my experiences and the issues that using CAQDAS have raised for me through an engagement with the way in which using CAQDAS is not and cannot be isolated from aspects of the broader identities, practices and power relations underpinning everyday research practice. All of the points I make above come from my own experience of the tensions and frustrations around identity and the process of generating codes in a team, and at the same time the pleasure of being able to have such thoughtful, timely and productive discussions with colleagues. Interestingly, perhaps, it is those issues of synthesis of views, and of managing that process of synthesis productively and respectfully, which have caused the 'headaches' generally. The technology has generally been easy to use and reliable in and of itself.

The one occasion I do recall having technology problems as such, was over an upgrade to *The Ethnograph* Version 5.0. Having five years of the MS-DOS version under my belt, we (the team I was working with in 1998) decided to upgrade to the new Windows version. This coincided with me taking on teaching accounting to undergraduates for the first time and I have to admit that I am not sure whether that upgrade had serious glitches or whether I simply did not have the time or the clarity of mind to work through what the problem might be. The pressure of getting the coding onto the system before Christmas and the horror of finding 'oddities' was certainly grim, in the context of having invested time in setting up and working through the upgrade and training up someone to use the new system to enter the codes for us when available time was almost non-existent. In fact, on reflection, it must have been so grim that it dissuaded me from going back at a later date to work through the problem, or maybe that has more to do with the continuing challenge of time management in occupying an academic role? That aside, I can no longer remember what the glitch was. I do know it was enough to send me scurrying back to what I knew had worked well for me for years, my good old MS-DOS version.

However, the issue of progress cannot be ignored forever. As mentioned earlier, my current institution only formally supports NVivo. I have *The Ethnograph* installed on my computer but the old MS-DOS version requires me to log out of the system, boot up and go to DOS. Then once searches have been performed they have to be sent to disk as, being logged out of the system, I cannot connect with the departmental printers. Then I have to boot up again and log back in (never a speedy a process it seems) in order to print any search output. Also, my snazzy laptop seems to have taken a dislike to such a simple package and heats up and closes down after a short amount of time working with the program. So, I think there is a bit of a message here and I do need to move with the times. The issue of technology progress will always have implications for the amount of time needed to keep CAQDAS skills efficient and effective to some degree, but I would argue that a new investment ten years on from my initial investment (and five years on from the 'glitch' episode) is not too much to ask. I would also anticipate reaping the same benefits from that investment and so face the task stoically. Rather scarily, however, I have discovered I have developed that defining trait of the 'old-hand' in that I find myself saying things like "it all sounds a bit complicated, now with *The*

Ethnograph...". However, I have not sat down and taken the time to learn properly, I am currently in delegation mode. I have been assured that it really is easier and less time consuming than my old MS-DOS program.

On the whole I have neither real horror stories (of lost or corrupted data etc.), nor a catalogue of stories where things went wrong in some way. As part of the everyday discussions and practices of research life, CAQDAS use itself has been smooth and rather unremarkable in that sense. As an end-note I would however like to return to the point I have tried to make throughout these reflections that although the use of CAQDAS is in some ways unremarkable at the level of using a computer to help manage the data and analysis, the issues that it relates to, the way CAQDAS gets 'lived', through the management of research and researcher identity, are far from unremarkable. When working with other researchers, decisions about whether to use CAQDAS, what codes to use, who does the coding, who is allowed to keep copies of the data, and what gets analysed and written about are decisions about who has a voice within the research. 'Forgetting' they are more than 'neutral' decisions about technology use masks one of the ways in which we are accountable to each other in research teams for good, respectful and productive, management practice.

References

Anderson-Gough, F. M. (2002). On becoming the new accounting expert: between formal and informal learning. Unpublished Ph.D. Thesis, The University of Leeds, U.K.

Anderson-Gough, F., Chatterjee, P., Gough, M., Hoskin, K., & Lucas, U. (2003). 'Mind the gap': bridging theory and practice in accountancy education and training. Paper presented at the 26th Annual Congress of the European Accountancy Association. Seville, Spain, April 2003.

Anderson-Gough, F. Grey, C., & Robson, K. (1998a). *Making up accountants: The organizational and professional socialization of trainee chartered accountants.* Ashgate: London.

Anderson-Gough, F. Grey, C., & Robson, K. (1998b). 'Work hard, play hard': an analysis of cliché in two accountancy practices. *Organization,* 5(4), 565–592.

Anderson-Gough, F. Grey, C., & Robson, K. (2000). In the name of the client: the service ethic in two international accounting firms. *Human Relations,* 53(9), 1151–1174.

Barthes, R. (1977). The death of the author. In: *Image-music-text* (pp. 142–148), [trans. Stephen Heath]. London: Fontana Press.

Beardsley, M. C., & Wimsatt, W. K. (1954). The intentional fallacy. In: W. K. Wimsatt (Ed.), *The verbal icon.* Lexington: The University Press of Kentucky.

Bryman, A. (1988). *Quantity and quality in social research.* London: Unwin Hyman.

Coffey, A. J. (1993). Double entry: the professional and organizational socialization of graduate accountants. Unpublished Ph.D. Thesis, University of Wales College Cardiff.

Gough, M. (1997). The death of the author and the life of the subject. In: K. Simms (Ed.), Language and the subject, *Critical Studies,* 9 (pp. 227–236). Amsterdam and Atlanta: Editions Rodopi.

Hanlon, G. (1994). *The commercialisation of accountancy: Flexible accumulation and the transformation of the service class.* Basingstoke: Macmillan.

Hoskin, K., & Anderson-Gough (forthcoming). The context of learning in professional work environments: insights from the accountancy profession. In: H. Rainbird, A. Fuller, & A. Munro (Eds), *Workplace learning in context.* London: Routledge.

Mello, R. A. (2002). Collocation analysis: a method for conceptualizing and understanding narrative data. *Qualitative research*, *2*(2), 231–243.

Miles, M., & Huberman, A. (Eds) (1994). *Qualitative data analysis: An expanded sourcebook.* London: Sage.

Ryan, G. W., & Bernard, H. R. (2000). Data management and analysis methods. In: N. K. Denzin, & Y. S. Lincoln (Eds), *Handbook of qualitative research.* Thousand Oaks, CA: Sage.

Seale, C. (1999). *The quality of qualitative research.* London: Sage.

Seidel, J., Friese, S., & Leonard, D. C. (1995). *The ethnograph v4.0: A user's guide.* Amherst, MA: Qualis Research Associates.

Weaver, A., & Atkinson, P. (1994). *Microcomputing and qualitative data analysis.* London: Avebury.

Weitzman, E. A. (2000). Software and qualitative research. In: N. K. Denzin, & Y. S. Lincoln (Eds), *Handbook of qualitative research.* Thousand Oaks, CA: Sage.

Weitzman, E. A., & Miles, M. B. (1995). *Computer programs for qualitative data analysis: A software sourcebook.* Thousand Oaks, CA: Sage.

Chapter 23

Qualitative Data Analysis: Illuminating a Process for Transforming a 'Messy' but 'Attractive' 'Nuisance'

Brendan O'Dwyer

"The real mystique of qualitative inquiry lies in the process of using data rather than in the processes of gathering data" (Wolcott 1990: 1).

Introduction

Qualitative research demands much of the researcher. He or she is the primary research instrument and is personally responsible for gaining access to sites and interviewees, maintaining good field relations, collecting/analysing data and writing in creative yet credible ways. This form of research has a strong craft-like element and competent field researchers acquire a significant amount of knowledge about their craft as a result of hands-on experiences (Leavy 1994; Baxter & Chua 1998). Furthermore, the burden of inference falls on the researcher as opposed to a statistical methodology which crunches inputs into outputs thereby effectively absolving the researcher of errors in inference (Ahrens & Dent 1998). Despite the plethora of books on qualitative research methods and analysis (see, for example, Wolcott 1990; King 1998, 1999; Symon & Cassell 1998; Cassell & Symon 1999; Silverman 2000; Patton 2002), the process of transforming this 'messy' data remains quite challenging. This chapter presents a personal, non-prescriptive, partial account of a process of analysis used to transform a set of data emanating from an interview-based study into a well-founded, coherent and illuminating narrative. It is intended both as an informed reflection and a potential guide for qualitative researchers in accounting entering the 'field' for the first time.

The analysis process I outline emanated from a larger, primarily exploratory PhD study investigating corporate social responsibility (CSR) and corporate social disclosure (CSD) in Ireland (O'Dwyer 2000). The study was guided by three core broadly based research questions informed by a critical analysis of the CSR and CSD literatures:

The Real Life Guide to Accounting Research: A Behind-the-Scenes View of Using Qualitative Research Methods
© 2004 Published by Elsevier Ltd.
ISBN: 0-08-043972-1

(1) What is the extent of CSD practice among listed companies in Ireland? (see O'Dwyer & Gray 1998)
(2) How do senior Irish executives in listed companies conceive of CSR and CSD? Why do they hold these conceptions? (see O'Dwyer 2003)
(3) Given that CSD is often perceived as a manifestation of CSR, do these conceptions of CSR together with conceptions of CSD, aid in explaining the motivations for CSD presence and absence in the Irish context? (see O'Dwyer 2002)

The study critically analysed the implications of the findings for the main theoretical interpretations of the motives for CSD.

Within this chapter I present a loose chronology recounting the analysis of the interview-based evidence gathered in order to answer the aspect of the second question above dealing with managerial conceptions of CSR. I also reflect on the interpretive analysis of this evidence using a specific lens aimed at constructing a more focused, theoretically informed narrative for an academic paper (see O'Dwyer 2003). This lens was drawn from prior CSR and CSD research and concentrated on identifying and reflecting on the nature of 'managerial capture'[1] of the CSR concept evident in the perspectives gained. The managerial capture lens (or theme) was implicit in my thinking at the beginning of the research process but it was not explicitly pre-selected. Twenty-nine in-depth semi-structured interviews with Finance Directors, Chief Executive Officers, Chairpersons and Company Secretaries in 27 Irish listed companies were undertaken over a four-month period. The questions addressed were open-ended and partially influenced by the CSR and CSD literature. The managers' conceptions were described in depth in the Ph.D. study while the subsequent academic paper considered the implications these conceptions had for social accounting scholars' attempts to engage with and transform business practice in the interests of the wider society.

The Ph.D. study was partially focused on describing and exploring meanings of CSR (and CSD) among these managers. I wanted to discover what was in and on their minds regarding CSR (and CSD) and to strive for some understanding of CSD practice (and non-practice) from this. Given I was keen to 'get inside the heads' of the managers in order to hear them speak and reflect, face to face interviews seemed the most obvious choice of research method. Consequently, I became engaged in a primarily subjective approach to the study of social science which felt extremely comfortable to me. As I undertook the interviews I dwelt in depth on the implicit methodological assumptions driving me to undertake qualitative research of this nature. I reflected carefully on my perception of the social world and this exposed my previously implicit inclination towards ideographic methodologies. However, I only became explicitly aware of my methodological assumptions after I had decided to use semi-structured interviews as my primary research method.

---

[1] The term 'managerial capture' refers to the means by which corporations, through the actions of their management, take control of the debate over what CSR involves by attempting to outline their own definition which is primarily concerned with pursuing corporate goals of shareholder wealth maximisation (Owen *et al.* 1997, 2000, 2001). This analytical theme allowed me to consider if the perspectives I gained displayed evidence (or otherwise) of managerial capture, and if so, how this manifested itself.

Prior to undertaking the interviews I had little idea as to how I was going to analyse the resultant data. I decided to tape and transcribe any interviews I could as my prior reading suggested there were specific methods for analysing qualitative data captured in this manner. Qualitative research method books and articles seemed to offer a plethora of possibilities for analysis (see Miles 1979; Tesch 1990; Miles & Huberman 1994; King 1998, 1999; Lillis 1999). Ultimately, I devised a rigorous process using advice from both texts and colleagues. As I shall recount, much of my attempt at analysis was initially intuitive and somewhat obsessive in its rigour.

The remainder of the chapter proceeds to describe and reflect on the post-interview data analysis undertaken in three distinct though somewhat overlapping phases. These phases encompass: data reduction; data display; and data interpretation and are outlined in more detail in Figure 1 — see below. The concluding section of the chapter reflects on my experiences throughout the analysis process.

The Process of Analysis

This section forms the core of the chapter and makes explicit the process of post interview analysis undertaken on the qualitative data emanating from the twenty-nine interviews. By focusing on post-interview data analysis, I present a partial picture of qualitative data analysis. This form of analysis constitutes a pervasive activity throughout a study's life and does not commence after interview evidence has been collected. It should originate and be ongoing during the *data collection* phase making use of various props such as journals/diaries and other reflections.

Huberman & Miles (1994) suggest that qualitative data analysis embraces three linked subprocesses: data reduction; data display; and conclusion drawing/verification (which I refer to as 'data interpretation'). In the succeeding sections, as Figure 1 outlines, I detail and reflect on the post interview analysis process in a chronological fashion under these three somewhat overlapping headings. Initially, the *data reduction* process is described. This involved interacting with the various tools of analysis gathered during the data collection process such as journal/diary reflections, interview notes, interview transcripts, and contextual and background information. This process was aimed at identifying key themes and patterns in the evidence collected. The core elements of this phase are summarised in the top three boxes in Figure 1. I then proceed to outline my attempts at visually displaying this reduced data (*data display*), primarily through the formulation of detailed matrices encompassing the key themes and patterns identified (see Figure 1). The final sub-section, dealing with *data interpretation*, deliberates on my efforts to interpret the reduced data sets emanating from the data reduction and data display phases. This is summarised in the final five boxes of the chronology outlined in Figure 1.

The process I describe reflects the two sides to qualitative analysis: the highly creative element depending on the insights and conceptual capabilities of the analyst; and a technical side that is analytically rigorous, mentally replicable, and explicitly systematic (Patton 1990).

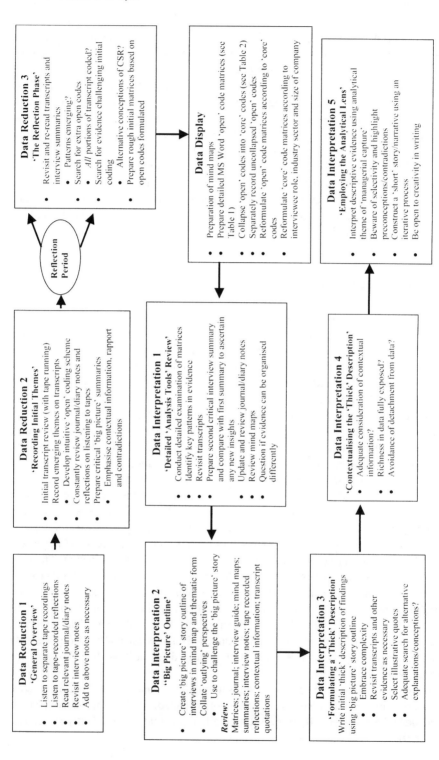

Figure 1: Path of post interview data analysis.

Data Reduction

Twenty-five of the twenty-nine interviews were tape-recorded and subsequently transcribed. Four interviewees declined to be tape-recorded and during their interviews I took detailed notes and developed linkages between the various issues being addressed. As with all interviews I took further notes immediately after these unrecorded interviews and also tape-recorded reflections in order to ensure that all issues raised were immediately recorded. I transcribed over half of the recorded interviews and had some assistance transcribing the remainder. This produced over 700 pages of transcribed evidence. Transcribing the interviews yourself enables you to analyse in depth as you transcribe and gives you a better 'feel' for the data as you progress. This is unavoidably time-consuming but in terms of obtaining insights and forcing you to think about the data, it can be invaluable.

Numerous sources from my data collection phase were available to aid the subsequent transcript analysis. These encompassed the interview guide, the interview tapes, journal notes and rough diagrams, tape-recorded reflections immediately after the interviews, interview notes relating to issues such as the rapport developed during each interview and the general attitude of the interviewee to the subject under study.[2] It was at this stage of the process that I became rather overwhelmed by the volume of transcript and other evidence. Before I could progress I needed to engage in some form of data reduction to further facilitate my analysis.

I briefly considered using some form of computer assisted qualitative data analysis software (CAQDAS) as this had been referred to in many of the research method books I had reviewed. I spoke to some colleagues about this but few had used the software either because they were not aware of it or because they did not undertake qualitative research. One close colleague had, however, undertaken extensive qualitative research and had reviewed the Nud*ist software package. She decided against using it as she felt there might be a danger that it might over-quantify her analysis or detach her too much from her data. Many of the approaches to data analysis I had studied did not deal in great depth with the use of CAQDAS and I had closely followed manual methods in these texts. My initial rush to commence post interview analysis, helped by my ignorance of what CAQDAS could really offer me, led me to discount its use at this early stage. This may have increased the time scale involved in the succeeding analysis but I cannot be certain of this. I have investigated CAQDAS in more detail since but have yet to use it despite its many advantages (see Barry 1998), although I am very open to doing so in the near future. Nevertheless, it should be highlighted that CAQDAS is merely a *tool* designed to assist analysis. It cannot do your thinking for you, it cannot formulate your conclusions for you, it is you, the individual researcher who has stored and interpreted many of the contextual factors that will influence inferences drawn from the analysis.

---

[2] This can vary and I had some experiences where interviewees were initially hostile to the idea of CSR being discussed at all, and questioned why I would want to study the issue given my background as an accountancy lecturer. These experiences were recorded and considered in my analysis as, to my mind, they formed part of my 'findings'.

Date Reduction 1 — General Overview

Before commencing to read the interview transcripts in depth, I proceeded to listen to the separate tape-recorded interviews in a relaxed manner. This was undertaken while reviewing my journal/diary and interview notes. As I listened to the tape recordings I added to these notes where new insights were gained. This gave me a general 'feel' for my interview findings and helped me to formulate some preliminary key findings before I proceeded to the detailed transcript analysis.

Data Reduction 2 — Recording Initial Themes

In approaching the detailed post interview analysis of transcripts (see Figure 1), the broad areas addressed in the interview guide provided a very rough initial framework/ template from which a detailed transcript analysis could proceed. Certain themes had also arisen consistently throughout each interview and were evident from my field notes. Consequently, the core element of my initial analysis involved coding the transcript evidence under the specific areas addressed in the interview guide. This, however, proved quite difficult given the differing issues/themes that seemed to arise from reading and listening to the data. Therefore, even though I was actively engaged in a search for new themes of interest these emerged more easily than I had envisaged. It is important to realise that while interview guide questions may act as a rough template, they cannot be allowed to constrain your openness to new or stand-alone themes emerging. In my case, of the initial four primary themes identified (see below), only two related directly to the nature of the questions asked.

Composing 'Open' Codes to Represent/Interpret Primary Themes   The first detailed in-depth reading of each interview transcript was undertaken with the tape of each interview running. This helped me to focus on emphasis, mood, and intonation in order to elaborate on any meaning I derived from the analysis. Each interview was then listened to and reviewed a second time. Numerous themes (what I refer to as 'sub-themes') were identified at this stage and were recorded beside the relevant section of each interview transcript in bright red marker using a set of intuitively derived 'open' codes or labels representing each apparent theme.

The sub-themes and the codes representing them were developed while referring to the initial notes taken at the interviews and the notes taken during the earlier readings of the transcripts. Each apparent sub-theme (along with its relevant code) was recorded separately in a hardback copybook file and cross-referenced to the marked page in the transcript. As I coded the transcripts in this manner, I maintained a second separate 'memo' file in order to record observations and reflections on the meaning of the data as a whole. This ensured I did not lose sight of the 'big picture' in the data as I became immersed in coding.

After a third detailed reading, four key or *primary* themes in need of detailed analysis/ explanation were derived. As I mentioned above, two of these evolved directly from the interview guide questions while the remainder emanated from the coding process. These encompassed:

(1) the rationales/motives driving the recognition of corporate social responsibilities;[3]
(2) the meanings ascribed to an absence of CSR (however defined);
(3) resistance to CSR;
(4) defences/rationalisations of narrow conceptualisations of CSR.

The initial 'open' codes (identified in the transcripts by bright red marker), representing the 'sub-themes', were compiled, where possible, under these 'primary' themes. To illustrate, during the transcript analysis above I derived numerous 'open' codes which were grouped under the first primary theme above — 'rationales/motives driving the recognition of corporate social responsibilities' (subsequently referred to as 'rationales/ motives') — (coded 'M'). Examples included: M/CEO — 'direct influence of CEO'; M/O — 'a sense of obligation or duty'; and M/S — 'a direct result of economic success'. The 'M' element of the code indicated that this was a perspective on the primary theme of *rationales/motives*. The latter part of the code (for example, /CEO) indicated the perceived rationale driving the recognition of social responsibilities (see Table 1) and this is what I term a 'sub-theme'. Any 'open' codes that did not illuminate the primary themes were recorded separately and remained an important part of my ongoing analysis.

While undertaking the analysis on the transcript evidence, I conducted a similar analysis on my notes from the unrecorded interviews. Obviously, these notes were much less detailed than the complete transcripts. However, I found that my anxiety at not being able to record these interviews manifested itself in more insightful interview notes and tape-recorded reflections. Themes presented themselves more readily. Moreover, as I identified themes in the transcribed interview transcripts, I revisited my notes and reflections on the unrecorded interviews to see if these themes were also evident in these interviews. In two of the four cases of unrecorded interviews, some quite controversial statements were made whereas in the other two, the individuals were reticent and rather aggressive in the tone of their responses. There is a danger that I might have underplayed the findings from the unrecorded interviews. However, given I was extremely conscious of this risk I may in fact have overcompensated for it in my final analysis.

Evoking the 'Big Picture'   A fourth reading of each transcript was subsequently undertaken in order to identify any further primary themes and accompanying sub-themes (and thus new codes representing these sub-themes). This led to additional sub-themes further illuminating primary themes being identified. After each interview transcript had been coded in the above manner, a two-page critical summary of each interview was prepared using all my notes and reflections to date along with the codes developed. This further highlighted the emerging themes, recorded general observations on the conduct of each interview, identified contradictions in individual interviews, and forced me to form an overall impression of each interview.

---

[3] I will focus on this primary theme in order to illustrate the analysis process in the forthcoming sections. I will also subsequently refer to this primary theme as 'rationales/motives'.

Table 1: Extract from matrix depicting 'open' coding of a primary theme.

Primary Theme = Rationales/Motives underpinning the Recognition of Corporate Social Responsibilities ('M')

Code/ Interviewee	M/C	M/N	M/Pu	M/O	M/Su	M/M	M/IRL	M/PA
FD1	9,8,1[4]	3,7	3	1	2	24	3,3	
FD2	2,3,5	4	1	4,5	1,3		5	
FD3	5	3		2,4,5	7	6	2	14
...	...	...	...	...	...	...	...	...
Total[5]	*7*	*10*	*17*	*15*	*5*	*3*	*21*	*22*

'Open' Code Index:
M/C   pressure from local communities
M/N   desire to be a 'good neighbour', respect for 'stakeholders' in the community
M/Pu   desire for publicity, good public relations
M/O   core obligation/duty owed to the wider society
M/Su   driven by the success of the company, dependent on economic success
M/M   media pressure
M/IRL   'goldfish bowl' environment in Ireland means you are constantly under scrutiny
M/PA   increased public awareness, changing attitudes

Examples of other 'Open' Codes identified within this Primary Theme:
M/P   Local community pressure
M/Ceo   Driven by personal interests or ego of chief executive officer
M/SI   Proactively driven by economic self-interest. Correlation perceived between economic success and CSR
M/Fam   Family ethos in certain older companies
M/Cu   Organisational culture
M/EF   Desire to influence screeners of ethical funds
M/R   Quasi religious/Christian ethic in Irish context
M/S   Size and consequent public exposure of company
M/Ind   More publicly exposed industry sector
M/PG   Influence of environmental and other pressure groups

---

[4] Numbers in boxes beside interviewee code (e.g. FD1) refer to pages of individual transcripts where the 'open' code was identified in bright red marker. These boxes could also be used to include examples of quotes from transcripts representing each sub-theme (for example, M/C).

[5] All twenty-nine interviewees are included in a complete matrix. The numbers in the 'total' row represent the number of interviewees addressing a specific sub-theme under this primary theme.

Data Reduction 3 — The Reflection Phase

After an interim of approximately two months, I undertook one further reading of all transcripts and interview summaries in order to ascertain if any 'new' perspectives could be gained. This led to the identification of some extra sub-themes which were coded and added to the file of 'open' codes representing sub-themes. At this stage, special emphasis was placed on locating cases that would tend to conflict with the sub-themes that had emanated from the data at the earlier stages of the analysis and with identifying new primary themes. Patton (1990) claims that perfect patterns and omniscient explanations are likely to be greeted sceptically in qualitative research. Therefore, I kept asking if my preceding analysis could be 'flawed' in seeking limited explanations and jumping to conclusions too readily. Effectively, I was searching for some challenge to my initial analysis.

Data Display   The initial 'open' codes (such as, M/C etc.) were recorded in tabular/matrix form in a Microsoft Word file. Each matrix summarised the sub-themes under an individual primary theme (see Table 1). Using this tabular/matrix format, I could visualise how many times various codes were identified both in individual transcripts and in the overall 700 pages of transcription. These matrices therefore summarised the open codes identified by each interviewee by visually *displaying* them, with each code and its page location in each individual transcript being easily ascertained (see Table 1). The displays also aided in identifying patterns in the interview evidence as a whole with the predominant sub-themes becoming evident partially by mapping the relative incidence of different codes. Examining the matrices therefore enabled me to recognise numerous regularities, patterns and explanations in the evidence collected and compelled me to refocus on the 'big picture' in my analysis.

I also experimented with drawing mind maps of individual interviews and the story imparted by the interviews as a whole. These represented rough attempts at visualising what I was unearthing in the coding and helped further in my search for contradictions within individual interviews and among interviewees. I possessed no particular skill in developing these maps but I discovered they did allow me to visually identify linkages between interviews and patterns in the evidence.

Developing 'Core' Codes from 'Open' Codes

Approximately 115 individual open codes were initially developed from the above open coding procedure. Roughly twenty of these codes were included under the primary theme of 'rationales/motives' ('M'). These codes were further refined by ascertaining where relationships between codes were evident. Similar 'open' codes (i.e. those that seemed to fit together by virtue of representing similar themes) were aggregated into what I termed 'core' codes in order to collapse the initial matrix data displays into something more manageable. This process is partially illustrated for the primary theme of 'rationales/motives' if one moves from the 'open' codes outlined in Table 1 to the core codes which evolved in Table 2 (representing the collapsed or merged 'open' codes). For example, a 'core' code that was developed relating to 'rationales/motives' was 'M2' - indicating a 'reactive enlightened self interest rationale' underpinning CSR. This was comprised of numerous initial 'open' codes (see Table 1) including, among others, M/P — 'local community pressure', and M/PA - 'increased public awareness'. These 'open' codes (along with numerous others) were therefore collapsed or merged into a single 'core' code, 'M2' (see Table 2). This was undertaken for all open codes under each primary theme.

Collapsing the Initial Matrix Displays

The initial 'open' code matrices were extremely detailed incorporating all of the 115 'open' codes developed under the separate primary themes. These matrices were also reduced on a piecemeal basis in conformance with the reduction of the initial 'open' codes into 'core' codes above. All of the 'core' codes were then displayed in tabular form as matrices with each matrix display representing a primary theme. These condensed matrices enabled me to visualise the relative incidence of 'core' codes under

Table 2: Collapsing 'open' codes into 'core' codes.

Example of Two 'Core' Codes (M1 and M2) under the Primary Theme: Rationales/ Motives underpinning the recognition of Corporate Social Responsibilities

M1 **Proactive** **Enlightened** **Self Interest**	Recognition of a broader social role by the company as it is seen as being in the company's self-interest to pursue a broader perspective. The company selects the social involvement in order to pursue its self-interest. Represents a perceived *proactive* approach on the part of a company to selected social issues.
Initial 'open' codes collapsed	M/SI; M/Su; M/N; M/Pu; M/EF; M/Ceo
M2 **Reactive** **Enlightened** **Self Interest**	Recognition of a broader social role by the company as external pressure is brought to bear on the company to recognise certain issues. A *reactive* stance taken by the company in its own self-interest.
Initial 'open' codes collapsed	M/P; M/PG; M/S; M/PA; M/IRL; M/M; M/Ind; M/C

each primary theme in all transcripts. Any 'open' codes that did not fit easily under 'core' codes were recorded separately and remained key elements of my analysis.

What I have described above is not only a partial management scheme for coping with masses of qualitative data, it is also a way of thinking about and getting close to the data. On reflection, I found that this process of analysis was, in effect, part of my writing process. My experience therefore suggests that as you organise, you analyse. However, the organisation/analysis process can seem never ending. One has to consider when to cease data reduction and display (which, in themselves form part of data interpretation) and proceed formally to considering the data interpretation. As is evident from the above, my analysis process took place over a long period (six to eight months for the PhD and two months for the ensuing paper).[6] The decision to cease data reduction and data display and proceed to write up a data interpretation was taken for two key reasons. First, I had set myself time deadlines I wanted to meet and I had exceeded these. Second, I felt I had exhausted the themes/insights in the data and found that few new insights were emerging. I had also presented some of my preliminary findings at research seminars in the United Kingdom and the research had been positively received by senior academics in my field. Hence, my confidence in the findings and the story they were imparting increased. Related to this point, I also became a little fed up with the data as I had come to know it 'inside out' and therefore any extra contributions further analysis would expose were likely to be minimal. When to stop analysing the data is not something I formally thought about during the process and it is therefore difficult to definitively advise novice accounting researchers as to when you reach this stage. This is essentially a judgement call on the part of the researcher and my judgement was influenced by the factors mentioned above. However, I do think that as a junior researcher, the long length of time I spent analysing the data was linked to my personally perceived inexperience. The next section reflects on the final interpretation and writing up of the preceding analysis.

Data Interpretation

The interpretation process was instigated in two main stages. Firstly, a long primarily descriptive representation of the key findings was prepared somewhat iteratively. This was principally organised under the primary themes identified (see O'Dwyer 2000) but themes not falling under these codes were also encapsulated in the description. Drawing on this initial detailed description, a second more interpretive narrative (see Llewellyn 1999) or short story representing the findings was crafted clustered around a core analytical theme. This led to the preparation of a more focused representation of the findings (see O'Dwyer, forthcoming) and allowed the craft-like element of the analysis process to come more to the fore.

---

[6] I was not always working full-time on the analysis but these periods represent the rough periods over which the post interview analysis took place.

Data Interpretation 1 and 2 — Detailed 'Analysis Tools' Review and 'Big Picture' Outline

I revisited and analysed the detailed field notes, mind maps, tape-recorded reflections, memos, interview summaries, and journal in conjunction with a study of the final summary matrices. The matrices provided me with a primarily content based 'big picture' of the overriding themes emanating from the data while an analysis of my other evidential sources gave me a sense of the richness and complexity of the data. I constructed an initial rough outline of the 'story' emanating from my data using the primary themes and sub-themes evident from the matrices. I then enriched this outline with my observations and conclusions drawn from the various other tools of analysis above as well as the evidence from themes not falling directly under the primary themes. This was an iterative and extremely enjoyable process. I also mapped out a theme based 'big picture' story on an A3 sheet in the form of a comprehensive mind map.

Data Interpretation 3 — Formulating a 'Thick' Description

Combining the now (almost) manageable data sets and the outlines above I wrote an initial "thick description" (Denzin 1994: 505) of the interview findings using the primary themes and sub-themes above as my (very) loose framework. This was, in itself, an iterative process given that as I wrote, I seemed to learn about and reflect even more on the evidence. This forced me to reassess certain insights or interpretations. Moreover, I found that despite all my preceding organisation and analysis, the initial descriptive write up threw up some new insights. I also became more aware of contradictions in the data especially within the sub-themes I had identified. These insights caused me to critique my initial analysis further. This process can prove frustrating given the continual questioning of your initial interpretation the writing process forces you into. My description made extensive use of direct quotations from the transcripts in order to enrich the narrative. The organisation of the transcript segments according to 'core' codes facilitated easy access to key quotations when required.

Data Interpretation 4 — Contextualising the 'Thick' Description

While writing this initial description, the contextual information collected throughout the analysis process was crucial in order to bring to light the insights gained. The reader has, in some instances, to be made feel as if they were present at the interviews. Interview evidence presented in an overly disconnected manner is not overly convincing. It appears to suggest some sense of detachment and objectivity by the writer, which is at odds with the richness and depth inherent in qualitative research data as well as the methodological underpinnings driving the use of this method. I was there, I conducted the interviews, therefore why shroud this in a detached writing style?[7] Much

---

[7] Admittedly, some academic paper reviewers have disagreed with my perspective on these issues.

of the richness in the data is lost if this emphasis on context is lost. Were certain interviewees hesitant? Did they contradict themselves? Were there contrasting viewpoints among different interviewees? Were there issues interviewees refused to elaborate on and why? Avoiding contextualisation of this nature can lead to sanitised reflections on the evidence and lead to less convincing expositions. The process of analysis can be 'messy' and the representation of the findings should, to some extent, reflect this 'messiness'. Essentially, your attempt at sense making is your attempt to tell a story that you have observed as honestly as you can. This focus on context helps engender trust in the reader.

Data Interpretation 5 — Employing the Analytical Lens

There is no universally accepted formula for writing up qualitative research. Among the many choices, as mentioned above, I focused on a process akin to narrating a short story clustered around an analytical theme. Once the descriptive process is complete, a narrative focusing on a key analytical theme can help to develop a story in a certain manner. In my case, I used the analytical theme of 'managerial capture' to make further sense of and focus my description (O'Dwyer 2003). The managerial capture theme was implicit in my thinking at the beginning of the research process but it was not explicitly pre-selected. The purpose of my narrative was not to illustrate the existence or otherwise of managerial capture. I merely used this theme as a lens that enabled me to narrate the intricacies, intrigue, contradictions, diversity and puzzling nature of the perspectives emanating from the preceding descriptive analysis. This introduced greater creativity into the analysis process but also challenged my 'honesty' as a researcher given there can be a temptation to 'cherry pick' from elements of your description to either support or refute the core constructs in your analytical theme. I was wary of any such tendency to try and make my description 'fit' into the lens being used as this would have necessitated excluding crucial insights and contradictions thereby ensuring that the emerging narrative 'failed' my analysis. Focusing on telling a story, albeit a complex and in some cases confused one, helps resist this temptation.

Whatever approach to writing a researcher adopts, the resultant narrative should ensure the reader encounters a 'resonant' and 'invocative' account (Baxter & Chua 1998). Therefore, my short story included extensive description/interpretation and liberal use of verbatim quotes from the interview transcripts (which can help enhance the 'trustworthiness' of the narrative) with heavy emphasis on the context within which the interviews took place. The liberal use of quotes is essential in order to allow the reader to hear the interviewees' voices. I also favour leaving in minor grammatical errors in speech, as well as pauses as this allows the richness of the data to shine through. We do not speak as we write (an analysis of any interview transcript will confirm this) and this should be reflected, where possible, in direct quotes used. Finally, I had to place my findings in their proper context. My interviews were undertaken at a certain point in time in the Irish context when issues surrounding CSR were viewed sensitively by many in the business community. This was explicitly recognised in the narrative and in the conclusions drawn from my evidence.

Reflections and Concluding Comments

The account of the analysis outlined above is a personal and partial one. It is intended to provide some general guidance to novice accounting researchers and, as such, deliberately avoids using much of the 'technical' language employed in qualitative research generally. While I do not wish to suggest that rigorous qualitative analysis entails correctly following a set of mechanical procedures, some organisation and method can support the creative aspects of the process. A keen awareness of your methodological assumptions is also crucial when trying to convince yourself of the sense you are making from your data. It is essential to bear in mind that qualitative research is not value free and mainly represents perspective rather than any form of absolute truth.

As I reflect on the process, I can see how obsessive I may have been about aspects of the analysis. It is very difficult to switch off totally from the process and I did find myself recording insights at all sorts of strange times. This led to a large intrusion in my personal life given I was undertaking the Ph.D. study part-time. On reflection, I think I could have engaged in less detailed analysis and avoided some of the personal invasion. However, large-scale research of this nature demands total immersion and commitment as well as a realisation that you, the researcher, are a key part of the analysis. You cannot be detached and this demands a commitment that can overtake many other aspects of your life.

Whatever process of analysis you use, there is no substitute for knowing your data intimately. While I found that my literature review tended to sharpen my initial probing in interviews, subsequent research I have undertaken suggests that while knowing your literature is important, you have to be careful that it doesn't constrain both the issues you explore in interviews and the themes you identify in your analysis. Qualitative research can challenge and/or further inform the literature underpinning a study. I used an approach that ensured I initially possessed a thorough knowledge of the CSR (and CSD) literature but evolved to place primary emphasis on knowing my data inside out and then seeing how the themes in the data were reflected in this literature. Reflecting on this, I didn't necessarily need the extent of literature knowledge I gained prior to my data collection and initial analysis. For example, when employing the lens of managerial capture to further interpret my descriptive analysis a detailed literature review of the social accounting literature focusing on the theme of managerial capture was undertaken after the data had been initially analysed and described in my Ph.D. study.

The core aim of the paper which evolved from the preceding analysis was to make a contribution to the CSR and social accounting literature. Examining the responsibility dimension of the social (stakeholder) accountability framework commonly used to guide and provide theoretical coherence to social accountants' research filled a gap in this literature as this component had been somewhat neglected. Undertaking a qualitative investigation into conceptions of CSR enabled me to bring forth the complexity and contradictions inherent in the managers' conceptions of CSR. This also exposed the complex clash between personal and corporate influences in determining these conceptions. The paper concluded by warning social accountants to be aware of these complexities when engaging with business interests.

The process I outline is laborious and at times tedious but there are a number of reasons it worked for me. First, attempting to code interview transcripts provided me with a discipline that enabled me to become immersed in the transcript evidence. Moreover, despite its imposition of structure, it was essentially a creative process. Second, sitting back from the data and using broad summaries, matrices and other props for analysis (such as diaries, etc.) enabled me to view the data as a whole, and exposed interrelationships and contradictions in the data that required further investigation. This combination of detailed coding and broad thoughtful overviews ensured I remained critical of all insights, themes etc. emanating from the data. Third, as a novice researcher I was sometimes unsure whether my interpretation of my research would be accepted by examiners and reviewers. Therefore, I felt I first had to convince myself of the thoroughness of my approach to interpretation before I could commence convincing others. This may be an issue for many individuals entering qualitative research but also means you must think carefully about your methodological assumptions. My rigour instilled me with much confidence during the defence of the Ph.D. thesis at both the internal and external viva stages.[8] I was quite robustly challenged on my methodology and methods in the internal viva and felt, with respect to my methods and their thoroughness, that I was more confident in my responses. In my external viva I was actively encouraged to write up much of what is included in this chapter as the examiners were impressed, and somewhat surprised, by the rigour and openness displayed in the write up of the analysis process.

In the field of CSR and social accounting, reactions to the process I used have been mixed. Some Ph.D. students were frightened off by the appendices to my Ph.D. which outline the matrices that I prepared.[9] Certain senior academics, while admiring the meticulousness displayed in the process, questioned whether such depth was required in order to derive key insights from qualitative data. They also expressed concerns as to whether such depth could cause one to lose sight of the 'bigger picture' in the data assembled. There were also expressions of shock at the depth of analysis compared to that undertaken in their own published interview based work. Many of these responses surprised me somewhat. Implicit in some of the views seemed to be a perspective that I was being "inefficient" in taking so long to develop a narrative reflecting the 'bigger' picture in the interviews. Rationalising post the analysis leads me to conclude that more experienced academics may have greater confidence in their ability to analyse and write publishable narratives from interview data. I cannot advise any novice researcher when to stop analysing (or even interviewing). For me, this is always a judgement call and is often based on initial findings emanating from interviews conducted. There is little doubt that your gut instinct influences this decision whatever formal research method texts might tell you.

---

[8] An internal viva represents an internal examination of a Ph.D. draft prior to its formal submission for examination. In effect, it is a mock external viva which subjects the thesis to a rigorous preliminary review. In my case, the Ph.D. could not be formally submitted and examined until it had successfully proceeded through this internal viva stage.

[9] In one instance, a Ph.D. student decided studying hermeneutics in depth might be less troublesome!

In my post-doctoral research I have not been as obsessed with detailed analysis as I was during my Ph.D. However, I always try to provide structure to any analysis that I undertake. I have become more drawn towards using mind mapping in common with core theme identification as a sense making exercise. Furthermore, I have undertaken collaborative work where my co-author and I have debates about themes in interviews and brainstorming sessions in order to help us analyse interview data (see Canning & O'Dwyer 2003). We have also used early interviews to inform the issues we want to probe in more depth in later ones. Some of my subsequent research has also had to rely less on transcripts as some of the issues studied have been sensitive for the interviewees (O'Dwyer 2004). Therefore, I have to depend less on the detailed extraction of themes from transcripts and be more trusting in my ability to identify themes without the need for constant re-visiting of transcript data.

There is never going to be one 'true' story from a set of qualitative data but the process described above indicates a rigorous attempt at being systematic and reflective. There is no best method of analysis and my process merely served as my analysis technique. I hope it will encourage and, in some small way, guide novice qualitative researchers in accounting and help them in their attempts "to capture the complexity of the field in a coherent way" (Ahrens & Dent 1998: 34).

References

Ahrens, T., & Dent, J. (1998). Accounting and organizations: realizing the richness of field research. *Journal of Management Accounting Research, 10,* 1–39.

Barry, C. A. (1998). Choosing qualitative data analysis software: Atlas/ti and Nudist compared. *Sociological Research Online, 3*(3), http://www.socresonline.org.uk/socresonline/3/3/4.html.

Baxter, J. A., & Chua, W. F. (1998). Doing field research: practice and meta-theory in counterpoint. *Journal of Management Accounting Research, 10,* 69–87.

Canning, M., & O'Dwyer, B. (2003). A critique of the private interest model of professional accounting ethics: an examination over time in the Irish context. *Accounting, Auditing and Accountability Journal, 16*(2), 159–185.

Cassell, C., & Symon, G. (1999). *Qualitative methods in organizational research.* London: Sage.

Denzin, N. K. (1994). The art and politics of interpretation. In: N. K. Denzin, & Y. S. Lincoln (Eds), *Handbook of qualitative research.* Thousand Oaks, California: Sage.

Huberman, M., & Miles, M. B. (1994). Data management and analysis methods. In: N. K. Denzin, & Y. S. Lincoln (Eds), *Handbook of qualitative research.* Thousand Oaks, California: Sage.

Jones, S. (1985). The analysis of depth interviews. In: R. Walker (Ed.), *Applied qualitative research.* Aldershot: Gower.

King, N. (1998). Template analysis. In: G. Symon, & C. Cassell (Eds), *Qualitative methods and analysis in organizational research: A practical guide.* London: Sage.

King, N. (1999). The qualitative research interview. In: C. Cassell, & G. Symon (Eds), *Qualitative methods in organizational research: A practical guide.* London: Sage.

Leavy, B. (1994). The craft of case-based qualitative research. *Irish Business and Administrative Research, 15,* 105–118.

Lillis, A. M. (1999). A framework for the analysis of interview data from multiple field sites. *Accounting and Finance, 39*(1), 79–105.

Llewellyn, S. (1999). Narratives in accounting and management research. *Accounting, Auditing and Accountability Journal, 12*(2), 220–236.

Maykut, R., & Morehouse, R. (1994). *Beginning qualitative research: A philosophical and practical guide.* London: The Falmer Press.

Miles, M. B. (1979). Qualitative data as attractive nuisance: the problem of analysis. *Administrative Science Quarterly, 24*(December), 590–601.

Miles, M. B., & Huberman, A. M. (1994). *Qualitative data analysis.* Beverly Hills, California: Sage.

Mintzberg, H. (1979). An emerging strategy of 'direct' research. *Administrative Science Quarterly, 24*(December), 246–275.

O'Dwyer, B. (2000). Corporate social reporting in the Republic of Ireland: a description and quest for understanding. unpublished Ph.D. thesis. University of Dundee, Scotland.

O'Dwyer, B. (2002). Managerial perceptions of corporate social disclosure: an Irish story. *Accounting, Auditing and Accountability Journal, 15*(3), 406–436.

O'Dwyer, B. (2003). Conceptions of corporate social responsibility: the nature of managerial capture. *Accounting, Auditing and Accountability Journal, 16*(4), 523–557.

O'Dwyer, B. (2004). The construction of a social account: a case study in an overseas aid agency. *Accounting, Organizations and Society,* forthcoming.

O'Dwyer, B., & Gray, R. H. (1998). Corporate social reporting in the Republic of Ireland: a longitudinal study. *The Irish Accounting Review, 5*(2), 1–34.

Owen, D. L., Gray, R. H., & Bebbington, J. (1997). Green accounting: cosmetic irrelevance or radical agenda for change? *Asia Pacific Journal of Accounting, 4*(2, December), 175–198.

Owen, D. L., Swift, T. A., Humphrey, C., & Bowerman, M. (2000). The new social audits: accountability, managerial capture or the agenda of social champions? *European Accounting Review, 9*(1), 81–98.

Owen, D. L., Swift, T. A., & Hunt, K. (2001). Questioning the role of stakeholder engagement in social and ethical accounting, auditing and reporting. *Accounting Forum, 25*(3), 264–282.

Patton, M. Q. (1990). *Qualitative evaluation and research methods* (2nd ed.). Beverly Hills, California: Sage.

Patton, M. Q. (2002). *Qualitative Evaluation and Research Methods,* Third Edition, Sage, Beverly Hills, California.

Silverman, D. (2000). *Doing qualitative research: A practical handbook.* London: Sage.

Symon, G., & Cassell, C. (1998). *Qualitative methods and analysis in organizational research.* London: Sage.

Tesch, R. (1990). *Qualitative research: Analysis types and software tools.* Basingstoke, Hampshire: The Falmer Press.

Van Maanen, J. (1979). Reclaiming qualitative methods for organizational research: a preface. *Administrative Science Quarterly, 24*(December), 520–526.

Wolcott, H. F. (1990). *Writing up qualitative research.* California: Sage.

Section Four: Publishing and Dissemination

One of the ultimate objectives of much research is to disseminate the key findings. There are a range of different publication sources and other means of dissemination that accounting academics may pursue in the course of their careers. One of the most important means of dissemination is the academic journal in which researchers will publish their findings for the benefit of their peers and others. Accounting is also a recognised profession with practitioners who possess and require refinement of a body of knowledge. Practitioners provide an alternative audience for researchers who explore the validity of such knowledge. Accounting is also an academic discipline that is taught in universities and other institutions of higher education. Consequently, both undergraduate and postgraduate students provide an audience for the outputs of accounting research.

In commissioning chapters for this section, we sought contributions from people who each have considerable expertise in dealing with one or other of the different audiences to which academics may present their work. The first two chapters about publishing in academic research journals are by leading accounting research journal editors – one is by James Guthrie, Lee Parker and Rob Gray and the other is by Kari Lukka. The third chapter, which is about conducting and publishing research for a practitioner audience, is written by Stuart Turley who is currently an academic member of the U.K.'s Auditing Practices Board and has considerable experience in working and communicating with practitioners. The fourth chapter about using research in teaching accounting as part of undergraduate and post-graduate programmes is by Susan Richardson and John Cullen who both have considerable experience in teaching accounting at all levels.

Chapter twenty-four by James, Lee and Rob provides insights into how the everyday experience of conducting research may be organised to realise the goal of publication. Drawing on their combined seventy years of editorial and related experience and starting from the premise that research scholarship distinguishes academics from other roles, James, Lee and Rob outline the range of possible publication outlets, identify sets of research questions and fit this into a more general art of writing and getting a research paper published. They close by placing such an outcome into a strategy for a research and publication career. In chapter twenty-five, Kari Lukka, the editor of *European Accounting Review*, considers the more specific issue of the dissemination of ideas through refereed articles in academic journals. Drawing on his editorial experience, Kari suggests that journals should be forums for credible knowledge and provides insights into the everyday workings of the review process that should lead to successful publication of articles that exhibit contributions to knowledge.

In chapter twenty-six, Stuart Turley starts from a recognition that dissemination is likely to involve more than the simple publication of research findings. He identifies potential difficulties in researching practice and suggests some ways of overcoming them as well as considering a range of ways of communicating with practitioners and the benefits that can come from this (while not forgetting the importance of preserving academic independence). In chapter twenty-seven, Susan Richardson and John Cullen consider the relationship between research and teaching and the ways in which case study research can be used to enhance the teaching experience, both for academics and students at all levels. Susan and John review a range of benefits of teaching through case studies and offer a number of practical tips, especially when academics, in the spirit of research-led teaching, draw on their own case-based research experiences.

Chapter 24

Requirements and Understandings for Publishing Academic Research: An Insider View[1]

James Guthrie, Lee D. Parker and Rob Gray[2]

Introduction

While Academe's primary distinguishing feature might very well be thought of as the pursuit of scholarship, the relationship between scholarship and research, publication and teaching is not always explicit. Thus, many teachers appear to see their principal role as one of inculcating and training students in received (usually professionally determined) 'knowledge', while making few, if any, attempts to challenge, develop or expand upon that 'knowledge' (Sterling 1973; Sikka 1987; Lehman 1988; Gray *et al.* 1987). However, the notion of scholarship, although by no means incompatible with the aspirations of the inspirational teacher, must be considered to be far broader than teaching, encompassing also the individual's pursuit of learning and understanding

[1] This chapter is a summary of our personal experiences gained over several decades of actively engaging with the scholar activities. However, it also draws extensively from a prior research project undertaken by the authors and, in particular, owes a great deal to two papers: Parker *et al.* (1998) and Gray *et al.* (2002). Although this chapter goes beyond the scope of those papers, many of the arguments and assertions presented here have been developed further in those articles.

[2] All three authors have considerable experience as both editors and members of various editorial boards. Lee and James have been joint founding editors of *Accounting Auditing and Accountability Journal* for the last 16 years. James has been a past editor of the *Social Accounting Newsletter,* in addition to being current Australasian editor of the *Journal of Intellectual Capital* and serving on 18 editorial boards. Lee is Principal International Editor of the recently launched *Indonesian Management and Accounting Research* journal and is also a member of 20 editorial boards. Rob Gray is currently editor of *Social and Environmental Accounting Journal* and serves on 10 editorial boards. He was editor and joint editor of *British Accounting Review* for 13 years.

through formal research, reading, reflection, discussion, and writing (Gray *et al.* 2002). The value of such scholarship is then tested and confirmed as it is disseminated by means such as teaching, workshops, conversation, conferences and, of course, publication (Parker *et al.* 1998).

It can be argued that scholarly research findings and insights that are never disseminated do not constitute true scholarship, on the grounds that they never add to humanity's accessible stock of knowledge. However, it must equally be recognised that equating scholarship dissemination solely with publication risks ignoring the contribution to knowledge made by outstanding teachers, research advisers, informed critics, journal articles or book referees, and unpublished research degree theses (Gray *et al.* 2002). Notwithstanding this, however, scholarship ultimately tends to be judged (for example, as useful, good or significant) through processes of peer and reader reactions to the content of published research itself. Despite the various attempts to measure elusive notions of 'quality' — in academe as anywhere else — it is the intrinsic notion of contribution to one's discipline that ultimately guides and rewards one's endeavours.

Publication can therefore be seen to be central to the scholarly process, and this chapter is concerned with the publication of research. Accordingly, the authors address issues including alternative forms of publication, the process of research writing, the task of dealing with editors and referees, issues relating to the quality of published work,[3] and the management of research. A processual and strategic view of the publication process is offered, targeted specifically towards the intending author.

Alternative Forms of Publication

First, it is necessary to briefly consider the forms of publication available to a scholar. The list provided here in Figure 1, below, is a familiar one and all the authors of this chapter have at some time published in one of these, including poetry and song writing about the topic area! One does not need to be just international referred journal focused to stay sane. The order of forms of publication is intentionally alphabetical, so as not to suggest priority of one form over others. This list highlights the range of vehicles through which scholarship can be disseminated.

Despite an ability to publish a range of material, in the accounting and management disciplines generally the refereed research journal and refereed research book are regarded as the pinnacle of research output publication. In research-oriented

---

[3] Central to scholarly publication and peer assessment is the process of 'refereeing'. The term refers to the process whereby an article or other piece of work is sent — by the editor of the journal or book, by the commissioning body or by whoever is overseeing the eventual publication — to recognised experts in the field for comment. It is central to the scholarly journals and helps determine "journal quality". In the case of the more influential journals the editor will send the submitted article to a number of experts for comment. This will typically be done 'double blind' in that the referees will not know the identity of the author and the author will not know the identity of the referees. The author will need (if they are lucky! — again see below) to amend their work to meet the referees' concerns before the work can be seriously considered for publication. As we explain below, this can be a long (and sometime painful) process.

departments, discussion papers and conference papers are invariably considered to be minor, 'work-in-progress' forms of research dissemination, and in our experience, therefore not 'counted' for promotion and other determinations of an academic's 'quality'. An example of this can be seen in Australia, where, under DEETYA (1997) requirements, such papers must be published at significant national and international conferences that meet a strictly defined set of DEETYA criteria, or else they are not recognised for purposes of determining research funding (Parker *et al.* 1998; Neumann & Guthrie 2001).

However, our experience suggests that an exclusive focus on refereed academic journals neglects other important channels of knowledge dissemination. For example, the textbook and its obvious contribution to knowledge dissemination may be seriously devalued within this framework. While textbooks may not be formally recognised as 'research', they nevertheless have a profound influence upon the ways in which academics and students construct concepts and practices. It is therefore appropriate to comment a little further on some of the other forms of publication, as listed in Figure 1 (above) and discuss their relevance to an academic starting to establish a publishing career. The focus of the discussion will be our observations of how they might be viewed by university appointment, tenure and promotion committees when attributing research significance (see, Parker *et al.* 1998).

- Academic Journals in the Discipline
- Academic Journals outside the Discipline
- Book Reviews
- Chapters in Texts
- Conference Papers and Conference Proceedings
- Consultants' Reports
- Discussion Papers
- Edited Texts
- InterNet
- Newspapers/Television/radio/videos
- Other (non-new-research) Monographs
- Other non-academic/popular journals
- Poetry
- Professional Journals in the discipline
- Professional Journals outside the discipline
- Research Degrees
- Research Monographs
- Submissions to government/regulators
- Textbooks (basic/conventional teaching)
- Textbooks (new approaches/research synthesis)

Figure 1: Forms of academic publication (adapted from Gray *et al.* 2002).

Books

Books can be conveniently divided into three principal categories: textbooks, research books and edited books.[4]

- Textbooks represent a major commitment of time and effort by authors who, in the process of writing, also become committed to subsequent revisions, new editions, associated teacher guides, manuals for students, case studies, short answer questions, multiple choice test banks and so on. Often very attractive to relatively junior faculty who (very properly) wish to collate and communicate their emerging understanding of their subject, textbooks are not something to be embarked upon lightly — not least because of the input time required and the opportunity costs (of time for the pursuit of other forms of publication).
- Research books are more focussed than textbooks, being typically oriented towards leading edge thinking and research in a highly specific subject area. Such books are less likely to require authors to engage in subsequent revised versions or new editions. They generally elicit high levels of recognition for scholarly achievement in the university community, contingent upon the quality of work done, the significance of their contribution to knowledge, and peer reviews.
- Edited books come in a very wide range of forms. What is common to all is that, typically, putative editors imagine that this will involve them in less effort than personally writing an entire book. In our experience, we have been involved as editors of a number of these and this is frequently not the case as the effort in pursuing errant contributors and editing pieces into a coherent whole may take as much effort as writing the whole thing oneself. The contribution to knowledge that such books make depends to a considerable degree on the specific case but, in terms of personal kudos, it may be wiser to consider them as not dissimilar to the textbook.

For the junior academic, commitment to a book early in one's research and publishing career is not typically considered advisable.

Regardless of type, all books involve a considerable personal commitment of time and energy. Other forms of research and publishing offer the opportunity to engage in more limited scope, shorter time frame projects. More focused forms of publication also allow the newer academic to build up a variety of experiences in researching, writing and publishing whilst assisting him or her in developing a publishing 'track record'. In our experience, a book project is for the more mature academic, from both an academic career perspective and from the standpoint of producing a high quality product, a book is better embarked upon after some publishing experience has been attained and credentials have been accumulated. One of the current ironies in the present research assessment environment as it applies to accounting and finance academics in the U.K. is that fewer experienced and mature academics in leading departments are finding the

---

[4] Our experience suggests that these categories are not precise or entirely discrete. For example, the dividing line between a high level textbook and a research book may be far from clear in practice (for example, see Gray *et al.* 1996). While Rob Gray has been involved across text and research books, James Guthrie and Lee Parker have preferred involvement in research and edited books, given that textbooks consume considerable time in production of allied resources, revisions and new editions.

motivation or time to undertake book projects and publishers are looking elsewhere for their new products.

Book Chapters

Contributing a chapter to a book, particularly an edited book of readings, represents a medium of research and writing that is attractive and suitable both to new and established scholars. We have participated in a number of these projects at various stages in our careers. These chapters can comprise a critical review, a theoretical treatise or a report of an empirical study. The chapter represents a credible venue for both teaching and research related publication, although peer refereeing is the norm for the research book chapter. It can also allow a greater degree of discretion in treatment of subject, format, and length than a journal article. Thus, whilst (typically) not attracting the same reputational value as a journal article, a request to contribute a chapter to a book with a good editor is something to be welcomed by most academics.

Commissioned Reports

In our experience, to participate in a professional, business, or government related projects commissioned by governments and other parties also represents an rewarding avenue for research and its dissemination. University committees and government research weighting systems take varying approaches to the standing they confer upon such reports. Generally they do not rate as highly as refereed research journal articles, research books and book chapters, but they still demonstrate a commitment and contribution to applied research with potential policy and community importance. Inevitably, there is also a downside to such reports: generally an academic has to operate under fairly strict guidelines and the potential loss of academic independence must be considered — especially at the editing stage if the report is to be a public document. The academic upside of such projects is that they can provide access to interesting research sites, engage contemporary policy issues and provide much needed research funds.

Research Monograph

A research monograph is normally a shorter, privately published (see below) book or booklet which reviews and reports upon a commissioned and/or funded piece of research. They are most commonly associated, especially in the U.K., with the professional accountancy bodies who fund and publish them. There is much to recommend them: they typically involve the acquisition of a research grant; they may be commissioned or the academic may make a bid for a subject area of their own choosing; they permit a wider exploration of the research topic than would typically be the case in a journal article and, frequently being refereed by independent experts, they can carry a reasonable scholarly quality. Many newer academics find the whole process of undertaking and publishing with a professional body a formative experience.

Professional Journal Articles

These represent an often-neglected opportunity for academics. We have found that the professional journal article represents an excellent training ground for young scholars in both the process of writing clearly and succinctly for a practitioner audience and in adhering to editorial and publishing requirements. It also represents an important medium through which scholars can communicate research findings and perspectives to the business and professional community. As such, it serves both as a technology transfer medium and as a bridge between academia and the profession. While individually often rated much lower in significance by academic gatekeepers (see Parker *et al.* 1998), professional journal articles nonetheless do demonstrate a commitment to publishing and business/professional linkages that universities are finding increasingly attractive. Such articles are much less demanding in terms of the level of effort required by the author than refereed research journal articles and book chapters, and involve shorter lead times from acceptance to publication.

Refereed Journal Articles[5]

Traditionally, the accounting and management disciplines have tended to treat refereed research journal articles as the most valued channel of scholarly dissemination. While we ourselves have strong reservations about this privileging, we would be remiss not to emphasise the status of refereed research journal articles, particularly for the aspiring researcher. Such articles require a high standard of research rigour — methodological specification and application, data analysis, communication, argument, critique and theorisation must all be of a high standard, regardless of the methodological tradition involved. Some positivist traditions require papers to be presented in particular formats, with the required length of a paper varying according to the methodology employed and the editorial requirements of the target journal. The ubiquity and importance of the refereed journal article means that much of what follows will relate especially (though not exclusively) to this medium.

Conference Papers

The conference paper is rarely an end in itself, but may find itself incorporated into a collection of published conference proceedings. Be careful not to get on the conference bandwagon, by submitting the same paper time and again. It might be great to visit

---

[5] It is impossible to give a precise statement of the levels of effort each form of publishing requires, but from our combined experiences, we suggest between one to three equivalent full time working days for preparing a professional article and between three to six months equivalent full time work for a first draft research article). If one thought of a professional article as taking a maximum of three weeks (alongside other normal academic duties) and a refereed journal article as taking up to two years, you would have some sense of the relative effort involved. Of course such timing varies greatly with project type and scope, and the experienced scholar will inevitably be managing several projects simultaneously.

another city or country, but continued conference presentations without publication does little for your scholarly career. Generally, the conference paper represents a partly, though substantially, finished piece of work, fit for public display, but still requiring critical comment and improvement to render it acceptable for publication in a refereed journal[6] (the role of the conference paper in the publication process will be considered more fully in the section on dealing with editors and referees, below).

The Art of Writing a Research Paper

Regardless of the nature of the research, the targeted publishing medium or the intended audience, the writing of material for publication is an art form. However, the execution of the writing process will have a major influence over the ultimate publication of the work. What follows are our reflections on some crucial facets of effective research paper writing.[7] It should be noted that these insights also apply to writing for other publishing media.

Identifying and Justifying Topics

Aspiring scholars often ask how one may identify fruitful areas of research work and writing. The avenues are multiple, and often point to the potential significance of the research as well. Fruitful and significant research topics can arise from discussions with colleagues, debates at conferences, observations made by presenters and commentators at seminars, contemporary discourses in the professional and business communities and so on.

However, the most common source of ideas lies in the literature. Our advice is to read the professional and research literatures around one's area of intended specialisation searching for:

(a) Questions already tackled but not yet satisfactorily resolved;
(b) Questions not yet tackled;
(c) Questions apparently or tentatively resolved but worth further investigation/ challenge;

---

[6] However we have encountered journal editors who take the view that the inclusion of a complete conference paper in published conference proceedings precludes its publication in their journal. Yet other editors regard this as part of the draft paper refining process that improves its quality prior to submission to a journal! We personally support the latter view. However it is important to check with target journal editors with regard to their policies in advance. We also counsel against building a list of conference papers that have not subsequently found their way into journal publication. This can be taken as a signal of inability to drive one's work though to the peak standard and accreditation signified by appearance in a refereed research journal. Attainment of such publication usually involves a significant advance in revision and development beyond the level of attainment required for acceptance at even an international conference!

[7] As mature scholars, the authors have learnt research and publication skills through a process of trial and error, that is, by actually writing, rather than by merely discussing research and publication in the abstract. While you can save some pain through accepting the counsel of scholars such as ourselves, there is still no substitute for the fire of personal experience.

(d) Questions raised in 'further research' sections at the end of some research articles;

(e) Issues being debated in the business and professional media;

(f) Theories that require testing or offer new perspectives in the accounting and finance domain;

(g) Practices about which we know little in terms of foundation, rationale or real effect;

(h) Phenomena or practices, which, as yet, remain largely, unexplained or inadequately theorised.

In addition, recognising that scholarship is both a deeply personal and collegiate activity, consider marrying this reading with two other strategies. First, have a good look at colleagues' current work and consider cooperative development of that work. Second, give careful attention to your own personal passions and concerns and, whilst it can be a more risky approach to early forays into research, bear in mind that research which draws on a deep and abiding personal motivation can often be more original and will certainly be more potentially satisfying over the longer term.

Writing Up One's Work

It is a rare author who can produce a first draft that turns out to be the final version of a paper. High quality papers are usually the product of many rounds of revision, building on the first draft. Indeed, on occasion, an author may find that critical review of earlier drafts prompts them to rewrite a paper almost from scratch.

In writing up one's work, it is important for a prospective author to be clear as to why a particular writing task is being undertaken — whether it is for a research degree, for students, for practitioners, for fellow researchers and postgraduate students, or for some other audience. Clarification of this point will determine the content, its length and structure, the language employed, the extent of referencing, and so on. If the intention is to write for publication, it will be necessary to decide at the outset for which conference and/or journal (or other medium) the writing is intended, as each individual journal will have a unique set of editorial board members, a previous literature and a certain academic style.

When writing, an abstract can provide an excellent indicator of adequate project focus and communicative clarity. That is, it should be possible for an author to summarise in a brief abstract what was done, why it was done, what was found, and why it matters. (Alternatively, these questions could be stated: How? What? Where? When? Why? and, importantly, So What?).

Regarding structure and planning, the most effective and efficient writers plan and structure their paper in advance of the detailed write-up. To assist in developing structure, a series of sections and section headings are often devised, being supplemented with brief notes outlining possible substantive content and the key points to be included in each section. Charts and flow diagrams are also often employed to this end. In general, it is considered unwise for an author to attempt to write a complete

paper without at least some idea of the overall argument having been developed, even though aspects of the argument may change in the course of writing the detailed paper.
   In general, academic papers tend to be constructed as follows:

- An introduction, including a review of the relevant background literature, summarising and critiquing prior research in the subject area. This section should also include an outline of the focal questions of the research project, demonstrating the significance of the chosen subject to the field of research. A brief outline of the paper is also generally supplied.
- A rationale for and description of the research method, outlining the theoretical and methodological perspective(s) being employed and the specific steps involved in data collection and analysis (including any relevant details on population and sample).
- The research findings clearly and succinctly summarised, focusing on material specifically related to the central objective(s)/research questions outlined previously; this section tends to vary in structure and length according to the nature of the project (for example, questionnaire survey, field research, historical study).
- An analysis and interpretation of the findings, their significance, latent meaning, relationship to findings in prior studies, and implications for contemporary practice or policy.
- A summary, providing conclusions and directions for further research.

The intention in outlining this model is not to suggest that all papers should follow a single structural model. There are many possible variants. Rather, the above structure can be considered a guide, outlining the components that might be relevant and require inclusion in a paper's uniquely designed structure. The structure must also conform to that required by the paper's intended destination.[8] In the case of a journal article, structural requirements could be ascertained by thoroughly checking a number of previous issues, therefore avoiding the need to restructure the paper at a later date.
   Upon finishing the draft of a paper, it is necessary to juxtapose the introduction and the summary and conclusion, to discern whether the paper has been successful in achieving the objectives set out for it in the introduction. A number of questions can be used to guide an author in this process, including: Are the research objectives/questions posed in the introduction addressed and answered in the summary and conclusion? Are any limitations to the study spelled out in the summary and conclusions or earlier in the introduction/ research method(ology)[9] sections? Has the significance of the subject,

---

[8] As editors of considerable experience, we are still surprised that authors still submit to a journal with which they are not fully familiar. Levels of familiarity vary, but a useful (if not immutable) rule of thumb is that one should really consider having access to key journals and thus be reading those journals on a very regular basis — their scope of subject areas, preferred methodologies, article format, preferred article length, bibliographic referencing style etc. We have seen a number of horror stories of authors submitting to journals with which they clearly have no familiarity at all. The outcomes are usually predictable — rejection!!

[9] Methods are the means whereby one collects and analyses data. Methodology refers to the philosophical issues which underlie those methods. The terms, thus, mean very different things — but journals vary in the extent to which they are exercised by that difference.

indicated in the introduction, been reinforced with an explanation of the significance of the findings later in the paper?[10]

Once this process has been completed, it is appropriate to write the abstract. The abstract should summarise in one or two paragraphs the primary objective of the study, the research method(ology) employed and the major finding(s). It cannot be simply a replication of the introduction.

Having successfully reached this point in the writing enterprise, the author has expended a major amount of effort and time constructing the paper. A natural pride and satisfaction flow from this concrete achievement. It is beneficial at this point to set the paper aside in favour of other activities, returning to it at least a week later. This allows a certain 'distance' to develop from the work, allowing the author to make a more dispassionate and critical review of the work. Flaws often become apparent at this stage. To help in this review process, a series of critical questions, such as follows, must be asked regarding the work:

- Does the writing communicate clearly and with an economy of words?
- Does the language fit the target audience?
- Are the conclusions supported in full by the evidence, or do they go beyond its scope?
- Does the paper meet the 'so what?' test? Why is the paper important?
- Does the paper tell a complete and plausible story?
- Does the paper develop its theme(s) in a logical manner?
- Are there further implications and theorisations that can still be developed in the paper's concluding analysis?

The process of ensuring that the paper adequately addresses these questions may involve the author in several redrafts of the paper.

Individual and Team Writing

As a general rule it is desirable to build a personal research and publishing record that includes both solo and jointly authored work. There are various reasons for this strategy. For example, appointment, tenure and promotion panels will at times consider the balance between these two authorship arrangements as an indicator of an applicant's ability both to conduct independent research and to co-operate with or lead a team of researchers.

Individual research and writing is important as it allows the author to build research and writing skills, to learn how to manage a project in its entirety from beginning to end, and because it provides a full experience of all facets of a research project. Some scholars find they prefer the total control over project scope, focus, methodology,

---

[10] One is seeking to bring the same level of critical appraisal to ones own work that one brings to the reading and assessment of student work and, especially, honours and postgraduate student dissertations. It is worth noting that many academics — even experienced ones — can provide superb critiques of the work of others, but seem quite incapable of applying that critique to their own work.

execution and write-up that accompanies solo authorship. However, solo authorship also requires (as well as helps to build) high levels of self-motivation and discipline in order to produce a successful outcome. As such it is an essential learning tool and a staple contributor to any scholar's track record.

For scholars who are by nature more highly motivated, disciplined and organised, the solo approach can be more effective and efficient than the team based approach, assuming the size and scope of project allows this. As a scholar's publishing record develops, many begin to show a preference for either individual or team based research and writing. It is still advisable, however, to maintain both approaches in a scholarly repertoire.

Joint authored research papers are frequently more appropriate for large-scale projects, or may be required in order to bring multiple research skills and disciplinary backgrounds to bear on a particular subject. They may serve to provide less experienced researchers with the leadership of more senior scholars. Finally, it is often found that the peer pressure exerted by team members helps ensure that work is done at a higher level of quality and in a timelier manner than an individual might sometimes manage.

Be it comprised of two, three, four or even five people, to be effective, the research team must contain people with an appropriate mix of expertise and experience. A certain degree of 'chemistry' (in the sense of mutual understanding, commitment and communication) is also essential. Co-authors must be able to easily relate and must have confidence in one another's abilities (both in terms of their potential contribution and in their ability to deliver quality work to agreed timelines!).[11] Such research partnerships arise for a myriad of reasons but amongst the most apparent, especially in one's early work, a shared passion for the subject and/or simply a developing friendship is as good a place as any to start.

Sundry Considerations

It is important to ensure that a paper's subject matter, length, structure, and bibliographic style are appropriate to the journal to which one intends to submit. If not, the editor(s) may assume that the paper has been rejected by another journal, or that the author is unfamiliar with their journal. A careful examination of, and compliance with, the journal's style guide, as well as an examination of prior work published in the target journal that may be directly relevant to the paper (including it in one's literature review as necessary) can circumvent these problems. It is also generally advisable to include a cross section of relevant prior publications in the literature review so as to demonstrate an acquaintance with seminal work, leading authors, latest developments and international sources transcending the author's own national location.

---

[11] As co-authors on this chapter and previous papers (with each other and with other colleagues) we feel well qualified to warn that choice of co-authors is a crucial and sensitive process. A successful co-author team is built on personal 'chemistry', equality of work input, and mutual commitment. Intending co-authorship teams can often fail these tests. We advise considerable care before committing yourself to a co-authorship which shows any risk of you becoming the author who ends up carrying most of the load!

Less experienced authors have been known to submit first draft work to journal editors in the hope of avoiding the redrafting process, as discussed above. This strategy is highly inadvisable — referees cannot be expected to do the work of the author. As highly experienced scholars themselves, the referees will detect a first draft submission without delay and recommend against the paper's reconsideration by the target journal. Similarly, the submission of incompletely proofed paper (for example, incomplete bibliography, poor grammar and paragraph cohesion, etc.) serves only to antagonise referees and editors, quickly earning the author a bad reputation.

In our experience the chances of a paper achieving publication in a refereed research journal will be enhanced by submitting drafts to various colleagues for critique, as well as by presenting the paper at research seminars in the academic's own and/or other universities and presenting the work widely at conferences. Publishing the work in a widely circulated Discussion Paper series or on specialist websites can also be warmly recommended as helpful intermediate steps towards submission to a journal. This exposure will benefit the author, pointing out errors, alternative perspectives, ideas for further improvement, methodological issues, findings requiring further address, areas requiring improved explanation and so on. The more work that an author puts into the paper and its dissemination before submission; the greater is the chance of a favourable reception by a journal and its referees.

Consequently, the names of persons, seminars and conferences to which the paper has been exposed should also be listed in the 'Acknowledgements' section of your paper, on the cover page, where paper title and authorship are also shown. Inclusion of this information also signals to the journal editor that the paper has indeed been thoroughly prepared and developed and may also impress the referees. However, editors are generally alert to this tactic and will remove the footnote so as to secure an uninfluenced opinion from the referee(s).

Dealing with Editors and Referees

In this section, our collective experiences as editors (*AAAJ* and *BAR*) are used to discuss how to (and how not to) deal with editors and reviewers, including the packaging of research into acceptable forms and dealing with referee advice or rejection in a constructive way. However, be aware that journal editors' change and that some journals are captured by a singular interest group. Recent research has indicated that accounting academic perceptions of 'quality' can be dependent on geographical location, research interest or academic ranks (Ballas & Theoharakis 2002). If one were to sit down and try and calculate how to manage a research paper taking all these variables into account, then there would be no time left to publish! While our experience suggests that you must "suck it to taste it", it is generally known that a lemon is bitter to the taste and that *Journal of Accounting Research* only publishes articles written from a strictly positivist methodological stance.

Of course you may be able to access journal editorials which give clear indications of the type of material that editors are seeking. An extract from a recent editorial by two of the authors in Issue 1 of the 2002 volume of *Accounting Auditing & Accountablity Journal*, gives an example:

> "As we commence the 15th year of *AAAJ*'s publication, we are pleased that in the last year *AAAJ* has been an important avenue for dissemination of scholarly research. It is only with the support of a community of scholars stretching around the globe that we have been able to active this. As editors, we have stated that the *AAAJ*'s mission is to give voice to subject areas and methodologies under-represented in the accounting research literature, and to promote the investigation and critique of accounting within its social, institutional, political and economic contexts. Our coverage includes: alternative explanations for observed practice; critical and historical perspectives on current issues and problems; field study based theory development; social and environmental accounting; public sector accounting; social and critical perspectives on accounting policy and practice; and the broadening scope of audit, management control and accountability." Lee Parker and James Guthrie — Editors

Where is the 'quality' accounting research published? This is a very controversial question, which involves many issues and also one's personal perspective. It is now necessary to return to the question of targeting journals appropriate to research output. Academics often discuss journals in terms of perceived 'quality' — often a code for the perceived status of the journal rather than the quality or significance of the work it publishes. Part of the problem is that the notion of 'quality' is ill defined and interpreted in a variety of ways, often being inadequately articulated (Tinker & Puxty 1995). Yet a number of published surveys of academics' rankings of journals appear to presume that 'quality' is a unidimensional construct (Gray *et al.* 2002). Some studies (for example, Brinn *et al.* 1996) appear to suggest that academics themselves are allowing, even encouraging, this singular interpretation of journal quality.

In contrast to this unidimensional construct, Figure 2, below, offers a list of possible factors that might influence one's judgement of the value of a particular journal. Unfortunately, only a few of these factors have been addressed in studies seeking to rank journals.[12] It is therefore important that the individual academic beware of excessive reliance upon journal rankings, which in any case vary quite dramatically between different published survey studies (Gray *et al.* 2002). Indeed, the present authors' own prior study of senior academics' views on what constitutes "quality" in research and publishing (Parker *et al.* 1998) suggests that academic appointment, tenure and promotion committee decisions are impacted far more by those senior academic 'gatekeepers' individual evaluations (as referees and committee members) than by published journal ranking studies alone.

---

[12] For us, crude measures of 'quality' do not measure what is important, namely the intrinsic general sense of satisfaction that one has contributed to ones' discipline. It is this that ultimately guides and rewards one's endeavours in academic scholarship and publication (see Guthrie & Parker, 2002).

Accepting that Figure 2 is not exhaustive, it still seems reasonable to suggest that any assessment of journal quality might reflect the personal influence of the journal, one's admiration for the journal, and/or one's perception of its reputation. These character-istics may be unrelated to factors that might in reality determine a journal's intrinsic quality (for example, the rigour of its refereeing system, its citation in the discipline, or its readership).

Now the process of dealing with editors and reviewers will be discussed in a little more detail, including the packaging of research into acceptable forms and dealing with referee advice or rejection in a constructive way.

Target Journals

The most appropriate target journals for a paper can be identified from a variety of sources, including the institutional library, bibliographic indexes, journals in which relevant papers in the literature review have been published, and internet searches, among others. It is important for the author to develop from discussions with colleagues (in one's own institution and at seminars and conferences) an understanding of the scope, style, quality and significance of work published in potential target journals. On this basis an assessment can then be made of the potential match between the paper and

---

- How often do you read an article in the journal?
- How often do you browse the journal?
- How often do you consult the journal?
- Do you subscribe to the journal?
- Does your departmental library subscribe to it?
- How often do you submit to it?
- How often do you publish in it?
- What is its actual rejection rate?
- What is its perceived rejection rate?
- What are your views of how others perceive the journal?
- How have previous ranking/reputation studies rated it?
- What is its subject/method/ideological orientation?
- What is the purpose of the journal (for example, to influence practice, teaching etc.)?
- What is the purpose of your publication?
- What has been your experience as a referee/editor for it?
- Does your library subscribe to it? Multiple copies?
- How often do you cite it?
- How often it is recommended reading for students?

Figure 2: Questions and potential factors involved in individual assessments of journal quality (adapted from Gray *et al.* 2002).

the target journals and the likelihood of gaining eventual acceptance for publication. It is important that an author is realistic in selecting a target journal — there is no point in aiming at a journal that does not publish in the paper's subject area or methodological tradition. A candid self-assessment of the quality of the paper and hence its probability of success in any particular target journal is also useful at this point.

It is important to note that a paper must never be submitted to more than one journal at a time. This is considered to be a highly unethical practice. Similarly, attempting to publish slightly varied versions of the same paper in more than one journal is inadvisable, unless it has been clearly disclosed to the editor that this is the case, and the editor's agreement to consider your paper on that basis has been given. Editors and referees are often able to identify such strategies, particularly as a paper can sometimes find its way to a referee who is evaluating papers for multiple journals. Attempting to use these strategies can seriously damage one's reputation as a scholar, having a long-term effect on the credibility of the author's work and future research and publishing career.

One further point with respect to targeting journals concerns the phenomenon of special theme issues which journal editors publish from time to time.[13] You should keep a watch for announcements and calls for papers by journals planning to publish issues devoted to specific subject areas. These are designed to focus attention on major or emerging areas of research which editors believe deserve high profile and encouragement. The issues may often be edited by guest editors. If such a planned issue addresses an area of research in which you are currently working, then it may offer a highly receptive avenue for your paper submission. All the usual refereeing standards and processes will still apply.

What Referees Expect

While it is not possible to generalise about how journal referees evaluate papers, a number of considerations are commonly taken into account, as follows:

(1) Is the paper well written and error free?
(2) Is the research question interesting?
(3) Does it fit the journal's scope?
(4) Does it make an original contribution to knowledge?
(5) Does it address an issue of significance?
(6) Does it reference and extend the relevant previous literature?
(7) Does it exhibit rigour in methodological execution and argument? Are the paper's findings and arguments credible and justified?
(8) Does it present its conclusions and implications clearly and convincingly?

---

[13] For example, *Accounting, Auditing & Accountability Journal* has for many years had a policy of publishing one and sometimes two special issues devoted to a particular theme each year. These are edited by carefully selected guest editors with expertise in the thematic area and are usually two to three years in planning and development. Guest editors usually send out and publish calls for paper submissions 18 months to two years in advance of the planned issue publication date.

Considerations such as these are frequently referred to in reports to authors and also in the confidential remarks made to editors.

Editor Decision Types

Depending upon an editor's appraisal of a paper, a number of different responses can be anticipated by the author, as follows:[14]

- *Editorial rejection without refereeing*: The paper is returned without having been forwarded to referees. Three premier causes exist for this type of rejection. First, (due to a lack of 'homework' on the part of the author) the subject matter lies beyond the journal's scope or the paper's style suits a different journal. Second, the paper is rejected on the grounds that it is not of a standard for consideration for publishing in a refereed research journal. Advice is also given that the paper is sent to a professional journal (in this case the author has clearly misread the paper's suitability for research vs. professional or business journal). Third, the editor may consider the paper to be so badly written, poorly conceived, or so replete with errors that it is unfit for refereeing or submission to a professional journal.
- *Outright rejection with referee reports*: The paper is returned on the grounds that the editor considers the referee reports to be so unfavourable as to preclude any hope of revision for successful publication in the journal. The author is left with no alternative but to undertake a major reworking of the research and/or the paper before contemplating resubmission to another journal.
- *Rejection with major revisions required*: This response indicates that the referees require major revision work for the paper to have any hope of success, however, the reports will be both constructive and detailed, outlining what needs to be done. The revisions may be so far reaching that they almost constitute a new paper, but, if the author is prepared to make the effort, success is possible — either in this, or another, journal.
- *Offer of revision*: This response indicates that the referees are favourably disposed towards the paper, but nonetheless consider it to need further work before they will recommend it be accepted for publication. Assuming an author is willing to take these comments seriously, a significant probability of eventual publication exists.
- *Accept with minor revisions*: The referees are basically recommending acceptance, with some minor editorial amendments before final acceptance by the editor. These are usually easily addressed and reviewed only by the editor without being returned to referees. The paper can be considered to be very close to acceptance.

---

[14] In our experience it is impossible to accurately generalise about what proportion of submitted papers fall into each category of decision although some journals do publish this data from time to time. As a very rough guide new authors might assume that the first two categories of decisions will be applied to about 20–30% of papers submitted, whilst 'minor revisions' will be applied to less than 5% and 'without revision' will be applied to less than 1%. About 50–60% of papers may fall into the 'rejection with major revisions required' or 'offer of revision'. Many authors with papers in these categories, still do not succeed either because they lack the ability or the grit and determination to see the revision process through to its conclusion. So it can be a tough process — but see the section on managing a research strategy, below.

- *Acceptance without revision*: This almost never happens. Papers are almost always capable of improvement and referees will invariably suggest revisions to improve the paper's credibility, significance and impact in the published literature. Such an outcome, however, can be considered to represent high praise by the editor and referees for the quality of one's work.

In high quality refereed research journals, papers will commonly be put through one, two or even three rounds of revision by the editor and referees before final acceptance.

Dealing with Delay and Rejection

The refereeing process for research journals is invariably time consuming. Editors make their best efforts, but referees can often be overwhelmed with refereeing tasks from multiple journals, under pressure from their own workloads, or (regrettably) rather casual in their approach to refereeing timelines. Patience on the part of the author is required. It is not advisable for an author to phone or email editors to check on the paper's progress, as editors are usually besieged with communications and contributing further to this may alienate them. If, however, the delay has been considerable and no word has been received for five or six months after the submission date, a carefully worded enquiry may be justifiable.

As noted above, an editor's response will most likely entail some form of revision request or rejection and it must be noted that this can present personal difficulties for the author. Initial reactions to rejection or any hint of negativity in referee reports can include disappointment, denial and even anger. This is not uncommon, even amongst experienced writers. Upon asking any well-published academic, one will discover similar experiences.

Upon receiving an outright rejection, it is highly inadvisable to dispatch the paper to the next-choice journal by return of post.[15] It is possible that the next journal editor might unwittingly send the paper to a referee who was one of the referees for your paper at the previous journal. If referees find that you have responded to none of their comments and taken up none of their advice, they are likely to both reject the paper and inform the editor of the second journal of your attempt, with serious damage to your long-term reputation as a researcher.

A more appropriate response to rejection is to consign the rejected article to a desk drawer and return to other tasks, until emotions have receded and a more rational response is possible. Only when one is able to read the referee reports in a calm and appropriately critical manner, recognising that at least some of the referee comments and suggestions are justified and can add value to the paper, is one ready to begin

---

[15] This is not uncommon. We have witnessed this author tactic both as journal referees and as journal editors. Our personal experiences include one of us receiving the same paper from four different journals. In each case the paper was identical — the author had implemented none of the previous revisions suggested. This suggested to the reviewer that the author(s) was lazy and unprofessional. This builds a most unfavourable reputation for such authors with those editors privy to their identities and hastens their paper's rejection yet again.

revising the paper. It must be noted that referees' comments are rarely without merit, making justifiable and valuable recommendations that can significantly enhance the paper.

When Referees Ask for Revisions

Some suggestions may help in addressing requests for revision:

(a) Identify the major and minor revisions required.

(b It is not necessary to agree with the referees on every point they make. Where an author does not agree or is unable to follow their advice (for example, data access limitations, ethical constraints, etc.), it is necessary to explain the reasons for this in a response sheet to each referee.

(c) It is necessary to move beyond 'window-dressing' revisions in response to significant issues. Substantive revisions are required to address major criticisms. Indeed, failure to respond seriously to substantive comments can kill the chance of the paper being admitted to that journal.

(d) Referee comments need to be addressed in a full, in depth manner. Superficial revisions sent back in quick turnaround time tend to meet with equally speedy rejection.

(e) A response sheet for each referee needs to accompany a resubmitted paper. This sheet must detail exactly what revisions have been undertaken and where in the paper they occur, in response to each point made. Inaction on any point must also be defended.

(f) In the event that two original referees submitted opposing recommendations, the editor will most likely have sent the paper and the referees' reports to a third arbitrating referee. As a result, the author is now in the position of addressing the comments of three referees. It is important for the author to discern (from the editor's comments) which, if any, of the three reviewer's opinions are dominant, and to pay special attention to meeting the criticisms of that particular referee.

(g) Where a referee identifies an irrecoverable methodological flaw it must be presented as a recognised weakness and must be carefully addressed and, where possible, ameliorated in the revised paper.

(h) If there are grounds for considering a particular referee to be hostile or unreasonable, or if a referee appears to be contradicting prior advice (for example, on a second round revision), it may prove necessary for the author to ask the editor concerned for a new reviewer or for an arbitrating decision/guidance from the editor him or her self.

If and when all/most of the major criticisms have been addressed, the revised article is ready to be resubmitted to the same journal. If, however, an author finds that there are major areas of disagreement with one or more referees, it may be better to withdraw the paper from consideration for that journal and to resubmit it, after revising as far as possible, to another journal. This withdraw should be done formally with a letter of explanation to the editor.

Returning to the original journal, the resubmission needs to be accompanied by a letter to the editor of the journal, acknowledging points at which previous referee reports have been particularly helpful and summarising for the editor the major changes made to improve the paper. Reports for each referee, addressing each of their individual points and explaining how each has been addressed, should be enclosed. The editor will normally return the revised paper to the original referees along with the comments provided by the author on the points raised. They may be satisfied and recommend publication, they may ask for more (on the same points), or they may identify further points to be addressed.

To summarise, the author is left with two fundamental choices in dealing with referee criticism:

(1) The recommended changes are so fundamental to the paper's message or argument that the author is not prepared to make them. If this is the case, the author must withdraw and submit to another journal.
(2) The changes while possibly not being absolutely convincing to the author, nonetheless do not really detract from (or may in fact augment) your primary message or argument and can therefore be incorporated.

The author must judge whether the referees and/or the editor appear sufficiently unsympathetic, such that the prospects of successful revision are too low to warrant the effort of resubmitting to this particular journal. If this is judged to be the case, it is most likely prudent to withdraw the paper, revise it to the extent possible and then resubmit it to another journal.

Preparation, Preparation, Preparation

Successful publication in refereed research journals is a time consuming business and an author must be prepared to accept and manage research and publisher timelines. As an example, a paper submitted to a research journal can incur the following time lags:

To prepare and submit:	1–3 years
1st referee reports:	3–6 months
Revision time:	3–6 months
2nd referee reports:	3–6 months
If accepted, lag to publication:	6–9 months
Total time elapsed from inception to publication:	2–5 years

The preparation time should include time for exposure of the paper to critique and comment, including workshops, seminars and conference presentations. In addition to the benefits noted above, such exposure helps improve the author's research presentation defence/explanation skills, broadens the author's scholarly networks and enhances the author's profile and reputation in the scholarly community.

Managing a Research Strategy

Experienced authors rarely put all their eggs in one basket. That is to say, whilst a new researcher may well spend three years or so on a single research project in the form of a doctorate, once the Ph.D. is completed it is inadvisable to spend similar amounts of time working exclusively on a single paper. Particularly for a younger researcher working on one of his or her first major (post doctoral) research projects, an exclusive focus on targeting a journal known to have an extremely high rejection rate (for example, 90%) is very high risk indeed. If the paper is unsuccessful in its pursuit of that journal, resubmission to another journal with further consequent revisions may delay eventual publication even further. In the early stages of one's publishing career, it is therefore advisable to have multiple targets and to include journals in which there is a reasonable chance of (ultimate) acceptance.

Continuing with the 'eggs in more than one basket' strategy, working on a sequential project-by-project basis can be boring, and involve long fallow periods between resulting publications. Experienced researchers and authors typically run 4 to 5 (or even more) projects concurrently.[16]

To run a number of projects at the same time is not as difficult as it first sounds. All are at various stages in the process of publication. For example, one project may be at the conceptual design stage, another may be at the literature review stage and another at the revision stage (this strategy is made easier by working with others). This allows the author to maintain a variety of research that is both enlivening and permits cross fertilisation of ideas. It also ensures a steady stream of published research over time.

As indicated above, conference papers are not a substitute for published articles in refereed research journals. As such, a published conference paper should not be treated as the end point publication of a research project. It is important for an author to refine and revise such a paper and pursue publication in a refereed journal. This inevitably involves the hurdle of even higher quality standards, but, positively, will result in a final paper that has even greater potential to make a significant contribution to the literature of the discipline. We have experienced numbers of scholars who lack the determination and persistence that is required in this process of finding a journal publisher and to persevere with the publishing game. In many cases their personal academic record is made up of conference presentations, teaching activities, and maybe professional articles, but lacks a quantity of international referred journal articles or books.

In managing a research strategy, another set of choices must be faced. Some academics write only research articles; others only write books. Still others only write professional articles. There are even some academics that only write research articles for one or two selected journals. What type of projects a particular academic elects to pursue and what publication venues and target audiences he or she favours are a matter

---

[16] This chapter's authors are typically involved in anywhere from 4 to 8 research projects simultaneously. Any one of us will have a project management profile that includes sole and joint researcher projects in the design phase through to papers at final revision for journal publication phase. So at any one point in time, some projects will be almost concluded, some just starting, and different projects having planned durations of between 6 months and 3 years.

of personal preference. Scholars build a whole variety of different publishing profiles. However, over time, a conscious decision based upon personal abilities and preferences, available opportunities and resources, and the marketability of one's long-term profile as an academic, needs to be made.

As experienced editors and authors, we wish to express a personal predisposition towards developing a personal publishing profile over time that includes theoretical and applied research, empirical and critical review studies, professional and research publications, and the journal and book media — an 'all rounder' profile. This, it seems to us, provides the author with variety as well as with the chance to develop a range of empirical and theoretical matters, in addition to the chance to engage with practical and policy issues. It should be said that, whilst it is not uncommon to find serious academics who have concentrated most, if not all, of their output in refereed journals, it is much less common to encounter an academic of standing who has created a publishing profile entirely out of professional journal publications or entirely out of books. The choice is clearly up to the individual academic but it is an important choice and one which should be made explicitly rather than by default.

A Concluding Reflection

In our experience, no matter how successful and experienced an author may be as a researcher and publisher, still referees and editors will still challenge one's self-esteem. Battle scars will be an inevitable badge of honour. It remains to ask whether, in this difficult process, the gains for the individual outweigh the costs. As researchers and publishers, we find ourselves driven by a passion to make a lasting if incremental contribution to the discipline; to continue to build a network of collegial scholars around the globe; to discover new knowledge; and to contribute to theoretical understandings, strategic policy and practical processes to the accounting and management fields. To develop a successful research and publishing career and to maintain one's momentum, it is vital that the emerging scholar develop his or her own rationale as to why he or she is engaged in research. That manifesto will inevitably change over time, but will remain an essential driver for the most productive and influential scholars.

In our experience, the most committed researchers and publishers continue to pursue research regardless of instrumental rewards and despite the personal costs in time, effort, energy, and sacrifice. Why? It is because such researchers are energised by the pursuit of the new and unfamiliar, enjoy the cut and thrust of academic and professional debate, and gain immense satisfaction from their contribution to society through the power of the printed word. To this end the authors extend an ongoing invitation to postgraduate students and academics to join in this work, and also offer the foregoing observations on the research and publishing process.

References

Ballas, A., & Theoharakis, V., (2002). Global perceptions of accounting journals. The European Accounting Association Conference, April 25–27 2002, Copenhagen, Denmark.

Brinn, T., Jones, J. J., & Pendlebury, M. (1996). UK accountants' perceptions of journal quality. *Accounting and Business Research*, *26*(3), 265–278.

Department of Employment, Education, Training and Youth Affairs (DEETYA) (1997). *1998 Higher education financial and publications research data collection specifications*. Canberra: DEETYA, December.

Gray, R. H., Haslam, J., & Prodhan, B. (1987). Academic departments of accounting in the U.K.: a note on publication output. *The British Accounting Review*, *19*(10), 53–73.

Gray, R., Parker, L., & Guthrie, J. (2002). Rites of passage and the self-immolation of academic accounting labour: an essay exploring exclusivity vs. mutuality in accounting. *Accounting Forum*, *26*(1, March), 1–30.

Guthrie, J., & Parker, L. (2002). Mobilise change by means of academic scholarship and publication. *Accounting, Auditing and Accountability Journal*, *15*(1), 7–11.

Lehman, C. (1988). Accounting ethics: surviving survival of the fittest. *Advances in Public Interest Accounting*, *2*, 71–82.

Neumann, R., & Guthrie, J. (2001). The corporatisation of research in Australian higher education. CPAJ Conference on Corporatisation in Universities, Symposium 2001: The University in the New Corporate World, Wednesday, July 18th 2001, Adelaide, South Australia.

Parker, L., Guthrie, J., & Gray, R. (1998). Accounting and management research: passwords from the gatekeepers. *Accounting, Auditing and Accountability Journal*, *11*(4), 371–402.

Sikka, P. (1987). Professional education and auditing books: a review article. *British Accounting Review*, *19*(3, December), 291–304.

Sterling, R. R. (1973). Accounting research, education and practice. *Journal of Accountancy*, *36*, September, 44–52.

Tinker, T., & Puxty, T. (1995). *Policing accounting knowledge*. London: Paul Chapman.

Zivney, T. L., & Bertin, W. J. (1992). Publish or perish: what the competition is really doing. *Journal of Finance*, *47*(1, March), 295–329.

Chapter 25

How Do Accounting Research Journals Function? Reflections from the Inside[1]

Kari Lukka

Introduction

Being an editor of an accounting research journal is tough and complicated. I expected this when I accepted the offer to become the editor of *European Accounting Review* in 1999, but — to be honest — I had no idea whatsoever how tough and vastly complicated it really could be. Firstly, there is a lot of more editorial work than I could ever imagine, and everything takes much more time than one can anticipate. Secondly, the editor's job is much more many-sided than I could have expected. This is probably particularly true in an association journal like *EAR*, where interests, scholarly and other, compete, making the arena rather political.[2] Being an editor is not only about processing papers — though that is the core activity, and takes most time — but it also includes many other things. In addition to running the review processes of submitted manuscripts, an editor needs to set up special section projects, deal with the publisher on production and marketing issues, organise and attend editorial team and board meetings, prepare presentations and reports on journal's activities for its various stakeholders, consider issues of editorial structure, attend conferences in order to represent the journal and find interesting papers, and last but not least, design and implement the strategy of the journal. This list is far from being a complete one. Most significantly, editing a research journal is about networking with people and technologies, and consequently there is a huge amount of communication that an editor needs to handle. Consequently, there is practically no single day without incoming e-mails or letters around the journal, for instance.

However, had I known all this in 1999, I think I still would have accepted the offered task. I accepted the invitation since I expected the editorship to offer an interesting and

[1] I would like to thank Markus Granlund and Pekka Pihlanto for their helpful comments.
[2] *EAR* is the research journal of the European Accounting Association.

exciting experience, hence primarily due to academic curiosity. And interesting and exciting has it been.

As I took charge of *EAR* in the beginning of 2000, I already had certain strategic targets in mind. I wanted to make the editorial policy of *EAR* clear and well known within the accounting academia, make the journal more globally international than before,[3] improve its scholarly quality (both inherent and perceived), and get its editorial processes in the new editorial office established and sound as quickly as possible. These strategic intents led me to launch a number of projects and raise several initiatives in order to develop the journal's activities and its networks. However, in 2000 the most immediate and urgent need was to pull a bigger number of submissions in, since the journal lacked ready-for-publication materials. Accordingly, to start with, I had to concentrate on very practical matters.[4] During the course of time, I have gradually learned how much more there is I need to pay attention to and take care of. Achieving one thing has led to the emergence of several other issues and new challenges, and in that way the playground has continuously enlarged. There appears to be no end to this. Becoming an editor of a research journal really changes one's life.

Despite the plethora of pressures that an editor of an accounting research journal faces, the central issue needs to be kept clear all the time. It is processing the submitted manuscripts in a professional manner. Running of the review processes has offered me a number of good lessons regarding what I should do, or not do, as an editor. But it has also made me aware that there are many researchers who do not quite understand how scholarly research journals (in accounting) tend to function. There are obviously misunderstandings around research journals and their editorship within the academia. For instance, submitting authors should understand all the potential reasons why providing editorial feedback for them normally takes several months, what it actually means when a journal applies a double-blind review system, or what is the appropriate role of the memo of revision when a manuscript is resubmitted. Sometimes misunderstandings are due to such simplistic images of journals' activities, in which the various relevant parties are depicted as acting against, not together with, each other. I believe we should rather consider journals as collaborative entities, formed by their stakeholders.

In this chapter I will examine in detail the ways accounting research journals function in order, hopefully, to help their current and potential stakeholders to co-operate better. The analysis has both descriptive and normative elements. My experiences as the editor of *EAR* are used as an illustrative device. In particular, this analysis is targeted for the help of younger researchers, with only limited, if any, experience in international scholarly publishing. This focus is particularly motivated by the fact that, probably due to short traditions in international scholarly publishing in accounting overall, junior researchers often get practically no training regarding how to deal with research journals.

---

[3] Currently I like to define *European Accounting Review* as a "Europe-based international scholarly journal of accounting".

[4] I would like to thank the former editors of *EAR*, and especially Anne Loft, for their great help in this 'getting started' phase.

The Nature of Research Journals

One central starting point of this chapter is that the functioning of a research journal should be viewed as a collaborative effort. Hence, it is argued that the coalition theory of firms (Cyert & March 1963) can be extended to apply to research journals, too.[5] The key stakeholders of a research journal are its editor and other editorial organisation, peer reviewers, contributing authors, readers, and the publisher. In line with the coalition theory, the inputs and outputs of each stakeholder needs to be in balance for the journal to do well. Similarly as other collectives, in order to be strong, also research journals need to be able to shape and enrol an adequate number of allies from many directions, by aligning their interests around their functioning (Latour 1987). To make sure that this continuously happens is, primarily, the responsibility of the editor.

There exist many different ideas what research journals are and what they should do. These go from cynical views of seeing them as "markets for promotion and tenure" (Frankfurter 2000),[6] to neutral views of regarding them as screening devices attempting to distinguish research with credible contribution from rubbish, to more idealistic views of considering journals vehicles to foster and develop new research paradigms.

All of these general ideas of journals have their pros and cons. I think journals can, in principle, function in line with all of them simultaneously. However, the real question is *how* they do that. Current tendencies to increase formal academic performance measurement put a lot of pressure for researchers to publish by whatever means — otherwise their academic careers are at risk to perish. And it is not any publication that matters: in many countries, the research assessment systems tend to distinguish different tiers of journals, which score very differently.

In the current situation, there is a very real current problem of just looking technically at the format and location of a publication, and bypassing the contents. This is precisely what Willmott (1995) is worried about when he raises the notion of 'commodification' of academic work, viewing it as a major current threat for genuine system of knowledge production to work through academic journals. Commodification implies that the 'exchange value' of academic publications becomes the primary issue for academics. Hence, they are primarily concerned about the extent to which the outcomes of their work can be transformed to produce a flow of resources back to them, through positive measurement results of formal research assessment systems, for instance. This can lead to dangerously instrumental attitudes towards publishing activities within the academia.

The findings by Parker *et al.* (1998) seem to reflect the dominance of the 'markets for promotion and tenure' idea of journals (Frankfurter 2000) and the 'commodity' role of

---

[5] In Latourian terms, we could also regard journals as 'networks of actants' or 'collectives' (Latour 1987, 1999).

[6] Frankfurter (2000) provides a practically and critically oriented guide for young researchers for publishing in financial economics. The issues he raises and analyses are, in my view, largely valid in the field of accounting, too.

academic work (Willmott 1995). Their results from the U.K. and Australia show that the most important criteria for assessing the quality of a journal are journal's rank in survey studies, research methods generally employed in them, rejection rate, personal experience gained as an author or reviewer, and topics covered. Though also these criteria make some sense, it is striking that the contribution the papers published in a journal make to our understanding is not even mentioned in this list, nor even in the list of other criteria normally considered.[7]

The findings of Parker *et al.* (1998) suggest that the accounting academia may already be quite deep in a trap constructed by itself: a trap of forgetting what was the original aim of research journal activities. For journals, the real question is, what does it mean to be, or become, prestigious, and for scholars, what is the essence of developing scholarly reputation.

It is my view that journals should genuinely keep to being forums for publishing articles that matter due to their contents, and that they should be viewed primarily like that within the academia. Hence, the primary criterion that peer reviewers and editors should apply in their evaluation is the extent to which manuscripts make credible contribution to our existing knowledge, and that the same principle should be applied when journals are evaluated as a whole.[8]

This comes down to what journals functionally are. Depending on their editorial policy, journals can aim at playing very different roles within the academia. Some journals tend to function safely within the established limits of the discipline, focusing on the accumulation of homogeneous knowledge (Zimmerman 2001; cf. Lukka & Mouritsen 2002). At the other extreme, there are journals, which attempt to be maximally open for new ideas and even research paradigms. The editors of these journals tend to adopt a proactive role. But whatever is the general policy of a journal, to be successful, it must anyway provide established and professionally run processes to evaluate research. In purely functional terms, arguably, the primary driver of a journal's quality is the goodness of its review process.[9] An ability to be functionally successful should, in the long run, result in an accumulation of the academic prestige of the journal (which is an institutional issue by nature), which further fosters the viability of the coalition.[10] On the other hand, if the review process of the journal does not work (and there are plenty of potential reasons for this), then, in the long run, the academic prestige

---

[7] Of these additional criteria, closest to scholarly contribution comes perhaps the criterion 'readability and understandability', still meaning something else.

[8] Of course I am aware that there can be and indeed are very different notions about what constitutes knowledge (see for examples, Hines 1988; Gross & Levitt 1994; Latour 1999; Hacking 1999). Since examining these various views would go far beyond the scope and purposes of the piece at hand, this claim should be taken as a very abstract general idea only.

[9] My concept of 'goodness of the review process' should be understood broadly here, encompassing for example the professional quality of the editor to select competent and suitable reviewers for the submitted manuscripts and draw appropriate conclusions on the basis of their reports.

[10] Robey (2002) argues that the drivers of the long-run reputation development of a scholarly journal are the quality of its editorial board, it review process, and its acceptance rate.

of the journal does not develop, but diminishes. The likely end result is a struggling coalition, which will be, over time, very difficult to keep in balance.

The Review Process of a Research Journal

The Structure of the Process

A researcher who wishes to publish in a good scholarly journal needs to understand its process. Two somewhat different publication process types can be distinguished: those of normal submissions and those of commissioned ones. The former means submissions which are based on the general invitations of journals for anyone interested to submit a manuscript, while the latter refers to manuscripts which are particularly invited from certain (typically highly distinguished scholars) in special occasions. The review processes of commissioned papers probably vary very much case by case and they should be regarded, overall, as exceptional cases. Therefore, and also since this piece is particularly targeted to younger researchers, I will concentrate here on the default process type, i.e. normal submissions.

The structure of a typical publication process is relatively simple. A researcher (or a group of them) submits a manuscript to a journal.[11] As the editor of the journal receives the submission, s/he either starts processing it (this is the typical case) or rejects the paper directly (this occurs, but relatively rarely, after all). If a process is started, the paper is sent out for peer review, normally to two reviewers. After having received the peer reviews, the editor draws editorial conclusions. Sometimes, if the reviewers' evaluations conflict, additional peer reviews are asked for at this point, which causes a delay in the process. The three major editorial decision options are: accepted without revision, revise and resubmit, or rejected.[12] The editorial decision is communicated to the submitting (or corresponding) author, and in the case of 'revise and resubmit' decision, the ball is again with the author(s).

If the manuscript will be revised and resubmitted, basically what took place in the first review round will be repeated.[13] The process goes on like this until the paper has become acceptable, withdrawn from the process by the authors, or rejected. If and once the paper is accepted for publication, the publisher takes care of the remaining parts of the process. In due course the author(s) will receive proofs in order to check that no mistakes have entered into the text at the publisher end. Finally the accepted paper will be published in the journal. In the following I will go through the phases of the review process in detail.

---

[11] In some (especially U.S.-based) accounting journals there is a submission fee, but in most (like *EAR*) there is not.

[12] True, as noted by Day (1983), editors normally try to avoid using the harshly sounding word 'reject'.

[13] Some journals apply deadlines for resubmissions, others, like *EAR*, do not.

Before Submitting a Manuscript

One of the major problems for journal editors is the (too) large number of prematurely submitted manuscripts.[14] Time is precious to all of us. In order not to waste each other's time, one really should be careful not to submit papers prematurely. There are two critical sides to this: technical issues and contents. As for the former, it should be self-clear for all authors considering submitting a manuscript to a refereed research journal to follow to the letter the technical instructions given to submitting authors. It is next to criminal to submit papers, which are not properly formatted and language polished before submission. Neither editors nor reviewers should be viewed as language editors of submitted papers, and they should definitely refuse to adopt such role. There must be a division of labour here, so that academic evaluation is kept separate from technical support, such as language and style editing. One should also note that this is the easier side of the issue.

What comes to contents, researchers should always invite comments from their peers before submitting their papers to refereed research journals. They also should present their papers in research seminars, workshops, and conferences before submission, thereby getting peer comments. Otherwise submissions, especially those by younger researchers, are typically premature. Researchers need to achieve first a certain quality level with the help of other means, and only after that the refereed research journals should enter the picture: they can help with their normal editorial routines to do the last bit in order to achieve a publishable paper. Therefore, I strongly encourage researchers to attend conferences and corresponding events, and do their best to acquire a network of researchers for mutual support around them.

For instance in *EAR*, it is still far too common that when I receive a manuscript I can see nowhere acknowledgement notes to colleagues who would have contributed to the paper by their comments, nor references to conferences or workshops, in which the paper would have been presented.[15] If a paper comes to a refereed journal directly from the author's desk, without having been read by anyone else, its probability of being in the publishable condition is very low indeed. Normally the end result is direct reject, and only rarely, if the author is very lucky, a 'revise and resubmit' decision.

Before submitting a paper to a refereed journal, the author should very carefully ponder what is the contribution the paper makes to prior understanding. S/he should make sure s/he offers to a potential reader a good opportunity to understand the message s/he has and that the linkage of the paper to prior literature becomes clear: does the paper test, refine, or illustrate prior theories, or does it attempt to construct a new theory? Beside the contribution of the paper, another major issue is the credibility of its findings. An author needs to ask him/herself whether the reader is offered a solid grounding for the arguments of the paper. Naturally the supporting evidence can vastly

---

[14] I bypass here the obvious and sometimes difficult question of choosing the right journal to fit the nature of the paper at hand, but refer to the insightful comments of Frankfurter (2000) in this regard.

[15] Acknowledgements are for several reasons important to know for the editor, but in my view peer reviewers should not get to know them, since that could potentially affect their neutrality. *EAR* instructs authors to place acknowledgements on the cover page, which of course is not sent to the reviewers.

vary by nature, going from creative reasoning based on relevant extant literatures to tightly designed empirical test settings.

Manuscript Received: What does the Editor do?

After the receipt of a new submission, the first thing the editor does is to check whether the topic of the manuscript fits to the scope of the journal. In some narrowly focused journals this can be a major issue, but in more general ones, such as *EAR*, this only seldom poses a problem. Even if the paper would fit to the journal by its nature, the editor can also immediately conclude that the paper is so obviously of low scholarly quality that it should not be sent out for peer review — editors tend to be careful not to waste their peer reviewers' time.[16] The editor also sees that a file is opened for the submission, to which all correspondence related to the manuscript is collected. Typically an acknowledgement message of the receipt of the submission is sent to the author. Nowadays the correspondence related to submissions between editors, reviewers, and submitting authors is increasingly taking place in the electronic form by e-mail, which has the potential of notably speeding up the process.[17]

If a manuscript passes these first checks, the editor selects reviewers for the paper. This is both one of the critical phases of the process and probably one of its most creative parts: there can be no clear rules as to how peer reviewers are chosen. The Editorial Board of the journal is the normal starting point, when reviewers are chosen. However, since one also needs to consider scholars' workloads, most journals also use so-called ad-hoc reviewers. *EAR* is doing that, too. If the finding of a reviewer turns out to be complicated, sources for ideas can be picked from the list of quoted authors of the paper itself, for example. More generally, the Internet and various databanks of published works offer vast possibilities for editors to relatively easily get leads to good reviewers for each paper. In *EAR*, I also now and then ask for the view of an Associate editor for the most suitable reviewers, which option is sometimes a great relief for me.[18]

A 'competent reviewer' is a many-sided notion, having both a general and a paper-specific aspect. Generally, reviewers' should have a solid scholarly publication record of their own. If they have been used before, their reviewer record should be good, too, in terms of review quality and delivery turnover. Paper-specific criteria include profound

---

[16] During my first years as the editor of *EAR* (2000–2001), 8.4% of papers have become directly (without peer review) rejected from further processing. In the toughest of these cases I tend to ask for the view of one of the members of the Editorial team of the journal (currently including, in addition to the Editor, eight Associate editors).

[17] *EAR* is currently running all of its editorial processes in the e-mode, whenever it only is possible.

[18] In some journals the running of the review processes is decentralised to associate editors. In *EAR* we do this only in the case of the so-called 'analytical papers', in which mathematical modelling plays a decisive role. Another case where the running of the process is typically decentralised are special issue/section processes, which are taken care by particularly invited guest editors. In *EAR*, for instance, there tends to be several ongoing special issue/section processes all the time.

knowledge of the substance area of the paper and command of the methods it applies. Normally the application of these criteria leads the editor to a group of potential people, and when the workload issue is considered, a reasonable choice can be made. However, there are many tougher cases as well, especially those papers, which seriously challenge our prior understanding of the topic. In such cases, sending the paper for review only to those who have published in the field before causes the journal a risk of missing the opportunity of pushing knowledge forward. As such reviewers may feel that their prior research is questioned (for example, their methodology, style of reasoning, or conclusions), they can be too eager to recommend rejection of a challenging paper. Hence, in addition to sending this type of papers to one of the current experts of the area in question, I also tend to send it to one reviewer who I expect to have sufficient knowledge of the area in question, but who I also expect to be open-minded enough to recognise if s/he faces a potential for a giant step in our knowledge.

Normally there are several potentially suitable academics, from which to choose the reviewers, and often it is just a matter of learning by doing to see how things work out. In Europe, there is a great temptation to send (too) many manuscripts to British scholars, since within Europe the U.K. appears to have the most developed tradition in preparing peer reviews. However, due to this, the more senior British academics tend to be overloaded with review tasks. In addition, for a Europe-based international scholarly journal, such as *EAR*, it would not be grounded, in the long run, just to take the easiest route. Hence, I have tried to constantly enlarge my ad-hoc reviewer base to include as much continental European reviewers as possible. All of these attempts do not work at the start, but I believe they anyhow contribute to developing a broader European culture of serious academic co-operation. In order to strengthen the unlimitedly international nature of *EAR* and to enhance its global visibility, I also tend to increasingly invite peer reviewers from the rest of the world, particularly from North America and the Australia-New Zealand region.

Participating in the review processes can be learning devices for the reviewers, too. For instance in *EAR*, if a manuscript survives the first review round and a resubmission is received, then the revised paper will be normally sent back to all first round reviewers, together with all first round reviews and the editorial letter. This will offer all reviewers a possibility for self-reflection through comparing their evaluations to those of the other reviewers and the summary evaluation of the editor. In the long run this should be healthy for the academia.

The Role of Reviewers

Peer reviewers form another very important stakeholder of a journal. All editors need a good network of helpful and timely delivering reviewers. Peer review processes can be open or blind. Many journals, like *EAR*, nowadays run a system called 'double-blind review'. One should note that the word 'double' does not refer to the number of peer reviewers, but to the bi-directionally blind nature of the system: neither does the author get to know the person of the reviewer, nor the other way round.[19] Despite the fact that also the double blind review system can be criticised of certain potential weaknesses (for example, Fogarty & Ravenscroft 2000), it is my view that such system is still the best we have been able to Figure out.[20] This view gets, in fact, indirect support by Fogarty & Ravenscroft (2000) themselves, too, since — after going through the negative sides of the double-blind review system — they cannot suggest a better alternative in replace.[21]

In *EAR*, what I expect from my peer reviewers relate to the quality and speed of their reviews. More specifically, I wish they would communicate openly with me regarding whether they are truly accepting the review task and whether they will be able to deliver their reviews in suggested time. By default, we suggest six weeks for peer reviewers to deliver, but this can naturally be discussed case by case.[22] I also expect that they will, of course, very carefully read the paper and then prepare a thorough and comprehensive review of the manuscript in as constructive way as possible. I am happy to say that what I expect is increasingly what I get, too.

However, having been working with some two hundred and fifty reviewers during the first years of my editorship, I have noticed the vast differences in peer reviewer behaviour from one scholar to another. Many reviewers fulfil my wishes, and even dreams, and provide me with excellent informative reviews in the suggested time. Many others do the same, but are a little bit delayed, and with many of them the deadline has been postponed by explicit agreement. However, unfortunately there are also scholars who do not seem to take review tasks seriously enough. Some of them seem to think time does not matter, and deliver their reviews very badly delayed. At worst, there are people who even never respond to our review queries. Some reviewers send very brief reviews: just one or two lines in which they either say that they think the manuscript is good and should be published, or that they do not like it, and recommend rejection. Often these least valuable reviews also come in very badly delayed. It may be needless to say I cannot put much weight on this type of reviews and that I tend not to bother these academics later on with review requests.

That said, perhaps one should not blame these people too much since normally journals do not pay anything for their reviewers. Also, as noted above, one of the reasons for large variation in review report quality is probably related to cultural factors. During my editorship in *EAR* I have become increasingly aware of the fact that in some European countries, for instance, the tradition of sincere commenting or evaluating colleagues' work is virtually inexistent. One should also pay attention to the fact that the

---

[19] What the notion of double-blind review actually means is far from being clear to everybody. For instance, I was once blamed (by the author of a paper that had got critical reviews) of not following the publicly announced double-blind review system of *EAR* as I had asked for the views of three reviewers on his/her paper!

[20] Fogarty & Ravenscroft (2000) provide a comprehensive critical analysis of the nature and implications of the peer review system within the accounting academia, drawing on the works of Giddens and Foucault in particular.

[21] For arguments for the double-blind review system, see, for example, Robey (2002).

[22] In *EAR* in 2000, the average review turnover time was 7 weeks, with the range of 1–25 weeks. In 2001 the corresponding figures were 8 weeks (average) and 1–26 weeks (range).

history of peer reviewing within the accounting academia has a surprisingly short history overall: the first journal to start this procedure was *The Accounting Review* in 1966 (Sheldahl 1992).

Normally editors wish that reviewers would try to be constructive and clear in what they say and ground their arguments with references to prior knowledge of the field or logic-based reasoning. Reviewers are also wished to pay attention to the importance of the research topic, the motivation and purposes of the study, its structure, integration to prior literature, credibility of the (potential) empirical work, clarity of language and style, and, most importantly, to the contribution the manuscript makes to prior understanding on the subject issue. In my view, evaluating the paper from the viewpoint of its contribution to prior knowledge should be crucial in review work. The issue of contribution cannot be compromised, and lacking contribution cannot be compensated by other qualities, however notable they would be.

However, though one can try to list the ingredients of a good review, what really constitutes one is a most complicated issue. Frankfurter (2000: 306) is worried about the rarity of clear standards for reviews: "Although some journals provide instructions for the reviewer, most do not, and there is no proof that ignoring the instructions would be cause to invalidate a negative review". I accept that peer reviewers can be broadly instructed regarding on what issues to focus when preparing their reviews, but I do not believe this type of activity can be thoroughly standardised. Similarly as the selection of peer reviewers, also the peer review evaluations themselves should be viewed as creative and subjective elements of the process. In my experience, for any given manuscript there can be an infinite number of both differing excellent and low-quality reviews. Preparing a useful review is an art in a fundamental sense: you can recognise a high quality review when you encounter it, but you cannot establish definite *a priori* criteria of goodness for it, nor can you program how to prepare it.[23]

Editorial Feedback

Normally within two or three months reviewers send their reports to the editor, who then takes a comprehensive evaluative look at the case and draws his/her editorial conclusions.[24] Though there are fine-tuning alternatives, the three major editorial decision options are: accept without revision (takes place extremely seldom in refereed journals), revise and resubmit (occurs quite often) or reject (occurs quite often, too).[25] Together with the editorial letter, the reviews and (sometimes) annotated copies of the manuscript are sent to the author.[26]

---

[23] This comes down to the difficulty of even defining the notion "quality", see Pirsig (1974).

[24] If a journal has not provided editorial feedback on a submission within 4–5 months, then I think it is quite appropriate to contact the editor and ask about the progress of the review process.

[25] In addition to the quality of submissions, of course the proportions of these major conclusion alternatives depend on the relationship between the number of submissions the journal receives per year and the number of pages the editor has in use.

[26] In *EAR* in 2000, the first editorial letter was sent, on average, in 12 weeks from receiving the submission, with a range of 1–26 weeks. In 2001 the corresponding figures were 12 weeks (average) and 1–29 weeks (range).

If the paper is rejected, normally that is the end of the case, though sometimes authors start arguing against the reviewers and the editor. This takes place quite seldom, and probably even more seldom leads to any change in the editorial decision. However, personally I think it is always good if the authors who feel they have become badly treated by a journal go back to the editor with their worries. Issues need to be settled in depth, and open dialogue should be viewed as a natural part of the functioning of the academia.

If the editorial decision is 'revise and resubmit', then it is up to the author what to do. Sometimes authors decide to withdraw the paper at this stage since they do not agree with the views of the reviewers and the editor, or they agree but think the required revision is beyond their resources. In the "revise and resubmit" decision there are many alternative ways open for the editor to control the intensity of encouragement offered. It may be informative to open my files from *EAR* at this point and illustrate the main options by a few sample quotes from my editorial correspondence.[27]

(1) *After consideration, I would like to leave the door open for revision and resubmission for you. This means that you should take a very careful look at the feedback you now receive, and consider whether you think you can solve the issues raised. It is clear to me a quite substantive elaboration will be needed here. In addition, you should pay attention that there is a risk that this study will not become publishable even after your serious revision work. So, this is up to you to contemplate. If you need further advice, please do not hesitate to come back to me.*

The way (1) of putting the decision means that reviewers and the editor have been critical towards the paper. The paper has been truly close to the edge, and the editor has contemplated rejecting it. However, at least one of the review reports has included some positive tones, signalling publication potential after substantial revision. This decision means basically only that resubmission is allowed (or not forbidden), but that is all from the editor's side. In this case the author should very seriously consider whether the paper really can be rescued, since there is a considerable risk that the revision effort will be wasted time (at least in the case of this journal).

(2) *I think the topic of your paper has interest value to the readers of EAR. However, I also think the concerns of the reviewers are important and worth consideration. Hence, I encourage you to take a very careful look at the feedback you now receive, make a serious attempt to revise the paper, and thereafter resubmit it to EAR.*

The decision of type (2) should perhaps be regarded as the most typical one, overall. Here the peer reviewers have regarded the paper as potentially publishable, but, on the other hand, they have raised concerns, too. The editor's attitude is quite positive as well and hence there is a clear encouraging tone. In this case the probability of rejection after

---

[27] These are of course just parts of my editorial letters. They normally include brief one-paragraph outlines of each peer reviewer's key points and then the editorial conclusion parts such as those quoted here. In the 'revise and resubmit' cases, this is often followed by more detailed editorial suggestions and hints regarding on which issues the author(s) should particularly focus in developing the paper towards becoming publishable.

revision is normally quite small. However, this assumes that the author will make a serious and careful revision job.

(3) *The topic of your paper is certainly of interest value to the readers of EAR, and given these peer reviews, I am happy to conclude that I see its future promising. However, the paper still needs some further elaboration, too. Hence, I would like to warmly encourage you to take a very careful look at the feedback you now receive, make an attempt to revise the paper along the suggested lines, and thereafter resubmit it to EAR.*

Decision of type (3) should be regarded as very positive indeed. The peer reviewers have signalled clearly that there is publication potential in the manuscript, the editor agrees with them, and the remaining elaboration need is considered quite small. These papers normally never become rejected during the rest of the process, given that the author makes a true attempt to improve the paper along the suggested lines.

There is one special type of situation, which needs particular commenting. One of my recent editorial letters offers an example of this:

(4) *In fact, you should already be familiar with the report of Reviewer 2 since you have probably seen it before: this review is prepared on your manuscript when your study was submitted to [name of another journal]. Accidentally I sent the paper to the same reviewer as [name of another journal] had used. However, since there is basically no difference in the editorial ambitions of [name of another journal] and EAR, nor in their editorial policies regarding the publication of this type of papers, and Reviewer 2 finds the paper practically, if not completely, equal to the version s/he had seen before, I did not see any obstacle for using the same review for my purposes as well.*

This was part of a reject letter on a paper, which was sent to *EAR* in practically, if not entirely, similar shape as it was rejected in another international refereed journal. By chance, I happened to send the paper to the very same reviewer who had recommended its rejection for that other journal's editor — it can be a small world! If I see no grounds for regarding the earlier prepared review (like differences in journals' policies or ambitions, or low quality of the review in question), as I did not in this case, then I tend to use these reviews as the basis for my editorial decision, too.[28] I need to add I wish to particularly counteract to the kind of gaming behaviour by accounting researchers this example illustrates: if a paper is rejected in one refereed journal based on well-grounded criticism, then its authors normally need to do something more than just trying to 'shop around' and find another victim.[29] At least I wish to signal this clearly to the market what comes to *EAR*.

---

[28] I am well aware there can be different opinions on what is ethical in this kind of situations (see Fogarty & Ravenscroft 1998, 2000). The policy I apply was raised at one of the Editorial team meetings of *EAR*, at which it was thoroughly analysed and discussed, and eventually unanimously accepted.

[29] Fogarty & Ravenscroft (1998) seem to assume that all authors make a true effort to tackle the clear weaknesses of their manuscripts identified in the first journal before submitting them to the next one. My experience yet tells this is not always the case.

Revising and Resubmitting

Most often papers are indeed revised and thereafter resubmitted. When reading editors' letters and peer reviewers' reports, there are risks to both directions: one can read the criticism too negatively and unnecessarily give up, but one can also read them too positively, and hence invest too little into its elaboration, and the paper will be rejected in the second round.

In my experience, younger researchers tend to have difficulties in understanding the meaning of editorial letters and reviews. I sense that they, likely to be inexperienced to open critique, quite often read them too pessimistically. What may at the first glance look like harsh criticism can very often be turned into most constructive comments, extremely useful in developing the paper further. Also, if one receives long reviewer reports, one should normally regard it as a positive signal. The worst papers get typically the shortest reviews. In addition, one needs to remember the old rule of publication processes: 'You only need to survive the first review round'. Accordingly, once a paper has passed the first review round without rejection, then the risk of its rejection during later review rounds has diminished considerably. However, one should remember that such risk still exists, and the more so the less the editor encourages the author in his/her editorial letter. In my view, just if possible, younger researchers should try to get help from more experienced colleagues regarding how to read editorial letters and review reports and what kind of revision policy one should adopt.

Revision needs can include just improving the language and style of the report. This is normally quite easy, even though professional language support may need to be hired. Very often revision requirements include making the motivation and purpose, and especially contribution, clearer to the reader. Another typical need for improvement is to better integrate the study with prior knowledge, or simply to make better job in reviewing prior literature in order to develop the hypotheses of the study, for instance. In the case of empirical studies, very often reviewers have concerns about model specification issues or the ways statistical analyses are conducted. Perhaps the most complicated improvement requirements are those in which reviewers think additional empirical data needs to be acquired. Often this turns out to be impossible, and the paper is withdrawn from the process, or rejected in the next review round.

Normally the resubmitted papers are sent back to the very same first round reviewers. What had taken place in the first review round is, more or less, repeated, though the reviews are normally much shorter in the second round. Typically they concentrate on whether the revised paper has improved in the dimensions expected by reviewers in their first round reviews. There can be several peer review rounds altogether.[30] Whatever are the elaboration needs, the fundamental question for the author to ponder is what s/he attempts to do in the paper itself, and what issues s/he just attempts to explain and clarify in the memo of revision. This is a most critical trade-off. Indeed, a carefully prepared memo of revision (normally a report to each reviewer and a summary to the editor) is of vast significance when a revised paper is resubmitted. However, one needs

---

[30] For instance in *EAR*, the papers accepted for publication during the years 2000 and 2001 needed, on average, 2.3 review rounds.

to be careful not to overestimate the potential such memos have. Quite often even experienced scholars fall into the trap of the so-called 'quick and easy' revision solution: they tend to make only the easy revisions to the paper itself, and believe they can avoid the more challenging revisions by just washing them away in the memo of revision. Normally this does not work.

Quote (5) from one of my recent editorial letters exemplifies what can take place during the second review round, at worst from the author's perspective:

(5) *The second round peer reviews indicate that both reviewers are far from being satisfied with the paper even after revision. In my editorial feedback letter after the first review round I emphasised that a quite substantial revision would be needed. I understand you made a true attempt to rescue the paper after the criticism in the first review round. However, the second round reviews offer me a consistent and definite view of the peer reviewers — who both are qualified experts of the field of research in question — that the paper is far from being improved enough. They also both think its problems remain to be large indeed. In sum, since the revision attempt suggests that the pursued improvement of this paper, measured by the criteria of EAR, cannot be accomplished, I have to unfortunately conclude that the publication process of this manuscript will no longer be continued.*

Hence, papers really *can* be rejected also during the further evaluation rounds. The reason can be that the paper was, after all, too difficult to rescue given the resources the author had in use. Another potential reason is that the author fell into the trap of the "quick and easy" revision attempt when the editorial decision letter and the peer reviews of the prior evaluation round required something more.

Happy End: Forthcoming Publication

Once a paper is accepted for publication, only a few routine issues remain to be done. These are mostly taken care by the publisher, which in due course sends the proofs to the author for final check. Often publishers offer only very little time (say 48 hours, for instance) for authors' proof checking, and they tend to be very dismissive to any attempts to touch the substance of the paper at this stage. So, this phase is meant to be a technical check only. Depending on the queue the journal has for ready-for-publication papers, in due course the paper will finally be published in the journal.

Concluding Comments

Based on the stakeholder notion of research journals and my own experiences as an actor in this field, I have examined and discussed the ways accounting research journals function. I believe an enhanced understanding of their process will help us collaborate better in the context of this kind of coalitions. I examined how editors and peer reviewers tend to do their tasks, and offered hints regarding how to 'read' their actions from the submitting author's perspective. My major argument was targeted against the currently very real threat of adopting purely instrumental notions of research journals and scholarly publishing — one can see a lot of indications of the 'commodity' perspective to academic work around nowadays, not least if one acts as an editor of a research journal. In contrast to this, I believe research journals should genuinely keep to being forums for publishing articles that matter due to their contents. Several examples and specific details from the journal for which I currently serve as editor, i.e. *European Accounting Review*, illustrated the analysis above. Much of what I argued should be viewed as reflecting my subjective aspirations rather than so far accomplishments with that journal. Research journals are complicated collectives to keep in balance and strong.

References

Cyert, R. M., & March, J. G. (1963). *A behavioral theory of the firm*. Englewood Cliffs, N. J.: Prentice-Hall.

Day, R. A. (1983). *How to write and publish a scientific paper*. Philadelphia: ISI Press.

Fogarty, T., & Ravenscroft, S. (1998). Ethical problems posed by the repeated reviewer in academic peer review. *Journal of Information Ethics*, *7*(2), 45–66.

Fogarty, T., & Ravenscroft, S. (2000). Making accounting knowledge: peering at power. *Critical Perspectives on Accounting*, *11*(4), 409–431.

Frankfurter, G. M. (2000). The young finance faculty's guide to publishing. Inspired by and after (rather loosely) Benjamin Britten. *International Review of Financial Analysis*, *9*(3), 299–314.

Gross, P. G., & Levitt, N. (1994). *Higher superstition: The academic left and its quarrels with science*. Baltimore and London: The Johns Hopkins University Press.

Hacking, I. (1999). *The social construction of what?* Cambridge, MA: Harvard University Press.

Hines, R. D. (1988). Financial accounting: in communicating reality, we construct reality. *Accounting, Organizations and Society*, *13*(3), 251–161.

Latour, B. (1987). *Science in action*. Cambridge, MA: Harvard University Press.

Latour, B. (1999). *Pandora's hope. Essays on the reality of social sciences*. Cambridge, MA.: Harvard University Press.

Lukka, K., & Mouritsen, J. (2002). Homogeneity or heterogeneity of research in management accounting? *European Accounting Review*, *11*(4), 805–811.

Parker, L., Guthrie, J., & Gray, R. (1998). Accounting and management research: passwords from the gatekeepers. *Accounting, Auditing and Accountability Journal*, *11*(4), 371–402.

Pirsig, R. M. (1974). *Zen and the art of motorcycle maintenance: An enquiry into values*. London: Corgi.

Robey, D. (2002). Is *Information and Organization* an A journal? *Information and Organization*, *12*(4), 213–218.

Sheldahl, T. (1992). *The American accounting association in its third quarter century 1966–1991: Central governance and administration*. New York: Garland Press.

Zimmerman, J. L. (2001). Conjectures regarding empirical managerial accounting research. *Journal of Accounting and Economics*, *32*(1–3), 411–427.

Willmott, H. C. (1995). Managing the academics: commodification and control in the development of university education in the UK. *Human Relations*, *48*(9), 993–1027.

Chapter 26

Research and Public Practice Accounting

Stuart Turley

Introduction

Many people have a general perception that accounting is a practical and technical discipline, an activity defined by established conventions and rules of practice rather than one associated with more profound philosophical questions. It is somewhat discouraging to be asked the question — "what kind of research can you possibly do on accounting?" Periodically events such as the restatement of the valuations in Marconi's financial statements or the failure of Enron will lead to greater awareness of both the significance and the limitations of practice, but the associated sense of surprise really serves to illustrate again the underlying perception that accounting is simply a routinised practical discipline. This chapter discusses some aspects of the links between research and practice in accounting. In particular, the chapter focuses on public practice accounting services and, based on experience of research in this field over several years, looks at issues researchers should expect to confront in developing projects and in communicating with practitioners about research.

For the purposes of the discussion, research concerned with public practice accountancy is taken as covering:

- The services provided by individuals and firms established as accounting practices;
- The practitioners and firms who act as suppliers of those services;
- The links between public practice and the organization and activities of professional associations; and
- The links between public practice and economic activities and policy agendas.

The primary focus is the organization, conduct and communication of research involving public practice, broadly defined as above. So the chapter does not address all aspects of the relationship between accounting research and accounting practice. The study of most areas of accounting in some senses involves investigation of how accounting is practiced, for example managerial accounting within organizations, financial statement analysis or the use of accounting techniques in relation to public

The Real Life Guide to Accounting Research: A Behind-the-Scenes View of Using Qualitative Research Methods
ISBN: 0-08-043972-1

services. Nor is the chapter specifically about the general topic of the relationship between research and practice and the debate between the merits of theoretical and applied research.

A significant feature of research on public practice is that it involves addressing and interacting with a more diverse audience than may be the case in some areas of research. Practitioners may themselves be the subjects of the research, they may be the source of information and control data about the subject of inquiry and they may be significant potential recipients and commentators on the research output. In other words, research involving public practice gives rise to issues regarding participation (persuading practitioners to act as research subjects), assistance (accessing resources and data provided by practitioners) and communication (informing those involved with public practice about research contributions and findings). For these reasons, it is important to consider how to address a practitioner audience at the same time as constructing credible academic research. Importantly, this applies not only when reporting results but also when devising topics and seeking participation and assistance in the conduct of the research. Thus this chapter is about interacting with practitioners about research, not just communicating results and findings.

The comments in this chapter are based on experiences of attempting to bring research into the domain of public practice over several years and are organized into four broad sections. The first section discusses possible general perspectives that underlie research concerned with public practice and the related underlying research questions. Identifying these motivations can be important in engaging the interest of those outside the academic community. The need for interaction between the researcher and practitioners has implications for the way in which research projects will be structured and conducted. The second main section of the chapter looks at these practical issues of design and negotiating access, while the third reflects on certain additional matters, particularly concerning the 'ethics' of research, confidentiality, maintaining independence and avoiding the research being captured by the practice agenda. Finally, some brief comments are offered regarding research topics where new studies have the potential to make a particular contribution at the present time.

Why is Research on Public Practice Accounting of Interest?

In constructing a new project, as well as the choice of specific topic and questions about theory and methodology, the researcher has also to consider the broader approach being applied in the investigation of public practice. That is, it is important to have a view regarding the underlying reasons why the topic is of interest. I have found that articulating these motivations can be of value in generating interest in the research and disseminating the results. Essentially the underlying perspectives reveal potential answers to the initial question of why research on public practice might be considered interesting and worthwhile, i.e. "why bother with this research area?" Three possible broad approaches are discussed below, reflecting motivations that have informed projects I have been involved in — the agendas of professional and public policy debates, researching public practice as an industry, and analyzing the practices and behaviours of individuals and firms engaged in public practice services. This is neither a comprehensive list of all possible approaches nor a rigorous research classification but draws on personal experience of a number of research projects in this field.

Before turning to the three broad approaches, however, it is important to emphasise that research concerned with analyzing the activities undertaken in public practice accountancy and their significance does not have to involve applied research conducted for the purpose of serving practice. It is not uncommon for questions in academic-practitioner forums to be phrased in terms of how the research, whether theoretical, empirical or applied, should influence or inform the manner in which accounting is conducted in practice. In the extreme, this approach can take impact on practice as almost the sole criterion by which the value of research should be judged — something that most academic researchers would take exception to. The practicing community often raises the call for relevance, but relevance in terms of immediate technical considerations such as guidance with respect to the choice of an accounting standard. While practical impact is undoubtedly an important issue for researchers to consider, has its own value and motivates many engaged in more applied research, it is important to be clear that this approach is not being assumed *or* advocated here. Rather the value of researching public practice accountancy is that it can make more transparent, and improve understanding of, an important area of human activity that is heavily implicated in many aspects of society and the conduct of economic transactions. That is, the focus of the discussion is research on practice and it is important to recognize the distinction between this and research for practice. While most researchers would of course hope that their work would have some impact, research on practice does not necessarily have an objective to change or 'improve' practice. Change or improvement may follow but that is not a necessary underlying objective — changed practice does not have to be the output of the research. Nor is it necessary to take a particular perspective on the difficult question of what exactly would constitute 'improvement'. Research concerned with practice can be approached from many perspectives — critical, reflexive, theoretical, practical — but a concern for understanding the manner in which accounting and related services are performed in practice and how this interacts with other policy debates in the economy and society is an underlying common theme.

Professional and Public Policy Agendas

Frequently ideas for research questions arise because an issue of practice is a matter of current or emerging debate. Thus, an important motivation behind much research on public practice is interest in aspects of the professional and public policy agendas. If one is concerned about how accounting and auditing practice contributes to economy and society, then issues on professional and public policy agendas provide important potential sources of evidence to investigate this contribution. For example, I became interested in research in the market for audit services because of apparent concern regarding the developing market power of the largest accounting firms, in investigating audit firm methodologies because of their relevance to how (and whether) auditing makes an effective contribution to financial reporting, and in studying the operation of audit committees because of their rising significance during the 1990s as a means of addressing corporate governance issues. The corporate reporting environment and the market for professional services have seen many significant developments in the period of the last few decades and continue to be areas of rapid change. Put simply, I have found that the variety of issues under consideration and the proposals for change at any point in time provide a rich source of potential research topics!

To illustrate this point, a short round up of the environment in the U.K. alone within the recent past, shows that several public or quasi-public policy reports have been published with various issues under consideration and proposals for change: the Higgs Report on non-executive directors (Higgs 2003), the Smith guidelines for audit committees (Smith 2003), the Coordinating Group on Accountancy and Auditing (DTI 2003a), the review of Regulation of the Accountancy Profession (DTI 2003b), the DTI consultation on Fair Values (DTI 2003c) and the EC Communication on Auditing (EC 2003). Many of the matters in these reports have implications for public practice, for example the relationship between audit committees and external auditors, communications between them, the overall regulatory structure in public practice accounting and auditing, and the responsibility for guidance on ethical behaviour in public practice.

Building links between research plans and policy agendas by investigating what are matters of current debate may well assist in improving access to data and individuals — that is, in constructing viable projects. Certainly a lack of awareness of developments in the professional and public policy arenas is likely to undermine confidence in the quality of the research amongst those practitioners with whom the researcher comes into contact. In practical terms it is therefore important to be aware of the current practicing environment. Even if the underlying interest is in broad general research questions, the best way of investigating may be to look at illustrative specific issues of current debate. Also, it is often the fact that a topic has become a matter of debate at a particular point in time that is of interest in itself. Part of the purpose of the research may be to reflect on the processes by which policy agendas are determined and what this tells us about the nature and significance of public practice.

Two potential pitfalls to watch for in this kind of research are worth mentioning. First, it is important to guard against the danger of being driven solely by a policy agenda in the choice of research topic and conduct of a project, and against the demand for definitive policy recommendations. Research on matters of debate in the professional, business and regulatory spheres does not necessarily have to produce the 'answer' to a policy problem. The researcher's approach should retain concern for the quality of the content of the research rather than the generation of recommendations, and it may well be that by illuminating a problem more fully the outcome of the research is to complicate choices rather than to simplify them. Second, with current policy debates, there is often a demand for quick results. The most extreme example I have experienced in this regard was while working at the Research Board of the Institute of Chartered Accountants in England and Wales, when I received a request to "produce some research" relating to insider dealing (then a subject receiving the kind of attention more recently given to executive compensation) in about ten days! The particular piece of work that resulted did end up being quoted in *The Times*, but it doesn't feature on my CV!

Public Practice as an Industry

In the mid 1980s, a large part of one summer was spent manually extracting data on auditors and audit fees from some 1000 sets of financial statements, either hard copy or microfiche copies. This was an extremely laborious task, but it was the only way to build up a sufficient data set of this information, due to the limitations of electronic databases at that time. The motivation behind this work was to investigate auditing as part of public practice services in terms of the economic transactions taking place — fees as evidence of pricing, related to size of the business being audited and the supplier firm, continuity of supply and how the market for audit services was changing (Moizer & Turley 1989). Although referring to the accountancy practice as an 'industry' is sometimes felt to be somewhat pejorative, this can simply mean that the provision of accounting and related services through public practice can be approached as a defined area of economic activity and analysed as such — as an industry. It is clear that some of the major suppliers in this industry, the largest accounting firms, and the services they supply, are of considerable economic and societal significance.

From this perspective, a number of aspects of the basic economics of public practice accountancy have now been investigated in order to identify, for example, market structure, pricing of services, and terms of competition. A considerable body of research has been built up following this type of approach. Measures have been established of the degree of concentration of supply in the auditing services market in many countries, possible pricing differentials between the major firms and other suppliers have been tested, and possible effects of reputation on many factors have been investigated. Currently a wider set of information is available relating to the economics of the auditor-client relationship, for example information on non-audit fees and even fees classified according to different types of non-audit service, and this type of information is more readily available electronically. However, as the quality of data improves it is important that research does not simply replicate what has already been well-established in the literature, such as the high level of market concentration, but rather uses the data to ask novel questions, for example focusing on the exceptions rather than the generality.

One aspect of the industrial economics of public practice where data has never been easily accessible and that consequently it has always been difficult to investigate is the production side of accountancy services. While it is now easy to undertake work on the pricing side of the activity, through published fees, the cost and production functions remain relatively uninvestigated. The necessary information is closely guarded by the practice firms, partly because they regard it as commercially sensitive. Some researchers have been successful in gaining access to firm records on time and staff grades assigned to different areas of an engagement, but such studies are still very few in number and there remains considerable scope for further contributions.

Firms, Practices and Behaviour

In addition to policy issues and the economics of public practice, a further possible focus for research investigation is the content of the activities that comprise practice and the practitioners themselves engaged in those activities. There are a number of possible aspects to looking at practice and practitioners. For example it is possible to view the judgements, decisions and other actions of accountants in terms of their ability to illustrate particular facets of individual and collective human behaviour. A considerable volume of research has been developed applying ideas drawn from the psychology of human judgement and decision-making to audit practitioners. Another aspect is the technical process that makes up a service such as auditing, facets of what might be called the 'product design' in public practice.

Clearly there would be potential difficulties in approaching practitioners with a research agenda that set out the objectives as evaluating how 'good' they are at making judgements and decisions or what is the quality of the product or services they offer. However much one might argue that practitioners should themselves be very interested in such matters, access might just be a problem! To research what is really happening in practice it may therefore be best to find specific topics of interest and currency, but which nonetheless have the ability to provide evidence relevant to more fundamental questions.

An example of an area of interest at the level of the firm is the study of the way in which services are developed and delivered, specifically the development of audit methodologies. Linking back to the idea of an industry mentioned above, this topic can be seen as 'product innovation' at the firm level. At two points in time I have embarked on projects investigating the audit methodologies of public practice firms (Turley & Cooper 1991; Lemon *et al.* 2000). I would have to confess that I do not find the detailed content of the audit evidence process the most interesting subject imaginable! However, my primary interest in this research is less the detailed aspects of the methodology *per se*, but rather the fact that the way in which the audit process is constructed and conceptualized in firms indicates something about how the role of the service and its place in society are understood by service providers. What I find of interest is the way in which audit firms and practitioners see their own 'product' and the service they provide, because ultimately this reveals something about the manner in which they understand their contribution to business reporting. I have found that practitioners are very willing to talk about, and listen to presentations about, the development of what they do. Sometimes this is because they perceive that they have discovered a new way of constructing the audit process, sometimes because they are interested to try to find out what other firms are doing in this area and sometimes because of genuine uncertainty about concepts and procedures. Investigating the development of methodology has revealed points of wider significance about how practitioners see the role of auditing, such as the significance of 'client service' objectives, the balance between ideas of attestation and assessing risk and whether the engagement is viewed in terms of the single set of financial statements or as a continuing relationship with the business organization. Thus, building projects around apparent current innovations and developments in methodology has provided an opportunity to consider broader questions, effectively by using what is changing in practice as a case study for the wider underlying issues.

Conducting Research on Public Practice

The basic principles for conducting a research study involving public practice accountancy are not fundamentally different from those that apply more generally to the design and execution of research work. General questions about research design, the choice of research methods and their execution are outside the consideration in this chapter. However, as commented earlier, I have found that a feature of research on public practice is that it often involves considerable contact with and cooperation from the practitioner community and possibly sponsorship from professional organisations. Conducting research in this context gives rise to a number of specific practical issues and potential pitfalls about constructing credible projects and engaging practitioners in research. These considerations — making projects work rather than general issues of methodology and methods — are discussed in this and the next section.

Negotiating Access

Achieving the desired level of access is frequently a problem in research design, largely because it is not easy for the researcher to determine exactly what kind of access is going to be obtained and what quality of data will be available for analysis. Research on public practice requires going beyond the kind of data that is readily available from published sources and established databases. Much of the research I have learnt from as well as that I have been involved with has involved the generation of new data, often through qualitative methods such as surveys, interviews and case studies. For certain types of data, access can be thwarted by the barrier of client confidentiality.

My experience is that access very much depends on what you are asking for! I have had significant assistance from practitioners through interviews, participation in surveys, support with access to case study sites and in forums to assist with the dissemination of project findings. Practitioners are in general quite willing to discuss their activities in the abstract, for example how they structure and conduct their audits, the rationale behind their methodologies and the benefits of their approach, but asking for access to real data on how assignments have actually been executed in practice will almost certainly result in refusal on the grounds of confidentiality. The position of practitioners on this point probably reflects both a legitimate concern for confidentiality and a certain amount of defensiveness about practice, but it certainly frustrates many potential research ideas.

Two examples of potential projects that failed because of denial of access illustrate this problem. In the late 1980s, I developed a study intended to gather data about audit firm liability. The idea was to go beyond the limited information available in the public domain through settled cases to look at evidence in insurance companies' files on out of court settlements and gather information about the underlying triggers for claims against accounting firms, the stated basis alleged for negligence, outcomes and scale of settlements etc. At the time only two brokerage companies acted for almost all the U.K. accounting firms. One, which represented most of the smaller firms and one of the international top tier, was happy to cooperate and agreed to complete a *pro forma* document (protecting the identity of the case) for a sample of claims. The second insurer represented the remainder of the top tier. Although initial responses gave some grounds for optimism, the barrier of confidentiality was eventually used to deny access, despite support for the study from the ICAEW. More recently, having undertaken a project documenting developments in the audit methodologies of large firms, I approached one firm for assistance in providing data disclosing what had changed when the methodology was implemented, as reflected in factors such as hours recorded against different areas of the audit and evidence activities, such as analysis and testing. Again, despite the fact that no specific identification of clients was needed, the argument of confidentiality prevented the project going ahead.

In contrast, experience tends to suggest that access to practitioners themselves is often comparatively straightforward. Requests to be able to talk to certain individuals about their experience and approach to public practice matters commonly meet with a favourable response. There can sometimes be an initial scepticism about what agenda is being pursued in the research and whether this carries any threats for practice firms, but this is often based on lack of information and too much attention to the pages of *Accountancy Age*. It has to be remembered that relatively few practitioners have actually been exposed to academic approaches and hence some lack of understanding is inevitable. In fact I have generally found that practitioners are often very willing to discuss aspects of their work with researchers, although the usual caveats with any interview study apply concerning the interpretation of what is said and the representativeness of views expressed.

There is no easy answer to overcoming the problem of insufficient access to information, but a few practical guidelines are:

- Try to establish contact and lines of communication with individuals within the organizations of interest rather than the organization as an institution, in order to build the kind of confidence that will facilitate access.
- Be prepared to make explicit what it is you want to do — for example, while a detailed list of specific questions may not be necessary, it is helpful to send interviewees an agenda of the topics and areas of questioning to be covered. Access is more difficult if there is uncertainty about what is being requested.
- Undertake appropriate background research, including knowledge of the organization, as this again can help build confidence about the authority of the proposed research.
- Be prepared to give some undertakings about the way in which data will be treated and disclosed, and to show reports, possibly make presentations etc. — although a commitment, these things are only likely to enhance the quality of the research.

Reporting to Multiple Audiences

A particular feature of much research on public practice is the need to communicate with different audiences. Indeed, it is desirable to be able to reach both practicing and academic communities with the output of research as this gives additional opportunities for the findings to be discussed and may also increase the potential for future research opportunities.

It may be relevant here to make some comments regarding the impact of the Research Assessment Exercise (RAE) on research activity. Although some policy discussions have argued that the RAE should take into account and reward research that has practical relevance and impact, in general individual accounting academics perceive that the demands of the RAE place emphasis on publication through refereed journals almost to the exclusion of all else. A possible effect of this perception is that academics are less willing to take time to write articles which might communicate the results of their research to wider audiences or to write reports in monograph form for publication as standalone documents. Yet it is precisely these types of output that will most engage practitioners in thinking about the contribution research makes to current issues. My point here is not really about how the RAE should approach the task of assessing the quality of research, but rather that there is still a need to promote academics' communication to practitioners, and thus the aspiration of encouraging practitioners to give more attention to research. In my view, there is still a place for varied forms of research output — monographs, short articles and research summaries as well as journal papers — and this is an important issue for the academic accounting community to recognize.

The manner of presentation of findings in reports or papers produced for different audiences is likely to vary, but it is important that the essential message of the research should stay the same. There is little purpose in producing one message for the practitioner community and another when addressing academics. It is often valuable to take advantage of opportunities to present research work in professional forums. This may be the only way of obtaining practitioner reaction to research and the additional perspectives and challenges that arise can lead to improvements in the research. Also, the contacts from such forums have the potential to assist with access to sites and information in the future. There are insufficient opportunities for interchange between the practicing and academic communities and those that are available should therefore be made the most of.

While researchers should make efforts to ensure their work reaches practitioners, it is also appropriate to make some demands on those readers to come to terms with the content of the research. When writing a research report that may be read by practitioners, it is sensible to be aware of the 'curse' of the executive summary. This kind of document is often advocated on the grounds of the time pressures on potential readers. However, if this is all that is read then the danger increases that a few selective points from the research will be taken out of context. In a monograph reporting a project on the audit expectations gap, my co-authors and I, conscious of the need to include some policy implications from the research, made reference to the potential for greater independent regulatory oversight of audit appointments (Humphrey *et al.* 1992). Perhaps unsurprisingly, this was the single comment given most attention in the professional press, with the report being described as containing a "ticking timebomb of revolutionary reform" (*Financial Times*, 1 October 1992) causing 'red faces' at the ICAEW, which had in fact sponsored and willingly published the research.

Funding and Cooperation with Professional Organisations

Mention was made earlier of the fact that looking at topics of current interest in policy agendas can have the advantage of opening doors and improving access to data, particularly qualitative. An additional link between the choice of topic and the feasibility of investigation is the fact that funding from sources such as the research committees of the professional bodies may be more easily available. The committees of all the U.K. professional bodies have only limited budgets to allocate and it is natural for them to see research relevant to current topics as the best way to have as much impact for the limited spend.

There is a tension but also a mutual dependence between the researcher and the research funding arm of a professional institute. The latter wants impact and probably prompt delivery of the project. Impact is frequently seen partly in terms of reaching the institute's membership, because that helps the administration to justify the spending of membership subscriptions (even though the funding may be drawn from charitable endowments rather than directly from subscriptions) and partly in terms of newsworthiness and giving a basis for representations to be made in policy debates.

The researcher probably wants to focus on fundamental issues, rather than be forced into headline conclusions and is probably juggling the demands of a number of projects as well as other academic responsibilities. There is a danger that the sponsoring organization can see itself as having "employed" the researcher to do something, rather than simply providing a grant for a project under the researcher's control with few strings attached. At the same time, alongside this tension there is an element of mutual benefit. As well as expertise, researchers offer credibility to a professional body's activities, and so the academic contribution is very valuable to the bodies. From the researcher's point of view, as well as the basic funds to make a project happen, funding from a professional body offers possible assistance with access and additional opportunities for publication because the bodies are generally interested in 'products' they can point to other than just academic journal papers.

Perhaps the biggest potential source of tension between professional sponsors and researchers is on the timeliness of delivery of the output of projects. The practitioners on sponsoring bodies genuinely find it difficult to understand why academics appear to be so poor at meeting deadlines and it has to be acknowledged that this is too often an area of valid criticism of researchers. A large proportion of those of us who have received sponsorship from professional bodies have to confess that at the least they have been over optimistic in their schedule for delivering reports! The only defence to offer is perhaps one that rushing the product is likely simply to result in compromises on quality, and therefore possibly longer delay in the end. However, this isn't a strong argument and really we should acknowledge that this is an area where we could do more to meet practitioner expectations, certainly for projects on topics which are going to date quickly.

Understanding between practitioners and researchers is helped by opportunities for dialogue and communication. This is an area where the professional bodies have played a useful role in providing funding for conferences and symposiums where both academics and practitioners participate. Having been involved in organizing such an event over several years up to the late 1990s (the Financial Accounting and Auditing Research Conference), I have always been struck by the extent to which people from both groups value the interaction. However, a weakness in this dialogue is the fact that it doesn't seem to penetrate very far into the profession. That is, the participation from the public practice community often seems to be from the same small group of people who are persuaded of the value of research. It would be more encouraging if a wider level of participation from practice could be mobilized but currently there are too few meetings when both groups participate to be optimistic on this front.

Ethical Issues

In addition to matters of access, communication and cooperation there are a number of potential issues that can provide more personal challenges for the individual researchers engaged in projects on accountancy in practice. Again these issues are not exclusive to this area of research but they do have particular significance in that context. In general the rule is that these points need not be a problem providing they are properly thought about in advance.

Confidentiality

The nature of much research on public practice involves consideration of confidentiality for two main reasons. First it may be that the research involves access to material that is not otherwise in the public domain. This could include material considered of proprietary value or data that must be treated with care for client confidentiality. Second, it is often the case that research in this area involves the use of methods such as interviews and survey work to collect the data. The quality of information collected by these means partly depends on creating conditions in which participants can give frank and open expression of their views and disclose relevant information. One of the necessary conditions for this to happen is confidence that the researcher will deal with information with the appropriate confidentiality.

Sometimes it may be necessary to give undertakings to protect identity, the anonymity of comments, etc. For example, in my work on audit methodologies some individual firms have required a signature against written undertakings that their material will be not be disclosed other than as agreed. This commercial sensitivity contrasts with others who have been willing to hand over computer disc versions and one firm that publicized its new methodology through a publication issued to members of the American Accounting Association before even staff in the U.K. offices (Bell *et al.* 1997)

A further factor can arise where access is obtained to a number of individuals within the same organization. Here it is not a case of protecting the firm's interest but rather ensuring that individuals are not constrained by fear that what they say will somehow be reported to others within their organization in a way that could be prejudicial to their interests. For example, it is not uncommon when undertaking case study research to provide a summary of the case to participants in order to confirm the understanding obtained by the researcher. However it may be better to dispense with this procedure if the effect will be that individuals' anonymity will be removed and consequently that they will be less forthcoming in their disclosure to the researcher. Nonetheless, where an undertaking has been given to obtain clearance before reporting something that has been said, or disclosing information that has been provided, it is appropriate to fulfil that commitment.

Maintaining Independence and Avoiding Capture by the Professional Agenda

When research involves an element of partnership with those engaged in professional activities, a potential issue that may be relevant is the need to avoid the project simply being used to serve the practitioner's agenda alone. This can happen because the researcher loses independence or because the project becomes 'captured' and this is something that applies to both the conduct and the reporting of the research. The benefits of partnership, in terms of assistance with access and the contribution of a non-academic perspective, are not to be underestimated, but the integrity of the research process has to be maintained.

In the case of the research project referred to earlier on developments in audit methodologies (Lemon *et al.* 2000), the cooperation with those involved in the standard setting process was critical to being able to undertake the research, but it also meant that as a group of researchers it was necessary to be aware of two factors. First, because the work had effectively been initiated through interest from the Auditing Practices Board staff, it was apparent that there was an interest in establishing research that could help influence international cooperation on standard setting and in placing the developments in practice on the International Auditing and Assurance Standards Board (IAASB) agenda. Second, the three researchers became members of a joint working group of standard setters and practitioners from the United States, Canada and the United Kingdom and so were not only providing an input of research evidence but also participated in the process of deciding on what kind of recommendation, if any, should be put forward to the IAASB. It was fascinating to be in a participant observer position and listen to the exchanges between practitioners from different firms and different countries talk frankly about what they do, and to have an insight into the politics of international standard setting. However, it was also a challenge to ensure that, even if the research was influential in the policy debate, that it also maintained an independent standing. In this situation it was important to ensure that the report on the research was a separate document from the report of the working group considering the standard setting implications. Also, while the research report benefited from the comments of both practitioners and academics before being finalized, it ultimately remained under the authorship and control of the three academics involved in the project.

Inevitably, the independence of the research is a matter of degree. It may be difficult to participate with practitioners in research and at the same time to be totally independent, but it is important to have freedom of investigation and expression. If practitioners were to challenge this, then it is always possible to point out that the research will be of little value for their purposes if it seen as less than independent. Few people will be convinced if they think the research has been 'bought' (rather like the audit!).

A Continuing Research Agenda

In this final section some suggestions are offered regarding a small number of issues on the agenda for continuing research on public practice accountancy. The issues are: assurance, the culture of accounting firm practices, internationalisation, and international professional structures and regulation. While these topics are not a complete programme for research, and indeed a number of comments about potential investigation have already been made in earlier sections, they do represent some personal views on fruitful areas for future research.

Assurance

Over recent years, the way in which public practice services have become defined has changed in many firms. This change is perhaps encapsulated in the adoption of the terminology of "assurance". While traditionally auditing stood as one of the main functional divisions within the organization of services provided by accounting firms, that position has changed to one where the more generic term of assurance is used to cover not only auditing but also a range of other services. This development is also reflected in standard setting, where in 2002 the International Auditing Practices Committee changed its name to the International Auditing and Assurance Standards Board.

The importance of this trend is that, first, it suggests that practitioners are keen to communicate externally that their expertise is not narrowly based on auditing alone, notwithstanding the fact that during the last few years the major firms have come under pressure to dispose of some of their consultancy activities and thus effectively to narrow their services somewhat. In addition, the move to the language of assurance could indicate something about the way in which auditing itself is viewed internally in firms — that it is seen as simply one of a package of services that are similar in character rather than as a distinct activity with its own defining activities and characteristics. If so, this development could have implications for the way in which auditing services are carried out in practice.

What is unclear at present, and therefore where research may be able to make a valuable contribution, is what is the practical significance of this development. Does it result in a different view of auditing; does it involve different organisational arrangements within practicing firms; does it lead to different competencies and expertise being applied in the audit process; does it change expectations; or is it simply a question of labelling that can be dismissed as little more than an exercise in marketing? These questions can be researched under each of the three general perspectives discussed earlier. The nature of public practice accountancy does not remain fixed and research that can illuminate our understanding of the ways in which the firms construct and develop their activities and what these developments convey regarding the underlying concepts being applied in service provision will be of particular interest and value.

The Culture of Public Practice Accountancy Firms

A related area for potential study is what can be referred to as the "culture" of the public practice firms. Simply, this is an area where only a limited amount of research has been conducted so far and therefore an open area of considerable potential for development. The basic issue here goes back to understanding the ways in which accountancy firms operate internally — work practices, reward systems and codes of behaviour — and the character of public practice that results. It also has to do with the relationship between individual practitioners, the firms that they work in as economic units, and broader relationships with those relying on the services provided. Traditionally, codes of ethics have emphasized individual behaviour, but as long as it is the firm that controls the pay cheque and promotional opportunities for individuals then there is a need to ensure that incentives do not conflict with appropriate behaviour.

Over recent years, emphasis has been given to the need to promote "professional scepticism" as a key element in enhancing the contribution that auditing makes to financial reporting. For example the Auditing Practices Board has stated the view that "auditor scepticism is driven more by auditor training and the cultures and attitudes within audit firms than by Auditing Standards" (APB 2001: 10). Many of the criticisms levelled at practice following scandals such as Enron, Worldcom and Ahold are also relevant to this point. Questions have been raised about how a culture can be promoted in public practice which ensures that there is an appropriate challenge to corporate management and that internal pressures within firms do not result in conflicts which in turn lead to compromised judgement. Again, research in this area could address issues of public policy on, for example, ethical standards, utilize economic analysis of incentives and behaviour at the individual and firm level, or focus on the content of what practitioners do.

Internationalisation

A specific aspect of the development of public practice accountancy is the way in which a relatively small number of firms have come to dominate the market for, at least some, professional services. Perhaps more than any other professional service sector, accountancy has been influenced by what is normally referred to as the 'globalisation' of business. A few firms, conventionally referred to as the Big (Six, Five) Four, and a small group of other international networks are seen as the market leaders in most countries.

Research can contribute here on two fronts. First, there is scope for new work analyzing the economics of the international firms. Most existing research on the public practice accounting 'industry' has focused on individual national markets. Further investigation of, for example, the patterns through which referral work is distributed, the manner in which profits are shared and the constitutional structures of the firms and networks is relevant to how we see the international firms as economic units. Following the problems facing the U.S. practice in the wake of Enron, the firm of Arthur Andersen effectively broke up. Choices were made about linking the various national firm practices with what had previously been Andersen's competitors. It appears, however, that most of the decisions about these arrangements were made at the level of the national practice. If one of the most internationally integrated firms is structured in a way that involves this level of local autonomy, then this surely has implications for the way in which we see the major firms as "accountancy multinationals."

The growth of the major international firms is sometimes seen as the 'MacDonaldisation' of public practice, whereby the same type of service is delivered wherever the brand name of the firm is applied. Investigation of the extent to which this kind of claim really holds true is a second area where further research on internationalization will be valuable. Again this relates to the question of firm culture and the extent to which a common set of values and service is associated with a single firm operating in many environments and to similar questions about whether common practices are implemented globally and how firm wide concepts, policies and methodologies are applied.

International Professional Structures and Regulation

Extending the consideration beyond the level of the practicing firms, a further set of research topics relates to the development of the international accountancy profession. This is of particular relevance to public practice because of the movement towards international standards as the primary source of regulation. The same position is emerging in auditing where International Standards on Auditing (ISAs) produced by IAASB are likely to achieve greater prominence than they have had in the past. There have been moves towards recognition of ISAs by capital market authorities and the European Commission has issued a statement indicating that it wishes to require from 2005 adherence to ISAs for the audit of financial statements of listed companies (EC 2003). There is insufficient space here to discuss all the potential avenues of research linked to this development, but a few illustrative issues of importance are:

- The development of the institutions of the international accountancy profession;
- The feasibility of universal interpretation and application of international standards;
- The debate between rule based and principles based approaches to setting standards;
- The link between international standards on services such as auditing and ethical guides.

Concluding Comments

This chapter has contained personal reflections on conducting research on (not for) public practice accounting, communicating with practitioners and encouraging them to become more informed about the research process and to see the value of the contribution research can make. A critical aspect of this is recognizing that we need to see "dissemination" of research on public practice as involving much more than just communication of research output and spreading news about results. Given the nature of public practice and the traditions of professional training in the United Kingdom, practitioners are not well informed about academic accounting research and it is therefore appropriate to see dissemination as encompassing interaction with practitioners in many ways — to promote understanding of research plans and to increase their engagement in research.

The chapter has tried to argue that there are fundamental reasons why research on public practice is of interest, primarily because of the way in which accounting affects economic activity and society, and many different perspectives from which issues affecting public practice can be analyzed. There is no shortage of potential research projects and no suggestion that the supply of interesting topics in this field will reduce. But success in investigating many of these topics requires cooperation from and interaction with practitioners and the chapter has discussed some of the practical issues and pitfalls to be aware of in attempting to achieve this.

References

Auditing Practices Board (APB) (2001). *Aggressive earnings management*. London: APB.

Bell, T. B., Marrs, F. O., Solomon, I., & Thomas, I. (1997). A*uditing organizations through a strategic systems lens*. Montvale, NJ, KPMG LLP.

European Commission (EC) (2003). *Reinforcing the statutory audit in the EU*. Brussels: Communication from the Commission to the Council of the European Parliament.

Department of Trade and Industry (DTI) (2003a). *Final report of the coordinating group on accounting and auditing issues*. DTI, URN 03/567, January.

Department of Trade and Industry (DTI) (2003b). *Review of the regulatory regime for the accountancy profession*. Report to the Secretary of State for Trade and Industry, DTI, URN 03/589, January.

Department of Trade and Industry (DTI) (2003c). *Fair value accounting*. Consultation Document, DTI, June.

Higgs Committee (2003). *Review of the role and effectiveness of non-executive directors*. DTI, January.

Humphrey, C., Moizer, P., & Turley, S. (1992). *The audit expectations gap in the United Kingdom*. Institute of Chartered Accountants in England and Wales, Research Report.

Lemon, M., Tatum, K., & Turley, S. (2000). *Developments in the audit methodologies of large accounting firms*. London: Auditing Practices Board.

Moizer, P., & Turley, S. (1989). Changes in the U.K. market for auditing services 1972–1982. *Journal of Business Finance and Accounting, 16*(Spring), 41–53.

Smith Committee (2003). *Audit committees combined code guidance*. Financial Reporting Council, London, January.

Turley, S., & Cooper, M. (1991). *Auditing in the U.K. — Developments in the audit methodologies of large accounting firms*. Prentice Hall International/Institute of Chartered Accountants in England & Wales Research Studies Series 1991.

Chapter 27

Disseminating Research Through Teaching

Sue Richardson and John Cullen

Introduction

Numerous pressures bear down on our work as accounting academics. On the one hand, in our teaching there are calls for accounting education to more closely relate to the demands of accounting practice itself (Albrecht & Sack 2000), with emphasis beyond practical skills and technical knowledge. For example, the Quality Assurance Agency (QAA) Accountancy Benchmark Statement (2000) for U.K. accounting undergraduate programmes highlights the importance of developing a combination of subject knowledge and skills, cognitive abilities and non-subject specific skills, as well as knowledge and understanding of contemporary theories and empirical evidence. In other words, teaching abstract theories, concepts and techniques is not enough. Ideally, our programmes should be underpinned by real examples and contexts, informed by empirical research, that challenge current practice and equip would-be practitioners for the demands of modern accounting practice. On the other hand, the Research Assessment Exercise (RAE) attempts to drive our research agenda. Interestingly, in a review of the RAE 2001, Otley (2002) emphasises the importance being attached to research relevance and the importance for future generations of U.K. academics to be able and willing to tackle issues of practical significance. Despite the potential for some convergence here, there is still a perceived gap between accounting education and practice (for example, Milne & McConnell 2001; Montano et al. 2001). Some promote the use of case studies in teaching to bridge this gap (Hassall et al. 1998; Boyce et al. 2001; Milne & McConnell 2001) and research informed case studies in particular (Cullen et al. 2001). Others (Coppage & Baxendale 2001, for example) argue the merits of integrating teaching, research and consulting, to the extent that accounting educators become more productive whilst enhancing the learning experiences of both the educator and the students. Also, if we want to effect real accounting practice reform, Humphrey (2001) believes we must disseminate our research further than just publishing in academic journals. At a deeper level, Mahoney (1997), in a personal reflection on his career, articulates that although academic teaching and research are often seen as joined yet divergent interests and pursuits, the two are inextricably intertwined. He reflects that the teaching he enjoys is not possible if one views teaching and research as separate endeavours. In fact, he concludes by arguing that teaching and research are but different emphases or stages of the same learning process.

Set in this context, and given our predilection for case studies, we reflect on our own practices in accounting education and recount excerpts from our experiences at work using case studies. Initially, we establish what a case study approach to teaching might entail, largely as a framework around which our readers might interpret and evaluate what we have done. Then we present a 'case study' of our experiences and conclude with tips for others following similar pursuits.

Case Studies for Teaching Purposes

The case method in management education and training is generally associated with the Harvard Business School, which developed and widely promoted this approach throughout the twentieth century. The philosophy was that formal education could not provide answers to every situation a manager would face, but the development of generic skills, such as analysis, clear reasoning, use of imagination and judgement, would equip them to deal better with specific and complex situations in the future (Zoll 1966). It has its critics, however. Not only was the method prescriptive, but the structure of the case studies also followed similar lines, providing information needed to complete predetermined tasks. Hopper *et al.* (2001) were critical of 'Harvard' type case studies as effective research tools and highlighted concerns that the cases were too brief, too managerial, too closed to behavioural and external factors, unduly atheoretical, and hence inadequate for unravelling managerial processes and problems.

Recommendations and practices have emerged showing 'best ways' to use and write case studies in teaching (for example, Leenders & Erskine 1973; Richardson *et al.* 1995) and a range of advice is given. We are urged to consider the different levels of difficulty across different dimensions to achieve predetermined outcomes. We are warned against having too narrow a view about what constitutes 'the case method'. We are advised about 'best types' for particular purposes. For example, they might be used to illustrate a theory, to practice techniques or concepts, to introduce or legitimise a theory, or as a live example (Scholes 1995). Fitting the case study to the learning context and audience is pronounced as important. For example, undergraduates with little experience might be more comfortable with plenty of data and an analytical focus, whilst postgraduates might be better equipped to develop a case further (Thompson 1995). It is suggested we choose case studies that students will find interesting and motivating, using household names, because these are familiar, and topical issues where plenty of media coverage is available to fill in the gaps.

Curzon (1980) was more prescriptive about the 'types' of case studies used. According to Curzon, the most common type of case study is the major issue case. This provides lots of material and the student must analyse the case, identify issues and problems and propose appropriate actions. This is probably closest to the 'Harvard' tradition. The case history has no specific problems to be solved, but provides a context in which to analyse why certain courses of action were followed or to evaluate options, or to illustrate and reinforce other teaching. The sequential case stops at certain points where students make decisions before the story continues. The critical incident case just gives a brief description of a situation with inadequate background and students must request further data, thus learning to ask the right questions. In the role play case, students take on particular roles and viewpoints and develop an argument. The live case, for Curzon, is a topical issue where the outcome is uncertain. Others see the live case as the verbal exposition by some member of the organisation.

In relation to specific learning outcomes from using case studies in accounting education, Boyce *et al.* (2001) consider that they can play a crucial role in developing deep learning and generic skills. In a similar vein, Milne & McConnell (2001) promote their use within a problem-based learning approach to motivate students to acquire new knowledge and to develop their own learning. The mirroring of real world activity encourages students to develop expertise in the way that would be utilised by a 'reflective' practitioner (Schon 1983, 1987).

So what have we personally deduced from all of these recommendations? In line with Mahoney (1997), we see our research and teaching as part of the same process. We are excited by opportunities to research inside organisations and understand their workings and we are excited by opportunities to pass on our understandings to our colleagues and students. We embrace the idea of research that is practice relevant and significant and that infiltrates our academic programmes to challenge accepted practice, since we are naturally inclined towards this through our case study research and research-informed case study teaching. We see this approach as a means of developing deeper learning in our students and we find ways to develop this approach further. We do not perceive boundaries around our research or our teaching — these are mutually informing processes. What this means for us is encompassed in Humphrey & Scapens' (1996) view that case study research should be driven by the problems and issues relating to accounting practice in its social context. This means focusing on factors that are intriguing, puzzling and contradictory, so that socially informed theories of accounting practice might develop. Whilst recognising the RAE pressures (Hopper *et al.* 2001; Humphrey 2001) for our research publications to make a contribution to knowledge through theoretical analysis, our use of 'messy' cases in teaching situations allows us to explore other dimensions that do not conform to a specific theoretical framework. This approach presents opportunities to engage present and future practitioners with different empirical contexts, and opens up possibilities to effect real changes in accounting practice and to reveal new directions for research.

Interestingly though, many emerging stories of case study teaching practices infer a deliberate, 'designed' process to writing and using case studies in teaching. Of course, we must consider the student group and the learning outcomes when using a case study approach. Similarly, case studies might be researched in different ways specifically for teaching, using publicly available materials, media coverage, personal experiences at work, other people's experiences reported to the author, or even made-up scenarios. We have done all these things. But our evidence collected in the field, originally intended as data for academic publication, is often adapted for teaching too. The difference between our research-informed case studies for teaching and our published academic work using researched case studies is generally the way in which our research evidence is presented. In academic articles we conform to accepted practice and mould our evidence around particular theoretical concepts to develop our knowledge of such concepts in context. Paradoxically, in so doing, this presents only a partial understanding of events. These articles are useful in certain teaching contexts, but many of our adapted research-informed teaching case studies present a rather more disjointed and less organised evidence set and allow students to construct their own interpretations. These case studies may be written in different ways, with different content, for different student groups and seek to develop different skills.

We enthusiastically seek opportunities to use our research in teaching, not least because it enriches our own experience in the classroom. It can be much more fun discussing topics and contexts that enthuse us and such enthusiasm should make the experience more engaging and enjoyable for our students too. When students have more professional knowledge about particular topics and contexts than us, we learn and develop new ideas, and often gain further research contacts.

However, we recognise there might be downsides to using case studies in teaching. Rees & Porter (2002) comment on possible resistance, particularly by those students used to more conventional methods of education. Some colleagues have commented that using a case study approach to teaching leaves the teacher less in control of the classroom situation. You have to manage a discussion, manage time given up to small group work and, in summing up, remember points made by a variety of people and, all in all, have to think a lot on your feet. The outcomes are much less certain than a structured lecture or tutorial and depend on many variables, such as group dynamics, the knowledge and experience of the students and the teacher, and the nature of the case study itself. Using our own case studies can provide greater control of some of these variables. For example, we have much more knowledge of the case study detail than the students; we have reflected on the issues from a certain theoretical perspective; and we can talk about the real people in the organisation. But, the danger is that we may form preconceived ideas and be less open to other views, being so closely connected with the context.

Having presented some ideas about case study approaches to teaching and what might be achieved, what follows is a reflection on our own personal experiences.

A 'Case Study' of our Experiences

Over the last decade, we have collaborated in case study research, pursuing what intrigued us, in an exploratory, continuous and emergent process (Otley & Berry 1994; Humphrey & Scapens 1996). Studying different contexts longitudinally, we have disseminated our work in a similar vein, reporting and using the data at different stages in different ways.

In narrating our experiences of using case studies in our work, the story embraces students from undergraduate programmes through to postgraduate and management development programmes. It covers a range of research projects that we have used for teaching with both non-specialist and specialist accounting students. Initially, we look at one particular research project in the National Health Service (NHS) and explore how teaching and research are indeed inseparable endeavours that become different stages of a learning process for us and our students. Then we go on to describe how, in similar ways, we use our other research and a case study approach more generally.

Our National Health Service Project

In 1992 we gained access to our first NHS research site through collaboration with a student working on an issue in a Trust Hospital. The introduction of an internal market was in its early stages and we wanted to understand the implication of accounting in the process and the emerging issues. Sue was particularly keen to learn about a public sector context as she was teaching undergraduate first year public sector students at the time and knew very little about the changes. From this initial collaboration, a case study, Penn Valley Hospital Trust (PVHT), emerged and was used in that teaching context to familiarise students with the newly emerging public sector and the concepts underpinning 'new public management'. The outcomes were measured (rather crudely through a small scale questionnaire) at the time and the evidence suggested that these students found it useful for the above purposes. It was certainly useful for Sue as it removed much of the 'uncertainty' surrounding that particular context.

During our investigations, we discovered intriguing evidence of entrepreneurial activity within the Pathology Department, which led to further investigations between 1993 and 1996. A detailed case study recorded the evidence and conference papers followed, revealing Chris (the Pathology Manager) as a public entrepreneur and showing how accounting was implicated. We used these conference papers to engage particular groups of postgraduate students in unpicking accounting's role in this modernisation process. These groups included specialist NHS and Social Services students and NHS medical consultants on management training courses. This triggered interesting reactions and critical debate about emerging issues in this context, such as, "this is not appropriate behaviour for a public sector manager"; or "pathology is just like 'canning beans', so you can be entrepreneurial and also use accounting — but this is not appropriate for most hospital activities". It created a particularly striking reaction from another Pathology Manager (Matthew) who suggested that if he (Matthew) took such a cavalier approach to investment decisions "I could finish up with egg on my face. It would be a real problem if it backfired". These comments illustrate emerging tensions between traditional public sector ethos and the modernisation agenda, as well as a recognition that analysis at the activity level rather than organisational level should determine the appropriate type of control mechanism and managerial style (Hofstede 1981).

From a learning perspective, our understanding of the problems and issues these particular students faced enhanced our credibility and encouraged critical debate on very topical issues (as evidenced above). Such feedback caused us to reflect on the development of our research and provided new research opportunities.

Matthew agreed to take part in further investigations within his Department at Moorstown Hospital Trust (MHT). This comparative study enabled us to tease out entrepreneurial and accounting potential within this particular period of change, using concepts packaged as 'new public management' as our framework for analysis published in an academic article (see Richardson & Cullen 2000). While the evidence had been recorded as a detailed case study, the academic article moulded case material around particular issues, leaving much of the original case detail redundant.

We proceeded then to use both pathology case studies when teaching together on an undergraduate final year module Management Accounting Control Systems for accounting and management control students. As students found the concepts underpinning this module difficult to grasp from the academic literature they were given to read, we used case studies to provide context. Our pathology case studies were among those used. These introduced students to a context that was not well understood generally and 'new' to most. The studies confronted them with contemporary issues with which the organizations themselves were struggling. The studies also exposed students to the social and political context of accounting and the unintended consequences that can emerge. They provided 'inside' detail about how accounting was socially constructed in the management of change, using the actual words of the characters involved. For example, Matthew at MHT describes two consultants as "Mavericks, acting in their own self interest, using blackmail tactics and being downright awkward". As a consequence of this Matthew was "...pulled over the coals for being vastly overspent last year — and I was not aware of it". We could also provide other details in discussions about the context. Thus, students were able to devise their own ideas about public sector change, the role of accounting, the behaviour of actors, and compare these with 'theory'.

John also used the published article on a finance module for a Health Service and Social Services Managers postgraduate course and it provoked critical debate. Initially this was about the problems students had encountered with 'academic' language in the theorising parts. But refreshingly, when they proceeded to relate and compare their own experiences to the contrasting case scenarios, they entered into a debate about "antecedent conditions of possibility inherent in practice" (Llewellyn 1996: 116) and debated their own experiences of different structures of accountability and control. They used their own language, but demonstrated clear understanding of these concepts. In many ways, these mature postgraduate students engaged in social constructionist perspectives of their reality (Gold & Holman 2001) and shared these experiences, which enhanced the learning process. It facilitated discussion around ongoing developments in the NHS (*Shifting the Balance of Power* 2001; *Reforming NHS Financial Flows* 2002) and associated changes in the Social Services relating to shared services and pooling of budgets. It also encouraged debates around power, trust and control and the continually developing public-private partnership arrangements. Further opportunities for new research also emerged here. Similar experiences occurred on medical consultant development programmes with interesting debates around professional clinical rivalry. This type of exposure has stimulated ideas and developed our research programmes. We are now undertaking further research with a Primary Care Trust, exploring how accounting is implicated in the development of new organisational forms in the NHS.

Elsewhere our colleagues have used an adapted version of one of the pathology case studies with undergraduate final year students of accounting and management control undertaking a Financial Decision Making (FDM) module. A full discussion about this module is provided in Hassall *et al.* (1998). The module uses case studies exclusively as its learning and teaching method and is formatively assessed through a combination of interactive small group presentations (with role play by both tutors and students) and group reports for each case study, plus individual learning diaries of the whole process. The learning outcomes of this module are geared to: students appropriately researching and assessing the social context of each case study and the way in which accounting practices are immersed; demonstrating their understanding through verbal and written communication and role play; analysing the context and the problem and making appropriate recommendations for change. As a corollary to these aims, students' understanding of accounting theory and practice might be further informed and challenged and post assessment reflections (recorded in individual diaries) should promote deeper learning.

We were not part of the teaching team, but a colleague on the team adapted our case study, removing some of the detail, particularly the departmental organization chart. This abridged 'story' still retained the authenticity and richness of the data, particularly in respect to social, political and behavioural issues, and included the original quotations from various characters. As with the original case study, the problems and issues remained ambiguous and student research was necessary to fill in the gaps about the general context.

We were interested to see what particular benefits might arise from using our research case study on this module, so we undertook a small-scale study conducted with one cohort of these students and tutors to get feedback. Some initial results from this study were reported in Cullen *et al.* (2001) at a management control workshop. The objective was to contribute empirical evidence to the debate surrounding the use of case studies in accounting education, stimulated by the perceived 'gap' between accounting education and practice (Milne & McConnell 2001; Montano *et al.* 2001) and the need to address generic as well as subject specific skills. We concentrated on a reflection on the type of case studies used and the teaching approach adopted (Hassall *et al.* 1998; Boyce *et al.* 2001; Milne & McConnell 2001). Building on ideas relating to problem-based learning (Milne & McConnell 2001) we explored notions about organising case material so that problems are more vague and unstructured. This is intended to encourage students to develop their problem-solving and researching skills because of the ambiguous and incomplete nature of the material provided. In support of this notion, Barrows (1986) typology of case studies suggested a need for problem-based case studies that present 'fuzzy' problems reflecting the ambiguity of reality. This leaves students free to self-direct their inquiries as they see fit, based on prior knowledge. This would go beyond the 'Harvard' model that Stilson & Milter (1996) considered too narrow and discipline focused for these purposes.

Our evidence showed that students and tutors involved strongly agreed that our pathology case study enabled the module's learning outcomes to be achieved. They liked the fuzzy nature of the case material and one student commented "there was confusion in the case study about relationships, but I realised that this matches reality". They talked positively about the 'learning by doing' opportunities provided by this case. Equally, they felt that it enabled them to develop their generic skills in terms of group work, role play, communication and research which link to the refocusing of accounting education (Albrecht & Sack 2000; Boyce *et al.* 2001). For example, one student said "*I spoke to a (medical) consultant as part of the research for this case*". Another added, "*It developed my understanding of new contexts but research was necessary — but a good learning process for me*".

In Cullen *et al.* (2001), we reflect on the way 'messy stories', along problem-based learning lines, not only provide a contextual understanding of accounting in action and exposure to contemporary issues, but also have the potential to mirror the ambiguity of reality and promote the development of generic skills. This might prepare students for practice more effectively. In this particular learning situation our researched case study was particularly useful in conveying the actual experience of 'being there' and did seem to promote deep learning.

Using other Research and a General Approach to Case Studies

An ethnographically researched case study, MIS Limited (reported in Richardson *et al.* 1996; Ritchie & Richardson 2000), has featured in many teaching situations. MIS is a small firm run as a personal fiefdom by the owner and the case study explores the impact of the introduction of a new accountant and new accounting systems. We have presented this as a live case to groups of part-time undergraduate final year students, part-time and full-time MBA students, Executive MBA students, and at academic seminars and conferences. It always engages the audience, perhaps because Sue actually worked in this difficult and emotionally charged firm and had access to minute detail and first hand emotional and social experiences. Often, students with working experience comment that they could recognise the firm — almost as if they had worked there themselves. For example, one person commented "it was just as if you were talking about me". Some postgraduates have commented that they found the case study particularly relevant to their own practices because of its realism. This case study is particularly useful for portraying the social context in which accounting is set and the power relations that existed in this small firm. It is a useful vehicle for getting students to reflect on issues of accountability, corporate governance and smaller business failure and how theories about these issues might be challenged. It has also provided the contextual background for a teaching case study featured in Ducker *et al.* (1998). These learning situations have provided further research opportunities and we have recorded informants' stories of similar experiences to that of MIS (some featured in Richardson 1993).

In taking a research informed approach to our teaching, we have combined our case study researched academic articles, research informed case studies and case studies constructed from other sources such as current affairs programmes, media coverage, official documents, for example, and designed an entire module around these. One such example is Sue's Issues in Financial Management module (IFM). This is a second year undergraduate module for accounting and financial management students. It is structured around 'real' cases, some illustrated by video, and interspersed with an occasional guest speaker as a live case. It seeks to engage students with contemporary practice and theory and encourages them to understand the failures of accounting and financial management, and to challenge existing theory and practice.

For Sue this was a particularly challenging experience. As she recalls, "Taking on this module was very risky for me. I was shifting from my comfort zone — moving universities to teach in a new subject area with new colleagues. I could have easily fallen flat on my face (or had a nervous breakdown!), particularly as my appointment appeared embedded in political conflict regarding the direction in which the accounting and financial management subject group was to develop. Having no track record there, I felt rather vulnerable. To add to my anxiety, I was assigned an additional tutor whose values were embedded in a traditional teaching approach to the subject. My remit was to develop a module that took an organisational perspective of financial management and, encouraged by my professor, I decided to build on my strengths as an ex-practitioner with lots of experience in different contexts and as a researcher of organisations. I felt that my major inadequacies lay in my lack of knowledge about the macro context in which organisations conduct their financial management practices and which impinges on these too. This meant many months scouring libraries, bookshops and friends' video collections, developing ideas and discussing these with others. It was a stressful and scary time. IFM hung over me like a black cloud, but I really wanted to make it something different and good for the development of my students and myself. I was terrified the first time I delivered the module. It wasn't ground breaking stuff, but it was something different for my students, many of whom had not been confronted by its delivery mode and content before. I was also concerned about what the external examiner would think of it. Fortunately, it was well received by both the external examiner and my students, who generally enjoyed it and put in good performances. My students recommended it to others following them and some asked me to run through and comment on their job interview presentations based on case studies from my module. One student said it was the best module he had taken and wanted more of the same. This type of spin off gives me a buzz and makes me feel that my students have engaged with the subject and learned something useful."

One problem with this approach is keeping abreast of current issues in financial management and business affairs and getting the material in a suitable case study form for teaching purposes. One might say it was fortuitous that during the first two years of this module there were some particularly interesting and pertinent 'cases' such as the Millennium Dome, Marconi, Enron, Andersen, Railtrack and Worldcom. These provided fascinating contexts in which to explore financial management issues. It does mean that you have to be vigilant in capturing current affairs programmes and news items on video, as stories unfold.

Students are given specific tasks to undertake with each case study and these are discussed in tutorials. They are encouraged to develop their own ideas about new and emancipatory practices and become researchers too, since they often have to gather further information about the case studies for tutorial tasks, assignment work and examination preparation. Some feel insecure because the case studies do not provide 'right answers' and they ask for specimen solutions (which we do not provide), whilst more able students research the context, analyse it, reflect on the issues, consider the theoretical debate, and draw their own conclusions. It does require students to engage with the topics and contexts, otherwise discussions are ill informed and shallow. According to Sue, "I do find this approach quite challenging, not least when I can't get the video equipment to work. Sometimes it's my own technical inadequacy and sometimes its poor equipment in the old lecture theatres that I get allocated. Either way, I find myself tearing down corridors on a regular basis seeking a telephone to get hold of a technician, returning hot and bothered and short of lecture time. Using guest speakers can be stressful too, especially if they withdraw at the last minute. On one occasion Andersen's Corporate Finance Division arranged to do a lecture but were forced to pull out as the Enron debacle unfolded and they weren't allowed to have external links. This really brought home how 'current' our issues were. I didn't pick up the telephone message until a couple of hours before the proposed lecture. Fortunately, I had an appropriate video in reserve".

Despite such risks, guest speakers are an excellent way to communicate a case. A good example is connected to one of John's research projects, Sportasia. We invited a director from 'Sportasia' to talk to the IFM students about the Community Company Model the company had developed. This Community Company exists primarily to enhance the lives of all those employed within it, that is, its members. In value terms, it strives to go beyond the notion of simply providing a means of sustenance and survival, and endeavours to fulfil the needs of individuals to derive satisfaction and enjoyment from their careers. The pillars underpinning the organisation are based around information and involvement, fair reward, shared prosperity, employment protection, application of the organisation's values and developmental opportunities. Thus, the Sportasia experience facilitates a critical debate as to whether conventional wisdoms of corporate governance are too simplistic an account of the actual processes at work and highlights the need to explore different ways of managing organisations through different processes of governance. Using this live case, students could question and challenge the ideas being promoted and John provided some theoretical underpinning to the contextual issues by means of a short presentation. We also distributed a conference paper (Coad & Cullen 2001), which provided more detail about the organisation and related academic frameworks. According to Sue, "I am always anxious when I have a guest speaker. I suppose it is because I have begun to develop some common ground with my students and then I introduce an outsider and I'm not sure how things will go or how it will fit with what I intended. I suppose I feel less in control. I also worry that the students won't ask questions too. Fortunately, it usually works out really well". It is interesting (from their questions and comments) that students seek to understand the financial management practices in different ways in this company. This understanding was evident when some students integrated ideas about the community company model into their assessed work and — particularly this year, i.e. 2003 — into their examinations. This is also a useful process for enhancing the research project as it exposes ideas to new audiences with different perspectives. One student, for example, suggested that the model closely resembled his cultural and religious context. Another questioned whether the model was sustainable as the company grew and linked it to issues of power and control studied on the module. Another questioned whether the company was susceptible to 'cultural rigidity' as studied on the module.

Comments noted from the formal student feedback process and from informal student comments suggest they do find the module challenging, but interesting and relevant. Many say that it is particularly valuable at job interviews because they can demonstrate their knowledge of real organisations and current issues. In fact, as Sue recalls, "This year a student with the top assignment mark (based on Marks & Spencer) suggested she might take her assignment with her to help her get a job there".

John has also used the community company model research case study, referred to earlier, with other undergraduate final year accounting students. Here, it facilitated particular discussion about culture and 'cults' and generated quite heated debate about how the organisation operated and the control mechanisms used. Some viewed the organisation as a 'cult' since the recruitment processes ensured that only 'like minded people' entered and were expected to continually follow certain behaviour patterns. In stark contrast, others felt that total employee involvement and an environment that encouraged questioning and debate, suggested a truly democratic organisation. Exposure to this alternative view of corporate governance structures facilitated a much richer understanding of alternative corporate behaviours.

Using your own research material on research methods modules can be rewarding too. John does this at a specialist finance postgraduate level. A majority of these students hold preconceived views of research approaches that tend to focus on surveys and the use of statistical analysis. Exposure to research that uses an inductive approach to theory generation, rather than a deductive approach involving hypothesis testing, opens up new opportunities for a wider range of research based dissertations. The fact that John is one of the authors of the papers under review seems to encourage the students to engage in critical debate around, for example, the appropriateness of the research methods being used and the limitations of different approaches in that particular context. They enjoy a critical dialogue with him concerning his work. However, the danger is that they are not exposed to the full range of research methods available, and this has to be guarded against by involving other tutors and their papers (utilising different epistemological and ontological perspectives) into the module programme.

Concluding Thoughts

Pursuing our predilection for case studies, we have developed our own ways to integrate our research and teaching. We have described how these activities are somewhat inseparable endeavours that can become simply different stages of a learning process for us and our students (Mahoney 1997). We describe how 'realism' and 'practice relevance' might be achieved, using case studies, and we provide evidence of how deep learning and the development of generic skills may occur.

The examples we provide engage students (with varying degrees of work experience) at undergraduate, postgraduate and professional development levels. Our case studies are not in the 'Harvard' style. Sometimes they are presented in written form and sometimes they are live presentations. These are 'messy stories' that give characters a voice. Our study of the FDM student group suggests that this type of messiness can promote deep learning and develop generic skills, whilst exposing students to contemporary issues and empirical evidence.

We have shown how we integrate our research and our research interests into modules. Sue's IFM module demonstrates how contemporary issues might be brought to life, and how students might develop various generic skills in researching and analysing case studies and critically evaluating the issues. Deep learning is implied when students feel sufficiently confident to use their learning in job interviews. This also suggests the learning is practice relevant too.

When using our own academic articles, we describe how these can provide the vehicle for critical debate about the issues and the research method used. When working with students we could expose the empirical evidence to other interpretations and understandings because of our access to further details of the case. Paradoxically, our academic articles might close down such wider learning opportunities for audiences elsewhere, without access to the whole picture and guided tightly along a narrow theoretical line (Humphrey 2001). This raises the question of whether there is more to be gained, in terms of progressive thinking and learning within the academic community, by publishing the 'messy' case studies instead?

Using a 'case study' of our own experiences, we have reflected on how we disseminate our research through teaching rather than just publishing in academic journals. We also provide evidence, with respect to both teaching and research, of how this approach can bridge the gap between accounting education and practice, as well as promoting the development of both subject knowledge and generic skills. Exposure to different empirical contexts and social settings provides opportunities to effect real changes in accounting practice. It can also be a very personally rewarding experience for teachers and researchers too.

For other interested in this approach, we suggest the following tips.

- Write up your case study evidence as a full and detailed messy story, use it in your own teaching and invite colleagues to use it too.
- Try to get your messy case study published, so that others might construct their own ideas about its relevance.
- In teaching, consider the required learning outcomes, the particular student group and don't simply use the case study (particularly your own) to occupy class time.
- Be aware of your own predisposition to your work and try to maintain balance and openness to other views.
- Grasp opportunities to invite external speakers to present case studies of 'live' issues — it is not only good for the students but it might develop your work too. Also, encourage your colleagues to do likewise.
- Always be alert to current issues and capture current affairs programmes on video — these provide excellent and engaging case studies in which to explore contemporary issues and practice.
- Develop your skills in using case studies with students — seek training if necessary. This allows you to feel more in control and is more likely to achieve good outcomes for all.

References

Albrecht, W. S., & Sack, R. J. (2000). *Accounting education: Charting the course through a perilous future*. Sarasota: American Accounting Association, Accounting Education Series, Vol. 16.

Barrows, H. S. (1986). A taxonomy of problem-based learning methods. *Medical Education*, *20*(6), 481–486.

Boyce, G., Williams, S., Kelly, A., & Yee, H. (2001). Fostering deep and elaborative learning and generic (soft) skill development: the strategic use of case studies in accounting education. *Accounting Education: An International Journal*, *10*(1), 37–60.

Coad, A. F., & Cullen, J. (2001). The community company: towards a competences model of corporate governance. Paper presented at The Fifth International Management Control Systems Research Conference, July. University of London.

Coppage, R. E., & Baxendale, S. (2001). A synergistic approach to an accounting educator's primary responsibilities. *Accounting Education: An International Journal*, *10*(3), 239–246.

Cullen, J., Richardson, S., & O'Brien, R. (2001). Contextualising management control: exploring the boundaries between accounting research and accounting education. Paper presented to The Management Control Association, September.

Curzon, L. B. (1980). *Teaching in further education* (2nd ed.). London: Cassell.

Department of Health (2001). *Shifting the balance of power within the NHS — Securing delivery*. July.

Department of Health (2002). *Reforming NHS financial flows: introducing payment by results*. October.

Ducker, J., Head, A., McDonnell, B., O'Brien, R., & Richardson, S. (1998). *Case studies in management accounting and control*. Sheffield: Sheffield Hallam University Press.

Gold, J., & Holman, D. (2001). Let me tell you a story: an evaluation of the use of storytelling and argument analysis in management education. *Career Development International*, *6*(7), 384–395.

Hassall, T., Lewis, S., & Broadbent, M. (1998). The use and potential abuse of case studies in accounting education. *Accounting Education: An International Journal*, *7*(4), 325–334.

Hofstede, G. (1981). Management control of public and not-for-profit activities. *Accounting, Organizations and Society*, *6*(3), 193–211.

Hopper, T., Otley, D., & Scapens, R. (2001). British management accounting research: whence and whither: opinions and recollections. *British Accounting Review*, *33*(3), 263–291.

Humphrey, C. (2001). Paper prophets and the continuing case for thinking differently about accounting research. *British Accounting Review*, *33*(1), 91–103.

Humphrey, C., & Scapens, R. W. (1996). Methodological themes: theories and case studies of organizational accounting practices: limitation or liberation? *Accounting, Auditing and Accountability Journal*, *9*(4), 86–106.

Leenders, M. R., & Erskine, J. A. (1973). *Case research: The case writing process*. London: University of W. Ontario.

Llewellyn, S. (1996). Theories for theorists or theories for practice? liberating academic research? Commentary on Humphrey, C., & Scapens, R. W. (1996). Methodological themes: theories and case studies of organizational accounting practices: limitation or liberation? *Accounting, Auditing and Accountability Journal*, *9*(4), 112–118.

Mahoney, T. A. (1997). Scholarship as a career of learning through research and teaching. In: R. Andre, & P. J. Frost (Eds), *Researchers hooked on teaching: Noted scholars discuss the synergies of teaching and research* (pp. 112–124). London: Sage.

Milne, M. J., & McConnell, P. J. (2001). Problem-based learning: a pedagogy for using case material in accounting education. *Accounting Education: An International Journal, 10*(1), 61–82.

Montano, J. L. A., Anes, J. A. D., Hassall, T., & Joyce, J. (2001). Vocational skills in the accounting professional profile: the Chartered Institute of Management Accountants (CIMA) employers' opinion. *Accounting Education: An International Journal, 10*(3), 299–313.

Otley, D. (2002). British research in accounting and finance (1996–2000). the 2001 research assessment exercise. *British Accounting Review, 34*(4), 387–417.

Otley, D. T., & Berry, A. J. (1994). Case study research in management accounting and control. *Management Accounting Research, 5*(1), 45–65.

QAA Accountancy Benchmarking Statement (2000). Gloucester: Quality Assurance Agency for Higher Education.

Rees, W. D., & Porter, C. (2002). The use of case studies in management training and development. Part 1. *Industrial and Commercial Training, 34*(1), 5–8.

Richardson, B., Montanheiro, L., & O'Cinneide, B. (Eds) (1995). *How to research, write, teach and publish management case studies*. Sheffield Hallam University: PAVIC Publications.

Richardson, S. (1993). Descriptions of some selfishly led organisation realities. In: B. Richardson (Ed.), *Managing in enterprise contexts* (pp. 67–83). Sheffield Hallam University: PAVIC Publications.

Richardson, S., & Cullen, J. (2000). Autopsy of change: contextualising entrepreneurial and accounting potential in the NHS. *Financial Accountability and Management, 16*(4), 353–372.

Richardson. S., Cullen, J., & Richardson, B. (1996). The story of a schizoid organization: how accounting and the accountant are implicated in its creation. *Accounting, Auditing and Accountability Journal, 9*(1), 8–30.

Ritchie, J., & Richardson, S. (2000). Smaller business governance: exploring accountability and enterprise from the margins. *Management Accounting Research, 11*(4), 451–474.

Scholes, K. (1995). Strategic issues for the management case writer. In: B. Richardson, L. Montanheiro, & B. O'Cinneide (Eds), *op cit* (pp. 157–162).

Schon, D. A. (1983). *The reflective practitioner: How professionals think in action*. New York: Basic Books.

Schon, D. A. (1987). *Educating the reflective practitioner: Towards a new design for teaching and learning in the professions*. San Francisco: Jossey-Bass.

Stilson, J. E., & Milter, R. G. (1996). Problem-based learning in business education: curriculum design and implementation issues. *New Directions for Teaching and Learning, 68* (Winter), 33–42.

Thompson, J. L. (1995). What goes into a management strategy case study? In: B. Richardson, L. Montanheiro, & B. O'Cinneide (Eds), *op cit* (pp. 147–156).

Zoll, A. A. (1966). *Dynamic management education* (2nd ed.). New York: Addison Wesley.

Section Five: Interdisciplinary Perspectives

A key objective of this book has been to promote greater understanding of qualitative research in accounting by providing insights into the informal (but often unarticulated) processes that in large part make up the every-day experiences of using qualitative research methods. In this final section, we change tack by considering whether the issues that we have encouraged accounting academics to discuss in earlier sections find any resonance in the experiences of researchers in other disciplines. Like accounting, a number of other social science disciplines have had dominant quantitative traditions. Yet, also like accounting, the potential exists to apply qualitative research methods to generate alternative forms of understanding, although the extent to which a qualitative tradition has developed does vary between disciplines. The point to which a discipline has advanced down such a path will be affected by a wide range of different factors. These include just how much the raw data lends itself to a quantitative or qualitative analysis, the ease with which it is possible to obtain different types of data, the openness and flexibility of the discipline in embracing change and new perspectives, the nature and range of publication outlets for new types of research, the initiative that researchers show in recognising and engineering opportunities for conducting new types of research, the bravery and application that researchers demonstrate when pursuing those opportunities and the extent to which they are able to find others who have similar interests from whom to draw support.

In this section, we include three chapters from researchers working in other social science disciplines, namely, the Sociology of Science, Organizational Psychology and Financial Economics. There is a clearly a wide range of other disciplines from which we could have sought contributions. However, in commissioning the chapters included in this section, we were fortunate to be able to obtain insights from three disciplines that have progressed to different points in their use of qualitative methods and to have such insights provided by authors who have played quite different roles in the development and adoption of such methods.

In chapter twenty-eight, Harry Collins — one of the pioneers of qualitative research in the Sociology of Science — recounts his investigations into scientific research into TEA-Lasers and Gravitational Waves. Starting from the premise that scientific practices are markedly different from the application of an idealised form of scientific method and procedures, Harry's chapter serves to illustrate the fortuitous and unpredictable nature of a research career and the value of having an active and open mind. He shows how the introduction of an existing method of research into a new area and the development of a new concept arose from unseen or unintended circumstances, and how he was able to benefit from such developments. He closes by providing some invaluable tips to young (and older) researchers in terms of the outlook they should seek to maintain with respect to their work and discipline. Catherine Cassell and Gillian Symon — whose books have popularised qualitative methods across a range of disciplines — outline how, as two friends, they wanted to challenge the dominant practices in their discipline by publicising the qualitative methods that existed. They show how they went from struggling to obtain a book contract to ending up producing a series of best-selling guides in the field. The clear message from their chapter is of the incremental nature of change as a discipline slowly becomes more responsive to qualitative research. Cathy and Gillian also show the importance of perspective in terms of not underestimating what is capable of being achieved when pushing against dominant traditions, of avoiding a 'bunker-like mentality' and retaining a fresh and constructive face when advocating and pursuing change. In chapter thirty, the final chapter of the book, Kevin Dowd — a leading financial economics researcher — considers the potential for qualitative research in his discipline. Starting from a premise that all research is ultimately qualitative because it is based on implicit, subjective judgements about the nature of the world, Kevin points out the importance for qualitative researchers of not being mystified by the technicalities of quantitative methods used by financial economists. He uses his own technical knowledge and experience of Financial Economics to suggest areas where qualitative research could make a notable contribution to the area. Kevin's chapter is particularly interesting as he writes from the perspective of someone who has a predominantly quantitative research background. For him, qualitative research methods can, at times, appear quite daunting and challenging but this does not prevent him from seeing the rich potential of applying in qualitative methods in a discipline that has hardly made use of them. This has some clear overlaps with the accounting (and related finance) disciplines and presents a very positive future message and agenda for qualitative accounting researchers. It is a highly appropriate way to end this book!

Chapter 28

Qualitative Methodology in Practice: My Experience

Harry Collins

Introduction

There is a tendency in the social sciences to be 'scientistic'. The definition of scientism, as found in my *Chamber's Dictionary*, includes the view that the methods of the natural sciences should be applied to the social sciences. But the notion of scientism can be defined more usefully in a way which is hinted at in the dictionary when it mentions 'pseudo-scientific language'. Defined this way, scientism is the view that the methods of the social sciences should ape the methods of the natural sciences, not as found in practice, but as described and idealised by certain philosophers and other commentators. Perhaps the *Chamber's* definition was written before it was realised that there was such a gulf between scientific method as a set of abstract principles and scientific method as a set of practices. Scientific practice, we now know, is nearer to Paul Feyerabend's 'anything goes' than to the 'logic of science' adumbrated in the 1950s and before. Over the last three decades and more this has been argued in principle and shown to be so by many case studies of the natural sciences at work.[1]

What I will not do here is provide yet more arguments or evidence to demonstrate the difference between the practice and the abstract description of science; by now it must

---

[1] The tradition of empirical and historical studies of the 'Sociology of Scientific Knowledge' type goes back at least as far as Ludwik Fleck's *Genesis and Development of a Scientific Fact*, which was published in German in 1935, though it was not recognised as a tradition until much later and Fleck was unknown to most Western analysts until the publication of his book in English in 1979. Thomas Kuhn was one person who knew the original Fleck and he cites it in the preface to his well-known *The Structure of Scientific Revolutions*. Kuhn's book might be said to have set the scene for the emergence of sociology of scientific knowledge though the empirical studies would have been said to owe more to Fleck if we had known of his existence. There were a number of philosophical and historical works that were important at the time but the first fieldwork-based studies include the books and papers mentioned in the text and the rest of the footnotes, for example, Latour & Woolgar (1979); Pickering (1981, 1984); Pinch (1981, 1986); Travis (1981) and Collins & Pinch (1982).

The Real Life Guide to Accounting Research: A Behind-the-Scenes View of Using Qualitative Research Methods
Copyright © 2004 by Elsevier Ltd.
All rights of reproduction in any form reserved.
ISBN: 0-08-043972-1

be one of the best-established findings in the whole of the social sciences. Instead I will give some examples of my own sociological practice in studies I conducted in the 1970s. As it happens the work I am going to describe was an investigation of natural science in practice. Nevertheless, from the point of view of my main argument, this is a coincidence.

I am going to describe the genesis of the first two papers I wrote. Both of these papers have been cited many times and continue to be cited up to the present, and both have been reprinted. The first was reprinted in 1982 and then again in 1999. The second was reprinted twice in 1982 (once in English, once in French), and twice in 1985 (once in English, once in Spanish). I'll take this history of citations and reprints as indicating that these two papers are examples of non-trivial work in the social sciences.

How the Papers Developed

In the case of neither paper did I know what I would produce when I set out to do the fieldwork. In the case of the first paper I had no 'hypothesis' and no idea of doing a 'test'. I was just finding out about something that looked interesting. It did turn out to be interesting but in a way which I did not predict at the outset. In the second case I began with something much closer to an 'experimental design' but the design was based on a simple mistake which should have been obvious from the outset. Fortunately, I overlooked the mistake until most of the fieldwork was finished. The result was that I was forced to do something with the data which would not have occurred to me otherwise. This, I think, turned out to be a lot more interesting than the original idea.

Paper 1: TEA-lasers

The first paper grew out of my MA dissertation — a short piece of work tacked on to the end of nine months of courses and essay writing. When I began the research all I knew was that I wanted to do fieldwork in science laboratories and a university was a good location to start. My supervisor introduced me to some university scientists who were working on the problem of the chemical origin of gels and slimes (part of the problem of the origin of life), but I couldn't think of anything to do with the material.

Someone — I can't remember who but it might have been one of the gel scientists — told me that in another lab they were trying to build a new kind of laser. So I wandered over there and they told me that they were trying to make models of a specially powerful laser that had been discovered a couple of years before in a Canadian laboratory. Powerful lasers, with their potential to shoot down airplanes, seemed exciting; the devices were two or three feet long and the crucial parts were mounted inside transparent tubes of glass or perspex with the electronics outside, so you could see the whole thing and you could see quite a lot of the ways in which one of them differed from another. Better still, it was very hard to make them work, and this made the science seem less forbidding. What I decided to do was study the British 'knowledge diffusion network' for this kind of laser.

There are a couple of things I want to say in my own defence to counterbalance my haphazard approach to research. The first is that I had a theoretically informed idea of what I meant by knowledge diffusion. I had, in my head, the Kuhnian idea of 'paradigm' which was in turn informed by the Wittgensteinian idea of 'form-of-life'. Thus, I knew I wanted to look at knowledge diffusion as though it were the spreading out of a new language rather than as the mechanical passing out of discrete 'bits of information'. The most well-known knowledge diffusion studies had to do with the spread of knowledge about new drugs among doctors. These took the 'discrete bits of information' approach and I knew I wanted do something different to that.

The second thing I want to say in my defence is that nearly all my fellow students on the MA course were writing dissertations which could be done without stirring from the library. These had titles such as 'Lucien Goldman's contribution to Louis Althusser's intellectual formation' and such students tended to be favoured by many of the tutors. I did not want to spend any more time in libraries and I found the idea of driving round the country talking to people much more appealing. So my approach was a kind of mini-rebellion against what counted as the paradigm of 'sociological' work at that time and place. The paradigm for an MA dissertation was to start with some kind of 'theory' and suffocate it to death in the library. I was starting with some kind of theory and taking it for a brisk 'constitutional' around the country. I still think my approach was better.

The theoretical framework I took to the field made me attend to certain features of my diffusion network more carefully than others might have done. First I was interested not so much in those to whom knowledge of the new kind of laser had spread but in those who had learned what we might call 'the language of laser-building'. Thus, in the typical knowledge diffusion network, concerning awareness of new drugs among doctors, the data concerned which doctors knew of the drug and how they had learned of its existence. The rather nice 'two step theory of communication' had grown out of these studies. This theory said that there were often knowledge 'gatekeepers' in an organisation whose role was mainly to read all the literature and keep their ears open to all the networks and inform their colleagues of what was going on in the world around them. If I had taken this idea into the field I could probably have found it operating among the laser-builders too. I could have found out all the names of those who knew that such-and-such a kind of laser had been invented based on such-and-such principles and how they found out about it and whom they passed the information on to.

My informing metaphor, however, did not fit very well with the two-step theory of communication. My metaphor was, as it were, becoming fluent in French (laser-building) rather than knowing that the French language existed and a few of its nouns and verbs. This meant that I was specially alert to the difference between those scientists who had successfully built models of the laser and had them working on their bench and those who knew of the laser's existence and principles and could build one 'if only they wanted to'. Incidentally, it was easy to know whether a laser of this kind was working because the beam was so powerful that if you put a lump of concrete in the way of it the concrete would start to smoke.

The second thing that the language-learning metaphor caused me to look at closely was aspects of interpersonal interaction that one would associate with learning a language — immersion in the culture of the language — in this case, personal contact between scientists rather than the exchange of documents. Fluency in French is not learned from dictionaries and grammar manuals, it is learned by talking to French people. Incidentally, the new kind of laser was the *'Transversely Excited, Atmospheric pressure, carbon dioxide laser'*, or 'TEA-laser' for short. My question was 'Who has learned to build a TEA-laser and how did they learn it?'

What I actually did was drive around the country interviewing scientists who had built TEA-lasers and recording their words on tape. *Inter alia* I seemed to have invented a new fieldwork approach to science since nearly all previous work on contemporary scientists involved visits to single laboratories, or to a few organisations, or doing some kind of representative survey, or studying the science citation index. My population was neither scientists, nor scientific organisations, nor the scientific literature, but the complete set of TEA-laser builders in the U.K. They were defined, in other words, by their interest in a specific scientific project rather than by an institutional affiliation or formal qualification. In retrospect there was more to this than finding a new way to draw a sample: doing the fieldwork this way emerged out of an interest in the way *scientific knowledge* worked rather than the way *scientists* worked so it too was linked to the whole language-learning metaphor.

As can be guessed, what I was asking the scientists was whether they had a working laser, how they had reached the point at which they could make it work, what sources of information they used to get to that point, and how they dealt with enquiries about their own work. I enjoyed the whole thing enormously — getting out of the library, seeing the inside of new kinds of institution and talking to new kinds of people, visiting distant parts of the country I would not otherwise have gone to, and learning things about other peoples' working lives. I wasn't entirely sure what I was doing but it felt 'right'.

I analysed the results primarily by drawing networks on transparent sheets which could be overlaid, and by cobbling together various of my essays on network analysis and so forth, I managed to produce something that looked like a dissertation with an argument supporting the notion that building a TEA-laser was more like learning a language than gathering discrete bits of information. In particular, it slowly dawned that the only people who had made the laser work (aside from the original inventor), had strong personal contacts with another laboratory who had made it work. Those who had tried to build one of the things from written sources alone had always failed until they developed personal contacts and had lots of conversations. This was a very clean finding — they always failed.

I thought it was a pretty good dissertation and I hoped it would earn me a distinction in my MA but it didn't. Those distinctions went to the Lucien Goldman and Louis Althusser people as I recall.[2] But I had my degree and was able to go on to my Ph.D. and that put me in a position to do still more travelling around. This was 1971.

---

[2] I don't want to give the impression that I was in any way discouraged from doing this empirical study, just that an empirical study was not the kind of thing that was expected to form the basis of such a short dissertation at the time I did it. This was nothing explicit, just the norm that had developed within the community of the time.

It was sometime later that someone (Richard Whitley), suggested I should publish the thesis — it had not occurred to me until that moment that I had done anything worth broadcasting and I still thought of myself as a student. By this time I had more data as I had pursued the TEA-laser study as part of my Ph.D. and had filled it out with interviews representing the North American beginnings of the network. I wrote the enlarged study up in article form. My self-confidence was still low and I wrote it up in a studenty kind of way, which meant framing it as being 'against something'. In this case it was against the prevailing and ever-more-dominant fashion of citation analysis in the study of science — the exploration of the scientific community as delineated by networks of citations. I said that since real scientific understanding was transmitted by personal interaction the citation analyses represented a very superficial model of the process of scientific knowledge building. The editor of the journal to which I submitted the paper (David Edge) was very encouraging and that was the beginning of my transformation from student to professional.

The eventual form of the paper owed a lot to the remarks of colleagues and referees but without going back to the early correspondence it would be hard to work out exactly who contributed what. What I do remember is that one of my referees (Mike Mulkay) pointed out my ignorance of a whole raft of relevant literature turning on the notion of 'tacit knowledge'. The physical chemist Michael Polanyi had written books on the tacit knowledge of scientists — knowledge that they possessed but could not express. Surely, said the referee, what I was revealing was more of this working out of tacit knowledge. So I re-wrote the paper using the terminology of tacit knowledge and the published version was called "The TEA-set: Tacit Knowledge and Scientific Networks".[3]

The change of title and the setting of the paper within the tradition of tacit knowledge was probably a good thing as it helped readers recognise what it was about and saved me from critics who would otherwise have said it had all been done before. On the other hand, Polanyi's version, which has a lot to do with preserving the autonomy of scientists in a 'republic of science', includes a lot of stuff about scientists' creativity and intuition. It does not lead in the same direction as the deeper and more general Wittgensteinian notion of form-of-life. So the Polanyi connotation, though I have stuck with it, has occasionally been a nuisance and led people to misunderstand what I was trying to do in subsequent work.

I wrote a follow up study to the 1974 paper in 1975 and in 2001 I wrote another paper that is very similar to the 1974 paper though it is about a different group of scientists. It is called "Tacit Knowledge, Trust, and the Q of Sapphire".[4]

Paper 2: Gravitational Waves

For my Ph.D. in 1971 I decided I would extend the TEA-laser study and do some comparisons with other areas of science. As I have intimated, anyone who was

---

[3] See Collins (1974). Shortly after this date, the journal *Science Studies* changed its name to *Social Studies of Science*.
[4] See Collins & Harrison (1975) and Collins (2001). I have also written lots of other papers trying to make the issue more clear.

interested in science in those days was bound to be thinking about Thomas Kuhn's book *The Structure of Scientific Revolutions* with its contrast between normal science and revolutionary science. The TEA-laser was very clearly normal science and I thought I should do some comparisons with some science that was a bit less normal. I picked two 'extraordinary' areas for comparison: parapsychology and the attempt to detect cosmic gravitational radiation. I picked them because I had just read articles about them in the *New Scientist* and they seemed intriguing. I think the vague idea was that I would find out whether people in these 'revolutionary' areas were more or less competitive, and hence secretive, than the TEA-laser scientists.

My supervisor insisted that I should also make a comparison with a theoretical area. As a result I carried out thirteen interviews with top scientists working on the theory of amorphous semiconductors but at the end of these I had to admit that I still had no idea what they were talking about. I did not even know who agreed with whom and who disagreed. This was a very valuable experience even though the data were worthless and it has given me much more confidence in doing work in areas where I do know what the scientists are talking about. Because I now have something against which to set my understanding and I have a better sense of the difference between understanding and not understanding. That is another advantage of bad fieldwork design.

Anyway, my first new tranche of fieldwork, conducted in 1972, saw me buying an old car and driving 5000 miles around and across America interviewing scientists working in these three new areas of science and the TEA-laser area. As can be imagined, the trip satisfied all my criteria for good fieldwork even though, as I should have realised, it was badly flawed in terms of experimental design. The work on parapsychology eventually led to various articles and quite a successful book but the 1975 paper I am going to talk about was about the detection of gravitational waves was what I still think of as my best ever publication (how sad!) and I'll talk about that case study and ignore the rest.

Joe Weber, a university of Maryland physicist, had pioneered the detection of gravitational waves. He had set up bars of aluminium weighing a couple of tons inside vacuum chambers and isolated them from all known forces. He claimed that the residual vibrations in the bars were evidence for the existence of gravitational waves.

Joe Weber found a lot of gravitational waves and other scientists were either sufficiently excited by his claims to want to join in the search or sufficiently irritated by the seeming unlikelihood of the claims that they wanted to disprove them. Whatever the motivation, about half-a-dozen other groups had built Weber-type detectors but were seemingly failing to see what Weber has seen. In interviewing all these scientists I had inadvertently invented what became known as the 'controversy study'.

Anyway, this is how I remember it: I had done the large majority of these interviews and was driving across Nevada on my way to a last interview in Stanford, and I was thinking about how I would write up all the interesting data I had gathered. In my head I was going through the paper I would write, modelling it on the TEA-laser study of knowledge-diffusion among scientists. Crucial, you will recall, was the transmission of real understanding not just bits and pieces of information. Suddenly the hair stood up on the back of my neck. Vital to the TEA-laser study was my ability to tell whether a group had a working laser on their bench — whether they really had developed 'fluency in the TEA-laser language'. But, disastrously, there was no equivalent in the gravitational wave field because no one could be sure whether they had detected gravitational waves. Whereas the TEA-laser scientists could make concrete smoke, or not make concrete smoke as the case may be, no one could agree what the gravitational wave detectors ought to be doing. Should they be seeing gravitational waves or not seeing gravitational waves? How could I have made such a huge mistake in my experimental design? How could I not have spotted this elementary error until after I had driven 4000 miles carrying out interviews? I was in a state of panic.

If I remember rightly it took me about another half-hour's driving to work out what to do and when I had worked it out I immediately knew I was 'on to something'. The point was this: If I didn't know when a gravitational wave detector was working, then neither did the scientists! In the case of the TEA-laser, scientists knew how long they had to go on making phone calls, visiting other's laboratories, and rebuilding their lasers in slightly different ways, because they had a clear criterion of when they had attained success — smoking concrete. Without this clear criterion some of them would have believed they had succeeded when they had not, and others would not have succeeded because they would not have known just how hard they had to try. Now, in the case of the gravitational wave detectors there were many scientists claiming they had built detectors that were failing to do the equivalent of making concrete smoke — detecting gravitational waves — but they could not be sure whether this failure was to do with their not being any gravitational waves to see or their failure to build a machine that was good enough to see them. In 'normal science' I realised, this problem did not arise because there was consensus about what any device ought to see when it was working. In 'extraordinary science' however, what the device should see when it was working was precisely what the scientists were building the devices to find out.

This dilemma, its working out in scientific controversies, and its meaning for the foundations of scientific knowledge became the subject of the paper. It seemed to be to be still more exciting than the topic of the transmission of scientific understanding that I originally thought I was investigating and that was how I wrote up the fieldwork in the 1975 paper (see Collins 1975). The idea subsequently became known as 'the experimenter's regress', though I did not invent that name until I wrote the whole study up in a subsequent book (see Collins 1985).[5]

Conclusions

Mostly this has been a tale of lucky accidents and it is hard to draw any systematic conclusions from a series of lucky accidents. But there is one big conclusion — 'Put yourself in the way of potentially lucky accidents'. One can be completely sure that nothing as lucky as what occurred to me will happen if you do not put yourself in a position to benefit from the luck.

So what do you have to do, and not have to do, to put yourself in the way of lucky accidents? I'd say you have to have some kind of idea that guides the way you look at the world and then you have to go out and look at the world. What you do not have to

---

[5] To see where this work is going today see my gravitational website: www.cf.ac.uk/socsi/gravwave

do is read everything that might have a potential bearing on your idea; one really clear way of looking at the world is good enough. There is a chance that you will 'rediscover somebody else's wheel' but in my experience this hardly ever happens. On a number of occasions people have told me that what I have done is only what so-and-so has already done but after an initial panic I invariably find that this is not so, or not quite so. Often what the other person has done is either different or enriches my understanding of what I have already done. Sometimes, if I had been too assiduous in reading all this other stuff and making sure that I took it into account before I started I would either never start, or, my view of the world would be so hedged about with other viewpoints that I would not have seen what I did see. In practice what this means is not giving up reading but changing the conventional order of investigation. Conventionally one reads first and investigates later. My model would suggest that having read enough to know what you think you then investigate and carry on reading at the same time.

Another conclusion is that you must investigate and preferably investigate something that interests you enough to keep you at it even when you are not quite sure why. What you should not do is confine the investigation into the scientistic 'hypothesis-and-test' straightjacket. Or at least, if a hypothesis-and-test is the guiding idea, which it can be, don't let it be too confining.

This leads to another conclusion which is — 'to stay light on your feet'. Be ready to change the subject of the investigation if the fieldwork pushes you in that direction. I would say that in addition to the two cases described, nearly every piece of fieldwork I have ever undertaken has turned out to be an initial disappointment. That is, it failed to fit my expectations of what I would find. But when I decided that I must have been looking for something else all along that something else turned out to be much more interesting. Indeed, nowadays, if I don't get some kind of disturbing surprise during the course of fieldwork, or thinking about the fieldwork, or writing up and analysing the fieldwork, I start to get worried. Nearly all the interesting things I come up with are different in a bigger or smaller way from what I set out to find.[6] In sum, the rules are as follows:

(1) Always be clear.
(2) Take a broad idea into the field.
(3) Don't suffocate the idea by too much reading prior to fieldwork.
(4) Stay light on your feet and don't be too disappointed by your disappointments; disappointments can often be turned to advantage if initial ideas are not too rigid.

Afterword

Under the loosest definition of 'scientism' that can found in the Dictionary — that the methods of the natural sciences should be applied to the social sciences — my work is

---

[6] Here we do not encounter the problem of 'statistical massage'. There is a danger that statistically significant results can be obtained by retrospectively fitting the hypothesis to the results. But here we are not engaged in statistical generalisation but discovering the internal logic or, what is the same thing, the cultural imperative, behind a social process. Here one should not go wrong by retrospectively adjusting the problem.

scientistic. That is, I believe the arguments and findings of the social sciences should be clear, logically consistent as far as possible, empirically verifiable, repeatable by suitably experienced others, and so forth. I think this remains the case even though the very studies of science that I have described reveal that these terms have very different meanings to what was once believed and that they are deeply invested with 'the social'. The circle is squared because the 'ought' of method does not not follow from the 'is'. We still have to try to be as scientific as possible in the sense of the values expressed a couple of sentences ago even as we avoid being stifled by scientism in its narrow definition. There is no better way to do science than the old fashioned way. In detail, of course, the methods of natural and social science vary widely. For example, there is no equivalent of interpretivism in the natural science (see Collins 1984).[7]

The editors of this volume asked me to comment on another two matters that arise out of the chapter. I imply that the researcher has, to some extent, to 'go native' in order to pick up on the equivalent of the 'learning French' that is going on among the respondents. The question I was asked was whether this involved a loss of objectivity. The answer is that the kinds of generalisation that social science makes transcend any one case study. It follows that if these generalisations are sound they will be equally observable by anyone else going native in the same way in some other case. This is what has happened in the sociology of scientific knowledge. For example, the observation about the experimenter's regress has been repeated by lots of other observers doing lots of case studies of other sciences. There remains a problem about how to bring these things back home to academic readers who have not gone native. I discuss this in the paper mentioned in the last footnote.

The other question the editors asked turned on my knowing the name of the influential referee on my early papers. This was not a matter of policy, the referee just told me. If I were in charge of policy for these things, however, I would make it the normal expectation that refereeing was transparent not anonymous. I would allow the following exceptions:

(1) When the status of the author is substantially higher than the status of the referee the referee should be anonymous whether the review is positive or negative.
(2) When the review is dismissively negative. Sometimes conscience dictates that the paper has to be described as 'rubbish' or the equivalent and then the referee ought to be entitled not to have to add another enemy to the list.

Nowadays I always confess who I am when refereeing even if my remarks are negative. I try to soften the blow by making positive suggestions about how problems can be rectified. There are some people who will hate you for criticising them even a little, but that can't be helped.

Incidentally, in the social sciences the idea of authors remaining anonymous is usually a nonsense. A paper contains too much of the 'signature' of the author's work if they are well-known, and if they are not well-know it does not matter anyway.

---

[7] For a complete misunderstanding of these points see Flyvbjerg (2001). Flyvbjerg thinks that because social science uses interpretation it cannot be scientific.

References

Collins, H. M. (1974). The TEA set: tacit knowledge and scientific networks. *Science Studies*, *4*(2), 165–186.

Collins, H. M. (1975). The seven sexes: a study in the sociology of a phenomenon, or the replication of experiments in physics. *Sociology*, *9*(2), 205–224.

Collins, H. M. (1984). Concepts and Methods of Participatory Fieldwork. In: C. Bell, & H. Roberts (Eds), *Social Researching* (pp. 54–69). Henley-on-Thames: Routledge.

Collins, H. M. (1985). *Changing order: Replication and induction in scientific practice* Beverley Hills and London: Sage (2nd ed., University of Chicago Press 1992).

Collins, H. M. (2001). Tacit knowledge, trust, and the *Q* of sapphire. *Social Studies of Science*, *31*(1), 71–85.

Collins, H. M., & Harrison, R. (1975). Building a TEA laser: the caprices of communication. *Social Studies of Science*, *5*(4), 441–445.

Collins, H. M., & Pinch, T. J. (1982). *Frames of meaning: The social construction of extraordinary science*. Henley-on Thames: Routledge and Kegan Paul.

Flyvbjerg, B. (2001). *Making social science matter: Why social inquiry fails and how it can succeed again*. Cambridge: Cambridge University Press.

Latour, B., & Woolgar, S. (1979). *Laboratory life: The social construction of scientific facts*. London and Beverly Hills: Sage.

Pickering, A. (1981). Constraints on controversy: the case of the magnetic monopole. *Social Studies of Science*, *11*(1), 63–93.

Pickering, A. (1984). *Constructing quarks: A sociological history of particle physics*. Edinburgh: Edinburgh University Press.

Pinch, T. J. (1981). The sun-set: the presentation of certainty in scientific life. *Social Studies of Science*, *11*(1), 131–158.

Pinch, T. J. (1986). *Confronting nature: The sociology of solar-neutrino detection*. Dordrecht: Reidel.

Travis, G. D. L. (1981). Replicating replication? Aspects of the social construction of learning in planarian worms. *Social Studies of Science*, *11*(1), 11–32.

Chapter 29

Raising the Profile of Qualitative Methods in Organizational Research

Catherine Cassell and Gillian Symon

Introduction

This chapter concerns our experience of trying to raise the profile of qualitative methods in a discipline that is dominated strongly by a positivist research model. It tells the story of two researchers within the field of organizational psychology who bemoaned the lack of information about how to use qualitative methods within their disciplinary area, as well as the status that such methods had, and tried to do something about it. Twelve years later, the researchers have grown up a bit and produced two books, two special issues of journals, numerous symposia at conferences, and have a third book on the way, all focusing on the use of qualitative methods in organizational research. Put like that it sounds a grand tale; in practice it is the story of two mates who shared a set of assumptions about how research should be done, who, then, perhaps somewhat naively, set off to change current practice, and about how their ideas changed and evolved as they learnt more through actively engaging with the subject.

The chapter is divided into four sections. The first three tie in with the three edited books we have produced for Sage Publications, and each focuses broadly upon the key issues with which we were concerned at various times. These issues were largely debated in our editorial introductions to the books (and in other papers and presentations we gave at the time) rather than in the overall compositions of the books. Each book consisted of a set of chapters where a contributor described their use of a particular qualitative method. Whilst we may have asked contributors to pay attention to different specific issues in each volume, the content of each chapter was largely dictated by the contributor.

The first section of this chapter concentrates on our efforts to promote qualitative methods; the second concerns more epistemological issues and the politics of the research process; and the third section considers issues of reflexivity and diversity within qualitative approaches. In the final section, we conclude by questioning the

The Real Life Guide to Accounting Research: A Behind-the-Scenes View of Using Qualitative Research Methods
Copyright © 2004 by Elsevier Ltd.
All rights of reproduction in any form reserved.
ISBN: 0-08-043972-1

extent to which change has occurred with regard to the use of qualitative methods in our disciplinary area. Within the chapter we refer to our disciplinary domain in a number of ways: organizational psychology, occupational psychology, or work psychology. All terms are in common usage for the same disciplinary domain.

Promoting Qualitative Methods

Organizational psychology focuses on individual and group experiences of work and organization. We felt qualitative methods of data collection and analysis provided more opportunities to access that rich variety of experience. However, like most psychology students, we had both been trained in the use of quantitative methodologies. We often bemoaned how difficult it was to access information about the application of qualitative methods in psychology. We shared the view that such methods were more appropriate to the kind of research questions we were asking: focusing on meaning and interpretation rather than identifying variables and causal relationships. We believed that qualitative methods were becoming more widespread within the discipline but were, we suspected, not reported as much as they could be. We wanted to know more about how our colleagues were using such methods and how we could access and utilise this rich seam of alternative approaches in our own research work. For example, we were both interested in the study of organizational change and how individuals understand and make sense of change processes in the workplace. Our argument was that the use of quantitative methods might tell us if change had occurred — through the use of pre-test and post-test measures, for example. However, these methods could not really access the lived experience of organizational change, in the way that qualitative methods could. This conclusion was based on our own experience. Gillian had used tracer studies and diary studies as a way of documenting the informal and political processes of change (Hornby & Symon 1994; Symon 1998). We argued that an in-depth analysis of political processes was difficult using quantitative techniques. Catherine had used repertory grids from a constructivist perspective to look at the various ways in which performance was constructed in the workplace and how male and female managers construed notions of effective performance differently (Walsh & Cassell 1994). The argument was again that it would have been difficult to access those subtle differences through the use of quantitative techniques. Indeed, in the latter case, the research had been commissioned by a client organization that specifically wanted us to use qualitative techniques. A number of surveys they had commissioned had indicated that women were less likely to achieve senior management positions, but they wanted to know more about: why this was the case; the potential for change; and about the experiences that men and women expressed in relation to progression opportunities. Our argument was that we were more likely to generate an in-depth understanding of change processes through the use of qualitative techniques (like repertory grid) that focused on respondents' reactions or activities in their own words. These approaches were rarely reported in the mainstream work psychology journals of the time.

After expressing our joint frustrations about the lack of information on how to use qualitative methods, we put together a proposal for a book contract with Sage

Publications. The book was to be entitled *Qualitative Methods in Organizational Research: A Practical Guide* (Cassell & Symon 1994a) and contained 12 chapters that focused on how to use different qualitative methods, plus an introduction from us. This was our first experience of trying to get a book contract and the whole process took about six months. Clearly we were 'untested' and the publishers wanted to make sure we could deliver what we promised. The editor, who was very supportive of qualitative approaches, gave detailed comments on chapter abstracts from each of the contributors. It took a period of lots of reviewing and questioning before our contract finally arrived.

The book eventually came out in 1994. It was about conducting qualitative research in organizations; the variety of qualitative methods available to researchers; and how these methods could be used in practice to provide quality research data. Specifically, we saw the book at the time as having three important aims. Firstly, to document the variety of qualitative methods currently used by occupational and organizational psychologists; secondly, to provide the researcher and the practitioner with an overview of a range of methods, together with examples of how they are currently being used in practice; and thirdly, to try to raise the profile of qualitative methods within the discipline.

One of the first issues we came across was how to define qualitative methods. This issue is one we were continually discussing while preparing the book and, as we discovered, is not as straightforward as it seems. There were, at that time, very few exact definitions and it seemed like there was no precise meaning associated with the term qualitative methods. We felt that the search for a 'one best' definition was a misguided endeavour and in approaching contributors for the book, we did not make any claims about, or constraints upon, what constituted a 'qualitative' method. Clearly, individuals had very different ideas about what the term meant. However, as editors, we needed some sort of scope to provide a sense of common purpose for the volume (see also Symon 2002). To address this problem we read other writings in the area and the chapters themselves to come up with our own list of the characteristics of qualitative methods. These were, first, that qualitative research was generally non-restrictive, in that it is usually the case that qualitative research is less likely to impose a priori classifications on the data. Secondly, there was a focus on subjectivity. It is often argued that one of the cornerstones of the qualitative approach is its acceptance of the inherent subjectivity of the research endeavour (Bryman 1988). It is the view of the world as the organizational actors perceive it that is of explanatory value and interest. Thirdly, we suggested that qualitative research was context-dependent. In one sense, this implies that qualitative research should be conducted in naturalistic settings, that is, on location in organizations rather than in laboratories or other artificially constrained settings (Guba & Lincoln 1984; Marshall & Rossman 1989). It also suggests that context should be taken into account as formative in our explanations rather than as background noise which needs to be controlled out. Another key characteristic was that of taking a holistic perspective. An important characteristic of qualitative approaches is that they seek to provide a holistic view of the situations or organizations that researchers are trying to understand (Bogdan & Taylor 1975; Patton 1980). In this context, the individuals or organizations are not reduced to an isolated variable but are, rather, seen as part of a whole. To illustrate this point we used an excerpt from our favourite TV programme, which was the focus of much of our everyday conversation at that time:

> "At this stage we would like to summarize what we see to be the difference between the two forms of enquiry by referring to a comment from Rita Sullivan, a character in Coronation Street (our favourite weekly soap opera on British television). Rita's husband has recently died of a brain tumour and a legal action has been brought by his relatives concerning whether he was of 'sound mind' when he wrote his will (in which his widow receives all the money). They are all gathered in court and the prosecuting lawyer states: 'So here we have a man who couldn't do up his own buttons, whose writing and speaking would lead you to believe he was drunk and who in the ordinary run of things was sometimes confused about his wife's identity....would that be a fair picture?' Rita replies: 'No. I would say it were more like one of them games where you join the dots up to make a face — you just don't get a true impression' (date of broadcast: 24.2.93). In the positivist tradition we are concerned with establishing what the dots (or variables) are and drawing lines (causal links) between them — a reductionist view of the situation. In the interpretivist tradition, we are concerned with taking a holistic viewpoint — seeing the whole picture" (Cassell & Symon 1994b: 5).

The metaphor of joining the dots is one that we still use a lot (for example, Symon 2000a). The final characteristic was that those contributing to the research were treated as participants not subjects. Because such methods take place in the original setting of the research participant, Kirk & Miller (1986) suggest that qualitative researchers are engaged in interacting with people in their own language and on their own terms as would be expected on someone else's territory.

Within work psychology at that time, any qualitative methods used tended to emanate from a neo-positivist framework. We attempted to examine the implications of the view that methods came from different philosophical positions in our introductory chapter. However, this was something with which we struggled at the time and did not examine in as much detail as some reviewers would have liked. Reviews of the book from people within the work psychology field were very positive, they generally saw it as a new and useful contribution to the field. What was interesting was that the couple of reviewers who suggested that the book should have paid more attention to epistemological issues were from outside work psychology, both from the field of management where epistemological debates were much more in evidence. We felt at this time that, as we were in a very conservative discipline, our priority was to produce a practical guide that researchers keen to engage with the area could use as a reference.

Apart from defining qualitative methods, we wanted to highlight and enhance the profile and use of qualitative methods within our discipline. In the U.K. at that time, new initiatives in qualitative methods were emerging as a result of discussions stimulated by *The Future of Psychological Sciences Report* (1988). For example, a symposium sponsored by the Scientific Affairs Board of the British Psychological Society (B.P.S.) at the 1992 London conference argued that researchers needed to pay much more attention to qualitative methods (Henwood 1993). Despite such 'official' interest however, research using qualitative techniques was rarely reported in the main journals in the field. When editing a special issue of *The Occupational Psychologist* on 'Qualitative Methods in Occupational Psychology' in 1991, we asked the editors of the then entitled *Journal of Occupational Psychology*, the most prestigious U.K. journal in the field, to give their comments on this matter. They pointed out that, although they wished to encourage papers documenting qualitative research in occupational and organizational psychology, very few such papers were ever submitted to the journal. Clearly there were a number of potential explanations for this. We argued at the time that perhaps qualitative researchers did not send reports of their research to the main journals in the field because traditionally that kind of research was viewed as unorthodox and unscientific and they did not think they would be accepted. The editors of the *Journal of Occupational and Organizational Psychology* (as it was called when the book came out) argued that this assumption was mistaken, and that what was important was 'excellence' in the methodology used.

We felt very strongly that it was issues of value and ideology that were really important in this context — the judgement of 'excellence' may be shaped by many underlying assumptions. We believed that within organizational psychology qualitative and quantitative techniques were evaluated in different ways. Value is placed in psychology on research that is perceived to be methodologically rigorous. This is usually equated with quantitative approaches that are constructed as hard and scientific. Useful and appropriate knowledge is produced by orthodox techniques. This clearly has implications for qualitative researchers. In choosing to focus on qualitative approaches the researcher is taking a risk. Not for them is the credibility of the hardnosed scientist searching for the truth, but rather vulnerability and uncertainty as to how their research will be interpreted and evaluated primarily as a result of their chosen method.

A consequence of this was that, in our experience, there was a high level of expectation that qualitative researchers could and would account for the methodological approach of their work. This was in stark contrast to positivist work where the legitimacy and relevance of the method adopted was rarely questioned. Most qualitative researchers have become well-practised in defending their research in the context of positivist notions of reliability, generalisability and validity.

Our own experiences in psychology departments at that time was of qualitative Ph.D. researchers being informed by staff members that their research was 'nothing but journalism' and a visiting discourse analyst being told by staff members in the audience that her methodology 'came out of a Blue Peter annual'. One of us was warned by a member of her own department to stay away from the 'evils' of discourse analysis. As universities have to search for money to fund research, it becomes increasingly difficult for researchers to 'take risks' (as taking a qualitative approach would be interpreted). We were advised by some that going down the qualitative route may have a negative impact on our careers. We responded to this at the time, by making the following claim for our book:

"In work psychology efforts to legitimise psychology as a scientific endeavour (in the positivist sense) have been translated as the search for the 'natural (field) experiment' or the adoption of 'quasi-experimental' techniques (Cook & Campbell 1979). In contrast, this book has the objective of legitimising the use of qualitative methods in organizational research by illustrating the insights which can be achieved through their use" (Cassell & Symon 1994b: 9).

The book sold well, and we were very pleased with ourselves. We continued to pursue our desire to publicize qualitative methods by organising symposia regularly at various conferences. In the mid-nineties, far more interest was developing in qualitative methods in psychological and management research generally and numerous other texts were emerging. When we did receive public criticisms of the book they were inevitably about the lack of attention that the book paid to epistemological issues. One particular critique came from Peter Dachler, an internationally renowned Professor of Organizational Psychology who wrote a fifteen page book review essay of our book in the inter-disciplinary journal *Organization Studies* (Dachler 1997). The essay addressed numerous issues and in particular the epistemological underpinnings of methods with the title of 'Does the distinction between qualitative and quantitative methods make sense?' We were invited to write a response to the essay. Catherine wrote the first draft and asked a colleague to read it. Her colleague then advised her that rather than writing an article that could be perceived as both dismissive and curt, we should actually instead engage with some of the interesting issues that Dachler had raised. This made us realise how defensive we had become: that we were so used to having to defend the use of qualitative methods in our discipline, that we were finding it hard to engage in constructive debate.

Whilst also providing an analysis of the book, Dachler wanted to take the opportunity to open up a debate concerning underlying epistemological and ontological issues in the research process. In his critique he provided what we believed was an excellent summary of an epistemological position that eschews an essentialist, realist ontology and accepts research itself as a social process (see also Latour & Woolgar 1979; Gilbert & Mulkey 1984). He then applied this perspective to the (very varied) chapters in the book, and found it rather wanting. Although he was very positive about the text, he basically wanted to see more attention paid to particular epistemological issues, hence his title emerged from the argument that the distinction between qualitative and quantitative methods is not the significant issue. It is the underlying epistemological assumptions of research that are more worthy of debate. And he clearly had a preferred epistemological position. His critique opened up further potential discussions about who 'owns' qualitative methods and how change could be brought about in our research community. It became apparent to us that our position was one of participants in a 'quiet revolution' rather than the architects of a 'radical transformation'. We justified our position at the time in the following way:

"Our objectives in editing the book were rather prosaic (as indeed the title of the book suggests). Within our discipline of psychology, we felt the need (and believed it was shared) for some kind of overview of the qualitative research methods our colleagues (and ourselves) were using in their organizational research. Prompted by our own research and teaching needs we wanted a handbook which would be illustrative, practical, and, perhaps most importantly, accessible. Sensitive to the politics of research work, we thought, pragmatically, that producing such a book would give ourselves and other researchers a reference point, something to justify our use of 'alternative' methods within our local research communities, which were dominated by positivist assumptions and methods" (Cassell & Symon 1998: 1040).

The latter objective highlighted one of the major issues raised by Dachler's review: how do we bring about the change in our research communities that would allow qualitative methods to 'become true alternatives to the privileged ontology of quantitative research phenomenon'? How can raising the status of qualitative methods be 'more effectively achieved'? We argued that we had chosen an incremental approach rather than all out revolution but there is clearly room to debate whether this is appropriate (indeed this has been debated in the organizational change literature in general). Dachler's view was that this change could only be brought about if we ignored 'the fundamental research agendas and the corresponding epistemological assumptions championed by a realist/ individualistically oriented quantitative methodology'. However, we argued that we were continually expected to defend our qualitative work against criteria associated with a realist ontology within our own research communities, and that, therefore, from a political standpoint, our colleagues and ourselves needed to be equipped with such arguments. Another danger was that if we ignored research generated from a realist research agenda, this would exclude nearly all of the research that used qualitative methods in the work psychology field at that time! In order to bring about our quiet revolution, we argued that we needed to start from the current discourses prominent within the community addressed, as well as promoting alternative philosophical arguments that suggest fundamental critiques. Our concern, of course, was that we became trapped in neo-positivism. However, the alternative was to alienate potential 'converts'. This raises another issue for debate: in producing volumes such as ours, are we only addressing our sympathetic colleagues or perhaps seeking to convert those who have rarely conducted or encountered qualitative work? What is the ultimate goal of the continuing debate between researchers of different methodological persuasions? Should it be to be accepted on equal terms, or for one or other to dominate? (See also Reed 1992, and Smith, Harre & Van Langenhove 1995). Our position on this was that we did not necessarily want to see one approach dominate, but that research from a variety of different perspectives should be allowed to flourish as that would enhance our discipline. This was not the case in work psychology at that time. Also we realized that there was little chance of converting those who were not interested, or whose career ambitions were enhanced by being tied in to the positivist agenda. Rather, we wanted to make tools available for those who were interested in using qualitative methods, to try to contribute towards the creation of a more level playing field from which research using qualitative methods could be assessed.

The debate in *Organization Studies*, about which we had initially been so defensive, highlighted a key issue that we still face today. How can you change things, in this context, to enhance the profile of qualitative methods and encourage other researchers to engage with them? Our strategy in our books has been to deliberately try to make some of this whole area more accessible, and to bring about incremental change. This is not to say that radical transformation may not be necessary, and this has certainly occurred in other areas of psychology. Within social psychology such debates have tended to lead to a sharp polarising of positions in that sub-discipline (Parker 1989). In organizational psychology, the 'quiet revolution' is only just beginning and others, in addition to Dachler, clearly feel frustrated that we have not been radical enough. For example, a couple of months ago, at a conference, Catherine was arguing that qualitative methods need to be evaluated using criteria appropriate to the epistemological position in which they are used, and then it would be more likely that research using qualitative methods would get published. When it came to time for questions a member of the audience stood up and accused her of providing a sanitised, soft and cuddly version of what qualitative methods were about, and therefore selling out radical researchers. He told her what she should be saying in keynote speeches such as that, was that all positivist research was a total load of rubbish and based on unfounded principles of scientific naturalism. His criticism again ties in with the notion of how change occurs. Our view was that we needed to work within our scientific community and persuade rather than rant. We needed to start from the current state of work psychology and focus on making qualitative methods more accessible and therefore more acceptable. We sought to be included as part of our discipline, rather than to be positioned on the sidelines as 'different'. In conversation with Dachler, he clearly felt that work psychology was so far behind in these debates, that it was probably better to take up a position on the sidelines and confidently assert one's own epistemological assumptions. Having said that, we think most psychologists who saw us talking about methods at conferences thought we were raving anti-positivists regardless of what we said!

The other issue we took away from this debate was the significance of paying attention to epistemological issues, which we turn to in the next section. On a final note, we finally got to meet Peter Dachler in 1998 and have had a number of happy evenings with him since, discussing epistemological issues (amongst other things!). We have also produced a joint conference paper (Symon *et al.* 2001).

Epistemological Issues and the Politics of the Research Process

In 1998, we produced another book with another 12 methods. In contrast to the problems we had in securing a contract for the first book, we simply met with the current (different) editor at a conference and said we wanted to do another one. Her reply was 'Write me a paragraph about it', and we had the agreement from Sage to do it within a week. Clearly we were now in the publishing game. If the first book had not sold very well, maybe things would have been different: perhaps we would not have had the confidence and credibility we needed to continue.

In the second book, *Qualitative Methods and Analysis in Organizational Research,* (Symon & Cassell 1998) we paid more attention in our editorial to epistemological issues. Previously we were used to talking about the labels 'qualitative' and 'quantitative' as if these were unproblematic. Dachler had argued that as long as we used these terms, qualitative methods would always be disadvantaged. We had a lot of sympathy with this view and in the new book our position had changed somewhat:

> "The distinction between qualitative and quantitative methods is only a small part of a far wider ranging debate about epistemology and ontology. In practice the focus on the qualitative/quantitative debate is almost a red herring" (Symon & Cassell 1998: 3).

We also engaged directly with the notion of the book's contributors coming from a variety of epistemological positions rather than those that may have been seen as wholly radical. In the introduction we stated that:

> "Our task here is to present practical demonstrations of the range of (researcher-defined) qualitative techniques available. In doing this we must recognise the many ways in which organizational researchers are using qualitative techniques within a range of philosophical frameworks. In common with many other commentators (for example, Reed 1992; Smith *et al.* 1995), we believe that 'it is important at this stage for many different voices to be heard' (1995: 3) and to aim for an inclusive discipline" (Symon & Cassell 1998: 4).

We argued that using the term 'qualitative methods' is not the privilege of those who would claim, for example, an interpretivist or social constructivist position. It was not our aim to privilege a particular account or epistemological position, but to open the field up to alternatives. This meant that epistemological considerations were far more apparent in the chapters of the second book.

There were also more chapters on analysis in this book. This was for two reasons. Firstly there seemed to be a demand for information about the processes of qualitative data analysis. Secondly, more and more techniques were becoming available. The area of data analysis seemed to be the one where individuals approaching the use of qualitative methods for the first time felt the most concern. Clearly having vast amounts of textual data can be quite overwhelming, particularly for those used to numerical data. Therefore systematic ways of analysing qualitative data are seen as very attractive. Having a particular label, and a set of procedures to follow, is almost like a security blanket for the researcher new to qualitative methods. Whether this kind of analysis is always appropriate or whether it fits well with all epistemological beliefs is another issue that we did not at the time address.

In addition to producing the second book, we were getting more demanding about the lack of attention still being paid to qualitative methods in the organizational psychology literature. We decided to analyse in detail why we thought qualitative methods were not being used. In Symon & Cassell (1999) we identified a number of different barriers to innovation in research practice that we suggested were interrelated and emanated from a variety of social-psychological processes. We argued that few articles describing qualitative research are published in top (international) organizational psychology journals. Schaubroeck & Kuehn (1992) presented a review of research designs utilised in studies published in what they considered the 'top' work psychology journals over the period 1980–1990 (for example, *Journal of Applied Psychology*). Coming from an overtly positivist perspective, they concluded that such journals had given little space to qualitative studies which were, at any rate, of "marginal value" (Schaubroeck & Kuehn 1992: 119). Additionally, a brief evaluation of studies published in the dominant U.K. organizational psychology journal *Journal of Occupational and Organizational Psychology* from 1990–1998, which Gillian had conducted, indicated that about 3% were "qualitative" studies. When we turned to the best-selling textbooks in the area, we found that Arnold, Cooper & Robertson (1995) argued that qualitative methods were under-utilized because they are: time-consuming; difficult to validate; and difficult to generalise. In other words, they do not conform to positivist ideals.

We felt that this lack of visibility and under-utilization of qualitative methods arose from severe difficulties in opposing the current dominant practice. These in turn impact upon the career needs of researchers, particularly in relation to the U.K. Research Assessment Exercise. We specifically identified the issues below:

• getting research past epistemological gatekeepers (journal editors and reviewers, conference committees);
• conforming to journal editorial criteria and constraints of other presentations (set up with quantitative studies in mind);
• pressure to justify research methods according to inappropriate (positivist) criteria;
• convincing organizations who associate quantitative methods with 'science' and 'truth';
• little exposure to alternatives in popular textbooks or organizational psychology courses.

Our argument was that a work psychology underpinned by positivism was based on the notion of an objective truth existing 'out there' discoverable by 'scientific' methods. Therefore research practices must be seen as untainted by subjectivity, and controlled and narrowly focused to get to and dissect that truth. We argued that, rather, we believed the research process was influenced by power relations, career politics and pressure to conform. In other words, the research process is not necessarily one of an objective search after 'truth' but can be viewed as the social practice of individuals engaged in pursuing career needs. The 'job' of being a researcher and the adoption of epistemological stances are not separate issues. Thus, for example, some colleagues told us that they would be interested in using qualitative methods, but the pressures of publication from the RAE meant they preferred to concentrate on tried and trusted quantitative techniques.

These arguments suggest a reason for why a set of insightful research techniques was not being used by researchers without attributing the cause to something inherent in the techniques themselves. Additionally they provide an account for why qualitative researchers are not publishing in the best journals that does not locate the problem with the researcher. It is not that qualitative research and those who conduct it are just inherently weaker but rather that judgements of 'good practice' in research cannot be made without reference to the social and political context. The recognition of this was increasingly important given the emphasis placed on publication within the U.K. RAE. Within psychology the most prestigious international journals are all U.S. based and they very rarely publish research using qualitative methods only. One way organizational psychologists who use qualitative methods have responded to this is by avoiding the mainstream work psychology journals and instead aiming to publish in the high status management journals that are more open to alternative approaches, for example the *Journal of Management Studies* and *Organization Studies*. Additionally some new journals have been published, for example the *Journal of Qualitative Inquiry*, which specifically cater to the needs of qualitative researchers. Of course, new journals rarely have the credibility or status of long-established publications. We, however, were still keen to see some change in the work psychology community, and to publish in work psychology journals, rather than simply go outside the discipline. The recognition of the politics of the research process encouraged us to continue to press for change within our own discipline. This has oriented us specifically to considerations of: criteria for assessing research 'quality' and specifically epistemological gatekeepers' perceptions of 'good' research; training in research methods; and reflexivity in research practice. The former two considerations will be further discussed in the concluding section where we describe a current ESRC-funded research project. For now, our attention turns to the issue of reflexivity.

Reflexivity and Diversity

In the spring of 1999, we decided it was time to start work on another volume of methods as we had come across many other new and innovative methods we felt could be more widely known. At this stage, we had become interested in issues of reflexivity in research, and particularly in work psychology. We were writing at the time about how the world of organizational psychology was changing rapidly in substantive terms, but that there needed to be more reflection on how research was being conducted. We argued that work psychologists were spending considerable time discussing the impact of changing times on work, manifested through new psychological contracts and career structures, more sophisticated methods of selecting, assessing, rewarding and training employees, advanced technologies and post-bureaucratic organizational forms. However, despite the recent developments in the concerns of work psychology, there had been little change in the underlying epistemological assumptions that influenced how research was construed. Other researchers were also suggesting that a lack of reflection and creativity in this respect was stifling to the discipline (Anderson 1998). In other words, quantitative studies driven by positivist concerns, were adopting an essentially conservative research strategy, concentrating on investigating minor variations of already established theoretical models (adding a variable here or there, trying the model out in a different context or with a different sample etc). This was not contributing to a vibrant and innovative research community. Qualitative approaches and research adopting alternative epistemological perspectives hold out the promise of new insights by adopting a critical stance on accepted practices and approaching research topics with different objectives.

An example comes from one of the areas regarded as fundamental to work psychology: selection and assessment. Herriot & Anderson (1997) suggest that there is a whole range of questions about the selection process that are rendered inaccessible by the positivist paradigm. However some of those questions lay themselves open to investigation from other epistemological approaches. Taking alternative epistemological approaches might lead to a focus on the processes of selection, as opposed to the validity of individual methods. The research questions could concern how individuals construe, make sense of, and experience the selection process. Rather than seeking to correctly represent those constructions from the perspective of a neutral observer, the emphasis would be on how individuals in their accounts draw on particular discourses to explain or legitimise the experience of different selection techniques. Additionally, a focus could be on the iterative nature of the processes of selection and the relationship between the assessor and the assessed. For example, attention could be upon how the notion of the 'ideal candidate' is produced and reproduced through the interview process. Other questions that alternative epistemological approaches could address include impression management within the selection process by recruiters and candidates, and how the psychological contract is formed and developed by both parties through the selection experience (Herriot & Anderson 1997). Therefore, exploration of different perspectives creates new and interesting ways of asking and investigating work psychology questions. Two key themes in our new book, accordingly, were to be the importance of demonstrating the range of epistemological alternatives and methods available, and to ask the contributors to be reflexive about their own epistemological commitments and research practices.

On approaching Sage, we discovered we had a new editor again. This individual was clearly unfamiliar with our previous work as she suggested that, although she was interested in the text, it would be enhanced by the inclusion of quantitative methods. Once we recovered from the shock, and she withdrew her suggestions about including quantitative techniques, we negotiated a very exciting project. The plan was to take a selection of the chapters from the first two books, plus a number of new chapters, and put together 'an essential guide' to the use of qualitative methods in organizational research. This was an attractive idea to us at the time, not least because we were feeling the need for some closure on the process. We felt we could not go on forever editing books that described different types of qualitative methods. It also felt important to highlight the wide range of qualitative techniques that were available to the researcher by bringing them together in one volume. For example, an interview can take many different forms. Rather than varying only along the dimension of structure, the focus can be very different. Examples are life history interviews, critical incident technique, repertory grid interviews, and numerous other formats. An interview transcript can also be analysed using a range of different approaches, for example grounded theory, attributional analysis, metaphorical analysis, or analytic induction. Again there are many other approaches. A full list of the various qualitative techniques outlined in our books are presented in Table 1, below. We have categorized them only into techniques of data collection and data analysis. It is recognised that this list is by no means exhaustive and even this simple categorisation somewhat problematic (i.e. seemingly suggesting that method and analysis are divorced from each other — in all chapters, consideration was given to both data collection and data analysis). Additionally some of the techniques have been used with quantitative analysis. The potential uses for each of the approaches are addressed by the contributors.

In 2001, we wrote a paper, with Peter Dachler, arguing for a move towards a more reflexive work psychology (Symon *et al.* 2001). Much of our writing and presenting since that paper has argued for greater epistemological reflexivity within work psychology, and the increased use of alternative epistemological approaches to positivism (for example, Cassell & Symon 2002). We have argued that this would have a number of advantages and have tried to 'sell' the message in relation to the different questions researchers could ask, and the different insights that could be provided into work psychology issues. This has proved quite a useful strategy as the level of analysis

Table 1: Qualitative techniques of data collection and analysis
(from Cassell & Symon 1994, 2004; Symon & Cassell 1998)

Data Collection	Data Analysis
Action research	Analysis of company documentation
Case studies	Analytic induction
Cognitive mapping	Archiving qualitative data
Co-research	Attributional coding
Electronic interviews	Conversational analysis
Hermeneutics	Critical analysis
Intervention techniques	Discourse analysis
Life histories	Grounded theory
Participant observation	Matrices analysis
Repertory grid technique	Stakeholder analysis
Search conferences	Template analysis
Soft systems analysis	
Stories	
Twenty statements test	
Participant Observation	
Critical incident technique	
Group methods	
Intervention techniques	
Research diaries	
Interviews	
Pictorial representation	
Observation	
Question-asking and verbal protocol techniques	
Tracer studies	

is located within the development of the discipline as a whole, and how the discipline can be enhanced and more ready to face the challenges created by the changing world of work. Perhaps this is a more attractive argument to organizational psychologists, than arguments that focus on issues of research politics and individual research methods. This reflects a journey. At the beginning our arguments were mainly about methods and research questions, whereas now we take that for granted and focus on epistemological issues, encouraging critical thinking and reflection in research, and conducting innovative, interesting research suited to current organizational concerns. Our third book with Sage, entitled 'The essential guide to qualitative methods in organizational research' is currently in the process of being published (Cassell & Symon 2004).

Conclusion

A key question in an account such as this is: has anything changed with respect to the use of qualitative methods in our area? Certainly there are now more texts about 'how to do' qualitative research and guidelines for how to assess the quality of qualitative research. However there is still resistance. An interesting tale highlights the current position. Gillian recently had an article published in the *Journal of Occupational and Organizational Psychology* (Symon 2000b). The article was a review that advocated different approaches to and understandings of the use of new technologies in organizations, including more social constructivist and symbolic analyses. However, in a seemingly unprecedented move, an article providing a response from a positivist perspective to some of the issues Gillian raised in her article was published alongside it (Sonnentag 2000). This could be interpreted in one of two ways. The first and perhaps the most charitable is that this is a sign of healthy debate. However an alternative view is that given articles from a constructivist perspective are rarely (if ever) published in this journal, the editors were unhappy to publish such work without the more traditional position also being stated.

There have been some changes within Masters courses within Occupational Psychology (the qualification needed in order to practise as a Chartered Occupational Psychologist). Most now include training in the use of qualitative methods. However limited this is, this was rarely in evidence twelve years ago. There is now slightly more recognition that qualitative methods can form the basis of a Masters dissertation, and that it is possible to do a Ph.D. based solely on qualitative methods, as long as you choose the right External Examiner. This reflects developments and changes within psychology generally, and we would not attribute it to our work, although we are both involved in examining on those courses, and our books are sometimes used on those reading lists.

We have changed in the last twelve years. We have learnt a lot about the research process and the underlying political issues that influence it. We have also learnt to develop an analysis that locates responses and resistance to particular methodological approaches in a view of the whole academic system, and associated power relations, rather than seeing it as reflecting problems with specific research techniques. Twelve years on we feel more in a position to influence debates about methodology through our curriculum development work, editorial work and external examining. We are also part of a growing network of qualitative researchers within the organizational psychology field, a network that has provided much support over the years.

Some of the things we have learned are hopefully of use to others who may be in similar positions in other disciplines, or in a similar stage in their research career. A key issue is that of being aware of the different political issues surrounding the different 'status' of different research methods and the implications this has for trying to publish your own research. Another is to find like-minded people and join networks with researchers with similar approaches. It is also important when dealing with editors or other epistemological gatekeepers to do homework about the types of methods that are usually published in a particular journal, and how 'friendly' a journal may be to alternative approaches. We also discovered a range of strategies that enabled us to become more confident in using qualitative methods in our own research. One was to ensure that a mode of analysis we were using, for example, had a particular label, title or reference point. This would enhance its perceived legitimacy (Symon & Cassell 2004). Another was to gain training in using particular techniques, such as computer-based packages for data analysis for example. Finally, as we suggested earlier, our preferred strategy of trying to encourage change in perceptions of methodology and methodological debates was that of gentle persuasion within our own discipline, though others may argue that this is not the best way to achieve our goals.

One current interest is in the criteria that peer reviewers use to assess the output of qualitative research. Our argument is that qualitative research is often assessed using inappropriate criteria, which prevents the publication of high quality qualitative research. Catherine has developed some sets of criteria that are now used by journal reviewers for qualitative papers submitted to some journals in the field for example the *Journal of Occupational and Organizational Psychology* (BPS 2000) and *Personnel Review* (Cassell & Redman 2001). The aim of this is to try and ensure that papers using qualitative methods are assessed using more appropriate criteria (although we realise that there is a wide range of criteria possible). We have secured an ESRC grant (with another sympathetic colleague) to enable us to benchmark appropriate criteria for the assessment of qualitative methods in management research. Part of this process involves interviewing a variety of stakeholders (for example, journal editors, practitioners, university departmental research directors) as to their perceptions of qualitative research and their beliefs about good quality research. This will enable us to bring out any underlying assumptions that may be influencing the spread of qualitative research. This grant will also allow us to provide training in qualitative methods for a range of academics and practitioners, so pursuing our objective of raising the profile of qualitative methods further and tackling the potential (political) accusation of poor practice in the area. Through these processes we hope the quiet transformation will continue. It is perhaps a mark of how far qualitative methods have come that we have been awarded this grant at all and clearly the ESRC has recognised that training in this area is necessary.

On a final note, this chapter inevitably talks about our work, but our major role, in relation to our books particularly, has been that of editors. Numerous contributors described how they used the methods in their own research. Therefore we were (and are) always part of an alternative community of researchers within our discipline interested in these kinds of methodological issues.

Although, in this chapter, we have probably constructed *post hoc* what seems like a rational and coherent story, it certainly did not feel like that at the time. This is the first time we have really looked back on what we have achieved over the last few years and we feel we have travelled a very long way. Organizational psychology has not altogether moved with us! But there has certainly been a positive shift and the issues can at least now be debated. We are confident that this situation will continue to improve and are pleased that we have had the opportunity and perseverance to influence theoretical debates in our discipline and maybe make a difference. Reflexivity encourages us to strive not to be complacent and to continue to review and critique our own research practice. It is our continuing objective to do so.

References

Anderson, N. (1998). The people make the paradigm. *Journal of Organizational Behaviour, 19*(4), 323–328.

Arnold, J., Cooper, C. L., & Robertson, I. (1995). *Work psychology: Understanding human behaviour in the workplace* (2nd ed.). London: Pitman.

Bogdan, R., & Taylor, S. J. (1975). *Introduction to qualitative research methods.* New York: Wiley.

British Psychological Society (1988). *The future of the psychological sciences report.* Leicester: BPS.

British Psychological Society (2000). *Journal of occupational and organizational psychology guidelines for reviewers for papers using qualitative methods.* Leicester: BPS.

Bryman, A. (1988). *Quality and quantity in social research.* London: Unwin Hyman.

Cassell, C. M., Close, P., Duberley, J., & Johnson, P. (2000). Surfacing embedded assumptions: using repertory grid methodology to facilitate organizational change. *European Journal of Work and Organizational Psychology, 9*(4), 561–574.

Cassell, C. M., & Redman, T. (2001). Editorial: editorial policy for papers using qualitative methods. *Personnel Review, 31*(1), 6–8.

Cassell, C. M., & Symon, G. (1994a). *Qualitative methods in organizational research: A practical guide.* London: Sage Publications.

Cassell, C. M., & Symon, G. (1994b). Qualitative research in work contexts. In: C. M. Cassell, & G. Symon (Eds), *Qualitative methods in organizational research: A practical guide.* London: Sage Publications.

Cassell, C. M., & Symon, G. (1998). Quiet revolutions and radical transformations: a reply to H. Peter Dachler. *Organization Studies, 19*(6), 1039–1043.

Cassell, C. M., & Symon, G. (2002). Extending the epistemological boundaries of work and organizational psychology. Paper presented to the International Congress of Applied Psychology, Singapore, July.

Cassell, C. M., & Symon, G. (2004). *The essential guide to qualitative methods in organizational research.* London: Sage Publications (In press).

Cook, T. D., & Campbell, D. T. (1979). *Quasi-experimentation: Design and analysis issues for field settings*. Boston: Houghton Mifflin.

Dachler, H. P. (1997). Does the distinction between qualitative and quantitative methods make sense? A review of C. Cassell, & G. Symon Qualitative methods in organizational research. *Organization Studies, 18*(4), 709–724.

Gilbert, N., & Mulkay, M. (1984). *Opening pandora's box: A sociological analysis of scientists' discourse*. Cambridge: Cambridge University Press.

Guba, E., & Lincoln, Y. (1984). Competing paradigms in qualitative research. In: N. Denzin, & Y. Lincoln (Eds), *Handbook of qualitative research*. Newbury Park CA: Sage Publications.

Herriot, P., & Anderson, N. (1997). *International handbook of selection and assessment*. Chichester: John Wiley.

Holland, R. (1999). Reflexivity. *Human Relations, 52*(4), 463–483.

Hornby, P., & Symon, G. (1994). Tracer studies. In: C. M. Cassell, & G. Symon (Eds), *op. cit* (pp. 167–186).

Kirk, J., & Miller, M. L. (1986). *Reliability and validity in qualitative research* (*qualitative research methods series 1*). Beverley Hills, CA: Sage Publications.

Latour, B., & Woolgar, S. (1979). *Laboratory life: The social construction of scientific facts*. Beverley Hill, CA: Sage Publications.

Marshall, C., & Rossman, G. B. (1989). *Designing qualitative research*. Newbury Park Ca: Sage.

Newton, T. (1996). *'Managing' stress — Emotion and power and work*. London: Sage Publications.

Parker, I. (1989). *The crisis in modern social psychology — And how to end it*. London: Routledge.

Patton, M. Q. (1980). *Qualitative evaluation methods*. Beverley Hills CA: Sage Publications.

Reed, M. (1992). Introduction. In: M. Reed, & M. Hughes (Eds), *Re-thinking organization: New directions in organization theory and analysis*. London: Sage Publications.

Schaubroeck, J., & Kuehn, K. (1992). Research design in industrial and organizational psychology. In: C. L. Cooper, & I. T. Robertson (Eds), *International review of industrial and organizational psychology* (Vol. 7, pp. 99–121). Chichester: Wiley.

Smith, J., Harre, R., & van Langenhove, L. (1995). *Re-thinking methods in psychology*. London: Sage Publications.

Sonnentag, S. (2000). Working in a network context: what are we talking about? Comment on Symon. *Journal of Occupational and Organizational Psychology, 73*(4), 415–418.

Symon, G. (1998). Qualitative research diaries. In: G. Symon, & C. M. Cassell (Eds), *op. cit* (pp. 94–117).

Symon, G. (2002). Positioning qualitative research: meaning and value. *Contemporary Psychology, 47*(2), 176–178.

Symon, G. (2000a). Talking about working in a network context: A reply to Sonnentag. *Journal of Occupational and Organizational Psychology, 73*(4), 419–422.

Symon, G. (2000b). Information and communication technologies and the network organization: a critical analysis. *Journal of Occupational and Organizational Psychology, 73*(4), 389–414.

Symon, G., & Cassell, C. M. (1998). *Qualitative methods and analysis in organizational research: A practical guide*. London: Sage Publications.

Symon, G., & Cassell, C. M. (1999). Barriers to innovation in research practice. In: M. Cunha, & C. Maques (Eds), *Readings in organization science — Organizational change in a changing context*. Lisbon: ISPA.

Symon, G., Cassell, C. M., & Dachler, H. P. (2001). Towards a reflexive work and organizational psychology. Paper presented to the European Congress on Work and Organizational Psychology, Prague, May.

Walsh, S., & Cassell, C. M. (1994). *Managing diversity for competitive advantage*. London: The Bentinck Group.

Chapter 30

Qualitative Dimensions in Finance and Risk Management Research

Kevin Dowd[1]

Introduction

This chapter looks at the qualitative dimensions of finance and risk management research, and it is probably best if I begin by explaining my qualifications (such as there are) to pontificate on this subject. By background I am a frustrated historian (which must be a plus in this context) who went on to become an academic economist (which is obviously be a negative). Admittedly, I have always been interested in methodological and organisational issues (which must have some merit), and I supervised a PhD not so long ago based almost entirely on an interview-based methodology. So I don't really know much about qualitative research, although that hasn't stopped me occasionally dabbling with it in the past. However, I do have some experience of quantitative research, and standard quantitative methodology looks to me to be a lot easier. For a (hopefully, small) set-up cost — you learn some statistics, work out how to run some specialist software, and so forth — you gradually get a feel for the basic procedure, and after some experience you get to be quite good at operating the sausage machine. You form your hypothesis, get your data, estimate some equation, carry out your tests, discuss your results, and that's more or less it.[2]

Yet, at a deeper level, the distinction between qualitative and quantitative methodology is highly misleading: at a fundamental level all research is ultimately qualitative (i.e. dependent on judgement). Even the most arcane quantitative research

---

[1] I would like to thank Stuart Hyde, Manchester School of Accounting and Finance, University of Manchester for his helpful comments on an earlier draft.
[2] For those academic purists who insist on defining everything, I would suggest that we take quantitative methods to be the sausage machine referred to in the text, and (as befits someone unencumbered by any real knowledge of the area) I take qualitative methods to be everything else. Alternatively, there is always the economists' traditional definition of quantitative methods as 'hard' methods and qualitative methods as 'soft'.

---

always hinges on qualitative judgements of some sort, even if those judgements are poor ones (which is bad enough) or made unconsciously by default (which, from a methodological point of view is worse). An article can look very intimidating, with lots of heavy-duty jargon and statistics that hardly anyone can understand, and yet be built on feet of clay that render it pretty much worthless — and even big-name authors can (and do) produce this sort of rubbish.[3] From a social point of view, there is undoubtedly an over-supply of bad research, and I suspect that the real purpose of much of it is, in reality, merely to bolster academic CVs.[4] My point, in short, is that good quantitative research requires good judgement and an awareness of qualitative issues, institutional factors, context and so on. After all, the difference between good and bad research is entirely one of quality.

There are also the dangers — which might not worry some academic purists, but should — of pointlessness and faddishness. Many of the 'best' (or, more accurately, most highly rated) journals produce issue after issue of research that might be 'correct' — and might even be 'interesting', at least to 1.5 other specialists working in the same arcane area — but is completely pointless and has no discernable social value. This is particularly a problem with research in the area of 'theory', whether the 'theory' concerned be in economics, accounting or any other social science. The reason for this is, I think, because many social theorists have long since lost sight of their primary purpose — that is, to explain social phenomena: so 'explanation' is out, and 'theory' is in, and 'theory' in practice is often no more than obfuscation. Then there is faddishness. Again and again, someone comes along with a new approach that wakes us all up and is initially very refreshing; unfortunately, it is subsequently replicated *ad nauseam* until everyone becomes sick of it — with the result that we are then all too ready to jump on the next bandwagon when it comes along. This faddishness is very apparent in academic economics, and is what gives rise to the old joke that economists recycle the same old exam questions year after year, safe in the knowledge that it is the answers, not the questions, that change over time. To give just one example, in the early 1960s the

---

[3] My favourite example concerns a paper that I had to review many years ago for a graduate econometrics assignment. The paper was written by two very prominent economists and purported to apply a new statistical method to estimate a consumption equation. I read the paper repeatedly, but could not understand any of it. However, I eventually noticed in a footnote that the authors pointed out that their method only worked if a certain parameter was greater than one. This was interesting because this parameter was the marginal propensity to consume, which all first-year economics students (should) know must be less than one. So either the statistical approach was valid and the economic application was not, or vice versa, but there were no conceivable circumstances in which the statistical method as applied to this economic problem could possibly make sense. The paper was therefore nonsense, although this did not stop it coming out later came out in a top economics journal.

[4] I suspect that much of this serves little real social purpose. In the US, the supply of research has traditionally been driven by academic tenure issues, but we in the UK were largely free of pressures to produce worthless research until the last fifteen years or so. Unfortunately, the Government then invented the Research Assessment Exercise (RAE) process, an absurd monstrosity that has presided over a huge but utterly pointless expansion of UK research output. In my experience, the good quality research would have been done anyway, and the extra research 'stimulated' by the RAE — that is, the extra research articles extracted with great difficulty from uncooperative colleagues who demand to be paid to do research, but take offence at the idea that they should actually deliver the research they are being paid to do — is not worth the paper it is written on.

fashion in applied economics was to use ordinary-least-square (OLS) regression methods to estimate economic relationships, and the journals were full of OLS results. In the late 1960s and afterwards, we were then told that OLS methods were inadequate, and we were told not to use them. However, a new fad — 'cointegration' — then came along in the late 1980s, and we were now told that the methods to 'correct' OLS should be avoided like the plague — and also that old-fashioned OLS wasn't so bad after all. So the economist who 'switched off' in the mid 1960s would have been doing better empirical research than the one who kept up — although he would have got little published, as he was not using the currently correct methods.

At the same time, qualitative specialists would often do well to acquire some familiarity with 'quants' (or other technical) methods. They need to protect themselves against a 'black box' mentality, and the researcher who has some understanding of what is in the black box always has a clear edge over the one who does not. If I am doing interview-based research on, say, the activities of derivatives traders, then I (usually) need to know a certain minimum about derivatives and derivatives markets, much of which is highly quantitative and technical in nature; if I am researching the introduction of activity-based costing in a bank, I need to know something about the technicalities of banking and bank products, as well as some basic technical accounting; and so forth. So I would suggest that qualitative researchers often need to get to grips with such methods, because good qualitative research requires them to understand the technical contexts of their subject matter.[5] But I would also suggest that they should come to terms with such methods for another reason: to ensure that quants 'experts' don't pull the wool over their eyes — which, human nature being what it is, they are generally only too happy to do if they can get away with it. It is for this reason that I like to advise students to read *How to Lie with Statistics* (Huff 1991) — so they know the most obvious tricks. Of course, I am not suggesting that qualitative researchers should become fully qualified quants themselves: they should simply know enough to be able to ask the right questions and to be confident enough to assess the answers themselves.

This inter-connection between the qualitative and quantitative aspects of research is also very clear in the area I have been looking at over the last few years — risk management and, in particular, the estimation and use of Value-at-Risk (VaR) as a measure of financial risk. This is a highly quantitative subject, but also one that is strongly underpinned by qualitative or judgemental issues that are frequently overlooked by the practitioners and researchers who work on it.

I would like to begin by providing some background context to explain where I am coming from: how I got interested in this area, my experiences and what I have learned working in it, and so forth. After that, I will try to convey an impression of what (I think)

---

[5] The need to understand context was brought home to me by a nice anecdote told to me by a friend. A sociologist by trade, he wrote a good paper on how the physical framework of derivatives trading (i.e. the layout of open-outcry trading pits, etc.) affected communication between traders, and presented this research to a seminar in a sociology department. Unfortunately, the audience were clueless, as they didn't understand any of the institutional context to his work. Instead of discussing the sociology of communication, which was what the paper was about, the only questions he elicited were about gender issues in derivatives markets, on which his research had nothing to say, but which was all his audience wanted to discuss. So the seminar was a farce.

the subject itself is really like. After taking a brief pause to discuss epistemology, I go on to suggest some areas where I think there is a great deal of scope for good qualitative research in finance and risk management, and the final section offers some conclusions and reading.

If I have a message, it is a simple one: that areas like these — which might superficially appear to be dominated by quantitative issues — are actually crying out for qualitative research, and offer many research (and, indeed, career) opportunities for people trained in such methods. However, if qualitative researchers are to succeed in these areas, they must also come to terms with them, and learn enough to find their way through the 'technical' detail involved, 'quantitative' or otherwise.

Working in Risk Management and VaR: A Personal Perspective

My interest in the risk management area began as an offshoot of an earlier interest in the financial health and stability of banks: their capital, credit ratings, and so on. I had been working on these issues for some time — without much success, by the way[6] — and in early 1995, I began to find references to the (to me, mysterious) notion of 'value at risk'.[7] When I looked into it, I gradually realised that VaR was probably the key to understanding the problems I was working on, so I decided to take a temporary detour from my bank capital research and get to grips with it. After some further thought, I decided to write a book on VaR, but had the handicaps of not being well up on financial derivatives — a subject that figured prominently in the emerging VaR literature — and of having almost no experience of spreadsheets, which were necessary for all but the most basic VaR calculations. So before I could master VaR, I had to tool up on financial derivatives and Excel, which I had been wanting to do in any case.[8] My book eventually came out in 1998, although looking back at it now makes me cringe. Still, I can say in partial mitigation that the subject was very new at the time, and looks much clearer now than it did then.

---

[6] Bank capital is a tough area to work in, and I had major problems getting my papers in the area published. My worst experience was the response from a referee who claimed that the maths in one particular paper was just plain stupid, and went on to say that if the paper had been an economics assignment, the student should be failed the course and advised to go into some other area. Charming. The other referee thought it was a reasonable paper, so the editor invited me to respond to the negative referee. I did, and the traditional exchange of pleasantries followed. Fortunately, the second referee largely agreed with me, and the paper was eventually published after some further changes. Nonetheless, I have to wonder whether the publication was worth the aggravation.

[7] The VaR itself is the maximum likely loss over some specified period, and is a statistical concept because the term 'likely' is defined in terms of a probability. The VaR can be estimated in many different ways, depending on the assumptions one is prepared to make, and much of the VaR literature is no more than an effort to weigh up the pros and cons of alternative estimation methods for different VaR applications.

[8] Learning Excel brought immense benefits to my teaching as well as research, and for some subjects (financial modelling, derivatives, investments, etc.) is now absolutely essential. I always encourage my students to learn it as quickly and as thoroughly as they can, and for those who learn it, it also helps them enormously with homework and dissertations. Unfortunately, my experience is that most students don't listen to this sort of advice — but then I rarely listened to any advice at their age either.

Shortly after the book came out, I decided to postpone my bank capital research a little longer because there were loose ends I wanted to clear up. I had become very interested in the uses of VaR for risk management purposes, and I felt that the way forward — if I could get enough of a run at it — was to write another VaR book, but this time one focusing on the uses of VaR for risk management and downplaying the measurement issues (the latter were harder, I thought, and therefore best left to technicians with nothing better to do). I then made several attempts to get this out of the way over 1998–1999, but each time university problems intervened, and I lost my momentum. In the meantime, I gradually realised that I was wasting my time: the more I thought about the project, the more demanding it became. But by now I was committed to a new VaR book of some description — mainly out of stubbornness, I guess, because I didn't want all my earlier efforts to go to waste.[9] However, at some point I realised that risk measurement was easier after all, and the pieces of the book then fell into place.

But then the cycle repeated itself again. As I was writing the second book, various further projects gradually suggested themselves — I became more confident of my ability to use the various estimation approaches I was writing about, and I became increasingly aware of the potential uses of these approaches to interesting and (dare I say it?) even useful risk measurement problems: the estimation of derivatives risks, energy risks, insurance risks, and so on. So I made various mental notes along the way, and promised myself that I would come back to these projects as soon as I could. Once again, I felt that I may as well do a little bit more work on VaR, as I had already come this far: sunk costs and all of that. However, I also realised that despite a lot of frustration — or, perversely, perhaps because of it — I quite liked the sense of accomplishment that comes from writing a software routine that does something that I hadn't seen done before. I found that it provided a sense of gratification that I had only very rarely enjoyed doing work in economics. So I now found myself working through a new research programme, applying different VaR estimation methods to different risk problems, and after a while I worked out the ropes. You focus your particular research question, write the software, play around with the results and work out what corners you can cut, and then write the paper around whatever is left — a finance sausage machine, rather than an economics one. However, it is also more fun than economics and a lot less frustrating — in particular, there are no maddening maths problems to worry about.[10]

---

[9] This is bad economics, by the way. We always teach our economics students that sunk costs are irrelevant. If the return on continuing with a project is not high enough, we should cut our losses and abandon it, regardless of sunk costs. To do otherwise is to throw good resources after bad. My message to students: do as I say, not as I do.

[10] The biggest technical problem working in economics is the frequent need to struggle through difficult mathematical and statistical problems. However, my sense is that finance practitioners are gradually liberating themselves from this latter problem, as they increasingly rely on numerical methods such as random number simulation instead of 'hard' mathematics or statistics that require raw brainpower. These methods are a lot less sophisticated than they look, but are immensely powerful and (after a little getting used to) are relatively easy to program. What I really like about them is that they enable the great mathematically unwashed to produce numerical answers much faster than professional mathematicians can produce them, and I particularly enjoy the exquisite pleasure of telling the mathematicians in advance what their answers should be. Naturally, real mathematicians hate these methods.

I still don't know when — or even if — I will ever get back to my earlier projects on bank capital. I haven't made much effort to follow the literature — no point really, since I haven't time to do much about it — although I did pick up a journal a few months ago and got a bit of a shock to see a paper there on bank capital that I had hoped years ago to write myself. But that's the way it goes, and I knew myself that if I didn't get a move on with the bank capital stuff, then other people would.

Risk Management and VaR: A Cursory Overview

Having explained where I am coming from, I would now like to say a little bit about the subject itself, and in particular, about the importance of judgmental factors in it. Of course, risk management is notorious for being anything but transparent: many practitioners get high on their (usually more imagined than real) mastery of difficult quantitative methods (stochastic calculus, etc.), weird products ('exotic' derivatives, etc.), impenetrable derivatives terminology, bizarre trading ritual, and other difficult subjects (derivatives accounting, taxation and law, etc.). But, daunting as it looks, much of this heady cocktail is no more than smoke and mirrors to keep outsiders out: lets frighten others off, so we can have the market to ourselves and make a lot of money. And perhaps the most effective of these entry barriers is to promote the idea that you have to be a quant, a rocket scientist, to be successful in the City: you play up people's fears of mathematics, and this stratagem is often effective because mathematics intimidates almost all of us.

This is all well and good for the rocket scientists, and it does have a grain of truth: you can rarely employ someone straight off the street to come in and price your exotic derivatives for you. However, this attitude obscures the point that the value and success of everything, the quants included, must ultimately depend on judgement. As one of the world's leading real rocket scientists, the late Richard Feynman, once nicely put it when commenting on the Challenger disaster, "If a guy tells me the probability of failure is 1 in 1,000,000, I know he's full of crap".[11] Feynman's point was that we should come to terms with the need to make judgements, and we should beware of those who duck the issue by offering us spurious precision instead. The danger here is obvious. In the words of Nassim Taleb, a well-known derivatives veteran:

> "You're worse off relying on misleading information than not relying on any information at all. If you give a pilot an altimeter that is sometimes defective he will crash the plane. Give him nothing and he will look out of the window" (Taleb 1997a: 37).

Indeed, I would say that all the interesting issues in risk management are judgemental ones: everything else is just number crunching, which can be programmed into a computer.

A good example, which recurs again and again in the risk management area, relates to the estimation of volatility: if you are trading derivatives, you need to estimate some

---

[11] Quoted in Adams (1995: 213).

of the parameters that go into your derivatives pricing equations, and the most important of these is the volatility, often known in the trade as sigma, which is closely related to the standard deviation of prices. However evaluating volatility involves a lot of judgement, and is definitely not a simple case of plugging some historical data into a spreadsheet to calculate a standard deviation. Any fool can use a spreadsheet to estimate the price of an option, but the resulting option price is only as good (or as bad) as the parameter values that are fed into it. And this is no mere academic matter, because a misjudged volatility will translate into a mispriced option, and a trader who misprices his or her options will, in effect, give away money to other traders with better judgement. Individual traders have lost hundreds of millions from such mistakes. A nice example was the loss of £77m announced by Natwest in 1997, which arose because a junior trader had used the wrong volatility values to price and trade interest-rate options — and also, of course, because the bank's risk controls didn't pick up the problem till it was too late.

This same problem — the danger of misjudging volatility — also figures very prominently in the VaR area. Volatility is as important to VaR as it is to option pricing, and the consequences of mistakes can be equally costly. The standard example in the VaR field is where we use some historical estimate of volatility — that is to say, some standard deviation estimated on past data — and then plug this into an equation to estimate the VaR of a foreign-exchange position just before an exchange rate crisis. If we use recent historical data, the exchange rate will appear to be stable (i.e. will have a low volatility), and the VaR of a position involving the foreign currency will appear to be low. Our position will then appear to be safe — and we will lose a fortune if the exchange rate suddenly devalues. This is exactly what happened to many American financial institutions in December 1994, among many other instances, when the Mexican peso crashed without warning and apparently safe peso-denominated positions were revealed — too late — to have been highly risky.

Another common VaR mistake is to make the wrong assumption about the statistical distribution of the data. The standard (and also oft-repeated) error here is to assume without any real factual basis that a particular profit/loss series follows a normal statistical distribution, the classic bell curve. Naturally, there is no harm in doing this if our profit/loss series actually does follow a normal distribution, but most empirical distributions do not, implying that a mindless assumption of normality can lead to a serious under-estimate of VaR. As many users have found to their cost, an otherwise sound VaR model can then give potentially disastrous answers once practitioners start using it to make real risk management decisions.

In fact, naïve volatility estimation and taking normality for granted are the worst offences that VaR practitioners can commit, and the list of those who have self-destructed (at least in part) because they ignored these elementary rules includes some of the biggest names in the business. Perhaps the most spectacular was Long-Term Capital Management in 1998. Here was a firm, the darling of Wall Street, brimful of rocket scientists, and with a board that included Robert Merton and Myron Scholes, who (rightly, in my opinion) received the Nobel Economics prize in 1997 for their pioneering work on option pricing, which laid the foundations of the financial derivatives industry. However, LTCM also had a VaR model, and this model indicated in early 1998 that the firm was extremely safe: the probability of the firm defaulting was so low as to be utterly negligible. The firm then suffered devastating losses in the summer and autumn of 1998, and only avoided failure by means of a humiliating bail-out in September 1998. It turned out that its losses were 14 times the standard deviation of its earlier profit/loss — in the language of the trade, the firm had suffered a 14-sigma event. Assuming statistical normality, the probability of such an event was so low that it shouldn't have occurred once in the entire history of the universe! So take your pick: either the firm was incredibly unlucky . . . or, alternatively, it just had a very bad risk model.[12] Essentially, LTCM broke both the cardinal rules mentioned earlier: it had used a naïve volatility estimator and it had implicitly (if not otherwise) assumed normality or something like it. All the rocket science in the world is of no use if you ignore the elementary ABCs of good risk management. Perhaps they just got carried away by their own earlier success or by the adulating press they were getting, and felt it couldn't happen to them. Well, guys, it did — and you aren't the first and won't be the last 'invincible' firm to make the same mistake.

This same issue — good judgement vs. bad quants — comes up again and again. A leading derivatives academic, Bill Margrabe (1998: 27), once observed that:

> "A good trader with a bad model can beat a bad trader with a good model. For example, a good trader using Black's model [a well-known simple model] to price bond options could fleece a bad trader using a proprietary model [which should be better, in theory] if the good trader knows how to get the right inputs from brokers and the bad trader doesn't make all the required adjustments. Also, I've seen a good trader with no model at all take millions of dollars from a bad trader with a fancy model that is satisfactory for the equity market, but fatally flawed for the crude oil futures market."

Nassim Taleb (1997a: 40) puts the same point in a more delicate way:

> "Anytime I take a street-smart kid with a strong Brooklyn accent and train him or her in quant methods, I develop a wonderful quant trader who knows how to squeeze the sitting ducks. When you take extremely quantitative trainees, particularly from the physical sciences, and try to make them arbitrage traders, they freak out and become pure gamblers. They can't see the edge, and they become the sitting ducks. The world has too much texture, more than they can squeeze into the framework they're used to."

In short, good judgment beats bad quants every time.

---

[12] Getting good VaR estimates is difficult even if one avoids elementary mistakes such as these. A famous study by Tanya Beder (1995: 22) found that estimates of VaR were "wildly dependent" on the particular methodology and assumptions used. She went on to say that "some firms have been lulled into a fall sense of security" and that firms' senior managers were sometimes "shocked" to realise that their risk reports could change dramatically under alternative assumptions. However, these sorts of problems merely underscore the importance of good judgement in the VaR area. After all, risk managers can't expect to be paid their enormous salaries merely for number crunching.

A related theme is the old one that the outputs of models are only as good as the data put into them. Garbage in, garbage out, as the old saying goes. If we want to ensure that our data systems — not to mention our risk management systems in general — have integrity, then there is no substitute for old-fashioned management control: good compliance systems, good risk control systems, good managers who stay awake, and so on. A perfect example of how not to do it is that old favourite, Barings Bank, which went belly up in February 1995 thanks to the unauthorized activities of its star trader, Nick Leeson, in its Singapore office. It was later estimated that by the end of February 1995, Barings had a daily VaR of £126m and probably more (Chew 1996: 248). This contrasts with JP Morgan — an institution with ten times the capital of Barings — which had a daily VaR of under £10m. Barings therefore had a VaR (or level of risk) that was, after adjusting for the differential capital base — and this is a conservative estimate — well over a hundred times that of Morgan. So the most rudimentary calculations would have shown that Barings was extremely vulnerable relative to comparable institutions. Unfortunately, Barings' own risk models didn't give any hint of this exposure: in fact, they couldn't have, because the data fed to the London head office did not include any information about Leeson's hidden derivatives gambles, which were the principal source of Barings' huge risk exposures in the first place. Even the best risk model is no good if we feed it with useless data.

Epistemology and Methodology

Before discussing opportunities for qualitative research in this area, I should come clean and explain where I stand on the underlying epistemology. My position on epistemology is basically practical — we should use whatever seems to work for the problem at hand, and we should avoid excessive dogmatism: methodology is not an exact science. I also believe that researchers should be aware of the pitfalls to which their preferred methodology might expose them, and also get some feel for the epistemologies/ methodologies used by other researchers so they have some idea where they might be coming from. So what are the relative strengths and weaknesses of alternative approaches? At the most simplistic level, the strength of scientific/quantitative approaches is that they are respectful of the notion of 'truth', in some sense of other, but their weakness is the difficulty they have often have handling consciousness, intention, and so on; the social/qualitative approaches score the other way round.

In this context, my main concern with (some) qualitative research is that it over-emphasises the subjective, relativistic status of knowledge, to the point where some practitioners deny point-blank that the notion of 'truth' has any truth altogether. Yes, we can all agree that everyone has their own, probably unique, perception of the world around them, so there is a sense in which we can never escape the notions of context-dependent subjective reality, and so on. And, yes, we can all acknowledge that this makes it well-nigh impossible to verify the results of certain types of research. However, I think it is a serious misjudgement to then draw the conclusion — as some Postmodernists do — that the very notion of truth itself has no objective reality or meaning whatsoever. To make 'truth' completely subjective is to rob it of its very essence, and to make truth, and its opposite, untruth, effectively the same: in other words, to do away with the notion of truth altogether. Taken to its extreme, I would suggest that the 'truth is relative' argument undermines research — all research, including that of those who take that view — and has potentially dangerous social consequences. It undermines research because it makes the work of any researcher completely solipsistic, and so (arguably) no different from, and no more important than, the ramblings of those inane newspaper columnists who like to tell the rest of us what they were thinking when they brushed their teeth that morning. It is socially dangerous because I believe there are things that we know, and on which people — or at least reasonable people — can and do agree. To give an important example, the Holocaust did happen, and I would hope that all readers would concur that the truth of that claim is not dependent on whether or not I agree with it. And the converse claim — that the Holocaust didn't happen — is false. The difference between the two claims is that one is true, and the other is false. What worries me about taking the 'truth is relative' argument too far is that it undermines the epistemological difference between the two positions, and gives a veneer of respectability to rubbish like Holocaust-revisionism and to the anti-social groups that spout it. The lesson to Post Modernists in particular? Don't throw the baby out with the bathwater.

Opportunities for Qualitative Research in Finance and Risk Management

So, granted that quantitative and qualitative approaches are each valid within their respective (but not mutually exclusive!) domains, where are the opportunities to do qualitative research in finance and risk management? The answer is: everywhere.

An excellent example of good qualitative research in this area is an article by Chris Marshall and Michael Siegel, published in the *Journal of Derivatives* in 1997. They set out to examine the issue of implementation risk — the risk of differences in risk estimates arising solely from differences in the ways in which models were commercially implemented. They did so by asking all the major vendors of VaR models to provide VaR estimates for a set of pre-specified positions, with follow-up discussions to investigate any major discrepancies that came to light. Their results were very interesting. They found that in no case did any two systems' implementations of the same model produce precisely the same estimated VaR. They also found that differences between VaR estimates could be important, which suggests that a lot hinges on 'details' and ancillary decisions made by users and developers. In addition, they found that the variation in VaR estimates increases as instruments become more complex — that is, implementation risk increases with complexity. These results are important, because they highlight the dangers of viewing VaR models as black boxes that always produce the same results, and because they suggest a strong need for independent advice, particularly on complex models and their implementation.

Another promising line of inquiry is to investigate perception gaps in the risk management industry.[13] After Barings, the question on everyone's lips was "Could it happen to us?" and many firms hurriedly carried out risk audits to satisfy themselves that they were covered. (These included Deutsche Morgan Grenfell, and others, who satisfied themselves they were covered, and later found out the traditional way that they weren't.) Around this time, Cap Gemini published the results of an interesting survey, which found that no less than three-quarters of risk managers thought that their organisation was immune to a Barings-style scandal, and yet the same proportion of traders (who, one would have thought, were presumably in a position to know) believed the opposite.[14] So someone was clearly wrong — and ominously, the Cap Gemini survey went on to reveal that some 85% of traders also thought that they could hide forbidden trades from their managers, if they were minded to do so. Research like this sheds light on an important but otherwise hidden world — it shows the gaps in mutual perception, which form the seedbed from which many other problems spring. No-one ever lost money merely because they mis-measured risks: they lost money because control systems didn't work, and because those who should have anticipated these problems failed to do so. Yet such problems (always?) occur against a background of communication breakdown or incompatible expectations, and good qualitative investigation is ideal for helping to identify them. There are also, of course, many other perception gaps that are worth investigating (for example, gaps between risk managers and senior managers, gaps between either of these and regulators, or shareholders, etc., and the gaps can cover perceptions of safety, responsibility, good practice, etc.), and it would be interesting to track how some of these change over time. For instance, if firms were genuinely getting a better handle on operational risk (for example, rogue trader risk, etc.), as they all claim to be doing, then such research would show that risk managers were increasingly confident that these problems were safely under control, and that traders would be increasingly inclined to agree with them. Speaking for myself, I would bet that the results of such a survey would still be worrying — but it would be nice to know all the same.

There are also some (good, I think) projects that I would very much like to see someone carry out, if they haven't been done already. We all hear of the headline cases

[13] In this context, Willman *et al.* (2001) looks at the behaviour of traders in financial markets, and compares the observed empirical behaviour with that predicted by the main theories in the area (i.e., conventional economics/finance theories, as well as Kahneman and Tversky's prospect theory). They use data from a combination of questionnaires and semi-structured interviews, and find substantial discrepancies between empirical and predicted theories (i.e. so the theories don't work well in practice). A related study by the same authors (Willman *et al.* 2002)) examines the attitudes and risk-taking behaviour of traders and their managers in investment banks, and also came up with some interesting conclusions (for example, that managers are more interested in averting losses than making profits).

[14] I know who I'd believe. One investigator asked managers if they could spot traders' tricks, and conversation went something like this: "No, they couldn't [hide trades]. But, you know, if the trader did ... but he'd never think of that" (Simon Nelson, quoted in S. Paul-Choudhury 1997: 21). This doesn't inspire a great deal of confidence in managers' abilities to prevent rogue trading. Moreover, as Paul-Choudhury also went on to observe, it was very difficult to find a trader who hadn't broken the rules at some point and got away with it. If traders think they can pull the wool over their managers' eyes, I am sure they can.

where institutions make spectacular losses: such losses can't be covered up, at least not indefinitely.[15] Those who read the trade press will usually pick up the many more cases where firms make smaller losses: after all, a few million lost here and there is still real money. But wouldn't it be interesting to have an idea of how many firms experience near misses that are then hidden up to avoid embarrassment? There is no doubt that such cases do occur, and I know of at least two cases myself. One of them involved our old friend Nick Leeson: it is now a matter of public record — made public because of Leeson's later exploits — that Leeson had racked up large losses on an earlier occasion, but had managed to gamble his way out of them without any of his managers noticing. However, for reasons best known to himself, he did it again, and wasn't so lucky the second time. The other one was an incident that occurred years ago related to me by a friend who used to work for a far eastern bank operating in London: one evening a trader (again, for reasons we can only guess at) decided to bet the bank's capital — all of it — on the U.S. Treasuries market, in the belief that Treasuries were going to rise in price. The bank then started to slide over the edge, as the prices of Treasuries began falling and the bank couldn't unwind its positions quickly for fear of pushing those prices further down and wiping out its capital in the process. All the bank management could do was unload their positions slowly and pray that prices didn't keep falling. Over the course of the next few days they managed to unload their positions successfully, and the bank survived. The senior management were naturally very embarrassed about the whole business, so the episode was hushed up and even their overseas head office was never the wiser. The irony was that the trader turned out to be right, and Treasuries prices did rise — but only just in time. So my first suggestion is this: wouldn't it be interesting to get some idea of how often this sort of thing occurs? I realise that extracting this sort of confidential information would not be easy, but dealing with such difficulties is exactly where questionnaire/interview methods excel. Relatedly, wouldn't it also be interesting to get to get some idea of how frequently, and when, institutions make losses that are then covered up? Again, what is needed is some sort of mass confessional, and qualitative methods provide the only way we could ever get it.

Another area crying out for further research is the development of 'early warning' systems to help us identify the firms that are most likely to get into serious difficulties. There must, surely, be noticeable differences between firms that get into difficulties, and firms that don't: it can't all be just a bolt out of the blue. It would be very interesting, therefore, to investigate these differences: what are the distinguishing characteristics — in terms of culture, attitudes, morale, governance structures, communication problems, turnover, or whatever — of firms that subsequently get themselves into serious financial difficulties, compared to 'good' firms that don't? In other words, what factors make

---

[15] Although one does wonder. In 1995, Daiwa Bank announced that Toshihide Igushi, a trader at their New York office, had managed to accumulate losses of $1.1 billion without anyone apparently noticing — and even that loss only came to light when Mr. Igushi wrote to the head office in Tokyo to apologise for the trouble he had caused them. One wonders whether Daiwa would ever have noticed the loss had Mr. Igushi not had the decency to point it out to them.

firms prone to succeed or to fail? And can we go even further, and identify the chief factors that make firms safe or vulnerable? There has been a great deal of interest in these issues over the years, of course, and there is a lot of anecdotal evidence (for example, that the combination of a Queen's Award and a fancy fountain in the head-office foyer is a sure sign of impending disaster, etc.), but a great deal remains to be done.

One final area I would like to mention is behavioural finance. The focus of this area is how people actually behave when they take financial risks, and this relates to the difficulties that economists have had squaring the postulates of 'rational economic man' with the empirical evidence (i.e. that he might not really exist). These problems have made financial economists distinctly uncomfortable because they suggest that their models are missing something important. Their attempts to deal with these issues have led them to stray over into psychology, and have in turn led to open warfare between the two disciplines. The debate on this issue is a particularly entertaining one to watch because the two disciplines have no real choice but to go for each other's throats: economics is based on the premise of full-bodied rationality, and psychology is based on the opposite premise, so presumably one or the other is fundamentally unsound. Or maybe both. This controversy is obviously going to run and run,[16] and does, I think, create many new opportunities for researchers in adjacent disciplines, particularly accountants and sociologists, and qualitative researchers in general, to make substantial contributions. The focal point is that old chestnut, the extent to which rationality is (or might be, or isn't) a social construct, but perhaps with a newer focus on the rationality (or otherwise) of risk-taking, backed up by suitable empirical evidence.

Conclusions

We all know that a great deal of research in this area is highly 'technical', in one sense or other, and there is also a huge amount of jargon, macho posturing, and other — to use the economics jargon — barriers to entry. Leaving aside the point that even the most obtuse technical work is always underpinned by qualitative judgements of one sort or another (i.e. so the 'quantitative vs. qualitative debate' is highly misleading), there is also much that can only be properly investigated by traditional qualitative methods.

The fact is that we know very little about what actually happens in the finance and risk management worlds: we know very little about the day-to-day lives of risk managers and other practitioners, what they do, what they perceive, the roles they play, their mores, conventions, their sub-cultures, and so on, and how they relate to the

---

[16] In this context, it is also interesting to note that the one of the winners of the 2002 Nobel Prize in economics, Daniel Kahneman, received his award for his pioneering work on the interface between economics and psychology — that is, to put it bluntly, for making psychology 'respectable' in economics terms. This recognition of Kahneman's work will no doubt stir up the argument for many years to come.

technology they use (for example, how they use their models in practice).[17] The area is full of opportunities for good qualitative research, and not least because these markets, and the financial instruments traded in them, are all recent developments that many qualitative researchers have yet to take much notice of.[18] But if qualitative researchers are to succeed, they need to become familiar with the technical context within which this social behaviour takes place, and which (presumably) has a key bearing on that behaviour.

So where do you start — assuming, that is, that you believe any of this? The answer I usually give, though I admit without much enthusiasm, is to begin by reading the financial pages of the newspapers. However, if I am honest about it, I have always found the financial press boring and generally try to avoid reading it myself. Personally, I prefer *Private Eye*: all the really interesting stuff finds its way there in any case, and I believe that it is the primary source of information for many who work in the area. But the best way to get a feel for what finance is really like in practice is to read some of the 'kiss and tell' financial best-sellers: not the boring stuff with statistics in it, but the racy stuff, such as *Liar's Poker* (the scoop on the bond marketing antics at Solomon Brothers in the 1980s), *Barbarians at the Gate* (the inside story of the biggest takeover in Wall Street history), *The Predators' Ball* (the story of Drexel Burnham, the junk bond kings: enough said), *F.I.A.S.C.O.* (my favourite: the story of how Morgan Stanley ripped off its derivatives customers in the mid-1990s) and *Monkey Business* (the dirt on the internet craze). Each of these is a brilliant and highly entertaining read — much better than some soporific statistical tome on Value at Risk. But for those who really want that sort of book, there is always *Measuring Market Risk*.

References

Adams, J. (1995). *Risk*. London: UCL Press.
Black, F. (1989). How to use the holes in Black-Scholes. *Journal of Applied Corporate Finance*, *1*(4), 67–73.
Burrough, B., & Helyar, J. (1991). *Barbarians at the gate: The fall of RJR Nabisco*. New York: Harper Collins.
Bruck, C. (1989). *The predators' ball: The inside story of Drexel Burnham and the rise of the junk bond raiders*. New York: Penguin Books.

[17] A nice example here is the famous 'holes in Black-Scholes': the fact that the standard option-pricing model, the Black-Scholes model, is based on some patently unrealistic assumptions (as recognised by one of its authors; see Black (1989)) and yet the model remains extremely popular. Part of the reason is that traders appreciate its limitations, and make ad hoc adjustments to compensate for them. A huge corpus of convention and practice — traders' lore — has since grown up around this very point. (For more on all this, the standard reference is Taleb (1997b)). So entrenched has traders' lore become, that superior new models — such as the stochastic volatility model of Hull & White (1987), which allows the volatility to move randomly, instead of treating it as fixed as in Black-Scholes — have had great difficulty getting accepted by practitioners, even though everyone acknowledges their superiority over the Black-Scholes model. Clearly, there is a more going on here than meets the eye.

[18] Although there are good exceptions, such as the studies by Willman and his co-authors mentioned in note 13.

Chew, L. (1996). *Managing derivative risks: The uses and abuses of leverage*. Chichester: John Wiley and Sons.

Dowd, K. (1998). *Beyond value at risk: The new science of risk management*. Chichester: John Wiley and Sons.

Dowd, K. (2002). *Measuring market risk*. Chichester: John Wiley and Sons.

Hull, J., & White, A. (1987). The pricing of options on assets with stochastic volatilities. *Journal of Finance, 42*(2), 281–300.

Huff, D. (1991). *How to lie with statistics*. New York: Penguin.

Lewis, M. (1990). *Liar's poker: Rising through the wreckage on Wall Street*. New York: Penguin.

Margrabe, W. (1998). Roundtable discussion on 'The limits of VaR and risk modelling'. *Derivatives Strategy, 3*(2), 27.

Marshall, C., & Siegel, M. (1997). Value at risk: implementing a risk measurement standard. *Journal of Derivatives, 4* (Spring), 91–110.

Paul-Choudhury, S. (1997). This year's model. *Risk, 10*(5), 18–23.

Partnoy, F. (1997). *F.I.A.S.C.O.* New York: W. W. Norton and Co.

Rolfe, J., & Troob, P. (2001). *Monkey business: Swinging through the Wall Street jungle*. New York: Warner Books.

Taleb, N. (1997a). The world according to Nassim Taleb. *Derivatives Strategy, 2* (December/January) 37–40.

Taleb, N. (1997b). *Dynamic hedging: Managing vanillla and exotic options*. New York: John Wiley and Sons.

Willman, P., O'Creevy, M. Fenton, Nicholson, N., & Soane, E. (2001). Knowing the risks: theory and practice in financial market trading. *Human Relations, 54*(7), 887–910.

Willman, P., O'Creevy, M. F., Nicholson, N., & Soane, E. (2002). Traders, managers and loss aversion in investment banking: a field study. *Accounting, Organizations and Society, 27*(1–2), 85–98.

Author Index

Subject Index